STRATEGY FORMULATION
AND IMPLEMENTATION
Tasks of the General Manager

STRATEGY FORMULATION AND IMPLEMENTATION
Tasks of the General Manager

Arthur A. Thompson, Jr.
and
A.J. Strickland III

both of
The University of Alabama

1983 · Revised Edition

BUSINESS PUBLICATIONS, INC.
Plano, Texas 75075

ISBN 0-256-02884-2
Library of Congress Catalog Card No. 82-72865
Printed in the United States of America

6 7 8 9 0 ML 0 9 8 7 6 5

PREFACE

This book plows a lot of fresh ground. It features an expansive, up-to-date survey of strategic management concepts and analytical approaches, plus a collection of readings which probe leading-edge techniques and applications. Those persons familiar with the text portion of our *Strategy and Policy: Concepts and Cases,* published in 1981, will quickly note the addition of many new features and treatments. We have undertaken a truly thorough revision—one that incorporates many of the pioneering ideas, analytical approaches, experiences, and empirical studies now surfacing. Our objective in preparing this edition has been to assemble a text-readings package that puts readers on the frontiers of current knowledge and thinking about strategic management—what it is, what it involves, and how to do a better job of it.

The book is intended for two audiences: one, senior-level and MBA students taking a course in business policy and, two, managers and executives interested in staying abreast of the fast-moving practices of strategy management. We envision this book being used in several different pedagogical formats. It can be used in conjunction with one of several strategy management casebooks now on the market (such as our own *Cases in Strategic Management*) to form a concepts-readings-cases package of instructional materials. It can be used as a companion text to support the instructor's own lectures and cases or to complement a management decision game. It can be used in management development programs to help bring practitioners up-to-date on the rapidly emerging array of analytical techniques and approaches to strategic management. Or it can be used as a thought-provoking, on-the-job guide for managers who are trying to come to grips with strategy formulation and implementation in their companies.

The Growing Relevance of the Strategy Management Literature

During the last decade there has been an explosion of interest in the broad concept of strategy. A whole literature has emerged on the meaning of strategy, on how to formulate a strategic plan, and on all the ramifications of aligning the internal organization to fit the needs of strategy. Techniques for evaluating corporate business portfolios and for matching business strategy closely to the firm's situation and capabilities have grown in use and are having a significant impact on the strategy-related decisions of managers. Managers are paying conscious attention to strategy formulation and strategy implementation. There is heightened managerial application of such strategic concepts as driving forces, competitive position, business strength, key success factors, strategic fit, and distinctive competences. The whole strategy management cycle—from defining the business *to* strategy formation *to* implementation and execution *to* evaluation of results *to* reformulation and fine tuning of the game plan—has come under scrutiny by practitioners, consultants, and business school academics. While the approaches to strategy management and the attendant methods of analysis have not yet coalesced into a theory of how to manage an enterprise, they very definitely do represent a powerful way of thinking about managing. The whys and hows of strategic management illuminate the basic economics of a business, the requirements of success, and whether a firm is both doing the right things and doing things right. The window of strategy opens a whole new perspective of the enterpreneurial and administrative spectrum of managing.

It is not stretching things too far, therefore, to suggest that *the fundamentals of strategic management are a fundamental part of management and managing.* This is true, we think, at all levels of the management process and for all types of managers. All managers (and perhaps all employees!) are in a better position to contribute to organizational activities and performance when they have an accurate sense of organizational direction, their role in accomplishing the overall strategic plan, and how the plan is to be executed in their area of responsibility—in other words, when they are alert to all that is meant by strategy management and why it is important to performance and results. How to acquire the perspective of a strategic thinker and how to weigh things from an organizationwide point of view are the intended contributions of this book and of business school courses in strategic management.

The Textual Material

As with the first edition, the text portion of the book continues to stress the basic aspects of strategy management—the tasks of defining business purpose and setting strategic objectives, the strategic options for building a corporate portfolio of businesses, the specifics of formulating and implementing business strategy, evaluating business portfolios and line of business strategy, creating alignment between strategy requirements and the variables of corporate culture, and reevaluating organization direction and strategy. This edition features some significant improvements in coverage:

- The six text chapters of the first edition have been expanded to seven in this edition. Every chapter has been extensively up-dated, and new treatments have been incorporated—in line with the fast-moving pace reflected in literature.
- Core concepts and methods of strategy analysis are developed in more detail and then put into a framework for applying them in practice. The strategy-related tasks of general managers are brought into sharper focus and examined at length.
- New sections have been added on the general manager as chief entrepreneur and chief administrator, the basic strategic questions,

situation analysis, generic strategies, diagnosing the underlying economics of a business, driving forces, SWOT analysis, and techniques
for competitive advantage identification.

- Both the situation-specific aspects and the evolutionary aspects of
  strategic management are repeatedly stressed throughout. The
  analytical/rational-choice approaches to strategy are used to illustrate the potential for solid strategy analysis and situation diagnosis.
  The process/behavioral features of strategy management account for
  why and how strategy evolves and why and how implementation is
  gradual and incremental.

- Much more attention is given to the "politics of strategy" and how
  managers go about building a consensus for what strategy to follow
  and how to make it work.

- Corporate portfolio analysis is accorded chapter-length treatment.
  Featured are expanded discussions of portfolio matrices, methods of
  evaluating the make-up of a firm's business portfolio, performance-
  gap analysis, and the tactical approaches to corporate strategy
  formation.

- The approach to business-level strategy evaluation has been greatly
  expanded and is grounded in industry analysis, competition analysis,
  diagnosis of the firm's own situation, and the Boston Consulting
  Group's latest approach to competitive advantage analysis. This
  chapter is one of the highlights of this edition and contains, we think,
  an unusually thorough rundown of how to conduct an in-depth business strategy evaluation.

- Even though strategy implementation still remains the foggiest and
  least-explored aspect of strategy management, we have tried to zero
  in on the central tasks of the general manager in implementing and
  executing strategy and to discuss the key issues that arise in performing these tasks. One chapter concerns the tasks of building a strategically capable organization and focusing resources and energies on
  strategic objectives. A second chapter deals with galvanizing organizationwide commitment to the strategic plan, aligning corporate
  culture with strategy, and exerting strategic leadership.

- In discussing strategy implementation, new sections have been included on matching structure to strategy, the role of budgets and
  programs, the importance of defining jobs in terms of achieving
  strategic objectives, the McKinsey & Company 7-S framework, aligning corporate culture and strategy, the political importance of building support for strategy execution, and creating a climate for strategy
  accomplishment.

- There are more examples of what managers and companies actually
  do in formulating and implementing strategy.

- The use of in-depth illustration capsules to highlight the experiences of companies and to show the application of important topics has been expanded; the number of capsules has been increased from 16 to 25—13 are brand new.

All in all, we think you will find the text material stronger, fresher, better presented, and as close to the "state of the art" as textbook discussions can be.

The Readings

The book contains 11 readings, written by business executives, consultants, and academicians. Every reading is new to this edition and all are current—only one was published prior to 1980, and it appeared in 1979. The readings themselves are primarily of two types. One type adds in-depth treatment to important topic areas covered in the text, thereby probing further into the details of particular approaches and analytical techniques. The second type emphasizes applications and illustrations of how particular companies have used strategy management concepts and tools to good advantage. In tandem, they create a powerful pedagogy for both reinforcing and expanding the text treatment.

Other Pedagogical Features

Two additional features are continued in this revision. Appendix A is devoted to a chapter-length discussion of case method pedagogy and suggestions for approaching case analysis. In our experience, many students are unsure about what they are to do in analyzing a case and how they learn from the case method. Appendix A is intended to lessen these uncertainties by focusing the students' attention on the traditional analytical sequence of (1) identify, (2) evaluate, and (3) recommend. We have specifically included a brief review of how to calculate and interpret key financial ratios, a discussion of the nature of cases and the case method, pointers on how to learn from cases, how to prepare a case for oral class discussions, and guidelines for written case analyses. These discussions should be particularly useful for students who want assistance in crossing to the case method of teaching/learning. Moreover, this chapter in conjunction with the conceptual framework, the examples, and the illustration capsules should give readers a solid foundation for doing a good job of case analysis.

Appendix B contains a listing and brief description of some recently written cases on strategic management. They have been grouped under three headings: (1) the general manager—tasks, responsibilities, style of managing, (2) strategy formation and evaluation, and (3) strategy implementation and execution. Inspection copies of the listed cases can be ordered directly from Harvard Case Services, Soldiers Field Post Office, Boston, MA 02163.

Acknowledgments

We have benefited from the help of many people in the evolution of this book. Our intellectual debt to the writers and strategic thinkers upon whose works and experiences we have drawn is plain to anyone familiar with the literature on strategic management. We are likewise indebted to the publishers and authors of the readings for permission to reprint their articles. Students, adopters of the first edition, and reviewers have kindly offered an untold number of insightful comments and helpful suggestions for improving the manuscript.

In preparing this edition, we are particularly grateful for the patient, painstaking work of Marsha Baines, Martha Shirley, and Pat Murphy—all of whom exerted praiseworthy efforts and were instrumental in pioneering the production of the book from start to finish on word processing equipment. It truly was a learning (and fun?!) experience.

As always, we value your thoughts and recommendations about the book. Your comments regarding content and emphasis will be welcomed, as will your calling our attention to specific errors. Please write us at P.O. Box J, Department of Management and Marketing, University, AL 35486.

Arthur A. Thompson, Jr.
A.J. Strickland III

CONTENTS

---

the Intensity of Competition. Sizing Up the Different Competitive Approaches of Rival Firms. The Strategies of Key Competitors. An Assessment of the Firm's Own Present Business Situation: *The SWOT Analysis. The Pluses and Minuses in One's Own Competitive Position. How Well Is the Present Strategy Working? The Firm's Own Strategic Issues and Problems.* Sizing Up the Business Strategy Options: *Searching for the "Right" Competitive Advantage. Screening the List of Strategic Options.* The Act of Strategic Commitment.

Reading

Competitive Advantage: The Cornerstone of Strategic Thinking, *Stephen E. South,* 294

The Central Tasks of Strategy Implementation and Administration. Building a Strategically-Capable Organization: *Matching Organization Structure to Strategy. How Structure Evolves as Strategy Evolves: The Stages Model. The Strategy-Related Pros and Cons of Alternative Organization Forms. Perspectives on Matching Strategy and Structure. Building a Distinctive Competence.* Allocating and Focusing Resources on Strategic Objectives: *Allocating Resources: Budgets and Programs. Focusing Work Efforts on Strategic Objectives.*

Reading

Structure Is Not Organization, *Robert H. Waterman, Jr., Thomas J. Peters, and Julien R. Phillips,* 348

Galvanizing Organizationwide Commitment to the Strategic Plan: *Motivating the Organization to Accomplish Strategy. Measuring and Evaluating Strategic Performance. Linking the Reward Structure to Actual Strategic Performance. The Role of Strategy-Related Policies and Procedures.* Monitoring Strategic Progress. Exerting Strategic Leadership: *Creating a Climate for Strategy Accomplishment. The Politics of Strategy and Playing the Power Game. Leading the Process of Making Corrective Adjustments.* A Strategy Implementation Checklist.

Readings

Strategic Human Resource Management, *Noel M. Tichy, Charles J. Fombrun, and Mary Anne Devanna,* 399

Chief Executives Define Their Own Data Needs, *John F. Rockart,* 420

Headquarters Influence and Strategic Control in MNCs, *Yves L. Doz and C. K. Prahalad,* 442

STRATEGY FORMULATION AND IMPLEMENTATION: THE FRAMEWORK OF GENERAL MANAGEMENT

1

"Cheshire Puss," she (Alice) began ... "would you please tell me which way I ought to go from here?"
"That depends on where you want to get to," said the cat.

Lewis Carroll

To be in hell is to drift, to be in heaven is to steer.

George Bernard Shaw

W hy are some enterprises outstanding successes, while others are only modest successes and still others are dismal failures? How is it that some organizations move forward with purpose and direction while others drift? Why is it that some organizations are adept at seizing upon new opportunities while others watch passively or let them slip through the cracks? What makes an organization a winner or a loser? What distinguishes a well-managed business from a not so well-managed business? Are there any approaches to managing an organization that seem to work better than others? Although what we have learned so far in trying to gain answers to these questions falls short of a genuine theory of management, the evidence does indicate that managers have a heavy hand in whether organizations perform well or not.[1]

Some extremely important managerial insights derive from contrasting the managements of successful organizations with the managements of unsuccessful organizations:

1. The managers of successful organizations tend to establish a clear-cut direction for their organization and take a proactive stance in shaping the organization's present and future mix of activities. The managers of unsuccessful organizations are often so caught up in "putting out brush fires" and tending to paperwork and administrative detail that they neglect the tasks of assessing where the organization is now, where it ought to be headed, and what it ought to be doing and not doing.

2. In successful organizations managers take the time to formulate an astute, opportune *strategic game plan* for achieving target objectives and then they zero in on how to implement the chosen strategy and make it work as planned. The managers of unsuccessful organizations seldom have a comprehensive game plan which is being deliberately and systematically pursued.

3. The managers of successful organizations strive to gain an insightful understanding of what business they are in, who their customers are, and why buyers want or need the organization's product/service; they are "tuned-in" to market trends, customer needs, and new opportunities. In unsuccessful organizations managers are typically less perceptive about the hows and whys of "the market" for their product/service; they follow market trends rather than initiate them.

4. The managers of successful organizations are performance-conscious and results-oriented; they measure success in terms of how well their organization is performing and its ability to compete in the marketplace. In less successful organizations, management preoccupation with bottlenecks, operating problems, policies, procedures, and rou-

[1]Joel Ross and Michael Kami, *Corporate Management in Crisis: Why the Mighty Fall* (Englewood Cliffs, N.J.: Prentice-Hall, Inc., 1973); Seymour Tilles, "How to Evaluate Corporate Strategy," *Harvard Business Review*, vol. 41, no. 4 (July-August 1963), pp. 111-21; Dan Schendel, G. R. Patton, and James Riggs, "Corporate Turnaround Strategies," *Journal of General Management*, vol. 3, no. 3 (Spring 1976), pp. 3-11; H. Igor Ansoff et al, "Does Planning Pay? The Effect of Planning on Success of Acquisitions in American Firms," *Long Range Planning* (December 1970), pp. 2-7; D. M. Herold, "Long Range Planning and Organizational Performance: A Cross Validation Study," *Academy of Management Journal*, vol. 14, no. 1 (March 1971), pp. 91-102; L. W. Rue and R. M. Fulmer, "Is Long Range Planning Profitable?" *Proceedings: Academy of Management Meetings, 1973*, pp. 66-73; S. Schoeffler, R. D. Buzzell, and D. F. Heany, "Impact of Strategic Planning on Profit Performance," *Harvard Business Review*, vol. 52, no. 2 (March-April 1974), pp. 137-45; S. S. Thune and R. T. House, "Where Long Range Planning Pays Off," *Business Horizons*, vol. 13, no. 3 (August 1970), pp. 81-87; and Alfred D. Chandler, *The Visible Hand* (Cambridge, Mass.: Harvard University Press, 1977).

tine chores leads to "doing a good job" being defined in terms of problem-solving administrative skills and not causing waves that disrupt "the system."

These contrasts in mindsets and approaches are striking and revealing. The managers of successful organizations seem to be "strategic thinkers" with an appreciation for focusing externally on customers, markets, and competitive positioning as well as internally on operations. They have a talent for entrepreneurship to go along with a talent for administration. The managers of unsuccessful organizations seem to lack both strategic awareness and an eye for long-term competitive positioning; their downfall seems to be getting caught up in the exercise of administration and in the never-ending task of solving internal "problems"—at the expense of entrepreneurial effectiveness.

The success-causing power of clear direction, astute business strategy, and effective implementation of the game plan is rooted in the familiar expression "if you don't know where you are going, any road will take you there." Somebody must think about the big picture, consciously shape what an organization does, and direct where it is headed. That somebody obviously must be an organization's managers—but most especially its *general managers*.

THE GENERAL MANAGER: RESPONSIBILITIES AND FUNCTIONS

The term *general manager* refers to a manager who is accountable for the *overall* activities and performance of an organization (or line of business subunit) as opposed to a manager who is in charge of a specialized part of a business. A general manager is thus the "executive-in-charge," with authority extending over all operating phases and functions of the unit. *A general manager is both chief administrator and chief entrepreneur.* As chief administrator, a general manager has authority over organizing, staffing, supervising, and controlling daily activities. As chief entrepreneur, a general manager has responsibility for giving direction to the organization, making sure it is doing the right things at the right times, and formulating a workable strategic game plan that is capable of producing good organizational results. Because of both the administrative and entrepreneurial leadership which a general manager is called upon to exercise, it is uniquely the general manager's function to reflect upon and evaluate things in terms of their impact upon the *whole* organization and to discern what decisions and actions are best from the standpoint of the *total* enterprise.

This feature of formal authority over multiple functions and operating activities is what distinguishes a general manager from other types of managers. Other kinds of managerial jobs are usually limited to a single area of specialized activity within an enterprise—as in the case of the managers in charge of manufacturing quality or personnel training or sales or design engineering or R&D or public relations or internal auditing or shipping or purchasing. The latter are *functional* area managers with in-depth, specialized technical and managerial expertise in a narrowly defined function. Their job focus, being limited to a particular functional specialty, extends only over a *part* of what the enterprise does, whereas the scope of a general manager's job extends over many functional areas to cover either the whole enterprise or one of its line of business units.

Obviously, the term general manager includes both the chief executive officer and the chief operating officer of an organization. But general manager type jobs are by no means restricted to a few senior executives. Most large organizations place a general manager in charge of each business unit and major operating division; if the business division includes several different product lines, it is common for the division-level general manager to create subordinate positions with general management authority over each separate product line. Diversified enterprises typically have a general manager with profit center responsibility in charge of each line of business. Where corporate diversification extends over so many different businesses that it is impractical for all the business-level general managers to report to a single executive, a new level of general management may be created between the chief executive and the line-of-business level; these positions usually carry the title group vice-president and entail the group VP having general management authority over a group of three to six businesses. In the business world there are, therefore, many rather than few general management positions. General managers are found at the corporate level, the group level, the line-of-business level, the division level, and the product line level—a direct outgrowth of the trend to decentralized approaches to large-scale corporate enterprise.

The same is true in not-for-profit organizations. For example, a multi-campus state university has four identifiable levels of general management: (1) the president of the whole university system is a general manager with broad budgetary, programmatic, and coordinative authority over all the campuses; (2) the chancellor for each campus is a general manager with campuswide authority over all academic, student, athletic, and alumni matters; (3) the deans of the various colleges are general managers with authority extending over the academic programs, budgets, faculty, and students in the college; (4) the heads of the various academic departments are general managers with first-line supervisory responsibility for the departmental budget, the department's undergraduate and graduate program offerings, the faculty, and students majoring in the department. In federal and state government the heads of local, district, and regional offices function as general managers because they exercise line authority over all aspects of the activities conducted in the geographical area their units serve. In municipal government, the heads of the police department, the fire department, the water and sewer department, the parks and recreation department, the health department, and so on are general managers in the sense that they are in charge of the entire operations (budgets, personnel, facilities, services offered) under their supervision.

The key point to be grasped here is that general management jobs exist up and down the management hierarchy in almost every organization of any real size and diversity. What distinguishes a general manager from other managers is that a general manager has authority over all of the activities and operations of the "total enterprise" rather than over just a single, specialized functional activity that makes up part of the enterprise. Given the different levels of general management jobs within the management hierarchy, the nature of the "total enterprise" under a general manager's direction can be an entire corporation, a decentralized business subsidiary, a government agency, a geographic unit, a major division or department, and so on. It will simplify our exposition if such terms as "the total enterprise" or "the whole organization" or just "the organization," are understood to refer specifically to the whole of the organization unit under the general manager's direction—whether this be an entire company, a government agency, a single business division, or an entire operating facility (such as a manufacturing plant or a regional office of a federal agency). Henceforth such usage will be adopted, thereby avoiding the awkward phase "the organization or organizational subunit" (or its equivalent) to indicate the several organizational levels of general management responsibility.

The Special Importance of the General Manager's Role

A general manager is more than just a manager. The job of a general manager is special. It is unique. Why? Because a general manager, more than any other kind of manager, is in position to influence and shape what the organization is now and what it will become, what it does now and what it will do later, and how well it performs now and will be in position to perform later. As both chief entrepreneur and chief administrator, the general manager is positioned to act as the driving force of the organization, with a capability of creating change, making things happen, and otherwise causing the organization to be better positioned in its environment. How well a general manager performs the roles of chief entrepreneur and chief administrator is thus of central importance to an organization's present and future well-being—the *quality* of management at the top does indeed make a substantial difference.

The perspective and viewpoint of the general manager is likewise special. The role of the general manager is to manage the *total* enterprise. The problems and issues that crop up cover the whole spectrum of management. Many variables and situational factors have to be dealt with at once. Weighing the pros and cons of alternatives entails putting *all* of the pieces of the organizational puzzle together, dealing with *all* of the complexities and constraints of the external environment in which the organization operates, and then judging how *all* of the relevant factors add up to what is best for the organization as a whole. It means looking at things from an overall company point of view (or, in the cases of not-for-profit enterprise, from an overall organization point of view) and then trying to figure out what course of action to follow. The concern of the general manager, therefore, is more with the nature of the forest than with individual trees.

For a real-life example of what being both chief entrepreneur and chief administrator is all about and the tasks, functions, and responsibilities of a general manager, see Illustration Capsule 1 on Ted Turner's success in building Turner Broadcasting System.

ILLUSTRATION CAPSULE 1
The Bold Entrepreneurial Style of Ted Turner*

As one observer expressed it, Ted Turner is "in the great tradition of the individual entrepreneur who had a dream and backed it with his money and his sweat." Robert E. (Ted) Turner III, age 42, and president and chairman of Turner Broadcasting System, Inc., a $60 million multibusiness enterprise headquartered in Atlanta, had the distinction of having built his business almost from scratch and having executed some creative changes in the direction and make-up of his business holdings along the way.

Ted Turner was, however, not only a bold entrepreneur and businessman but also a character and public figure. His incongruous exploits include attending a state dinner at the White House; riding in an ostrich race at Atlanta Stadium, reading the Bible twice from cover to cover; permitting the screening of pornographic movies for the Atlanta Braves baseball players and their wives on a bus ride from Plains, Ga., to Atlanta; nudging a baseball around the base paths with his nose; arriving drunk at a news conference following his victory in the 1977 America's Cup race; being named "Yachtsman of the Year" four times; chewing Beechnut tobacco; and quoting and paraphrasing classical literature. In 1976, Turner was suspended from baseball for a year by Commissioner Bowie Kuhn for "conduct unbecoming to baseball." He was nicknamed by yachtsmen as "Captain Courageous" and featured as such in national ads touting Cutty Sark scotch. He was presented the 1980 "Private Enterprise Exemplar Medal" by the Freedom Foundation at Valley Forge.

*Source: Excerpted from the case study "Turner Broadcasting System" by Arthur A. Thompson and published in A. J. Strickland and Arthur A. Thompson, *Cases in Strategic Management* (Plano, Texas: Business Publications, Inc., 1982).

ILLUSTRATION CAPSULE 1 *(continued)*

Building the Company

Ted Turner, at age 24, found himself in charge of his late father's struggling outdoor advertising business that was short of cash and $6 million in debt. Bankruptcy appeared imminent. The company's bankers advised Ted that they didn't believe the business could survive under his unseasoned management and expressed reluctance at financing further operations. Turner was given an opportunity to sell out, but refused and ended up persuading the lenders to stick with him a while longer. He then sold off some assets to improve the company's cash position, arranged for some innovative financing, reworked contracts with customers, hired a sales force, and proceeded to turn things around. Within two years, the company was making its loan payments on time, and by 1969, the debt was paid off.

With Turner Advertising now secure, Turner began to look for new growth prospects. He felt that the billboard business had only limited growth potential and was not challenging enough (it took only about half of his time to run things), so he elected to diversify into something more exciting. The first acquisitions were two radio stations in Chattanooga (WGOW-AM and WYNQ-FM), a move which prompted adoption of the name Turner Communications Corporation. Turner wanted to buy a radio outlet in Atlanta but nothing attractive was available at the right price. In 1970 he settled for acquiring financially-strapped WTCG-TV, Channel 17, a two-year old independent UHF station that was losing $50,000 per month trying to compete with Atlanta's 3 network affiliates WSB-TV, WAGA-TV, and WXIA-TV. In the process of completing the acquisition of Channel 17, Turner Communications Corp. went public and its stock was traded in local over-the-counter markets; Ted Turner held about 47% of the stock.

Trying to turnaround Channel 17's operations provided Turner with some tough problems, the main one being the strategic issue of how to get Atlanta TV viewers to watch Channel 17 programs instead of the programs carried on the three major network stations. In a series of moves, Turner

- Convinced advertisers to buy time on Channel 17 because (1) their color commercials would have more shock value and catch viewer's attention given that most of Channel 17's programs (at that time) were in black and white and (2) people with UHF sets had higher incomes on average.

- Strengthened Channel 17's signal.

- Offered Atlanta viewers an alternative to the typical network programming by showing lots of old movies and reruns of such popular shows as *I Love Lucy, Gilligan's Island, Leave It to Beaver, Petticoat Junction, Gomer Pyle,* and *Andy Griffith; Star Trek* was positioned to show at 6:00 p.m. against the news programs of the local network affiliates.

- Seized the opportunity to air five NBC network shows which WSB-TV, Atlanta's number-one station and local NBC affiliate, elected not to show;

ILLUSTRATION CAPSULE 1 *(continued)*

Turner's outdoor advertising company then quickly put up billboards announcing "the NBC network moves to Channel 17" with a listing of the five shows.

- Stole a second march on WSB-TV, shortly thereafter, by acquiring rights to televise the Atlanta Braves major league baseball games. (At the time, the Braves were paying WSB-TV to telecast 25 games a year; Turner offered $2.5 million for the rights to games for five years. The Braves games were the top-rated locally-produced program in the Atlanta market.)

Atlanta-area residents were attracted by Channel 17's new style of sports-movies-reruns; with viewers and advertising revenues picking up steadily, Atlanta went from a three-station market plus Channel 17 to a four-station market. Then in 1975, when the Federal Communications Commission lifted its ban forbidding cable-TV operators from bringing in signals from distant TV stations over that of a local independent station and RCA launched its first communication satellite into orbit, Turner moved swiftly to transform Channel 17 into a "SuperStation" with nationwide geographic coverage. He joined the cable operators association and got to know the operators personally, and he initiated transmission of Channel 17 (now WTBS-TV) on the RCA satellite network. The number of full-time cable-TV subscribers receiving the WTBS signal soared from 462,000 in 1976 to over 9,000,000 in 1981; forecasts called for growth of about 3 million new households per year during the 1981-1985 period. A Nielsen survey in March 1981 showed a one-week cumulative audience of 9,800,000 persons, making WTBS the most viewed TV station in the U.S.

While Channel 17 was still in the red, Turner acquired (at a bankruptcy sale) a second UHF station, WRET-TV in Charlotte, N.C. It was purchased with Turner's personal funds because the directors of Turner Communications were not willing to risk corporate funds on the deal, given Channel 17's still unprofitable status and the high risk of being able to make a success of WRET-TV's situation. To help turn around the Charlotte station, Turner himself conducted a series of televised "Beg-a-thons" asking Charlotte viewers for financial support; over 36,000 contributions were received, ranging from 25 cents to $80. Turner collected a total of $25,000 and used the proceeds to help finance the same movie-sports-rerun programming emphasis that he had pioneered in Atlanta. By 1975 the Charlotte station was breaking even and Turner sold a controlling interest in the station to Turner Communications. Subsequently, WRET-TV became an affiliate of the NBC network.

In 1975, the billboard advertising operations were spun off from Turner Communications and made a separate company, Turner Advertising, with Ted Turner as majority stockholder. Turner Advertising succeeded in becoming the largest billboard firm in the Atlanta and Chattanooga markets; the remaining branches were sold. Meanwhile, Turner Communication began repurchasing its stock on the open market and reduced the number of

ILLUSTRATION CAPSULE 1 *(continued)*

shares outstanding from 1.65 million in 1970 to 980,000 in 1976; the reduction increased Ted Turner's ownership percentage to about 85% of the shares outstanding.

Turner's 1972 bid to televise the Atlanta Braves baseball games on Channel 17 not only was the first step in the company's major sports involvement but it also established a business relationship with the Braves owners, Chicago-based Atlanta LaSalle Corporation. In 1975 Atlanta LaSalle's management approached Ted Turner about buying the Braves club. Turner moved quickly and in January 1976 Turner Communications acquired the Braves through a newly-formed, wholly-owned subsidiary, Atlanta National League Baseball Club (ANLBC); the purchase price was $9.65 million, to be paid over 12 years at 6% interest.

In 1977, the Company acquired, through Atlanta Hawks, Inc., a 95% limited partnership interest in Hawks, Ltd., owner of the Atlanta Hawks professional basketball team which competed in the National Basketball Association. Live telecasts of the Braves' and Hawks' games became feature attractions on Turner's Channel 17 (which, naturally, had the telecasting rights). In 1978, Turner Communications acquired a limited partnership interest in Soccer, Ltd., the owner of the Atlanta Chiefs professional soccer team. Also in 1978, the company sold its AM and FM radio stations in Chattanooga for $1,050,000 cash, realizing a pre-tax gain of $395,000.

Three important developments occurred in 1979. The company launched plans for the Cable News Network (CNN), the first 24-hour all news programming network for cable television operators, to begin operations in June 1980; by the end of 1979 the Company had invested $6,816,000 in the news network venture, acquired and begun renovations of a headquarters facility, hired key personnel, and obtained purchase commitments to provide the programming. The second development was to change the name of Turner Communications Corporation to Turner Broadcasting System, Inc. The third involved an agreement to sell WRET-TV in Charlotte to Westinghouse for $20,000,000 cash plus the assumption by Westinghouse of the station's obligations for film programs; the proceeds were used to help finance CNN's costly startup.

In 1981, the business of Turner Broadcasting System (TBS) consisted of (1) the operations of WTBS-TV, whose signal was transmitted by an independent common carrier to cable television systems throughout the United States, (2) the Cable News Network (CNN), a 24-hour comprehensive news channel available to U.S. cable television systems, (3) 100 percent ownership of the Atlanta Braves professional major league baseball team, (4) equity interests in limited partnerships operating the Atlanta Hawks professional NBA basketball team and the Atlanta Chiefs professional soccer team, and (5) a management service contract (including all personnel) to operate Turner's outdoor advertising business, with operations based in Atlanta and Chattanooga, Tennessee.

ILLUSTRATION CAPSULE 1 *(continued)*

Ted Turner's Style of Managing

Ted Turner's approach to business and to dealing with people was both colorful and controversial. He was frequently interviewed by the media and seldom hesitated to say exactly what he thought. This, of course, delighted reporters and when they printed his quotes a swirl of discussion often ensued. During the 1981 baseball strike, it was rumored and reported in the *Atlanta Constitution* that Turner, at one of the owners' meetings to discuss the strike situation, remarked that all the players should be drowned and the teams restaffed from scratch. Over the years, writers and journalists appended Turner with such labels as Captain Outrageous, Terrible Ted, the Mouth of the South, honest, petulant, loud, profane, impulsive, egotistical, flambuoyant, ruthless, money-grubbing, sincere, and chauvinistic.

Turner was highly motivated, energetic, and willing to do what it took to achieve his goals. He told one interviewer, "I have such a distaste for people who can't roll up their sleeves and get the job done . . . My father always said to never set goals you can reach in your lifetime. After you accomplished them, there would be nothing left."[1] He valued and appreciated money—"Life is a game, but the way to keep score is money."[2] And he sought out success—"I've always been encouraged since I was a little kid to be a top competitor, and to be a worker, not a shirker."[3] Turner was known for being candid and honest with everyone. Honor, truth, and sincerity were his bywords.

Close associates described Turner as having a strong sense of what to do and when to do it. As one of his vice-presidents expressed it, "He's a good concept man. He's got a good eye for where profitable growth lies, where growth potential is. He has ability to put things together that make sense."[4]

Complementing Turner's sense of direction and sense of timing was a knack for picking capable managers to work under him. He delegated authority readily. Administrative matters and day-to-day operating details were left to his vice-presidents and lower-echelon managers. He did not, as a general rule, supervise them closely, preferring instead to let them do their jobs with a minimum of interference as long as things seemed to be progressing satisfactorily. The executives under Turner were regarded as devoted to him and seemed motivated by his leadership. A friend and sailing partner observed, "He is always winning, never losing and he gives that same feeling to people sailing or working with him."

Turner's approach was to throw 100 percent of his energies into a project until he felt he could go on to something else. He got bored sitting still doing

[1] As quoted in Curry Kirkpatrick, "Going Real Strawwng," *Sports Illustrated*, October 14, 1977, p. 78.
[2] Ibid., p. 75.
[3] As quoted in Bruce Galphin, "Other Things to Do," *Atlanta*, Spring 1978, p. 40.
[4] As quoted in Wayne Minshew and DeWitt Rogers, "A Winner," *Atlanta Constitution*, January 8, 1977.

ILLUSTRATION CAPSULE 1 *(concluded)*

the same things over and over and handling routine matters. As one writer described it:

> When he approaches a project, he demonstrates great powers of positive thinking and an even greater innocence. ("It can't be done? Let's find out.") If things aren't going particularly well, Turner is capable of short temper tantrums and brief flurries of petulance. When a project bores him, Turner is quick to turn his back on it and move to something fresh, leaving to his corporate subalterns the job of seeing the project through— as well as the task of pouring oil on the inevitable troubled waters he has left in his wake.[5]

By Turner's own admission, the thing that turned him on was trying to win, the playing of the game, the competition, the matching of wits. He liked to turn losers into winners, in sports and in business. The general manager of WTBS-TV described his perception of Turner:

> He has a tremendous desire to win. He doesn't like to lose. If he does he is one of the few people I know who benefits from the loss. He asks himself, "why did I lose?" I don't know why he has to win so. It's a compulsion with him.
>
> One of my responsibilities is, if I know he is doing something wrong, try and stop him. But did you ever try and stop a speeding train?
>
> If he wants something he is going to get it. The problem is, he will pay more than it's worth. And the other guy knows it.[6]

However, Turner did not look at himself as a "win at all costs" practitioner:

> I don't think winning is everything. It's a big mistake when you say that. I think *trying* to win is what counts. Be kind and fair, and make the world a better place to live, that's what's important. . . . I think the saddest people I've ever met were people with a lot of wealth. If you polled 90 percent of the people and asked them what they want most, most would want to be millionaires. I'll tell you, you've got to be one to know how unimportant it is.
>
> I'm blessed with some talents. I've made a lot of money, more than I ever thought I would . . . But if I continue to be successful, I would like to serve my fellow man in some way other than doing flips at third base.
>
> . . . People want leadership, somebody to rally around, and I want to be a leader.[7]

[5]As quoted in Kim Chapin, "The Man Who Makes Waves," *United Mainliner*, May 1980, p. 85.
[6]As quoted in Minshew and Rogers, "A Winner."
[7]Ibid.

THE TASKS OF STRATEGY FORMULATION AND STRATEGY IMPLEMENTATION

If one were to record the activities and functions which make up a typical day or week in the job of being a general manager, the resulting picture would be one of *variety, fragmentation,* and *brevity.* Studies of "what general managers actually do" indicate that during the course of their schedules they (1) deal with many different people and events each day; (2) play a variety of different roles; (3) spend only a few minutes (rarely more than half an hour) on any one activity at any one time; and (4) rarely conclude final action on a matter at one sitting. Professor Mintzberg in his landmark study described the general manager's job in terms of ten functional roles:[2]

Three Interpersonal Roles

- **Figurehead role**—representing the organization on ceremonial occasions.

- **Liaison role**—interacting with other managers and groups outside the organization unit.

- **Leader role**—establishing relationships with subordinates (motivating, supervising) and exercising formal authority within the organizational unit.

Three Informational Roles

- **Monitor role**—receiving and collecting information from both inside and outside the organizational unit.

- **Disseminator role**—transmitting information to members within the organization unit.

- **Spokesman role**—informing those outside the organization unit.

Four Decision-Related Roles

- **Innovator role**—initiating change.

- **Resource allocation role**—deciding where efforts and energies will be directed.

- **Negotiator role**—dealing with situations involving negotiations on behalf of the organization.

---

[2]Henry Mintzberg, *The Nature of Managerial Work* (Englewood Cliffs, N.J.: Prentice-Hall, Inc., 1980), Chapter 4.

- **Disturbance handler role**—taking charge when crises arise and the organization is threatened.

Mintzberg's study, along with other researchers' studies of what managers do, is valuable in categorizing general management activities and in correctly conveying the diverse, broad-ranging makeup of the general manager's job. But it is not particularly helpful in gaining a perspective view and command over the myriad of tasks and roles which "come with the territory" of being a general manager. A descriptive listing of all the things a general manager does fails to clarify which tasks are more important and which are less important and why. Nor is it of much help in establishing a framework and guide by which to manage the total enterprise.

What sense, if any, can be made out of all the different activities and tasks that a general manager performs? How does the performer of ten roles avoid the "activity trap" and get a good grip on what to concentrate on and why? What are the main priorities beyond degree of urgency? What really must be accomplished? How can one judge whether a general manager is doing a good job or not? Before reading on, take the test in Illustration Capsule 2.

ILLUSTRATION CAPSULE 2
Ted Turner and Managing the Total Enterprise: A Short Exercise on What General Management Is and Is Not*

> While the job of managing the total enterprise does indeed involve a heavy and varied menu of activities, some things a general manager does are more important to the health and well-being of the organization than are others. Being a general manager is a distinct kind of work—not better, not superior, but distinct.
>
> To understand how and why general management is distinct and to be able to discern the difference between *general* management and other kinds of management, read/reread Illustration Capsule 1 and then do the exercise below.
>
> *Exercise*
>
> In building Turner Broadcasting System from a regional outdoor advertising firm into a multi-business enterprise approaching national TV network status, Ted Turner has undoubtedly had a busy schedule. Was Ted Turner performing the tasks of a general manager when he:
>
> *The content of this Capsule is inspired by and adapted from material in Steven C. Brandt, *Strategic Planning in Emerging Companies*(Reading, Mass.: Addison-Wesley Publishing Co., 1981), Chapter 11.

ILLUSTRATION CAPSULE 2 *(continued)*

		Yes	No
1.	Spent an afternoon with the president of the largest cable-TV company in the U. S., a company which offered both WTBS and the Cable News Network to its 2,000,000-plus subscribers?	___	___
2.	Visited with the senior loan officer of the New York bank where TBS was negotiating a major loan to finance the startup of CNN?	___	___
3.	Solved the knotty programming problem of finding something to replace the telecasts of the Atlanta Braves baseball games on WTBS-TV during the major league baseball strike in 1981?	___	___
4.	Discussed with a sporting goods salesman the colors and fabrics for new uniforms for the Atlanta Hawks professional basketball team?	___	___
5.	Gave a speech to the Atlanta Chamber of Commerce concerning the contribution of professional sports teams to the local economy?	___	___
6.	Went to the Omni in Atlanta to watch the Atlanta Hawks play the Boston Celtics?	___	___
7.	Flew to New York to try to recruit former New York Yankees' free agent Reggie Jackson to play baseball for the Atlanta Braves?	___	___
8.	Held a staff meeting with the TBS financial officers and CNN managers to discuss when CNN would reach breakeven and stop needing cash infusions?	___	___
9.	Interviewed several candidates to become the new general manager of WTBS-TV, and made an offer to one of them?	___	___
10.	Accompanied the recently promoted Vice-President for Advertising at WTBS-TV to a convention of the top advertising executives of the largest U.S. corporations in order to introduce the VP to some of the people whose companies were big advertisers on WTBS-TV?	___	___

To help you decide on your answers to the above questions, think about the following:

1. Was Ted Turner "managing" during that afternoon with the largest cable-TV operator or was he "selling?" Is selling a part of a general manager's job of managing the *total* enterprise?

2. Was Ted Turner managing when he visited with the loan officer of the New York bank or was he doing the work of a chief financial officer? Is attending to loan arrangements part of a general manager's job?

ILLUSTRATION CAPSULE 2 *(concluded)*

3. Was Ted Turner managing when he had the idea of how to fill the vacant programming slot created by the major league baseball strike or was he doing the work of a programming executive?

4. Was Ted Turner doing the work of an owner/general manager when he watched the Hawks play basketball?

5. What is the difference between "doing" (working to achieve a result by oneself) and "managing" (achieving planned results *through* others)?

Now, do the exercise (again?) and, when you have finished, read the next section.

Understanding the Job of the General Manager: An Analogy

In a very real sense, the job of a general manager in managing the total enterprise is much like that of a football coach. A football coach has ultimate responsibility for the team's performance and win-loss record but cannot function as a player; to get the team to perform, a coach organizes, staffs, motivates, plans, directs, evaluates, confers with the team, and, in general, *works through others* to achieve results.

Admittedly, a general manager cannot and probably should not spend full time managing *through* people and "coaching" the organization. The job of being a general manager is that of both coach and player—both managing through people and achieving results by oneself. Ted Turner probably did need to visit with the president of the largest cable-TV company and sell. He probably did need to be closely involved in the loan negotiation with the New York bank and he probably did need to be personally involved in trying to negotiate a contract to sign star player Reggie Jackson to play for the Atlanta Braves. Clearly, occasions arise when a general manager, by taking a leading-active-doing role, can make a special contribution to organization performance. In football parlance, a general manager may have to assume the role of a scrambling quarterback who, when faced with a broken play, twists and turns upfield for a first down that keeps a potential touchdown drive alive. But the general manager is not *managing* in this role.

The issue between playing and coaching, or doing and managing, is one of mix and balance. As a rule, the larger and more diversified is the organization being managed, the greater is the proportion of time spent on *managing* (achieving organizational results through the activities of others) rather than *doing* (achieving organizational results through one's own personal actions).

The Three Basic Strategic Questions

The approach we shall take here is to view *the general manager* as an organization's *chief entrepreneur* and *chief administrator,* with primary responsibility and authority for formulating and executing the organization's strategic plan. If the general manager happens to be the president or chief executive officer of an organization, then the strategic plan in question encompasses the *whole* organization. If the general manager is the head of an organizational subunit (line of business, division, product line, plant), then the strategic plan embraces only the general manager's organizational subunit.

The *strategic plan* of an organization or organizational subunit is a composite, systematic blueprint of management's answers to the three basic strategic questions facing any enterprise:

1. *What* will we sell and *to whom* will we sell it?

    (*Note*: A thoughtful answer to this question defines the organization's purpose and mission and decides the issue of "what is our business, what will it be, and what should it be?")

2. What *objectives* do we want to achieve?

    (*Note*: The setting of objectives reveals what priorities are to be observed, what kind of performance is expected, and what results are to be accomplished through the organization's chosen activities.)

3. *How* are we going to manage the organization's activities so as to achieve the chosen objectives?

    (*Note*: A comprehensive answer to this question indicates the *strategy* of how the organization will be positioned in its overall environment and what "the game plan" is for approaching markets, competing against rivals, and otherwise operating the organization in a successful manner.)

Taken together, the answers to these three strategic questions set forth what an organization intends to do and to accomplish. They define a strategic plan for managerial action. The answer to "what will we sell and to whom will we sell it" delineates an organization's service mission to customers, its purpose for being, and the scope and make-up of the organization's portfolio of activities and interests. By setting objectives management establishes the organization's priorities and its commitment to specific results, thus guarding against drift and aimless actions. The third question addresses the issue of precisely *how* the desired results are to be accomplished; *strategy is management's "game plan" for positioning the organization in its overall environment and for managing its portfolio of activities*. Strategy serves as a guideline for what entrepreneurial and competitive approaches will be taken and as a roadmap for getting the organization where it wants to go and achieving what it wants to become.

Managing the Strategic Plan

The job of managing an organization's strategic plan has two distinct elements:

1. The task of formulating the strategic plan (and reformulating it when-
    ever circumstances dictate).
2. Implementing and executing the strategic plan.

Strategy Formulation and Entrepreneurship.   The managerial task of
formulating a strategic plan for an organization is primarily *entrepreneurial*
in character and focus. The essence of strategy formulation is an entrepreneurial size-up of whether an organization is *doing the right things* and how
it can be *more effective in what it does*. As chief entrepreneur, the general
manager has to strive to move the enterprise in the right direction at the
right time, to set the right priorities, and to fund their pursuit. The basic
entrepreneurial tasks are (1) to *position* the organization so that it can enjoy
superior performance and (2) to keep the organization responsive to
change and capable of further growth and success. This specifically means
devoting managerial time and attention to such key entrepreneurial concerns as identifying opportunities to enter new markets, developing new
and improved products and services, figuring out better ways to meet
customer needs and wants, evaluating how to meet emerging environmental or competitive threats, deciding upon when and how to diversify, and,
ultimately, choosing which businesses to get out of, which to continue with,
and which new ones to enter. Of equal importance is an entrepreneurial
alertness for internal opportunities to redirect resources away from areas of
low or diminishing results toward areas of high or increasing results. The
managerial posture in strategy formulation thus combines an internal scrutiny of "how can we do better what we're already doing?" with an external
alertness to "what sorts of *new* or *different* activities should we undertake?" The hoped-for outcome is to come up with insightful, timely, and
creative ways to strengthen the organization's mix of activities and to
improve performance in each of the activities it undertakes.

Strategy Implementation and Administration.   The second piece of
the general manager's job—that of implementing and executing the strategic plan—has a sharply different flavor and is essentially *administrative*
in character. Putting the strategy into place and building an organization
which is capable of executing the chosen strategy entails all the usual kinds
of administrative activities: structuring and organizing the necessary daily
activities, devising policies and procedures and monitoring how well they
smooth the flow of operations, dealing with a wide assortment of "people
problems," making sure that schedules are set and timetables met, enhancing employee morale and productivity, initiating corrective action when
actual performance does not measure up to expectation and so on *ad
infinitum*. Virtually all of the administrative activities and tasks implied
and hinted at in Mintzberg's ten roles cited above are involved in implementing and administering the strategic plan. It helps establish perspective, however, to view the *administrative* tasks a general manager must
perform as falling under the umbrella of managing pursuit of the strategic

plan. The ultimate administrative aim must be to see that (1) the chosen strategy works as well as circumstances allow and (2) the strategic plan is implemented and executed in ways which achieve internal efficiency, a smooth flow of operations, and in general, the condition of *doing things right*.

Entrepreneurship versus Administration.   What is the more crucial determinant of organization success: good entrepreneurship (strategy formulation) or good administration (strategy implementation)? This is a relevant question because it helps establish a perspective view about the relative importance and contribution of the many roles and facets of the general manager's job.

As a general rule, the entrepreneurial task of strategy formulation is more crucial to organization performance than is the administrative task of strategy implementation.[3] The reason is powerful and simple: *An organization simply cannot be successful or outstanding or a winner if it is doing the wrong things—irrespective of how efficient and well-administered it may be*. An extreme example illustrates the point. A firm might well be the world's most efficient and best-managed producer of coated paper for copying equipment, but in the absence of much demand for coated paper (now that the majority of copiers use plain paper) there is no way for efficient operations and competent administration alone to produce spectacular growth and profitability. Consequently, even the most efficiently administered organization is unlikely to succeed for long when its efficiency is attached to doing the wrong things; the most that superior administrative efficiency and competence can do is to delay a decline in performance. *It takes entrepreneurial effectiveness and a strategy predicated on doing the right things at the right time to keep an organization positioned to achieve superior performance over the long-term*. Or, to put it a bit differently, the foundations of organizational success rest *first* on an entrepreneurially astute strategy keyed to doing the right things; once an organization is entrepreneurially positioned, the *second* general management priority is administrative efficiency in executing the strategic plan and a concern for doing things right.

It follows, then, that two things lie at the root of what separates truly successful organizations from not-as-successful enterprises:

1.   Superior entrepreneurship (a shrewd, well-formulated strategic plan that positions the organization in its environment in the right way at the right time).
2.   Competent implementation and execution of the strategic plan.

---

[3]Peter F. Drucker, *Management: Tasks, Responsibilities, Practices* (New York: Harper and Row Publishers, 1974), pp. 45-48; Chester I. Barnard, *The Functions of the Executive* (Cambridge, Mass: Harvard University Press, 1938), pp. 26-32, 55-61.

It takes both to produce superior performance. A great strategic game plan which is subsequently marred and flawed with poor execution reduces performance. Likewise, a subpar strategic plan which is flawlessly executed doesn't qualify for a gold star award either. The optimal condition is plainly superior entrepreneurship and strategy formulation combined with superb strategy implementation and execution. Such are the standards for judging the performance of a general manager. The chances are excellent that when these standards are met, or nearly so, the organization will be a high performer—a winner. This is management!

Now, having set the stage with these introductory remarks, let's probe the central tasks of strategy formulation and implementation more deeply.

THE JOB OF THE GENERAL MANAGER: STRATEGY FORMULATION AND ENTREPRENEURSHIP

As chief entrepreneur, the general manager necessarily presides over and has a heavy hand in all direction-setting decisions for the organization or organizational unit. There are three key components that comprise the process of giving direction and performing the entrepreneurial function:

1. Defining the organization's purpose and mission.
2. Establishing objectives.
3. Formulating a strategy to achieve the objectives.

All three not only have important roles in shaping the organizational outcome of success or failure but they are also basic to creating a comprehensive strategic plan for the organization, as shown in Figure 1-1.

Defining Organization Purpose and Mission: The First Step in Setting Direction

The starting point in formulating strategy is to develop a concept of what the organization's scope and make-up will be, now and in the future. The fundamental questions are: Who are we and what will we do? What activities should we engage in? What products or services do we want to provide? In what kinds of markets and technologies do we want to be involved? Who should our customers be and why should they buy *our* products and/or services? What, if anything, will we do that is distinctive or better or otherwise different from other organizations? The essence of these questions is to establish "what is our business, what will it be, and what should it be." The choices thus made are central to the molding of an organization's identity and character and make-up.

As we shall use the term, an organization's *purpose* and *mission* refers to management's concept of what the organization seeks to do and the

FIGURE 1-1
Setting Organization Direction and Performing the Entrepreneurial Function

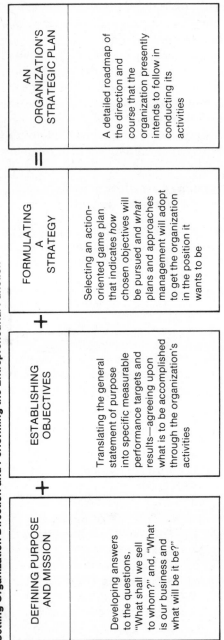

DEFINING PURPOSE AND MISSION		ESTABLISHING OBJECTIVES		FORMULATING A STRATEGY		AN ORGANIZATION'S STRATEGIC PLAN
Developing answers to the questions, "What shall we sell to whom?" and, "What is our business and what will be it be?"	+	Translating the general statement of purpose into specific measurable performance targets and results—agreeing upon what is to be accomplished through the organization's activities	+	Selecting an action-oriented game plan that indicates *how* chosen objectives will be pursued and *what* plans and approaches management will adopt to get the organization in the position it wants to be	=	A detailed roadmap of the direction and course that the organization presently intends to follow in conducting its activities

markets and customers it intends to serve. Expressing organization purpose and mission *in managerially meaningful terms* provides a view of what activities the organization as a whole intends to pursue now and in the future. It says something about what kind of organization it is now and is to become and, by omission, what it is not to do and not to become.[4] It depicts an organization's character, image, and scope of activities in ways that are detailed enough to distinguish the organization from other types of organizations. In short, it defines the business of the organization.

Presented below are examples of how several prominent companies have expressed their purpose and mission:

Standard Oil of Ohio.   The Standard Oil Company is an integrated domestic petroleum company engaged in all phases of the petroleum business including the production of crude oil and natural gas and the transportation, refining and marketing of crude oil and petroleum products. Through its ownership of oil and gas leases at Prudhoe Bay on the North Slope of Alaska and the development of the Prudhoe Bay oil reserves, the Company is the largest holder of domestic proved crude oil reserves and it is one of the leading producers of domestic crude oil. In addition, the Company is engaged in the mining and marketing of coal and uranium and the manufacture and marketing of chemical and plastic products.

Polaroid.   Polaroid manufactures and sells photographic products based on inventions of the Company in the field of one-step instant photography and light polarizing products, utilizing the Company's inventions in the field of polarized light. The Company considers itself to be engaged in one line of business.

General Portland Cement Co., Inc.   It's long been a business philosophy of General Portland that "we manufacture and sell cement, but we market concrete." Our job, as we see it, is to manufacture top quality cement and to work with our customers to develop new applications for concrete while expanding current uses.

General Motors.   General Motors is a highly integrated business engaged primarily in the manufacture, assembly and sale of automobiles, trucks and related parts and accessories classified as automotive products. Substantially all of General Motors' products are marketed through retail dealers and through distributors and jobbers in the United States and Canada and through distributors and dealers overseas. To assist in the merchandising of General Motors products, General Motors Acceptance Corporation and its subsidiaries offer financial services and certain types of automobile insurance to dealers and customers.

Fuqua Industries.   Fuqua Industries . . . is a multi-market manufacturing, distribution and service company with businesses in the areas of Recre-

---

[4]C. Roland Christensen, Kenneth R. Andrews, and Joseph L. Bower, *Business Policy: Text and Cases*, Fourth Edition (Homewood, Illinois: Richard D. Irwin, Inc., 1978), p. 125. For a more extended discussion see Kenneth R. Andrews, *The Concept of Corporate Strategy*, Revised Edition (Homewood, Illinois: Richard D. Irwin, Inc., 1980), Chapters 1 and 2.

ational Products and Services, Farm and Home Products, Transportation, Petroleum Distribution and Other Operations.

In each of these market areas, Fuqua prides itself upon providing high quality products and services. Recreational Products and Services include photofinishing, entertainment and sporting goods. The Farm and Home Products segment covers lawn and garden equipment, shelter products and retail farm, home and auto stores. Interstate Motor Freight System and the Direct System comprise Fuqua's Transportation group. In the area of Petroleum Distribution, Fuqua is a wholesale distributor of refined petroleum products. Fuqua's Other Operations include Industrial Services and Food products . . .

Fuqua Industries has grown by acquiring well-managed businesses and providing them with the financial resources and management support for internal expansion. Although widely diversified, Fuqua's companies generally have a high market share and low capital intensity.

Tandy Corporation.   Tandy Corporation is engaged in consumer electronics retailing and manufacturing with more than 6,500 Radio Shack retail outlets in all 50 United States and Canada. The Company also conducts retail operations in England, Belgium, Holland, West Germany, France, Australia and Japan through approximately 650 outlets under the Tandy name. The average Radio Shack store is slightly over 2,100 square feet and stocks more than 2,400 different items. Radio Shack stores carry a multitude of electronic products including antennas, radios, receivers, magnetic tape, speakers, turntables, public address systems, intercoms, calculators, electronic and scientific toys, games and kits, citizens band radios, scanners and electronic parts. The TRS-80 ™ Microcomputer System introduced in August 1977 is the most successful product category innovation in Radio Shack's history.

Cummins Engine Company.   Cummins Engine Company manufactures and sells a diversified line of in-line and V-type heavy-duty diesel engines, components and replacement parts in worldwide markets. Substantially all of the company's sales are attributed to engines, parts and related products. The company's principal market is the U.S. on-highway truck industry, with every major U.S. truck manufacturer offering Cummins engines as standard or optional equipment.

Cummins also manufactures and markets crankshafts, turbochargers and related components for diesel engines and industrial equipment; oil, fuel, air and water filters for truck and passenger car engines; and reconditioned diesel engines and parts.

The Importance of a Clear Purpose.   Observe that these statements of "who are we and what do we do" are both broad and narrow. They are broad in the sense of cutting across several distinct types of products, customers, and markets to be served, but they are narrow in the sense of delimiting the nature and character of the organization's business interests. This is as it should be. It serves no useful function for an organization's purpose to be so narrowly conceived that it confines the enterprise's growth and development or else restricts its adaptation to changing market and economic conditions.[5] On the other hand, there is little to be gained from management's conceiving organization purpose and mission in such broad and ambiguous language as to obscure what the firm's central character and range of operations really is and is going to be. An umbrella-like statement that "our purpose is to serve the food needs of the nation" can mean anything from growing wheat to operating a vegetable cannery to delivering milk to manufacturing farm machinery to running a Kentucky Fried Chicken franchise. A sweeping statement of purpose may occasionally have public relations value, but it is certainly *too broad to guide management action*. It does not establish direction nor does it narrow down and focus management attention on what the firm is actually trying to do. It offers no guidance to the firm's managers in developing sharply-focused, results-oriented objectives, strategies, and policies—and this is where the real value of a carefully reasoned purpose comes into play.

A clear understanding of "what is our business and what will it be" is the necessary first step in setting a direction for the organization and in avoiding the trap of trying to march in all directions at once and its counterpart, the trap of being so confused that one does not know when or where to march at all. Or, to put it another way, managing and deliberately shaping an organization's future wisely begins with clarity of organization purpose—with an in-depth understanding of the central character of the organization, where it is now and where it is headed, and what it should and should not be doing and for whom.

The Focus of Purpose Is External.   Notice also that the focus of organization purpose is external rather than internal. While it is tempting to view the purpose of a business firm as one of "making a profit," this typifies all profit-seeking enterprises and thus distinguishes none.[6] Profit is best viewed as a *result* of doing something; to look upon business purpose as "making a profit" poses the immediate question of "what will we *do* to make a profit?" It is the answer to "make a profit doing what and for whom?" that identifies and defines business purpose. Ultimately, therefore, the definition of business purpose is always grounded in "what shall we sell and to whom will we sell it?"

Defining purpose in terms of markets and customers to be served and, even more fundamentally, in terms of the wants or needs customers satisfy when they utilize the organization's product or service is a step forward.

---

[5]Of course, any "danger" of an organization "locking itself in" with an overly narrow concept of purpose is contrived rather than real. Organization purpose is always subject to revision and is not something "carved in stone." Many, if not most, organizations fundamentally change the scope of their activities (and hence their purpose) from time to time. This is particularly true of firms which, for one reason or another, diversify into activities well outside their original business (as when a cigarette manufacturing company diversifies into brewing beer).

[6]Philip Kotler, *Marketing Management: Analysis, Planning, Control* (Englewood Cliffs, N.J.: Prentice-Hall, Inc., 1976), p. 52.

This is more than incidental. Peter Drucker, in *Management: Tasks, Responsibilities, Practices*, maintains:

> To know what a business is we have to start with its *purpose*. Its purpose must lie outside of the business itself. In fact, it must lie in society since business enterprise is an organ of society. There is only one valid definition of business purpose: *to create a customer.*[7]

Drucker's insightful point about purpose is that unless an organization can develop a sufficiently large clientele for its product/service, it is destined to wither and die. The customer is the foundation of an organization and keeps it in existence.[8] What would happen to General Motors if no one bought GM cars? What would happen to a university if there were no students? What would happen to a church if no one wanted to be a member? This alone is reason enough to define the purpose of an enterprise in terms of the clientele to be served and the customer wants and needs to be satisfied. To do otherwise is to risk not having a perceptive answer to "what is our business?"

Establishing Objectives: The Second Step in Setting Direction

Objectives are the specific results which management seeks to achieve in pursuing the organization's purpose and mission.[9] Ideally, organizational objectives should relate (1) *externally* to the desired impact upon the organi-

---

[7](New York: Harper and Row Publishers, 1974), p. 61.

[8]Ibid. Moreover, according to Drucker, every organization, profit-seeking or not-for-profit, has an implied contract with society that calls not only for the organization's purpose to be ratified by its customers but also for the organization's activities to be consistent with the expectations of society at large. Society has, after all, entrusted a portion of its pool of scarce, productive resources to the organization and thus has a right to expect they not be misused. For this reason, failure to act in socially responsible ways or to perform socially useful functions quite properly tends to trigger serious societal scrutiny of an organization's activities and, usually, a reevaluation by the organization of its purpose and behavior.

[9]The literature of management is filled with references to *goals* and *objectives*. These terms are used in a variety of ways, many of them conflicting. Some writers use the term goals to refer to the *long-run* results which an organization seeks to achieve and use the term objectives to refer to immediate, *short-run* performance targets. Other writers reverse the usage, referring to objectives as the desired long-run results and goals as the desired short-run results. Still other writers use the terms interchangeably, as synonyms. And still others use the term goals to refer to *general* organizationwide performance targets and the term objectives to mean the specific targets set by subordinate managers in response to the broader, more inclusive goals of the whole organization. In our view, the semantical confusion over the usage of the terms goals and objectives is secondary; the important thing is to recognize that the results a firm seeks to attain vary both in scope and in time perspective. In nearly every instance, those organizations which are results-oriented will tend to establish a hierarchy of both long-range and short-range performance targets. Practically speaking, it makes no difference what labels one attaches to these targets. Thus we have deliberately chosen to use the single term *objectives* to refer to the performance targets and results which an organization seeks to attain. We will use the adjectives long-range (or long-run) and short-range (or short-run) to identify the relevant time frame and we will endeavor to describe objectives in such a way as to indicate their intended scope and level in the organization.

zation's customers in terms of satisfaction, product performance, and meeting individual and societal wants and needs and (2) *internally* to the desired organizational performance and results—i.e., market share, growth, profitability, cash flow, return on investment, and so on. By delineating the specific results which are to be achieved, objectives become the second step in setting a direction for the organization.

This second direction-setting step is essential. Unless and until the direction an organization is headed is converted into *specific* targets and *specific* commitments, there is great risk that organization purpose will remain a statement of good intentions and unrealized achievement. Setting objectives reduces this risk in managerially useful ways. When the desired results are made concrete and measurable, it is more likely that (1) resources can and will be allocated to their attainment, (2) priorities can be agreed upon and deadlines set, and (3) responsibility can be assigned and somebody held accountable for producing the desired results. *The hard knocks of experience tell a powerful story about the use of objectives: managements that establish objectives for themselves and for their organizations are more likely to achieve them than managements that operate without performance targets.*

In very real ways *managing with objectives* is safer and easier: it helps prevent organization drift; it helps promote and instill a results-orientation; and it focuses organizationwide attention on making the right things happen. Indeed, *managing with objectives implies deliberately selecting and making the right things happen.* Concrete action commitments are a necessary element in the entrepreneurial task of setting direction for the organization.

What Kinds of Objectives.   Objectives are needed in *all areas* on which the *survival* and *success* of the organization depend and they are needed at all levels of management from the corporate level on down to the first-level of supervision.[10] Moreover, it is normally desirable to develop both long-range objectives and short-range objectives. *Long-range objectives* keep management alert to what has to be done *now* to attain the desired results later. *Short-range objectives* serve to indicate the speed and momentum which management seeks to maintain in accomplishing longer range objectives and purpose; they direct the attention of managers and organizational subunits toward the desired standards of performance and behavior in the near term.

From a long-run corporatewide perspective, most organizations have need for:

1. *Sales, growth, and marketing objectives*—so as to create a viable, sustainable customer base and market for its products/services;

---

[10]Ibid., p. 100. See, also, Charles H. Granger, "The Hierarchy of Objectives," *Harvard Business Review*, vol. 42, no. 3 (May-June 1963), pp. 63-74.

2. *Technology-innovation objectives*—so as to keep products/services up-to-date and competitive (thereby avoiding obsolescence);

3. *Profitability and financial objectives*—so as to cover the risks of economic activity, test the validity of the organization's contributions, and generate the financial capital requisite for preserving (and enhancing if necessary) the organization's productive capability;

4. *Efficiency objectives*—so as to remain cost competitive and to make judicious use of the economic resources entrusted by society to its care;

5. *Resource supply objectives*—so as to work toward the availability of whatever human, capital, and natural resources are needed for continuing to supply customers (society) with the organization's products/services; and

6. *Social responsibility objectives*—so as to keep the organization in tune with societal expectations and priorities and, in particular, to keep management alert to the positive and negative impacts which organizational activities can have on the environment at large.

The foregoing list is, of course, by no means exhaustive. An organization may wish to have long-run objectives relating to industry leadership, competitive position, overall size and degree of diversification, technological capability, the financial payoffs it seeks to provide stockholders in the form of dividends and capital gains, and its degree of vulnerability to recession. The essential consideration is that the chosen *set* of objectives signify, in specific terms, just what kinds of performance and results management wants the organization to produce.

Because long-run objectives relate to the ongoing activities of an organization, their achievement tends to be open-ended in the sense of not being bounded by time. For example, the objective of survival is never completely attained since failure and bankruptcy are always future possibilities. A long-run objective of 10 percent growth in sales and profits continues on into the future even though it may have been successfully reached in the past.

An organization's short-run objectives act as the intermediate quantitative and qualitative performance targets which management wishes to attain in moving toward long-run objectives. Because short-run objectives are inherently keyed to the pursuit of longer-run objectives, they should (1) relate to some specific long-run objective or set of long-run objectives; (2) be measurable and reflect the progress being made in achieving long-run objectives; (3) be internally consistent such that any conflicts that pit the achievement of one against another are resolved; and (4) be within the reach of organizational capability and within what market and competitive conditions will allow. Once short-run objectives are agreed upon both for the organization as a whole and for each subordinate level and activity, then they should be ranked according to priority. The following statements are illustrations of short-run objectives:

1. We intend to reduce new store openings by 10% this year.
2. Our immediate target is to increase private donations and charitable contributions by 20%.
3. Our aim is to cut back staffing requirements by 5% each of the next three years.
4. We seek to gain enough new accounts this year to reach $50 million in deposits.
5. We aim to reduce infant mortality rates to less than 1 per 100 births within 12 months.
6. The plant's annual production objective is an output rate close to 95 percent of rated capacity.

Observe that these statements all reflect a short-range target level of achievement.

ILLUSTRATION CAPSULE 3
Stating Objectives: How to Tell a "Good" One from a "Bad" One

If the managerial purpose of objectives is to be fulfilled as well as it might, objectives have to be stated properly. There are five specifications for a well-stated objective:

1. An objective should relate to a single, specific topic. (It should absolutely *not* take the form of a vague abstraction or a pious platitude—"we want to be a leader in our industry" or "our objective is to be more aggressive marketers.")
2. An objective should relate to a result, not to an activity to be performed. (The objective is the result of the activity, not the performing of the activity.)
3. An objective should be measurable (stated in quantitative terms whenever feasible).
4. An objective should contain a time deadline for its achievement.
5. An objective should be challenging but achievable.

Consider the following examples:

- *Poor:* Our objective is to maximize profits.
  Remarks: How much is "maximum?" The statement is not subject to measurement. What criterion or yardstick will management use to determine if and when actual profits are equal to "maximum" profits? No deadline is specified.

ILLUSTRATION CAPSULE 3 *(concluded)*

Better: Our total profit target in 1983 is $1,000,000.

- *Poor:* Our objective is to increase sales revenue and unit volume.

    Remarks: How much? Also, because the statement relates to *two* topics, it may be inconsistent. Increasing unit volume may require a price cut and, if demand is price inelastic, sales revenue would fall as unit volume rises. No time frame for achievement is indicated.

    Better: Our objective this calendar year is to increase sales revenues from $30,000,000 to $35,000,000; we expect this to be accomplished by selling 1,000,000 units at an average price of $35.

- *Poor:* Our objective in 1984 is to boost advertising expenditures by 15%.

    Remarks: Advertising is an activity, not a result. The advertising objective should be stated in terms of what result the extra advertising is intended to produce.

    Better: Our objective is to boost our market share from 8% to 10% in 1984 with the help of a 15% increase in advertising expenditures.

- *Poor:* Our objective is to be a pioneer in research and development and to be the technological leader in the industry.

    Remarks: Very sweeping and perhaps overly ambitious; implies trying to march in too many directions at once if the industry is one with a wide range of technological frontiers. More a platitude than an action commitment to a specific result.

    Better: During the 1980s our objective is to continue as a leader in introducing new technologies and new devices that will allow buyers of electrically-powered equipment to conserve on electric energy usage.

- *Poor:* Our objective is to be the most profitable company in our industry.

    Remarks: Not specific enough; by what measures of profit—total dollars or earnings per share or unit profit margin or return on equity investment or all of these? Also, because the objective concerns how well *other* companies will perform, the objective, while challenging, may not be achievable.

    Better: We will strive to remain atop the industry in terms of rate of return on equity investment by earning a 25% after-tax return on equity investment in 1983.

The Hierarchy of Objectives.   Well conceived objectives are a potentially powerful management tool for keeping the whole organization's attention focused on making the right things happen. Objectives point to what is important and to where resources and energies should be aimed. Thus, from a management perspective, objectives should be formulated and stated in such a way that they point directly to specific tasks, assignment of responsibility, and deadlines. Moreover, objectives are needed not only at the corporate level for the organization as a whole but also for each of the specific lines of business and products in which the organization has an interest and, further, for each functional area and department within the organization structure. When every manager, from the chief executive officer on down to the first-line supervisor, is involved in formulating objectives at his/her level of job responsibility and is committed to achieving the agreed-upon objectives, chances are that managers will understand what they need to accomplish and what their expected role and contribution to organizational performance is.

An example may make clearer why this is so and how it works. Suppose the senior executives of a diversified corporation establish a corporate profit objective of $5 million for a given year. Suppose further, after discussion between corporate management and the general managers of the firm's five different businesses, that each business is given the challenging but achievable profit objective of $1 million (the plan being that if the five business divisions can contribute $1 million each in profit, the corporation as a whole can reach its $5 million profit objective). Observe so far, with respect to profit only, that corporate executives have set a priority of $5 million in total profit for the year and that the general managers of each business division have been assigned responsibility for $1 million in profit by year-end. A concrete result has thus been agreed upon and translated into measurable action commitments to achieve something at two levels in the managerial hierarchy. Next, the general manager of business unit X may, after some analytical calculations and discussion with functional area subordinates, conclude that reaching the $1 million profit objective will require selling 100,000 units at an average price of $50 and producing them at an average cost of $40 (the $10 profit margin multiplied by 100,000 units yields a $1 million profit). Consequently, the general manager and the manufacturing manager may settle upon manufacturing objectives of producing 100,000 units at a cost of $40; and the general manager and the marketing manager may agree upon a sales objective of 100,000 units and an average target selling price of $50. In turn, the marketing manager may break the sales objective of 100,000 units down into unit sales targets for each salesperson, for each sales territory, for each customer type, and/or for each item in the product line. In similar fashion, objectives can be discussed and agreed upon for every other relevant area of concern and priority.

The key thing to recognize and understand from this example is that the managerial process of establishing objectives at each level of the organization and for each manager leads to a clearer definition of what results are expected and what is to be accomplished. If done right, *setting objectives energizes the organization*, heads it down the chosen path, and creates a results-oriented organizational climate. At the same time, a hierarchy of objectives that transcends and links the levels within an organization serves to clarify and expand the answers to "who are we and what are we trying to do." The effect is to add both meaning and specificity to the necessarily general concept of organization purpose and mission. By defining in concrete, measurable terms what contribution and results are expected from each manager and unit within the organization, everyone in the managerial hierarchy comes to understand the direction of the total enterprise and their role in it—an essential second step in the direction-setting task of managing the total enterprise. It shouldn't take much imagination to see why managing with objectives is likely to produce better organizational performance than managing without objectives.

ILLUSTRATION CAPSULE 4
The Alternatives to "Managing with Objectives"

One way to be convinced of the usefulness and power of *managing with objectives* is to consider the alternatives:*

1. *Managing by Extrapolation (MBE)*—rely upon the principle "if it ain't broke, don't fix it." The basic game plan is: keep on doing about the same things in about the same ways because, judging from how things are going, we've pretty well got it figured out—our act *is* together.

2. *Managing by Crisis (MBC)*—based upon the belief that the forte of any really good manager is solving problems. Given that there are plenty of crises around—enough to keep everyone occupied full time, managers ought to bring their time and creative energy to bear on solving whatever the most pressing problems are today. MBC is, essentially, a form of reacting rather than acting and of letting events dictate the whats and whens of management decisions.

3. *Managing by Subjectives (MBS)*—in the absence of any general consensus or directives on which way to head and what to do, then do the best you can to accomplish what *you think* should be done—in short, a "do your own thing, the best way you know how" approach. (This is sometimes referred to as "the mystery approach to decision-making" because subordinates are left to figure out what's happening and why—explicit guidelines and decision criteria are conspicuously absent.)

4. *Managing by Hope (MBH)*—recognize that the future is laden with great uncertainty and that if what we try at first doesn't succeed, then, hopefully, we will get it right the second (or third) time. Decisions are predicated on the *hope* that they will work and that good times are just around the corner (after all, luck and good fortune may be on our side). Failing that, if we try hard enough and long enough, then we are bound to get somewhere. Much time, therefore, is allocated to hoping and wishing that things will get better.

*These alternatives were inspired by and adapted from Steven C. Brandt, *Strategic Planning in Emerging Companies* (Reading, Mass.: Addison-Wesley Publishing Co., 1981), Chapter 2.

ILLUSTRATION CAPSULE 4 *(concluded)*

All four of the above styles represent "muddling-through" types of approaches—ways of *managing by wandering around* (MBWA). There is a notable absence of calculated incremental effort to shape or to influence where an organization is headed and what its activity mix is. It is very doubtful whether managers who rely heavily upon them can consistently outperform managers who select performance targets and then formulate a timely, astute game plan to achieve them.

Formulating Strategy: The Third Step in Setting Direction

In almost every instance, an organization will have several viable ways for achieving its objectives—as the old adage goes "there's more than one way to skin a cat." *An organization's strategy is the managerial game plan for how the organization is to be positioned in its overall environment and for how the organization's portfolio of activities is to be managed in the light of all the relevant internal constraints and external conditions.* As such, strategy makes a clear statement about how management intends to try to achieve the organization's target objectives, given all the ramifications of the firm's situation.

General Electric, one of the pioneers in the development and use of the concept of strategy, views strategy as "a statement of how what resources are going to be used to take advantage of which opportunities to minimize which threats to produce a desired result." This view emphasizes an essential concern of strategy: *how* are we going to strengthen our position? Specifically, strategy must deal with four ever-present managerial issues:

1. How to respond to changing conditions (how to take advantage of new opportunities, how to lessen the impact of externally-imposed threats, and how to strengthen the mix of the firm's activities by doing more of some things and less of others).

2. How to allocate resources among the various businesses, activities, divisions, and organizational subunits (given that all things are not equally important, what priorities and guidelines will be observed?).

3. How to compete in each one of the businesses in which the organization is engaged (how to approach the marketplace and survive the competitive struggle, which customer groups and customer needs to emphasize and which to de-emphasize, which technologies to use to offer which products, and so on).

4. Within each line of business, how to manage each of the major functional areas and operating departments so as to support the overall

business strategy and create a unified strategic effort throughout the business unit.

Just as there is a direction-setting logic for establishing a hierarchy of objectives that span the organization from top to bottom, there is a concomitant rationale for developing a strategic game plan at each level of the organization to achieve the objectives set at that level. Thus, corporate-level objectives are the basis for formulating corporate-level strategy; line of business objectives are the basis for formulating line of business strategy; functional area objectives are the basis for formulating functional area strategies; and departmental and work unit objectives are the basis for formulating operating-level strategies. We shall have more to say about the levels of strategy in Chapter 2; suffice it here to say that the establishment of a hierarchy of objectives (the second step in giving an organization direction) needs to be followed by creating a hierarchical web of strategies to achieve them (the third step in giving direction).

As an example of what strategy is and how it works, consider the game plan which corporate-level managers at Beatrice Foods used to transform the company from a local dairy operation into a diversified corporation with $5 billion in sales:[11]

> Originally a local butter and egg company in Beatrice, Nebraska, the company began an effort to diversify its product line and reduce its dependence on local conditions. It started by acquiring a string of small dairies. From the outset, Beatrice followed two key principles—diversification and decentralization. Only firms headed by independent-minded entrepreneurs were brought into the fold. Although Beatrice found that the dairy business had the disadvantage of low profit margins, it had the advantage of generating a lot of excess cash (mainly because inventories of milk are provided by nature and do not require endless financing). Thus, having acquired dairies coast to coast and grown into a $200 million dairy company, Beatrice began to invest some of its cash in higher-margin food companies. LaChoy Food Products was the first acquisition and, when it worked out well, Beatrice began to push into other food lines at an accelerating rate. In the 1960s Beatrice acquired some non-food firms and by the 1970s owned several different kinds of manufacturing operations, a warehousing division, and an insurance company. Among its acquisitions were Samsonite (luggage), Meadow Gold (dairy products), Martha White (flour), Dannon (yogurt), Clark (candy bars), Eckrich (meats), Gebhardt's (chili and tamales), and LaChoy (Chinese foods).
>
> Beatrice's acquisition strategy followed some strict guidelines. Commodity-oriented firms were excluded because of the unpredictable price swings. Companies in head-on competition with such powerhouses as Kellogg's and Campbell Soups were avoided. In the non-food areas, Beatrice

---

[11]For a more complete discussion of Beatrice's strategy and operating philosophy, see Linda Grant Martin, "How Beatrice Foods Sneaked up on $5 Billion," *Fortune* (April 1976), pp. 118-29.

shied away from labor-intensive companies because of the risks of inflation of labor costs. Industries like steel and chemicals were avoided because of their heavy capital demands.

The basic acquisition strategy was to go after companies with at least five years of sales and profit increases, and to eliminate from consideration any firm so large that failure could seriously damage Beatrice's overall profitability. Between 1952 and 1962 most of the acquired firms had sales of about $2 million. While Beatrice sought companies with a growth rate higher than its own, it insisted on a purchase price keyed to a price-earnings multiple about one-third below Beatrice's own current price-earnings ratio. Beatrice was generally successful in buying firms it wanted at a "discount" because the Beatrice stock it was offering in return had performed so very well over the years.

Once acquired, the new businesses were managed under a decentralized structure; the general managers of each unit were given broad-ranging authority and turned loose to formulate and implement their own strategies, thereby allowing each one to be tailored to the specifics of its own market environment.

In 1977 Beatrice Foods overtook Kraft and Esmark to become the largest food processing firm in the United States.

Another example of the use of strategy to accomplish objectives is presented in Illustration Capsule 5.

ILLUSTRATION CAPSULE 5
Northwest Industries' Strategy for Coping with Inflation and Producing Real Growth*

In November 1978, Northwest Industries gave a public account of what its strategies were for lessening the impact of inflation on its operations and on its stockholders:

No company can control or even completely foresee the rate of inflation. But at Northwest Industries we're always trying to lessen its influence on our operations. We do this by sticking with longstanding management strategies that are particularly helpful in uncertain times.

Our goal is to produce real growth. And that means to maximize the total return to our stockholders—including dividend income.

Vertical Integration
One tool we use is vertical integration. It doesn't just provide cost efficiencies. It also helps insulate our operating companies from price volatility in purchased materials and services. For instance, our General Battery Corporation's integrated production processes include everything from secondary lead smelting and plastic case manufacturing to the delivery of batteries by the company's own truck distribution

*Source: Ad appearing in *Business Week*, November 20, 1978, pp. 168-9.

ILLUSTRATION CAPSULE 5 *(concluded)*

system. This kind of control helps keep our product costs both reasonable and comparatively predictable.

We also have a conscious policy of making forward commitments on key raw materials well into the future—far longer than many of our competitors. Occasionally we guess wrong and miss out on falling prices. But we like the advantage of having known costs for an extended period of time. For instance, by settling now on future cotton costs, Union Underwear Company can stabilize an important cost element. This helps Union plan production and price its goods sensibly. But be sure of this: we are *not* speculators or commodity traders. We are manufacturers.

Efficient Production

Efficient production also helps us fight inflation. Almost all of our companies are industry leaders. That allows us advantages many competitors do not have, so we can make good products at lower costs. And when it comes to maintaining or increasing margins in an inflationary environment, our companies frequently do the job through cost reduction rather than by relying simply on price increases.

Another way our companies maintain margins without price increases is by upgrading product mix. They drop lower margin goods to concentrate on more profitable items. This ensures our facilities are utilized for maximum profitability. An example is Acme Boot Company getting out of the manufacturing of golf and dress shoes to make and sell more western boots. A simple move, but effective.

Acquisition Criteria

That we seek stability in an unstable economy is also evident in our acquisition criteria. These criteria generally rule out companies subject to unusually large cyclical swings. We avoid companies that are dependent on a single supplier or customer. We never want to be in a position where a customer or supplier can control our bottom line. Also, we avoid highly labor intensive businesses. We believe we can control the availability of capital more easily than the availability of labor.

U.S. Orientation

Another way we have tried to insulate our stockholders from uncertainty is by keeping Northwest's earnings coming essentially from the U.S., and for good reason. With 95% of our earnings U.S. based, we have avoided the comparatively high rates of inflation and the unstable economies of many countries, not to mention the damaging effects of fickle policy changes by foreign governments. In so doing, we have largely avoided the vagaries of foreign currency fluctuations.

Every policy we follow—whether it pertains to management, manufacturing, or marketing—seeks to add stability to our rates of growth. And not just growth at the rate of inflation, but at a considerably higher rate.

Two Key Features of Strategy Formulation.   Strategy formulation is inherently *situational* and *evolutionary*. It is situational because the substance underlying good strategy formulation is an entrepreneurial skill for positioning an organization in its overall environment so as to keep it on the track of doing the right things. What is the right thing and the right strategy for one organization need not be the right thing or the right strategy for another organization—even one in the same business. Why? Because situations differ from organization to organization, as well as from time to time. A good strategy is one which is right for the organization, given all of the relevant specifics of *its* situation. The entrepreneurial task of formulating strategy thus requires a heavy dose of "situational design and analysis" where the strategic objective is to achieve "goodness of fit" with all the relevant internal and external considerations.

A second strategy formulation characteristic is that *strategy evolves*. This is a logical consequence of the need to match strategy with the situation. As an organization's situation evolves, so also does its strategy. Hence, strategic plans are normally the product of incremental adjustments to unfolding events. Rarely does strategy stand as the result of a single unique analytical brainstorm by the general manager (or a group of managers) which subsequently is used to guide the firm unerringly. Far more frequently, an organization's strategic plan *continuously evolves* from a combination of external events and an internal moving of information and ideas up and down the organization in a continuous dialogue. Strategy gradually gets refined and finetuned from management's "hands-on" experience with the organization's situation and with events as they unfold. Strategy thus stands as an incrementally arrived-at product of guiding and orchestrating daily events and of the cumulative impact of all the little insights, ideas, and information that come from salespeople, workers, customers, actions of competitors, and economic events, all contributing bit-by-bit and piece-by-piece to a coherent strategic course that is adjusted from time to time by new events and circumstances and managerial choices.

THE JOB OF THE GENERAL MANAGER: STRATEGY IMPLEMENTATION AND EXECUTION

Once the entrepreneurial and analytical aspects of strategy formulation have been settled for the time being, the general manager's priority is one of putting the strategic plan into operation and making it work as well as conditions allow. This is always much more time consuming than formulating strategy, and the variety of administrative tasks involved sweep across a wide front. Implementation raises all kinds of administrative and policy issues concerning the specifics and details of what it will take to put the chosen strategy into place and achieve acceptable results. A brief overview of some important managerial aspects of strategy implementation is offered below.

Structuring and Organizing Key Activities

Successful strategy execution is assisted when tasks and activities are linked directly and clearly to accomplishing the strategic plan. What is entailed here is a process of taking objectives and strategies and breaking them down into key activities, assignments, jobs, and deadlines. The central issues are:

1. What key activities, what organization units, what specific tasks, and what jobs are needed to implement the strategy and to reach the target objectives?

2. What skills, expertise, authority, and budgets are needed to allow individuals and organization units to do their part in contributing to the target levels of organization performance?

3. How should all of the various activities and organization units be structured and authority delegated?

In dealing with these issues, two considerations are worth keeping in mind. The first is that structure should be supportive of strategy and serve its peculiar needs, meaning that organization structure should be built squarely upon and center around those few, critical *key activities* upon which strategic success or failure depends. The second is that the functions of organizational units and the nature of individual jobs need to be defined in terms of the objectives to be achieved, not simply in terms of the activities to be performed. Why? Because it puts emphasis on what is to be accomplished (the strategic plan), rather than on descriptions of activities to be worked on. The advantage of a results-focused approach to delegating authority, establishing budgets, and making work assignments is that it helps keep the whole organization trained on implementing and executing strategy. It draws organizationwide attention to the right things to shoot for, rather than risking inadvertent drift and creating a climate where people are so engrossed in performing tasks and activities that they lose sight of why they are doing them.

Developing a Distinctive Competence

In most high-performing organizations, management will be found to have worked hard at figuring out how the organization can be not only just good at what it does but also how it can be *better* than rival organizations. Management may accomplish this by hiring superior technical talent, by striving to be more innovative, by focusing energies on some neglected but important facet of furnishing a product/service and translating this into a competitive edge, by figuring out ways to make good employees perform over their heads, or maybe even by out-managing other organizations. When an organization is *uniquely good in performing a strategically relevant activity*, it can be said to have a *distinctive competence*. Deliberately ferreting out a strategically useful distinctive competence and then building, staffing, and otherwise nurturing the internal creation of this distinctive competence can greatly enhance performance and strategic success. A distinctive competence can be the basis for gaining a significant competitive edge and/or for carrying out the strategic plan in a more efficient and effective manner. In either case discerning the contribution of a particular distinctive competence and then doing what it takes to install the distinctive competence within the organization is one of the "trade secrets" of first-rate general management.

It is difficult to overstate the contribution which a well conceived *distinctive competence* can make to organization success. IBM's distinctive competences in computer software and service have given the company a major competitive edge over other computer manufacturers even though IBM's computer hardware is not generally viewed as "superior." McDonald's distinctive competence in its system of controls and procedures for operating hamburger and french fry outlets produce profit margins which are the envy of the fast food industry. Experiences such as these teach that attending to the development of a useful distinctive competence is one of the traits of effective strategy management.

Setting and Monitoring Policy

Policies prescribe how internal organization activities will be administered. They specify the organization's "standard operating procedures," communicate "how we do things around here," and set boundaries on independent action. Ideally, policy flows from an organization's strategy and is explicitly designed to help execute the strategy.[12] The strategy-

---

[12]In management literature, definition and actual use of the term *policy* is far from uniform. In years past, it was common and customary to refer to "policy" to describe company purpose, company direction, and ways of doing business—a usage which makes policy and strategy indistinguishable. However, this overlap in usage is giving way to a conceptual difference between strategy and policy much like we have used and defined them here. Nonetheless, there are times when both academicians and practitioners use the term policy to refer to top management pronouncements on what course of action a company will follow (it is our "policy" not to diversify into markets where we lack technological proficiency) and on statements of management intent (it is our "policy" to pay dividends equal to 50 percent of net earnings per share). It is important for the reader to be alert, therefore, to the fact that policy is sometimes used in a much broader sense than we have defined it here; our definition is a relatively narrow one. The definition we presented tends to equate "policy" with those managerial actions and decisions relating specifically to strategy implementation and execution. We think this is advantageous since it permits a sharper conceptual distinction to be made between those actions and decisions relating primarily to strategy formulation and those relating to strategy administration.

implementing features of policy relate chiefly to developing methods and procedures conducive to internal efficiency and to an operating mode supportive of accomplishing the strategic plan. For example, General Motors' policy of trying to standardize as many parts as possible in producing its many different models of Chevrolets, Pontiacs, Buicks, Oldsmobiles and Cadillacs was aimed at achieving greater mass production economies and minimizing the working capital tied up in parts inventories.

Measuring and Evaluating Performance

Obtaining timely and appropriate information about external conditions and internal operations is an obvious aspect of strategy administration. Current performance has to be carefully and thoroughly monitored; this specifically includes looking at profitability, financial status, market share and sales growth, customer satisfaction, operating efficiency, employee productivity and job performance, and other significant areas which indicate the tempo of how well things are going and the pace of strategy implementation. Such information gives direct indication of what results the strategy is producing and the extent to which objectives are being attained. Deviations from plan can thus be identified and corrective action taken on an "as needed" basis.

There are several elements to this phase of strategy implementation and execution. One is insisting that contributions and results be documented and rigorously compared against objectives. A second is bringing the full range of rewards and incentives (pay, promotion, the parceling out of coveted assignments, the use of fear and pressure to perform, instilling some anxiety about job security, and so on) to bear upon making the achievement of objectives and strategy the basis for deciding who has done a good job or not. Tightly linking tasks to objectives to rewards helps counteract tendencies for individuals and organizational units to resist or reject strategy and objectives. A third is the design and installation of a network of management controls with clear reporting channels and timely, reliable feedback on daily operations and overall organization performance. By staying armed with information on what's happening, managers are in position to intervene and take corrective actions when negative deviations from plans appear.

Exerting Strategic Leadership

There is an obvious role for general managers in communicating the priorities of objectives and strategy and in securing the emotional commitment of the organization's members to the strategic plan. Besides clarifying and defending objectives and strategies against internal erosion (and external attack as well), occasions will arise where the general manager has to persuade, to inspire confidence, to propose, to listen, and to take command of difficult situations. In presiding over the strategy implementation process, the general manager has an opportunity to infuse flair and distinction into the organization's activities and to help set the tone of enthusiasm and motivation that go into making up an organization's "personality." By his or her energy, integrity, character, and example, the general manager keynotes the degrees of energy and ethical behavior that is expected of others.

KEY TERMS AND CONCEPTS

Purpose—consists of a long-term vision of what an organization seeks to do and what kind of organization it intends to become; answers the strategic questions of "what shall we sell to whom?" and "what is our business and what will it be?"

Objectives—define the specific kinds of performance and results which an organization seeks to produce through its activities.

Long-range objectives—the desired performance and results on an ongoing basis.

Short-range objectives—the near-term organizational performance targets which an organization desires to attain in progressing toward its long range objectives.

Strategy—refers to management's "game plan" for achieving the chosen objectives; specifies *how* the organization will be operated and run and indicates what actions will be taken to get the organization in the position it wants to be.

Strategic Plan—a comprehensive statement of an organization's purpose and mission, objectives, and strategy; a detailed roadmap of the direction and course that the organization presently intends to follow in conducting its activities.

Strategy Formulation—the process whereby management develops an organization's purpose and mission, derives specific objectives, and chooses a strategy; includes all of direction-setting components of managing the *total* organization.

Strategy Implementation—embraces the full range of managerial activities associated with putting the chosen strategy into place and supervising its pursuit.

There is another side to the strategic leadership role, though. Organizational politics always creeps into the picture. One has to be sensitive about when to push hard, when to go slow, when to compromise, and how to size-up what people are capable of doing and not doing. The people who comprise an organization are, at once, the major constraint to strategy implementation and the vehicle through which the strategy must be made successful. Not only will there be occasions to be an astute practitioner of organizational politics but it is also useful to work hard at stimulating and encouraging a flow of ideas and proposals from the bottom to the top of the organization. Aside from the fact that general managers cannot take it upon themselves to do all of the important thinking and to handle personally all of the important administrative matters, there are only a limited number of one's own ideas that a general manager can get adopted. Thus, it is essential to involve as many people as feasible in originating ways to translate the strategic plan into daily action and make it work. Then the trick is to become skillful in arousing support for the better of these ideas and proposals.

Broadly viewed, therefore, the general management task of strategy implementation is one of shaping and tailoring the formal organization structure, its informal relationships, and task-authority-budget-reward-incentive schemes to the specific requirements of the organization's strategic plan. The aim is to keep organization resources and energies focused squarely on objectives and strategy and to avoid the trap of letting work, assignments, and functions become activity-focused and problem-focused. One cannot safely assume that just because people are busy and working hard that the hoped-for results and performance will occur. Hence, the job of strategy implementation and execution is inherently one of translating the strategic plan into definition and organization of key activities, into authority and assignments, into operating budgets, and into schedules and deadlines—with the overriding criterion for judging whether individuals and organizational subunits have done a good job or not being "Did we achieve the agreed-upon objectives and has the strategy worked as well as it could under the circumstances?"

SUMMARY AND PERSPECTIVES

This introductory survey of the tasks of the general manager has stressed the basic elements in managing the total enterprise—and, in particular, how performance of the management function contributes to making an organization successful and effective in what it does. The job of managing the total enterprise has five identifiable phases:

1. Defining organization purpose and mission.

2. Establishing objectives.

3. Formulating a strategy.

4. Implementing and executing the chosen strategic plan.

5. Evaluating and reformulating the strategic plan in the light of actual experience, changing conditions, and new priorities.

Taken together, they form a "model" of the strategic management process, shown in Figure 1-2. Phases 1, 2, and 3 comprise the direction-setting function of management and are entrepreneurial in character; combined, they constitute an organization's strategic plan. The fourth phase embraces all of the managerial tasks and responsibilities associated with putting the strategic plan into place and generating the target results. The fifth phase, strategy evaluation and strategy reformulation, is called for because changing external conditions, emerging market and competitive developments, and new internal priorities and circumstances combine to make reappraisal of the present strategy a regular occurrence. In this sense, strategy evaluation is both the end and the beginning of the strategy management cycle.

FIGURE 1-2
The Ongoing Process of Strategy Management

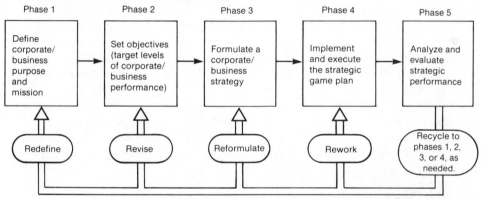

While the five phases or tasks of defining purpose, establishing objectives, formulating strategy, implementing and executing the strategic plan, and analyzing and evaluating strategy go to the heart of what managing the total enterprise is all about, there are four points about the actual practice of strategic management which need to be stressed:

1. *In actual situations it is not always easy to distinguish sharply between purpose and objectives, between objectives and strategy, and between strategy formulation (entrepreneurship) and strategy implementation and execution (administration).* We have tried to maintain a fairly clear-cut separation in our definitions and conceptual descriptions, so as to better expose the elements inherent in charting an organization's course and in describing the task of general management. But such careful distinctions in terminology are not uniformly understood and strictly adhered to in practice. Words like purpose, objectives, strategy, strategic plan, entrepreneurship, and administration are "accordionlike" in the sense that they include statements which can span the

spectrum from broad to narrow, very important to comparatively unimportant, and general to specific. Moreover, statements of purpose and mission shade into objectives, objectives shade into strategies, and strategies shade into ways of executing them. An indication of the possibility for overlap is given by the statement "Our major objective is to be a diversified, growing, and profitable company with emphasis on manufacturing electronic products and components for worldwide use in industry, government, and the home." This statement, which is not an uncommon form of expression, contains an indication of what the company is trying to do (its purpose and mission); it suggests the existence of several objectives (diversification, growth, profitability); and it has hints of strategy (the emphasis on manufacturing electronic products and the identification of target markets).

2. *The sequence of steps from purpose to objectives to strategy to implementation and execution to evaluation and reformulation is not something that general managers actually do in this neat, exact order.* In practice, these steps are intertwined, with two-way cause and effect. Take the case of the three direction-setting components—purpose, objectives, and strategy. The how of strategy is plainly predicated upon the whats of an organization's purpose and objectives; at the same time, though, strategy (especially one which is either highly successful or a dismal failure) bends back to raise/lower objectives and expand/contract the scope and mix of organizational activities.

3. *The tasks of strategy formulation and strategy implementation are seldom accomplished in planned, systematic fashion in isolation from everything else.* As previously discussed, a general manager's schedule is fragmented, varied, and often hectic, subject to the press of daily events, meetings, one-of-a-kind problems, and brushfires. The really *key* entrepreneurial and administrative tasks have to be performed in the midst of all the other things falling within the purview of the general manager's job. Thus, it is incorrect to narrowly construe the job of managing the total enterprise as *purely* one of managing the formulation and pursuit of the organization's strategic plan—this is the essential function of the general manager but it is not the only function.

4. *The needs of strategy management are irregular and the progress made in both formulation and implementation of strategy usually take the form of incremental adjustments rather than grand designs and giant leaps forward.*[13] Strategic issues, new opportunities, and "bright

[13]Robert N. Anthony, *Planning and Control Systems: A Framework for Analysis* (Boston: Division of Research, Graduate School of Business Administration, Harvard University, 1965), pp. 38-39. James B. Quinn, *Strategies for Change: Logical Incrementalism* (Homewood, Ill.: Richard D. Irwin, Inc., 1980), Chapter 2, especially pp. 58-59.

ideas" do not appear according to some neat timetable; they have to be dealt with as they arise, using both judgment and whatever analytical techniques may be handy. Certain strategic decisions are motivated by problems forced on the manager; others result from an active, deliberate entrepreneurial search for new and better opportunities; others emerge from the ongoing flow of ideas and information up and down the organization structure; and still others are the product of a good brainstorm.[14] In addition, each strategic decision tends to be made in a different context at unpredictable intervals and with new information and changed circumstances; precise evaluation is seldom feasible.[15] The result is that strategy stands more as the product of a Darwinist evolutionary approach than it does as a precise, systematically analyzed, once and for all time Biblical grand design.[16] Similarly, strategy implementation is the product of incremental improvements, internal finetuning, and the pooling effect of many administrative decisions and contributions of both managerial subordinates and employees; it is not something that happens in one fell swoop, the result of managerial decree and design.

Nonetheless, the process of strategic management depicted in Figure 1-2 is a useful framework for pinpointing the central elements of general management which bear most heavily on organization success or failure. The five phases of defining purpose, establishing objectives, formulating strategy, implementing strategy, and evaluating strategy may not be something that general managers do precisely, sequentially, systematically, or exclusively, but they do accurately spotlight what strategic management involves. When these tasks are done well, the chances are much better that the organization will be one which is engaged in doing the right things, which is entrepreneurially effective, which is well administered, and which performs. This is what managing the *total* enterprise is all about. In the succeeding chapters and readings, we shall add flesh to this skeletal outline of the general management tasks of strategy formulation and strategy implementation.

SUGGESTED READINGS

Andrews, Kenneth R. *The Concept of Corporate Strategy*. Revised Edition. (Homewood Ill.: Richard D. Irwin, Inc., 1980), Chap. 1.

Barnard, Chester I. *The Functions of the Executive*. (Cambridge, Mass.: Harvard University Press, 1938), Chaps. 15, 16, and 17.

---

[14]Henry Mintzberg, "The Science of Strategy-Making," *Industrial Management Review* vol. 8, no. 2 (Spring 1967), pp. 73-74.

[15]Ibid., p. 74.

[16]Ibid., p. 80.

Boettinger, Henry M. "Is Management Really an Art?" *Harvard Business Review*, vol. 53, no. 1, January-February 1975, pp. 54-64.

Drucker, Peter F. *Management: Tasks, Responsibilities, Practices.* (New York: Harper and Row, Publishers, Inc., 1974), Chaps. 2, 4, 30, 31, and 50.

Granger, Charles H. "The Hierarchy of Objectives." *Harvard Business Review*, vol. 42, no. 3, May-June 1964, pp. 63-74.

Katz, Robert L. "Skills of an Effective Administrator." *Harvard Business Review*, vol. 33, no. 1, January-February 1955, pp. 33-42.

Koontz, Harold. "Making Strategic Planning Work." *Business Horizons*, vol. 19, no. 2, April 1976, pp. 37-47.

Livingston, J. Sterling. "Myth of the Well-Educated Manager." *Harvard Business Review*, vol. 49, no. 1, January-February 1971, pp. 79-87.

McConkey, Dale D. *How to Manage by Results* (New York: Amacom, 1976), Chapters 4, 5, 10, 11, and 13.

Mintzberg, Henry. "The Manager's Job: Folklore and Fact." *Harvard Business Review*, vol. 53, no. 4, July-August 1975, pp. 49-61.

Quinn, James B. *Strategies for Change: Logical Incrementalism* (Homewood, Ill.: Richard D. Irwin, Inc., 1980), Chapters 2 and 3.

Raia, Anthony P. *Managing by Objectives* (Glenview, Ill.: Scott, Foresman & Co., 1974), Chapters 1 and 3.

Ross, Joel, and Kami, Michael. *Corporate Management in Crisis: Why the Mighty Fall.* (Englewood Cliffs, N.J.: Prentice-Hall, Inc., 1973).

Tilles, Seymour. "The Manager's Job: A Systems Approach." *Harvard Business Review*, vol. 41, no. 1, January-February 1963, pp. 73-81.

Wrapp, H. Edward. "Good Managers Don't Make Policy Decisions." *Harvard Business Review*, vol. 45, no. 5, September-October 1967, pp. 91-99.

READING

Strategic Planning—Myth or Reality?—A Chief Executive's View*

T. MITCHELL FORD

T. Mitchell Ford is Chairman, President and Chief Executive Officer of Emhart Corporation, Hartford, Connecticut.

There is evidence that only 10 percent of all U.S. companies with strategic plans use them effectively—and rare is the company that would confess to not having one. It is, perhaps, because we Americans are prone to being trendy, we adopt popularized managerial techniques often without fully understanding their genesis, their underpinnings, or their application.

Strategic planning is a buzz-word (soon to be eclipsed by 'reindustrialization'). How does it differ from what companies have been doing for years? Does it, indeed, differ? Why is it so difficult to do well?

I would like to discuss these issues as a chief executive who has been engaged in the process for 3 years and one who has committed his company to a long-range strategic plan.

I define strategic planning as the 'management of change.' It is a decision-making process, based on empirical evidence and analytical studies, that provides the basic direction and focus of the enterprise.

WHERE TO BEGIN?

One begins, as we did, by defining what business we are in. That is so fundamental as to seem ludicrous. But the failure to ask that question is said to be the most single cause of business failure. Management literature in the U.S. is chock full of examples of companies that did not raise the question, did not answer it thoughtfully and thoroughly and suffered.

Of course, we knew the answer right off. But our opinion was subsequently validated and refined, by 3 years of some hard-nosed audits of our planning and activities.

The rationale for our existence as a corporation, we believe, is to provide shareholders with a better than average return on their investment; to provide a pleasant working environment for our employees, with opportunities for personal and financial growth, and to be a good neighbor.

Nothing startling here.

---

*This article is reprinted from *Long Range Planning*, vol. 14, no. 6 (December 1981), pp. 9-11.

How can we guarantee to do that over the long haul? We produce products basic to anyone's standard of living (glass and shoe machines; hardware) product lines that are long-lived cash generators and relatively resistant to technological obsolescence, yet at the same time, susceptible to technological improvement.

Decisions on how capital and manpower resources should be deployed had been made at Emhart more by intuition than by scientific analysis over the years. But intuitive judgments cannot be passed along to the next generation of managers. What we needed, we believed, was a formal set of guidelines. Further, our company had grown in dimension and its multinational character had out-stripped the ability to cope with informal decision-making.

TRYING TO MANAGE CHANGE

The world, too, is caught up in such a maelstrom of change that long-range planning is no longer an option but a matter of survival.

Strategic planning, as I learned, is not a financial plan. That is too narrow. The whole idea is to think broadly and thoughtfully about trends and developments that could affect the business . . . to evaluate the options, to identify the issues that might impinge on these options and to choose the best course.

Strategic plans often go awry, in my opinion, by over-emphasis on short-term gains. The year ahead, even two, is generally set before you even begin planning. The company will run more or less on its momentum for at least that long. You have to look ahead, to 3-5 years.

It is also not generally recognized that effective strategic planning requires a great deal of time, a lot of mental effort and some skillful and tactfully introduced education. As chief executive you are responding to change, by planning to manage it, but implicit in this is the change that you will create.

In so doing, you will undoubtedly disrupt comfortable ways of doing things. You will break the thread of continuity with the past that provides security for many people. The culture shock can be great unless the entire organization recognizes and accepts the necessity of the planning process and appreciates the benefits to all concerned. This is easy to say and hard to do. This is why I add four new roles to the traditional functions of the chief executive as decision-maker, planner, economist and strategist. He must, today, also be a counselor, arbitrator, company philosopher and chief worrier!

This points up yet another flaw in some strategic plans. Too often the initiative and the concept are delegated to line management in the absence of a well understood process for planning. Immediately, they get intertwined in the inevitable corporate bureaucracy, or worse, are perceived as a conventional business plan with only financial objectives coming through loud and clear.

The chief executive *must* be the chief executive officer of the strategic plan. It is he who approves the final strategy that commits the company to a course of action. And it is he who is accountable to the Board of Directors and to the shareholders for the results of the basic strategy direction.

PRIORITIES FOR FUNDS

Before we went public at Emhart with our own plan we forced ourselves through extensive and probing self-analysis. Our plan may not be letter-perfect but we have confidence in its concepts.

We know better who we are and where we are going. We have specific financial goals, of course, (a 20 percent return on equity, or 10 percent in real terms) but these are part, not the whole, of the strategic plan.

We want businesses that have a strong competitive advantage, either by expertise, uniqueness, being a low cost producer or market share. In our case, businesses that fit that form at will, will receive funds to vigorously maintain their position.

Businesses that presently do not measure up but can present a strategy that will eventually achieve the desired returns, will also be funded if the time frame is reasonable.

Those businesses which have low odds of ever fitting into this framework will be managed in such a way as to minimize their impact on the corporation as a whole, divested in some cases and the assets redeployed.

Venture management risk-taking is by no means excluded. We recognize that new businesses may take as long as 10 years to develop and, under the proper circumstances, we are prepared to fund the venture for this period.

The psychological impact of the strategic plan is perhaps as critical as its criteria. The organization as a whole begins to share in the process. The confusion that shrouds some decisions lifts. The pieces start to fall into place. We become more comfortable with our decisions because they can finally be seen from the perspective of the worldwide company rather than from the narrow parochial view of a strategic business unit.

SOME PRACTICAL SUGGESTIONS

Even with 3 years of preliminary planning and analysis behind us, we are still very much in the embryonic stage of a case study of strategic planning. The results will not be in for some years to come. If the insights of one who has personally spent thousands of hours on the process are valid, perhaps I can offer some practical suggestions to potential long-range planners. To wit:

- Be patient. It takes time, more than you would expect. Serious management education must accompany any strategic plan if you are to achieve widespread understanding and acceptance.

- Do not overlook the critical necessity to develop a human resources development plan in conjunction with and in support of the strategic plan.

- Do not develop the strategic plan apart from such other planning efforts as operating and capital budgets. Dovetail them.

- One must tie the plan into the incentive compensation program or it will falter.

- Recognize that the strategic plan is not cast in stone; it must be flexible and adjust to changes, too. Changes in the company's composition; in the environments; in the financial arena and in changes in shareholder requirements.

- Integrate current, competing and future technologies into the planning process.

- Do not fail to develop and articulate a strategic philosophy to accompany the proposed strategy.

Finally, while the plan bears the imprint of the chief executive—and he, the ultimate responsibility, it will never fully succeed unless and until line management see it as *their* plan!

READING

Top Management's Role in Strategic Planning*

DONALD R. MELVILLE

Donald R. Melville is President and Chief Executive Officer, Norton Company.

The 1970s were a successful decade of growth and diversification for Norton Company. In 1979, sales exceeded \$1 billion, ranking Norton 261 on the list of *Fortune's* 500 industrial companies. Half of Norton's sales were made outside the United States. In 1979, the company's return on equity was 20 percent. Norton maintained a leading market position in its historical business, abrasives, and in half a dozen other industries.

One of Norton's most significant acts in this decade of growth was to disband its corporate planning department. While the planning department was doing a very effective job, top management perceived that the planners were the wrong people to be doing the job.

At Norton Company, strategy is the business of line managers. The line manager's knowledge, experience, skill—even his gut feel—are indispensable to realistic planning. In addition, the best-conceived strategy is worthless if it's not well implemented. People are much more likely to wholeheartedly implement a plan if they have played the leading role in developing it.

THREE KEY ROLES

At Norton, top management plays three important roles—guide, interpreter, and asker of difficult questions—in the planning process. In his guiding role, the top manager must keep an eye on long-range goals for the total corporation, to see that a line manager's strategy fits into the overall direction of the company. He must have a view of the company in general, a concept of what he wants it to be, as well as an understanding of all its particulars.

As an interpreter, he must try to understand, and help others in the company understand, the social, political, and economic trends outside the company and how those trends could influence the company's future.

As an asker of difficult questions, the top manager must continually challenge the prevailing orthodoxy, the conventional wisdom. By its very nature, an organization becomes bureaucratic, and its people will devise

---

*This article is reprinted by permission from *The Journal of Business Strategy*, vol. 1, no. 4 (Spring 1981), pp. 62-65. Copyright 1981, Warren, Gorham and Lamont Inc., 210 South Street, Boston, Mass. All rights reserved.

the obvious solutions. The top manager must be prepared to ask the probing, the difficult, even the embarrassing questions.

Norton Company uses well-known planning techniques but top management probably spends more time and has greater involvement in both the planning and implementation process than at many other companies.

MANAGING THE PORTFOLIO

The heart of the process is the portfolio management concept. By working with portfolio charts, such as growth/market share matrices, managers answer the questions: What are we now? What are we trying to become? Can we get there and, if so, how will we do it? Every business is, of course, a portfolio of many businesses. At Norton, there are about forty separate strategic business units among seven major businesses. To understand the position of each individual unit you have to know its position in its industry's life cycle, its rate of growth, and its market share relative to that growth. Then, with knowledge of the experience curve and an evaluation of future trends, perceived competitive patterns, and available resources, one can predict its potential return and the optimum strategic path to follow. To evaluate the unit, one must see it in terms of the direction in which the corporation is moving as a whole. What might be good business for Norton might not fit at all in the plans of another company.

Additionally, it is important to weigh the attractiveness of the industry in which the SBU is operating. There can, after all, be greater differences in profitability between industries than between companies in the same industry.

HOW THE STRATEGY GUIDANCE COMMITTEE WORKS

In 1972, Norton formed a top management committee whose job is to continually look at the company's businesses, and to develop and monitor the portfolio, from the viewpoint of achieving Norton's corporate objectives.

At the moment, this committee, the Strategy Guidance Committee, has fourteen members—the CEO, the financial vice-president, eight top vice-presidents in charge of operations, the controller, assistant controller, vice-president for corporate development, and an assistant vice president. Each of these individuals spends at least 10 to 20 percent of his time on strategic planning. When top managers clearly define strategy with and for the line manager, top managers do not then have to spend as much of their time actually running the business. Consensus has been found and, therefore, delegation will work.

The line manager in charge of each strategic business unit comes before the committee about every two years with a detailed strategy for each major segment of the unit's operations. A review every two years is about right for top management to be assured that the unit's strategy is viable and that it is still in harmony with overall corporate objectives.

The Strategy Guidance Committee looks at a strategic business unit from many viewpoints—return on net assets, return on sales, asset turn-over, market share strategy. The committee might test sales growth rate against market growth rate against market share strategy. The committee also looks at competition, relative strengths and weaknesses, and cash generation plotted against market share strategy. It also places the unit on a balloon chart or growth/market share matrix for the entire company, to see how this unit fits in with all the others.

ASKING THE RIGHT QUESTIONS

While looking at the unit from all possible angles, the committee asks a lot of questions:

- How does this unit contribute to the overall scheme of things?
- Does it help to balance the total?
- Does it increase or decrease the cyclical nature of the company?
- How does it relate to other Norton technologies, processes, or distribution systems?
- How successfully does it compete?
- How is it regarded by its customers and by its competitors?
- Does it hurt or improve the company's image with the investment community?
- What are its mission and mode of operation in terms of build, maintain, or harvest?
- Is its current strategy appropriate?
- Can we win and, if so, how?
- If it has changed its strategy or performance since the last review, why has it changed?
- What does our analysis suggest about the unit's profitability in comparison with similar businesses?

The Strategy Guidance Committee meets about twenty-five times a year—an average of about two meetings per month—for two to five hours, to review line managers' strategies and, if necessary, to discuss acquisition candidates. Once a year, the committee updates Norton's regular five-year financial model, which provides a major progress check on planning, and discusses the overall corporate mission and objectives.

While this top management committee is obviously very powerful, it takes no votes, approves no capital expenditures or budgets. Its most important role is to keep everybody moving in the same corporate direction.

The company's overall strategies are presented annually to Norton's Board of Directors to ensure that there is agreement with the general direction being charted by the management of the company. The board, by asking searching questions, provides an important check to ensure objectivity.

CASE STUDY: THE COATED ABRASIVE DIVISION

The recent experience of the Coated Abrasive Division is a good illustration of this process at work. Norton was founded nearly 100 years ago as a grinding wheel manufacturer. In the 1930s, it acquired a coated abrasive business. By 1970, Norton's abrasives businesses had good market share in slow-growth markets. The abrasives businesses were seen as cash generators for Norton's growing portfolio of nonabrasive businesses which would be the key to future growth. The company hoped that the nonabrasive businesses would offset the cycles of abrasives, which follow the ups and downs of the manufacture of durable goods.

In the early 1970s, the Coated Abrasive Division in the United States was having difficulties. Market share and profitability were declining. The company undertook a major restructuring program in 1974 that emphasized substantial cost reductions to make the division more competitive. In spite of this restructuring, market share and profitability continued to decline for another two years.

In 1976, the Strategy Guidance Committee decided to evaluate again the long-term strategy for the Coated Abrasive Division. The corporate objectives were twofold:

- Norton intended to remain the worldwide leader in abrasives.
- Management wanted to increase overall profitability by diversifying into nonabrasive businesses, using abrasives as the cash generator for this diversification.

It wasn't clear to the Committee that the Coated Abrasive Division could fulfill its corporate role as a cash generator.

PICKING THE STRATEGY

The line manager of the division, who thought it could, had developed a strategy for maintaining market share. He wanted to complete the restructuring and cost-reduction programs that had been launched two years before. He thought that with some more time the organization could be consolidated into a coherent team, and a focused marketing effort through segmentation could be pursued on the basis of some strengths that had emerged during the restructuring. He also recommended directing a larger percentage of research resources into an emerging new product line and technology. He thought that this strategy would eventually allow the division to be the cash generator it was intended to be, and also allow it to continue as the technical focal point for coated abrasive operations overseas.

A PIMS (Profit Impact of Marketing Strategies) analysis, which Norton received as a subscriber to the Strategic Planning Institute, suggested a different strategy. It suggested a moderate harvest strategy.

During its discussion, the Strategy Guidance Committee looked at what the future would probably be for the coated abrasive industry. The consensus was:

- It would experience low growth and only gradual change.

- There would be no major changes in manufacturing technology, but the division could slowly develop some important new abrasive products.

- Except for one significant competitor, the return of most companies in the business was below the U.S. industrial average.

The committee studied a summary of the market share strategies for all the businesses in Norton's portfolio. A growth share matrix showed the division to lie well in the undesirable low-growth/smaller-than-competitor quadrant, which meant that it was not a very desirable business. When the committee applied its cash generation versus market share test to the line manager's proposed strategy, it found that the combination of maintaining market share and generating cash was acceptable if the market share could be maintained.

To maintain or to harvest? In the end, the committee decided not to harvest the division, but to take the approach of careful segmentation, building on some strengths, and harvesting only those portions where position was irretrievably weak. There were several reasons for this decision.

First, and most important, coated abrasives complemented Norton's grinding wheel business and therefore strengthened the company's distribution network. It didn't seem wise to harvest, at that time, such an important part of the abrasives business which is still the guts of the. company.

Another reason for the decision to maintain was that continuing research and development efforts in the United States would benefit Norton's large overseas coated abrasives operations.

BACK ON TRACK

Since that 1976 decision, the restructuring of the division continued with additional emphasis on organization development—getting the right people into the right positions. Norton is now successfully building some of its coated abrasives businesses and has introduced new products by capitalizing on advances in product development and manufacturing technology. The company is also successfully harvesting parts of the business. The division's line manager has developed the appropriate segmentation and the appropriate strengths.

The repair of the Coated Abrasive Division is still in progress. Since 1976, its profits have at least doubled. It is moving toward a positive cash flow. It seems clearer now that it would have been a mistake five years ago to harvest the whole division. The line manager saw this, from his close knowledge of the strategic segments of the business and the division's strengths relative to its competitors. The top managers on the Strategy Guidance Committee also saw this, from their perspective on overall corporate strategy.

PLANNING IN THE 1980s

How will Norton's planning process change in the 1980s? Top management's involvement—and line management's—will remain much as it is. If a planning department is reinstituted, the planners will work closely and intensely with the line people on current planning operations. Top management's role will still be to guide, to interpret, to question, and to challenge.

It is important that top management continues to be involved and to provide leadership to the strategic planning effort. If top managers believe in the process and spend time and effort in making it as effective as possible, then strategic planning will become a way of life throughout the company.

During the 1980s, Norton will put more emphasis on human resource planning as part of its strategic planning. It takes an entrepreneur to build a business, an administrator to maintain one, and an economizer to harvest one. It is important to find the right person for the right job and reward people appropriately for attaining their individual goals. Helping to choose the right people must become part of the top manager's functions, along with the continuing role of reconciling all strategies with corporate objectives.

During the 1980s, it will be increasingly important that top managers study public issues and how that will affect planning for the future. At Norton, we already do some scenario building when we review our five-year financial model. In the 1980s, we expect the scenarios to include social and political issues as well as economic ones and to reach out ten or more years rather than the five that has so far seemed appropriate.

During the 1980s, top management will have to ensure that the organization remains sufficiently flexible and resilient to respond effectively to the unforeseen change which produces a discontinuity. None of us foresaw in 1970 the impact that OPEC was to have on every business in every country.

Some companies, and some countries, responded to the challenging change in the economic, political, and social climate better than others. We must be prepared to respond appropriately to the next profound discontinuity when it occurs.

In the 1980s, Norton's strategic planning system will rest, as it did in the 1970s, on the premise that the job of planning is the business of line managers. So far, that has been the most important factor in our success.

FORMULATING
ORGANIZATION
STRATEGY

2

"... there is a growing suspicion that the more relevant criterion of organizational effectiveness is not, as it used to be, that of efficiency, but rather that of adaptability to changes in the environment."

Dennis W. Organ

"Without a strategy the organization is like a ship without a rudder, going around in circles. It's like a tramp; it has no place to go."

Joel Ross and Michael Kami

While it is easy enough to grasp the concept of strategy as a managerial "game plan" or roadmap for achieving organizational objectives and for getting the organization where it wants to go, it is another thing to understand what a general manager needs to consider and to do in order to forge a full-blown strategic plan. This chapter explores the task of strategy formation and offers an in-depth look at the components of strategy and how they join together. Specific attention is given to how to define a business, the concept of strategic fit, the levels of strategy, the kinds of factors which shape strategy, and mechanics of how organizations actually go through the process of strategy formation. The purpose of this chapter is twofold: one, to highlight the considerations that go into formulating strategy and, two, to explore how and why strategy spans all levels of the managerial hierarchy.

THE VALUE OF CONSCIOUSLY FORMULATED STRATEGY

Every organization can be said to have a strategy, however imperfect or unconscious it may be. Its strategy may be openly stated by management or it may have to be deduced from management actions and the ways in which an organization operates and behaves. The present strategy may have been carefully calculated and regularly assessed from every angle or it may have emerged haphazardly and be mainly a product of chance and circumstance. Or, in the most frequent case, it may have evolved gradually over time, standing as a result of trial and error, managerial judgments, and market feedback regarding what worked and what didn't.

It is fair to inquire, though, whether a consciously formulated strategy is better than one which has been arrived at by "muddling through." Can better strategies and better performance result if management takes the time and trouble to do a thorough strategic review and analytically arrive at a strategic game plan? The answer may not be as obvious as it seems because there are organizations which have done well by their fortuitous possession of key raw materials, superior finances and/or labor skills, good products (or services), key patents and proprietary technical knowhow, or outstanding location or even just the luck and coincidence of having been in the right place at the right time. Nonetheless, the current research evidence to date does point to effective strategy management and formal strategy analysis as having a positive impact on organization performance.[1] The significance of leading edge strategy management has been underscored by the chief executive officer of a very successful company which has been a longstanding leader in its industry:

> In the main, our competitors are acquainted with the same fundamental concepts and techniques and approaches that we follow, and they are as free to pursue them as we are. More often than not, the difference between their level of success and ours lie in the relative thoroughness and self discipline with which we and they develop and execute our strategies for the future.[2]

The advantages of an organization having a consciously formulated strategy, rather than one which just evolves from freewheeling improvisa-

---

[1] For a representative sample of studies, see Stanley Thune and Robert House, "Where Long-Range Planning Pays Off," *Business Horizons*, vol. 13, no. 4 (August 1970), pp. 81-87; Joseph O. Eastlack and Phillip R. McDonald, "CEO's Role in Corporate Growth," *Harvard Business Review*, vol. 48, no. 3 (May-June 1970), pp. 150-63; David M. Herold, "Long-Range Planning and Organizational Performance: A Cross-Validation Study," *Academy of Management Journal*, vol. 15, no. 1 (March 1972), pp. 91-102; Dan Schendel, G. R. Patton, and James Riggs, "Corporate Turnaround Strategies," *Journal of General Management*, vol. 3, no. 3 (Spring 1976), pp. 3-11; S. Schoeffler, Robert Buzzell, and Donald Heany, "Impact of Strategic Planning on Profit Performance," *Harvard Business Review*, vol. 52, no. 2 (March-April 1974), pp. 137-45; and Donald W. Beard and Gregory G. Dess, "Corporate-Level Strategy, Business-Level Strategy, and Firm Performance," *Academy of Management Journal*, vol. 24, no. 4 (December 1981), pp. 663-88.

[2] Dick Neuschel, "The Chief Executive's Strategic Role and Responsibilities," a Special Study prepared for The Presidents Association, the Chief Executive Officers' Division of the American Management Association, 1977, p. 5.

tion or drifting along, include: (1) the guidance it provides to the managers of organizational subunits, (2) the contribution it makes to identifying strategic issues and to coordinating management's direction-setting decisions, (3) the rationale it provides top management in deploying organizational resources among various activities and in evaluating competing requests from organizational subunits for corporate funds, and (4) the desirability of trying to *influence* rather than merely *respond* to product-market-technological-environmental change.[3] The fourth advantage is of acute importance. A well-managed enterprise will always seek to *impact* its target market with a timely, perceptive, and opportunistic strategy. Indeed, a major thrust of business strategy formation revolves around how to *initiate* and *influence* rather than just *respond* and *react*—although, obviously, it is sometimes useful to employ adaptive and defensive strategies as well as offensive strategies. But it can be fairly said that *the acid test of a powerful strategy is the extent to which it successfully impacts buyers, rival firms, a firm's own position in the marketplace, and the directions of product-market-technological change.* The desired outcome is one where the firm's strategy becomes the *trend-setter* for the whole industry, the benefit of which is that its products/services become better differentiated and stronger buyer preferences for them are created.

In the final analysis, of course, the value of conscious strategy formation and careful strategy analysis hinges upon whether and how much organizational performance is improved. Whether better performance is realized depends upon how much is learned from the process of developing a full-blown organizational strategy, the quality of the strategy (the assumptions, predictions, and business savvy on which it is based), and the skill with which it is implemented. By itself, strategy formulation—while clearly a step forward—is still only a prelude to effective action.

WHERE STRATEGY FORMULATION BEGINS—WITH A CONCEPT

The logical starting point in formulating strategy is with a clear concept of "what is our business, what will it be, and what should it be?"—that is, with a concept of the organization's overall purpose and business mission. The following questions are fundamental: Should we be a single-business enterprise or a diversified enterprise? If we are to be diversified, should our lines of business be related or unrelated? In what kinds of industries should we have an interest? Who should our customers be and which of their needs should we try to meet? What products/services should be provided to meet these customer needs? In what ways should we try to be distinctively good at what we do such that enough buyers will be motivated to purchase *our*

---

[3]Kenneth R. Andrews, *The Concept of Corporate Strategy*, Revised Edition (Homewood, Ill.: Richard D. Irwin, Inc., 1980), pp. 15-16, 46, 123-29; and Seymour Tilles, "How to Evaluate Corporate Strategy," *Harvard Business Review*, vol. 41, no. 4 (July-August 1963), p. 116.

products/services? Normally, an organization's answers to these questions are a product of its own specific situation and the choices and judgments of its managers. Moreover, its answers to "who are we and where are we headed?" are not final—they *evolve* out of changing circumstances, experiences, and new priorities.

There are several ways that organizations approach the questions of "what is our business, what will it be, and what should it be?" Some organizations build the concept of their purpose and mission around the dominant characteristics of their products or services. Thus, a trucking company may think of itself as being in the trucking business, a chemical company as in the chemicals business, and a shoe manufacturer as being in the shoe business. Similarly, in the non-profit sector an agricultural extension service may define its business as agriculture-related technical assistance and information, and the local fire department may view its business as fire-fighting and fire prevention.

Other organizations define their business by the principal ingredient in their products, as with steel companies, aluminum companies, and paper companies. Technology can also serve as the basis for conceptual definition, an example being General Electric, whose thousands of products have sprung from the technology of electricity.

Still other organizations prefer a concept based on a *broad* view of the customer groups and customer functions their products serve. Thus, a government welfare agency may view its purpose and mission as one of providing many kinds of assistance to almost anyone in need of help. An agricultural machinery manufacturer may define its business mission as supplying farm equipment to farmers. The business of small appliance manufacturers may be thought of as offering a variety of effort-saving and time-saving conveniences to household members.

Yet another alternative is for a firm to define its business in terms of a specific product aimed at a specific product-market *segment* or distinguishable group of customers having some common (and strategically relevant) characteristic—location, usage of product, timing of purchase, volume bought, service requirements, and so forth. For instance, typewriters sold as office equipment define a buyer segment quite distinct from portable typewriters sold to individuals through retail channels. Likewise, the educational program offerings of a two-year community college are intended for a narrower clientele than those of a major multi-campus state university. And the business of a neighborhood convenience food mart is intended to meet a fewer number of needs for a narrower customer group than is a large supermarket. In such cases, an organization's concept of its business combines a definition of its product with a definition of the class of customer or market segment to which that product is sold.

Finally, an enterprise may have a business concept that is predicated on the scope of its operations. For a small company, just part of an industry may constitute its sole field of endeavor; such would be the case of a firm whose entire business consists of drilling offshore oil wells. This type of firm is often labeled as "specialized" and such a firm may well perceive its economic mission as none other than a specialty-type enterprise performing a limited service. Larger firms may, for reasons of scale economies, have activities extending across several stages of the process of getting a product to the final consumer (mining, manufacturing, distribution) and are thus said to be "integrated." An example would be an oil company which drills its own oil wells, pipes crude oil to its own refineries, and sells gasoline through its own network of branded distributors and service station outlets. Still other firms, large or small, are said to be "diversified" because their operations extend into several different industries—either related or unrelated. In the case of "purely" diversified or conglomerate firms, which by design are in a number of *unrelated* businesses, the answer to "what is our business?" is stated in terms of risk, financial objectives, growth, and earnings stability rather than in terms of a conceptual theme that links different businesses in customer-industry-technology terms.[4]

"What Is Our Business?"

Peter Drucker, one of the most perceptive authorities on the whys and hows of an organization clearly defining its purpose and mission, has noted that while nothing may seem simpler or more obvious than "What is our business?" managerial neglect of this question is the most important single cause of organization frustration and failure. He argues forcefully that the theory of an organization's business should be thought through and spelled out clearly; otherwise it will lack a solid foundation for establishing realistic objectives, strategies, plans, and work assignments.[5] Drucker offers the following approach to defining "what is our business":

> A business is not defined by the company's name, statutes, or articles of incorporation. It is defined by the want the customer satisfies when he buys a product or a service. To satisfy the customer is the mission and purpose of every business. The question "What is our business?" can, therefore, be answered only by looking at the business from the outside, from the point of view of customer and market. What the customer sees, thinks, believes, and wants, at any given time, must be accepted by management as an objective fact . . . .
>
> . . . to the customer, no product or service, and certainly no company, is of much importance . . . The customer only wants to know what the product or service will do for him tomorrow. All he is interested in are his own values, his own wants, his own reality. For this reason alone, any serious attempt to state

---

[4]See, for example, Richard F. Vancil and Peter Lorange, "Strategic Planning in Diversified Companies," *Harvard Business Review*, vol. 53, no. 1 (January-February 1975), pp. 81-90.

[5]Peter F. Drucker, *Management: Tasks, Responsibilities, Practices* (New York: Harper and Row, Publishers, 1974), pp. 77-79.

"What our business is" must start with the customer, his realities, his situation, his behavior, his expectations, and his values.[6]

The Three Dimensions of Defining "What Is Our Business?"   Derek Abell has expanded on the importance of a customer-focused concept and suggests defining a business in terms of three dimensions: (1) customer groups, or *who* is being satisfied, (2) customer needs, or *what* is being satisfied and (3) technologies, or *how* customer needs are satisfied.[7] Figure 2-1 illustrates this three-dimensional approach to business definition. Abell

FIGURE 2-1
Defining a Business

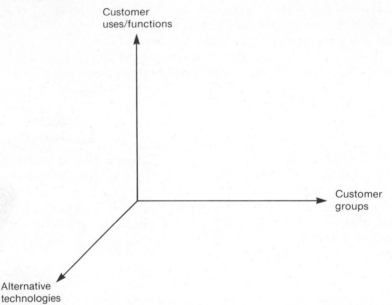

points out that viewing "what is our business" in terms of just products and markets obscures essential understanding. A product, in reality, is only a physical manifestation of the application of a particular technology to the satisfaction of a particular function or need for a particular customer group. The business choice, therefore, is a joint one of technologies, functions, and customers to serve, not simply of products to offer. Thinking of a business solely in terms of markets is also deficient because served markets are usually described only in terms of customer groups and customer

---

[6]Ibid., pp. 79-80.
[7]Derek F. Abell, *Defining the Business: The Starting Point of Strategic Planning* (Englewood Cliffs, N.J.: Prentice-Hall, Inc., 1980), p. 169.

functions, with little or no mention of technological options. Abell's points here are telling. The products offered and the markets served are *results* of choices of customer needs and functions, customer groups, and technologies; hence, it is the specific combination of the three choices which *reveal the most* about "what is our business."

As an illustration of the analytical power of the three-dimensional approach to defining a business, consider the electric utility industry. As shown in Figure 2-2, electric utility companies serve many customer groups—residential, commercial, industrial, rural cooperatives, and municipal electric systems. And the electricity that is supplied serves many functions (heating, cooling, water heating, cooking, lighting, and powering appliances, tools, and equipment) and meets a variety of customer needs (comfort, convenience, improved quality of life, and energy to operate business-related equipment and facilities). Yet, there are technological alternatives to generating and supplying such electricity: (1) conventional central station generation (coal, nuclear, hydro-electric) which is then transmitted over an elaborate distribution system directly to individual customers, (2) on-site generation (solar, windmills, fuel cells, gasoline-

FIGURE 2-2
Defining a Business: The Case of the Electric Utilities

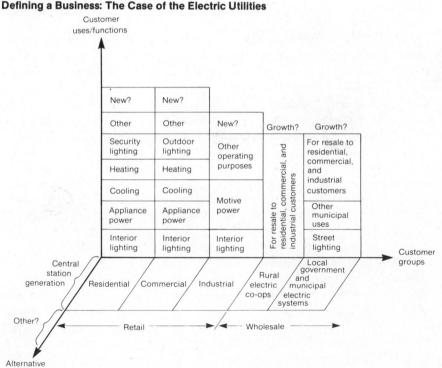

powered generators), and (3) co-generation of electricity as a by-product of industrial processes. Up to now, nearly every electric utility company has defined its business in terms of serving all customer groups in its territory and meeting all electric energy needs of these customers but using only the technology of central station generation and transmission to do so.

However, the sharp, sustained increases in the price of supplying electricity in this manner are raising issues about whether the electric utility business can long continue with its current definition. More industrial customers are turning to co-generation as a source of electricity. Residential customers are beginning to install solar equipment. Alternative generating technologies are undergoing rapid research and development. A whole host of energy-saving and energy-efficient devices are appearing in the marketplace. A number of municipalities and rural cooperatives are forming joint ventures to build their own generating stations and thus to supply their own electric energy needs rather than buy it at wholesale from the electric utilities. All of these developments have strong implications for how conventional electric utility companies define their business: Should they stick with only central station technology or move to adopt new technologies? Should they get into the business of making and installing energy-saving devices? Should they seek out new customer groups? Should they develop new uses for electricity? Is it time to begin thinking about diversificaton?

"What Will Our Business Be?"   Sooner or later, as the electric utility example shows, today's answer to "what is our business?" becomes obsolete. Therefore, in considering the question of "what is our business?" management is well-advised to add "and what *will* it be?"[8] This latter question forces the organization to look ahead and try to anticipate the impact of changing customer needs, changing technology, changing customer uses, and changing customer markets on the organization's business. It lays the basis for conscious redirection of the organization. It reduces the chances of becoming smug and complacent. It directs attention to "What are the customer's *unsatisfied* wants?"—the response to which may offer clues as to what direction a firm ought to pursue in modifying, extending, and developing its existing business concept. The analytical framework in Figure 2-1 offers an effective means of addressing how a firm might alter its business definition and decide the issue of "where do we go from here."

"What Should Our Business Be?"   Finally, it is pertinent to inquire "What *should* our business be?"[9] How can innovations be converted into new businesses? What technologies are opening up or can be created that offer attractive prospects for serving new and different customer functions and customer groups? Should diversification be pursued and, if so, what kind and how much diversification makes sense? Which things should the

---

[8]Ibid., p. 88-89.
[9]Ibid., p. 82.

organization continue doing and which should it plan to abandon? As examples, should electric utilities pursue interests in other energy fields such as coal, nuclear fuel, solar power, fuel cells, and other such "wave of the future" energy technologies? Should electric utilities be suppliers of electricity or suppliers of energy? Should electric utilities continue to be monopolies in supplying all electric customers within their geographic territory or should they begin to focus more narrowly on selected customer groups, letting other suppliers take on those customers which the electric utility ought to give up? Should electric utilities serve every conceivable customer need for electricity (or energy) or should it concentrate on serving a narrower range of needs? Should electric utilities begin to diversify outside of energy altogether?

Avoiding Broad or Vague Answers to "What Is Our Business?"

In approaching the question of "what is our business, what will it be and what should it be?" it is best to avoid answers that fail to clarify "who are we and where are we headed" or that are so all-encompassing an organization falls into the trap of trying to march in too many directions at once.[10] No contribution to direction-setting and to effective strategy formation comes from concepts so sweeping that they can mean almost anything. For example, if a state university perceives its business as "higher education," is this to mean it should offer the *full* range of programs in "higher education"—including technical training, associate degrees similar to those of junior colleges, adult and continuing education, as well as undergraduate and graduate programs in *all* disciplines and professions? A railroad company may decide to view itself as a "transporation company," but does this mean it should get into long-haul trucking or air-freight services or fleet car leasing or intercity busing or urban transit? The broader the language used to answer "what is our business and what will it be?" the less focus it directs to customer groups, customer needs, technologies, and types of products. Broad generalities may be okay from a public relations or annual report perspective but they are very dysfunctional when it comes to the needs of managers to have a sharp understanding of the firm's business and where it is headed.

Generally speaking, top management's concept of an organization's business should (1) avoid the ambiguity of organizational direction that flows from broad statements about purpose and scope, (2) be reasonably specific about the customer groups to be served, the customer needs to be satisfied, the range of technologies to be employed, and the types of products to be offered, and (3) not be so confining as to give managers tunnel vision in examining how to adapt the firm's business to changing circumstances and new priorities.

---

[10]H. Igor Ansoff, *Corporate Strategy* (New York: McGraw-Hill, 1965), pp. 105-108.

THE CONCEPT OF STRATEGIC FIT

In trying to define "what is our business, what will it be and what should it be?" many companies have a distinct preference for building some degree of "relatedness" into their different activities. This is an especially pertinent consideration in resolving "what kind and how much diversification?" When an organization's several activities have some form of "strategic fit," organizational effectiveness and efficiency are often enhanced.

As it has come to be thought of, *strategic fit* is a measure of the relatedness and synergistic match among different businesses or activities. Strategic fit can produce a $2 + 2 = 5$ phenomenon because of certain benefits that emerge from a "goodness of fit" among different activities.[11] The nature of the benefit varies according to the nature of the fit.

Product-market fit exists when different products follow common distribution channels, utilize the same sales promotion techniques, are bought by the same customers, meet related customer needs and functions, and/or can be sold by the same sales force. This type of strategic fit generally enhances the firm's overall effectiveness in the marketplace.

Operating fit results from purchasing and warehousing economies, joint utilization of plant and equipment, overlaps in technology and engineering design, carryover of R&D activities, and/or common labor requirements. This type of fit tends to yield gains in internal operating efficiency.

Management fit emerges when different kinds of activities present managers with comparable or similar types of entrepreneurial, technical, administrative, or operating problems, thereby allowing the accumulated managerial know-how associated with one line of business to spill over and be useful in managing another of the organization's activities. Management fit tends to reduce the myriad of management problems and complications, thus making diversification easier to manage.

Is Strategic Fit Necessary?   Because the synergistic benefits of strategic fit can be considerable and because there is a unifying value to building diversification around a conceptual customer-technology-product theme, many firms have chosen to pursue mostly *related* types of diversification efforts. Other firms, however, have not been guided by strategic fit considerations. The so-called conglomerate firms are built upon the principle of *unrelated* diversification and thus are by design without real customer-technology-product fit among their different businesses. Textron, for example, is the corporate parent of such diverse businesses as Bell helicopters, Gorham silver, Homelite chain saws, Sheaffer pens, Fafnir bearings, Speidel watchbands, Polaris snowmobiles, Sprague gas meters and fittings, Bostitch staplers, air cushion vehicles, iron castings, milling machines, rolling mills, industrial fasteners, insurance, and

---

[11]David T. Kollat, Roger D. Blackwell, and James F. Robeson, *Strategic Marketing* (New York: Holt, Rinehart & Winston, Inc., 1972), pp. 23-24.

missile and spacecraft propulsion systems—among others. (Illustration Capsule 6 describes the logic underlying Textron's diversity.)

ILLUSTRATION CAPSULE 6
Textron's Concept of Conglomerate Diversification

In its *1976* and *1977 Annual Reports*, Textron made the following statements about its corporate purpose, objectives, and strategy:

Textron is founded on the principle of balanced diversification, designed on the one hand to afford protection against economic cycles and product obsolescence and on the other to provide a means for participating in new markets and new technologies. The key elements are balance and flexibility in a rapidly changing world.

Textron, . . ., has established a versatile business organization with a presence in many markets, geographic areas and technologies, and a management style and philosophy that has generated a proven record.

Textron seeks to be distinctive in its products and services—distinctive as to technology, design, and service and value. Superior performance will be achieved by way of excellence and quality. These, plus motivated people of high standards, are the essential ingredients for achievement of an overall goal of superior performance on a continuing basis.

Through more than two dozen Divisions in five Groups—Aerospace, Consumer, Industrial, Metal Product, and Creative Capital—Textron's decentralization of day-to-day operations is coupled with corporate coordination and control to assure consistency of standards and performance. The operating Divisions are provided with the capital and planning assistance to meet demonstrated needs for growth. This business structure combines the enthusiasm and quick response of moderate-sized enterprises with the planning and financial resources available on a consolidated basis.

Textron has three important priorities: *People development. Internal profit growth. New initiatives.* Emphasizing these priorities, Textron seeks to accomplish quantitative objectives set in 1972 for the ten-year period ending 1982. These specific targets for compound rates of growth are:

Sales: 8% per year, to $3.5 billion in 1982.
Progress, 1972 to date: 11% to $2.8 billion in 1977.

Net income: 10% per year, to $200 million in 1982.
Progress, 1972 to date: 11% to $137 million in 1977.

Net income per common share: 10% per year, to $6.00 in 1982.
Progress, 1972 to date: 9% to $3.65 in 1977.

Another pioneer of the conglomerate or pure diversification concept is International Telephone and Telegraph (ITT), which has grown from a medium-sized telecommunications company into the nation's fourteenth largest industrial corporation with 1981 annual sales exceeding $17.3 billion. At one juncture, "the world of ITT" consisted of some 350 companies having an additional 700-plus lower-tier subsidiaries of their own; ITT products and companies included telephone equipment, Sheraton hotels, Wonder Bread, Smithfield Hams, Bobbs-Merrill Publishing Co., Hartford Insurance Co., Aetna Finance Co., Jabsco Pump Co., Gotham Lighting Co., Speedwriting Inc., Transportation Displays, Inc., Rayonier chemical cellulose, Bramwell Business School, South Bend Window Cleaning Co., and Scott lawn care products.

Textron and ITT, along with several other conglomerates, have been successful enough to cast doubt upon the *necessity* of unified themes and strategic fit. But the experience to date *does* indicate that managing widely diversified companies presents big demands on corporate-level management.[12] Broadly-diversified conglomerates have had difficulties in profitably operating so many unrelated businesses—chiefly because corporate managers, not having firsthand experience in each one of the firm's varied business interests, find themselves short on the grassroots customer-technology-industry knowledge requisite for avoiding bad decisions.[13] The greater the number of diverse businesses that corporate managers must oversee the harder it is for them to keep close watch over the real strategic issues in each line of business and thereby remain in position to probe deeply into the strategic actions and plans of business-level managers. As one president of a diversified firm expressed it:

> . . . we've got to make sure that our core businesses are properly managed for solid, long-term earnings. We can't just sit back and watch the numbers. We've got to know what the real issues are out there in the profit centers. Otherwise, we're not even in a position to check out our managers on the big decisions. And considering the pressures they're under, that's pretty dangerous for all concerned.[14]

THE LEVELS OF STRATEGY

Once an organization's managers have a conceptual grip on "who are we and where are we headed?" and a working understanding of "what is our business, what will it be, and what should it be?" then they have a basis for setting challenging but achievable performance objectives and for formu-

---

[12]For an interesting discussion of some of the issues involved, see Lewis Meman, "What We Learned from the Great Merger Frenzy," *Fortune* (April 1973), pp. 70-73, 144-40 and Dan Cordtz, "What Does U.S.I. Do: Why, Almost Everything," *Fortune* (February 1973), pp. 73-77.

[13]This point is explored further in Chapter 3.

[14]Carter F. Bales, "Strategic Control: The President's Paradox," *Business Horizons*, vol. 20, no. 4 (August 1977), p. 17.

lating strategies to achieve them. The desired outcome is the creation of a hierarchy of objectives that spans the organization from top to bottom and the formation of a corresponding hierarchy of strategies to achieve the objectives at each organization level. Thus, corporate-level objectives underlie the formation of *corporate-level strategy*; line of business objectives underlie the formation of *line of business strategy* (or just *business strategy*); functional area objectives (in manufacturing, marketing, finance, and so on) underlie the formation of *functional area support strategy*; and departmental and work unit objectives underlie the formation of *operating-level strategy*.

Corporate-Level Strategy.   *Corporate-level strategy* is top management's game plan for directing and running the organization as a whole; it focuses squarely on "how shall we manage the *set* of businesses we are in and intend to be in" to achieve the target levels of corporate performance. Corporate-level strategy is the pattern of entrepreneurial actions and intents underlying all of an organization's strategic interests—its different businesses, divisions, product lines, technologies, buyer groups, and buyer needs. At the corporate level, there are two overriding strategic concerns:

1. *How should we manage the scope, mix, and emphasis among our various activities?* This embraces such strategic issues as: When and how should we get into new businesses? Which of our existing businesses should we get out of, and should we do so quickly or gradually? Which of our existing businesses should be given greater emphasis and which should be given lesser emphasis? What general strategic approach should we employ in each one of our different activities—grow and build, or hold and maintain, or overhaul and reposition, or shrink and manage for decline, or what? What can we do to improve the performance of our overall business portfolio?

2. *How shall corporate resources be allocated across our activities?* The essential issue here is which organizational unit shall get how much and in what order of priority.

The strategic importance of an organization's scope and mix of activities is that it determines not only the organization's health and well-being but also its "position" in the external environment. Which customer needs a firm is meeting and is moving to meet, which customer groups it serves and is moving to serve, which technologies it employs and is becoming capable of employing, and which products it is offering and is capable of offering (all of which, combined, define the scope and mix of organizational activities) are excellent barometers of how well-situated an organization is to capitalize on opportunities and how vulnerable it may be to emerging threats. For example, a diversified firm whose business portfolio is weighted heavily with so many young, promising businesses that it is short of capital to undertake aggressive grow-and-build strategies in each one is weakly positioned to take advantage of the opportunities before it.

The second concern of corporate-level strategy—how to allocate corporate resources—is crucial because it supplies a much-needed management rationale for evaluating competing requests for corporate resources. Corporate-level managers need to work through the issue of what kind of match between internal resource capability and scope/mix of activities will yield a level of performance and results commensurate with corporate objectives. This is central to the corporate game plan because if a high level of organizational performance is to be achieved, then both the availability of internal resources and the patterns with which they are deployed need to be in close alignment with the success requirements of each line of business the corporation is in.

The concept of corporate strategy has classic application in multi-product, multi-industry, multi-technology organizations since their top managements are continually under the gun to make a workable whole out of numerous activities, some or many of which are not related. But it also applies to single-business enterprises which are contemplating some kind of diversification and/or shift in corporate direction. Thus, in either single-business or multi-business enterprises, corporate strategy formulation entails consideration of what new businesses (if any) to get into, which current businesses to give greater or lesser emphasis to, which existing activities to divest or close down, and what general strategic approach to follow in each chosen line of business. Necessarily, then, corporate strategy is concerned with the issue of strategic fit and with how the pros and cons of related/unrelated diversification pertain to the specifics of the firm's own situation. It is concerned with how much and what kind of diversification to pursue. It is concerned with the whys and hows of acquisition and divestiture and, more generally, with a strategic rationale for evaluating a portfolio of businesses. It is concerned with how generally to manage each different business it is in. And it is concerned with the criteria and priorities to be used in allocating financial capital and organizational skills among the chosen lines of businesses.

Consider the abbreviated statements of corporate-level strategy:

Corporate Strategy Statement	*Remarks*
1. The strategy of Morris Steel Co. is to become a fully integrated steel producer over the next five years, with emphasis on manufacturing those steel products which have the fastest-growing uses.	This is a good beginning statement but it is incomplete. It says something about direction, scope, and emphasis but nothing about (1) resource allocation among the stages of vertical integration, (2) how the firm intends to compete successfully, and (3) specific customer groups, customer needs,

Corporate Strategy Statement	*Remarks*
	and product offerings. It is silent about whether a marketing focus on fast-growing product categories is compatible with the need for manufacturing efficiency. (Is there any risk of potential fragmentation of manufacturing and technological resource associated with using growth rates as the sole criterion for product line selection?) Among the literally hundreds of "steel products," is it really feasible in terms of plants and equipment and distribution channels to restrict attention only to the fastest-growing items? More specifics are thus badly needed to flesh out the statement and give it real strategic content.
2. PWB Company's strategy is to retain all of its profits to finance diversification into the leisure time industry and thereby raise its annual growth rate of sales and profits from 5 to 10 percent. Diversification will emphasize acquiring young, rapidly-growing companies which have proven management and which have demonstrated the ability to manufacture and market a quality product.	Although the strategy suggests a wider scope of operation and the means to finance it, as well as relating strategy to specific objectives, it omits mention of PWB's existing business. Who is PWB and what does it do now? Also, the notion of "leisure time industry" needs to be pinned down; it could mean anything from manufacturing slot machines to making scuba diving gear to selling hiking and camping equipment—all of which have different business requirements.
3. Our strategy for the next two years is to compete in the low price segment of the women's apparel business, with a limited line of fashion conscious items that can be sold	This strategy statement is the most complete and detailed of the three statements. It describes the intended scope of operations, the deployment of resources, and the competitive approach to the

Corporate Strategy Statement ·   *Remarks*

on the basis of style and low price directly to national retail chains catering to budget-conscious women. During this period, no diversification efforts will be undertaken and all available internal funds will be allocated to debt retirement, increased marketing efforts, and improved production methods—in that order of priority.	market. Yet it could be improved upon by adding references to distinctive competence, sought for competitive advantages, and what types of women's apparel it intends to make.

Observe that the more specific and detailed the strategy statement is, the more clear it is what kind of organization is being described, where it is headed, and how it is going to get there. Unless strategy reveals these things about an organization, it is too vague to provide guidance to lower-level managers and it may reflect a fuzzy or incompletely formulated strategic plan.

Illustration Capsule 7 explores some aspects of how corporate-level strategy is formulated and discussed within the top management structure.

ILLUSTRATION CAPSULE 7
Corporate Strategy: Out in the Open or Kept under Wraps?

There are several issues concerning how open the discussion of corporate-level strategy ought to be: To what extent should the details of corporate strategy be expressly articulated to the board of directors, to the various levels of management, to stockholders, and to the outside world? Should a large, multibusiness corporation's board of directors be involved in formulating corporate strategy or is its role the more narrow one of reviewing it and monitoring the process that produces it? What is the best clue of a success-producing corporate strategy—a clearly thoughtout strategy that is articulated, questioned, and evaluated before it is approved and used as a basis for decisions *or* an entrepreneurially astute chief executive officer *or* the circumstances of being in the right place at the right time? How can one know what a firm's corporate strategy *really* is?

There are no nice, neat, pat answers to the questions posed. But partial answers, at least, are emerging. As Professor Edward Wrapp cogently observed in a recent *Harvard Business Review* column, there can be four different perspectives about what a firm's corporate strategy is:[1]

[1]As quoted by Kenneth R. Andrews in "Corporate Strategy as a Vital Function of the Board," *Harvard Business Review*, vol. 59, no. 6 (November-December 1981), p. 176.

ILLUSTRATION CAPSULE 7 *(continued)*

1. *Corporate strategy for the annual report.* Usually the discussions of corporate strategy in annual reports are sterilized by top managment and carefully edited by the public relations staff. Nonetheless, pressures for such statements are growing because they give stockholders a sense of direction about where the company is headed and convey an assurance that management has a conscious game plan for directing and running the enterprise.

2. *Corporate strategy for the board of directors, middle managers, and outside securities analysts.* The articulation of corporate strategy for these groups is more comprehensive and detailed than annual report statements. It includes more information about the hows and whys of corporate direction, gives some details on growth opportunities, offers information about specific businesses and markets, and contains more documentation of top management's plans for the company. Yet, even these audiences get only part of the strategy; discussions and documentation are kept simple and somewhat superficial—possible pitfalls and drawbacks are seldom explicitly discussed.

3. *Corporate strategy for top management.* In organizations of much size or complexity, all of the key top executives usually participate in comprehensive, in-depth discussions of basic corporate direction, corporate strengths and weaknesses, emerging threats and opportunities, and what moves and countermoves are under contemplation. Typically, special studies and analyses may be prepared as a basis for deciding what course to follow. A full airing of the pros and cons and the various ramifications of each option often precede strategic decisions. The chief executive/ general manager, needing the support of key subordinates, may strive to reach broad consensus on strategy. In the process, key executives come to understand, question, evaluate, and formalize the chosen corporate-level strategy.

4. *The chief executive's own private version of corporate strategy.* The chief executive/general manager commonly mulls a range of moves that are disclosed to almost no one. The reasons for keeping one's own counsel on strategy may be dictated by a belief that he/she has the best entrepreneurial instincts to sort out the pros and cons and to decide how best to proceed; or it may be because of the risks of premature disclosure of sensitive maneuvers; or it may reflect his/her own perception of needs and circumstances that others have not yet recognized and diagnosed; or it may stem from a desire to maneuver informally and flexibly. Given that the chief executive bears ultimate responsibility for corporate strategy and must preside over the strategy formulation process, it should come as no surprise that his/her own personal vision of the game plan (which no doubt undergoes constant change as events unfold and new information is assimilated) is an authentic and highly relevant "source" of what an organization's corporate strategy really is and is going to be. The importance of the top executive's private version of strategy ex-

ILLUSTRATION CAPSULE 7 *(continued)*

plains why "strategy-watchers" both inside and outside the organization pay so much attention to his/her actions and pronouncements for whatever "signals" they may contain.

How much one knows about corporate strategy is thus a variable: it depends on who you are, how much an organization elects to reveal about its strategy, and what can be deduced and inferred from the organization's actions.

As concerns the role of the board of directors in the corporate strategy formulation process, this too is a variable. Some organizations involve board members much more heavily in corporate strategy decisions than do others. Texas Instruments, for example, has its board members attend a four-day strategic planning conference each year to discuss business opportunities over the next ten years; some members stay on for another two days of meetings with 500 managers from all the company's activities. In addition, there is a corporate objectives committee composed of board members and each director is furnished a wealth of strategy-related information. The outcome is that the TI board is heavily involved in reviewing and monitoring the TI strategy. In other companies, though, corporate executives prefer to keep board members "splashing around in the shallow end of the pool, never letting them venture into deep water." As one former chief executive officer of a multibusiness firm expressed it, "The idea of exposing my strategy for a full discussion by the board never crossed my mind."[2] Another chief executive related, "My board members spent too much time talking about how they did things in their own companies. We listened to their stories, but for the most part they had remote relevance . . . ."[3]

One of the originating pioneers of the concept of corporate strategy, Kenneth R. Andrews, argues:

The board must sense at least how well the chief strategic officer of the company (in almost all cases the CEO) has investigated market opportunity, appraised and invested in the distinctive competence and total resources of his company, and combined opportunity and resources, consistent with the economic resources, personal values, and ethical aspirations that define the character of the company.

Since no one has a monopoly on insight, not only should top management agree on what it will try to accomplish, but so should the board.[4]

[2]Ibid., p. 180.
[3]Ibid.
[4]Ibid.

ILLUSTRATION CAPSULE 7 *(concluded)*

Andrews' point is that board review and discussion of strategy presents individual directors the opportunity (1) to test whether top management has done a creditable job of formulating a durable corporate strategy, however sparsely stated, (2) to get some idea of its validity and feasibility, (3) to relate it to individual project and capital investment decisions, and (4) to ask strategically relevant questions.

While Andrews and others argue that the cause of corporate strategy formulation is enhanced when it is brought out of the closet and becomes a candidly participative process, the contrary view is that so long as the chief executive and other important general managers are creative entrepreneurs and skilled strategic thinkers, they can find ways to make businesses healthy and keep them that way—a consideration that outweighs the issue of whether the strategy is articulated and made explicit or not.

(*Note*: As you may have surmised, the focus of this book is on the third item in Professor Wrapp's list—corporate strategy for top management.)

Line of Business Strategy. *Line of business (or business) strategy* is management's game plan for directing and running a particular business unit. Business strategy deals expressly with the issues of (1) how the organization intends to compete in that specific business, (2) what the role/thrust of each key functional area of the business will be in contributing to the success of the enterprise to the marketplace, and (3) resource allocation *within* the business unit.

The external aspects of line of business strategy concern how the organization can be entrepreneurially effective in that particular business—what sort of competitive edge to strive for, which customer needs and customer groups to emphasize, whether and how to differentiate the firm's product offerings from those of rivals, how to "position" the business in the marketplace vis-a-vis rivals and to appeal to customers, and what must be done to keep the firm's market approach abreast of the evolutionary aspects of industry trends and direction, societal changes, and economic conditions. The internal character of line of business strategy suggests how the different pieces of the business (manufacturing, marketing, finance, R&D, and so on) ought to be aligned and coordinated so as to be responsive to those market factors upon which competitive success depends. In the latter regard, line of business strategy provides guidance for organizing and funding the performance of subactivities within the business and for doing so in ways which speak directly to what is needed for strategic success. Perhaps the key internal concern is what kind of distinctive competence to develop and how to develop it. Being truly and uniquely good at some key aspect of creating, producing, and marketing the firm's product/service can be *the vehicle for establishing a competitive advantage* and, in turn, translating this into successful business performance.

Observe that for a single-product, single-business enterprise, corporate strategy and business strategy are one and the same, except for when a single-business firm begins to contemplate diversification. Our distinction between corporate and business strategy is most relevant for multi-business firms—that is, for firms which are sufficiently diversified to have more than one line of business or which have different strategies for separate customer-technology-product segments.

A good example of line of business strategy is Kellogg's approach to the ready-to-eat cereals business. Since 1906, when Will Keith Kellogg formed the company after accidentally discovering a way to make ready-to-eat cereal, Kellogg has aimed its strategy at being the dominant leader in the ready-to-eat cereal business. Kellogg's strategy for competing is based on product differentiation and market segmentation. The company's product line features a diverse number of brands, differentiated according to grain, shape, form, flavor, color, and taste—a something for everyone approach. Competing on the basis of low price has been deemphasized in favor of nonprice strategies keyed to extensive product variety, regular product innovation, substantial TV advertising, periodic promotional offers and prizes, and maintaining more space on the grocery shelf than rivals have. Much of Kellogg's sales efforts are targeted at the under-25 age group (the biggest cereal eaters with an average annual consumption of 11 pounds per capita), and 33 percent of its cereal sales are in presweetened brands promoted almost totally through TV advertising to children. Kellogg endeavors to sidestep industry maturity and product saturation with introductions of fresh, "new" types of cereals (presweetened cereals in the 1940s, "nutritional" cereals in the 1950s, "natural" and health conscious cereals in the 1960s and early 1970s, and adult cereals in the late 1970s) and also by advertising a variety of times and places for eating cereals other than at the morning breakfast table. Product line freshness is additionally enhanced by introduction of brands which differ only slightly from existing brands (flakes vs. shredded, plain vs. sugar-frosted, puffed vs. cocoa flavored). In 1979, Kellogg introduced five new cereal brands—more than it had ever launched in a single year—as part of a stepped-up and redirected effort to attract consumers in the 25-50 age group (where consumption levels were only half those of the younger age groups). Kellogg also introduced its cereals in four additional countries in South America and the Middle East using campaigns that featured free samples, demonstration booths in food stores, and heavy local advertising so as to promote the use of ready-to-eat cereals as a substitute for traditional breakfast foods (corn meal and bulgur). Both of these moves were aimed at changing the eating habits of adults who had shied away from cereals or who had spurned breakfast altogether. In further support of its attempt to appeal to more customer groups, Kellogg continued to up its research budget (already the industry's most extensive) by 15 percent annually in an effort to develop more nutritional, health conscious cereals and breakfast foods for the older consumer segment. The whole of Kellogg's strategy in cereals had three strategic objectives: (1) increasing Kellogg's 42 percent market share, (2) increasing sales by 5 percent annually (compared to an industry growth of 2 percent), and (3) boosting annual cereal consumption from 8.6 pounds per capita to 12 pounds by 1985.

Functional Area Support Strategy.   *Functional area support strategy* concerns the game plan for managing a principal subordinate activity *within* the business. Functional strategies undergird overall business strategy and consist of even more details and specifics about how a business will be managed. There is a functional area support strategy for the production part of the business, for marketing, for finance, for human resources, for R&D—indeed for every major subpart of the whole business. Functional area support strategies are thus major corollaries of the line of business strategy; their role is to flesh out the overall game plan and give it more substance, completeness, and concrete meaning as applied to a specific part of the business. They are important because they explicitly indicate how each major subactivity in the business is to contribute to accomplishing the overall business strategy. In addition, when each of the principal activities within a single business, and most especially the activities crucial to successful strategy execution, are integrated and fit together to form a smoothly-functioning, consistent business unit, the success of business strategy is enhanced.

Whereas formation of line of business strategy is the responsibility of the general manager of the business unit, responsibility for formation of functional area support strategy is typically delegated by the business-level manager to his/her principal subordinates who are charged with running the functional areas in question. And just as the business-level manager is obliged to establish a set of objectives and a strategy that is deemed by corporate management to contribute adequately toward corporate-level performance objectives, it follows that functional area managers need to establish performance objectives and strategies that will promote accomplishment of business-level objectives and strategy. Moreover, just as business-level strategies and objectives tend to be approved via negotiation between corporate managers and business managers, the close tie between line of business strategy and functional area support strategies argues for the business manager's ratification of the functional area objectives and support strategies which are proposed by functional managers.

Illustration Capsule 8 provides a detailed look at a sample functional area support strategy—IBM's marketing approach.

Operating-Level Strategy.   *Operating-level strategies* refer to the even more specific strategy-related actions and practices of departmental and supervisory level managers—how they intend to manage the day-to-day

ILLUSTRATION CAPSULE 8
IBM's Marketing Approach—A Sample Functional Area Strategy*

IBM's strategic approach to marketing its products during the 1967-1972 period is considered by industry observers to be a prime reason for the firm's success in capturing about a 65-70% share of the computer systems market. At the heart of the IBM approach was the "systems selling" concept whereby IBM salespeople were encouraged to sell customers a complete data-processing system. The IBM package included a central processing unit, peripheral equipment (tape storage, disk storage, high-speed printers, card readers, keypunch machines), software, maintenance, emergency repairs, applications support, and consulting services to train the customer's personnel. By offering a total systems package IBM attempted to supply the full range of a customer's data-processing needs.

IBM encouraged customers to lease rather than purchase its products. The advantage to the customer of a leasing arrangement was protection against rapid technological obsolescence. As new equipment was introduced and/or as customer requirements changed, the old system could be turned in for a bigger, better (albeit, generally more costly) new system. In introducing new systems, IBM priced the new equipment *lower* than the older system on a performance/price basis; thus for a given set of jobs, the new system represented a savings to the customer over the old system. However, because the customer's usage of the new system expanded to cover more tasks and applications, the upgrading to the new system produced higher rentals for IBM.

Initially, IBM charged rentals for hardware and provided service, software, and consulting free to its customers—a pricing strategy which motivated customers to accept the total IBM package (to the exclusion of rivals who offered only a partial package—just service or just hardware and software). When IBM was charged by the Justice Department in the late 1960s with monopolizing and attempting to monopolize the computer market (one complaint being the "one-price" rental system), IBM's marketing strategy shifted to one of pricing its equipment rental and services separately. IBM began using a standard base contract for all equipment which provided for a monthly rental and required a 30-day notice for cancellation (a feature which facilitated upgrading of customers as new products were introduced). The base rental fee covered the use of equipment for a specified number of hours per week; usage beyond this amount (usually 40 to 50 hours) resulted in "additional use" rental fees of up to 40% of the base rental. All rented equipment was serviced by IBM under a separate service contract, with the amount of the service fee being pegged to equipment usage.

However, when IBM's competitors began to introduce attractively-priced peripheral equipment (printers, tapes, disks, and memories) that were com-

*The content of this capsule has been extracted and synthesized from Derek F. Abell, *Defining the Business: The Starting Point of Strategic Planning* (Englewood Cliffs, N.J.: Prentice-Hall, Inc., 1980), pp. 32-48.

ILLUSTRATION CAPSULE 8 (concluded)

patible with IBM central processing units, IBM adopted a Fixed Term Plan (FTP) leasing approach for its tape, disk, and printer products. Under the FTP, customers were allowed an 8% discount on 1-year leases, a 16% discount on 2-year leases, and all extra use charges were eliminated; the penalty for canceling an FTP was 2 1/2 times the monthly rental for 1-year contracts and 5 times the monthly rental for 2-year contracts. The FTP not only made IBM products more price competitive but it also shielded IBM's leased products from competition for a longer period. To make up for the lost revenues under the FTP price discounts, IBM raised its prices for products not covered by the FTP and, also, raised prices for maintenance and services. The net effect was that while most customers ended up paying IBM about the same total amount as before FTP, they paid less for those IBM products which faced active competition.

When the peripheral equipment manufacturers responded to the FTP with price cuts of their own, IBM initiated a second round of price cuts, along with product design changes. IBM's basic marketing strategy continued to be to induce customers to trade up to progressively higher performance computers.

requirements of functional area support strategies. Thus, operating strategy deals with the nuts and bolts of how the various facets of each functional area strategy will be carried out. The scope of the operating manager's job is, of course, more limited than that of the functional area manager to whom he/she reports and the operating strategy statement which guides his/her activities is accordingly narrower and more specific.[15] However, since operating managers have the task of devising and executing actions that will partially implement the functional area strategy and, ultimately, the business strategy, the need for operating managers to have their own specific game plans for their respective areas of responsibility is every bit as great as it is for higher-ranking managers.[16]

Several examples of operating-level strategy are indicated below:

- A cosmetics firm relies upon ads placed in magazines as an integral part of its marketing effort to inform women about its product line. The firm's advertising director elects to run ad campaigns during the month prior to each of the company's three peak sales periods of Christmas, Easter, and Mother's Day, with full page ads to be placed in *McCall's*, *Cosmopolitan*, and *Ladies Home Journal* and quarter-page ads to be placed in *Seventeen*, *Family Circle*, and *Woman's Day*.

[15]Richard F. Vancil, "Strategy Formulation in Complex Organizations," *Sloan Management Review*, vol. 17, no. 2 (Winter 1976), p. 12.
[16]Ibid.

- A company with a low-price, high-volume business strategy supports its efforts at the manufacturing level with a production worker strategy that stresses achieving high levels of labor efficiency via (1) careful selection and training of new employees, (2) unhesitating purchases of time-saving tools and equipment, and (3) a wage-fringe benefit package that promotes high morale and employee retention.

- A distributor of heating and air-conditioning equipment emphasizes quick, reliable parts delivery as the feature component of its dealer service package. Accordingly, the inventory strategy of the warehouse manager is to maintain such a sufficiently ample supply of parts that the chance of a stockout on a given item is virtually nil, and his warehouse staffing strategy is to maintain a large enough work force to service each order within 24 hours.

Note that in each example cited the logic of the operating-level strategy flowed directly from a higher-order strategic requirement and that responsibility for the operating strategy was assigned to the lower echelons of the management hierarchy where the day-to-day details of a firm's activities are administered.

The Hierachical Web of Strategy

Ideally, corporate strategy, business strategy, functional area support strategy, and operating-level strategy are developed in sufficient detail that each manager in the organization has a confident understanding of how to manage his/her area of responsibility in accordance with the total organizationwide game plan. This is why many layers of strategy are typically needed (especially in large, diversified organizations), with each layer being progressively more detailed to provide strategic guidance for the next level of subordinate managers. In addition, the separate pieces and layers of strategy should be consistent and interlock smoothly—like the pieces of a puzzle. When the various parts of an organization's strategic plan are in harmony and mutually supportive, organizational cohesiveness is enhanced. Diverse activities are welded together in a more coherent fashion, and individuals are more likely to have a shared commitment to accomplishing the overall game plan. A unified strategic plan wherein all the various elements of strategy are "pulling together" acts to keep the pet projects of individuals and the viewpoints of functional specialists from blurring organizationwide strategic priorities.[17] In a sense, the links between and among the levels of strategy become the conceptual glue that binds an organization's activities together.[18]

[17]The ease with which functional areas can get at cross purposes with business strategy is illustrated by the case of a well-established foundry which initiated a strategy to build up a new customer base for industrial castings but found that work orders for castings were given the lowest priority in the milling and shipping departments because they were a new item and required different handling procedures; the strategic importance of the castings had simply not been impressed upon these two functional subunits.

[18]Vancil, "Strategy Formulation in Complex Organizations," p. 18.

Figure 2-3 depicts a hypothetical composite strategy and the several levels of directional actions and decisions requisite for making it operationally complete. Note the logical flow from corporate strategy to business strategy to functional support strategies to operating-level strategies. It should be evident from an examination of this figure that an organization's strategic plan is the sum total of the directional actions and decisions it must make in trying to accomplish its objectives. *The* strategy of an organization is really a collection of strategies—one for each facet of an organization's activities and perhaps even one for each manager. These strategies form a hierarchical network encompassing the broad-ranging to the very specific and they are linked together by analysis and soul-searching, as well as by an interactive, iterative process of negotiation and agreement on objectives, approaches, practices, policies, and constraints.

One final word about the levels of strategy. No matter how layered and specific a given strategy is, it should still be regarded as something which changes and which evolves.[19] While an organization's business purpose and long-term strategic objectives may not change significantly over long periods of time (particularly if they are carefully drawn), the overall make-up and emphasis given to its various product-customer-technological activities are certain to change in response to new internal priorities and to a fairly constant flow of new circumstances in the industry and its larger macro-environment. As a consequence, fine tuning-type changes in strategic plans, and an occasional major change in strategic thrust, are normal and expected. The *inevitability of an evolving strategy* means that any strategic plan stands only for a finite time—until either internal or external circumstances warrant a change.

WHAT KINDS OF FACTORS SHAPE STRATEGY

Many, many factors have to be considered in formulating strategy. In general, the aim is to achieve a match between the organization's internal skills, capabilities, and resources on the one hand and all of the relevant external considerations on the other hand. Although the determinants of strategy will be thoroughly explored in Chapters 4 and 5, it is useful at this point to review the general considerations that shape strategy.

Where a Firm's Best Opportunities Lie

Opportunity is always a factor in determining strategy.[20] Most of the time it is a pivotal strategic consideration, for unless one perceives that an

---

[19]Ibid, pp. 2-5.

[20]As cogently pointed out by Philip Kotler, there is a difference of opinion in the literature of management regarding whether the strategy formulation process should begin with the identification of opportunities or with the defining of business purpose and objectives. Those who say the first step should be to identify opportunities argue that (1) many organizations

FIGURE 2-3
The Levels of Strategy for a Hypothetical Petroleum Company

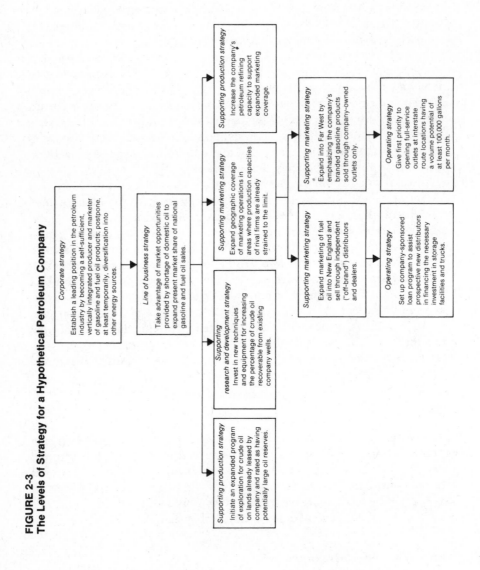

Corporate strategy

Establish a leading position in the petroleum industry by becoming a self-sufficient, vertically integrated producer and marketer of gasoline and fuel oil products; postpone, at least temporarily, diversification into other energy sources.

Line of business strategy

Take advantage of market opportunities provided by shortage of domestic oil to expand present market share of national gasoline and fuel oil sales.

Supporting production strategy

Initiate an expanded program of exploration for crude oil on lands already leased by company and rated as having potentially large oil reserves.

Supporting research and development strategy

Invest in new techniques and equipment for increasing the percentage of crude oil recoverable from existing company wells.

Supporting marketing strategy

Expand geographic coverage of marketing operations in areas where production capacities of rival firms are already strained to the limit.

Supporting production strategy

Increase the company's petroleum refining capacity to support expanded marketing coverage.

Supporting marketing strategy

Expand marketing of fuel oil into New England and sell through independent ("off-brand") distributors and dealers.

Supporting marketing strategy

Expand into Far West by emphasizing the company's branded gasoline products sold through company-owned outlets only.

Operating strategy

Set up company-sponsored loan program to assist prospective new distributors in financing the necessary investment in storage facilities and trucks.

Operating strategy

Give first priority to opening full-service outlets at interstate route locations having a volume potential of at least 100,000 gallons per month.

opportunity exists there is little point in proceeding. But on occasions, opportunity is just a necessary presence. For instance, when market demand is growing rapidly, it is virtually certain that firms in the industry will pursue the avenues for increased sales and profits; the gut issue is thus not whether opportunity exists but rather how to capture it.

In general terms, an organization's attempt to relate its strategy to opportunity consists of an assessment of any influences or trends in the external environment which may make a difference in what it elects to do or not do. This assessment of the external environment entails many facets: analyzing it; predicting it; attempting to change it; deciding how best to adapt to it; electing to get into or get out of some parts of it (in terms of specific customer groups, customer needs, technologies, and products). It means looking at all relevant external aspects: market trends, where an industry is headed, how and why customers use the products in question, market size, competitive forces, competitor's strategies, trends in technology, R&D potentials, government policies and regulations, buyer demographics and profiles, competition from substitute products, economic trends and conditions—essentially anything and everything that can have a bearing on the firm's business opportunities.

In viewing the role of opportunity in the strategy formulation process, it is important to distinguish between *environmental opportunities* and *company opportunities*.[21] It is fair to say that there are always business opportunities in an economy as long as there are unsatisfied needs and wants backed up by adequate purchasing power. But none of these necessarily represent opportunities for a specific company. New forms of health care delivery are probably not an opportunity for Texaco, nor is a growing popularity of skiing a likely opportunity for General Motors. The environmental opportunities that are most likely to be relevant to a particular

have gotten their start because they recognized the existence of a major opportunity (Xerox, Polaroid, Holiday Inns, IBM, and Coca-Cola, among others); (2) many organizations which lack sharply-defined objectives and are unable to articulate what they are really trying to do have nonetheless compiled a good record of seizing opportunities; and (3) a number of organizations have changed their focus and their objectives when their opportunities change (as did the March of Dimes in shifting to a concentration on birth defects when the Salk vaccine virtually eliminated polio). Those who argue that the setting of purpose and objectives should logically precede a search for opportunity point out that (1) a number of organizations have been observed to look for opportunities that will allow them to achieve sales, profit, and growth objectives, (2) the environment is simply too full of opportunities for companies to look merely for opportunities without a guiding purpose and set of objectives, and (3) organizations can and do, from time to time, change their objectives—an event which, subsequently, leads them to search for new and different opportunities.

Both viewpoints have merit in theory and in practice. Quite clearly there is a close two-way link between an organization's search for opportunity and its definition of purpose and objectives. As long as this is recognized, there is little need to become embroiled in a "chicken or egg—which comes first" type of controversy.

See Philip Kotler, *Marketing Management: Analysis, Planning, and Control,* 3rd ed. (Englewood Cliffs, N.J.: Prentice-Hall, Inc., 1976), p. 46.

[21]Ibid., p. 47.

company are those where the company in question will be able to enjoy some kind of strategic fit or competitive advantage.

A number of companies have been observed to pursue business opportunities in a particular strategic sequence. Starting from a single-product, limited-market base, a firm first seeks to increase its sales volume, improve its market share, and build customer loyalty in the business in which it first started. In essence, this strategic phase represents an attempt to grow and to build a stronger position in the business it is already in. Price, quality, service, and promotion are fine tuned to respond more precisely to a detailed market need, often including the introduction of a full product line to meet minor variations in customer tastes and preferences. As this single-business strategy approaches its full exploitation in the current geographic target market, a growth-minded company will next begin to assess the opportunities for geographical market expansion. Normally, the strategy of wider geographical coverage proceeds from local to regional to national to international markets, though the degree of penetration may be uneven from area to area because of varying profit potentials and may, of course, stop well short of global or even national proportions. When the opportunities for profitable geographic market area expansion start to peter out, the focus of organization strategy may shift toward opportunities for vertical integration—either backward to sources of supply or forward to the ultimate consumer. For some companies this is a natural strategic move, owing to the close relationships to the organization's main product line and to the potential for realizing economies of scale. Once a firm has reached the limits of geographical market expansion for its original product line and has also come to terms with the possibilities of forward and backward integration, the strategic options are either to continue in the same lines of business and attempt a more intensive implementation or to shift the focus to diversification opportunities.

No set standard procedure can be prescribed for how an organization ought to conduct its search for opportunity. These remain somewhat unique to each organization and its particular circumstances. Suffice it to say that ferreting out and validating opportunities must be a constant concern of top management, and that the task requires daily enterpreneurial alertness to what is happening and what the implications are for the organization.

Organizational Competence and Resources

No matter how appealing or how abundant a firm's business opportunities may be, a strategist is forced to validate the viability of each "opportunity" by inquiring into whether the organization has the means to capitalize upon it, given the opposing forces of competition and organizational circumstance. Opportunity without the organizational skills and resources competence to capture it is an illusion. An organization's strengths (demonstrated and potential) may make it particularly suited to seize some opportunities; likewise, its weaknesses may make the pursuit of other opportunities excessively risky or else disqualify it entirely.

The point is that a firm's internal strengths and weaknesses (what it is good at doing and what it is not so good at doing) make it better suited to pursue some opportunities than others. A good strategy must be doable as well as tuned to opportunity. Therefore, there is a clear cut imperative to gear a firm's strategy to its skills and resources and to evaluate what a firm can do and what it shouldn't try to do. Experience shows that in seeking an attractive match between a firm's opportunities and its capabilities, there is wisdom in trying to build upon what the firm is good at doing and in avoiding things whose key requirements involve what the firm does poorly or what it has never done at all or what goes heavily against the ingrained corporate culture. *In thinking comprehensively about what strategy to select, one must take into account the problems of carrying it out.* This means looking at strategy alternatives in light of the firm's past history, its experiences, its internal culture, its approach to doing things, and its specific competences. If one would have to turn an organization upside down and inside out to make a particular strategy doable, then it probably should be ruled out as a viable alternative. An example of why it is crucial to match strategy with internal capabilities is described in Illustration Capsule 9.

ILLUSTRATION CAPSULE 9
AM International: The Case of a Company Where Strategy Was Not Matched to Internal Capabilities*

In the mid-1970s Addressograph-Multigraph Corp. was a marginally profitable manufacturer of traditional duplicators and addressing machines. AM was confronted with vigorous competition from several Japanese firms and from growing popularity of xerographic copiers. As one A-M executive put it, "we needed more products that hummed and whirred and fewer that clinked and clanked."

To liven up the growth prospects at AM, the company hired Roy L. Ash, well-known as the co-founder of Litton Industries and as budget director in the Nixon Administration, as chairman and chief executive officer and gave him the task of creating a new future for the company and its mature product line. Ash moved quickly to establish a new direction and a new corporate strategy for AM. The plan was to reposition AM alongside Xerox, IBM, and Wang as a major supplier of sophisticated equipment for the "office of the future." A dozen young companies with promising products and glamour

*Source: "AM International: When Technology Was Not Enough," *Business Week*, January 25, 1982, pp. 62-68.

ILLUSTRATION CAPSULE 9 *(continued)*

technologies were acquired; among them were a maker of point-of-sale recording systems for the food service industry, a manufacturer of microfilm and microfiche equipment, a producer of equipment for monitoring copying equipment, a specialty plastics firm, and a manufacturer of word processing equipment and small office computers. The grand strategy was to acquire foothold positions in a number of specific technological areas and try to develop them with aggressive "build and grow" business-level strategies; not all of these were expected to turn out as successes, but the hope was that enough would to make the overall effort worthwhile. It was felt that AM's older products, although mature and without a great future, would nonetheless generate enough profits and cash flows to fund the new technological ventures. Moreover, it was felt that when AM's capable worldwide sales organization was provided all the hoped-for modern, automated, electronic office products, the company could quickly establish itself as a major contender in the fast-growing office equipment market.

In addition, the new corporate strategy included a different corporate image. The company's name was changed from Addressograph-Multigraph Corp. to AM International; corporate headquarters was moved from Cleveland to Los Angeles, and new buzzwords were coined to hype the advertising of the new products—AM was dubbed "the informationists" and the company's market niche was billed as "where the computer meets the paper."

The new strategy was well-received by both Wall Street and stockholders. But the company's perceived new opportunity in office products proved to be an illusion because the strategy was not well matched to AM's ability to execute it:

- The technologies of the young companies which were purchased were unfamiliar to AM's management. This, coupled with the fact that the companies' technologies were unproven and needed considerable development to keep pace in fast-moving competitive markets, made it hard for AM management to assess what really needed to be done in each of the newly acquired companies and how best to allocate corporate funds to finance their needs.

- Because AM lacked the executive skills and depth to manage so many new acquisitions, additional managers had to be hired. But the people doing the hiring, partly because of their lack of familiarity with the technologies and products and partly because of their rush to reposition AM in the office equipment market, did not match the skills of many of the new managers they hired to the jobs they were assigned. Much time and energy was spent in replacing them and management turnover was high at a time when AM could ill afford the confusion and wheel-spinning that accompanied frequent management changes.

ILLUSTRATION CAPSULE 9 *(continued)*

- AM's financial resources were inadequate to fund all of the new ventures. AM's corporate strategy called for the cash flows and profits from the sale of the older, mature products to be used to finance the newly-acquired businesses, supplemented with debt if necessary. The combined financial needs of the new ventures turned out to be much greater than anticipated. To deal with the cash bind, AM squeezed all of the funds it could out of its older businesses (to the point that they were allowed to deteriorate) and pushed its debt (including capital leases) up to $228 million in 1980, more than double the 1978 amount and nearly equal to AM's equity investment. In 1980, AM's cash available was only $4 million, down from $56 million three years previous.

- AM did not have the financial expertise to install the information and reporting controls needed to monitor divisional performance. Consequently, corporate management was often surprised by the sizes of the financial needs of the divisions, by the lack of progress made in their achieving profitability, and by the financial toll the investments in the business-level projects were having on the company's overall financial picture. Inadequate financial controls caused sales for two divisions to be overstated by $10 million in 1980. In its 1981 10-K report filed with the Securities and Exchange Commission, AM admitted "extensive inaccuracies" in its financial records and noted that it had made "certain apparent errors in the preparation of financial statements" in its 1980 and 1981 annual reports. The adjustments totaled some $203 million and led to charges that the assets of virtually every major division were "substantially misstated."

A specific example of AM's inability to manage its new acquisitions involved the purchase of Infortext, Inc. for $4.8 million in 1978. Infortext made electronic equipment that monitored, controlled, and tabulated the use of duplicators and copying machines. In an interview with *Business Week*, Roy Ash commented on AM's experience with Infortext, ". . . we defined the market too broadly. We thought the market was all the users of copiers and duplicating machines that could benefit by controlling the use of their machines." Actually, the sales potential proved much smaller because many customers placed very low priority on investing funds for copier controls. AM invested more than $20 million trying to make a success out of Infortext before deciding to give up on the effort.

In the case of its Jacquard unit, AM's corporate management misjudged the technological readiness of products and the amount of time and money it would take to realize the unit's potential. AM acquired Jacquard in late 1978 for $18 million, although its sales at the time were only $2 million, in the belief that Jacquard's "new generation" word processing equipment was ready to go into production. However, several serious technological problems re-

ILLUSTRATION CAPSULE 9 *(concluded)*

mained to be worked out. Over the next two years, AM invested another $60 million in product development, production facilities, and expanded marketing and distribution capability. Jacquard's sales jumped to a rate of $40 million in early 1981, but losses were in the $20-$30 million range. Operating inefficiencies were extensive (the accounting department had a staff of 105 people—enough to handle $250 million in sales, yet some customers were billed before they received their equipment, while others were not invoiced until several months after delivery). Key operating personnel, disillusioned by the push for excessively rapid growth, were leaving at such a rate that replacements often did not have anyone with experience and understanding to train them and offer guidance.

At the same time, in the rush to become a broad-line office equipment supplier, AM began to overlook its mainstay businesses. The Multigraphics division which made duplicators was plagued with mistakes. A new production control system was put in place, but it failed to do an adequate job of matching parts inventories with production schedules; not only were production lines faced with stockouts of necessary parts but also service personnel got so desperate for parts that order clerks would remove parts from newly-produced machines and send them to field personnel for use in repairs. At times unfinished machines were shipped, with final assembly work left to service technicians. Field representatives were sometimes sent to install new automated equipment without having been through a training course to explain to customers how the new products worked. The Multigraphics division had six presidents in five years and more than 30 people passed through the seven top jobs below the president. As a consequence, AM fell to second place in sales (behind A.B. Dick Co.) in its bread-and-butter product—mechanical offset duplicators selling at prices in the $10,000-$20,000 range.

Not surprisingly, AM International's performance suffered during the years following the adoption of its new corporate strategy:

Year	Sales ($ millions)	Net Income ($ millions)	Total Debt ($ millions)	Net Worth ($ millions)
1978	666	21	92	218
1979	754	12	144	228
1980	909	6	228	232
1981	857	(245)	250	14

Moreover, because of the strategic relevance of organizational strengths, weaknesses, and resource capabilities, it is always worthwhile for an organization to ponder what *distinctive* skills and capabilities it can bring to bear that will allow it to either gain a competitive advantage or give it unique capability to pursue an attractive opportunity. In practice, there are many possible types of distinctive skills. For instance, some organizations excel in manufacturing a "quality product," others in creative approaches to marketing, and still others in such areas as technological innovation, new product development, support services for customers, low-cost production efficiency, or clever advertising. An organization's *distinctive competence* goes beyond just what it does well—*it is what it does especially well in comparison to rival enterprises.*[22] The importance of distinctive competence to strategy formation rests with (1) the unique capability it gives an organization in capitalizing upon a particular opportunity, (2) the competitive edge it may give a firm in the marketplace, and (3) the potential for building a distinctive competence and making it the cornerstone of strategy.

The concept of distinctive competence is especially relevant in formulating business-level strategy. Successful business strategies are usually built around a product-market approach that will set a firm apart from its rivals and give it some kind of strategic advantage. Generally, this means (1) following a different course from rival firms, (2) conceiving of a plan which will have quite different (and more favorable) consequences for one's own organization than for competitors, and (3) making it hard for rivals to imitate the strategy should it succeed.[23] Obviously enough, strengthening one's competitive position in this manner is facilitated when an organization has some kind of distinctive competence around which to build its strategy. It is always easier to develop strategic advantage in a market when a firm has a distinctive competence in one of the key requirements for competitive success, where rival organizations do not have offsetting competences, and where rivals are not able to attain a similar competence except at high cost and/or over an extended period of time.[24]

Even if an organization has no distinctive competence (and many do not), it is still incumbent upon a firm to shape its strategy to suit its particular skills and available resources. It never makes sense to adopt a strategic plan which cannot be executed with the skills and resources a firm is able to muster.

Environmental Threats

Very often, certain factors in a firm's overall environment pose *threats* to its strategic well-being. These externally imposed threats may stem from possible new technological developments, the advent of new substitute products, adverse economic trends, government action, changing consumer values and lifestyles, projections of natural resource depletion, unfavorable demographic shifts, new sources of strong competition, and the

[22]Philip Selznick, *Leadership in Administration* (Evanston, Ill.: Row, Peterson & Company, 1957), p. 42.

[23]Bruce D. Henderson, "Construction of a Business Strategy," reprinted in Daniel J. McCarthy, Robert J. Minichiello, and Joseph R. Curran, *Business Policy and Strategy: Concepts and Readings* (Homewood, Ill.: Richard D. Irwin, Inc., 1975), p. 290.

[24]Kollat, Blackwell, and Robeson, *Strategic Marketing*, p. 24.

like. Such threats can be a major factor in shaping organizational strategy and a wise strategist is as much alert to the threats of environmental change as to the opportunities that it may present.

An example of the technological threat which solid-state digital watches presented to Timex is described in Illustration Capsule 10. Other instances of strategy-related environmental threats are cited below:

- The potential of nationalization and government takeover threatens the investment strategy of transnational corporations whenever they locate facilities in countries having a record of political instability.

ILLUSTRATION CAPSULE 10
Strategic Implications of the Solid-State Technology Threat to Timex

In 1975, Timex ranked as the world's largest maker of finished watches. Its sales of some 40 million watches a year gave it a commanding 50 percent of the U.S. mechanical watch market and 70 percent of the electric watch market. The core of Timex's strategy was (1) to mass-produce a simple pin-levered movement watch in highly efficient plant facilities, and (2) to market them at rock-bottom prices through some 150,000 outlets—drugstores, variety stores, department stores, and even auto supply dealers. With eye-catching point-of-sale displays and skillful television advertising (the "torture test ads" narrated by John Cameron Swazy) to go with its low prices, Timex watches made steady market inroads to become the leading brand.

But, unexpectedly in 1975, Timex found itself confronted with a major technological challenge to its market position: how to develop a strategic response to the digital watch and the technology of solid-state electronics—a technology that was on the verge of sweeping the watch industry and undermining the cost advantage Timex enjoyed with its simple pin-levered mechanical watches. To complicate matters, Timex had little, if any, digital technology capability of its own.

The solid-state revolution in digital display watches was spearheaded not by established watch companies (Timex, Bulova, Benrus, Gruen, and others), but by semiconductor companies, including Texas Instruments, National Semiconductor, Litronix, Hughes Aircraft, and Fairchild Camera & Instrument. These firms, although newcomers to the watch industry, moved aggressively to dominate the market. Accustomed to competing in an industry where technological breakthroughs change things almost overnight, they quickly began to ignore traditional watch business practices (such as financing the watch inventories of retail jewelers and considering a 50 percent margin of selling price over cost as standard). They initiated bold price cuts

Sources: "The Electronics Threat to Timex," *Business Week*, August 18, 1975, pp. 42 ff; "Digital Watches: Bringing Watchmaking Back to the U.S.," *Business Week*, October 27, 1975, pp. 78 ff; "Timex Corporation," in H. Uyterhoeven, R. W. Ackerman, and J. W. Rosenblum, *Strategy and Organization: Text and Cases in General Management* (Homewood, Ill.: Richard D. Irwin, Inc., 1973), pp. 309-20; and "The $20 Digital Watch Arrives a Year Early," *Business Week*, January 26, 1976, pp. 27-28.

ILLUSTRATION CAPSULE 10 *(continued)*

even though demand seemed to be outstripping supply. Whereas the strategy of several semiconductor firms was, originally, to seek to enter into joint ventures with the traditional watchmakers, when the latter reacted so slowly, the strategy was changed to one of beating them head-on in the marketplace. Developments were so fast-paced that by mid-1975 jewelers were worried about the digital watch killing their watch business—not only because of the sharply lower profit margins but also because the semiconductor companies planned to furnish what little service or repair was needed on digitals from the factory, rather than at the point of sale.

Digital watch technology represented a radical departure from the Timex pin-levered watch. The digital watch had no moving parts to wear out and was far more accurate (within a minute per year) than even the most expensive mechanical watch. It operated with just four components: a battery, quartz crystal, an integrated circuit, and a digital display. The battery caused the quartz crystal to vibrate at 32,868 cycles per second (in most watches). The integrated circuit divided the vibrations into one pulse per second, accumulated the pulses to compute minutes, hours, days, and months, and transmitted signals to the display to illuminate the digits showing the time and date.

When the first digital watches appeared in 1972, Timex was not unduly alarmed. It, together with most other watch manufacturers, viewed digital as a fad or at most a specialty watch. Moreover, the first digitals were poorly designed, big and ugly, and experienced 60 percent defective returns. The biggest problem was in the digital time displays which were unreliable and often unreadable. Within three years, however, the semiconductor firms had made rapid progress in making the displays dependable and easy to read; styling was much sharper; and components had been made much smaller. Then in a move reminiscent of their strategy in the calculator business, the semiconductor firms in early 1975 slashed the prices of components in half— to as low as $20 per watch. Lower digital watch prices quickly followed (about half of what prices were in 1974). The move caught Timex and other traditional watch manufacturers off guard. The apparent pricing strategy of the semiconductor firms was based on the "experience curve" whereby the prices of watches and component modules were to be lowered as production efficiency increased through the learning that comes with experience. But, at the same time, the digital watch firms were finding ways to reduce the number of parts in the module, ways to squeeze more of the electronic circuitry onto the main circuit, and ways to cut assembly costs. These savings permitted large price cuts to be made even sooner than planned.

As late as 1975, Timex had done little more than dip its toe into the digital market, with mediocre results. Solid-state technology was new to Timex. The company had no in-house capacity to produce such components as integrated circuits and digital displays, although it had introduced a digital watch line back in 1972.

Previously, Timex had rejected several contractual offers from semicon-

ILLUSTRATION CAPSULE 10 *(concluded)*

ductor firms to supply it with digital-watch components. Hughes Aircraft Company, for example, which produced integrated circuits for Timex analog quartz watches, offered in 1971 to build a digital watch to sell under the Timex label if Timex would guarantee a minimum production run of 1 million units. The Hughes offer was for watches with light-emitting diode readouts which had to be turned on by pushing a button. Timex rejected the offer. Meanwhile, Timex's own efforts to develop in-house electronic watch capability progressed slowly. The head of its program to develop both digital and analog quartz watches left in 1973 to become director of watch operations at Rockwell International Corporation; his departure reportedly was due to Timex's failure to move rapidly in building up a digital capability.

The solid-state technology threat thus raised several strategy issues of vital concern to Timex's future:

1. Was the digital watch just a fad or was solid-state circuitry the wave of the future in watchmaking technology? (In 1974, digital watch sales totaled 650,000; some forecasts called for digital sales of 2.5 million units in 1975, and as much as 10 million in 1976.)

2. How quickly and to what extent would the rapidly falling prices of digital watches begin to create strong competitive pressures for Timex? (The prices of digital watches fell from $125 in 1974 to $50 in 1975, and to as low as $20 in early 1976.)

3. When and to what extent should Timex begin to push its own line of digital watches?

4. Should it purchase digital watch components from suppliers or should it develop its own digital component manufacturing capability? If the latter, then should the capability be developed internally or should Timex seek to acquire a firm with the technological know-how and experience?

In the minds of many observers, there was little doubt that Timex would soon have to offer a wide range of digital watches and, because of its carefully nurtured image as a producer of economy-priced watches, that the new digital watches would also have to be low priced. Otherwise, its market position would be in serious jeopardy.

- The business of the manufacturers of coated copying paper was threatened and eventually ruined by technological developments which allowed the use of plain paper in copying equipment.

- Scientific discoveries that fluorocarbon-based aerosol sprays damaged the ozone layers on the earth's atmosphere (and the subsequent likelihood of future government bans) caused aerosol chemical manufacturers and aerosol can users to initiate a high priority search for substitute forms of technology and packaging.

- Increased costs of regulatory compliance and public concerns about the safety of nuclear generation of electric power threatened both the viability of the business of the manufacturers of nuclear generating equipment and the financial ability of power companies to install and operate nuclear powered plants—indeed, during the 1978-1981 period no new nuclear facilities were ordered and many previously contracted-for units were cancelled. A market once thought to be promising dried up quickly.

For the most part, organizations appear to *react* to environmental threats rather than to plan for or to anticipate them. Actually, this is not a strong criticism of managers; many strategically important environmental changes seem to occur at random or are not readily subject to prediction. Some occur without warning and with few, if any, advance clues; others are "bound to happen" but the uncertainty is when. And still others are simply "unknowable." Moreover, even when threatening signals are detected early, it is not always easy to assess the extent of their strategic significance. Trying to forecast the strategic significance of future events is scarcely an exact science. Nonetheless, staying in close touch with the threatening developments and shaping a strategy capable of coping with adverse environmental change is something managers have to try to do.

Personal Values and Aspirations

Strategy formulation is rarely so objective an analytical process that the personal values and aspirations of managers are excluded. Both casual observation and systematic studies indicate that the backgrounds, influences, experiences, beliefs, and personal goals of managers can have an important influence on strategy.[25] As Professor Andrews has noted in characterizing why personal values are relevant to strategy, "Some people have to have their hearts in it."[26]

Most managers have their own concepts of what their organization's strategy is or ought to be. These concepts are certain to reflect, in part, a manager's own values and opinions—especially when he/she has had a hand in formulating the strategy. There is a natural human tendency for managers to draw upon their own personal values, background experiences, preferences, and ambitions when choosing among alternative strategies and shaping strategic plans. Sometimes the influence of one's own values and experiences is conscious and deliberate, at other times it may be unconscious. Whichever, the important point is that managers do not dispassionately assess what their organization can do or should do; they

---

[25]See, for instance, William D. Guth and Renato Tagiuri, "Personal Values and Corporate Strategy," *Harvard Business Review*, vol. 43, no. 5 (September-October 1965), pp. 123-32; Kenneth R. Andrews, *The Concept of Corporate Strategy*, Revised Edition (Homewood, Ill.: Dow Jones-Irwin, Inc., 1980), Chapter 4; and Vancil, "Strategy Formulation in Complex Organizations," pp. 4-5.

[26]Andrews, *The Concept of Corporate Strategy*, p. 85.

often are influenced by what they personally want the company to do and to be.

Two well-known instances can be cited.[27] The publishers and editors of the *New York Times* have a strong, long-standing commitment to reporting the news intelligently, accurately, and without bias or sensationalism. Their dedication to this style of journalism has caused them to reject changing the nature and character of the *New York Times*, even though their decision to stick with this strategic approach may have restricted circulation and produced a lower return on investment. Hugh Hefner, the founder and publisher of *Playboy*, worked initially for several other magazines, but he found himself wanting to strike out on his own and create a magazine which reflected his own preferences and lifestyle. As he soon discovered, there was indeed a market for *Playboy* and Hefner, guided partly by his own sense of values and aspirations, pioneered a new concept in magazine publishing.

Societal Obligations and Ethical Considerations

The ethical, political, social, and moral aspects of the external environment obviously enter into strategy formulation. Although the interaction between strategy and societal factors is a two-way street, here we wish to focus on how societal values and expectations, together with a firm's perceived social and ethical obligation, impinge on strategy. That consumerism, truth-in-packaging, equal opportunity employment, occupational health and safety, open housing, product safety, beliefs about ethics and morals, pollution control, and other similar societal-based factors have an impact on organization strategies requires no discussion. Adapting strategy to accommodate these factors is commonplace. Food processors have altered their use of sugar and preservatives in food products and begun to promote nutritional content and "natural" flavors. The cigarette manufacturers have dramatically reduced the tar and nicotine content of cigarettes and are aggressively marketing new low-tar, low nicotine brands. The growers of agricultural products and the manufacturers of national defense-related items have had to adjust their strategic approaches in international markets to conform to emerging U.S. foreign policy and to the unfolding of international "crises." The efforts of the Moral Majority and other such groups have not gone unnoticed by the major TV networks in their programming or by the publishers of textbooks marketed to public schools. When some banks and insurance companies were charged with systematically turning down mortgage loans to qualified applicants because the properties were in slum districts or other "undesirable" locations (a practice labeled "redlining"), the whole mortgage industry was forced to reexamine its lending policies and investment portfolio make-up.

---

[27]Guth and Tagiuri, "Personal Values and Corporate Strategy," p. 128.

Some firms, since they can exercise but little influence over societal values and expectations, view the ethical-moral-societal dimensions of strategy formation as constraints and sometimes as a threat. This view is not without some justification; changes in social mores and preferences can indeed be potentially threatening to an organization's business. But, what is threatening to one enterprise may, at the same time, open new doors to another organization. For instance, while public concern about cancer-causing food additives poses obvious strategic threats to some food manufacturers, there arises simultaneously major new market opportunities for organizations with expertise in health and nutrition research and for producers of food items thought to be safe. While depletion of oil and natural gas reserves poses obvious long-run strategic threats to the oil and gas companies, it also creates major new market opportunities for manufacturers of energy efficient devices and for firms which come up with new energy producing technologies.

Irrespective of whether changes in societal values and requirements destroy or create strategic opportunities, managerial alertness to the strategic implications of societal forces and social concerns is an essential ingredient of the strategy formulation process. Indeed, the desirability (if not the imperative) of relating an organization to the needs and expectations of society is, today, a fairly noncontroversial issue. The notion of what management ought to do to make an organization "socially responsible" includes (1) endeavoring to keep organizational activities in tune with what is generally perceived as the public interest, (2) responding positively to emerging societal priorities, (3) demonstrating a willingness to take needed action ahead of regulatory confrontation, (4) balancing stockholder interests against the larger interest of society as a whole, (5) being a "good citizen" in the community, and (6) making the corporation's social and ethical obligations an explicit and high priority consideration in the way the enterprise conducts its affairs.

Being "socially responsible" has both carrot and stick aspects. There is the positive appeal for all organizations to pursue strategies that will improve their public standing at the same time that it enhances their own performance opportunities—and these are always inexorably tied to the generally healthy well-being of society.[28] And there is the negative burden of public criticism and potentially onerous regulation if firms ignore the changing priorities and expectations of society.

Strategy and Organization "Personality"

Every organization has a personality and modes of behavior which are

---

[28]Those who doubt the general principle that high levels of organization performance are closely tied to the general well-being of society should take note of the remarkably good correlation between changes in the levels of business profits and changes in the level of economic activity. Comparatively few businesses will be found to enjoy higher levels of performance during periods of social and economic decline.

somewhat unique to itself. Some organizations are noted for being aggressive and exhibiting leadership; others are clearly more complacent and slow-moving, often quite content to assume a follow-the-leader role. Still others are noted for "conservatism," or technological proficiency, or financial wheeling and dealing, or hard-hitting competitive style, or an emphasis on growth via acquisition, or a strong social consciousness, or a desire to avoid risk.

Quite clearly, these "personality" traits are a component of strategy and, in some cases, can even dominate the formulation of strategy. To some extent, they create a corporate culture and they become imbedded in how a firm's executives think and act, how the firm responds to external events, and what skills and expertise it builds into its structure. All of these facets of a corporation's culture and personality shape perceptions of what strategy to select and, also, what strategy a firm may be most capable of executing with some proficiency.

THE SITUATIONAL DESIGN AND ANALYSIS ASPECTS OF STRATEGY FORMULATION

One way of illustrating where and how the preceding factors come into play in shaping strategy is presented in Figure 2-4.[30] This simple "model" suggests that formulating strategy entails a fairly complex synthesis of many factors and considerations—nearly all of which are *situation specific*, nearly all of which are *subject to change* as new events unfold, and at least some of which are subject to alternative managerial judgment. Said a bit differently, what is involved in formulating strategy is a heavy dose of "situational analysis" and "situational design" whereby managers take into account *all* of the relevant specifics of an organization's situation.

How each strategically relevant factor weighs into the formation of strategy is conditional upon a specific organization's situation at a specific time and upon the entrepreneurial skills and judgment of those managers who are formulating strategy. Situations differ from time to time and from organization to organization in terms of external opportunities and threats, internal strengths and weaknesses, managerial priorities and performance objectives, competitive realities, societal and governmental constraints, scope and diversity of operations, and so on. At the same time, organization strategy is inherently the product of managers and thus bears the marks of their own particular values, priorities, aspirations, perceptions, analysis, entrepreneurial skills, and judgment. Consequently, there can be no formula-like specification of exactly what determines strategy and no

---

[30]More elaborate diagrammatics are, of course, possible. For two such elaborate strategy formulation models, see Ansoff, *Corporate Strategy*, p. 202; and Charles W. Hofer and Dan Schendel, *Strategy Formulation: Analytical Concepts* (St. Paul, Minnesota: West Publishing Company, 1978), Chapter 3.

FIGURE 2-4
A Simple Model of the Primary Factors Which Shape Strategy

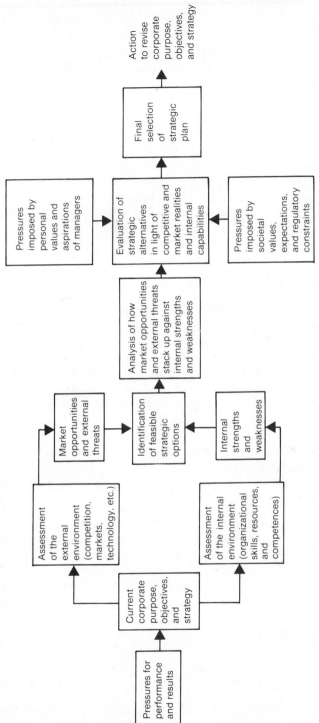

single model of what steps to follow and what to do at each step. Each organization's strategic plan is governed by the specifics of its own situation and by managerial judgment. The strategy that represents a "good" fit with one organization's situation may be a "poor" fit with a different organization's situation. The strategy that produces a good fit with today's situation may not fit tomorrow's situation nearly as well. What one manager views as the "best" strategy may be perceived by another manager as "inferior" to some other strategy.

A generalized and detailed presentation of some step-by-step, how-to-do-it methodology for arriving at a strategy, therefore, has much less to offer practicing managers (and to successful strategy formulation) than does a heightened managerial consciousness about what *kinds* of considerations to take into account and the importance of creative, perceptive, timely entrepreneurship.

MANAGING THE STRATEGY FORMULATION PROCESS

Companies approach the task of formulating strategy differently. Some firms arrive at their strategic game plans *informally* rather than according to prescribed times and formal procedures. This is particularly true of companies where either a single individual or a small group of key people make the key strategic choices. An advantage of the informal approach is that it gives managers added flexibility to adjust to changing market and environmental conditions, and some managers believe they are more effective strategists when they are free to maneuver unfettered by a formal strategic planning procedure. On the other hand, more and more firms (especially large corporations) are opting for formalized strategic planning that is time bound and that is carried out in a prescribed manner, complete with forms, calculation procedures, and meetings to gain approval.

Four different patterns of strategy formulation have been identified:[31]

1. **Bottom-up approach**—Strategy formulation initiatives are taken at the business unit level and then passed upward through the structure for approval and for aggregation with the strategies made in other units. Corporate-level strategy, thus, is a composite of the strategies of the various business units. At the business level, strategy is tailored to match its particular circumstances, with the dominant strategic focus being the unit's *existing* areas of activity and consolidation of its position; any new business initiatives tend to be extensions of present activities.

    Moreover, a large number of managers in the business unit are conversant with the strategic and operating details of the unit; partici-

---

[31]R. McLellan and G. Kelly, "Business Policy Formulation: Understanding the Process," *Journal of General Management*, vol. 6, no. 1 (Autumn 1980), pp. 38-47.

pation in the formulation of strategy is broad rather than narrow. Corporate-level management may be informally involved during the strategy formulation phase, exerting some downward influence on strategy as it is being assembled. Top management often expects all business units to use the same standardized documentation for supporting the chosen strategy and for presenting it for approval. When the business unit strategies are finalized, they are passed upwards through the organization for approval; corporate-level approval is usually forthcoming because the informal, downward influences exerted earlier tend to ensure that business strategy is in an approvable state when presented. The chief drawback of bottom-up strategy formulation is that because each business unit's strategy is specific to its own situation, the aggregation of business strategies into a corporate strategy can easily result in a hodgepodge that lacks coherence, unity, and consistency and that does not fit the environmental and resource demands placed on the organization as a whole. There is, after all, little reason to expect several business strategies, each formulated in isolation from the others and in accordance with the specifics of its own situation, to converge into a common corporate purpose and corporate direction.

The bottom-up formulation process tends to be undertaken regularly (usually annually). Between formulation phases, business unit managers are mainly concerned with the tasks of strategy implementation. They may also be reflecting upon the appropriateness of the approved strategy in readiness for the next round of strategy formulation.

2. **Top-down approach**—This approach evolves in organizations where the formulation of strategy is seen as the province of corporate management. Unlike the bottom-up approach, only a small fraction of the firm's managers are intimately involved in the actual formulation process. Strategy is thus a reflection of senior management's judgment about how best to achieve corporate objectives, and any inconsistencies and conflicts that may be present across different business units are thrashed out and settled at the corporate level (although advice and recommendations from lower-level managers may be asked for and considered). In general, the top-down approach results in a unified, coherent strategic plan that is not vague with respect to either corporate direction or corporate objectives and performance targets. Corporate strategy is then disaggregated into strategies and guidelines for each business unit and handed down to the business units for implementation. Business unit implementation of corporate and business strategy is ongoing, pausing or changing only in response to new strategies from corporate headquarters. Managers at the business/ functional area levels implement their assigned pieces of the strategic

plan, raising additional questions when needed and gaining approval to modify or embellish corporate directives as may be necessary. The objectives and performance targets included in the corporate plan may provide the basis for evaluating the performance of the business unit.

3. **Interactive or negotiated approach**—Here, corporate and business unit managers jointly formulate business strategy and corporate strategy, with influences moving both upward and downward. The strategic plan is neither the sole product of corporate managers as in the top-down approach nor solely that of business unit managers as in the bottom-up approach. Rather, the formulation process is participative and negotiated, reflecting a linkage between corporate objectives and expectations and business-level managers' knowledge of their specific business situations. Negotiations and deliberations during formulation may be more lengthy and exhaustive but this may be compensated for by the speed of the approval and implementation phases.

    This formulation process involves short bursts of activity in each business unit as corporate management turns successively to negotiate each unit's strategy. Again, corporate management may specify that the format and documentary support for the unit's strategy be relatively standard from unit to unit. Basically, corporate management's role is not so much to second-guess the strategy proposals of the business unit managers as to shape the pattern of the separate business strategies into a corporate portfolio of strategies that is compatible with corporate resources, corporate objectives, and corporate direction. Any conflicts that emerge between corporate strategy and the business unit's proposed strategy are resolved through negotiation. The strategies of newly acquired business units are usually singled out by corporate management for detailed scrutiny and negotiation, a process which tends to facilitate assimilation and coordination of the new business with that of the new parent.

4. **Semi-autonomous approach**—This approach is distinguished by relatively independent strategy formulation activities at both the corporate and business levels. At the business unit level, strategy is formulated to suit each unit's particular set of circumstances and objectives. Once formulated, the strategic plan is submitted for corporate approval. The formal strategy review and proposal activity takes place periodically, usually once a year.

    At the corporate level, strategy formulation and re-evaluation is more or less continuous, with the emphasis placed on identifying new directions for the corporation, evaluating emerging threats and opportunities, and deciding which new businesses to enter, which existing businesses to divest, and what priorities to attach to the businesses which are to remain in the corporate portfolio. The emphasis of corporate-level managers is on evaluating the portfolio of business units and trying to improve the performance of the portfolio as a whole, but not to the extent of becoming intimately involved in detailed evaluation and formulation of business unit strategy. When new corporate direction or new corporate strategy emerges, it may be fed into the activities of existing business units and/or it may lead to new acquisitions and divestitures and/or to a reordering of resource priorities among the business units. Absorption of these corporate decisions by the business units may result in business unit objectives and strategies being revised. Such occasions, as well as the exercise of reviewing and approving business unit strategies, sometimes provide corporate managers with new ideas for corporate strategy.

All four approaches to managing the strategy formulation process can be observed in actual practice. Which one a particular organization uses is a matter of management preference and decision.

An organization's strategy, when formulated, may or may not be boldly and comprehensively laid out in some document called "the strategic plan." Written versions, though highlighting and summarizing the primary elements of strategy, may for any of several reasons not contain a complete level-by-level, detail-by-detail account of what the current strategy is (see the discussion in Illustration Capsule 7). Many aspects of strategy typically remain couched in verbal discussions, the unspoken thoughts of the strategists themselves, and the implicit consequences of managerial actions and decisions. Outsiders may be able to deduce parts of an organization's strategy from such visible actions as acquisitions, divestitures, and behavior in the marketplace. Other pieces of strategy may appear in annual reports, speeches of top executives before meetings of securities analysts, and interviews and articles in the business press and in trade journals.

From the standpoint of the practicing general manager, however, the important part of the strategic plan is not what is on paper or what can be seen by others. It is what is in the general manager's mind—his mental game plan, the continuing dialogue that he has with himself and that is a composite of what is on paper, what has been settled orally, what is already being done, and what adjustments are needed in the light of unfolding events and circumstances. It is this "mental" game plan that is the general manager's basis for charting the course to follow.

CHARACTERISTICS OF "GOOD" STRATEGY FORMULATION

How well the task of strategy formulation has been done can be appraised from two angles.[32] One is from the perspective of whether the strategy is right for the organization in its particular situation. Does it offer a

---

[32]Vancil, "Strategy Formulation in Complex Organizations," p. 3.

viable and potentially effective fit between the organization's internal and external environments? Does it allow the enterprise to exploit attractive product-market opportunities and/or to escape the impact of externally imposed threats? Is it compatible with the organization's perceived strengths and weaknesses? Does it fully utilize internal competences and resources? Is it timely? All things considered, how well does the strategy exemplify "goodness of fit" among the relevant external/internal considerations?

The second angle involves the more subtle issue of whether the strategy has been sufficiently delineated. Is the strategy complete enough to allow managers to proceed confidently in managing their areas of responsibility according to the game plan? Has the strategy been developed and articulated in sufficient detail, beginning at the corporate level and continuing in ever more detailed layers down to the operating level? The whole of an organization's strategy is always a compound of many distinct actions and decisions, rather than a single point of attack.

Ultimately, though, the test of good strategy formulation is whether the chosen strategy produces the desired levels of performance and culminates in the achievement of corporate objectives.

SUGGESTED READINGS

Andrews, Kenneth R., *The Concept of Corporate Strategy*, Revised Edition (Homewood, Ill.: Dow Jones-Irwin, Inc., 1980), Chapters 2, 3, 4, and 5.

Ansoff, H. Igor, *Corporate Strategy* (New York: McGraw-Hill Book Co., 1965), Chapter 6.

Drucker, Peter F., *Management: Tasks, Responsibilities, Practices* (New York: Harper & Row, Publishers, 1974), Chapters 6 and 7.

Hofer, Charles W. and Dan Schendel, *Strategy Formulation: Analytical Concepts*, (St. Paul, Minn.: West Publishing Co., 1978), Chapter 2.

Levitt, Theodore, "Marketing Myopia," *Harvard Business Review*, vol. 38, no. 4 (July-August 1960), pp. 45-56.

McLellan, R. and G. Kelly, "Business Policy Formulation: Understanding the Process," *Journal of General Management*, vol. 6, no. 1 (Autumn 1980), pp. 38-47.

Quinn, James Brian, *Strategies for Change: Logical Incrementalism* (Homewood, Ill.: Richard D. Irwin, Inc., 1980), Chapters 2 and 4.

Stephenson, Howard H., "Defining Corporate Strengths and Weaknesses," *Sloan Management Review*, vol. 17, no. 3 (Spring 1976), pp. 51-68.

Tilles, Seymour, "Making Strategy Explicit," *Business Strategy*, edited by H. Igor Ansoff (New York: Penguin Books, 1970), pp. 180-209.

Vancil, Richard F., "Strategy Formulation in Complex Organizations," *Sloan Management Review*, vol. 17, no. 2 (Winter 1976), pp. 1-18.

Vancil, Richard F. and Peter Lorange, "Strategic Planning in Diversified Companies," *Harvard Business Review*, vol. 53, no. 1 (January-February 1975), pp. 81-90.

READING

Managing Strategic Change*

JAMES BRIAN QUINN

James Brian Quinn is the William and Josephine Buchanan Professor of Management at the Amos Tuck School of Business Administration, Dartmouth College.

"Just as bad money has always driven out good, so the talented general manager—the person who makes a company go—is being overwhelmed by a flood of so-called 'professionals,' textbook executives more interested in the form of management than the content, more concerned about defining and categorizing and quantifying the job, than in getting it done. . . . They have created false expectations and wasted untold man-hours by making a religion of formal long-range planning."[1]

H. E. Wrapp, New York Times.

Two previous articles have tried to demonstrate why executives managing strategic change in large organizations should not—and do not—follow highly formalized textbook approaches in long-range planning, goal generation, and strategy formulation.[2] Instead, they artfully blend formal analysis, behavioral techniques, and power politics to bring about cohesive, step-by-step movement toward ends which initially are broadly conceived, but which are then constantly refined and reshaped as new information appears.[3] Their integrating methodology can best be described as "logical incrementalism."

But is this truly a process in itself, capable of being managed? Or does it simply amount to applied intuition? Are there some conceptual structures, principles, or paradigms that are generally useful? Wrapp, Normann, Braybrooke, Lindblom, and Bennis have provided some macrostructures incorporating many important elements they have observed in strategic

---

*This article is reprinted from *Sloan Management Review*, vol. 21, no. 4 (Summer 1980), pp. 3-20. Copyright © by Sloan Management Review Association. All rights reserved.

[1]See H. E. Wrapp, "A Plague of Professional Managers," *New York Times*, 8 April 1979.

[2]This is the third in a series of articles based upon my study on ten major corporations' processes for achieving significant strategic change. The other two articles in the series are: J. B. Quinn, "Strategic Goals: Process and Politics," *Sloan Management Review*, Fall 1977, pp. 21-37; J. B. Quinn, "Strategic Change: 'Logical Incrementalism'," *Sloan Management Review*, Fall 1978, pp. 7-21. The whole study will be published as a book entitled *Strategies for Change: Logical Incrementalism* (Homewood, IL: Dow Jones-Irwin, 1980). All findings purposely deal only with strategic changes in large organizations.

[3]See R. M. Cyert and J. G. March, *A Behavioral Theory of the Firm* (Englewood Cliffs, NJ: Prentice-Hall, 1963), p. 123. Note this learning-feedback-adaptiveness of goals and feasible alternatives over time as organizational learning.

change situations.[4] These studies and other contributions cited in this article offer important insights into the management of change in large organizations. But my data suggest that top managers in such enterprises develop their major strategies through processes which neither these studies nor more formal approaches to planning adequately explain. Managers *consciously* and *proactively* move forward *incrementally*:

To improve the quality of information utilized in corporate strategic decisions.

To cope with the varying lead times, pacing parameters, and sequencing needs of the "subsystems" through which such decisions tend to be made.

To deal with the personal resistance and political pressures any important strategic change encounters.

To build the organizational awareness, understanding, and psychological commitment needed for effective implementation.

To decrease the uncertainty surrounding such decisions by allowing for interactive learning between the enterprise and its various impinging environments.

To improve the quality of the strategic decisions themselves by (1) systematically involving those with most specific knowledge, (2) obtaining the participation of those who must carry out the decisions and (3) avoiding premature momenta or closure which could lead the decision in improper directions.

How does one manage the complex incremental processes which can achieve these goals? The earlier articles structured certain key elements;[5] these will not be repeated here. The following is perhaps the most articulate short statement on how executives proactively manage incrementalism in the development of corporate strategies:

Typically you start with general concerns, vaguely felt. Next you roll an issue around in your mind till you think you have a conclusion that makes sense for the company. You then go out and sort of post the idea without being too wedded to its details. You then start hearing the arguments pro and con, and some very good refinements of the idea usually emerge. Then you pull the idea in and put some resources together to study it so it can be put forward as more of a formal presentation. You wait for "stimuli occurrences" or "crises," and launch pieces of the idea to help in these situations. But they

---

[4]See: H. E. Wrapp, "Good Managers Don't Make Policy Decisions," *Harvard Business Review*, September-October 1967, pp. 91-99; R. Normann, *Management for Growth*, trans. N. Adler (New York: John Wiley & Sons, 1977); D. Braybrooke and C. E. Lindblom, *A Strategy of Decision: Policy Evaluation as a Social Process* (New York: Free Press of Glencoe, 1963); C. E. Lindblom, *The Policy-Making Process* (Englewood Cliffs, NJ: Prentice Hall, 1968); W. G. Bennis, *Changing Organizations: Essays on the Development and Evolution of Human Organizations* (New York: McGraw Hill, 1966).

[5]See respectively: Quinn (Fall 1977); Quinn (Fall 1978).

lead toward your ultimate aim. You know where you want to get. You'd like to get there in six months. But it may take three years, or you may not get there. And when you do get there, you don't know whether it was originally your own idea—or somebody else had reached the same conclusion before you and just got you on board for it. You never know. The president would follow the same basic process, but he could drive it much faster than an executive lower in the organization.[6]

Because of differences in organizational form, management style, or the content of individual decisions, no single paradigm can hold for all strategic decisions.[7] However, very complex strategic decisions in my sample of large organizations tended to evoke certain kinds of broad process steps. These are briefly outlined below. While these process steps occur generally in the order presented, stages are by no means orderly or discrete. Executives do consciously manage individual steps proactively, but it is doubtful that any one person guides a major strategic change sequentially through all the steps. Developing most strategies requires numerous loops back to earlier stages as unexpected issues or new data dictate. Or decision times can become compressed and require short-circuiting leaps forward as crises occur.[8] Nevertheless, certain patterns are clearly dominant in the successful management of strategic change in large organizations.

CREATING AWARENESS AND COMMITMENT—
INCREMENTALLY

Although many of the sample companies had elaborate formal environmental scanning procedures, most major strategic issues first emerged in vague or undefined terms, such as "organizational overlap," "product proliferation," "excessive exposure in one market," or "lack of focus and motivation."[9] Some appeared as "inconsistencies" in internal action patterns or "anomalies" between the enterprise's current posture and some perception of its future environment.[10] Early signals may come from any-

---

[6]See J. B. Quinn, *Xerox Corporation (B)* (copyrighted case, Amos Tuck School of Business Administration, Dartmouth College, Hanover, NH, 1979).

[7]See O. G. Brim, D. Class et al., *Personality and Decision Processes: Studies in the Social Psychology of Thinking* (Stanford, CA: Stanford University Press, 1962).

[8]Crises did occur at some stage in almost all the strategies investigated. However, the study was concerned with the attempt to manage strategic change in an ordinary way. While executives had to deal with precipitating events in this process, crisis management was not—and should not be—the focus of effective strategic management.

[9]For some formal approaches and philosophies for environmental scanning, see: W. D. Guth, "Formulating Organizational Objectives and Strategy: A Systematic Approach," *Journal of Business Policy* (Autumn 1971): 24-31; F. J. Aguilar, *Scanning the Business Environment* (New York: Macmillan Co., 1967). For confirmation of the early vagueness and ambiguity in problem form and identification, see H. Mintzberg, D. Raisinghani, and A. Theoret, "The Structure of 'Unstructured' Decision Processes," *Administrative Science Quarterly* (June 1976): 246-75.

[10]For a discussion on various types of "misfits" between the organization and its environment as a basis for problem identification, see Normann (1977), p. 19.

where and may be difficult to distinguish from the background "noise" or ordinary communications. Crises, of course, announce themselves with strident urgency in operations control systems. But, if organizations wait until signals reach amplitudes high enough to be sensed by formal measurement systems, smooth, efficient transitions may be impossible. [11].

Need Sensing: Leading the Formal Information System

Effective change managers actively develop informal networks to get objective information—from other staff and line executives, workers, customers, board members, suppliers, politicians, technologists, educators, outside professionals, government groups, and so on—to sense possible needs for change. They purposely use these networks to short-circuit all the careful screens[12] their organizations build up to "tell the top only what it wants to hear." For example:

> Peter McColough, chairman and CEO of Xerox, was active in many high-level political and charitable activities—from treasurer of the Democratic National Committee to chairman of the Urban League. In addition, he said, "I've tried to decentralize decision making. If something bothers me, I don't rely on reports or what other executives may want to tell me. I'll go down very deep into the organization, to certain issues and people, so I'll have a feeling for what they think." He refused to let his life be run by letters and memos. "Because I came up by that route, I know what a salesman can say. I also know that before I see [memos] they go through fifteen hands, and I know what that can do to them."[13]

To avoid undercutting intermediate managers, such bypassing has to be limited to information gathering, with no implication that orders or approvals are given to lower levels. Properly handled, this practice actually improves formal communications and motivational systems as well. Line managers are less tempted to screen information and lower levels are flattered to be able "to talk about the very top." Since people sift signals about threats and opportunities through perceptual screens defined by their own values, careful executives make sure their sensing networks include people who look at the world very differently than do those in the enterprise's dominating culture. Effective executives consciously seek options and threat signals beyond the *status quo*. "If I'm not two to three years ahead of my organization, I'm not doing my job" was a common comment of such executives in the sample.

---

[11]For suggestions on why organizations engage in "problem search" patterns, see R. M. Cyert, H. A. Simon, and D. B. Trow, "Observation of a Business Decision," *The Journal of Business* (October 1956): 237-48; for the problems of timing in transitions, see L.R. Sayles, *Managerial Behavior: Administration in Complex Organizations* (New York: McGraw-Hill, 1964).

[12]For a classic view of how these screens operate, see C. Argyris, "Double Loop Learning in Organizations," *Harvard Business Review*, September-October 1977, pp. 115-25.

[13]See Quinn (copyrighted case, 1979).

Amplifying Understanding and Awareness

In some cases executives quickly perceive the broad dimensions of needed change. But they still may seek amplifying data, wider executive understanding of issues, or greater organizational support before initiating action. Far from accepting the first satisfactory (satisficing) solution—as some have suggested they do—successful managers seem to consciously generate and consider a broad array of alternatives.[14] Why? They want to stimulate and choose from the most creative solutions offered by the best minds in their organizations. They wish to have colleagues knowledgeable enough about issues to help them think through all the ramifications. They seek data and arguments sufficiently strong to dislodge preconceived ideas or blindly followed past practices. They do not want to be the prime supporters of losing ideas or to have their organizations slavishly adopt "the boss's solution." Nor do they want—through announcing decisions too early—to prematurely threaten existing power centers which could kill any changes aborning.

Even when executives do not have in mind specific solutions to emerging problems, they can still proactively guide actions in intuitively desired directions—by defining what issues staffs should investigate, by selecting principal investigators, and by controlling reporting processes. They can selectively "tap the collective wit" of their organizations, generating more awareness of critical issues and forcing initial thinking down to lower levels to achieve greater involvement. Yet they can also avoid irreconcilable opposition, emotional overcommitment,[15] or organizational momenta beyond their control by regarding all proposals as "strictly advisory" at this early stage.

As issues are clarified and options are narrowed, executives may systematically alert ever wider audiences. They may first "shop" key ideas among trusted colleagues to test responses. Then they may commission a few studies to illuminate emerging alternatives, contingencies, or opportunities. But key players might still not be ready to change their past action patterns or even be able to investigate options creatively. Only when persuasive data are in hand and enough people are alerted and "on board" to make a particular solution work, might key executives finally commit themselves to it. Building awareness, concern, and interest to attention-getting levels is often a vital—and slowly achieved—step in the process of managing basic changes. For example:

> In the early 1970s there was still a glut in world oil supplies. Nevertheless, analysts in the General Motors Chief Economist's Office began to project a developing U.S. dependency on foreign oil and the likelihood of higher future oil prices. These concerns led the board in 1972 to create an ad hoc

---

[14]Cyert and March (1963) suggest that executives choose from a number of satisfactory solutions; later observers suggest they choose the first truly satisfactory solution discovered.

[15]See F. F. Gilmore, "Overcoming the Perils of Advocacy in Corporate Planning," *California Management Review* (Spring 1973): 127-37.

energy task force headed by David C. Collier, then treasurer, later head of GM of Canada and then of the Buick Division. Collier's group included people from manufacturing, research, design, finance, industry-government relations, and the economics staff. After six months of research, in May of 1973 the task force went to the board with three conclusions: (1) there was a developing energy problem, (2) the government had no particular plan to deal with it, (3) energy costs would have a profound effect on GM's business. Collier's report created a good deal of discussion around the company in the ensuing months. "We were trying to get other people to think about the issue," said Richard C. Gerstenberg, then chairman of GM.[16]

Changing Symbols: Building Credibility

As awareness of the need for change grows, managers often want to signal the organization that certain types of changes are coming, even if specific solutions are not in hand. Knowing they cannot communicate directly with the thousands who could carry out the strategy, some executives purposely undertake highly visible actions which wordlessly convey complex messages that could never be communicated as well—or as credibly—in verbal terms.[17]. Some use symbolic moves to preview or verify intended changes in direction. At other times, such moves confirm the intention of top management to back a thrust already partially begun— as Mr. McColough's relocation of Xerox headquarters to Connecticut (away from the company's Rochester reprographics base) underscored that company's developing commitment to product diversification, organizational decentralization, and international operations. Organizations often need such symbolic moves—or decisions they regard as symbolic— to build credibility behind a new strategy. Without such actions even forceful verbiage might be interpreted as mere rhetoric. For example:

> In GM's downsizing engineers said that one of top management's early decisions affected the credibility of the whole weight-reduction program. "Initially, we proposed a program using a lot of aluminum and substitute materials to meet the new 'mass' targets. But this would have meant a very high cost, and would have strained the suppliers' aluminum capacity. However, when we presented this program to management, they said, 'Okay, if necessary, we'll do it.' They didn't back down. We began to understand then that they were dead serious. Feeling that the company would spend the money was critical to the success of the entire mass reduction effort."[18]

---

[16]See J. B. Quinn, *General Motors Corporation: The Downsizing Decision* (copyrighted case, Amos Tuck School of Business Administration, Dartmouth College, Hanover, NH. 1978).

[17]See E. Rhenman, *Organization Theory for Long-Range Planning* (New York: John Wiley & Sons, 1973), p. 63. Here author notes a similar phenomenon.

[18]See Quinn (copyrighted case, 1978).

Legitimizing New Viewpoints

Often before reaching specific strategic decisions, it is necessary to legitimize new options which have been acknowledged as possibilities, but which still entail an undue aura of uncertainty or concern. Because of their familiarity, older options are usually perceived as having lower risks (or potential costs) than newer alternatives. Therefore, top managers seeking change often consciously create forums and allow slack time for their organizations to talk through threatening issues, work out the implications of new solutions, or gain an improved information base that will permit new options to be evaluated objectively in comparison with more familiar alternatives.[19] In many cases, strategic concepts which are at first strongly resisted gain acceptance and support simply by the passage of time, if executives do not exacerbate hostility by pushing them too fast from the top. For example:

> When Joe Wilson thought Haloid Corporation should change its name to include Xerox, he first submitted a memorandum asking colleagues what they thought of the idea. They rejected it. Wilson then explained his concerns more fully, and his executives rejected the idea again. Finally Wilson formed a committee headed by Sol Linowitz, who had thought a separate Xerox subsidiary might be the best solution. As this committee deliberated, negotiations were under way with the Rank Organizations and the term Rank-Xerox was commonly heard and Haloid-Xerox no longer seemed so strange. "And so," according to John Dessauer, "a six-month delay having diluted most opposition, we of the committee agreed that the change to Haloid-Xerox might in the long run produce sound advantages."[20]

Many top executives consciously plan for such "gestation periods" and often find that the strategic concept itself is made more effective by the resulting feedback.

Tactical Shifts and Partial Solutions

At this stage in the process guiding executives might share a fairly clear vision of the general directions for movement. But rarely does a total new corporate posture emerge full grown—like Minerva from the brow of Jupiter—from any one source. Instead, early resolutions are likely to be

---

[19]See R. M. Cyert, W. R. Dill, and J. G. March, "The Role of Expectations in Business Decision Making," *Administrative Science Quarterly* (December 1958): 307-40. The authors point out the perils of top management advocacy because existing polities may unconsciously bias information to support views they value.

[20]See J. H. Dessauer, *My Years with Xerox: The Billions Nobody Wanted* (Garden City, NY: Doubleday, 1971).

partial, tentative, or experimental.[21] Beginning moves often appear as mere tactical adjustments in the enterprise's existing posture. As such, they encounter little opposition, yet each partial solution adds momentum in new directions. Guiding executives try carefully to maintain the enterprise's ongoing strengths while shifting its total posture incrementally—at the margin—toward new needs. Such executives themselves might not yet perceive the full nature of the strategic shifts they have begun. They can still experiment with partial new approaches and learn without risking the viability of the total enterprise. Their broad early steps can still legitimately lead to a variety of different success scenarios. Yet logic might dictate that they wait before committing themselves to a total new strategy.[22] As events unfurl, solutions to several interrelated problems might well flow together in a not-yet-perceived synthesis. For example:

> In the early 1970s at General Motors there was a distinct awareness of a developing fuel economy ethic. General Motors executives said, "Our conclusions were really at the conversational level—that the big car trend was at an end. But we were not at all sure sufficient numbers of large car buyers were ready to move to dramatically lighter cars." Nevertheless, GM did start concept studies that resulted in the Cadillac Seville.

> When the oil crisis hit in fall 1973, the company responded in further increments, at first merely increasing production of its existing small car lines. Then as the crisis deepened, it added another partial solution, the subcompact "T car"—the Chevette—and accelerated the Seville's development cycle. Next, as fuel economy appeared more saleable, executives set an initial target of removing 400 pounds from B-C bodies by 1977. As fuel economy pressures persisted and engineering feasibilities offered greater confidence, this target was increased to 800-1000 pounds (three mpg). No step by itself shifted the company's total strategic posture until the full downsizing of all lines was announced. But each partial solution built confidence and commitment toward a new direction.

Broadening Political Support

Often these broad emerging strategic thrusts need expanded political support and understanding to achieve sufficient momentum to survive.[23] Committees, task forces, and retreats tend to be favored mechanisms for accomplishing this. If carefully managed, these do not become the "garbage cans" of emerging ideas, as some observers have noted.[24] By selecting

[21]See: H. Mintzberg, *The Nature of Managerial Work* (New York: Harper & Row, 1973). Note that this "vision" is not necessarily the beginning point of the process. Instead it emerges as new data and viewpoints interact; Normann (1977).

[22]See Mintzberg, Raisinghani, and Theoret (June 1976). Here the authors liken the process to a decision tree where decisions at each node become more narrow, with failure at any node allowing recycling back to the broader tree trunk.

[23]Wrapp (September-October 1967) notes that a conditioning process that may stretch over months or years is necessary in order to prepare the organization for radical departures from what it is already striving to attain.

[24]See J. G. March, J. P. Olsen, S. Christensen et al., *Ambiguity and Choice in Organizations* (Bergen, Norway: Universitetsforlaget, 1976).

the committee's chairman, membership, timing, and agenda, guiding executives can largely influence and predict a desired outcome, and can force other executives toward a consensus. Such groups can be balanced to educate, evaluate, neutralize, or overwhelm opponents. They can be used to legitimize new options or to generate broad cohesion among diverse thrusts, or they can be narrowly focused to build momentum. Guiding executives can constantly maintain complete control over these "advisory processes" through their various influences and veto potentials. For example:

> IBM's Chairman Watson and Executive Vice President Larson had become concerned over what to do about: third generation computer technology, a proliferation of designs from various divisions, increasing costs of developing software, internal competition among their lines, and the needed breadth of line for the new computer applications they began to foresee. Step by step, they oversaw the killing of the company's huge Stretch computer line (uneconomic), a proposed 8000 series of computers (incompatible software), and the prototype English Scamp Computer (duplicative). They then initiated a series of "strategic dialogues" with divisional executives to define a new strategy. But none came into place because of the parochial nature of divisional viewpoints.
>
> Learson, therefore, set up the SPREAD Committee, representing every major segment of the company. Its twelve members included the most likely opponent of an integrated line (Haanstra), the people who had earlier suggested the 8000 and Scamp designs, and Learson's handpicked lieutenant (Evans). When progress became "hellishly slow," Haanstra was removed as chairman and Evans took over. Eventually the committee came forth with an integrating proposal for a single, compatible line of computers to blanket and open up the market for both scientific and business applications, with "standard interface" for peripheral equipment. At an all-day meeting of the fifty top executives of the company, the report was not received with enthusiasm, but there were no compelling objections. So Larson blessed the silence as consensus saying, "OK, we'll do it"—i.e., go ahead with a major development program.[25]

In addition to facilitating smooth implementation, many managers reported that interactive consensus building processes also improve the quality of the strategic decisions themselves and help achieve positive and innovative assistance when things otherwise could go wrong.

Overcoming Opposition: "Zones of Indifference" and "No Lose" Situations

Executives of basically healthy companies in the sample realized that any attempt to introduce a new strategy would have to deal with the

[25]See: T. A. Wise, "I.B.M.'s $5 Billion Gamble," *Fortune*, September 1966, pp. 118-24; T. A. Wise, "The Rocky Road to the Marketplace (Part II: I.B.M.'s $5 Billion Gamble)," *Fortune*, October 1966, pp. 138-52.

support its predecessor had. Barring a major crisis, a frontal attack on an old strategy could be regarded as an attack on those who espoused it—perhaps properly—and brought the enterprise to its present levels of success. There often exists a variety of legitimate views on what could and should be done in the new circumstances that a company faces. And wise executives do not want to alienate people who would otherwise be supporters. Consequently, they try to get key people behind their concepts whenever possible, to co-opt or neutralize serious opposition if necessary, or to find "zones of indifference" where the proposition would not be disastrously opposed.[26] Most of all they seek "no lose" situations which will motivate all the important players toward a common goal. For example:

> When James McFarland took over at General Mills from his power base in the Grocery Products Division, another serious contender for the top spot had been Louis B. "Bo" Polk, a very bright, aggressive young man who headed the corporation's acquisition-diversification program. Both traditional lines and acquisitions groups wanted support for their activities and had high-level supporters. McFarland's corporate-wide "goodness to greatness" conferences (described in earlier articles) first obtained broad agreement on growth goals and criteria for all areas.
>
> Out of this and the related acquisition proposal process came two thrusts: (1) to expand—internally and through acquisitions—in food-related sectors and (2) to acquire new growth centers based on General Mills' marketing skills. Although there was no formal statement, there was a strong feeling that the majority of resources should be used in food-related areas. But neither group was foreclosed, and no one could suggest the new management was vindictive. As it turned out, over the next five years about $450 million was invested in new businesses, and the majority were not closely related to foods.

But such tactics do not always work. Successful executives surveyed tended to honor legitimate differences in viewpoints and noted that initial opponents often shaped new strategies in more effective directions and became supporters as new information became available. But strong-minded executives sometimes disagreed to the point where they had to be moved or stimulated to leave; timing could dictate very firm top-level decisions at key junctions. Barring crises, however, disciplinary steps usually occurred incrementally as individual executives' attitudes and competencies emerged vis-a-vis a new strategy.

---

[26]For an excellent overview of the processes of co-optation and neutralization, see Sayles (1964). For perhaps the first reference to the concept of the "zone of indifference," see C. I. Barnard, *The Functions of the Executive* (Cambridge, MA: Harvard University Press, 1938). The following two sources note the need of executives for coalition behavior to reduce the organizational conflict resulting from differing interests and goal preferences in large organizations: Cyert and March (1963); J. G. March, "Business Decision Making," in *Readings in Managerial Psychology*, H. J. Leavitt and L. R. Pondy, eds. (Chicago: University of Chicago Press, 1964).

Structuring Flexibility: Buffers, Slacks, and Activists

Typically there are too many uncertainties in the total environment for managers to program or control all the events involved in effecting a major change in strategic direction. Logic dictates, therefore, that managers purposely design flexibility into their organizations and have resources ready to deploy incrementally as events demand. Planned flexibility requires: (1) proactive horizon scanning to identify the general nature and potential impact of opportunities and threats the firm is most likely to encounter, (2) creating sufficient resource buffers—or slacks—to respond effectively as events actually unfurl, (3) developing and positioning "credible activists" with a psychological commitment to move quickly and flexibly to exploit specific opportunities as they occur, and (4) shortening decision lines from such people (and key operating managers) to the top for the most rapid system response. These—rather than pre-capsuled (and shelved) programs to respond to stimuli which never quite occur as expected—are the keys to real contingency planning.

The concept of resource buffers requires special amplification. Quick access to resources is needed to cushion the impact of random events, to offset opponents' sudden attacks, or to build momentum for new strategic shifts. Some examples will indicate the form these buffers may take.

> For critical purchased items, General Motors maintained at least three suppliers, each with sufficient capacity to expand production should one of the others encounter a catastrophe. Thus, the company had expandable capacity with no fixed investment. Exxon set up its Exploration Group to purposely undertake the higher risks and longer-term investments necessary to search for oil in new areas, and thus to reduce the potential impact on Exxon if there were sudden unpredictable changes in the availability of Middle East oil. Instead of hoarding cash, Pillsbury and General Mills sold off unprofitable businesses and cleaned up their financial statements to improve their access to external capital sources for acquisitions. Such access in essence provided the protection of a cash buffer without its investment. IBM's large R&D facility and its project team approach to development assured that it had a pool of people it could quickly shift among various projects to exploit interesting new technologies.

When such flexible response patterns are designed into the enterprise's strategy, it is proactively ready to move on those thrusts—acquisitions, innovations, or resource explorations—which require incrementalism.

Systematic Waiting and Trial Concepts

The prepared strategist may have to wait for events, as Roosevelt awaited a trauma like Pearl Harbor. The availability of desired acquisitions or real estate might depend on a death, divorce, fiscal crisis, management change, or an erratic stock market break.[27] Technological advances may have to await new knowledge, inventions, or lucky accidents. Despite otherwise complete preparations, a planned market entry might not be wise until new legislation, trade agreements, or competitive shake-outs occur. Organizational moves have to be timed to retirements, promotions, management failures, and so on. Very often the specific strategy adopted depends on the timing or sequence of such random events.[28] For example:

> Although Continental Group's top executives had thoroughly discussed and investigated energy, natural resources, and insurance as possible "fourth legs" for the company, the major acquisition possibilities were so different that the strategic choice depended on the fit of particular candidates—e.g., Peabody Coal or Richmond Insurance—within these possible industries. The choice of one industry would have precluded the others. The sequence in which firms became available affected the final choice, and that choice itself greatly influenced the whole strategic posture of the company.

In many of the cases studied, strategists proactively launched trial concepts—Mr. McColough's "architecture of information" (Xerox), Mr. Spoor's "Super Box" (Pillsbury)—in order to generate options and concrete proposals. Usually these "trial balloons" were phrased in very broad terms. Without making a commitment to any specific solution, the executive can activate the organization's creative abilities. This approach keeps the manager's own options open until substantive alternatives can be evaluated against each other and against concrete current realities. It prevents practical line managers from rejecting a strategic shift, as they might if forced to compare a "paper option" against well-defined current needs. Such trial concepts give cohesion to the new strategy while enabling the company to take maximum advantage of the psychological and informational benefits of incrementalism.

SOLIDIFYING PROGRESS—INCREMENTALLY

As events move forward, executives can more clearly perceive the specific directions in which their organizations should—and realistically can—move. They can seek more aggressive movement and commitment to their new perceptions, without undermining important ongoing activities or creating unnecessary reactions to their purposes. Until this point, new strategic goals might remain broad, relatively unrefined, or even unstated except as philosophic concepts. More specific dimensions might be incrementally announced as key pieces of information fall into place, specific unanswered issues approach resolution, or significant resources have to be formally committed.

---

[27]Cyert and March (1963) also note that not only do organizations seek alternatives but that "alternatives seek organizations" (as when finders, scientists, bankers, etc., bring in new solutions).

[28]See March, Olsen, Christensen et al. (1976).

Creating Pockets of Commitment

Early in this stage, guiding executives may need to actively implant support in the organization for new thrusts. They may encourage an array of exploratory projects for each of several possible options. Initial projects can be kept small, partial, or ad hoc, neither forming a comprehensive program nor seeming to be integrated into a cohesive strategy. Executives often provide stimulating goals, a proper climate for imaginative proposals, and flexible resource support, rather than being personally identified with specific projects. In this way they can achieve organizational involvement and early commitment without focusing attention on any one solution too soon or losing personal credibility if it fails.

Once under way, project teams on the more successful programs in the sample became ever more committed to their particular areas of exploration. They became pockets of support for new strategies deep within the organization. Yet, if necessary, top managers could delay until the last moment their final decisions blending individual projects into a total strategy. Thus, they were able to obtain the best possible match among the company's technical abilities, its psychological commitments, and its changing market needs. By making final choices more effectively—as late as possible with better data, more conscientiously investigated options, and the expert critiques competitive projects allowed—these executives actually increased technical and market efficiencies of their enterprises, despite the apparent added costs of parallel efforts.[29]

In order to maintain their own objectivity and future flexibility, some executives choose to keep their own political profiles low as they build a new consensus. If they seem committed to a strategy too soon, they might discourage others from pursuing key issues which should be raised.[30] By stimulating detailed investigations several levels down, top executives can seem detached yet still shape both progress and ultimate outcomes—by reviewing interim results and specifying the timing, format, and forums for the release of data. When reports come forward, these executives can stand above the battle and review proposals objectively, without being personally on the defensive for having committed themselves to a particular solution too soon. From this position they can more easily orchestrate a high-level consensus on a new strategic thrust. As an added benefit, negative decisions on proposals often come from a group consensus that top executives can simply confirm to lower levels, thereby preserving their personal veto for more crucial moments. In many well-made decisions people at all levels contribute to the generation, amplification, and inter-

---

[29]Much of the rationale for this approach is contained in J. B. Quinn, "Technological Innovation, Entrepreneurship, and Strategy," *Sloan Management Review*, Spring 1979, pp. 19-30.

[30]See C. Argyris, "Interpersonal Barriers to Decision Making," *Harvard Business Review*, March-April 1966, pp. 84-97. The author notes that when the president introduced major decisions from the top, discussion was "less than open" and commitment was "less than complete," although executives might assure the president to the contrary.

pretation of options and information to the extent that it is often difficult to say who really makes the decision.[31]

Focusing the Organization

In spite of their apparent detachment, top executives do focus their organizations on developing strategies at critical points in the process. While adhering to the rhetoric of specific goal setting, most executives are careful *not* to state new goals in concrete terms before they have built a consensus among key players. They fear that they will prematurely centralize the organization, preempt interesting options, provide a common focus for otherwise fragmented opposition, or cause the organization to act prematurely to carry out a specified commitment. Guiding executives may quietly shape the many alternatives flowing upward by using what Wrapp refers to as "a hidden hand." Through their information networks they can encourage concepts they favor, let weakly supported options die through inaction, and establish hurdles or tests for strongly supported ideas with which they do not agree but which they do not wish to oppose openly.

Since opportunities for such focusing generally develop unexpectedly, the timing of key moves is often unpredictable. A crisis, a rash of reassignments, a reorganization, or a key appointment may allow an executive to focus attention on particular thrusts, add momentum to some, and perhaps quietly phase out others.[32] Most managers surveyed seemed well aware of the notion that "if there are no other options, mine wins." Without being Machiavellian, they did not want misdirected options to gain strong political momentum and later have to be terminated in an open bloodbath. They also did not want to send false signals that stimulated other segments of their organizations to make proposals in undesirable directions. They sensed very clearly that the patterns in which proposals are approved or denied will inevitably be perceived by lower echelons as precedents for developing future goals or policies.

Managing Coalitions

Power interactions among key players are important at this stage of solidifying progress. Each player has a different level of power determined by his or her information base, organizational position, and personal credibility.[33] Executives legitimately perceive problems or opportunities differ-

---

[31]See March (1964).

[32]The process tends to be one of eliminating the less feasible rather than of determining a target or objectives. The process typically reduces the number of alternatives through successive limited comparisons to a point where understood analytical techniques can apply and the organization structure can function to make a choice. See Cyert and March (1963).

[33]For more detailed relationships between authority and power, see: H. C. Metcalf and L. Urwick, eds., *Dynamic Administration: The Collected Papers of Mary Parker Follett* (New York: Harper & Brothers, 1941); A. Zaleznik, "Power and Politics in Organizational Life," *Harvard Business Review*, May-June 1970, pp. 47-60.

ently because of their particular values, experiences, and vantage points. They will promote the solutions they perceive as the best compromise for the total enterprise, for themselves, and for their particular units. In an organization with dispersed power, the key figure is the one who can manage coalitions.[34] Since no one player has all the power, regardless of that individual's skill or position, the action that occurs over time might differ greatly from the intentions of any of the players.[35] Top executives try to sense whether support exists among important parties for specific aspects of an issue and try to get partial decisions and momenta going for those aspects. As "comfort levels" or political pressures within the top group rise in favor of specific decisions, the guiding executive might, within his or her concept of a more complete solution, seek—among the various features of different proposals—a balance that the most influential and credible parties can actively support. The result tends to be a stream of partial decisions on limited strategic issues made by constantly changing coalitions of the critical power centers.[36] These decisions steadily evolve toward a broader consensus, accceptable to both the top executive and some "dominant coalition" among these centers.

As a partial consensus emerges, top executives might crystallize issues by stating some broad goals in more specific terms for internal consumption. Finally, when sufficient general acceptance exists and the timing is right, the goals may begin to appear in more public announcements. For example:

> As General Mills divested several of its major divisions in the early 1960s, its annual reports began to refer to these as deliberate moves "to concentrate on the company's strengths" and "to intensify General Mills' efforts in the convenience foods field." Such statements could not have been made until many of the actual divestitures were completed, and a sufficient consensus existed among the top executives to support the new corporate concept.

Formalizing Commitment by Empowering Champions

As each major strategic thrust comes into focus, top executives try to ensure that some individual or group feels responsible for its goals. If the thrust will project the enterprise in entirely new directions, executives often want more than mere accountability for its success—they want real commitment.[37] A significantly new major thrust, concept, product, or problem

---

[34]See J. D. Thompson, "The Control of Complex Organizations," in *Organizations in Action* (New York: McGraw-Hill, 1967).

[35]See G. T. Allison, *Essence of Decision: Explaining the Cuban Missile Crisis* (Boston: Little, Brown and Company, 1971).

[36]See C. E. Lindblom, "The Science of 'Muddling Through'," *Public Administration Review* (Spring 1959): 79-88. The author notes that the relative weights individuals give to values and the intensity of their feelings will vary sequentially from decision to decision, hence the dominant coalition itself varies with each decision somewhat.

[37]Zaleznik (May-June 1970) notes that confusing compliance with commitment is one of the most common and difficult problems of strategic implementation. He notes that often organizational commitment may override personal interest if the former is developed carefully.

solution frequently needs the nurturing hand of someone who genuinely identifies with it and whose future depends on its success. For example:

> Once the divestiture program at General Mills was sufficiently under way, General Rawlings selected young "Bo" Polk to head up an acquisition program to use the cash generated. In this role Polk had nothing to lose. With strong senior management in the remaining consumer products divisions, the ambitious Polk would have had a long road to the top there. In acquisitions, he provided a small political target, only a $50,000 budget in a $500 million company. Yet he had high visibility and could build his own power base, if he were successful. With direct access to and the support of Rawlings, he would be protected through his early ventures. All he had to do was make sure his first few acquisitions were successful. As subsequent acquisitions succeeded, his power base could feed on itself—satisfying both Polk's ego needs and the company's strategic goals.

In some cases, top executives have to wait for champions to appear before committing resources to risky new strategies. They may immediately assign accountability for less dramatic plans by converting them into new missions for ongoing groups.

From this point on, the strategy process is familiar. The organization's formal structure has to be adjusted to support the strategy.[38] Commitment to the most important new thrusts has to be confirmed in formal plans. Detailed budgets, programs, controls, and reward systems have to reflect all planned strategic thrusts. Finally, the guiding executive has to see that recruiting and staffing plans are aligned with the new goals and that—when the situation permits—supporters and persistent opponents of intended new thrusts are assigned to appropriate positions.

Continuing the Dynamics by Eroding Consensus

The major strategic changes studied tended to take many years to accomplish. The process was continuous, often without any clear beginning or end.[39] The decision process constantly molded and modified management's concerns and concepts. Radical crusades became the new conventional wisdom, and over time totally new issues emerged. Participants or observers were often not aware of exactly when a particular decision had been made[40] or when a subsequent consensus was created to supersede or modify it; the process of strategic change was continuous and dynamic. Several GM executives described the frequently imperceptible[41] way in which many strategic decisions evolved:

---

[38]See A. D. Chandler, *Strategy and Structure: Chapters in the History of the Industrial Enterprise* (Cambridge, MA: MIT Press, 1962).

[39]See K. J. Cohen and R. M. Cyert, "Strategy: Formulation, Implementation, and Monitoring," *The Journal of Business* (July 1973): 349-67.

[40]March (1964) notes that major decisions are "processes of gradual commitment."

[41]Sayles (1964) notes that such decisions are a "flow process" with no one person ever really making the decisions.

We use an iterative process to make a series of tentative decisions on the way we think the market will go. As we get more data we modify these continuously. It is often difficult to say who decided something and when— or even who originated a decision. . . . Strategy really evolves as a series of incremental steps. . . . I frequently don't know when a decision is made in General Motors. I don't remember being in a committee meeting when things came to a vote. Usually someone will simply summarize a developing position. Everyone else either nods or states his particular terms of consensus.

A major strategic change in Xerox was characterized this way:

How was the overall organization decision made? I've often heard it said that after talking with a lot of people and having trouble with a number of decisions which were pending, Archie McCardell really reached his own conclusion and got Peter McColough's backing on it. But it really didn't happen quite that way. It was an absolutely evolutionary approach. It was a growing feeling. A number of people felt we ought to be moving toward some kind of matrix organization. We have always been a pretty democratic type of organization. In our culture you can't come down with mandates or ultimatums from the top on major changes like this. You almost have to work these things through and let them grow and evolve, keep them on the table so people are thinking about them and talking about them.

Once the organization arrives at its new consensus, the guiding executive has to move immediately to insure that this new position does not become inflexible. In trying to build commitment to a new concept, individual executives often surround themselves with people who see the world in the same way. Such people can rapidly become systematic screens against other views. Effective executives therefore purposely continue the change process, constantly introducing new faces and stimuli at the top. They consciously begin to erode the very strategic thrusts they may have just created—a very difficult, but essential, psychological task.

INTEGRATION OF PROCESSES AND OF INTERESTS

In the large enterprises observed, strategy formulation was a continuously evolving analytical-political consensus process with neither a finite beginning nor a definite end. It generally followed the sequence described above. Yet the total process was anything but linear. It was a grouping, cyclical process that often circled back on itself, with frequent interruptions and delays. Pfiffner aptly describes the process of strategy formation as being "like fermentation in biochemistry, rather than an industrial assembly line."[42]

Such incremental management processes are not abrogations of good

[42]See J. M. Pfiffner, "Administrative Rationality," *Public Administration Review* (Summer 1960): 125-32.

management practice. Nor are they Machiavellian or consciously manipulative maneuvers. Instead, they represent an adaptation to the practical psychological and informational problems of getting a constantly changing group of people with diverse talents and interests to move together effectively in a continually dynamic environment. Much of the impelling force behind logical incrementalism comes from a desire to tap the talents and psychological drives of the whole organization, to create cohesion, and to generate identity with the emerging strategy. The remainder of that force results from the interactive nature of the random factors and lead times affecting the independent subsystems that compose any total strategy.

An Incremental—Not Piecemeal—Process

The total pattern of action, though highly incremental, is not piecemeal in well-managed organizations. It requires constant, conscious reassessment of the total organization, its capacities, and its needs as related to surrounding environments. It requires continual attempts by top managers to integrate these actions into an understandable, cohesive whole. How do top managers themselves describe the process? Mr. Estes, president of General Motors, said:

> We try to give them the broad concepts we are trying to achieve. We operate through questioning and fact gathering. Strategy is a state of mind you go through. When you think about a little problem, your mind begins to think how it will affect all the different elements in the total situation. Once you have had all the jobs you need to qualify for this position, you can see the problem from a variety of viewpoints. But you don't try to ram your conclusions down people's throats. You try to persuade people what has to be done and provide confidence and leadership for them.

Formal-Analytical Techniques.   At each stage of strategy development, effective executives constantly try to visualize the new patterns that might exist among the emerging strategies of various subsystems. As each subsystem strategy becomes more apparent, both its executive team and top-level groups try to project its implications for the total enterprise and to stimulate queries, support, and feedback from those involved in related strategies. Perceptive top executives see that the various teams generating subsystem strategies have overlapping members. They require periodic updates and reviews before higher echelon groups that can bring a total corporate view to bear. They use formal planning processes to interrelate and evaluate the resources required, benefits sought, and risks undertaken vis-a-vis other elements of the enterprise's overall strategy. Some use scenario-techniques to help visualize potential impacts and relationships. Others utilize complex forecasting models to better understand the basic interactions among subsystems, the total enterprise, and the environment. Still others use specialized staffs, "devil's advocates," or "contention teams" to make sure that all important aspects of their strategies receive a thorough evaluation.

Power-Behavioral Aspects: Coalition Management.   All of the formal methodologies help, but the real integration of all the components in an enterprise's total strategy eventually takes place only in the minds of high-level executives. Each executive may legitimately perceive the intended balance of goals and thrusts differently. Some of these differences may be openly expressed as issues to be resolved when new information becomes available. Some differences may remain unstated—hidden agendas to emerge at later dates. Others may be masked by accepting so broad a statement of intention that many different views are included in a seeming consensus, when a more specific statement might be divisive. Nevertheless, effective strategies do achieve a level of understanding and consensus sufficient to focus action.

Top executives deliberately manage the incremental processes within each subsystem to create the basis for consensus. They also manage the coalitions that lie at the heart of most controlled strategy developments.[43] They recognize that they are at the confluence of innumerable pressures—from stockholders, environmentalists, government bodies, customers, suppliers, distributors, producing units, marketing groups, technologists, unions, special issue activists, individual employees, ambitious executives, and so on—and that knowledgeable people of goodwill can easily disagree on proper actions. In response to changing pressures and coalitions among these groups, the top management team constantly forms and reforms its own coalitions on various decisions.[44]

Most major strategic moves tend to assist some interests—and executives' careers—at the expense of others. Consequently, each set of interests serves as a check on the others and thus helps maintain the breadth and balance of strategy.[45] To avoid significant errors some managers try to ensure that all important groups have representation at or access to the top.[46] The guiding executive group may continuously adjust the number, power, or proximity of such access points in order to maintain a desired balance and focus.[47] These delicate adjustments require constant negotiations and implied bargains within the leadership group. Balancing the focuses that different interests exert on key decisions is perhaps the ulti-

[43]See R. James, "Corporate Strategy and Change—The Management of People" (monograph, The University of Chicago, 1978). The author does an excellent job of pulling together the threads of coalition management at top organizational levels.

[44]See Cyert and March (1963), p. 115.

[45]Lindblom (Spring 1959) notes that every interest has a "watchdog" and that purposely allowing these watchdogs to participate in and influence decisions creates consensus decisions that all can live with. Similar conscious access to the top for different interests can now be found in corporate structures.

[46]See Zaleznik (May-June 1970).

[47]For an excellent view of the bargaining processes involved in coalition management, see Sayles (1964), pp. 207-17.

mate control top executives have in guiding and coordinating the formulation of their companies' strategies.[48]

Establishing, Measuring, and Rewarding Key Thrusts

Few executives or management teams can keep all the dimensions of a complex evolving strategy in mind as they deal with the continuous flux of urgent issues. Consequently, effective strategic managers seek to identify a few central themes that can help to draw diverse efforts together in a common cause.[49] Once identified, these themes help to maintain focus and consistency in the strategy. They make it easier to discuss and monitor proposed strategic thrusts. Ideally, these themes can be developed into a matrix of programs and goals, cutting across formal divisional lines and dominating the selection and ranking of projects within divisions. This matrix can, in turn, serve as the basis for performance measurement, control, and reward systems that ensure the intended strategy is properly implemented.

Unfortunately, few companies in the sample were able to implement such a complex planning and control system without creating undue rigidities. But all did utilize logical incrementalism to bring cohesion to the formal-analytical and power-behavioral processes needed to create effective strategies. Most used some approximation of the process sequence described above to form their strategies at both subsystem and overall corporate levels. A final summary example demonstrates how deliberate incrementalism can integrate the key elements in more traditional approaches to strategy formulation.

In the late 1970s a major nation's largest bank named as its new president and CEO a man with a long and successful career, largely in domestic operating positions. The bank's chairman had been a familiar figure on the international stage and was due to retire in three to five years. The new CEO, with the help of a few trusted colleagues, his chief planner, and a consultant, first tried to answer the questions: "If I look ahead seven to eight years to my retirement as CEO, what should I like to leave behind as the hallmarks of my leadership? What accomplishments would define my era as having been successful?" He chose the following as goals:

1. To be the country's number one bank in profitability and size without sacrificing the quality of its assets or liabilities.

2. To be recognized as a major international bank.

---

[48]For suggestions on why the central power figure in decentralized organizations must be the person who manages its dominant coalition, the size of which will depend on the issues involved, and the number of areas in which the organizations must rely on judgmental decisions, see Thompson (1967).

[49]Wrapp (September-October 1967) notes the futility of a top manager trying to push a full package of goals.

3. To improve substantially the public image and employee perceptions of the bank.

4. To maintain progressive policies that prevent unionization.

5. To be viewed as a professional, well-managed bank with strong, planned management continuity.

6. To be clearly identified as the country's most professional corporate finance bank, with a strong base within the country but with foreign and domestic operations growing in balance.

7. To have women in top management and to achieve full utilization of the bank's female employees.

8. To have a tighter, smaller headquarters and a more rationalized, decentralized corporate structure.

The CEO brought back to the corporate offices the head of his overseas divisions to be COO and to be a member of the Executive Committee, which ran the company's affairs. The CEO discussed his personal views concerning the bank's future with this Committee and also with several of his group VPs. Then, to arrive at a cohesive set of corporate goals, the Executive Committee investigated the bank's existing strengths and weaknesses (again with the assistance of consultants) and extrapolated its existing growth trends seven to eight years into the future. According to the results of this exercise, the bank's foreseeable growth would require that:

1. The bank's whole structure be reoriented to make it a much stronger force in international banking.

2. The bank decentralize operations much more than it ever had.

3. The bank find or develop at least 100 new top-level specialists and general managers within a few years.

4. The bank reorganize around a "four bank" principle (international, commercial, investment, and retail banks) with entirely new linkages forged among these units.

5. These linkages and much of the bank's new international thrust be built on its expertise in certain industries, which were the primary basis of its parent country's international trade.

6. The bank's profitability be improved across the board, especially in its diverse retail banking units.

To develop more detailed data for specific actions and to further develop consensus around needed moves, the CEO commissioned two consulting studies: one on the future of the bank's home country and the other on changing trade patterns and relationships worldwide. As these studies became available, the CEO allowed an ever wider circle of top executives to critique the studies' findings and to share their insights. Finally, the CEO and the Executive Committee were willing to draw up and agree to a statement of ten broad goals (parallel to the CEO's original goals but enriched in flavor and detail). By then, some steps were already under way to implement specific goals (e.g., the four bank concept). But the CEO wanted further participation of his line officers in the formulation of the goals and in the strategic thrusts they represented across the whole bank. By now eighteen months had gone by, but there was widespread consensus within the top management group on major goals and directions.

The CEO then organized an international conference of some forty top officers of the bank and had a background document prepared for this meeting containing: (1) the broad goals agreed upon, (2) the ten major thrusts that the Executive Committee thought were necessary to meet these goals, (3) the key elements needed to back up each thrust, and (4) a summary of the national and economic analyses the thrusts were based upon. The forty executives had two full days to critique, question, improve, and clarify the ideas in this document. Small work groups of line executives reported their findings and concerns directly to the Executive Committee. At the end of the meeting, the Executive Committee tabled one of the major thrusts for further study, agreed to refined wording for some of the bank's broad goals, and modified details of the major thrusts in line with expressed concerns.

The CEO announced that within three months each line officer would be expected to submit his own statement of how his unit would contribute to the major goals and thrusts agreed on. Once these unit goals were discussed and negotiated with the appropriate top executive group, the line officers would develop specific budgetary and nonbudgetary programs showing precisely how their units would carry out each of the major thrusts in the strategy. The CEO was asked to develop measures both for all key elements of each unit's fiscal performance and for performance against each agreed upon strategic thrust within each unit. As these plans came into place, it became clear that the old organization had to be aligned behind these new thrusts. The CEO had to substantially redefine the CEO's job, deal with some crucial internal political pressures, and place the next generation of top managers in the line positions supporting each major thrust. The total process from concept formulation to implementation of the control system was to span three to four years, with new goals and thrusts emerging flexibly as external events and opportunities developed.

CONCLUSIONS

In recent years, there has been an increasingly loud chorus of discontent about corporate strategic planning. Many managers are concerned that despite elaborate strategic planning systems, costly staffs for planning, and major commitments of their own time, their most elaborately analyzed strategies never get implemented. These executives and their companies generally have fallen into the trap of thinking about strategy formulation and implementation as separate, sequential processes. They rely on the awesome rationality of their formally derived strategies and the inherent power of their positions to cause their organizations to respond. When this does not occur, they become bewildered, if not frustrated and angry. Instead, successful managers in the companies observed acted logically and incrementally to improve the quality of information used in key decisions; to overcome the personal and political pressures resisting change; to deal with the varying lead times and sequencing problems in critical decisions; and to build the organizational awareness, understanding, and psychological commitment essential to effective strategies. By the time the strategies began to crystallize, pieces of them were already being implemented. Through the very processes they used to formulate their strategies, these executives had built sufficient organizational momentum and identity with the strategies to make them flow toward flexible and successful implementation.

IDENTIFYING THE MAJOR CORPORATE AND BUSINESS STRATEGY OPTIONS

3

"Markets are not created by God, nature or economic forces but by businessmen.

     Peter Drucker

". . . there is no such thing as a growth industry. . . . There are only companies organized and operated to create and capitalize on growth opportunities.

     Theodore Levitt

As discussed in Chapter 2, business-level strategy and corporate-level strategy are two different animals. The central concerns of business strategy are with (1) how a firm should position itself to compete in a distinctly identifiable, and strategically relevant, market—which types of products to offer to which groups of customers to meet which user functions and needs and (2) how to manage the internal aspects of the business in support of the chosen competitive approach. On the other hand, corporate strategy deals with the game plan for managing diversified enterprises whose activities cut across several lines of business, thus posing the ever-present issues of: How should we manage our business portfolio? What existing businesses should we get out of? What new businesses should we get into? What priority and role should each of the businesses we are currently in have in our portfolio?

Because of the differences in scope and focus between corporate and business strategy, there are basic differences in the strategy alternatives at each level. Corporate strategy alternatives deal directly with the various options for (1) shaping what an organization does and does not do and (2) selecting the emphasis to be placed upon each of the organization's chosen business activities and the role each is to have in the makeup of the portfolio. Business strategy alternatives, on the other hand, concern the different ways of trying to compete in a given market and the different postures and approaches for handling a particular kind of business, given its particular situation and circumstances.

In identifying and discussing the various strategic alternatives open to an enterprise, it is therefore desirable to proceed at two levels: the basic alternatives of corporate strategy and the basic alternatives of business strategy. We begin with corporate strategy alternatives.

THE BASIC ALTERNATIVES OF CORPORATE STRATEGY

In trying to decide upon a corporatewide strategic plan, an organization has essentially nine basic corporate strategy options to select from:

1. concentration on a single business
2. vertical integration
3. concentric or related diversification
4. conglomerate or unrelated diversification
5. joint ventures
6. retrenchment
7. divestiture
8. liquidation
9. combination strategies

Each of these merit discussion.

Concentration on a Single Business

The number of organizations which have made their mark specializing in a single-product, single-market, or single-technology business is impressively long. The power and achievement which attaches to a strategy of concentrating on the right business at the right time is testified to by the blue-chip performance of such familiar companies as McDonald's, Holiday Inn, Coca-Cola, BIC Pen Corp., Campbell Soup Co., Anheuser-Busch, Xerox, Dr Pepper, Gerber, and Polaroid. In the non-profit sector specialist strategies have proved successful for the Boston Pops Orchestra, the Red Cross, the Girl Scouts, Phi Beta Kappa, and the American Civil Liberties Union.

A concentration strategy offers numerous strengths and advantages. To begin with, a specialized business is more manageable. Simplicity breeds clarity and unity of purpose. With the efforts of the *total* organization focused sharply on a particular technology-customer-product combination, objectives can be made precise and competitive strategy can be fine tuned to market conditions and emerging threats and opportunities. There is less chance that limited organizational resources will be spread thinly over too many activities. Corporate management has ample opportunity to develop first-hand, in-depth knowledge of the business, the market, the organization, its customers, its technology, and major competitors. As a consequence, a concentration strategy offers excellent potential for an organization to:

1. Focus on doing *one* thing *very well*, thereby building a distinctive competence.

2. Zero in on the specific needs of specific customer groups, thus enhancing market visibility and reputation.

3. Anticipate changes and trends in customer needs and to be in position to respond effectively as they occur.

4. Achieve a proficiency in developing fresh approaches to customer groups and needs, in meeting stiffer competition, and in reacting to industry trends and developments.

5. Create a differential strategic advantage via the market reputation and the competitive strength that come from specialization and having a distinctive competence.

The advantages of a concentration strategy cannot be taken lightly. That they are well recognized and important is acknowledged by the widespread attempt of diversified firms to decentralize their activities into well-defined lines of business so that a special opportunity in a particular niche can be brought into sharp strategic focus. The power of a concentration strategy is also suggested by the fact that the managers of large, diversified companies often view their strongest competitors in a particular business as being smaller, specialized enterprises with concentrated, in-depth expertise in particular products and market segments. When a given product or customer group is only one among many of a company's interests, then it may not receive the same degree of attention and management priority as when it is the organization's sole business.

A concentration strategy need not be boring in the sense that it requires an enterprise to continue to do the same thing in the same ways. Ten examples of how to keep a concentration strategy fresh and effective are given below:

1. *Create and promote more uses for the product.* Arm & Hammer

baking soda sales increased markedly after the product was promoted for freshening refrigerators, cat litter boxes, and swimming pools.

2. *Take a commodity item and make a broader differentiated product out of it.* Frank Perdue succeeded in convincing people that his brand of chickens tasted better; Sunkist has done the same with oranges and lemons.

3. *Use advertising and promotional efforts to stimulate demand.* International Playtex and Johnson & Johnson discovered that tampons were "underadvertised" and scored major sales gains with increased television advertising.

4. *Attract nonusers to buy the product.* Procter & Gamble reversed declining Ivory soap sales in 1971 after promoting it for adults, instead of just for babies.

5. *Turn an apparent disadvantage into an advantage.* J. M. Smucker put its funny-sounding name to good use with an advertising slogan: "With a name like Smucker's, it has to be good."

6. *Use price cuts to build volume, market share, and profitability.* Johnson & Johnson made its Tylenol analgesic a market success after it reduced Tylenol's price to match what Bristol-Myers was charging for Datril. The Bell System has increased the use and profitability of its long-distance call business by giving substantial rate discounts on night and weekend calls.

7. *Seek market outlets for complementary by-products.* Several lumber and wood products firms have marketed pine bark for landscaping purposes, and cat litter and wood shavings for household pets.

8. *Develop a more compelling sales appeal.* Procter & Gamble's Pampers disposable diapers were only a modest success when touted as a convenience item for mothers, but sales took off after ads were changed to say that Pampers kept babies dry and happy.

9. *Capitalize on social concerns.* Sales of Dannon Yogurt rose sharply after ads helped health-conscious consumers "discover" the product.

10. *Make the product available through additional types of distribution channels.* Hanes captured additional sales and market share when it began to sell L'eggs panty hose in supermarkets.

Still other concentration strategy options include (1) convincing current customers to use more of a product via quantity discounts and faster rates of product innovation, (2) expansion into additional geographic markets, (3) improving quality, (4) offering more support services to customers, and (5) introducing a wider variety of models, sizes, and features to cater to specific buyer needs and preferences.

The corporate strategy of concentrating on a single business does pose a major business risk, however. By specializing, an enterprise puts all its eggs in one basket. If the market for the enterprise's product or service declines, so does the enterprise's business. Changing customer needs, technological innovation, or new substitute products can undermine or virtually wipe out a highly specialized, single-business firm in short order. One has only to recall what television did to the profitability and markets of the once-powerful Hollywood movie producers and what IBM electric typewriters did to the manual typewriter business formerly dominated by Royal-McBee, Underwood, and Smith Corona. And if the product/service is particularly vulnerable to recessionary influence in the economy, then the enterprises's fortunes are subject to wide swings and, consequently, a normally lower stock market appraisal.

Furthermore, by concentrating its expertise in a narrow area, an organization may find itself without the entrepreneurial competence and know-how to break out of its shell and diversify if and when the time arrives to cast off a fast-obsolescing concentration strategy. Every product, every service, every technology eventually loses its market grip.[1] Sales volume may still be there, but profitability and growth opportunities shrivel as market saturation sets in. When this occurs a single-business enterprise will need some fresh options to break out of its low growth or no-growth situation. This entails an entrepreneurial alertness for doing something new and different—an alertness that, like any skill, must be kept sharp by practice. Otherwise the capacity for shifting to new strategies and new businesses is never developed or else withers away.

Vertical Integration

Two factors tend to trigger serious corporate-level consideration of a vertical integration strategy: (1) diminishing profit prospects associated with further expansion of the main product line into new geographic markets and (2) being the wrong size to realize scale economies and performance potentials. Market saturation and the impracticalities of an oversize market coverage give rise to the first factor cited. A variety of causes underlie being the wrong size but the symptom is easy enough to spot: one (or a few) of the organization's production or distribution activities are out of proportion to the remainder, thereby making it difficult for the organization to support the volume, the product line, or the market standing requisite for economical operations and long-run competitive survival.[2]

Vertical integration has much to recommend as a strategy for dealing with these two factors. Consider first the benefits of integrating backward.

---

[1] It has been estimated that 80 percent of today's products will have disappeared from the market ten years from now and that 80 percent of the products which will be sold in the next decade are as yet unknown. See E. E. Scheuing, *New Product Management* (Hinsdale, Ill.: The Dryden Press, 1974), p. 1.

[2] Peter F. Drucker, *Management: Tasks, Responsibilities, Practices* (New York: Harper and Row Publishers, 1974), pp. 666-67.

To begin with, backward integration offers the potential for converting a cost center into a profit producer. This potential may be very attractive when suppliers have wide profit margins. Moreover, integrating backward allows a firm to supersede market uncertainties associated with supplies of raw materials. Where a firm is dependent on a particular raw material or service furnished by other enterprises, the door is always open for requisite supplies to be disrupted by strikes, bad weather, production breakdowns, or delays in scheduled deliveries. Furthermore, the cost structure is vulnerable to untimely increases in the prices of critical component materials. Stockpiling, fixed-price contracts, or the use of substitute inputs may not be feasible ways for dealing with such market uncertainties. When this is the case, bringing supplies and costs under its own wings may be an organization's most profitable strategic option for securing *reliable deliveries* of essential inputs at *reliable prices*. In short, sparing itself the uncertainties of being dependent upon suppliers permits an organization to coordinate and routinize its operating cycle, thereby (1) avoiding the transient, but upsetting, influences of unreliable suppliers and wide swings in supply prices, (2) realizing the cost efficiencies of a stable operating pattern, and (3) insulating itself from the tactical maneuvers of other firms regarding raw material sources. In so doing, an organization can become more a master of its own destiny than a slave to fortuitous market circumstances beyond its control.

While backward integration may be justified by an economic need to assure sources of supply, it may also be the best and most practical way to obtain a workable degree of commitment from suppliers. The case of Sears offers a prime example.[3] A large portion of the merchandise which Sears sells is made by manufacturers in which Sears has an ownership interest. While this might stem from Sears' desire to "control" its suppliers, it is as probable that Sears was concerned that it could not get reputable suppliers to commit themselves to making goods especially for Sears unless assured of a long-term relationship. The reasoning is not hard to understand: for a firm to become the chief supplier of one of Sears' big-ticket or volume items is likely to make Sears the supplier's main customer and major channel of distribution. For a supplier to allow itself to become a "captive company" of Sears without some sort of guarantee that the relationship would be a continuing one would be foolhardy and unduly risky. Thus for Sears to get major suppliers to forego their independence and agree to orient most or all of their business of manufacturing products to Sears' specifications to be sold under Sears' brand names and to be delivered according to Sears' demands very likely meant in some cases that Sears had to go beyond the offering of a "long term" contract. Without ties as permanent as those of ownership, some key suppliers could have balked,

---

[3]Ibid., p. 686.

leaving Sears with uncertain sources of supply and fluctuating quality in its lines of merchandise. Given Sears' merchandising strategy, being the "wrong size" to assure itself of dependable supplies of goods at the right price and quality could have been a serious strategic flaw. The strategic impetus for forward integration has much the same roots. Undependable sales and distribution channels can give rise to costly inventory pileups and frequent production shutdowns, thereby undermining the economies of stable production operation. Loss of these economies may make it imperative for an organization to gain stronger market access in order to remain competitive. Sometimes even a few percentage point increases in the average rate of capacity utilization can make a substantial difference in price and profitability.

For a raw materials producer, integrating forward into manufacturing may help achieve greater product differentiation and thus allow for increased profit margins. In the early phases of the vertical product flow, intermediate goods are "commodities," that is they have essentially identical technical specifications irrespective of producer (wheat, coal, sheet steel, cement, sulfuric acid, newsprint). Competition is extremely price-oriented. Yet, the closer the production stage is to the ultimate consumer, the greater are the opportunities for a firm to differentiate its end product via design, service, quality features, packaging, promotion, and so on. Marketing activities become more critical and the importance of price shrinks in comparison to other competitive variables.

For a manufacturer, integrating forward may take the form of building a chain of closely supervised dealer franchises or it may mean establishing company-owned and operated retail outlets. Alternatively, it could entail simply staffing regional and district sales offices instead of selling through manufacturer's agents or independent distributors. Whatever its specific format, forward integration is usually motivated by a desire to realize the higher profits that come with stable production, larger-scale distribution, and product differentiation and to enjoy the security that comes with having one's own capability for accessing markets and customers.

There are, however, some strategic disadvantages of vertical integration which warrant mention. The large capital requirements that sometimes accompany a vertical integration strategy may place a heavy strain on an organization's financial resources. Second, integration introduces more complexity into the management process. It requires new skills and the assumption of additional risks since the effect is to extend the enterprise's scope of operations. It means bearing the burdens of learning a new business and coping with the problems of a larger organization. While this may all be justified if it remedies a disparity between costs and profits, it can so increase a firm's vested interests in its technology and production facilities that it becomes reluctant to abandon its heavy fixed investments. Because of this inflexibility a fully integrated firm is vulnerable to new technologies and new products. Either it has to write off large portions of its fixed investments or else it must endure a competitive disadvantage with innovative enterprises having no proprietary interests to protect.

Third, vertical integration can pose problems of balancing capacity at each production stage. The most efficient sizes at each phase of the vertical product flow can be at substantial variance. This can mean exact self-sufficiency at each interface is the exception not the rule. Where internal capacity is deficient to supply the next stage, the difference will have to be bought externally. Where internal capacity is excessive, customers will need to be found for the surplus. And if by-products are generated, they will require arrangements for disposal.

All in all, therefore, a vertical integration strategy has both important strengths and weaknesses. Which direction the scales tip on vertical integration depends upon (1) how compatible it is with the organization's long-term strategic interests and performance objectives, (2) how much it strengthens an organization's position in its primary business, and (3) the extent to which it permits fuller exploitation of an organization's technical talents. Unless these issues are answered in the affirmative, vertical integration is likely to be an unattractive corporate strategy option.

Corporate Diversification Strategies

A number of wide-ranging factors account for the strategic appeal of corporate diversification:[4]

1. An organization may consider diversification because market saturation, competitive pressures, product line obsolescence, declining demand, or fear of antitrust action no longer allow profit objectives to be met solely through an expansion of its current product-market activities.

2. Even if appealing expansion opportunities still exist in its current business, an organization may diversify because its free cash flow exceeds the cash needs of expansion.

3. An organization's diversification opportunities may have a greater expected profitability than that of expanding its present business.

4. An organization may consider diversification because of a desire to spread risk and increase the stability and security of its operations. This desire may stem from uneasiness about "overspecialization" in partic-

[4]H. Igor Ansoff, *Corporate Strategy* (New York: McGraw-Hill, 1965), pp. 129-30; Drucker, *Management*, p. 684; George A. Steiner, "Why and How to Diversify," *California Management Review*, vol. 6, no. 4 (Summer 1964) pp. 11-17; J. F. Weston and S. F. Mansinghka, "Tests of the Efficiency Performance of Conglomerate Firms," *Journal of Finance*, vol. 26, no. 4 (September 1971), pp. 919-36; and Ronald W. Melicher and David F. Rush, "Evidence on the Acquisition-Related Performance of Conglomerate Firms,"*Journal of Finance*, vol. 29, no. 1 (March 1974), pp. 141-49.

ular products or technologies, the risks of having a disproportionately large fraction of sales to a single customer, dwindling supplies of a key raw material, the threat of new technologies, or vulnerability to swings in the economy.

5. A firm may diversify because of a perceived financial serendipity associated with certain kinds of acquisition. This search for financial-related advantages is said to account for (a) attempts by firms with depressed earnings to diversify into areas of higher average earnings performance level, (b) the pursuit of "instantaneous profits" whereby an acquiring firm buys out firms having lower pre-merger price-earnings ratios in an effort to immediately realize a higher stock price and earnings per share, and (c) the attempt to increase one's access to capital by acquiring enterprises with large cash flows and/or low debt to equity ratios.

6. An organization may pursue diversification because owners/managers enjoy the challenges of something new and something different.

One viewpoint even goes so far as to make diversification a condition of survival—"in the long run an organization must diversify or die."[5] The argument here is that a concentration strategy eventually falls victim to the new obsoleting the old. Be that as it may, the wealth of organizational experiences with diversification strategies clearly demonstrates that there is *right* diversification and *wrong* diversification.[6] Drucker's analogy to the musician illustrates the point well:

> An accomplished and well-established concert pianist will as a matter of course, add one new major piece to his repertoire each year. Every few years he will pick for his new piece something quite different from the repertoire through which he has made his name. This forces him to learn again, to hear new things in old and familiar pieces, and to become a better pianist altogether. At the same time, concert pianists have long known that they slough off an old piece as they add on one new major one. The total size of the repertoire remains the same. There are only so many pieces of music even the greatest pianist can play with excellence. If and when corporate diversification appears on the strategy agenda, the question of what kind of diversification—how exactly to apply the musician's rule—becomes paramount.[7]

There are two basic kinds of corporate diversification: *concentric* and *conglomerate*. Concentric diversification is *related* diversification; that is, the organization's lines of business, although distinct, still possess some meaningful kind of strategic fit. In concentric diversification, the related nature of the various lines of business can be keyed to common technology, customer usage, distribution channels, methods of operation, managerial know-how, or product similarity—virtually any strategically meaningful

---

[5]George A. Steiner, "Why and How to Diversify," p. 12.
[6]Drucker, *Management*, p. 692.
[7]Ibid., p. 685.

facet. In contrast, conglomerate diversification is *unrelated* or *pure* diversification; there is no common thread or element of true strategic fit among the organization's several lines of business.

Concentric Diversification Strategies.   Concentric diversification is a very attractive corporate strategy. It allows an enterprise to preserve a common core of unity in its business activities, while at the same time spreading the risks out over a broader business base. But more importantly, perhaps, when an organization has some kind of distinctive competence in its present business, concentric diversification offers a way to build upon what it does best. Diversifying with the express intent of extending the firm's expertise to related businesses may carry with it a competitive advantage and above-average profit opportunities.

Specific types of concentric diversification include:

1. Moving into closely related products (a bread bakery getting into saltine crackers).

2. Building upon company technology or know-how (a supplier of agricultural seeds and fertilizers diversifying into chemicals for insect and plant disease control).

3. Seeking to increase plant utilization (a window manufacturer deciding to add shower doors to its product line).

4. Utilizing available sources of raw materials (a pulp and paper products firm elects to devote some of its timberland to plywood production).

5. Making fuller utilization of the firm's sales force (a wholesaler of electrical wiring supplies adds electric heating and cooling equipment to its line of products).

6. Building upon the organization's brand name and goodwill (a successful coffee firm diversifies into tea).

Numerous actual examples of concentric diversification abound. Procter & Gamble has been eminently successful in building a diversified product line (Crest toothpaste, Ivory Snow, Tide, Duncan Hines cake mixes, Folger's coffee, Jif peanut butter, Pringles potato chips, Head and Shoulder's shampoo, Crisco shortening, Comet cleanser, Charmin toilet tissue—to mention a few) around its expertise in marketing household products through supermarket channels. Pepsi-Cola practiced concentric diversification when it bought Frito-Lay, Pizza Hut, and Taco Bell, as did Coca-Cola in purchasing Minute Maid Orange Juice and Taylor Wine, and Lockheed in encircling the needs of the Department of Defense with its product line of airframes, rocket engines, missiles, electronics, defense research and development, and shipbuilding. Sears learned that the diverse nature of TV sets, auto repair centers, men's suits, draperies, refrigerators, paint, and homeowner's insurance posed no difficulty to its corporate strategy because the same customer buys them, in very much the same way, and with the same value expectations, thereby providing the essential link for its version of customer-based concentric diversification.

Technology-based concentric diversification has proven successful in process industries (steel, aluminum, paper, and glass), where a single processing technique spawns a multitude of related products. The same paper machines which produce newsprint are equally adept at turning out stationery, notebook paper, and specialty printing paper for books and magazines.

Other firms (in chemicals and electronics particularly) have pursued a technology-linked diversification strategy because their expertise in a given scientific area led to the discovery of new technological branches having practical market application. Often, in the early stages of a major technology, it is not feasible to exploit an innovation fully by concentrating on just one or a few product markets. Simultaneous, or else closely-sequenced, R&D efforts into several product areas may be optimal.[8]

A further indication of the use and preference for concentric diversification strategies is shown in Illustration Capsule 11.

ILLUSTRATION CAPSULE 11
Pillsbury's Shift in Diversification Strategy

During the 60s many companies initiated strategies for broadly diversifying their activities. During the 70s, when it became painfully apparent that many of the newly-acquired businesses were not performing up to expectations or else did not "fit in" very well, a sizable number of these very same companies changed their strategies from pure diversification to one of related diversification. Pillsbury was one of the companies which retreated from a conglomerate approach to a conceptual approach to diversification.

When William H. Spoor became chairman of the board of Pillsbury in January 1973, he moved quickly to narrow Pillsbury's product base to the area he felt the company knew best—food. In short order Pillsbury moved to divest its low-growth, cyclical business in poultry, its minority housing unit (Pentom Builders), its interest in magazine publishing (*Bon Appetit*), its com-

---

[8]However, beyond some stage the progressive branching out of a common technology can spread an enterprise so thin and push it in so many different directions that further technological-based diversification dilutes what once was clear advantage. According to Peter Drucker:

That this might be the case is indicated by the fact that most of these giant extended technological families have a few areas in which they have strength and maintain their leadership position: GE and Westinghouse in heavy electrical apparatus, Philips in consumer electronics, Union Carbide in metallurgical chemistry, DuPont in textile fibers and so on. In these areas they also maintain their innovative capacity. The reason for the relative sluggishness and vulnerability of these companies is not "poor management" but "spotty management." It is not that they are in too few "good" businesses but that they are in too many that do not "fit." See Drucker, *Management*, p. 705.

ILLUSTRATION CAPSULE 11 *(continued)*

puter services business, and its money-losing wine business (Souverain Winery). Mr. Spoor was quoted as saying, "I am only interested in businesses that fall into three categories. We should only be in consumer foods, food away from home, and agri-products."

Pillsbury's original base of businesses from which it first launched its diversification efforts revolved around flour milling (it is the largest miller in the U.S.), producing bakery mixes (some 300 varieties), commodity merchandising, grain exports, and grocery items for consumers (including flour, cake mixes and frostings, pancake mix, quick bread mixes, and a wide assortment of refrigerated dough products). Most of these businesses generated healthy profits and cash flows but were in markets where growth was slower. Volume gains, particularly in the consumer products categories, were largely dependent on taking business away from rival brands—a costly process with little prospect of major gains in profitability. This was what motivated the original diversification strategy.

Under Spoor's leadership, however, Pillsbury's acquisitions reverted to a more focused direction and reflected the decision to become an international food company participating in the three major areas of agribusiness, household food items, and restaurants. Firms acquired by Pillsbury under its new corporate concept included:

1. Wilton Enterprises, Inc. (acquired in 1973)—the nation's leading marketer of cake decorating products.

2. Totino's Pizza (acquired in 1976)—the second largest maker of prepared pizzas, with just over a 20 percent market share.

3. Fox Deluxe Foods (acquired in 1976)—operator of a pizza manufacturing plant in Joplin, Missouri.

4. American Beauty Macaroni Company (acquired in 1977)—manufacturer of a broad line of quality pasta products.

5. Speas Company (acquired in 1978)—a manufacturer of apple juice, cider vinegar, and pectin.

6. Green Giant Co. (acquired in 1978)—maker of frozen and canned foods.

The Green Giant acquisition was a major strategic effort by Pillsbury to gain a product mix that would put the company on a par with Kellogg Co. and H. J. Heinz, and to prepare it for a later capability to compete more broadly with General Mills and General Foods. By acquiring Green Giant, Pillsbury gained some strategic leverage in capturing shelf space in supermarkets for Pillsbury's less widely distributed lines (cake decorating sets, Funny Face and Squoze powdered drink mixes, Erasco food products, American Beauty pasta, and Sprinkle Sweet artificial sweetner). Green Giant's canned and frozen foods lines were popular and thus attractive lines for supermarkets to carry. A key to success in gaining distribution through supermarkets is for a

ILLUSTRATION CAPSULE 11 *(concluded)*

manufacturer to have products with dominant first or second positions in fast-growing sales areas—something Pillsbury had not been able to accomplish as well as some other manufacturers. Green Giant products were tagged to fill this gap.

Besides its new acquisitions, Pillsbury continued to be active in expanding its interests in the restaurant business. Burger King Corp., acquired in 1967, was turned into the company's main revenue producer. Shortly after the acquisition, when Burger King failed to keep pace with its fast-growing market, Spoor hired the No. 3 man at McDonald's, Donald Smith, to revitalize the chain—specifically to double the number of outlets and triple earnings by 1983. During the 1973-1978 period, 70 percent of Pillsbury's capital improvements budget, or $385 million, was allocated to the Burger King division. A grow-and-build strategy was also used in Pillsbury's Steak and Ale restaurants (some of which operate under the names of Jolly Ox and Bennigan's) where the number of outlets rose from 52 in 1973 to 165 in 1978. At the same time, Pillsbury pushed forward in expanding its Poppin Fresh Pie Shops business; the number of units open increased from 6 in 1974 to 45 in 1978. The pie shops are mid-priced family restaurants, seating about 135 persons, featuring 27 varieties of pies and offering a limited menu of sandwiches, soups, and salads.

In its *1977 Annual Report*, Pillsbury announced that its current corporate strategy and diversification programs were aimed at producing a "repetitive, predictable, and growing" stream of earnings. The company's quantitative targets were (1) an average annual sales growth rate of 10 percent, (2) a minimum annual earnings per share growth rate of 10 percent, (3) a pretax return on average invested capital of 20 percent, (4) an after-tax return on stockholders' equity of 16 percent, and (5) an "A" credit rating.

Conglomerate Diversification Strategies. While one might expect an overwhelming majority of organizations to favor concentric diversification because of the greater likelihood of good strategic fit, the conglomerate strategy has nonetheless attracted some important companies. A simple criterion of "will it meet our minimum standard for expected profitability?" captures the essence of the corporate strategy of such firms as Textron, Whittaker, ITT, Litton, Gulf + Western, U. S. Industries, Fuqua Industries, and Northwest Industries.

However, other organizations have opted for unrelated diversification because their distinctive competence either was so narrow as to have little in common with other businesses or was so lacking in depth that any diversification move was inherently a move into something new and different. And still others have viewed unrelated diversification as the optimal way of escaping a declining industry or overdependence on a single product-market area. Possible options for conglomerate diversification strategies include:

1. Seeking a match between a cash-rich, opportunity-poor company and an opportunity-rich, cash-poor firm.

2. Diversifying into areas with a counterseasonal or countercyclical sales pattern so as to smooth out sales and profit fluctuations.

3. Attempting to merge an opportunity-poor, skill-rich company with an opportunity-rich, skill-poor enterprise.

4. Seeking out a marriage of a highly leveraged firm and a debt-free firm so as to balance the capital structure of the former and increase its borrowing capacity.

5. Gaining entry into new product markets via licensing agreements or purchase of manufacturing or distribution rights.

6. Acquiring any firm in any line of business so long as the projected profit opportunities equal or exceed minimum criteria.

Aside from the pros and cons of being in businesses not having either a common thread or strategic fit, an unrelated diversification strategy has several other important advantages and limitations. First, while unrelated diversification can lead to improved sales, profits, and growth when an organization diversifies into industries where the economic potential is stronger than its existing businesses, it is wise to be skeptical of "promising opportunities" in businesses where one has no skill or prior experience. Sooner or later every business gets into trouble. Thus, whenever a firm's management contemplates diversifying into new unrelated areas, it should ask, "If the new business got into trouble, would we know how to bail it out?" If the answer is no, it likely represents diversification of the wrong kind even though the lure of above-average profitability is tempting.[9]

Second, despite the fact that its consolidated performance may improve, the price which a conglomerate pays to buy its way into a growth industry may impair stockholder earnings. This holds whether diversification takes place from within or through acquisition since some kind of $2 + 2 = 5$ effect is frequently needed to offset the premium price paid to get into the business. The high price-earnings multiples which many conglomerates have paid for their acquisitions, as well as the millions of dollars of purchased "goodwill" which appear on corporate financial statements, are ample evidence of the added costs of "buying in."

Third, unless there is some kind of strategic fit, consolidated performance of a conglomerate enterprise will tend to be no better than if its divisions were independent firms, and it may be worse to the extent that

---

[9] Of course, management may be willing to assume the risk that trouble will not strike before it has had time to learn the business well enough to bail it out of most any difficulty. See Drucker, *Management*, p. 709.

centralized management policies hamstring the operating divisions. This implies that the best which conglomerates can generally expect is to be at no cost/efficiency disadvantage in trying to compete against nonconglomerates.[10] Fourth, although in theory a conglomerate strategy would seem to offer the potential of greater sales-profit stability over the course of the business cycle, in practice the attempts at countercyclical diversification appear to have fallen short of the mark. Conglomerate profits have evidenced no propensity to suffer milder reversals in periods of recession and economic stress.[11] In fact, during times of adversity, the staying power of conglomerates may be weaker than that of concentrically-diversified firms.[12] Finally, the "financial synergism" of trying to marry businesses with a high cash throw-off to businesses with a large cash appetite often goes awry because of a lack of "fit" and expertise in other key respects. For a conglomerate diversification strategy to be truly successful, a great deal more resources are needed than money alone.[13]

A Perspective View of Corporate Diversification Strategies.   Diversification—whether concentric or conglomerate—can be neither recommended nor condemned *per se*. Many organizations are actively pursuing diversification strategies of some sort, and are doing so for what they view as good and sufficient business reasons. It plainly makes sense for a firm to *consider* diversification when its existing business has been expanded to its practical limits and/or when it is severely threatened by outside forces; it may or may not make sense to diversify before this occurs.

In addition, the pros and cons of what kind and how much diversification an organization needs to get the best performance and results weigh differently from case to case. A logical place for an organization's management to begin its evaluation of diversification alternatives is with consideration of "what is the least diversification we need to attain our objectives and remain a healthy, viable entity, capable of competing successfully?" At the other extreme, though, management is equally obliged to examine the question of "what is the most diversification we can manage given the complexity it adds?"[14] In all likelihood, the optimal answer lies in between. And after deciding what to include and what to exclude, the next step is to make the diversification strategy specific enough to define the

[10]Evidence to this effect is given in Stanley E. Boyle, *Economic Report on Conglomerate Merger Performance: An Empirical Analysis of Nine Corporations*, Staff Report to the Federal Trade Commission, reprinted in *Mergers and Acquisitions*, vol. 8, no. 1 (Spring 1973), pp. 5-41; Ronald W. Melicher and David F. Rush, "The Performance of Conglomerate Firms: Recent Risk and Return Experience," *Journal of Finance*, vol. 28, no. 2 (May 1973), pp. 381-88; and Robert L. Coun, "The Performance of Conglomerate Firms: Comment," *Journal of Finance*, vol. 28, no. 3 (June 1973), pp. 754-58.

[11]Drucker, *Management*, p. 767.

[12]See H. I. Ansoff and J. F. Weston, "Merger Objectives and Organization Structure," *Quarterly Review of Economics and Business*, vol. 2, no. 3(August 1962), pp. 49-58.

[13]Drucker, *Management*, pp. 707-8.

[14]Ibid., pp. 692-93.

role of each line of business within the total organization. The reverse approach of letting corporate strategy be merely an aggregation of each line of business strategy is risky—it can quickly deteriorate into marching in too many directions at once.

The Achilles heel of unrelated diversification is the strain it places on corporate-level management to cope with the variety of problems encountered in a widely diversified business portfolio. Not many corporate managements are truly capable of managing many different businesses at once. Such capability is seldom demonstrated by successfully managing one or two different businesses since the experiences and know-how gained in one often do not transfer to another. Just as the skills of an all-pro basketball player do not transfer to playing professional ice hockey, so also may the skills of a television manufacturer be lacking in managing a newly-acquired fast food chain. One simply cannot count upon being clever enough to hire "good management" to run many kinds of entirely different businesses and, in addition, to be clever at staying on top of how well all of the different business-level managers are doing their jobs—such cleverness is easier to conceive of in theory than it is to carry out in practice. The wisdom of related diversification as contrasted to unrelated diversification is that in related diversification a firm can seek to extend and build upon something it knows about whereas in unrelated diversification a firm is entering "a whole new ball game" where its prior skills and experience count for little.

The investor disfavor which conglomerates have acquired, the poor performance of several prominent conglomerates, and the inherent difficulty of managing a diverse number of businesses over the long run have caused many highly diversified firms to avoid or discard the conglomerate label by developing "corporate unity themes." Multi-business firms have resorted to comprehensive labels like leisure-time, high technology, consumer products, materials processing, total communication systems, and energy services to describe their business portfolios; businesses that no longer fit are being divested. The idea seems to be to convey the image of being diversified around a concept ("a conceptually-oriented conglomerate") rather than projecting the image of a "free-form" conglomerate with interests extending across many unrelated businesses.

ILLUSTRATION CAPSULE 12
Using Mergers and Acquisitions to Accomplish Corporate Strategy

A given merger or acquisition can be motivated by a desire to expand within the same type of business, by a move to integrate vertically, or by an effort at diversification. In this sense, merger/acquisition is a tactic for accomplishing a larger strategic objective and one which is often used—

ILLUSTRATION CAPSULE 12 *(continued)*

sometimes with drama, stress, and marketwide impact. Some firms use merger/acquisition as the exclusive means for entering new businesses they want to be in: indeed, entire companies (nearly all of the large conglomerates) have been put together via mergers and acquisitions.

A *merger* can be thought of as combining two (or more) firms into a new enterprise. An *acquisition* is when one firm (the parent) acquires another and either "absorbs" it into its own operations or establishes it as an operating subsidiary or semi-autonomous business unit.

There are five types of mergers and acquisitions:

1. *Horizontal acquisition* is when one firm acquires or merges with another firm in the same industry. Examples are National Steel's acquisition of Granite City Steel, Honeywell's acquisition of General Electric's computer division, and Atlantic Richfield's acquisition of Sinclair Oil. Horizontal acquisitions are an offshoot of a concentration strategy since the acquiring firm remains in much the same business (unless the firm which is acquired has other business interests as well). The chief constraint in horizontal acquisition is staying clear of Section 7 of the Clayton Act which forbids acquisition of competitors where the effect "may be substantially to lessen competition, or to tend to create a monopoly." Horizontal mergers tend to raise issues of market power because they eliminate side-by-side competition between the two firms. Because the Antitrust Division of the Justice Department will normally challenge a horizontal merger when the firms involved have a combined market share greater than 10 percent, the use of horizontal acquisition as a corporate strategy is constrained.

2. *Vertical acquisition* occurs in an effort to create a more vertically integrated enterprise. Examples include Pacific Power and Light's backward integration into coal mining and U.S. Plywood's merger with Champion Paper. In some instances vertical mergers have been held to raise barriers to entry, to produce unfair control over sources of critical inputs, and to allow vertically integrated firms to put a profit squeeze on nonintegrated firms. As a consequence, vertical acquisition resulting in 10-20 percent market shares at both levels will usually be given close scrutiny by antitrust officials.

3. *Market extension acquisition* involves two firms in the same industry which do business in different *geographical* areas. This type of acquisition strategy is a common one; many firms seek to enter new geographical areas by acquiring a firm (young or mature, large or small, successful or not so successful) which operates in the desired location. Examples include Winn-Dixie's acquisition of a retail grocery chain in Texas, Standard Oil of California's acquisition of Standard Oil of Kentucky, and the merger of Southern Airways and North Central Airlines into Republic Airlines.

ILLUSTRATION CAPSULE 12 *(continued)*

4. *Product extension acquisition* arises when Firm A adds a product related to its existing product line by acquiring Firm B. According to the Federal Trade Commission, these are the most common types of acquisitions. Examples include Pepsico's acquisition of Pizza Hut, Rheingold Beer, and Taco Bell, Colgate-Palmolive's acquisition of Helena Rubenstein, and Dr Pepper's acquisition of Canada Dry Corporation.

5. *Conglomerate acquisition/merger* is used to accomplish entry into a new and entirely unrelated business—pure diversification. Roughly 30 percent of the merger activity since 1960 has consisted of conglomerate merger—a direct reflection of the wide use of conglomerate diversification strategy. Some prominent examples include U.S. Steel's acquisition of Marathon Oil, DuPont's acquisition of Conoco Oil, and American Tobacco's acquisition of Sunshine Biscuits.

Pros and Cons of Acquisition Strategies

There are several reasons why an organization may prefer acquisition of an existing enterprise to launching its own grassroots development of a new business. The factors involved are those implicit in any "buy or build" situation, but often the most important considerations are time and money.[1] Acquiring existing organizations, products, technologies, facilities, or talent and manpower has the strong advantage of much quicker entry into the target market while, at the same time, detouring such barriers to entry as patents, technological inexperience, lack of raw material supplies, substantial economies of scale, costly promotional expenses requisite for gaining market visibility and brand recognition, and establishment of distribution channels. Internally developing the knowledge, resources, and reputation necessary to become an effective competitor can take years and entails all the problems of startup. Internal entry can also result in oversupply conditions in the market. For instance, if existing firms already have the production capability to supply customer's needs and/or if entry must be on a large scale to take advantage of scale economies, then the added presence of a new, large supplier can produce an acute surplus of capacity. The likely outcome would be a spirited and profitless battle for market share. The prospect of such situations effectively reduces the number of viable options to two: entry via acquisition versus no entry at all.

Yet, acquisition is not without its own drawbacks. Finding the right kind of company to acquire can sometimes present a problem. Conceivably, an

[1] A study of firms' experiences with diversification from within is reported in Ralph Biggadike, "The Risky Business of Diversification," *Harvard Business Review*, vol. 57, no. 3 (May-June 1979), pp. 103-11. Methods for evaluating how much to pay for an acquisition are contained in Alfred Rappaport, "Strategic Analysis for More Profitable Acquisitions," *Harvard Business Review*, vol. 57, no. 4 (July-August 1979), pp. 99-110.

ILLUSTRATION CAPSULE 12 *(continued)*

acquisition-minded firm may face the dilemma of buying a successful company at a high price or a struggling company at a low price. In the first case, the seller is in position to demand a generous compensation for the risks that have been faced and for the effort expended in putting together a successful product, technology, market, organization or whatever key feature (distinctive competence) is being acquired. If the buying firm has very little knowledge about the industry it is seeking to enter but has ample capital, then it may be better off acquiring a capable firm—irrespective of the higher price. On the other hand, it can be advantageous to acquire a struggling firm at a bargain price when the new parent sees promising ways for transforming the weak firm into a strong one and has the money and know-how to back up a turnaround strategy.

Mergers and acquisitions can be accomplished via any of several financial strategies: purchase of stock on the open market, tender offers, an exchange of stock, a purchase of assets, or by a pooling of interests. They can occur amicably or with conflict and tension, intermingled with proxy fights, bidding wars, and complex legal maneuvering. One of the most dramatic of these is the takeover.

Takeover Strategies

A *takeover* is the surprise attempt of one firm to acquire ownership or control over the management of another firm against the wishes of the latter's management (and perhaps some of its stockholders). In recent years, takeover strategies have been used increasingly as a means of acquisition. The motives for takeover and the types of takeover mergers (horizontal, vertical, conglomerate) are the same as for any kind of merger/acquisition; what makes takeover unique is its unfriendly nature and the mechanics by which it is carried out.

A takeover strategy can follow many different paths and sequences. Typically, the acquiring firm or its investment banker conducts a search for likely takeover candidates which meet management's criteria; hundreds or even thousands of firms may be looked at via computerized procedures. When the takover target is selected, an offer price is chosen—usually 20-30 percent above the current stock price, and other specific details are worked out. The takeover target may be approached openly at this point (in hope of a friendly merger or a quiet surrender) or the tender offer may be sprung publicly as a surprise. The terms of the tender offer are frequently announced at a news conference, followed up quickly with newspaper ads and personal contacts with known large shareholders of the target firm.

The takeover target may initiate a vigorous defensive strategy: denouncing the offer as too low, urging all shareholders not to accept the tender offer, making special attempts to convince major stockholders to reject the bid for their stock, requesting the Justice Department or other government agencies

ILLUSTRATION CAPSULE 12 *(concluded)*

to intervene to stop the merger, seeking out a more attractive merger partner, filing lawsuits to block the takeover, and trying quickly to arrange some acquisitions of its own—to force a revision of the takeover offer. In launching its defense, top management may be trying both to get better offer terms and to protect its own jobs and independence.

The struggle may last a few days, a few weeks, or a few months. The original tender offer may be raised one or more times—especially if another bidder enters the fray, attracted by the action and seeing an interesting takeover possibility of its own. The market price of the target firm's stock often fluctuates up and down as the tender offer changes and prospects of merger brighten or darken. Speculators may trade heavily in the stocks of the firms, buying, selling, or selling short according to their estimates of the situation.

The outcome can go either way and depends on many factors. If the takeover target escapes, its management is likely to make numerous changes in strategy and internal operations to avert future takeover attempts and, especially, to improve performance and results. Dividends may be increased to try to solidify stockholder support of present management. The firm may become bolder, more innovative, and more competitive in outlook. If the takeover is successful, the acquiring firm may absorb the acquired firm and parcel its activities among various subunits; or it may operate the acquired firm as a separate and fairly autonomous division, keeping the original management or replacing all or part of top management with its own team. Either way, changes in the acquired firm can be expected in the way of revised objectives, new strategies, attempts to improve operating efficiency and profit performance, transfers of assets, closing or selling of marginal plants, expansion or pruning of the product line, new policies and procedures—in general, new direction.

The significance of takeover strategies, for our purpose, is two-fold: one, it is a new and increasingly used vehicle for accomplishing a merger/acquisition that might otherwise not occur, thereby opening up strategic opportunities for giving an organization new direction and different focus. Two, fears of takeover are prompting management to adjust corporate strategies so as to make their firms less vulnerable to takeover. Examples of defensive moves being undertaken to help thwart a takeover include (1) stock splits (to broaden and splinter ownership and thereby make it harder for an outsider to gain control by secretly negotiating the purchase of large blocks of shares), (2) keeping liquidity to a safe minimum (to avoid large cash reserves which may be viewed as a desirable target in itself by "cash-poor" or "opportunity-rich" firms), (3) discarding "conservative" policies and strategies in favor of more innovative, aggressive ones, and (4) making special efforts to remain efficient and as profitable as possible (thus eliminating takeover attempts motivated by the potential for sharply higher profits).

Joint Venture Strategies

A joint venture is the right corporate strategy for several types of organizational and business situations.[15] It is, first, a device for doing something which an organization is not well-suited to doing alone. Entering into a "consortium" kind of arrangement is a means of making a workable whole out of otherwise undersized levels of activity. In such cases, the whole is greater than the sum of its parts because alone each part is smaller than the threshold size of effectiveness. The Alaskan pipeline, for instance, is a joint corporate venture in raw material supply which not only is beyond the prudent financial strength of any one oil giant but which also is, in its most economic size, designed to carry more crude oil than one company could produce from its reserve holdings. For each oil company owning oil reserves on the Alaskan North Slope to build its own pipeline geared to the size of its own production capability would make little business or environmental sense. But for them all to contribute to a jointly-financed and jointly-operated pipeline allows the group to make economic fits out of misfits, enhancing the value of their Alaskan oil reserves. At the same time, the strategy of joint venturing carries the advantage that risk is shared and therefore reduced for each of the participating firms. This is no small matter in a relatively large undertaking.

A second type of joint venture emerges when the distinctive competence of two or more independent organizations is brought together to form a jointly-owned business. In this joint venture format each company brings to the deal special talents which, when pooled, give rise to a new enterprise with features quite apart from the parents. The complementarity of two or more distinctive competences can create a degree of synergy that spells the difference between success and near-success. For example, when in the 1920s General Motors developed tetraethyl lead to cure engine knocking problems, it decided not to start its own gasoline production and distribution business to exploit the advantages of tetraethyl lead but, instead, chose to enter into a joint venture with Standard Oil of New Jersey (now Exxon) which already knew the gasoline business and had the missing expertise. Thus was born Ethyl Corporation which grew into a worldwide supplier of tetraethyl lead for all the large gasoline marketers. With its joint venture strategy GM, in effect, made money on every gallon of tetraethyl lead gasoline sold--an effective outcome as compared to that of entering the gasoline business on its own and trying to compete directly against the oil companies.[16]

---

[15]Drucker, *Management*, pp 720-24. Information regarding the joint venture activities of firms can be found in *Mergers and Acquisitions: The Journal of Corporate Venture*.

[16]General Motors and Standard Oil, N.J. sold Ethyl Corporation in the 1960s largely because Ethyl had become too big and too successful to be continued as a joint venture. Likewise, when Sears decided it was time for Whirlpool not only to supply Sears but also to

Lastly, there are joint ventures created chiefly to surmount political and cultural roadblocks.[17] The political realities of nationalism often require a foreign company to team up with a domestic company if it is to gain needed government approval for its activities. At the same time, there are added pressures for a foreign company to seek out a domestic partner to help it overcome language and cultural barriers. So powerful are nationalistic interests in developing nations such as Brazil, Chile, Peru, and India that it is not unusual for foreign companies to find themselves restricted to a minority ownership position. Indeed, local businesses in Brazil and India, even though deeply engaged in joint ventures with multinational corporations based in the U.S. and in Europe, have been quite vocal in demanding protection from multinational domination, advocating not just controlling ownership but the closing off of whole economic sectors to multinationals as well.

Retrenchment Strategies

The conceptual thrust of a corporate retrenchment strategy is to fall back and regroup.[18] It is a common short-run strategy for organizations during periods of uncertainty about the economic future, recession, tight money and corporate financial strain, and poor corporate performance. Retrenchment at the corporate level can assume either of two variations: one, stringent across-the-board internal economies aimed at wringing out organizational slack and improving efficiency and, two, a selective pruning and revamping of the weakest performing businesses in the corporate portfolio.

---

sell appliances under the Whirlpool brand, Sears took the company public while retaining a controlling majority interest; gradually, then, Sears sold its holdings of Whirlpool shares as the company began to make it on its own. Such a spinning off of joint ventures into independent companies is not uncommon—either with or without the parent companies retaining an ownership interest.

To extend the life of a successful joint venture beyond some point in its development can have the effect of stunting its growth. Moreover, conflicts begin to arise between objectives of the parent companies and the mission of the joint venture. Hence, at some point it becomes propitious for a successful joint venture company to begin to develop its own mission, objectives, and strategy and for its management to become autonomous.

Alternatively, a joint venture can be liquidated with the parents splitting up the business and absorbing it into their own operations. This was the fate of Standard Vacuum, a joint venture of Standard Oil, N.J. and Mobil Oil begun in the World War I era to produce, refine, and market petroleum products in the Far East. In the 1950s Standard Vacuum's petroleum business in the Far East had expanded to a size where it was more desirable for each of the parents to proceed on their own rather than to continue a joint venture where their strategies and objectives were beginning to clash.

See Drucker, *Management*, 722-24.

[17]Philip Kotler, *Marketing Management: Analysis, Planning, and Control*, Fourth Edition, (Englewood Cliffs, N.J.: Prentice-Hall, Inc., 1980), pp. 671-73.

[18]A retrenchment strategy can be (and is) used at both the levels of corporate strategy and business strategy. This section focuses on retrenchment at the corporate level—primarily as concerns diversified firms; business strategy retrenchment is discussed later in this chapter along with the other types of business level strategies.

In the first instance, an organization which finds itself in a defensive or overextended position elects to hold onto most or all of its business activities and weather the storm with various internal economy measures. Ordinarily this type of corporate retrenchment strategy is highlighted by corporatewide directives to reduce operating expenses, improve productivity, and increase profit margins. The specifics of this approach to retrenchment vary according to the situation but may include reduced hiring of new personnel, trimming the size of corporate staff, postponing capital expenditure projects, stretching out the use of equipment and delaying replacement purchases so as to economize on cash requirements, retiring obsolete equipment, dropping marginally profitable products, closing older and less efficient plants, internal reorganization of work flows, inventory reductions, revised purchasing procedures, and so on.

The second variation of corporate retrenchment singles out the weak performing parts of the corporate business portfolio for major strategy revisions, internal overhaul, and whatever else may be necessary to restore them to good health. Performing radical surgery on those units that are least profitable is nearly always a by-product of poor overall corporate performance and/or persistently poor performance in the targeted business units. Many diversified firms have found it necessary to launch drastic cutbacks in one or more of their business units because of severe trouble managing so many different businesses which do not "fit," or because of operating problems in one or more divisions which proved intractable or beyond their expertise, or because of a lack of funds to support the investment needs of all the businesses in their corporate portfolios.

Corporate retrenchment is a typical reaction to adversity from within or without the organization. Ordinarily, it is a temporary or short-run strategy for riding through bad times; once it becomes feasible to renew growth and pursue expansion opportunities, retrenchment strategies are usually discarded in favor of some other strategy.

Divestiture Strategies

Even a shrewd corporate diversification strategy can result in the acquisition of businesses that just do not work out. Misfits or partial fits cannot be completely avoided, if only because it is impossible to predict precisely how getting into a new line of business will actually work out. Moreover, market potentials change with the times and what once was a good diversification move may later turn sour. Subpar performance by some operating units is bound to occur, thereby raising questions of whether to continue. Other operating units may simply not mesh as well with the rest of the organization as was originally thought.

Sometimes, a diversification move which originally appeared to make good sense from the standpoint of common markets, technologies, or channels turns out to lack the compatibility of values essential to a *temper-*

amental fit.[19] The pharmaceutical companies had just this experience. When several tried to diversify into cosmetics and perfume they discovered that their personnel had little respect for the "frivolous" nature of such products as compared to the far nobler task of developing miracle drugs to cure the ill. The absence of "temperamental unity" between the chemical and compounding expertise of the pharmaceutical companies and the fashion-marketing orientation of the cosmetics business was the undoing of the pharmaceutical's diversification move into what otherwise was a business with related technology and logical product fit.

Partial misfits and poorly performing divisions can also occur, despite the presence of some strategic fit, owing to an organization's inability to manage the business or to the overload placed on internal cash resources. In still other cases, the market changes slowly but surely to where the product consumers want to buy differs from what the producer is trying to sell, thereby breaking up what once was a good strategic fit with the seller's other products. Likewise, technological branching can progress to a point where pruning becomes a wise course of action if not a necessary one.

When a particular line of business loses its appeal (for any of the preceding reasons), divestiture may be the most attractive corporate strategy for that part of the organization. Normally such businesses should be divested as fast as is practical. To drag things out in hopes of a breakthrough or a turnaround is liable to be futile and risks draining away valuable organization resources. This explains why every diversified organization needs a systematic "planned abandonment" strategy for divesting itself of poor performers, losers, and misfits. A useful guide for determining if and when to divest a particular line of business is to ask the question "If we were not in this business today, would we want to get into it now?"[20] When the answer is "no" or "probably not," then divestiture ought to become a strategic consideration.

Divestiture can take either of two forms. In some cases, it works fine to divest a business by spinning it off as a financially and managerially independent company, with the parent company retaining partial ownership or not.[21] In other cases, divestiture is best accomplished by selling the unit outright (perhaps because this will yield more benefit to the corporation's stockholders or because the business may not be able to survive as an

---

[19]Drucker, *Management*, p. 709.

[20]Ibid., p. 94.

[21]One of the more unique approaches to divestiture involved Ling-Temco-Vought's reorganization of the Wilson Company in 1967. Shortly after it acquired Wilson, LTV split Wilson into three separate corporations: Wilson and Company (meats and food products), Wilson Sporting Goods, and Wilson Pharmaceutical and Chemical Company. LTV then sold off a substantial minority portion of the stock of each of the three new companies at price-earnings ratios higher than it initially paid for the total Wilson operation. LTV was attracted to this approach because it allowed LTV to improve its return from the Wilson acquisition by recovering part of its initial investment, while retaining control over all three of the new Wilson companies. For a more complete discussion, see Robert S. Attiyeh, "Where Next for Conglomerates," *Business Horizons*, vol. 12, no. 6 (December 1968), p. 42.

independent operation), in which case a buyer needs to be found. This is a "marketing" rather than a "selling" problem.[22] As a rule, divestiture should not be approached from the angle of "who can we pawn this business off on and what is the most we can get for it?" Instead, it is wiser to proceed by addressing "for what sort of organization would this business be a good fit and under what conditions would it be viewed as a sound bet?" In identifying organizations for whom the business is a "good fit," one also finds the buyers who will pay the highest price.

Liquidation Strategy

Of all the strategic alternatives, liquidation is the most unpleasant and painful, especially for a single-business enterprise where it means terminating the organization's existence. For a multi-product firm to liquidate one of its lines of business is less traumatic; the hardships of suffering through layoffs, plant closings, and so on, while not to be minimized, still leave an ongoing organization, and perhaps one that eventually will turn out to be healthier after its pruning than before.

ILLUSTRATION CAPSULE 13
Corporate Liquidation: A Case of Being Worth More Dead than Alive

Rarely does a healthy company pursue a liquidation strategy—especially if it is a large company listed No. 357 on the *Fortune 500*. But in early 1979 the board of directors of UV Industries, at the urging of board chairman and major stockholder Martin Horvitz, voted unanimously for a resolution to sell or distribute all of the company's assets to stockholders.

During the 1960s and 1970s UV Industries—formerly U.S. Smelting, Refining, and Mining Co.—used an aggressive acquisition strategy to increase sales from $31 million to over $600 million and profits from $2.3 million to nearly $40 million. After approval of the liquidation resolution, UV's stock price jumped from $19 a share to about $30 a share, and a successful liquidation was projected to yield shareholders $33 or more a share.

UV's business interests included copper, gold, and coal operations, oil and gas properties, a lead-refining company, and a manufacturer of electric generating equipment. The sale of the latter, Federal Pacific Electric Co.— UV's largest business (60 percent of sales and earnings), was arranged in late 1978; Reliance Electric offered UV a handsome $345 million in cash for Federal Pacific, a price which represented a p/e ratio of 13 at a time when UV's common stock was selling at 5 times earnings. The sale price produced a sizable capital gain—and a tax liability of some $45 million. Liquidation

Source: Peter W. Bernstein, "A Company That's Worth More Dead than Alive," *Fortune* (February 26, 1979), pp. 42-44.

---

[22]Drucker, *Management*, p. 719.

ILLUSTRATION CAPSULE 13 *(concluded)*

offered a way to avoid this tax since under Section 337 of the Internal Revenue Code any corporation that liquidates itself in the space of one year pays no *corporate* capital gains tax on the sale of its assets (however, shareholders are subject to capital gains taxes on any appreciation in the common stock price). Liquidation was also a good defensive strategy against a takeover, given that UV would be flush with some $500 million in cash from the Federal Pacific sale and from funds generated by various other securities transactions.

Management's liquidation plan was to sell off those divisions and businesses where attractive prices could be obtained and, where the offers to buy were deemed too low, to spin the divisions off into independent companies, distributing shares to current UV stockholders. Liquidation was not expected to produce a hardship because UV only had 40 employees at its New York City headquarters and its operating divisions would presumably continue to exist—albeit under new owners and managers.

In hopeless situations, an early liquidation effort often serves owner-stockholder interests better than an inevitable bankruptcy. Prolonging the pursuit of a lost cause merely exhausts an organization's resources and leaves less to liquidate; it can also mar reputations and ruin management careers. Unfortunately, of course, it is seldom simple for management to differentiate between when a cause is lost and when a turnaround is achievable. This is particularly true when emotions and pride get crossways with sound managerial judgement—as often they do.

Combination Strategies

The eight corporate strategy alternatives discussed above are not mutually exclusive. They can be used in combination, either in whole or in part, and they can be chained together in whatever sequences may be appropriate for adjusting to changing internal and external circumstances. Moreover, there are endless variations of each of the eight "pure" alternatives themselves. These variations allow ample room for organizations to create their own individualized blend of corporate purpose, objectives, and strategies. As a consequence, the difficulty of determining corporate strategy concerns not so much figuring out what options are open as evaluating the various viable alternatives.

When Some Corporate Strategies Are More Logical Than Others

A firm's market position and competitive strength is often such that some corporate strategy alternatives offer a stronger logical fit than do others.[23] Consider, for instance, Figure 3-1 where a firm's competitive position is plotted against the rate of market growth to create four distinct strategic situations. Firms which fall into quadrant I (rapid market growth and strong competitive position) are clearly in an excellent strategic position. In such circumstances a concentration strategy has powerful appeal and one can logically expect quadrant I firms to push hard to maintain or increase their market shares, to develop further their distinctive competences, and to make whatever capital investments may be necessary to continue in a leadership position. In addition, a quadrant I company may find it desirable to consider vertical integration as strategy for undergirding its market standing and protecting its profit margins. It may also make sense for an organization to look into concentric diversification as a means of spreading its business risks and capitalizing on its distinctive competence.

Firms falling into quadrant II should, first of all, direct their attention to a concentration strategy (given the high rate of market growth) and address the questions of (1) why their current approach to the market has resulted in a weak competitive position and (2) what it will take to become an effective competitor. With the market expanding rapidly, there should be ample opportunity for even a weak firm to carve out a viable market niche, provided strategic and organizational shortcomings can be overcome and the needed resource base developed. Certainly, a young, developing company has a better chance for survival in a growing market where there is plenty of new business than it does in a stable or declining industry. However, if a quadrant II firm lacks one or more key ingredients for a successful concentration strategy, then either horizontal merger with another company in the industry that has the missing pieces or else merger with an outsider having the cash and resources to support the organization's development may be the best corporate strategy alternative. Failing this, the most logical strategies would entail getting out of the industry: divestiture in the case of a multi-product firm or liquidation in the case of a single-product firm. While getting out may seem extreme, it is well to remember that a company which is unable to make a profit in a booming market probably does not have the ability to make a profit at all and has little prospect of survival—particularly if recession hits or competition stiffens.

Quadrant III companies with their weak competitive position in a more or less stagnant market would do well to consider (1) retrenchment—so as to free up unproductive resources for possible redeployment, (2) diversification—either concentric or conglomerate, depending on existing opportunities elsewhere, (3) getting out of the industry (divestiture of this line of business), or even (4) liquidation—if profit prospects are nonexistent and other opportunities fail to materialize.

---

[23] C. Roland Christensen, Norman A. Berg, and Malcolm S. Salter, *Policy Formulation and Administration*, 7th ed. (Homewood, Ill.: Richard D. Irwin, Inc., 1976), pp. 16-18.

FIGURE 3-1
Matching Corporate Strategy Alternatives to Fit a Firm's Circumstances

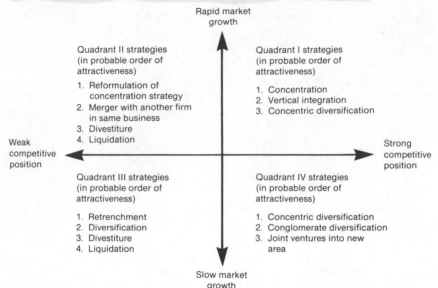

Quadrant IV organizations, given their dim growth prospects, are likely to be drawn toward using the excess cash flow from their existing business to begin a program of diversification. A concentric approach keyed to the distinctive competence that gave it its dominant position is an obvious option, but conglomerate diversification should be considered if concentric opportunities do not appear especially attractive. Joint ventures with other organizations into new fields of endeavor are another logical possibility. Whichever, the firm will likely wish to minimize new investments in its present facilities (to do little more than preserve the status quo), thereby freeing the maximum amount of funds for new endeavors.

Comparing firms on the basis of competitive position and market growth rate (or any other two variables) is useful for the insight it provides into why companies (even those in the same industry) may have good reason to pursue different corporate strategies. The nature of a firm's market standing, its competitive capabilities, its cash flow, its capital investment requirements, its ability to respond to emerging market opportunities, its distinctive competences, and so on all combine to shape its strategic position and its strategic alternatives. Sometimes a company's situation is such that a radical change in corporate strategy is called for; at other times, though, maintaining the status quo or just fine tuning will suffice.

ALTERNATIVE LINE OF BUSINESS STRATEGIES

The focus of strategy at the business level is "how do we compete effectively in this particular business?" Strategic analysis at the business level consists primarily of (1) assessing opportunities and threats in particular markets and for particular products, (2) determining the keys to success in that particular business, (3) evaluating the competitive strategies of rival organizations, (4) searching for an effective competitive advantage, (5) identifying organizational strengths and weaknesses, and (6) trying to match specific product-market opportunities with internal skills, distinctive competences, and financial resources. The *essential* concern is finding an approach to the market and a competitive strategy that is capable of being effective and producing the desired performance and results.

Numerous types of business strategies abound. We shall discuss the following categories and classifications to indicate the rich array of varieties and options:

1. Strategies for underdog and low market share businesses.
2. Strategies for dominant firms.
3. Strategies for firms in growth markets.
4. Strategies for weak or failing businesses.
5. Strategies for firms in mature or declining businesses.
6. Turnaround strategies.
7. Strategies to be leery of.
8. Strategies to avoid.

Strategies for Underdog and Low Market Share Businesses

In many cases the most important strategic concern is how a firm can increase its market share and transform a trailing position into a more profitable position or a "middle-of-the-pack" position into a leadership position. A sizable (10 percent or more) market share is sometimes necessary to realize scale economies, to generate an ample R&D budget, to gain good distribution, and, in general, to establish a viable long-run competitive niche in the industry. Normally, if an underdog firm is to be "outstandingly successful" it will need some sort of differentiating strategy aimed at building a competitive advantage; rarely can an underdog achieve real success by imitating what leading firms in the industry are doing.

The stage of the product-market life cycle often dictates just where the right kind of competitive advantage is likely to be located.[24] During the

---

[24]Most discussions of product-market life cycles speak of five stages: (1) introduction and development, (2) take off and rapid growth, (3) maturity, (4) saturation, and (5) stagnation

product development stage of a young industry, the competitive spotlight tends to center on product design, product quality positioning, and technical capability. Later, during the maturity-shakeout phase, the keys to competitive success tend to turn to product performance features, pricing, service, effectiveness of distribution channels, and market segmentation. Even so, underdog firms must still figure out just what strategic approach to product design, product positioning, product performance, market segmentation, and so on they ought to employ. No dependable generalizations can be offered. Each situation is sufficiently unique that creativity and sensitivity to market forces will be required. In some cases, a low market share business faces only two strategic options: fight to increase its share or withdraw from the business (gradually or quickly). In other cases, though, companies having a low market share may be able to remain small, compete effectively, and earn healthy profits.

There are several business strategies which can work well for underdog and low market share companies:[25]

1. *Vacant Niche Strategy*—Search out and cultivate customers and product-use applications that major firms have bypassed or neglected. An ideal market niche would be of sufficient size and scope to be profitable, have some growth potential, and be well-suited to a firm's own capabilities and skills. An example of successful use of a vacant niche strategy is the small tire manufacturers which have managed to survive competing with Goodyear, Firestone, B.F. Goodrich, and Uniroyal.

2. *Specialist or Focus Strategy*—Aim efforts at only a few carefully chosen product-customer *segments*, rather than trying to compete for all types of customers with a full product line catering to all different

---

and decline. The period of introduction and development entails slow growth as initial inertia, product debugging, and start-up must all be overcome. Growth is a period of rapid market acceptance and substantial profit improvement. Many new firms may be drawn into the market to try to capitalize upon the opportunities present whereas other firms, unable to keep pace, fall by the wayside. Maturity is characterized by a slowing down in sales growth, proliferation of products, attempts at intense market segmentation, and increased competition; there is often an industrywide *shakeout* of weak, inefficient, and ineffective firms. Saturation brings on negligible sales growth and pressure on profit margins, as price cutting and competition heat up—the struggle is much like a "survival of the fittest" type of contest. Stagnation and decline is the period where new and better substitutes begin to appear, sales erode and begin a downward drift, and profits decline rapidly toward the zero level.

The point here is that the nature of competition shifts in important ways over the course of the cycle. What it takes to compete effectively in the early part of the product-market life cycle is not the same as in the latter part of the cycle. For an excellent treatment of product-market life cycles see Robert D. Buzzell, "Competitive Behavior and Product Life Cycles," in *New Ideas for Successful Marketing*, ed. by John S. Wright and Jac L. Goldstucker (Chicago: American Marketing Association, 1966), pp. 46-68; and Kotler, *Marketing Management*, pp. 289-309.

[25]For more details, see Kotler, *Marketing Management*, pp. 281-84 and R. G. Hamermesh, M. J. Anderson, Jr., and J. E. Harris, "Strategies for Low Market Share Businesses," *Harvard Business Review*, vol. 56, no. 3 (May-June 1978), pp. 95-102.

needs and functions. Focus on segments where the company has or can develop special expertise and where such expertise will be highly valued by customers. Be alert to the fact that a market can be segmented by stage of production, price-quality-performance characteristics of the product, the cost and speed of distribution, geographic location, credit and service arrangements, and manufacturing capability as well as by types of products and customers. Companies which have successfully used a specialist or concentration approach include Control Data (which developed a better computer for scientific research), and Crown Cork and Seal (which concentrated on metal cans for hard-to-hold products and on aerosol cans).

3.   *"Ours-Is-Better-Than-Theirs" Strategy*—Try to capitalize on opportunities to improve upon the products of dominant firms and develop an appeal to quality-conscious or performance-oriented buyers. Be more innovative. Work closely with major customers to develop a better product. Some examples: Chivas Regal's approach to selling Scotch, Zenith's attempt to overtake RCA with its "the quality goes in, before the name goes on" strategy, and Mercedes-Benz's appeal to luxury car buyers.

4.   *Content Follower Strategy*—Follow rather than challenge the market leaders. Avoid overt attempts to steal customers away from leading firms and grab market share. Define one's own path to growth and market share maintenance, using approaches and tactics that will not provoke competitive retaliation. Burroughs (in computers) and Union Camp (in paper products) have been successful market followers by relying upon conscious concentration on limited product-customer uses, effectively focused R&D, profit emphasis rather than market share emphasis, and strong top management.

5.   *Guppy Strategy*—Focus the firm's competitive energies on the products and customers of smaller rivals and grow by taking away their market share. Several major beer firms owe their sales and market share growth to having beaten out or acquired small regional and local breweries.

6.   *Distinctive Image Strategy*—Seek to develop a differential competitive advantage via some distinctive and visible appeal. This may take the form of lower prices achieved through cost reductions, prestige quality at a good price, improved customer services, more product variants, innovative distribution channels, leadership in new product introduction or unique and creative advertising. Examples include Dr Pepper's combined strategy of distinctive taste and "We're different" advertising slogans; Miller's introduction of Lite Beer; and Avis' "We're No. 2, we try harder" campaign to provide cleaner rental cars and more personal attention.

Without a doubt, in some industries low market share companies have serious obstacles to overcome—less access to economies of scale in manufacturing or distribution or sales promotion, smaller R&D budgets, less opportunity to distribute through internal channels, difficulties in attracting capital, keeping good managerial and technical personnel, and gaining public and customer recognition.[26] But it is erroneous to classify all low share businesses as "dogs." The handicaps can be surmounted and a viable competitive position established. The most promising strategic guidelines seem to be: (1) compete only in carefully chosen market segments where particular strengths can be developed and avoid attacking dominant firms head-on with price cuts and increased promotional expenditure; (2) focus R&D budgets on developing a distinctive competence in new product development or technical capabilities, but only for the target market segments; (3) be content to remain small and emphasize profits rather than sales growth or market share; (4) push specialization rather than diversification (but if diversification is needed, enter closely related markets); and (5) manage the business in an innovative/"dare to be different"/"beat-the-odds" type of mode as opposed an all-out grow-and-build strategy that attacks the market leaders across a wide front. However if the economics of the business is such that large market share is the key to profitability, then a low market share firm has to employ a grow-and-build type strategy that emphasizes developing a competitive advantage and that extends over many market segments. Of course, a trailing firm may be able to make major market share gains without a real competitive advantage if it makes a sudden technological breakthrough, or if the leaders stumble or become complacent, or if it is willing to make major investments over long periods of time to secure incremental gains in its products and customer base.

Business Strategies for Dominant Firms

The strategic position of a dominant firm is more enviable. As a leader, it has a well-established and well-known market position. The main issue of business strategy thus tends to revolve around how best to harvest what has been achieved and how to maintain or improve upon the present position. Several different strategic postures are open:[27]

1. *Keep-the-Offensive Strategy*—Refuse to be content with just being a leader. Seek to continue to outperform the industry by breaking records the firm itself has already set. Become *the* source of new product ideas, cost-cutting discoveries, innovative customer services, and better means of distribution. In general, exercise initiative, set the pace,

---

[26]Hamermesh, Anderson, and Harris, "Strategies for Low Market Share Businesses," p. 102.
[27]Kotler, *Marketing Management*, pp. 273-81.

and exploit the weaknesses of rival firms. Apply the principle that the best defense is a good offense.

2. *Hold and Maintain Strategy.* Surround key products with patents; foreclose the attractiveness of entry by introducing more of the company's own brands to compete with those already successful company brands; introduce additional items under current brand names; keep prices reasonable and quality attractive; preserve the level of customer service. Peg the level of reinvestment in the business high enough to maintain production capacity, to remain technologically progressive, and to capture at least the firm's existing share of new market growth, thus staving off any market share slippage and decline. Any extra cash flow may, however, be shifted to more profitable opportunities elsewhere.

3. *Confrontation Strategy.* Make it hard for aggressive-minded smaller firms to grow and prosper. Meet all competitive price cuts promptly—with even larger price cuts if necessary. Be quick to launch large-scale retaliatory promotional campaigns if lesser-sized firms seek to increase their market shares; offer major customers more or better deals. Should the occasion seem to require it, resort to harassment tactics and teach small firms a lesson regarding who should lead and who should follow; such tactics may include pressuring distributors not to carry rivals' products, having salespersons bad-mouth the products of aggressive small firms, or trying to hire away the better executives of firms which "get out of line."

Business Strategies for Firms in Growth Markets

Two crucial strategic issues confront firms trying to participate in a rapidly growing market: (1) how to acquire the resources needed to support a *grow and build strategy* aimed at maintaining or improving the firm's current market position and (2) how to develop the sort of distinctive competence and competitive stamina that will be needed as growth slows and a competitive shake-out of rival firms ensues.[28] Again, no neat prescriptions can be given for just how these two issues should be resolved. The form of the grow and build strategy has to be geared to match the firm's situation and the character of market expansion. Nonetheless, the following strategic guidelines can be offered:[29]

1. Manage the business in an entrepreneurial mode with the aim of building the business for its future potential.

---

[28]Charles W. Hofer and Dan Schendel, *Strategy Formulation: Analytical Concept* (St. Paul, Minnesota: West Publishing Co., 1978), pp. 164-165.
[29]Kotler, *Marketing Management,* p. 296.

2. Be alert for product development opportunities keyed to product quality, performance features, styling, additional models and sizes, and improved design.

3. Search out new market segments and new geographical areas to enter.

4. Shift the focus of advertising and promotion from building product awareness to increasing frequency of use and to creating brand loyalty.

5. Seek out new distribution channels to gain additional product exposure.

6. Watch for the right time to lower prices to attract the next layer of price-sensitive buyers into the market.

7. Although the priorities may be on growth, market share, and a strengthening of competitive position, recognize that during the growth stage market-expanding activities usually come at the expense of higher current profits. If the profits foregone now to capture growth are to be recaptured later, then any market share or dominant position gained at the expense of profitability in the growth stage should offer the prospect of a higher than otherwise return on investment.

However, one caution can be urged. The strategic imperative of how to maintain/improve competitive market position during the takeoff stage should not blind management to the longer-range strategic need to prepare for the different types of competition that will occur when the market matures and a rigorous market share struggle sets in.[30] The temptation to neglect the latter for the former can be great when current market growth is in the 15-50 percent range and management must spend much of its energies figuring out ways to continue to achieve rapid growth—how to supplement internal cash flows with debt and equity capital, where to build new plants, how many personnel to add, which way to push R&D and market development efforts, how to respond to the product developments of rival firms, and so on. Moreover, it may be hard to foresee what twists competition may take as the market matures.

Nonetheless, the longer-range needs of strategy ought to be balanced against the immediate needs. This can be accomplished most easily in multi-industry enterprises that have had experience in managing young businesses through the early stages of product-market evolution. A single-business enterprise in a rapid growth situation does have some strategic substitutes for experience: it can gain guidance via wise selection of members for its board of directors; it can hire skilled management personnel from firms that have recently passed through the shakeout stage or else are in the early maturity phase; or it can try to gain functional skills via acquisition or merger.

---

[30]Hofer and Schendel, *Strategy Formulation*, pp. 164-65.

Strategies for Weak or Failing Businesses

Management has essentially four options for handling a weak business (whether it be a division, product line, or product).[31] It can employ a *grow and build strategy* and pour enough money and talent into the business to make it a stronger performer. It can use a *hold-and-maintain strategy* and assign enough resources to the business to keep sales, market share, profitability, and competitive position at present levels. It can opt for an *abandonment strategy* (divestiture or liquidation) and get out of the business— quickly or gradually. Or, it can resort to a *harvest strategy* whereby reinvestment in the business is held to a bare bones minimum and the main objective is to "harvest" reasonable short-term profits and/or maximize short-term cash flow. The first three options are self-explanatory. The fourth deserves added treatment.

A *harvesting strategy* steers a middle course between maintenance and abandonment. It entails a level of resource support in between what is required for maintenance and a decision to divest or liquidate. It is a phasing down or endgame approach. Kotler has suggested seven indicators of when a business should become a candidate for harvesting:[32]

1. When the business is in a saturated or declining market.

2. When the business has gained only a small market share, and building it up would be too costly or not profitable enough; or when it has a respectable market share that is becoming increasingly costly to maintain or defend.

3. When profits are not especially attractive.

4. When reduced levels of resource support will not entail sharp declines in sales and market position.

5. When the organization can redeploy the freed-up resources in higher opportunity areas.

6. When the business is not a major component of the organization's overall business portfolio.

7. When the business does not contribute other desired features (sales stability, prestige, a well-rounded product line) to the total business portfolio.

The more of these seven conditions which are present, the more ideal the business is for harvesting.

The features of a harvesting strategy are fairly clearcut. The operating budget is reduced to a bare bones level; stringent cost-cutting is under-

---

[31] Ibid., p. 166.

[32] Philip Kotler, "Harvesting Strategies for Weak Products," *Business Horizons*, vol. 21, no. 5 (August 1978), pp. 17-18.

taken. The business is given little, if any, capital expenditure priority—depending upon the current condition of fixed assets and upon whether the harvest is to be fast or slow. Price may be raised, promotional expenses cut, quality reduced, customer services curtailed, equipment maintenance decreased, and the like. The mandate, typically, is to maximize short-term cash flow—for redeployment to other parts of the organization. It is understood that sales will fall to some core level of demand, but it may be that costs can be cut such that profits do not suffer much—at least immediately. Ideally, though, sales and market share will not fall far below their preharvest level in the short run. If the business cannot make money and/or generate positive cash flow at the lower core level of demand, then it can be divested or liquidated. A harvesting strategy thus clearly implies the sunset or twilight stage of a product or business in its life cycle.

Although a harvesting strategy calls for reduced budgets and cost-cutting, it is useful to implement these moves in ways which do not alert competitors and customers to the harvesting intention.[33] To do so merely precipitates the decline in sales and reduces the potential harvest. Generally, the first cutbacks should be in expenditures for R&D and for plant and equipment. Later, marketing expenditures can be reduced and prices raised slightly. Still later, product quality and customer services can be trimmed. Management may also elect to splash some advertising occasionally; since such sporadic bursts will recapture customer and dealer attention, thereby slowing sales decay. Such an approach may result in a smaller gain in cash flow, but one which lasts over a longer period. A fast harvest, where deep cutbacks are made across the board, produces a large cash flow increase, but it doesn't last long.

Although it may not seem so at first, harvesting strategies have much to recommend, especially in diversified companies having products in the mature or declining stages of the life cycle. Different lines of business deserve different levels of resource support depending on their profit potential, their life cycle stage, and their rank in an organization's overall corporate portfolio. Businesses which are fading or on the verge of decline are logical candidates for a harvesting strategy. Reducing resource support and commitment to a line of business (or division or product) makes strategic sense when costs can be decreased without proportionate losses in sales. The result can be improved profitability and cash flow in the short run—the very things at which a harvesting strategy aims.

Strategies for Firms in Mature or Declining Industries

Many firms do business in industries where demand is declining or else growing at rates well below the economywide average. Although such

---

[33]Ibid., p. 20.

businesses may be prime candidates for harvesting, divestiture, or even liquidation, other alternatives exist and may in fact be more appealing.[34] The difficulty of finding a buyer who will pay an acceptable price often makes divestiture impractical, and stagnant or declining demand by itself is not enough to warrant liquidation. For example, even though the demand for coffee has trended downward for over 15 years, General Foods still derives 40 percent of its sales and 33 percent of its profits from its line of coffee products. Even more importantly, a decision to drop certain product lines just because they are in tough, slow-growth markets is not always best since, without the contribution margin generated by the sales of such products, a firm may find itself unable to cover overhead costs and its whole operation may become unprofitable.

A first step in formulating a successful strategy for a slow-growth/declining business is to accept the difficult realities of a continuing stagnant demand and then adopt a set of target objectives consistent with market opportunities.[35] Cash flow and return on investment criteria are more appropriate than growth-oriented performance measures. Furthermore, head-to-head competition is usually more intense in markets where demand is stagnant than where expansion is vigorous. So long as industry demand grows rapidly, there tends to be enough new business that firms need not launch aggressive attacks on rivals to gain higher sales; the major concern is with how to take advantage of market growth, not with how to outmaneuver rival firms. However, as industry growth slows to a halt, increases in volume have to come at the expense of one's competitors. The ensuing battle for market share frequently drives weaker firms out of the market and market shares of the remaining companies rise. For instance in the cigar industry, where unit volume has been declining at a 5 percent annual rate since the mid-60s, the number of manufacturers declined from 283 in 1958 to 132 in 1972; in coffee, not only did the number of companies decline but the combined market shares of the top three firms rose from 47 percent in 1960 to 67 percent in 1976.[36]

In general, three themes characterize the strategies of firms which have succeeded in stagnant industries:[37]

1. *Identify, create, and exploit the growth segments within the industry.* Most industries are composed of numerous segments and subsegments (whether the segments are best identified by price, product use, geographic location, customer type, product features, or service requirements varies from case to case). Nearly always at least one of these segments is growing rapidly. The skill, then, is to collect and analyze

---

[34]R. G. Hamermesh and S. B. Silk, "How to Compete in Stagnant Industries," *Harvard Business Review*, vol. 57, no. 5 (September-October 1979), p. 161.
[35]Ibid., p. 162.
[36]Ibid.
[37]Ibid., pp. 163-65.

industry information in such a way as to seek out and identify the segments with faster growth potential. By concentrating its efforts in the emerging or growth segments, a firm thus escapes being victimized by the declining industrywide trends. Such a conscious redefinition of what business to compete in is precisely what the strategy formulation task is all about.

2. *Emphasize quality improvement and product innovation.* A key point to be recognized here is that stagnant demand does not preclude significant innovation; indeed, innovation can rejuvenate demand by creating important new growth segments or otherwise postponing further stagnation in sales. From the standpoint of competition, successful product innovation allows a firm to escape competing mainly on the basis of selling price. In addition, it can be difficult and expensive for rival firms to imitate. An example is General Foods' introduction of freeze-dried coffee. Because many people viewed freeze-dried instant coffee as better tasting, demand grew rapidly (even though total consumption of coffee declined). Yet, with the notable exception of Nestlé, other producers were unwilling or unable to invest in the more expensive freeze-dry technology; as a consequence, the profit margins which General Foods has earned on its freeze-dried business are the highest of all coffee products.

3. *Work diligently and persistently to improve production and distribution efficiency.* When increases in sales cannot be counted upon to generate increases in earnings, an alternative is to improve profit margins and return on investment by reducing operating costs. This can be achieved by (1) improving the manufacturing process via automation and increased specialization, (2) consolidating underutilized production facilities, (3) adding more distribution channels to ensure the unit volume needed for low-cost production, and (4) shifting sales away from low-volume, high-cost distribution outlets to high-volume, low-cost outlets.

Plainly enough, these three strategic themes are not mutually exclusive. They can be used simultaneously and can reinforce one another.[38] For instance, attempts to introduce new innovative versions of a product can result in *creating* a fast growing market segment. Similarly, concentrating on operating efficiencies can stimulate an increased emphasis on catering to emerging growth segments.

In any event, since it is a rare company that competes only in rapidly growing markets, strategies for competing successfully in stagnant or declining industries warrant close management attention.

---

[38]Ibid., p. 165.

Turnaround Strategies

Turnaround strategies come into play when a business worth saving has fallen into disrepair and decline. The goal is to arrest and reverse the situation as quickly as possible. Assuming that it is possible to avoid failure and/or bankruptcy, the first task of a turnaround is diagnosis. What is the cause of the decline? Is it bad strategy? Or poor implementation and execution of an otherwise workable strategy? Is it weak management? Or are the causes of decline beyond management control? One must know what is wrong before a plan for cure can be formulated. Moreover, one must learn what internal skills and resources need to be protected so as to preserve them as a base for launching a turnaround strategy. Generally speaking, there are six approaches to turnaround: (1) a fundamental rebuilding and repositioning of the enterprise via major revisions in strategy, (2) a replacement of top management and other key personnel, (3) revenue-increasing strategies, (4) cost-reduction strategies, (5) asset reduction/retrenchment strategies, and (6) a combination of these.[39]

When the cause of weak performance is diagnosed as "bad" strategy, the focus of a turnaround centers on *rejuvenating the firm's business strategy*, and "saving" the business then hinges upon making the "right" kinds of strategic changes. The changes can assume several forms: (1) shifting to a new way of trying to compete in the marketplace and thus repositioning the business in its competitive environment, (2) overhauling key functional area strategies to produce better support of the same basic overall business strategy, and (3) efforts to enter a new business or businesses. The details of what the new strategic action plan should be depend on conditions prevailing in the industry and on the firm's strengths and weaknesses vis-a-vis rival firms. This entails doing an intensive "situation analysis" of the industry, major competitors, and the firm's own competitive position.

Replacing key management personnel is an obvious turnaround alternative. Management is responsible for successful performance of a business. It is obliged to take whatever actions are deemed advisable to accommodate internal and external changes and to ensure efficient, effective performance. It is reasonable to infer that when decay sets into a business, management has either taken no action to ward off poor performance or else it has taken inappropriate actions. Whichever, one corrective approach is to install new management.[40] Only when the circumstances underlying

---

[39]For an excellent survey discussion of all the ins and outs of turnaround strategies, see Charles W. Hofer, "Turnaround Strategies," *Journal of Business Strategy*, vol. 1, no. 1 (Summer 1980), pp. 19-31.

[40]One study of corporate turnaround reports the occurrence of significant management changes, including chief executive officers, in 39 out of 54 firms attempting to reverse a downturn in performance. See Dan Schendel, G. R. Patton, and James Riggs, "Corporate Turnaround Strategies," *Journal of General Management*, vol. 3, no. 3 (Spring 1976), pp. 3-11.

decline are beyond management control should no change in management be seriously contemplated.

Revenue-increasing turnaround strategy focuses on how to increase sales volume (increased promotion, more emphasis on marketing, added customer services) and whether and how much of a price increase can be instituted. It is a necessary strategic approach when there is little or no room in the operating budget to cut back on expenses and still reach breakeven and when the key to restoring profitability is an increased utilization of existing capacity.

Cost-reduction turnaround strategies work best when the firm's cost structure is flexible enough to permit radical surgery, when operating inefficiencies are identifiable and readily correctable, and when the firm is relatively close to its breakeven point. Accompanying a general belt-tightening can be an increased emphasis on budgeting and cost control, elimination of jobs and hirings, modernization of existing plant and equipment to gain greater productivity, and capital expenditure cutbacks.

Asset reduction/retrenchment turnaround strategies are necessary when cash flow is a critical consideration and when the most practical way to generate cash is (1) through sale of some of the firm's assets (plant and equipment, land, patents, divisions, or inventories) and (2) through retrenchment—pruning of marginal products from the product line, closing or sale of older plants, a reduced work force, withdrawal from outlying markets, cutbacks in customer service, and the like. A divestment of assets may not only be needed to improve cash flow but it may also represent the best way to unload money-losing activities and restore profitability. Thus asset reduction may not signify liquidation and retrenchment as much as it does an attempt to eliminate losses and cash drains.

Combination turnaround strategies are usually the most effective, especially in grim situations where fast action on a broad front is required. This is because the results to be gained from using several or all of the approaches to turnaround tend to be better than depending on an intensive application of just one approach.[41]

No matter which variety of turnaround strategy is chosen, attention will tend to center on those actions which have the greatest short-term cash flow impact and which will move the business toward breakeven the quickest. The urgency and limited resources of a near-bankrupt business make these considerations imperative. The key to turnaround is early management action to rebuild and to reposition the business in the marketplace. Specifically, it is important to diagnose whether the prevailing strategy is suitably matched to the external environment and to internal resources. If so, the difficulties probably lie in operating inefficiency and poor internal management. But if strategy is at the root of the decline in performance, the spotlight of turnaround must be on strategy reformulation.

---

[41] Hofer and Schendel, *Strategy Formulation*, p. 174.

Many turnaround efforts prove unsuccessful. A recent study of 64 companies found no successful turnarounds among the most troubled companies in eight basic industries.[42] Many waited too late to begin a turnaround and others found themselves short of both cash and entrepreneurial talent to compete in a mature industry characterized by a fierce battle for market share; their stronger rivals simply proved too strong to defeat in head-to-head combat for the market share needed to survive. This study found that as market maturity approaches and competitive hostility intensifies the range of strategic options narrows. For an underdog firm to be successful in a turnaround effort, its management has to be alert to the signs of the coming competitive shakeout and launch an early effort to strategically reposition the firm in the marketplace.

Strategies to Be Leery of

On occasion managers may be pulled toward the adoption of a strategy which is risky and lacks the potential for real success. This can occur out of desperation or poor analysis or simply lack of creativity. The following strategies are offered as examples of those which managers should be cautious about adopting:[43]

1. *"Me Too" or "Copy-Cat" Strategy*—Imitating the strategy of leading or successful enterprises; trying to play catch-up by beating the leaders at their own game. *Weakness*: Ignores development of firm's own personality, image, strategy, and direction.

2. *Take-Away Strategy*—Trying to achieve greater market share and market penetration by attacking other firms head on and luring away their customers via a lower price, more advertising, and other attention-getting gimmicks. *Weakness*: Invites retaliation and risks precipitating a fierce and costly battle for market share in which no one wins—including the firm trying to play take-away.

3. *Glamour Strategy*—When a firm gets seduced by the prospects of a new idea for a product or technology which it thinks will sweep the market. *Weakness*: The best laid plans. . . .

4. *Test-the-Water Strategy*—Often arises when an enterprise is engaged in developing new opportunities or is relating to market-technological-environmental changes which call for a fundamental reformulation or redesign of strategy. In such cases, firms may "test-the-water" in venturing out into new fields of endeavor. *Weakness*: A half-way effort or "sideline stepchild" seldom succeeds for lack of adequate corporate commitment; it's usually best to either get in or stay out entirely.

---

[42]William K. Hall, "Survival Strategies in a Hostile Environment," *Harvard Business Review*, vol. 58, no. 5 (September-October 1980), pp. 75-85.

[43]Kotler, *Marketing Management*, Second Edition, Chapter 8; and Joel Ross and Michael Kami, *Corporate Management in Crisis: Why the Mighty Fall* (Englewood Cliffs, N.J.: Prentice-Hall, Inc., 1973).

5. *Hit-Another-Home-Run Strategy*—This strategy is typified by a firm which has hit one "home run" (pioneering a very successful product and strategy) and which is urgently looking for ways to hit a second home run (by getting into a new line of business either related or unrelated to its first home run), so as to continue to grow and prosper at its former rate. A second "home-run" business may be necessary because growth of the initial business is rapidly slowing down and becoming more competitive. *Weakness*: Trying to repeat the same strategy in a new business may not work out because of differing circumstances and subtle differences in key success factors.

6. *Arms-Race Strategy*—May emerge when firms of relatively equal size enter into a spirited battle for increased market share. Commonly, such battles are waged with increased promotional and advertising expenditures and/or aggressive price cuts and/or increased R&D and new product development budgets and/or extra services to customers. As one firm pours more money into its efforts, other firms feel forced to do likewise for defensive reasons. The result is escalating costs, producing a situation much like an arms race. *Weakness*: Seldom do such battles produce a substantial change in market shares, yet they almost certainly raise costs—costs which must either be absorbed in the form of lower profit margins or else passed on to customers via higher prices.

Strategies to Avoid

Experience has shown that some business strategies seldom if ever work. An alert management, for obvious reasons, will seek to avoid use of the following strategies:[44]

1. *Drift Strategy*—When strategy is not consciously designed and coordinated but rather just evolves out of day-to-day decisions and actions at the operating level.

2. *Hope-for-a-Better-Day Strategy*—Emerges from managerial inertia and tradition and is exemplified by firms which blame their subpar sales-profits-market share performance on bad luck, the economy, unexpected problems, and other circumstances "beyond their control." Such "entrepreneurial coasting" until good times arrive is a sure sign of a dim future and managerial ineptness.

3. *Losing-Hand Strategy*—Arises in companies where a once successful (and perhaps spectacularly so) strategy is fading and no longer viable. Nonetheless, management, blinded by the success-breeds-success syndrome, continues to be reluctant to begin to reformulate its strategy, preferring instead to try to rekindle the old spark with cosmetic changes—in hopes of reversing a downhill slide.

---

[44]Ibid.

4. *Popgun Strategy*—Seeking to go into head-to-head competition with proven leaders when the firm has neither a differential competitive advantage nor adequate financial strength with which to do battle.

Business Strategies: A Perspective View

The foregoing survey of business strategy alternatives is by no means exhaustive. For example, concentration or specialist strategies, joint venture strategies, retrenchment strategies, divestiture, and liquidation, all of which were discussed under the heading of corporate strategy, also have their counterparts in line of business strategy. Moreover, as has been pointed out, whether a particular business strategy is "right" for an organization depends upon the stage of product-market evolution, the competitive position a firm has, the competitive position it seeks, the business strategies being used by rival firms, the internal resources and distinctive competences at a firm's disposal, the prevailing market threats and opportunities, the type and vigor of competition that characterizes the marketplace, customer needs and how they use the product—to mention only the more important considerations.

How a firm should try to compete—the overriding issue in line of business strategy—is therefore variable from situation to situation and from time to time. Competition is a dynamic process which assumes many forms and comes in many different shades of intensity. The situations of firms change and so do those of their customers. Thus, just as with corporate-level strategy, line of business strategy is something which must be tailor-made to fit the situation at hand. There can be no one best strategy for all times and circumstances. There are only strategies that *fit* certain situations and those that don't, those that are *right* for a given company at a given time and those that aren't. Our sampling of strategic alternatives is intended to highlight the variety of approaches and to demonstrate the need for creative strategy formulation.

A Concluding Point.   Every organization ought to be wary of becoming a prisoner of its present strategy. Sooner or later, all strategies grow stale or obsolete. They need either fine tuning or major overhaul or radical surgery. Thus, while it is by no means necesssary for the incumbent strategic plan to be shunted aside in favor of new alternatives at each time of reappraisal, an alert management will guard against letting strategic reevaluation be little more than a time for rationalizing why the status quo should be maintained.

The real managerial purpose behind regular reappraisal of strategy is to help management avoid the complacency of viewing the prevailing strategy as too much of a given rather than as only one among several practical, and perhaps more attractive, possibilities. True, taking a creative, entrepreneurial approach to strategy reformulation may threaten those in the organization who have vested interests in the current strategic plan. But for an enterprise which aspires to continued success and high performance, this is the way things must be. Imaginative strategy formulation and reformulation is virtually a prerequisite of sustained high performance. Nostalgic and inopportune adherence to existing strategy merely paves the way for other organizations which, lacking strong attachment to strategies of the past or present, will surely be less reluctant to seize upon a fresh strategy if they view the entrenched firms' strategies as vulnerable to attack. For this reason alone, a strong commitment to regular strategic reappraisals and, further, to creative identification of strategic alternatives is an essential ingredient of entrepreneurially effective management.

SUGGESTED READINGS

Ansoff, H. Igor and John M. Stewart, "Strategies for a Technology-Based Business," *Harvard Business Review*, vol. 45, no. 6 (November-December 1967), pp. 71-83.

Bloom, Paul N. and Philip Kotler, "Strategies for High Market Share Companies," *Harvard Business Review*, vol. 53, no. 6 (November-December 1975), pp. 63-72.

Cooper, Arnold C. and Dan Schendel, "Strategic Responses to Technological Threats," *Business Horizons*, vol. 19, no. 1 (February 1976), pp. 61-69.

Drucker, Peter, *Mangement: Tasks, Responsibilities, Practices* (New York: Harper & Row, 1974), Chapters 55, 56, 57, 58, 60, and 61.

Guth, William D., "Corporate Growth Strategies," *Journal of Business Strategy*, vol. 1, no. 2 (Fall 1980), pp. 56-62.

Hall, William K., "Survival Strategies in a Hostile Environment," *Harvard Business Review*, vol. 58, no. 5 (September-October 1980), pp. 75-85.

Hamermesh, R. G., M. J. Anderson and J. E. Harris, "Strategies for Low Market Share Businesses," *Harvard Business Review*, vol. 56, no. 3 (May-June 1978), pp. 95-102.

Hamermesh, R. G. and Silk, S. B., "How to Compete in Stagnant Industries," *Harvard Business Review*, vol. 57, no. 5 (September-October 1979), pp. 161-68.

Hofer, Charles W., "Turnaround Strategies," *Journal of Business Strategy*, vol. 1, no. 1 (Summer 1980), pp. 19-31.

Kotler, Philip, "Harvesting Strategies for Weak Products," *Business Horizons*, vol. 21, no. 4 (August 1978), pp. 15-22.

Lauenstein, Milton and Wickham Skinner, "Formulating a Strategy of Superior Resources," *Journal of Business Strategy*, vol. 1, no. 1 (Summer 1980), pp. 4-10.

MacMillan, Ian, "How Business Strategists Can Use Guerilla Warfare Tactics," *Journal of Business Strategy*, vol. 1, no. 2 (Fall 1980), pp. 63-65.

Porter, Michael E., *Competitive Strategy* (New York: Free Press, 1980), Chapters 9-16.

READING

Formulating a Strategy of Superior Resources*

MILTON C. LAUENSTEIN AND WICKHAM SKINNER

Milton C. Lauenstein is President of Telequip Corporation, Littleton, MA. Wickham Skinner is James E. Robison Professor of Business Administration, Harvard University Graduate School of Business.

The grass may seem greener in another field, but take a long, hard look before your company diversifies. The pitfalls of scattering your resources—technology, knowledge, management, human skills, and finances—can mean disaster. Concentrate instead on focusing your energies and gaining competitive advantage.

The organization with superior resources—technology, knowledge, management, human skills, and finances—usually wins. A key objective of management is to develop those key resources to be better than those of competitors. This basic tenet of strategy is perhaps the one most frequently violated as managers so often spread and divert vital, limited resources instead of concentrating and focusing them so as to achieve a clear, overwhelming competitive advantage.

The advantages of focusing assets and energies on a narrow enough sector of objectives to be able to achieve competitive superiority are obvious enough in the management of both military and corporate operations. They are clear in personal careers as well. "Don't spread yourself too thin" is accepted as sound advice for managers. Rare is the executive who has not learned that trying to do too much at once usually results in success in nothing.

The disciplined corporate organization concentrates its resources and attention on a limited sector of technology, product, or market and, thus, gains a telling competitive advantage. Many such companies, in a successful reinforcing cycle, have grown even stronger and, gaining experience, financial strength, and market share, then develop even more powerful resources and a position of industry dominance. The unfocused company—with resources spread thin, talents stretched tight, and lacking a clear edge of superiority in key resource sectors—ends up struggling to survive. Its market share, profit margins, and cash flows are typically smaller than those of the dominant focused producers. The poor get poorer. Lucky or brilliant breakthroughs in technology or product or marketing may pull it out, but the firm plays catch-up ball when its resources are inferior.

Why, then, is the truly focused company or division so rare? There are, in fact, many factors that tend to scatter and diffuse a company's activities, skills, and resources and start it down the slide to a weakened strategic position. Analysis of companies whose results have deteriorated because they lost focus over a period of time suggests that identifying the causes for weakening resources can lead to a more positive posture for an effective strategy for developing superior resources.

THE TEMPTATIONS OF DIVERSIFICATION

The position of every company in each of its markets is subject to a continuing series of threats from competition, changing customer demands, new technologies, government regulations, and a host of other factors. Managers are usually properly sensitive to these vulnerabilities and are rarely completely sure that positions will not be eroded. When a company or division is primarily dependent on one market, product line, or technology, it is especially nervous. The results of losing its position would be so serious as to constitute a strong motivation to diversify.

Obviously, a disaster in any one area is less serious to a firm that operates in several. However, when diversification results in a company's resources being spread weakly over several areas, the chances that it will not be able to compete effectively may be very much higher in each area in which it participates. A study of the Fortune 500 companies indicates that nondiversified companies on the average not only achieved faster growth and superior return on investment but also were considered safer by a noted published investment advisory service.

Salter and Weinhold[1] cite the low capital productivity of widely diversified companies. The return on equity of a broad sample of such companies was 18 percent below the Fortune 500 average in 1975 and 20 percent below in the ten-year period 1967-1977. They state that

> the acquisitive diversifiers had low price-earnings ratios. On December 31, 1977, the average P/E of the sample was 30 percent below that of the New York Stock Exchange stocks as a whole. The situation has changed little over several years. Even higher return-on-equity performers like Northwest Industries, Teledyne, and Textron have P/E's well below the market's average.

These facts suggest that the reduced vulnerability to reverses in any one sector was more than offset by the negative effect of diffusing effort in the diversified companies.

"MEETING THE PLAN"

In many situations where superior resources have not been built, current operating problems have dominated management thinking. Especially in

---

[1]Malcolm S. Salter and Wolf A. Weinhold, "Diversification via Acquisition: Creating Value," *Harvard Business Review*, 166-176 (July-Aug. 1978).

the case of divisions of large corporations, results in the relatively short run are critically important to the careers of the division managers. Pressure to "meet the plan" (i.e., the annual and monthly or quarterly budget) is the engine of a short-term point of view. Immediate customer requirements, competitive moves, production and cost problems get priority attention.

As a result, planning efforts are typically concentrated on the current year. Strategic issues receive superficial attention at best, and the long-term development of resources needed to achieve leadership in a specific market gets almost none at all. Every effort is made to live within the short-term operating plan and to overcome variances occasioned by operating problems, economic conditions, competitive moves, or unexpected actions by customers. Identification of key resources is not made explicit, and investment in those resources is neglected.

Many chief executive officers were successful practitioners of that approach when they were at lower levels of management. They have learned through their experience as operating executives that advancement comes from improving profit margins, taking customers away from competition, meeting forecasts by squeezing out every dollar rather than from sacrificing current earnings to build the capabilities that may be more decisive in the long run. This leads to opportunism and scattered actions rather than effort focused on long-term objectives. If things are not going well, pressure is exerted to seek a "quick fix."

Equally common is the tendency in the large, portfolio-managed, financially dominated company to "dump the losers" and move to greener fields, without thoroughly considering what it would take to build the resources necessary for success. In the smaller or medium-sized company, the syndrome is to merge or acquire companies in new fields, reducing their focus and potential competitive advantage in the market they know best but about which they are discouraged or feel impotent.

UNDERESTIMATING OPPORTUNITIES
IN PRESENT FIELDS

Many companies move away from a single-minded concentration on their present lines of business because, discouraged with their performance, top management concludes that their markets, products, or technologies have too-limited growth or profit futures. Sometimes this is a valid judgment. But often the real problem is a failure to manage effectively the present business. The failure may be derived from current marketing, manufacturing, or product design policies or activities. The difficulty may be more basic. The firm may have failed to develop the unique capabilities needed to compete successfully in its industry. When critical resources are already spread thin, it is easy to conclude that the future looks bleak—and that diversification is the only way out.

For example, a medium-sized inorganic chemical specialty company reached pessimistic conclusions about its future and subsequently embarked upon a lengthy program to diversify and grow in other fields. Over several years, it acquired four companies in a variety of growing industries. Ultimately, however, its original business began to increase in volume and profitability while its acquisitions floundered along and finally fell by the wayside. This occurred after considerable time, capital, and management effort were consumed. The happy ending was delayed, in fact, for over five years while the management diverted scarce resources to the new fields, which seemed to offer attractive industry growth and higher profit than their own. But they learned that they were better off to compete effectively in a field they knew thoroughly than to come in last in several different growth industries.

BUCKLING UNDER THE PRESSURE TO GROW

Companies and divisions are under great pressure to grow. There are financial reasons, managers' ambitions, career opportunities, and rewards in the stock market. This set of forces constantly exerts inducements to expand and leads almost inevitably to a rosy view of opportunities for the company outside of its present sphere of activities.

A high-technology company waited patiently in a "crouching position" for several years as potential customers only slowly discovered and began to take advantage of its unique technological skills. Impatience set in for the managers, whose personal finances depended principally on market appreciation of company stock, and who believed the company to be too small to attract market attention. Growth itself became a primary objective.

For this reason the company made a large acquisition in a low-to-medium-technology industry that was totally different from the business it knew well. The acquisition doubled sales. The purchase price was modest, however, because the newly acquired company had not performed well in recent years. The new parent believed it could turn matters around with its own management skills and superior technical competence.

The diversification proved disastrous. Management was poor and, hence, the company lost more money than the parent could earn. The parent's management was unable to be in enough places at once either to anticipate or to control the losses. After absorbing substantial management and financial resources, the acquisition had to be sold. Meanwhile, the firm's patient but thorough development of superior resources in its own high-technology field finally began to pay off as new, large, and profitable business was developed. Growth as a primary, overriding objective had proved dysfunctional when it led the management into a situation it could not manage.

THE OVERCONFIDENCE SYNDROME

When a company is doing well, its managers often believe that they have superior ability and can, therefore, succeed in almost any business. The merger candidate "only needs the good management we can bring it." They lose sight of the fact that their specialized knowledge of the particular practices, products, and people of their own industry, which took years to acquire, represents an important basis for the competitive success they have achieved. In a new market, where they do not have the background and experience-bred wisdom required for success, they often fail, or at best do not succeed. Worse still, by diverting attention from their main business, they may wreck or at least seriously injure it.

MISJUDGING THE SUCCESS REQUIREMENTS

A repeated cause of disappointment in investment in a new field by firms successful in their own traditional areas is simply miscalculation or poor judgment of a new area. Problems encountered in the new business often turn out to be more complex, knotty, and resistant to solution than originally anticipated.

Analysis of such problems suggests that these misperceptions occur most often when a clear connection appears to exist between the old business and the new—when there is a common customer or market, or a familiar technology or similar product. For instance, in the example given earlier of the high-technology firm, the parent company and the company acquired both served the same general market area, along with other markets. But such connections are often merely superficial. Managers hastily say, "We're familiar with that," only to find that even with the same customer there are often major differences in what it takes to sell a new product. Based on some familiarity, the company is overconfident, and fails to check deeply enough into the whole set of resources, knowledge, and expertise it takes to be successful in the new sector or business. What appears contiguous and realizable in one dimension may be far removed and difficult in other vital success elements.

THE RUSH TO USE IDLE CAPACITY

The factors mentioned above combine to create an almost overwhelming pressure to enter new fields if a company has idle capacity. This pressure may be most pronounced when the idle capacity is in unused manufacturing facilities, but it also occurs when the company perceives it has the marketing capability to sell other products, managers ready for promotion into new challenges, engineers without full work loads, or other forms of underutilized resources.

When a company is paying the fixed costs for production facilities that are not being used, the pressure for increased earnings is frequently acute and the incremental effect of putting the facilities to work is obviously modest. For these reasons a task force is then organized to find a product, to locate subcontract work, or to do almost anything to employ the excess capacity. Too often the result is an operation that does not fit the facilities, skills and style of current manufacturing. Run lengths may be different. Skill levels and wage rates that are appropriate for the new operation may be quite different from what the company has been doing. Ultimately, the intangible costs to the present operation may far exceed the incremental margin gained on the additional operation.

Similar phenomena characterize taking on new lines to sell. Almost inevitably there are new things for the sales force to learn, not only about the products and their uses but also about the way the new products are marketed. Efforts on the present line are diluted. Sometimes the expected increased potency of having a broader line ultimately results in a new way for the customer to split his business with competition. Or the customers use the greater volume with the supplier as an additional lever to get lower prices.

Whether in manufacturing, marketing, or technology, taking on new activities usually involves unforeseen costs and often requires the development of additional capabilities at considerable cost. Thus, efforts to fill idle capacity, like the Trojan Horse, easily infiltrate an organization, but they frequently succeed only in absorbing a good deal of time and effort while diverting managers from more profitable activities.

THE SIREN SONG OF INTEGRATION

The managements of many companies have yielded to the siren song of integration, which very often sounds like a successful strategic approach. In concept, forward integration can help assure markets, broaden horizons, and get the supplier "closer to the customer." And backward integration promises to protect sources of supplies, save profit paid to vendors, and afford better control over quality and delivery.

Too often, however, the more highly focused supplier or customer has learned to do a job far more efficiently than the company which takes it on as part of an integration strategy. At the same time, management attention is diffused and the company moves into a position of managing businesses that it does not understand well and about which it must learn the hard way over time. Moreover, the company is probably carrying on these activities on a scale far lower than that of its suppliers and/or customers, which usually represents a built-in economic disadvantage. Keeping up with changing technology in these new fields often requires investments and resources not available to the company. Often enough, the final decision is a retrenchment.

LACK OF A SOUND STRATEGIC POLICY

The factors prompting diversification and diffusion of effort are particularly virulent in the many situations where companies do not have a well-thought-out strategy. Those companies that have analyzed their prospects and determined the field in which they are likely to grow fastest and make the highest return on investment are much less likely to be tempted into an unwise diversification. In contrast, those that have been simply concentrating their attention on operations have no real basis for resisting the lure of the various defocusing factors which push, pull, or seduce them away from effective focus.

When a firm lacks a sound strategy, it is vulnerable to whims and often tries to copy the patterns of the successful. Thus, small- and medium-sized firms are prompted to look at giant corporations as models to emulate. Since they are often diversified, it appears that entering new fields is a good way to expand.

Similarly, top management nearly always watches competitive moves closely. When a competitor takes a new task, a company's management is naturally apprehensive lest that give the rival a telling advantage. As a result, one frequently sees the companies in a given industry play follow-the-leader. The temptation to imitate a competitor often has a more decisive influence on the decision of whether or not to diversify than an analysis of whether the move is sound and appropriate to the situation of the company.

THE DANGERS OF PRIDE

When a chief executive has been responsible for a company's entering a new field, it may become a matter of personal pride and identification and prevent or delay an otherwise wise divestiture when it fails or does not clearly succeed. Disposing of the unsuccessful new venture would, of course, appear to reflect adversely on the reputation of the executive's management.

As a result of pride, many companies are held back from shedding operations years after they have demonstrated that those operations offer neither an attractive return on investment nor even a growth opportunity for the enterprise. Thus, even when there are valid reasons for a company to spin off sidelines and drop some unfocused activities so that it can concentrate its resources on its better opportunities, the acquisition process turns out to be irreversible because of personal motives.

STAYING IN FOCUS: WHAT CAN BE DONE?

A company's operating resources—facilities, technology, distribution channels, personnel, market knowledge, management skills, reputation—

have been designed and developed for the businesses in which the enterprise is already active. It will normally be able to earn the greatest return on investment in those businesses in which its operating resources are the most outstanding. Therefore, the first and usually the best place to find opportunities for expansion and attractive returns is in the very sectors where the company has already focused. Until top management is satisfied that this has been thoroughly accomplished, it should not permit other areas to be explored.

Often this is not done, simply because managers have grown stale in a business area. They tend to conclude that their limited success should be blamed on the business area and not on themselves. Managers lose objectivity about their own industry and business and "know things" which, if analyzed or tested, are no longer, or perhaps never were, true. Sometimes this happens because the very familiarity with an area of business (which should be an important asset) becomes a liability when it leads to false assumptions of how things "must" be done and "what cannot succeed in this industry."

This occurs most often when business conditions, costs, consumer habits, or technology, for example, change from the situations in which the firm has been successful. Such changing conditions can make it more difficult to find opportunities to grow in the field in which an enterprise is already engaged as long as it retains its traditional approach to the business. The management becomes discouraged and begins to look for new fields instead of recognizing and overcoming the challenges in the present business area that have altered its earlier pattern of success.

The company's present scope of operations may be too broad for it to be able to achieve a leadership position. If so, the firm would be well advised to identify a segment of its present industry in which to focus its resources, rather than to continue to spread them thinly and across areas in which they are not better than those of competitors. The capabilities of a company are more likely to represent competitive strength in a narrow segment of its own field than in other areas.

Early success carries the seeds of future problems in other ways as well. Not only does a management become wedded to its particular winning approaches to business, but often the excellent results are produced for a period of time despite levels of efficiency and effectiveness that could not be permitted in more competitive situations. The high costs and low productivity that sometimes develop in businesses with an unusually strong proprietary position eventually catch up and hurt. Disappointing results deter the company's full exploitation of its current opportunities by inducing management to look outside rather than inside.

Recognizing this syndrome is the first step in counteracting it. Before abandoning an early success turned sour, the managers must determine whether the business requires a new approach or simply a higher level of operating effectiveness. While it may be difficult for a company already in the field to recognize its own problems, thereby leading it to falsely based discouragement, a strong dose of self-analysis may prevent the abandonment of a business area in which it actually has the basic elements needed for success.

ARE THE GREEN FIELDS REALLY GREENER?

In evaluating business possibilities outside of the fields in which it is already operating, a company must be doubly careful. First, it must be sure it thoroughly understands the requirements for success in the new field. Since the company has not been active there before, this may be an expensive and hazardous undertaking.

New business territories are often alluring. At first the venture seems so easy that to resist is difficult. "If we get only x percent of the market, it still looks like a good deal." Potential customers give encouraging reports to attract new suppliers. Once the commitment is made, however, the situation is different. Having succeeded in attracting a new supplier, the customer is now interested only in the best value it can get.

Now the new supplier finds itself pitted against well-entrenched competitors in an uneven contest. With greater volume, years of experience, and a depreciated plant, the established supplier often has lower cost. New competition often causes old high prices to disappear, so that only the low-cost producer can earn a reasonable return on its investment. With capital already committed, it is too late to withdraw without large losses.

For these reasons a company should determine whether or not its resources really do qualify it to compete successfully with the well-established firms already supplying the market. Often, present competitors have important strengths that are not readily apparent to the newcomer. As the newcomer enters the field, requirements for business success that were not immediately apparent rise to the surface. A field service organization may be needed. Large inventories may be essential. Discounts and special terms may make prices significantly lower than they appear to be. Continual technical development and new products at high cost may be an inherent feature of the business. Failure to meet any of these requirements may result in winning too small a share of the market to be profitable. The analysis and research required to surface these realities is expensive and painstaking. But there is really no other way to combat the "green field" temptation.

WHAT ARE THE EXPANSION CRITERIA?

To decide whether or not to undertake or expand in a given area, it is useful to have a list of strategic criteria against which to evaluate the opportunity. Such criteria should direct attention to factors influencing how attractive the new activity is likely to be in the long run. They may include:

- *Expected return on investment over the long term, with reasons.* It is important to analyze the reasons given to determine whether in fact they represent an adequate basis for anticipating attractive financial results.
- *Evaluation of the company's resources for being in the business compared with those of actual and potential competitors.* Such factors as manufacturing and distribution costs, technical competence, financial requirements, knowledge of and access to markets, raw material position, and business relationships must be reviewed. It is essential to identify those factors that are critically important for success in the business in question and to be sure that the company is adequately prepared in these areas. If other firms are better qualified for the business in question, it is not likely to provide an attractive return.
- *Anticipated share of relevant market segments.* Most often, the leading company in a market enjoys economies of scale and has inherent cost advantages. If a company is unable to identify one or more segments in which it has a good chance of gaining a leading position, it should be cautious about entering a new area. If "only x percent market share of the business even looks profitable," it is unlikely to remain a good opportunity in the face of competition from firms with larger shares.
- *Business trends.* A business area may be changing so as to become either more or less attractive to a given entrant. These changes may be in any phase of business: technology, market size, buying habits, marketing tactics, or whatever. Before investing in a new area, management should consider the impact of likely changes on results in the longer term.
- *Effect on other operations.* New business relationships can be either helpful or harmful to other divisions. Entering a new field inevitably draws management attention and often other resources away from other corporate activities. Nevertheless, companies diversifying often expect synergies to contribute to building resources, such as technology or marketing programs in one operation which could contribute to the success of other activities. More often than not, however, these synergies do not take place because they are simply very difficult to achieve in an administrative sense. People and cultures get in the way; they have different objectives; they have different reward systems. These factors result in focusing on their separate operations rather than on something of joint interest.

REWARDING MANAGERS FOR RESISTING SEDUCTIVE DIVERSIFICATION

Performance measures that reward executives for developing long-term resources are essential to provide incentives to spend more effort on activities that can be decisive with respect to longer-term results. Such a reward system is likely to lead to greater corporate focus and is less conducive to seductive diversification. For example, programs to develop outstanding depth in a technical field, to achieve market leadership, or to become the low-cost producer require a concentration of effort in relatively narrow areas rather than spreading efforts over a wide diversity of business activities.

But the reward and measurement system must identify and encourage these kinds of long-term investments, because the payoffs are apt to be beyond the tenure of the particular manager who pays the costs and makes the investment. That manager pays the definite cost for an indefinite outcome, usually years ahead. Therefore, only an unusually long time horizon reward system will encourage long-term behavior rather than a "meet the plan" mentality.

Using "resource development" as one element on which to base incentive compensation has been effective in motivating managers to give weight to building the capabilities that will make for long-term profitable growth as well as current results.

SUMMARY

The advantages of a strategy of superior resources are easy to recognize. However, many powerful factors lead to executive decisions that tend to diffuse efforts and resources so as to seriously impair the buildup of the corporate strength necessary to achieve leadership in any field.

Operating executives often tire of concentrating and simply "trying harder" to achieve attractive results in the execution of current programs. Performance, however, usually depends on the relative quality of assets available to the various competitors. A major determinant of success in the long run is the quality and quantity of effort applied to develop formidable personnel and organization, technology, marketing expertise, manufacturing know-how, brand name acceptance, sales techniques, and customer behavior. Instead of seeking "greener fields," therefore, managers would usually do better by investing in building resources in present fields or a segment of present fields. But incentives and performance measurement commonly reward executives primarily for current results. By encouraging the pursuit of short-term opportunities, these policies and procedures often discourage investments aimed at building the long-term resources needed to achieve competitive success.

Top management can secure the advantages of corporate focus by demanding full exploitation of opportunities in areas in which the company is already active, establishing strategic criteria for evaluating business segments the company might enter, and providing incentives to develop resources for the long term.

READING

How Business Strategists Can Use Guerilla Warfare Tactics*

IAN C. MACMILLAN

Ian C. Macmillan is a professor in the Graduate School of Business at Columbia University.

There is a real possibility that in the next decade several of the following events will occur:

- Inflation rates greater than in the past decade.
- Increasingly uncertain supplies of raw materials.
- Decelerating real growth rates.
- Consumer and government pressure to keep selling prices from increasing as fast as raw material prices.
- Increasing government intervention in business.
- Increased competition from overseas coupled with increased difficulty in expanding into overseas markets.
- An increased inability to treat labor as a variable cost.
- Decelerating productivity improvements and decelerating rates of innovation.

If even a few of these trends do in fact occur, it appears that one of the key characteristics of management problems in the future will involve finding ways of improving performance with fewer options, fewer managerial prerogatives, more uncertainty, and fewer resources.

LESSONS FROM MAO

Consideration of these conditions, which require the successful securing of a competitive position with very limited resources, leads to the conclusion that there is a distinct parallel to the problem of a general attempting to secure military dominance via guerilla warfare. Here also, positions have to be secured under conditions that are resource constrained and fraught with high uncertainty.

It so happens that many of the principles of guerilla warfare as espoused by Mao Tse Tung (Mao Zedung) in his communiques (in particular those written during the Second World War) are, after some modificaiton,[1]

---

*This article is reprinted by permission from the *Journal of Business Strategy*, vol. 1, no. 2 (Fall 1980), pp. 63-65. Copyright ©1980 by Warren, Gorham and Lamont Inc., 210 South Street, Boston, Mass. All rights reserved.

[1]See the *Selected Military Writings of Mao Tse Tung* (Peking Press, 1966).

translatable into a set of principles for developing business strategies under resource-constrained conditions.

CHOOSE WHERE TO FIGHT

Essentially Mao envisioned two theatres of operations which he named "guerilla base" operations and "guerilla front" operations. His fundamental principle was to establish and consolidate guerilla bases in militarily secure areas where surplus resources were available, and to then use these surplus resources to attack on guerilla fronts, where he engaged the enemy under conditions that suited him rather than them. In times of adversity, he would retreat, if necessary, all the way back to his guerilla bases. The major point of interest about this strategy was his specification of the conditions in which he would decide that the situation suited him rather than the enemy. In this regard, he specified several conditions that he sought and took the position that unless at least three of these conditions were present, he would rather retreat than engage the enemy. This strategy is clearly designed to enhance the probability of success without wasting vitally scarce resources.

AVOID WARS OF ATTRITION

Turning now to the problem of formulating business strategy, it is clear that if we are to face more adverse circumstances than in the past, in which resources are severely constrained, then it may be wise to attempt to apply similar strategic thinking. This is not to say that we must do it, or that we can do it, but rather that we should seek to do it so that every opportunity is grasped to secure a position at minimum expenditure of resources and maximum probability of success. Those organizations that can do this more often than their competitors will in the long run avoid the enormously costly "wars of attrition" in which one literally tosses resources away in head-to-head confrontations with one's opponents. In this regard, it is interesting to note that an analysis by Liddell Hart of all the military campaigns that were turning points in Western history, from the Greek Wars up to 1914, indicates that there were only six campaigns in which the use of direct, massive frontal assault achieved a decisive result.[2] In general, wars of attrition leave the "victors" exhausted, with resources depleted, and sometimes painfully vulnerable.

SET UP GUERILLA BASES OR MARKET NICHES

The question then is how the principles of guerilla warfare apply in business strategy. It appears that the business equivalent of the guerilla

---

[2]See Liddell Hart, *Strategy*, (Signet Books, 1967).

base is the market segment or niche.[3] For such segments or niches to serve as a guerilla base, they must meet two conditions. First, they must be competitively secure either because competitors cannot or will not enter. The instances when they cannot enter are rare (patent protection and legal injunction being cases in point). The more common situation is where competitors will not enter because the cost of entry is high or the direction of entry is counter strategic. In fact, competitors, particularly those with large long-run resource or managerial commitments, are often inclined not to enter particular segments aggressively because they are otherwise engaged.

The second condition for an appropriate market niche to act as a guerilla base is that it provides surplus resources which can be used to survive times of adversity or to engage in competition elsewhere. In most instances, these surplus resources have been profits; but there have also been cases where a company has occupied a break-even segment to secure future technology, to develop top quality technical or marketing talent, or to develop a powerful distribution system. Some companies have even been prepared to operate below the breakeven point in order to secure these resources. It seems that the key difference between the military guerilla base and the market segment is that the geography of the military guerilla base is constant, whereas the demography and technology of the market are changing. Thus, no segment or niche is ever permanent. This calls for the business strategist to follow one additional maxim: Current segments should be employed to develop the surplus resources required to establish segments for the future.

ATTACK ON COMPETITIVE FRONTS

It is in the establishment of future segments and niches that the "second theatre" of Mao is germane. For the sake of terminology, let us call the business equivalent of a guerilla front a competitive front. The third maxim of the business strategist should be to attack on competitive fronts, that is, in product/market segments in which we can compete under conditions that suit us rather than our competitors.

To determine the feasibility of an effective competitive front, one should attempt to take as many of the actions specified below as possible since each of them enhances the probability of success and reduces the amount of resources required to achieve that success.

- *Find allies who are willing and able to commit resources to the endeavor.* Mao made astute use of Russian aid as well as taking advantage of

---

[3]A market niche is a segment of the market that is defensible with limited resources. Niches, therefore, usually make excellent guerilla bases, although not all of them generate sufficient resources to serve this purpose. Segments, by contrast, usually generate the resources needed to serve as guerilla bases but are not always competitively secure.

local warlords in campaigns. A number of perceptive chief executives refuse to spend a dollar in accomplishing their purpose until they have exhausted the possibilities of getting others to commit funds and human resources to that purpose. Their own resources can then be saved for the really critical efforts. Suppliers, key customers, bankers, foreign competitors, and government bodies should all be viewed with the express purpose of identifying who else will benefit by the move being contemplated and seeking their assistance in accomplishing that move.

- *Concentrate one's efforts to a greater degree than the opposition.* Mao said, "Though I fight one against ten, I engage ten against one." This is the oldest of military maxims, even in conventional war. Focusing effort on a narrow, well defined segment or niche that is weakly defended by competitors enhances the probability of success.

- *Centralize ideology but decentralize decision making.* Mao gave a great deal of attention to the development of an ideology—a set of principles and policies to be followed by his officers—which was continuously reinforced, yet which also allowed enormous autonomy in local operations. In the same way, to the extent that we can lay out a clear "ideology (and strategy) of the business" to managers in the field that will shape their local decisions, but at the same time give them local autonomy of action, we create ideal conditions for them to defeat bureaucratic competitors.

- *Seek environmental support.* Mao expressly forbade looting and ill treatment of the peasantry he was attempting to convert. His competitors did not. Thus, if he had to retreat from an area, his return was welcomed by the peasants. Successful entry to a product/market segment or niche involves the development of a "cause," a position that requires support of the customer, supplier, and distributor, and which the competitor finds hard to refute. Similarly, successful exit from a product/market segment seeks to ensure that our temporary departure is viewed with regret by the customers, suppliers, and distributors.

- *Seek decisive results.* Mao argued that if an engagement was expected to last more than two days he would prefer not to engage. The longer the engagement took place, the more likely that opponents would have time to deploy increasing amounts of resources to the engagement, slowly locking him into a local war of attrition. In the same way, any competitive engagement that results in the securing of a dominant competitive position in the target niche in less than eighteen months is preferable to an engagement in which the position will not be achieved for years, since in the latter circumstance competition has time to deploy resources and a "war of attrition" could ensue.

- *Build superior commitment.* Mao would rather not engage if he felt that his troops' morale was lower than that of the enemy. In the same way, it is more important to build morale, particularly of the sales force, to a level that exceeds those of the competitors before even attempting to attack a new segment or a niche. Low morale feeds defeatism, and to send out salespeople with low morale is to invite defeat. Rather build morale via small successes first.

- *Seek areas where opponents have overextended resources.* Mao argued that a key opportunity for a decisive result arises whenever the enemies' logistical systems are strained. Indications that the competitor has stretched its resources are reductions in service, delayed delivery, and decreases in quality. Whenever competitors have overextended themselves, particularly if we can concentrate our effort on those segments where they have spread their resources most thinly, the probability of success with minimum use of our resources is enhanced.

- *Seek opportunities for capturing opponent's resources.* Mao largely supplied himself with equipment captured from defeated enemy forces. If the result of a competitive engagement leaves us with some of the competitor's resources (the plant, key marketing, technical or management personnel, distribution channels, and so on), this is doubly advantageous. Often such resources are obtained at less cost than developing them ourselves and at the same time they are resources now denied to competitors.

- *Retain the initiative.* The company that retains the initiative controls the competitive arena. Competitors are forced to respond to the initiator's moves defensively and under conditions not of their choosing. Even a strategic exit from a market should be controlled in such a way that competitors are responding to the tactics of the strategic retreat. In many cases, Mao was able to convert a strategic retreat into a victory by enticing the enemy forward until their logistical lines were overextended and then advancing with devastating effect.

- *Build superior intelligence systems.* Mao continuously stressed the value of intelligence, i.e., superior knowledge of terrain and climate, of the deployment, morale, and strengths of opposing forces, and of the opposing officers. This kept the initiative in his hands since it reduced the enemy's ability to surprise him. In business strategy, superior competitive intelligence, i.e., knowledge of the local product/market conditions, the plans of the competitors, and the local management of the competitors, reduces the probability that the competitors can inflict surprises and thus start to gain the initiative.

SUMMARY

Although Mao spelled out several other principles of guerilla warfare, the ten listed above appear to be the major ones that are transferable to the field of business strategy. As noted earlier, the major reason for applying such principles is to enhance the probability of competitive success, while at the same time reducing the amount of resources that must be used to achieve that success. In this regard, firms should seek product/ market opportunities where as many of the conditions for effective guerilla action as possible are present. Those companies that develop these skills are more likely to achieve their growth and profit objectives in the coming resource-constrained decade. In particular, if they can succeed in securing future product/market segments and niches by application of the above principles, they are more likely to emerge from the next decade ahead of the game.

ANALYZING AND EVALUATING CORPORATE-LEVEL STRATEGY

4

If we can know where we are and something about how we got there, we might see where we are trending—and if the outcomes which lie naturally in our course are unacceptable, to make timely change.

Abraham Lincoln

The preceding chapter surveyed the major corporate and business strategy alternatives. The task of this and the next chapter is to examine the analytic considerations which make up a thoroughgoing strategy evaluation and which thus form the basis for deciding which strategy to choose. This chapter concentrates upon the analysis and evaluation of corporate-level strategy in a multibusiness organization; Chapter 5 deals with the task of analyzing business-level strategy.

APPROACHING THE TASK OF CORPORATE STRATEGY EVALUATION

A major task of top management in any organization is developing a coherent response to such questions as: What is the organization's current position? If we stay in the same activities we are in today and don't alter the mix of our businesses or the priorities among them, where will we be in another five to ten years? Do we like the answer to this question? If not, what can we and what should we do about it? How top management deals with questions of how to improve the organization's business portfolio and enhance long-term performance sums up very neatly what strategic management at the corporate level is all about.[1]

Managerial approaches to strategy evaluation at the corporate level can and do vary to some extent with the type of company. In a multibusiness enterprise, the central tasks of corporate strategy evaluation revolve around (1) determining whether the enterprise is headed in the right direction and doing the right things, (2) determining the relative attractiveness of each of the firm's current businesses, and (3) figuring out how the performance of the total business portfolio can be upgraded via better strategic management of existing businesses, further diversification, and/or divestiture. The development of specific *business* strategies in multi-industry companies tends to be delegated to lower-level general managers who have profit-and-loss responsibility for particular business units and product lines. Corporate and business strategies are then joined and dovetailed by negotiation between corporate managers and business-unit managers, usually according to the priorities and objectives of corporate strategy. Consequently, in a multi-industry enterprise business strategy tends to be fashioned to the needs of corporate strategy (rather than the other way around).

In contrast, in single-line or dominant-product-line companies, the strategy of the base business is the center of attention, after which diversification and other portfolio questions relating to corporate strategy are addressed. Such firms generally do not divorce corporate strategy evaluation and business strategy evaluation because (1) activities outside the base business contribute minimally to sales and profits and (2) the issue of "which way do we go from here" is so closely related to the main business. Thus in dominant-business companies corporate strategy is heavily keyed to business strategy instead of being the other way around. But whatever approach to corporate strategy formulation best fits a company, sound strategy evaluation starts with explicit and detailed information about the realities of the organization's present condition and situation.

Identifying the Present Corporate Strategy

Identifying an organization's present corporate strategy is an obvious first step in strategy analysis and evaluation. Understanding where a company is now and what strategy is being followed logically precedes any serious judgments as to whether the "right" strategy or an appropriate strategy is being pursued and whether any changes in corporate strategy are called for.

Although identifying "what the strategy is" comes before recommend-

---

[1]George Odiorne, *Management and the Activity Trap* (New York: Harper & Row, Publishers, 1974), p. 12.

ing "what the strategy should be," this is easier said than done. Seldom will management have formally articulated the firm's corporate strategy fully and completely. Some, or even much, of the strategy commonly has to be deduced or inferred from the ways the firm's operations have been and are being conducted—that is, from its past behavior and pattern of doing business and from its major policies, plans, and objectives. On occasions, there may be contradictions and inconsistencies between what is said and what is done, thus further confounding what the reality of the strategy is. The analyst thus has the task of interpreting and evaluating both the actions of the firm and the statements of various managers in identifying the current strategy.

Areas for Analysis in the Strategy Identification Process.   A full identification of an organization's corporate strategy requires an assessment of both external and internal factors. The relevant external factors include:

1. The present scope and diversity of the firm's activities and business interests as concerns customer groups, customer needs, technologies, and major product categories.

2. The nature of the firm's recent acquisitions and divestitures.

3. The *relative* priorities placed on each of the firm's business activities and strategic interests, together with the recent trends in these proportions and the apparent factors underlying any changes in priorities and approaches.

4. What "opportunities" the firm is apparently trying to pursue and capitalize upon.

5. How the firm seems to be trying to minimize the impact of perceived external "threats."

The most important internal factors include:

1. The firm's objectives (stated or implied), especially with respect to growth, profitability, and financial performance targets.

2. The stated criteria for allocating investment capital to proposed projects and the actual pattern of investment expenditures across the firm's various lines of business.

3. The organization's attitude toward risk, as stated by management and as reflected by policies governing debt-equity ratios, liquidity, financing of new investments and growth, and overall financial structure and financial condition.

4. Where the firm is focusing its R&D efforts.

Figure 4-1 is a summary portrayal of these factors and considerations; the totality of how they interact constitutes a picture of the present corporate strategy and where the organization is now. As previously stated, this picture may reveal a company and a management which is simply "muddling through," or at the other extreme, it may reflect a timely, opportunistic organizationwide game plan which gives every evidence of having been shrewdly thought out and carefully integrated into a consistent, powerful companywide action plan. Whichever is the case, a skillful identification of the present corporate strategy lays the foundation for conducting a thoroughgoing strategy analysis and, subsequently, for reformulating the strategy as it "should be."

FIGURE 4-1
Angles from which to Determine Corporate Strategy

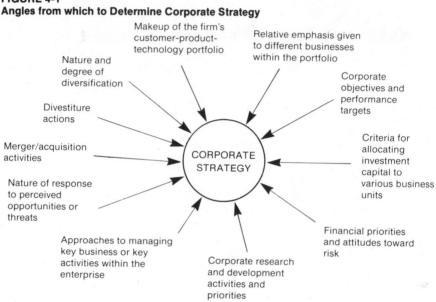

CORPORATE PORTFOLIO ANALYSIS

Our discussion of corporate strategy evaluation will focus upon *corporate portfolio analysis* which, currently at least, is the prevailing method of strategy analysis at the corporate level in diversified firms and in multi-product firms. In less diversified firms, the portfolio approach is also applicable, provided it is modified slightly to take account of the fact that the main strategic issue is not so much how to realign the mix and proportions of the firm's business to improve overall performance as it is what kind of new businesses—if any—the firm should attempt to get into to go along with its base business.[2]

---

[2]However, the portfolio approach turns out to be just as valid for a multi-product firm as for a multi-business firm when the former manages each product and/or market segment as if they were independent businesses.

Growing use of corporate portfolio analysis as a tool of strategy management is based largely on the relative simplicity and clarity it offers in making an *aggregate assessment* of a firm's several lines of business. The popular centerpiece of this analysis is the construction of a *business portfolio matrix*. Such a matrix graphically portrays and compares the positions of different businesses on the basis of such strategically relevant variables as market growth rate, relative competitive position, stage of product/market evolution, market share, and overall industry attractiveness. Any two-variable comparison can be used.

The Four-Cell BCG Growth-Share Matrix

The most publicized business portfolio matrix is a four-square grid pioneered by the Boston Consulting Group (BCG) and depicted in Figure

FIGURE 4-2
The BCG Growth-Share Business Portfolio Matrix

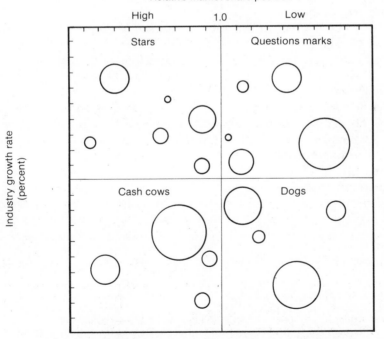

Relative market share position

Industry growth rate (percent)

High   1.0   Low

Stars   Questions marks

Cash cows   Dogs

Note: *Relative* market share is defined by the ratio of one's own market share to the market share held by the largest *rival* firm. The only way a firm can thus achieve a star or cash cow position in the growth-share matrix is to have 1.0 or greater relative market share; this requires having the largest marekt share.

4-2.[3] Each of the company's businesses is plotted in the matrix based on the industry or market growth rate and its own relative market share position. The size of each circle in the matrix is proportional to the sales revenues generated by each business in the firm's portfolio. The dividing line between "high" and "low" market growth is, arbitrarily, set at 10 percent. The border between "high" and "low" relative market share is typically set at 1.0; relative market share is defined as the ratio of the business's market share (in units, not dollars) to the market share held by the largest rival firm.[4] For instance, if business A has a unit market share of 15 percent and the share held by the largest rival is 30 percent, then the relative market share for A is 0.5. A firm will have relative market shares of more than 1.0 for those of its business units which are market share leaders in their respective industry and ratios below 1.0 for those businesses which trail rival firms in market share. Observe, then, that those circles in the two leftside cells of the matrix represent businesses in the firm's portfolio that are leaders in their industry; those falling in the two rightside cells trail the leaders, with the degree to which they trail being indicated by the size of the relative market share ratio (a ratio of .10 indicates that the business has a market share only one-tenth that of the largest firm in the market whereas a ratio of .80 indicates a market share that is four-fifths or 80 percent as big as the leading firm's share).

The merit of using relative market share instead of simply market share to construct the growth-share matrix is that the former is a better indicator of comparative market position—a 10 percent market share is much stronger if the leader's share is 12 percent than if it is 50 percent; the use of relative market share captures this difference. An equally important consideration in using relative market share is that it is also likely to be a reflection of relative cost based on experience in producing the product and on economies of larger scale production. The potential of larger businesses to operate at lower unit costs than smaller firms because of technological and efficiency gains that attach to larger size is a well-understood possibility. But personnel from the Boston Consulting Group accumulated evidence that the phenomenon of lower unit costs went beyond just the effects of economies of scale; they found that as the cumulative volume of production increased, the resulting knowledge and

---

[3]For a readily available, more extensive treatment, see Barry Hedley, "A Fundamental Approach to Strategy Development," *Long Range Planning* (December 1976), pp. 2-11. The original presentation is Bruce D. Henderson, "The Experience Curve—Reviewed. IV. The Growth Share Matrix of the Product Portfolio," (Boston: The Boston Consulting Group, 1973), Perspectives No. 135.

[4]There is nothing sacred about setting the dividing lines at 10 percent and 1.0, respectively. In the case of the market growth rate, the idea is to place the line such that businesses above the line can fairly be said to be in the growth phase whereas those below the line are in the mature-saturation-decline phase. In the case of relative market share, the dividing line should be placed such that businesses to the left enjoy positions as market leaders (though not necessarily *the* leader) and those to the right are in trailing or underdog market share positions.

experience gained led to the discovery of additional efficiencies and ways to reduce costs even further. The relationship between cumulative production experience and lower unit costs was labeled by BCG as *the experience curve effect*—a more complete discussion of which is presented in Illustration Capsule 14. The strategic significance of the experience curve effect is that it places a premium on market share: the firm that gains the biggest market share tends to realize important cost advantages which, in turn, can be used to lower prices and gain still additional customers, sales, market share, and profit.

With these points in mind, we are ready to explore the portfolio implications for businesses falling into each cell of the BCG growth-share matrix.

ILLUSTRATION CAPSULE 14
The Experience Curve: A Basis for Strategy Analysis?

The Boston Consulting Group (BCG) has in recent years gotten the attention of businessmen with a concept it calls "the experience curve." The experience curve derives from the well-known learning curve (a phenomenon discovered by an Air Force officer in the 1920s) which holds that the time needed to perform a task decreases by a constant percentage the more often it is done. The power of the learning curve is such that in some firms unit labor costs have declined 10% to 15% each time output is doubled.

In the late 1960s, Bruce D. Henderson, founder and president of Boston Consulting Group, observed that the learning curve principle seemed to apply to the *overall* unit costs of making a product as well as to just unit *labor* costs. On the basis of BCG's experiences with client firms, Henderson claimed that each time the number of units produced doubled there was a *tendency* for unit costs to also decline by a fixed percentage—usually in the 20% to 30% range. He attributed this decline in cost with each doubling of experience to the combined effect of learning, specialization, increased scale of operation, and increased intensity of capital investment. The relationships were deemed predictable enough that the declines in unit cost, relative to volume, could be accurately plotted—BCG labeled the resulting graphical relationship "the experience curve."

In BCG's view, the experience curve can be a "powerful and universal tool for strategic planning," as well as a simple means of predicting and controlling a firm's costs. The rationale is as follows: the firm which produces the most units will probably have the lowest average costs. If that firm also has the largest market share, then it should earn the greatest profits. Therefore, a firm should strive to gain a dominant market share in as many products as possible, even if that means temporarily lower profit margins.

The usefulness of the experience curve concept is that it permits the

Sources: "Selling Business a Theory of Economics," *Business Week* (September 8, 1973), pp. 85-90, and Derek F. Abell and John S. Hammond, *Strategic Market Planning* (Englewood Cliffs, N.J.: Prentice-Hall, Inc., 1979), pp. 106-21.

ILLUSTRATION CAPSULE 14 *(continued)*

profitability of an increase in market share for a particular product to be calculated with more precision than otherwise. An experience curve based on actual statistics shows the decline in costs that can be anticipated with increases in volume and market share. And, as volume grows, prices can be reduced because of lower realized unit costs. Then it is merely a matter of weighing the worth of the increased market share against the investment it takes to achieve it and the probable reaction of competitors. The strategic implication of the experience curve effect is, according to BCG, that a company should strive to become a dominant force in the markets for its products, either by introducing new product variations, segmenting the market, or discouraging competitors by keeping prices low.

BCG found that some companies ignore these principles, even though they seem elementary. This particularly applies to a firm which finds itself with early leadership in market share of a product but then tries to translate lower costs into higher profit margins instead of lower prices; in BCG's view it is better to increase profits through greater volume rather than wider profit margins—as depicted in the accompanying graph. When price does not follow cost down, the door is open for rival firms to begin to gain on the market leader.

<table>
<tr><td align="center">(a)</td><td align="center">(b)</td></tr>
<tr><td>A relatively level introductory price, if held too long, encourages competitors to enter the market, triggering a steep price decline, or competitive shakeout.</td><td>If prices are lowered in step with unit costs as projected via the experience curve, entry may be discouraged and market share increased; profit margins are smaller, but long-run profits tend to be more secure.</td></tr>
</table>

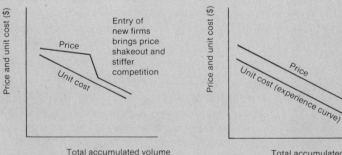

One of BCG's first efforts at applying experience curve theory was with Norton Company of Worcester, Massachusetts. Norton was having trouble profitably penetrating the market for pressure-sensitive tape—a market dominated by 3M Company. Norton had successfully cut production costs and lowered prices, but still was unable to make a dent in increasing its

ILLUSTRATION CAPSULE 14 *(concluded)*

market share. BCG's experience curve analysis showed that Norton, in effect, was chasing 3M Company down the cost curve, and that so long as 3M followed pricing and growth strategies to maximize market share, it was a fruitless struggle for Norton. Subsequently, Norton concluded that it could not compete successfully against 3M by trying to produce a broad range of products sold in a large number of markets; rather, the company decided it was better off concentrating in selected areas. In BCG's view the Norton situation illustrated an important experience curve commandment: if you cannot get enough market share to be cost-competitive, then get out of the business. Another instance where the same lesson applied was the effort of Allis-Chalmers Company to compete against General Electric and Westinghouse in steam turbine engines. Between 1946 and 1963 Allis-Chalmer's market share was too small to give it a chance to be competitive on cost and therefore on price with large-volume manufacturers; thus, A-C's best decision was to withdraw from the industry.

Black & Decker, Texas Instruments, and Weyerhaeuser are among the companies which at one time or another have utilized the experience curve philosophy. In 1973, Texas Instruments described its strategy for expanding market share this way: "Follow an aggressive pricing policy, focus on continuing cost reduction and productivity improvement, build on shared experience gained in making related products, and keep capacity growing ahead of demand."

A word of caution, however. Before embarking on a strategy based on the experience curve effect, one should understand the full implications. The selection of a corporate/business strategy based on sustained cost reduction due to experience or scale entails a strategic emphasis on cost-price-efficiency over differentiation-market effectiveness considerations. For an "efficiency" strategy to succeed, one must affirm that there are significant numbers of customers that want low price as opposed to quality/service/product innovation/specialized use and other such differentiating features. Moreover, once it is decided to pursue an efficiency or price-cost leadership strategy, a firm has to guard against losing its ability to respond to product-technology-customer changes; strategies based on tight adherence to experience curve effects frequently result in creating a highly specialized work force and in relatively inflexible facilities and technologies. The outcome can be an increased difficulty and cost in (1) responding to changes in customer needs and product uses, (2) matching or bettering the product innovations of rival firms, (3) accommodating major changes in process technology and implementing technological breakthroughs, and (4) initiating these changes on one's own to drive the market in new directions.

Question Marks and Problem Children.   Businesses falling in the upper right quadrant of the growth-share matrix are tagged by BCG as "question marks" or "problem children." Rapid market growth makes the business attractive from an industry standpoint, but low market share makes it questionable whether the profit potential associated with market growth can realistically be captured—hence, the "question mark" or "problem child" designation. According to BCG, question mark businesses are typically "cash hogs"—so labeled because their cash needs are high (owing to the investment requirements of rapid growth and product development) and their internal cash generation is low (owing to low market share and less access to scale economies). BCG reasons that the most rational strategic options for a question mark business are (1) an aggressive grow-and-build strategy to capitalize on the high growth opportunity or (2) divestiture, in the event that the costs of strengthening its market share standing via a grow-and-build strategy outweigh the potential payoff and financial risk.

Stars.   Businesses with high market share positions in high growth markets are labeled as "stars" by BCG on the premise that their market position offers both excellent profit and excellent growth opportunities. As such, they are the businesses that an enterprise needs to nurture and groom for the long-run owing to the effects of the "experience curve"—see Illustration Capsule 14. Given their dominant market share position and the rapid growth environment, stars typically require large cash investments for expansion of production facilities and for working capital, but they also tend to generate large internal cash flows due to the low-cost advantage that attaches to economies of scale and cumulative production experience.

Star-type businesses vary as to whether they can support their investment needs from within or whether they require external infusions of investment funds to support continued rapid growth and high performance. According to BCG, some stars (usually those that are well-established and beginning to mature) are virtually self-sustaining in terms of cash flow and little investment will be needed from sources *external* to the business. Young stars, however, often require substantial investment capital *beyond what can be generated internally* in order to secure and maintain their high growth/high market share ranking and may thus be "cash hogs."

Cash Cows.   Businesses with a high market share in a low growth market are called "cash cows" by BCG because their entrenched position tends to yield substantial *cash surpluses* over and above what is needed for reinvestment and growth in the business. Many of today's cash cows are yesterday's stars. Cash cows, though less attractive from a growth standpoint, are nonetheless a valuable corporate portfolio holding because they can be "milked" for the cash to pay corporate dividends and corporate overhead, they help finance new acquisitions, and they provide cash flow to support investment in the next round of stars (cash cows provide the dollars to "feed" the cash hogs). "Strong cash cows" are not "harvested" but are maintained and managed for cash flow. The idea is to preserve market position while efficiently generating dollars to reallocate to business investments elsewhere. "Weak cash cows," however, may be prime candidates for harvesting and, eventually, divestiture.

Dogs.   Businesses with low growth and low market share are referred to as "dogs" by BCG because of their weak competitive position (owing, perhaps, to high costs, low quality products, less effective marketing, and the like) and the low profit potential that can be associated with slow growth and impending market saturation. Another characteristic of dogs is the lack of attractive cash flow on a long-term basis; sometimes they do not produce enough cash to maintain their existing position—especially if competition is stiff, profit margins are thin, or inflation is causing sharply higher costs. Consequently, except in unusual cases, BCG recommends that dogs be harvested, divested, or liquidated, depending on which alternative yields the most attractive cash flow.

Implications for Corporate Strategy.   The chief contribution of the BCG growth-share matrix is the attention it draws to the cash flow and investment characteristics of various types of businesses and how corporate financial resources can be used to optimize the long-term strategic position and performance of the whole corporate portfolio. According to BCG analysis, the foundation of a sound, long-term corporate strategy is to utilize the excess cash generated by cash cow business units to finance market share increases for cash hog businesses—the young stars still unable to finance their own growth internally and those problem children which have been singled out as having the best potential to grow into stars. If successful, the cash hogs eventually become self-supporting stars and then, when the markets of the star businesses begin to mature and their growth slows down, they will become the cash cows of the future. The "success sequence" is thus problem child/question mark to young star (but perhaps still a cash hog) to self-supporting star to cash cow.

The weaker, less attractive "question mark" businesses not deemed worthy of the financial investment it would take to fund a long-term grow-and-build strategy are often a portfolio liability because of the higher-cost economics associated with a low relative market share and because internal cash flows are too small to keep the business abreast of fast-paced market growth. These "question marks" should, according to BCG prescriptions, be prime divestiture candidates *unless* they can be kept profitable and viable with their own internally generated funds (all "problem child" businesses are not untenable cash hogs; some may be able to generate the cash to finance a "hold and maintain" strategy and thus contribute enough to corporate earnings and return on investment to justify retention in the portfolio). Even so, such low-priority "question marks" still have a dim future in the portfolio; as market growth slows and maturity-saturation sets in, they will move vertically downward in the matrix, becoming "dogs."

"Dogs" should be retained only as long as they can contribute positive cash flow and provided they do not tie up assets and resources that could be more profitably redeployed. The BCG recommendation for managing a weak "dog" is to employ a harvesting strategy. If and when a harvesting strategy is no longer attractive, then a weak "dog" business becomes a candidate for elimination from the portfolio.

There are two "disaster sequences" in the BCG scheme of things: (1) when a star's position in the matrix erodes over time to that of a "problem child" and then falls to become a "dog" and (2) when a "cash cow" loses market leadership to the point where it becomes a "dog." Other strategic mistakes include overinvesting in a safe "cash cow"; underinvesting in a "question mark" such that instead of moving into the "star" category it tumbles into a "dog"; and spreading resources thinly over many "question marks" rather than focusing resources on selected "question marks" to turn them into "stars."

Weaknesses in the Growth-Share Matrix Approach.   The BCG business portfolio matrix has considerable appeal in evaluating different businesses and reaching strategic decisions on how to manage a corporate portfolio. Yet, several legitimate shortcomings exist:

1.   A four-cell matrix based on high-low classifications hides the fact that many businesses (the majority?) are in markets with an "average" growth rate and have relative market shares which may be best characterized as neither high nor low but rather "in-between" or "intermediate." Which cells do these "average" businesses belong in?

2.   While viewing all businesses as being stars, cash cows, dogs, or question marks does indeed add a useful element of flavor and communicative appeal, it is a misleading simplification to think of the corporate portfolio in terms of just four types of businesses. All market leaders cannot be neatly categorized as "stars" or "cash cows"—more than a few market leaders have encountered hard times and some have ended up in bankruptcy as "dogs." Some market share leaders have never really been stars in terms of profitability. All businesses with low relative market shares are not "dogs" or "question marks"—a number are proven star performers in terms of growth, profitability, and competitive ability.

3.   The BCG matrix is not very helpful in comparing relative investment opportunities across business units. For example, is every "star" better than a "cash cow"? How should one "question mark" be compared to another in terms of whether it should be built into a "star" or divested?[5]

4.   Being a market leader in a slow-growth industry is not a surefire guarantee of "cash cow" status because (a) the investment requirements of a hold-and-maintain strategy, given the impact of inflation on

---

[5]Derek F. Abell and John S. Hammond, *Strategic Market Planning* (Englewood Cliffs, N.J.: Prentice-Hall, Inc., 1979), p. 212.

the costs of replacing wornout facilities and equipment, can soak up much or all of the available internal cash flows and (b) as markets mature, competitive forces often stiffen and the ensuing vigorous battle for volume and market share acts to shrink profit margins and cash flows.

5. The connection between market share and profitability is not as tight as the experience curve effect implies. The importance of cumulative production experience in lowering unit costs varies from industry to industry. In some cases a larger market share can be translated into a unit cost advantage; in others it cannot. In a number of industries, companies with a low market share are able to earn consistently high profits with strategies geared to product innovation, product differentiation, and careful market segmentation; cost leadership is only one dimension on which to base competitive advantage and long-term performance. Hence, it is wise to be cautious in depending upon the variables of market growth rate and relative market share to be sufficient indicators of a business's profitability, cash flow, and overall chances for competitive success in the marketplace.

6. A thorough assessment of the business portfolio usually requires an examination of more than just market growth and relative market share variables. Other relevant factors in evaluating where a business stands in the corporate portfolio and how it should be managed include size of the market, the existence of competitive advantages and distinctive competences, abilities to capitalize on emerging opportunities and to ward off threatening market developments, vulnerability to ups and downs in the economy, ease of entry into and exit from the business, the form and intensity of competitive pressures, stage of product-market evolution, capital requirements, and degree of strategic fit with other businesses in the portfolio. In short, the task of portfolio analysis embraces a number of strategic considerations not directly reflected in the growth-share matrix.

The Nine-Cell GE Matrix

An alternative matrix approach which avoids some of the shortcomings of the BCG growth-share matrix has been pioneered by General Electric, with help from the consulting firm of McKinsey & Company. The GE effort is a nine-cell portfolio matrix based on the two dimensions of long-term product-market attractiveness and business strength/competitive position.[6] In this matrix, depicted in Figure 4-3, the area of the circles is proportional to the size of the industry, and the pie slices within the circle

---

[6]For an expanded treatment, see Michael G. Allen, "Diagramming G.E.'s Planning for What's WATT," in Robert J. Allio and Malcolm W. Pennington, editors, *Corporate Planning: Techniques and Applications* (New York: AMACOM, 1979).

FIGURE 4-3
General Electric's Nine-Cell Business Portfolio Matrix

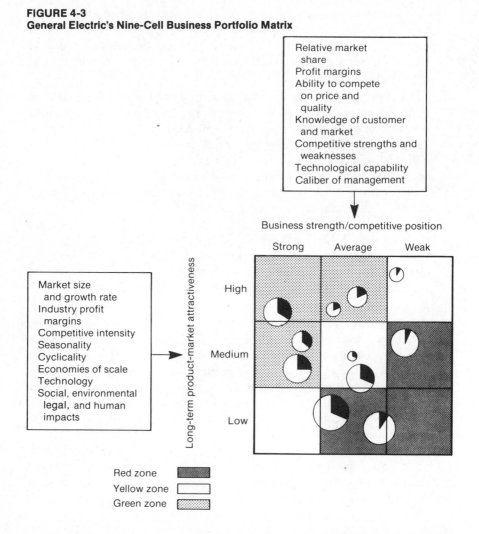

reflect the business's market share. The vertical axis represents each industry's long-term attractiveness, defined as a composite weighting of market growth rate, market size, historical and projected industry profitability, market structure and competitive intensity, scale economies, seasonality and cyclical influences, technological and capital requirements, and social, environmental, and regulatory influences. The procedure involves assigning each industry attractiveness factor a weight according to its perceived importance, assessing how the business stacks up on each factor (using a 1 to 5 rating scale), and then obtaining a weighted composite rating as shown on the following page.

Industry Attractiveness Factor	Weight	Rating	Value
Market size	.15	5	0.75
Projected rate of market growth	.20	1	0.20
Historical and projected profitability	.10	1	0.10
Intensity of competition	.20	5	1.00
Emerging opportunities	.15	1	0.05
Seasonality and cyclical influences	.05	2	0.30
Technological and capital requirements	.10	3	0.30
Environmental impact	.05	4	0.20
Social, political, regulatory factors	Must be acceptable	-	-
	1.00		2.90

To arrive at a measure of business strength/competitive position, each business is rated, using the same approach shown above, on such aspects of business strength/competitive position as relative market share, success in increasing market share and profitability, ability to match rival firms on cost and product quality, knowledge of customers and markets, how well the firm's skills and competences in the business match the various requirements for competitive success in the industry (distribution network, promotion and marketing, access to scale economies, technological proficiency, support services, manufacturing efficiency), adequacy of production capacity, and calibre of management. The two composite values for long-term product-market attractiveness and business strength/competitive position are then used to plot each business's position in the matrix.

Corporate Strategy Implications.   The nine cells of the GE matrix are grouped into 3 categories or zones. The green zone (vertical lines) consists of the three cells at the upper left where long-term industry attractiveness and business strength/competitive position are favorable—the general strategic prescription here is "grow-and-build" and businesses in these zones are accorded a high priority in the allocation of investment funds. The yellow zone (unshaded) consists of the 3 diagonal cells stretching from the lower left to the upper right; businesses falling into these cells usually carry a medium investment allocation priority in the portfolio and are managed with "maintain and hold" type strategies. The red zone (horizontal lines) is composed of the three cells in the lower right corner of the matrix; the strategy prescription for red zone businesses is typically harvest or divest (in exceptional cases it can be "rebuild and reposition" using some type of turnaround approach).[7]

The strength of the nine-cell GE approach is threefold. One, it allows for intermediate rankings between high and low and between strong and

[7]At General Electric, each business actually ended up in one of five types of categories: (1) *high-growth* potential products deserving top investment priority, (2) *stable base* products deserving steady reinvestment to maintain position, (3) *support* products deserving periodic investment funding, (4) *selective pruning* or *rejuvenation* products deserving reduced investment funding and (5) *venture* products deserving heavy R&D investment.

weak. Two, it incorporates explicit consideration of a much wider variety of strategically relevant variables. Three, and most important, the powerful logic of GE's approach is its emphasis on channeling corporate resources to those businesses that combine medium to high product-market attractiveness with average to strong business strength/competitive position, the thesis being that it is in these combinations where the greatest probability of a superior performance payoff lies.

However, the nine-cell GE matrix, like the four-cell growth-share matrix, provides no real clues or hints as to the specifics of business strategy; all that matrix analysis can suggest are *general* prescriptions: grow-and-build or hold-and-maintain or harvest-divest. Such prescriptions are perhaps adequate insofar as corporate-level strategy formulation is concerned, but the issue of what specific types of grow-and-build or hold-and-maintain or harvest-divest strategies to use in the case of each different business remains wide open. Another weakness has been pointed out by Professors Hofer and Schendel: the GE approach does not depict as well as it might the positions of businesses that are about to emerge as winners because the product/market is entering the takeoff stage.[8]

The Product/Market Evolution Matrix

To better identify a *developing winner* type of business, Hofer and Schendel propose a 15-cell matrix in which businesses are plotted in terms of stage of product/market evolution and competitive position, as shown in Figure 4-4.[9] Again, the circles represent the sizes of the industries involved and pie wedges denote the business's market share. Looking at the plot in Figure 4-4, business A would appear to be a *developing winner*, business C might be classified as a *potential loser*, business E might be labeled an *established winner*, business F could be a cash cow, and business G a loser or a dog. The power of this analytical matrix is the story it tells about the distribution of the firm's businesses across the stages of product-market evolution.

Actually, there is no need to force a choice as to which type of portfolio matrix to use; any or all can be constructed to gain insights from different perspectives. Each matrix type has its pros and cons. The important thing is analytical accuracy and completeness in describing the firm's current portfolio position—all for the larger purpose of how to manage the portfolio as a whole and get the best performance from the allocation of corporate resources.

---

[8]Charles W. Hofer and Dan Schendel, *Strategy Formulation: Analytical Concepts* (St. Paul, Minnesota: West Publishing Co., 1978), p. 33.
[9]Ibid., p. 34. This approach to business portfolio analysis was reportedly first used in actual practice by consultants at Arthur D. Little, Inc.

FIGURE 4-4
A Product/Market Evolution Portfolio Matrix

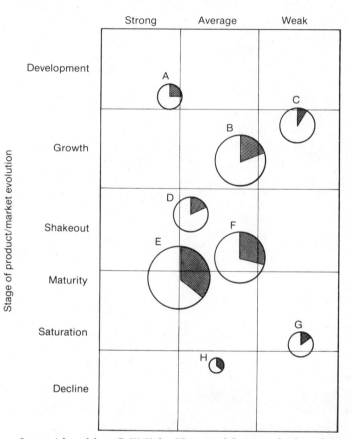

Source: Adapted from C. W. Hofer, "Conceptual Constructs for Formulating Corporate and Business Strategies," (Boston: Harvard Case Services, #9-378-754, 1977), p. 3.

ILLUSTRATION CAPSULE 15
What Corporate Executives Think about the Value of
Business Portfolio Analysis

Business portfolio matrix analysis has spread rapidly among large, diversi-fied corporations. A 1979 survey, the results of which were recently reported by Phillippe Haspeslagh in a *Harvard Business Review* article, indicated that 45 percent of all *Fortune 500* firms and 36 percent of all *Fortune 1000* firms

Source: Phillippe Haspeslagh, "Portfolio Planning: Uses and Limits," *Harvard Business Review*, vol. 60, no. 1 (January-February 1982), pp. 58-73.

ILLUSTRATION CAPSULE 15 *(continued)*

had introduced this analytical approach to some extent and their ranks are growing at about 25 to 30 firms per year. The use of portfolio analysis was more prevalent in some industries than in others:

Prevalent use	Occasional use	Rare or no use
Chemicals	Motor vehicles	Aerospace
Industrial farm equipment	Metal products	Muscial instruments, toys, and sporting goods
Electronics and appliances	Measuring, scientific, and photographic equipment	Tobacco
Paper and fiber products	Pharmaceuticals	Shipbuilding and railroads
Food	Office equipment, including computers	Soaps and cosmetics
Metal manufacturing	Publishing and printing	Mining and crude oil production
Petroleum refining	Rubber and plastic products	Furniture
Glass, concrete, abrasives, and gypsum	Beverages	Leather
	Textiles and vinyl flooring	Jewelry and silverware
	Apparel	Broadcasting and motion picture production

Portfolio analysis was found to be more widely employed by large, diversified firms—about 75 percent were utilizing the technique in one way or another. From the time the technique is first introduced until it becomes an integral, accepted, and formal part of the of the strategic management process was found to average 5 years.

Corporate executives reported the following perceived benefits:

1. A noticeable improvement in the quality of strategies at both the corporate and business levels.

2. More selective and focused allocation of corporate resources in a capital-constrained environment.

3. A stronger framework for tailoring "how we manage" to the needs of each business in the portfolio.

4. A greatly improved capacity for performing the tasks of strategic management and exerting firmer control over strategy at both the corporate and business levels.

5. Less reluctance to face the problem of marginal businesses.

The impetus for adopting portfolio analysis was the sheer number of different businesses—so many that corporate-level managers could not realistically even hope to be intimately familiar with all of the relevant strategic aspects of each line of business. The appeal of the portfolio analysis technique was its formal recognition that diversified companies are a collection of businesses, each of which makes a distinct contribution to overall corporate performance and which should be deliberately and intentionally managed to optimize this

ILLUSTRATION CAPSULE 15 *(concluded)*

contribution. Executives reported that portfolio analysis tended (1) to sharpen understanding of the role and potential contribution of each business unit, (2) to help build a rational framework for making resource commitments, and (3) to prescribe general types of strategies to each business unit—in sum, to clarify what the firm ought to do with each of its businesses.

One of the most interesting and telling impacts of portfolio analysis was found to be a shift in emphasis away from short-term profits and sales objectives toward competitive analysis and the achievement of long-term profit and sales targets, as shown below:

Issue	Rank without portfolio analysis	Rank with portfolio analysis
Next year's profit objectives	1	6
Long-range profit objectives	2	1
Next year's capital investment plan	3	4
Next year's sales objectives	4	8
Long-range sales objectives	5	3
Long-range resource allocation	6	2
Competitive analysis	7	5
Milestones for implementation	8	7
Contingency plans	9	9

The consensus among executives was that business portfolio analysis is not a passing fad; rather, it is here to stay because it represents an important step forward in the practice of management in multibusiness enterprises.

EVALUATING A FIRM'S CURRENT BUSINESS PORTFOLIO

While the construction of business portfolio matrices is a revealing way to identify the make-up and character of a firm's business portfolio, it by no means constitutes the whole evaluation process. As noted by Hofer and Schendel, other relevant perspectives include:[10]

---

[10]Hofer and Schendel, *Strategy Formulation: Analytical Concepts*, p. 71 and pp. 81-86. The remainder of this section is drawn from Hofer and Schendel's discussion of their procedural approach, particularly pp. 72-86.

1. A searching assessment of each industry in which the firm does busi-
    ness to determine key trends and market direction, the nature and
    strength of competition, important technological developments, cost
    and raw material supply conditions, labor conditions, capital require-
    ments, and profit prospects—all with an eye towards how worthwhile
    it will be to have a strategic interest and business stake in the industry.

2. An evaluation of the firm's competitive position in each industry and
    how the business ranks on the key factors underlying competitive
    success. This is crucial to picking out those product-customer-technol-
    ogy opportunities best suited to the firm's strengths and competitive
    capabilities.

3. An identification of opportunities and threats that might reasonably
    arise in each of the firm's businesses.

4. A consideration of what corporate resources and skills could improve
    the competitive strength of each business unit.

5. A comparison of short-run profit potential and risk with longer-term
    profit potential and risk for each of the different businesses in the firm's
    portfolio.

6. An examination of the overall portfolio to determine whether the mix
    of businesses is adequately "balanced"—not too many losers or ques-
    tion marks, not so many mature businesses that corporate growth will
    be slow, enough cash producers to support the stars and developing
    winners, too few dependable profit performers, and so on.

Assessing Industry Attractiveness

A business is seldom much more attractive than the industry or industry
segment of which it is a part.[11] Hence an integral step in corporate strategy
evaluation is a systematic assessment of the risks and potential of each
industry in which the firm has a strategic interest. The main concerns here
center around (1) whether the industry has enough of the positive attributes

---

[11]As an example of the relevance of assessing industry attractiveness, consider the following long-range strategy issues now confronting the major oil companies in their oil business.
Given the apparently dwindling world oil supplies and the rapidly rising price of crude oil,
what is the long-range future of the petroleum industry? How soon and how fast can rising
crude oil prices and a dependence on foreign oil imports be expected to propel a switch to
other forms of energy? When and what kinds of new substitute energy sources are likely?
What kinds of cost and supply advantages are they likely to have over currently known energy
alternatives? Will the established oil companies have access to these new energy technologies
or will antitrust factors make them the exclusive province of new companies? How probable
is it that large industrial energy-users will be able to integrate backward and supply their own
energy needs? What should the oil companies be doing *today* to prepare for the future of the
oil business? How the oil companies answer these questions can scarcely fail to weigh heavily
on whether they choose to invest heavily in oil or whether they begin to divert funds into other
energy or nonenergy businesses.

that management is looking for (such as growth, profitability, or export opportunities), (2) the extent to which the industry is characterized by traits that management wants to avoid (such as a history of labor strife, highly cyclical or seasonal demand, or major pollution control problems), and (3) the risk that industry conditions and trends will not be favorable enough to allow the firm's business to contribute its "fair share" toward the achievement of overall corporate objectives.

The method which Hofer and Schendel recommend for determining industry attractiveness entails a five-step procedure:[12]

1. Decide which traits and factors are most relevant as criteria for judging industry attractiveness. (Table 4-1 lists some of the commonly considered factors; however, in comparing different industries, it is probably not practical to develop more than ten attractiveness criteria, so as to escape getting bogged down in detail.)

TABLE 4-1
Factors to Consider in Assessing
Industry Attractiveness

A. *Industry Characteristics and Trends*

  1. Market size and growth rate

  2. Profitablilty in comparison to other industries and businesses

  3. Stage of life cycle (infancy, early takeoff, rapid growth, early maturity, saturation, or decline)

  4. Barriers to entry and exit

  5. Composition of buying side of market (number and size of segments, segment growth rates, buyer demographics)

  6. Demand patterns and conditions (seasonality, vulnerability to recession or other adverse economic conditions, importance and value of product to users, stability of demand side of market)

  7. Projected balance between buyer demand and seller capacity to supply

  8. Structure of supply side of market (number and sizes of sellers)

  9. Importance of economies of scale (importance of volume and market share to profitability)

---

[12]Hofer and Schendel, *Strategy Formulation: Analytical Concepts*, pp. 72-75. For some other approaches, see D. E. Hussey, "Portfolio Analysis: Practical Experience with the Directional Policy Matrix," *Long Range Planning*, vol. 11 no. 4 (August 1978), pp. 4-5; Derek F. Abell and John S. Hammond, *Strategic Market Planning*, pp. 212-219; and William E. Rothschild, *Putting It All Together: A Guide to Strategic Thinking* (New York: AMACOM, 1976), Chapter 8.

TABLE 4-1 *(concluded)*

10. Capital requirements
11. Cash flow features (a cash cow or cash hog business)
12. Labor availability, union-management relationships
13. Role and influence of government regulations and policies
14. Industry outlook—emerging opportunities and threats
15. Skills and resources needed to succeed in marketplace (technological, manufacturing, marketing, and so on)
16. Import/export barriers

B. *Competitive Forces and Pressures*

1. Intensity of rivalry among firms
2. Competition from substitute products
3. Competition from foreign firms
4. Power of suppliers
5. Competitive strength and positions of leading firms
6. Key factors, forces, and variables around which competition is centered
7. Difficulty of achieving and holding an attractive competitive position
8. Overall intensity and strength of competitive pressures

C. *Other Factors*

1. The role and influence which social mores, lifestyles, attitudes, and societal expectations and concerns have regarding the industry and its practices
2. The attractiveness of the industry from the standpoint of strategic fit with other of the corporation's businesses
3. Impact of the industry's activities on the environment, on energy usage, on the quality of human life (health, safety), and on human values and beliefs (war, nuclear power, morals)
4. Impact of the industry's activities on relations with foreign nations and foreign governments
5. Importance of the industry to the economy and to overall national welfare
6. How Wall Street and the banking and investment community in general view the industry.

2. Attach priorities or weights to each of the factors on which overall attractiveness depends.

3. Gather information relevant to each one of the industry factors selected as being important considerations.

4. Rate the industry on each of the attractiveness factors and compute a weighted overall attractiveness "score." (The assigned rating may be a simple go/no go type or a numerical score that ranges from highly positive down to highly negative.)

5. Check the weighted overall ranking against informed managerial opinions and perceptions about the industry and its potential, and attempt to resolve any significant disparity.

This procedure parallels that used by GE and draws its strength from the systematic manner in the way each strategically relevant aspect of industry attractiveness is formally considered.

Table 4-2 provides a rundown of major sources of information for assessing industry attractiveness and for finding out about specific companies.

TABLE 4-2
**Sources of Information for Assesing Industry
Attractiveness and Evaluating Companies***

A. *Population, the Economy, and Current Business Conditions*

1. U.S. Department of Commerce, Bureau of the Census, *Census of Population, Census of Housing, County Business Patterns, Census of Governments*—for periodic, but comprehensive and detailed, data on population characteristics, housing conditions, and various business and governmental statistics.

2. U.S. Department of Commerce, *Survey of Current Business* (monthly), *Business Conditions Digest* (monthly), *U.S. Industrial Outlook, Statistical Abstract of the United States* (annually)— for current and historical statistics on the economy and business conditions.

3. Council of Economic Advisors, *Economic Report of the President* (published annually)—contains a good variety of statistics relating to GNP, income, employment, prices, money supply, and governmental finance.

*For an additional classification and survey of information sources, see C. R. Goeldner and Laura M. Dirks, "Business Facts: Where to Find Them," *Business Topics,* vol. 24, no. 3 (Summer 1976), pp. 23-36.

TABLE 4-2 (continued)

4. United Nations, *Statistical Yearbook*—for various economic statistics of foreign countries.

5. OECD, *Economic Outlook and Main Economic Indicators*—for international economic data.

6. Board of Governors of Federal Reserve System, *Federal Reserve Bulletin* (monthly)—for data on banking, money supply conditions, interest rates, and credit conditions.

7. U.S. Department of Labor, Bureau of Labor Statistics, *Monthly Labor Review* (monthly), *Employment and Earnings* (monthly), *Handbook of Labor Statistics* (annually)—for data on employment, hours worked and earnings, productivity, wholesale and consumer prices, labor turnover, and area unemployment characteristics.

8. Editor and Publisher, *Market Guide* (annually)—contains rankings of cities, counties, and SMSA areas based on individual income population, total retail sales, and food sales as well as pertinent local area information.

9. *Sales Management* magazine's "Annual Survey of Buying Power"— for rankings on the amount spent for selected products/services by geographical location.

B. *Industry Information*

1. U.S. Department of Commerce, Bureau of the Census, *Census of Manufactures, Annual Survey of Manufacturing, Census of Business, Census of Transportation*—for statistics relating to the volume of manufacturing activity, size and structure of firms, retail and wholesale trade, and transportation.

2. Federal Trade Commission, *Quarterly Financial Report for Manufacturing, Mining, and Trade Corporations* (quarterly)—for sales, profit, balance sheet, and income statement statistics by industry division and size of firm.

3. U.S. Department of the Treasury, Internal Revenue Service, *Business Income Tax Returns* (annually) and *Corporate Income Tax Returns* (annually)—for breakdowns on revenues, operating expenses, and profits by type of business organization and industry division.

4. National Industrial Conference Board: research and statistical reports issued periodically and the *Conference Board Record* (monthly).

5. Securities and Exchange Commission: quarterly reports of finance and capital expenditures.

6. Trade association and industry publications such as *Commercial and Financial Chronicle, Banking, Advertising Age, Automotive*

TABLE 4-2 *(concluded)*

> *News, Public Utilities Fortnightly, Engineering News Record, Best's Insurance Review, Progressive Grocer*, and *Electronic News*.

C. *Company-Oriented Information*

1. Annual reports of companies.

2. Investment services and directories: Standard and Poor's, Moody's, *Value Line*.

3. Financial ratios: Dun & Bradstreet Annual Surveys, Robert Morris Associates *Annual Statement Studies*.

4. Securities and Exchange Commission, Form 10-K reports.

5. Periodicals: *Fortune, Barron's, Forbes, Wall Street Transcript, Dun's Review, Business Week, Financial World, Over-the-Counter Securities Review*.

Evaluation of Competitive Position

The value of competitive position analysis is to arrive at a measure of a firm's potential to capitalize upon the opportunities that exist in each of the industries in which it has a stake.[13] A favorable judgment on industry attractiveness is necessary but not sufficient to warrant keeping a business in the firm's portfolio; in addition, a firm must be (or be capable of becoming) a viable competitor in that industry—being relegated to an also-ran in an attractive industry is usually not a "go" proposition.

There are two main dimensions to an evaluation of a business's competitive position and competitive strength. One involves a determination of where the firm's business stands in relation to that of its rivals, with particular emphasis on comparisons of market share, prices, breadth and quality of product line, profit margins, technology and cost differentials, facilities locations, proprietary know-how, key accounts advantages, and overall image with buyers. The second involves an explicit identification of the key factors underlying competitive success in the industry and an evaluation of how well the firm rates on each of these *key success factors*. A clear understanding of what specific competences, competitive advantages, and strategic approaches have produced leading positions in the marketplace is an essential part of assessing the competitive potential of the firm's own business.

Key success factors, as the label implies, are the answers to the question of "how do you make money in this business?" They point directly to the

---

[13]Hofer and Schendel, *Strategy Formulation: Analytical Concepts*, pp. 75-77. A much more complete discussion of how to analyze the competitive position of a given business is presented in Chapter 5.

things a firm must be good at doing if its business is to be truly successful. Key success factors vary from industry to industry but they always relate to the pivotal economic and technological characteristics of the business and to those particular competitive variables which unlock the door to building a successful strategy. Examples of key success factors include an ability to manufacture a superior quality product in a market where customers are quality-conscious, a talent for developing unusually effective advertising campaigns in a business where clever ads have a big effect on sales, using low-cost manufacture as the basis for outcompeting rival firms on price in a market where buyers are very price sensitive, having a more complete product line in a market where customers place a high value on broad product selection, and having proficiency in R&D in a high technology business. Ordinarily, there are only a few key success factors that have a substantial impact on competitive position. Thus it is more useful to limit the analysis to the five or so most important key success factors and how the business ranks on each of them, than it is to attempt a comprehensive identification and evaluation of 10 to 15 factors.[14] A check against how the business ranks on an industry's key success factors can be made by using the firm's current market share and recent changes in its share as yardsticks in judging the reasonableness of the evaluation results.

ILLUSTRATION CAPSULE 16
Teledyne's Corporate Portfolio Strategy

Under the guidance of its founder and chairman, Henry E. Singleton, Teledyne Inc. employed two different corporate strategies over a two decade period. In the 1960s Teledyne followed an unrelated diversification strategy, and via acquisition assembled a base of some 150 companies, many of which were cash cows. During the 1970s, only a small portion of the cash flows and earnings from the operating companies were reinvested in plant and equipment and R&D; rather, funds were diverted to acquiring a portfolio of common stock holdings in other companies.

In 1981, Teledyne reported revenues of $4.3 billion, net income of $412 million, and a stock portfolio with a market value of $2.9 billion. Some $326 million of Teledyne's $734 million in 1981 operating profits came from dividends on its stock investments, interest payments, and Teledyne's equity in profits earned by companies in which Teledyne owned more than 20% of the stock. The operating company portion of Teledyne's corporate portfolio consisted of 5 major groups:

1. *Industrial products and services* (1981 revenues of $1.2 billion)—diesel

Source: "A Strategy Hooked to Cash Is Faltering," *Business Week*, May 31, 1982, pp. 58-62.

---

[14]Ibid., p. 78.

ILLUSTRATION CAPSULE 16 (continued)

engines for tanks, offshore oil drilling, geophysical services, solid rubber tires, toxic waste disposal, and machine tools.

2. *Insurance and finance* (1981 revenues of $1.1 billion)—life insurance, property and casualty insurance, and consumer finance.

3. *Specialty metals* (1981 revenues of $870 million)—zirconium, steel alloys, tungsten, titanium, and casting and forging.

4. *Aviation and electronics* (1981 revenues of $865 million)—piston and turbine engines, robot aircraft, relays, navigation systems, and flight control computers.

5. *Consumer products* (1981 revenues of $299 million)—Water Pik dental appliances, Shower Massage, swimming pool heaters, dental supplies, and electronic retailing.

The common stock portion of Teledyne's corporate portfolio included the following:

Companies	Number of shares owned (thousands)	Percent of ownership	Market value Dec. 31, 1981 (millions of dollars)	Percent change in value since Dec. 31, 1980*
Aetna Life	4,445	6%	$196	24
Borden	1,481	5	41	9
Brockway	2,275	33	33	4
Colt Industries	1,145	8	64	24
Connecticut General**	2,269	6	113	8
Crown Cork	1,204	8	36	6
Curtiss-Wright	2,602	52	107	Unchanged
Dart & Kraft	2,376	4	121	16
Exxon	4,046	****	126	−14
Intl. Harvester***	5,497	6	47	−59
Kidde	3,898	21	91	3
Kimberly-Clark	888	4	58	23
Litton Ind.	10,400	26	586	−35
Mobil	2,375	1	57	−29
National Can	1,227	14	26	−6
Reichold Chem.	1,535	22	17	−4
Security Pacific	1,310	5	53	19
Texaco	5,633	2	186	−9
Travelers	2,251	5	99	13
Wells Fargo	1,103	5	28	−11
60 other companies	NA	NA	838	−5
TOTAL	NA	NA	$2,923	−11

*Adjusted for purchases during 1981
**Merged into CIGNA on March 31, 1982
***Includes 1.7 million common-equivalent shares of convertible preferred stock
****Less than 1%
NA Not available

ILLUSTRATION CAPSULE 16 *(continued)*

Teledyne's two-phase portfolio strategy has worked well and been timely. In the 1960s when conglomerate diversification was the vogue, Teledyne built its business portfolio by using Teledyne stock to acquire a long string of small companies; the earnings of the newly acquired companies provided a steady boost to Teledyne's profits. Then when unrelated diversification fell from favor, Teledyne milked its new business base of cash and used the funds to launch a major program of common stock acquisition. Each of Teledyne's 130 profit centers is expected to be a net generator rather than user of cash.

Many of the stocks that Singleton chose to buy with this cash rose in value and he won the reputation of being something of a financial genius. Although Teledyne never paid dividends, the rise in the stock price from $10 in 1972 to $175 in mid-1981 made Teledyne one of the top U.S. companies in total stockholder rewards (dividends plus the capital gains from stock price increases). The rise in Teledyne's stock price was helped along when Teledyne used part of its cash to repurchase 75% of its outstanding common shares between 1972 and 1980, thereby greatly enhancing earnings per share and the ownership value of the remaining shares outstanding (some 7.8% were owned by Singleton).

In 1982, there were signs that Teledyne's corporate strategy might be on the verge of entering a third phase, partly because of necessity:

- Water Pik, Teledyne's best-known consumer products business, had experienced a 50% decline in sales—from $130 million in 1976 to $65 million in 1981. The division's two main products, the Water Pik dental appliance and the Shower Massage pulsating showerhead, were hit hard by rapid market saturation and attempts at new product development had fizzled.

- The Continental Motors Division, maker of diesel engines for tanks, was described by outsiders as "stagnating." Pentagon officials were said to have been relieved when Continental was not awarded the contract for engines for the new M-1 tank. A scheduled 1,000-hour test of Teledyne's proposed engine for the M-1 was halted after 218 hours because the engine had in that time failed 51 times.

- Teledyne's offshore oil drilling unit, one of the company's best cash cows, failed to expand its six-rig fleet during the boom years of the late 1970s. Moreover, a new $45 million rig was purchased for early 1982 delivery—a time when an oil surplus cut deeply into the rates which drilling rigs could charge.

- Teledyne's zirconium unit when acquired had a virtual monopoly on free-world production of zirconium (a crucial metal in building nuclear reactors); in 1982, with no new production capacity since its acquisition, the unit's market share was projected to fall under 50%.

- Teledyne's Fireside Thrift and Loan, a consumer finance business in California, lost $4 million before taxes in both 1980 and 1981, one of the worst performances among California's 50 thrift operations.

ILLUSTRATION CAPSULE 16 *(concluded)*

- United Life Insurance Co. of America, Teledyne's major life insurance subsidiary, fell from 47th in 1970 to 68th in 1980 in premium revenues. The property and casualty units dropped from 33rd to 40th by the same measure.

- In recent years Teledyne has spent less than 1.5% of manufacturing sales on R&D, more than 25% below the all-industry average of about 1.9%.

- Teledyne tried unsuccessfully to acquire Chrysler Corp.'s military tank business (losing out to General Dynamics). This was Teledyne's first big acquisition bid in 13 years.

- The market value of Teledyne's common stock portfolio declined $380 million in 1981. Its investment in International Harvester was particularly shaky in light of IH's huge losses in 1981 and its grim financial picture (bordering on bankruptcy).

Teledyne was thought to have three strategic options for reviving its performance. The company could, once again, make new acquisitions to boost sales and earnings (the bid for Chrysler's tank business could signal the beginning of such an effort). Two, Teledyne could begin to reinvest more of its cash in its existing businesses to restore their vitality. Or, three, as a short-run financial boost to the firm's stock price, it could repurchase more shares of its own stock. As of mid-1982, Singleton was offering no clues as to which, if any, of the three options might be pursued. Officially, all Singleton would say was that Teledyne's troubles were largely due to the economic recession and that the 12% decline in first-quarter 1982 earnings reflected the company's heavy mix of capital-good businesses—businesses that are typically hard hit by widespread recessionary conditions.

Identifying Opportunities and Threats in the Industry

Some of the opportunities and threats present in the industry environment may have been identified and included in the assessment of industry attractiveness. But there is merit in a separate and explicit identification and evaluation of industrywide opportunities and threats.[15] Managerial alertness to the specific opportunities/threats in an industry is useful in two respects, namely in understanding how they impinge on the industry's relative attractiveness and in suggesting the whys and hows of adjusting the firm's business-level strategy to meet whatever challenges they pose.

The thrust at this stage should be to concentrate on pinpointing how industry-specific opportunities and threats might significantly strengthen or weaken the competitive position of each business in the firm's portfolio. All firms in an industry are not equally capable of capitalizing on a given

---

[15]Ibid., p. 79.

opportunity or of dealing with a given competitive threat. Hence, explicitly considering the ability of the firm to cope with the opportunities and threats prevailing in each industry adds an important element in sizing up the potential and risk inherent in each business in the portfolio. Not only do these considerations add to the determination of a business's overall strength but they also serve as a basis for ranking the various businesses in terms of investment priority.

Resource/Skills Analysis

This aspect of corporate strategy evaluation entails a realistic appraisal of whether the organization has any resources and skills that could materially alter the firm's competitive standing in the industry under study.[16] This is especially important where the business is judged to be in a less than desirable competitive position and/or where improvement in some key success area is indicated. In particular, what needs to be considered here is whether the organization has any skills, competence, or strengths that it is willing to devote to the business in an effort to develop a competitive edge and make its market position more viable.

Comparing the Attractiveness of Different Businesses

After each of the businesses in the firm's portfolio has been assessed in terms of overall industry attractiveness, competitive position in the industry, unique opportunities and threats, and the availability of special skills and resources, it is time to compare and rate their relative attractiveness and to factor any considerations about strategic fit into this assessment. The groundwork for this has been done in the form of the ratings and scores calculated in assessing each business. These scores could, of course, be used to construct any of several different types of business portfolio matrices. But the summary picture provided by such a matrix (or matrices) usually will need supplementing. This means more than considering "the intangibles" and explicitly examining some of the underlying details. Two additional factors are pertinent. One is whether any difference exists between the assessments of short-run and long-run attractiveness and how this affects the comparisons across the portfolio. The second is the importance that management attaches to building a portfolio that has good strategic fit and how this will alter the relative rankings within the portfolio.

Overall "Balance" in the Portfolio

The focus here is on an evaluation of the *mix* of businesses in the

---

[16]Ibid., p. 80.

portfolio.[17] The kinds of key questions to be answered include: Does the portfolio contain enough businesses in "attractive" or "very attractive" industries? Does it contain too many "losers" or "question marks"? Is the proportion of mature or declining businesses so great that corporate growth will be sluggish? Does the firm have enough "cash cows" to finance the "stars" and emerging winners? Are there enough businesses that generate dependable profits and/or cash flow? Is the portfolio overly vulnerable to inflation or recessionary influences? Are there too many businesses which it is time to get out of or divest? Does the firm have its share of businesses with strong competitive positions or is it burdened with too many businesses in average to weak competitive positions?

PERFORMANCE GAP ANALYSIS

The final phase of the corporate strategy evaluation process involves determining whether the aggregate performance of the businesses in the portfolio can be expected to produce achievement of corporate objectives and, if not, what kinds of corporate strategy changes can be devised to close the performance gap. If a performance gap is found to exist, then there are at least five basic types of actions that top management can take to reduce or close the gap between the projected levels of corporate performance:[18]

1. *Alter the business-level strategies of some (or all) of its businesses.* This option essentially involves special corporate efforts to improve the competitive position of selected business units. The attempt may entail not only a shift in business-level strategy but also shifts in corporate financial support of the business and in functional area support (R&D, manufacturing, marketing, and so on) so as to enhance the chances of building a distinctive competence and, in turn, an improved standing in the market.

2. *Add new business units to the corporate portfolio.* The alternative of an acquisition or internal start-up of a new business raises several corporate strategy issues, namely: (1) What kind and size of new business and having what kind of strategic fit? (2) How would the new business fit into the present corporate structure? (3) What specific features should be looked for in an acquisition candidate? (5) Are acquisitions compatible with the present corporate strategy?

3. *Delete one or more businesses from the corporate portfolio.* The most

---

[17]Barry Hedley, "Strategy and the Business Portfolio," *Long Range Planning*, vol. 10, no. 1 (February 1977), p. 13 and Hofer and Schendel, *Strategy Formulation: Analytical Concepts*, pp. 82-86.

[18]Hofer and Schendel, *Strategy Formulation: Analytical Concepts*, pp. 93-100.

likely candidates for divestiture are those businesses which are in a weak competitive position, or in a relatively unattractive industry, or in an industry which does not "fit."

4. *Use political action to alter conditions which are responsible for sub-par performance potentials.* In some situations, concerted actions with rival firms, trade associations, suppliers, unions, customers, or other interested groups may help ameliorate adverse conditions and improve the business climate. Joining forces to form a political action group may be an effective way of dealing with import-export problems, tax disincentives, regulatory matters, or environmental requirements.

5. *Change corporate performance objectives.* On occasion, changing circumstances render corporate objectives unreachable. Closing the gap between actual and desired performance may then require revision of corporate objectives to bring them more in line with reality. As a practical matter, though, this tends to be a "last resort" option, being used only after other options have been explored and tried.

MANAGING THE CORPORATE STRATEGY FORMULATION PROCESS

Although formal analysis and entrepreneurial brainstorming are important contributors to corporate strategy selection, there is more to where corporate strategy comes from and how it evolves. The process used to arrive at major strategic decisions is typically fragmented, incremental, and the product of a widely shared consensus for action among key members of corporate-level management.[19] Rarely is there an all-inclusive grand formulation of the total corporate strategy. Instead, corporate strategy in major enterprises emerges incrementally from the unfolding of many different internal and external events, the result of probing the future, experimenting, gathering more information, sensing problems, building awareness of the various options, developing ad hoc responses to unexpected "crises," communicating partial consensus as it emerges, and acquiring a "feel" for all the strategically relevant factors, their importance, and their interrelationships.[20]

One should not think, therefore, of corporate strategy evaluation as a time executives set aside to undertake a single comprehensive review. Such big reviews may be scheduled, but the evidence is that major strategic decisions emerge gradually rather than from periodic, full-scale analysis followed by a prompt decision. Typically, the process of corporate strat-

---

[19]James Brian Quinn, *Strategies for Change: Logical Incrementalism* (Homewood, Ill.: Richard D. Irwin, Inc., 1980), p. 15.
[20]Ibid., p. 58 and p. 196.

egy formulation in large enterprises is one where top executives move toward strategic decisions incrementally, often starting from broad, intuitive conceptions and then embellishing, fine tuning, and modifying their original thinking as more information is gathered, as formal analysis clarifies understanding of the situation, and as confidence and consensus builds for how to manage the corporate portfolio. Astute strategists are aware of this gradual, evolutionary process and they consciously intervene in it to improve the analysis and information available for decisions, to broaden support and comfort levels for action, to keep options open and keep the organization flexible to change, and to sense developing strategic needs.[21] The most effective process seems to be one where management concentrates its attention and organizational resources on a few critical strategic thrusts which illuminate and integrate organization direction, objectives, and strategies—it is a conscious, proactive approach to the management of change.[22] The outcome is a continuously evolving consensus about what the corporate strategy is and should be and the process has no precise beginning or end. Formal analysis, like that described earlier in this chapter, is conducted and contributes to the outcome, but it does not constitute the whole process.

"Tips" for Effective Corporate Strategy Management

How does one manage such a process? How can one be "wise" in proceeding in such an ambiguous, uncertain setting to try to formulate a corporate strategy capable of coping with the predictable, the unpredictable, and the unknowable changes that may occur in the most important environments surrounding an enterprise? Several "tips" can be offered based on evidence of what works and what doesn't:[23]

- Keep early responses to a crisis broadly formative, tentative, and subject to later review. Keeping one's options open and making initial decisions vague and tentative encourages more participation from subordinates, allows specialists to develop more information, and buys the time to build commitments to solutions.

- Recognize that formal strategic analysis is more likely to contribute to significant change when it is set up as a "special study" on some important aspect of corporate strategy.

- Make final strategic commitments as late as possible consistent with the information available, thus avoiding undue inflexibility and stimulating others' creativity.

---

[21]Ibid., p. 58 and p. 196.
[22]Ibid., p. 203.
[23]Adapted from James Brian Quinn, *Strategies for Change: Logical Incrementalism*, pp. 20, 21, 39, 52, 53, 84, 85, 107, 119, and 182.

- Attempt to build a resource base and a corporate portfolio that are so strong in selected areas that the enterprise can survive and prosper in all but the most devastating events; consciously select customer/technology/product segments in which the enterprise can be a "dominant force" and place some "side bets" to decrease the risk of catastrophic failure and to increase future options.
- Try to invest corporate strategy with a "dream" or "vision" that can provide a galvanizing, motivating, morale-boosting force for subordinate personnel.
- Remember that organizations with no sense of direction and no coherent strategy can precipitate their own demise by ignoring major problems and overlooking strategic alternatives.
- Make an effort to sense impending issues, problems, opportunities, and threats ahead of the rest of the organization. (This can be accomplished by actively engaging in a variety of different social and intellectual circles, reading, listening, and searching out options beyond simple extrapolations of the status quo.)
- Help bring the full force of the enterprise behind a new strategy by enlisting the support of key people, coopting or neutralizing serious opposition (if necessary), identifying zones of indifference where the strategy will not be opposed, and seeking out no-lose strategies that will be positively received by all key personnel.
- Work at gaining a "feel" and intuitive "sixth sense" for what the various strategic factors and variables are, their importance, and their relationships.

The role of formal, systematic analysis (such as was outlined earlier) in corporate strategy formation is to assist the evolutionary strategic decision-making process along. Thorough corporate portfolio analysis clarifies managerial understanding, identifies relationships and relevant factors to be considered, and promotes consensus-building on which way to go—as discussed in Illustration Capsule 15.

CONCLUDING PERSPECTIVE

To contribute fully to corporate strategy formation, formal portfolio analysis must be iterative and ongoing, incorporating reappraisal of each business as it develops and takes a new position in the portfolio matrix. Moreover, reassessments of the mix of businesses in the corporate portfolio should be routinely conducted. At General Electric, reappraisal is initiated not just at regular intervals but also when a strategic "trigger point" (an external development projected to have a significant impact on a business's performance) occurs.[24] Such an approach is one way of keeping a close

---

[24]William K. Hall, "SBUs: Hot, New Topic in the Management of Diversification," p. 22.

watch on whether a business will actually contribute its expected weight toward the achievement of corporate objectives.

One final point. Even when the portfolio has been systematically evaluated and strategic decisions reached on generally how to handle each business, the strategy formation process is not concluded. Simply deciding to manage a business as a star or a cash cow will not make anything happen.[25] Detailed business strategies, functional area support strategies, and operating-level strategies still need to be devised and implemented. And numerous business-level alternatives exist—there is more than one strategy for managing a cash cow and more than one way to harvest a dog. It is at this juncture that business strategy and corporate strategy come together and can be dovetailed.

Suggested Readings

Bales, Carter F., "Strategic Control: The President's Paradox," *Business Horizons*, vol. 20, no. 4 (August 1977), pp. 17-28.

Bettis, Richard A., and William K. Hall, "Strategic Portfolio Management in the Multibusiness Firms," *California Management Review*, vol. 24, no. 1 (Fall 1981), pp. 23-38.

Emshoff, James R., and Arthur Finnel, "Defining Corporate Strategy: A Case Study Using Strategic Assumptions Analysis," *Sloan Management Review*, vol. 20, no. 3 (Spring 1979), pp. 41-52.

Hall, William K., "SBUs: Hot, New Topic in the Management of Diversification," *Business Horizons*, vol. 21, no. 1 (February 1978), pp. 17-25.

Haspeslagh, Phillippe, "Portfolio Planning: Uses and Limits," *Harvard Business Review*, vol. 60, no. 1 (January-February 1982), pp. 58-73.

Hedley, Barry, "A Fundamental Approach to Strategy Development," *Long Range Planning*, vol. 9, no. 6 (December 1976), pp. 2-11.

_____, "Strategy and the Business Portfolio," *Long Range Planning*, vol. 10, no. 1 (February 1977), pp. 9-15.

Hofer, Charles W., and Schendel, Dan, *Strategy Formulation: Analytical Concepts* (St. Paul, Minnesota: West Publishing Co., 1978), Chapters 2 and 4.

Hussey, D. E., "Portfolio Analysis: Practical Experience with the Directional Policy Matrix," *Long Range Planning*, vol. 11, no. 4 (August 1978), pp. 2-8.

Kiechel, Walter, "Playing by the Rules of the Corporate Strategy Game," *Fortune* (September 24, 1979), pp. 110-18.

Koontz, Harold, "Making Strategic Planning Work," *Business Horizons*, vol. 19, no. 2 (April 1976), pp. 37-47.

Lorange, Peter, *Corporate Planning: An Executive Viewpoint* (Englewood Cliffs, N.J.: Prentice-Hall, Inc., 1980), Chapters 1-3.

Paul, Ronald N., Neil B. Donavan, and James W. Taylor, "The Reality Gap in Strategic Planning," *Harvard Business Review*, vol. 56, no. 3 (May-June 1978), pp. 124-30.

Quinn, James B., *Strategies for Change: Logical Incrementalism* (Homewood, Ill.: Richard D. Irwin, Inc., 1980).

---

[25]Ibid.

Salter, Malcolm and Wolf Weinhold, *Diversification through Acquisition* (New York: Macmillan, 1979).

Robinson, S. J. Q., R. E. Hitchens, and D. P. Wade, "The Directional Policy Matrix: Tool for Strategic Planning," *Long Range Planning*, vol. 11, no. 3 (June 1978), pp. 8-15.

Wilson, Ian H., "Environmental Scanning and Strategic Planning," *Business Environment/Public Policy: 1979 Conference Papers* (St. Louis: American Assembly of Collegiate Schools of Business, 1980), pp. 159-63.

READING

Designing Product and Business Portfolios*

YORAM WIND AND VIJAY MAHAJAN

Yoram Wind is professor of marketing and director of the Center for International Management Studies at the Wharton School, University of Pennsylvania. Vijay Mahajan is associate professor of marketing and director of the Center for Strategic Marketing at the Wharton School.

In our complex business environment, companies big and small continually assess the compatibility of their strategy for each product or service—existing or planned—with the needs, resources, and objectives of the organization. Should we be in this business? Should we add a new business? How can we win and hold a substantial share of the market?

In seeking answers to such probing questions, many companies view product mix decisions as portfolio decisions. A company offers a variety of product lines, each requiring a certain investment and promising a certain return on that investment. In this view of operations, top management's role is to determine the products (or businesses) that will comprise the portfolio and to allot funds to them on some rational basis.

A number of product portfolio models have appeared over the past several years to assist management in this task. Examples are the growth/share matrix, the business profile matrix, the business assessment array, and the directional policy matrix. *Exhibit I* classifies these four models as well as five others that have also gained acceptance. Conceptually the models differ in three ways:

- Whether the model offers a general prescriptive framework or a framework tailored to that particular company's needs and its top officers' preferences.

- The dimensions used to construct the model.

- The degree to which the model imposes rules for allocating resources among products.

Exhibit II compares the nine illustrative portfolio approaches according to these three characteristics.

The question facing management is which approach, if any, to select. To the extent that the models yield the same results (strategic guidelines), the choice may not matter much. Recently, however, one of us compared three

---

*This article is reprinted from the *Harvard Business Review*, vol. 59, no. 1 (January-February 1981), pp. 155-65. Copyright © by the President and Fellows of Harvard College. All rights reserved.

EXHIBIT I
Selected Product Portfolio Models and Approaches

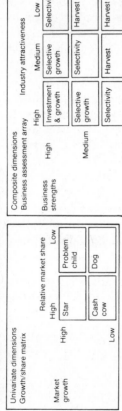

Univariate dimensions
Growth/share matrix

Market growth	Relative market share	
	High	Low
High	Star	Problem child
Low	Cash cow	Dog

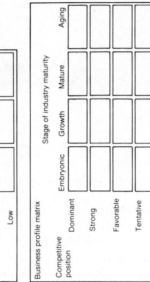

Composite dimensions
Business assessment array

Business strengths	Industry attractiveness		
	High	Medium	Low
High	Investment & growth	Selective growth	Selectivity
Medium	Selective growth	Selectivity	Harvest
Low	Selectivity	Harvest	Harvest

Business profile matrix

Competitive position	Stage of industry maturity			
	Embryonic	Growth	Mature	Aging
Dominant				
Strong				
Favorable				
Tentative				
Weak				

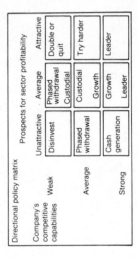

Directional policy matrix

Company's competitive capabilities	Prospects for sector profitability		
	Unattractive	Average	Attractive
Weak	Disinvest	Phased withdrawal / Custodial	Double or quit
Average	Phased withdrawal	Custodial / Growth	Try harder
Strong	Cash generation	Growth / Leader	Leader

EXHIBIT I (*concluded*)

Customized models

Financed-oriented models

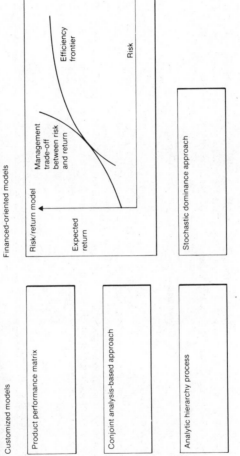

Product performance matrix

Conjoint analysis-based approach

Analytic hierarchy process

Risk/return model

Management
trade-off
between risk
and return

Expected
return

Efficiency
frontier

Risk

Stochastic dominance approach

EXHIBIT II
Key Characteristics of the Nine Portfolio Models

Growth/Share Matrix

Dimensions
1. Relative market share (cash generation).
2. Market growth (cash use).

Degree of Adaptability
None; a rigid framework.

Allocation Rules
1. Allocation of resources among the four categories (move cash to problem child).
2. Consideration for product deletion (e.g., dogs).
3. No explicit portfolio recommendations (as to the optimal mix of stars, cows, and dogs, etc.) except with respect to the balance of cash flows.

Comments
Widely used but conceptually questionable given the forcing of two dimensions, the unique operational definition, and lack of rules for determining a portfolio of dogs, stars, and so forth. No consideration of risk. No weighting of dimensions.

Business Assessment Array

Dimensions
1. Industry attractiveness.
2. Business strengths.

Each of the dimensions is a composite of a number of variables.

Degree of Adaptability
More flexible than growth/share matrix but limited to two composite dimensions.

Allocation Rules
In its basic use, it offers slightly greater precision than the growth/share matrix. (Nine cells versus four; better definition of dimensions.) In its more sophisiticated uses (as by GE), classification of products on these two dimensions in used only as input to an explicit resource allocation model.

Comments
Forcing of two dimensions that might not be the appropriate ones. Empirical determination of the correlates of the two dimensions is superior to the growth/share matrix. Yet, given the tailoring of factors to each industry, comparability across industries is difficult. No consideration of risk.

Business Profile Matrix

Dimensions
1. Competitive market position.
2. Industry maturity.

Degree of Adaptability
Same as business assessment array.

Allocation rules
Same as business assessment array.

Comments
Same as business assessment array.

Directional Policy Matrix

Dimensions
1. Profitability of market segment
2. Competitive position in the segment.

Degree of Adaptability
Same as business assessment array.

Allocation Rules
Same as business assessment array.

Comments
Same as business assessment array.

Product Performance Matrix

Degree of Adaptability

Considerable, the specific dimensions are selected by management.

Dimensions

No general dimensions; International Harvester, for example, has used four dimensions:

1. Industry sales.
2. Product sales.
3. Market share.
4. Profitability.

The data are calculated and analyzed by market segment.

Allocation rules

Some as growth/share matrix but based on *projected* results in response to alternative marketing strategies.

Comments

Applications are limited; offers the conceptual advantage of management-determined performance dimensions and allocation of resources based on projected rather than historical performance. No weighting of dimensions.

Analytic Hierarchy Process

Degree of Adaptability

Fully adaptable to management needs.

Dimensions

As with conjoint analysis, dimensions are determined by management.

Allocation Rules

Optimal allocation among all items of the portfolio, (e.g., products, market segments) is determined algorithmically.

Comments

Conceptually and mathematically very appealing, but not widely used. Allows management to evaluate strategic assumptions and allocate resources across products, market segments, and distribution networks under different scenarios. Weighting of dimensions considered.

Conjoint Analysis-Based Approach

Degree of Adaptability

Fully adaptable to management needs.

Dimensions

No general dimensions; they and their relative importance are determined by management.

Allocation Rules

Based on computer simulation which incorporates management utility functions and product performance data (supplemented by management judgment on the performance of current and new products and businesses). No optimal allocation is offered, but any portfolio can be evaluated on the basis of performance on all dimensions.

Comments

Limited applications, also time consuming. The approach is analogous to consumer choice of new products based on the relative importance of the key attributes and perception of the product's performance on these attributes.

Risk/Return Model

Degree of Adaptability

Limited. It is a theory-derived model.

Dimensions

1. Expected return (mean).
2. Risk (variance).

Allocation Rules

Determination of optimal portfolio.

Comments

Conceptually the most defensible, yet difficult to make operational for the product-portfolio decision. Limited real-world applications.

Stochastic Dominance

Degree of Adaptability

Same as risk/return model.

Dimensions

The entire distribution of return.

Allocation Rules

Same as risk/return.

Comments

Same as risk/return.

of these models and found that a set of products can be classified quite differently depending on the model adopted. And, more disturbing, product classification can also depend on the measures a model uses to construct the dimensions and evaluate the products.

The importance of the measurement aspect of portfolio analysis is evident even from a cursory examination of the diverse dimensions and definitions various approaches use. But surprisingly, most of the literature on portfolios has focused not on the fundamental issues of definition and measurement but on the selling of one approach over another and on the strategic implications of, for example, the "dog" or "cash cow" status of a certain product.

We contend that, in selecting a portfolio approach or evaluating a model already in place, management should pay more attention to the construction of the model and the likely sensitivity of the results (and hence the strategic conclusions) to the dimensions employed and their measures. The selection of the correct dimensions (and a careful evaluation of their measures) is a critical matter.

FRAMEWORK FOR DESIGN

Analysis of a product portfolio requires seven major steps:

1. Establishing the level and unit of analysis and determining what links connect them.

2. Identifying the relevant dimensions, including single-variable and composite.

3. Determining the relative importance of the dimensions.

4. To the extent that two or more dimensions are viewed as dominant, constructing a matrix based on them.

5. Locating the products or businesses on the relevant portfolio dimensions.

6. Projecting the likely position of each product or business on the dimensions if (a) no changes are expected in environmental conditions, competitive activities, or the company's strategies and if (b) changes *are* expected.

7. Selecting the desired position for each existing and new product (as a basis for developing alternative strategies to close the gap between the current and new portfolios) and deciding how resources might best be allocated among these products.

Not present, the reader will notice, is the strategy recommendations step. Despite their attractiveness as a ready cure for any ailment, standardized guidelines such as "all-out push for share" and "hold position" are very dangerous. If a prescription ignores any relevant dimensions or the projected position of the business under alternative scenarios, it will be quite misleading. Portfolio analysis can be an effective vehicle for analyzing and evaluating strategic options only if it exploits management's creativity and imagination—instead of conforming to some general prescription.

Establishment of the Level & Unit

At what level of the organization should the analysis be conducted? Ideally, at all the strategic business levels. And at the lowest level it should include each product (by its positioning, if possible) by market segment. Such thoroughness, however, takes much management time and requires huge quantities of data.

On the other hand, the aggregation of product-market segments may mean that they fall into a misleading "average" position in the portfolio, which, in turn, may cause inappropriate strategy designation. Consider the case of a manufacturer of (among other products) shampoo, shaving cream, bath soap, toothpaste, and other personal care items for which a single strategic business unit (SBU) is responsible. The company has constructed a growth/share matrix designating this SBU as a cash cow. Now, clearly this designation may be inappropriate for each line in the product mix and, further, for each item in the line. So aggregation may lead to erroneous positioning in the portfolio matrix as well as to poor resource allocation and strategy recommendations.

A hierarchical structure of portfolios would start at the level of the product line (or product group or division), proceed through the product mix of one SBU to the mix of several SBUs, and culminate at the corporate level, which would, of course, include all lower-level portfolios. This would permit evaluation of relevant strategies at the different levels of analysis and assist in designation and allocation of resources to SBUs and product lines. General Electric has a five-level portfolio approach: product, product line, market segment, SBU, and business sector.

Whereas such a hierarchy represents a considerable improvement over a single portfolio for the entire company, the complexities of modern business, particularly with respect to competition among large corporations (increasingly on a global basis), suggest the need for development of a dual hierarchy—a domestic hierarchy plus a worldwide one. Furthermore, both hierarchies should be examined not only according to patterns of competition among brands and businesses but also according to potential cooperation. That is, the company should ask itself: Which companies or businesses should we consider as candidates for merger or acquisition?

Related to the analysis level is the desired extent of market segmentation and product positioning. Portfolio analysis should be undertaken first in every relevant market segment and product position, then at higher levels across the positionings of the various product-market segments, and finally—if the company is multinational—across countries and modes of entry (such as export, licensing, and joint ventures).

The issue here is: When does it become meaningful to divide the total market into segments? And when to divide the products into specific positionings? The answers become complicated when the market boundaries cannot be identified easily. The risk of aggregating market segments and product positionings is high. Detailed positioning/segment-level portfolio analysis is necessary for higher-level portfolio examination. Without it, the value of recommendations for corporate-level portfolios is questionable, especially when the units are heterogeneous with respect to their perceived positioning and intended market segments.

According to one authority, segmentation should be limited to grouping those buyers who share strategically relevant situational or behavioral characteristics. (In such cases the company must use different marketing mixes to serve the identified segments, which will result in different cost and price structures.) Other manifestations of a strategically important segment boundary are a discontinuity in growth rates, share patterns, distribution patterns, and so forth.[1]

The marketer must take into account consumers' perceptions, their preference for and usage of the various products, their desire for variety, their inventorying activity (for example, hoarding when they expect a price increase), and the multiperson nature of consumption in most households. Traditional approaches to portfolio analysis tend to ignore the consumer and concentrate on product performance. The two focuses of analysis are not alternatives but complementary diagnostic tools.

After adding the second dimension of investigation—markets—to its portfolio analysis, management should evaluate and then settle on the most attractive combination of products and markets. Identification of a product-market portfolio and subsequent selection of the target markets and products are consistent with the concept and findings of market segmentation, which suggest that the demand for any product varies by segment. Resource allocation decisions should not be limited, therefore, only to allocation among products; they should also take into account the trade-offs of investing in various market segments.

In cases where the distribution system figures importantly in the company's marketing mix, management can extend the analysis to include distribution as a third dimension. Of course, acquisition or development of new distribution outlets is often used to improve a company's portfolio.

As a rule, the portfolio should be constructed to include all major options management has for using its resources. The company, however, may not

---

[1] See George S. Day, "Diagnosing the Product Portfolio," *Journal of Marketing*, April 1977, p. 29.

be organized in terms of resource allocation units. If it isn't, it should consider reorganizing so that resource allocation needs will match portfolio levels and units.

Identification of the Dimensions

The most common portfolio approach is based on the dimensions of market share and market growth. In contrast, the directional policy matrix is based on sector profitability and competitive position, while the product performance matrix allows selection of other dimensions as management deems appropriate.

The four standardized portfolio models rely on a matrix in which one axis represents the strength of the product or business in terms of market share or some broader characteristic while the other represents industry or market attractiveness. These models use two approaches to measure the axes: one relying on a single measurable criterion along each axis (for example, relative market share and market growth), the other using composite measures consisting of a number of objective and subjective factors to label each axis (for example, business strengths and industry attractiveness).

The factors defining the composite dimensions naturally vary among companies and even (though not often) among different businesses of the same company. Furthermore, the factors can change over time. In 1980 GE reduced its original 40 factors to 15. Six of these factors define industry attractiveness—market size, growth, profitability, cyclicality, ability to recover from inflation, and world scope—while nine define business strengths. Business strengths, in turn, have two components: market position (domestic market share, world share, share growth, and share compared with the leading competing brand) and competitive strength, defined according to leadership in five respects (quality, technology, cost, marketing, and relative profitability).

The members of top management who select the portfolio dimensions naturally assume that they are choosing dimensions related to their corporate (and hence portfolio) objectives. Unfortunately, justification for this assumption is often unconvincing or hard to document.

Consider the market share dimension. Its inclusion in product portfolio models reflects the general acceptance of the relationship of share with competitive strength, with profitability, and with the market response function. Indeed, research for the PIMS (profit impact of market strategy) project, which examines the correlates of profitability in the modern corporation, found businesses with large market shares to be more profitable than those with small shares.[2]

---

[2]Sidney Schoeffler, Robert D. Buzzell, and Donald F. Heany, "Impact of Strategic Planning on Profit Performance," *Harvard Business Review*, March-April 1974, p. 137.

This correlation is not perfect, however, and its causes are not completely understood. Is it due to the benefits of the learning curve, with respect to both product and marketing economies of scale for large-share businesses, or due to the fact that many large-share products compete on a nonprice basis and hence command higher margins and profits?

Moreover, studies of industries—for example, brewers and banks—have contradicted the positive relationship between share and profitability found by PIMS.[3] Also, a number of banks that reduced their unprofitable segments thereby boosted their profitability. Whatever the relationship between market share and profit, it is important to examine not only the relationship between share (and its measures) and profitability but also the relationship between a change in share (that is, investment in share) and a change in the resulting profitability.

The connection between market share and the product's market response function is even less understood. Supposedly, a dollar increase in the marketing effort for a low-share brand will yield a smaller return than that achieved by a dollar increase in the marketing effort for a large-share brand.

This supposed relationship, illustrated in *Exhibit III*, assumes that the low-share brand will have lower sales at zero incremental marketing effort, a lower saturation level, and probably also a less effective marketing effort (a gentler slope of the response function). Why? Because a larger-share brand can achieve greater economies of scale and because the advertising and other marketing efforts of well-known, high-share brands often spill over to benefit less-familiar brands.

If this relationship does exist, the marketer of a low-share brand must work harder to differentiate that brand. This relationship further suggests the importance of assessing the response elasticities of the company's various brands and, if it is not closely correlated with another portfolio dimension, adopting elasticity as one of the portfolio dimensions.

Operational Definitions

Before settling on an existing product portfolio model or designing a new one, management must define the dimensions selected. The importance of operational definitions for the chosen dimensions, both single-variable and composite, should not be underestimated. They could significantly alter results.

---

[3]Dan E. Schendel and G. Richard Patton, "A Simultaneous Equation Model of Corporate Strategy," *Management Science*, November 1978, p. 1611; and Jean-Claude Larreche, "On Limitations of Positive Market Share-Profitability Relationships: The Case of the French Banking Industry," *1980 Educators' Conference Proceedings* (Chicago: American Marketing Association, 1980), p. 209.

EXHIBIT III
Hypothesized Relationship Between Market Share and Market Response Function for Competing Brands

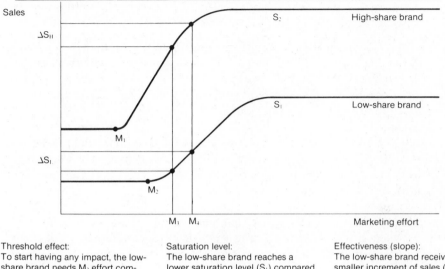

Threshold effect:
To start having any impact, the low-share brand needs M_2 effort compared with the lower level (M_1) required by the high-share brand.

Saturation level:
The low-share brand reaches a lower saturation level (S_1) compared with the high-share brand (S_2).

Effectiveness (slope):
The low-share brand receives a smaller increment of sales (ΔS_1) than that of the high-share brand (ΔS_{11}) for each one-unit increase in marketing effort (a move from M_3 to M_4).

Single-variable dimensions: Take account of a relative share measure, such as the one employed in the growth/share matrix (the most notable example of measurement of single-variable dimensions), and then compare it with other possible share measures based on:

1. Different units of measurement, such as dollar sales, unit sales, units purchased, or users.

2. Product definition (product lines and brands in various sizes, forms, and positionings).

3. Definition of the served market that defines the competitive arena (competitors, customers, and technology) within which the product is sold, including markets defined in terms of geography, channel, customer segment, or usage occasion.

4. The time horizon involved.

5. The nature of the denominator in the share calculation. Usually the definition of the denominator is based on either: (a) all the brands in the particular market, whether defined by the product category or preferably the perceived position of the brand; or (b) a selected number of

brands—an option that includes all brands within a subcategory (like national brands), the leading competitor, or the leading two or three competitors. A third approach, less popular but conceptually more defensible, defines the denominator on the basis of all products serving the same consumer need or solving the same problem.

Clearly a marketer must make some critical decisions before selecting a definition of market share. Similar complexity faces him with the definition of any dimension. Think of product sales, of which there are at least four measures: absolute level, rate of growth, level by industry or by product class, and industry or product class rate of growth.

Whatever measure is used, it is necessary to establish the relevant instrument in terms of units (such as dollar sales or unit sales), necessary adjustments (such as per capita sales), time (such as quarterly or annually), and data sources used (such as company shipments, wholesale and retail audits, or consumer diaries and reports).

Different yardsticks can, of course, produce different results. A pharmaceutical manufacturer found that sales generated by a promotion varied from success to failure depending on the data used—company shipments, physician panel, drugstore survey, and third-party payments. It is essential, therefore, that top management understand the selected measures and their properties.

Composite dimensions: Several portfolio models use composite dimensions to designate the matrix axes. The business assessment array, for example, labels one axis "business strengths" and the other "industry attractiveness." Each is a composite of a number of objective and subjective factors. The rationale is that the factors and their relative importance depend mainly on customer behavior, the nature of the product, the industry, the characteristics of the company, and the preference of its management.

Unlike the growth/share matrix approach, portfolio models using composite dimensions rely heavily on managerial judgment to identify the relevant factors and determine their relative importance. Identifying those factors requires assumptions about the relationships among them and how they will change over time. This process has the healthy result of nurturing strategic thinking, but unlike the growth/share matrix framework, it makes considerable demands on management's time.

Composite-dimension models have other limitations:

• They may mask important differences among products. Suppose a manufacturer evaluates three products on a composite dimension (say, business strengths) consisting of two factors. The scale is 1 (low) to 10 (high). The results might be like those in *Exhibit IV*. Obviously the performance characteristics differ markedly. Yet on this particular composite dimension (assuming equal weight for the two factors) the products would be assigned identical positions in the portfolio matrix.

EXHIBIT IV
Two-Factor Rating of Three Products

	Market Share Rating	Product Technology Rating	Composite Dimension Score
Product A	9	1	10
Product B	1	9	10
Product C	5	5	10

- The subjective evaluation that is to an extent necessary raises questions as to who the respondents should be or how any discrepancy in their evaluations should be treated. Should we seek consensus, as in a Delphi approach? Or would any lack of consensus suggest the need to weight the judges' views according to their expertise or importance? Should we even exclude the disputed factor from the analysis?

- A weighting system that does not take into account close correlations among factors can produce a misleading product classification. This will hold true even if no weights are used to obtain the composite score. In this case, if the company employs five measures of sales and one measure of product technology to define business strengths, the relative weight of the two factors is not equal but 5 to 1.

- If the weights of the factors that are combined to develop a composite measure are to be determined empirically, based on the historical relationships among the factors, the calculation imposes heavy data requirements because of the type of statistical analysis required—like multiple regression analysis (if a dependent variable can be identified) or factor analysis.

Determination of Relative Importance

Most portfolio matrices, like the growth/share approach, assume equal weight for the dimensions. As we said, in composite dimensions the factors are often weighted, but rarely are differential weights placed on the two major dimensions that constitute the matrix.

In contrast, most customized portfolio models, the analytic hierarchy process (AHP) for one, allow for management's assessment of weights. Conjoint analysis has been used in the design of other customized portfolio models as a way of assessing weights assigned to the risk/return dimensions and other relevant dimensions.

To the extent that weighting calls for subjective evaluation, management must decide who the evaluators will be and how conflict among them will be resolved. These decisions cannot be left to staff members involved in the construction or implementation of the portfolio.

Construction of the Portfolio Matrix

Portfolio models differ in the degree to which they offer a general, rigid, and normative framework or a flexible format reflecting the user's characteristics. The growth/share framework is the most rigid, followed by the risk/return model (which takes into account differences in managers' trade-offs between risk and return). Both the directional policy matrix and the product performance matrix are flexible—the former in the factors determining the dimensions and the latter in the number and definition of the dimensions.

The simplicity of a 2x2 or 3x3 matrix makes it very attractive. It is easy to communicate and it is typically accompanied by some generalized strategic guidelines. But it becomes simplistic and misleading if (a) it ignores major dimensions and the conditions under which the recommended strategy is most likely to be effective or if (b) the grouping of continuous variables, like market share or growth, into two or three categories leads to loss of pertinent information.

Limitations like these make portfolio models not in matrix form attractive. The AHP, the most recently developed model, uses a hierarchical structure and permits complete flexibility in selecting dimensions. The risk-return approach relies on generation of efficient frontiers graphically or mathematically.

LOCATION IN THE PORTFOLIO

In any portfolio analysis, the most time-consuming task is the collection of data on the products or other items in the portfolio and on their performance in terms of the selected dimensions. This evaluation requires hard data from company records (for instance, on sales and profitability) and from outside sources (for instance, market share, industry growth, and perceived positioning). And of course there is the key element of management's judgment.

Care should be given to collecting valid data. If the company uses consumer surveys, it should examine the projectability of the sample and the accuracy of the measurement instruments. Naturally, obtaining data and measures from several sources will help safeguard the reliability of the data.

PROJECTION OF THE PRODUCT POSITION

In analysis of the positions of products in the portfolio, should the dimensions be measured only on the basis of historical data or should they also reflect projected positions? Most product portfolio models rely on historical data.

Measuring, say, the sales growth rate in terms of the historical growth rate in the past x years is satisfactory if that growth rate is expected to continue. If, however, the company anticipates deviation from it, the historical data should be supplemented with projected performance and, where possible, conditional forecasts. Such forecasts—also used in the product performance matrix approach—consist of, for example, a series of projections conditional on certain marketing activities.

A corporation can also forecast performance for a number of environmental scenarios. The analysis should include at least three scenarios: (1) continuation of the current trend, (2) a scenario in which all environmental, market, and competitive conditions are favorable, and (3) a disaster scenario. Sensitivity analyses for both the short and long term can ascertain the sensitivity of results to these (and perhaps other) scenarios. General Electric, Monsanto, Shell Oil, and Atlantic Richfield, among other companies, use scenarios in strategy formulation.[4]

A variety of econometric forecasting procedures are in use for projecting the performance of existing products. Simulated test market is one of the new-product forecasting models available.

At this stage, management evaluates the projection procedure and the likely future scenarios. As evaluators, the executives should be asking such questions as: Do the assumptions of the approach make sense? Do the projections meet our expectations? As devil's advocates, they can help those designing the portfolio to make sense out of the approach and the projections.

SELECTION OF THE DESIRED PORTFOLIO

It goes without saying that the most critical aspect in portfolio analysis is a decision on what changes, if any, are necessary. Unfortunately, most of the standard portfolio models do not offer explicit guidelines for establishing an optimal portfolio. For example, classifying certain products as dogs, problem children, cash cows, and stars does not help determine their optimal mix.

Obviously management wants many stars and no dogs. Yet in many cases the cash cows, not the stars, provide the funds necessary to fuel growth and yield profits. Furthermore, at times dogs may be essential as insurance against the risk of certain contingencies. A multinational may cherish its foreign dogs as hedges against currency fluctuations, likely government restrictions, or materials shortages.

The standardized portfolio models are useful primarily for analyzing

---

[4]For a description of how GE uses environmental scenarios for this purpose, see Ian H. Wilson, "Reforming the Strategic Planning Process: Integration of Social and Business Needs," *Long Range Planning*, October 1974, p. 2.

the relationships among business units and products. They do not offer answers to questions like: When should a cash cow be milked of its cash? When should a dog be disposed of? Which stars should be selected for investment and which de-emphasized? At the same time, by suggesting simple strategies such as "harvesting," the standard models may constrain management's motivation to try alternative solutions like repositioning products or developing new domestic or international market segments.

Furthermore, most of the current portfolio models, designed to accommodate existing product-market relationships, lack guidelines to deal with corporate directional changes. These models do not answer such questions as: How can we convert a problem child to a star? How can we find new stars? What characteristics should a new product line have to balance the company's portfolio?

Sometimes the way the portfolio model is constructed suggests an unwise change. Conceivably, for example, a low-market share business in a low-growth market may be very attractive in cash flow terms if it is also low in capital intensity. Since the growth/share matrix does not explicitly consider capital intensity, a dog may be inappropriately considered a candidate for divestment.[5] Similarly, a business identified as high in market attractiveness that also has a strong position in the business assessment array could produce a good ROI but not a good cash flow.

In shaping the portfolio, top officers should not leave the generation of strategy options to the staff. Often top managers prefer to position themselves as evaluators, but their involvement in the creative process is critical to the enterprise. The staff members who develop the portfolio should incorporate a resource allocation procedure to guide management in apportioning financial and material resources among the existing and new portfolio parts.

In a portfolio context there are two approaches to resource allocation:

- General Electric's approach, which uses GE's business assessment array as a product classification device. The company combines information from this process with other data to build a resource allocation model.

- The analytic hierarchy model, which includes a resource allotment algorithm in the portfolio model.

WHAT KIND OF APPROACH?

Since its emergence in the early 1970s, the portfolio technique—along with related concepts like the SBU and the experience curve—has become the framework for strategic planning in many diversified companies. Now the art has advanced enough to give a diversified company a variety of

---

[5]See Derek F. Channon, "Commentary on Strategy Formulation," in Dan E. Schendel and Charles W. Hofer, eds., *Strategic Management* (Boston: Little, Brown, 1979).

approaches when it is considering installing such a system or substituting one that evidently meets its needs better than the current portfolio.

Conceptually, we think, the tailor-made approaches are superior because they:

- Permit inclusion of the conceptually desirable dimensions of risk and return, plus any other idiosyncratic elements viewed by management as important.
- Stimulate creativity by forcing management's involvement in developing strategic options.
- Help to gain an advantage over competitors, who are ignorant of the company's portfolio framework and so cannot "read" it with the aim of anticipating the company's strategic moves.
- Can offer explicit guidelines for resource allocation among the portfolio items.

But a tailor-made system costs more, mainly in data requirements and management time. Even if top management decides not to implement an idiosyncratic approach (based on a cost-benefit analysis), an evaluation of currently used portfolio models, using the seven steps we have described, should add to the value of the portfolio analysis and the quality of the strategies designed to build a new portfolio.

ANALYZING AND EVALUATING LINE OF BUSINESS STRATEGY

5

The best way for a firm to be lucky is to make its own luck. That requires knowing what makes a business successful.

Theodore Levitt

Tomorrow's competitive environment is of more import than today's.

Anonymous

Once a "go" decision has been reached on continuing in or entering a particular industry, the action and work of strategy analysis and evaluation shifts to the business-unit level and below. It is at the line of business level that one finds the real bread and butter of strategic analysis. Accurately appraising business strategy requires in-depth understanding of what makes a business successful and a size-up of what it will take to keep the business successful in the future. This chapter examines the essentials of conducting a full-scale business strategy evaluation.

THE ESSENTIAL ELEMENTS OF BUSINESS STRATEGY EVALUATION

Assessing whether and how a firm's present line of business strategy can be improved entails a host of considerations. To be comprehensive, strategy analysis at the business level needs to be conducted on three fronts:

1. *An examination of industry conditions and characteristics*—The specific analytical objectives here are to ascertain or confirm (a) the strategically relevant features of the industry's structure, (b) the direction the industry is headed and the forces pushing it in this direction, (c) the underlying economics of the business, with emphasis on how a firm makes money in the business and the particular skills and competencies required for market success, and (d) what strategic issues and problems are confronting the industry and must be dealt with.

2. *An analysis of competition and key competitors*—Here the focus is on getting answers to three key strategic questions: (a) What are the forces driving competition in the industry? (b) How do the competitive approaches of rival firms differ? and (c) What are the competitive positions and relative competitive strengths of key rivals (what are their strategies and how well are they working)?

3. *An assessment of the firm's own present business situation*—The aim of this analytical piece is to size-up (a) the firm's internal strengths and weaknesses, (b) its external opportunities and threats, (c) the pluses and minuses in its competitive market position—is the firm gaining ground or losing out and why, (d) how well the present business and functional area strategies are working and why, and (e) any special strategic issues and problems unique to the firm and its business.

Out of these analyses should come a clearer picture of what the firm's strategic options are and what it can do better and/or do different to improve upon its market position and overall business performance. The indicated changes thus become the new and revised strategic game plan for the business.

Figure 5-1 presents a schematic of this approach to strategy evaluation at the business level. The remainder of this chapter is devoted to describing and explaining this analytical process.

Identifying the Present Strategy

In an ongoing business, strategy evaluation logically begins with what the present strategy is. As is the case with corporate strategy, identification of the current strategy of a business-unit entails sorting out what management has said the strategy is, the firm's actual behavior in the marketplace, and various plans and actions in the main functional areas of the business. In a new start-up situation, the evaluation process is, of course, aimed at what the strategy of the business ought to be; since there is no existing strategy, the analysis can usefully begin with what the preliminary strategic plan for the business is. In either instance, it is important for the strategic game plan to be completely identified and fully understood.

FIGURE 5-1
Framework for Analyzing and Evaluating Business-Level Strategy

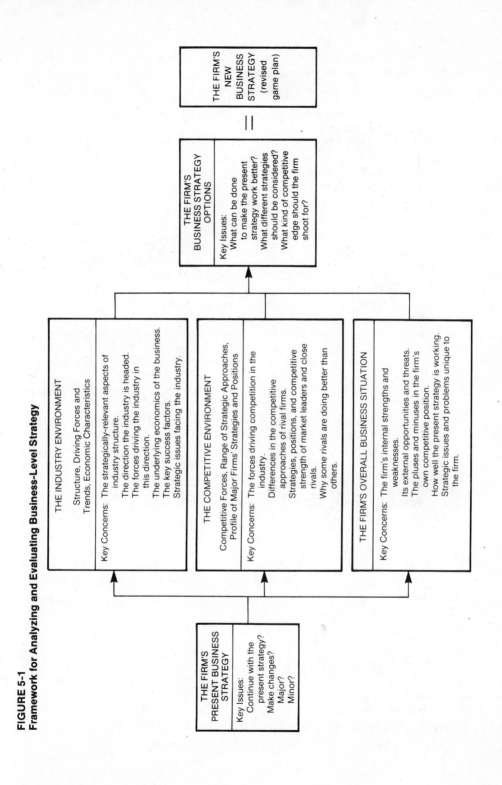

THE INDUSTRY ENVIRONMENT

Structure, Driving Forces and Trends, Economic Characteristics

Key Concerns: The strategically-relevant aspects of industry structure.
The direction the industry is headed.
The forces driving the industry in this direction.
The underlying economics of the business.
The key success factors.
Strategic issues facing the industry.

THE COMPETITIVE ENVIRONMENT

Competitive Forces, Range of Strategic Approaches, Profile of Major Firms' Strategies and Positions

Key Concerns: The forces driving competition in the industry.
Differences in the competitive approaches of rival firms.
Strategies, positions, and competitive strength of market leaders and close rivals.
Why some rivals are doing better than others.

THE FIRM'S OVERALL BUSINESS SITUATION

Key Concerns: The firm's internal strengths and weaknesses.
Its external opportunities and threats.
The pluses and minuses in the firm's own competitive position.
How well the present strategy is working.
Strategic issues and problems unique to the firm.

THE FIRM'S PRESENT BUSINESS STRATEGY

Key Issues:
Continue with the present strategy?
Make changes?
Major?
Minor?

THE FIRM'S BUSINESS STRATEGY OPTIONS

Key Issues:
What can be done to make the present strategy work better?
What different strategies should be considered?
What kind of competitive edge should the firm shoot for?

=

THE FIRM'S NEW BUSINESS STRATEGY (revised game plan)

ILLUSTRATION CAPSULE 17
A Failure in Business Strategy Evaluation

Recently, Greyhound and Trailways took on one another in a fierce and profitless strategic maneuver over passenger bus fares. Greyhound, in an effort to boost passenger traffic on its intercity bus routes, in early 1978 announced a $50 fare applying to all trips extending more than 1,000 miles. Trailways responded with a series of commercials on national television proclaiming the cheapest rates from New York to Los Angeles.

However, the promotional war drew in little new business, mainly because it took no account of the changing market for intercity bus service. The reduced fares were aimed at long-distance travelers—despite the fact that fewer than 5 percent of all bus passengers ride 1,000 miles or more. Most of the passenger market for distances over 500 miles is captured by the airlines. Even though air fares are roughly 50 percent higher than bus fares, the travel time is much less on long trips. For instance, at the height of the Greyhound-Trailways price war, the lowest one-way bus fare from Chicago to Miami was $69 and involved travel time of a day and a half; by airplane the fare was $99 and flight time was two and a half-hours—a comparison which pinpoints the strategic folly of the bus lines' attempt to attract long-distance business.

At the same time, both Trailways and Greyhound failed to focus their business strategy on the short-haul market of less than 200 miles, the segment containing 40 percent of all intercity travel. Moreover, they ignored the airlines' long-standing and successful strategy of structuring their routes into networks of short-haul markets, where each major city serves as the hub of spokes or corridor routes radiating out for 100-200 miles to smaller cities and other key hubs. Instead, buses were often run on a continuing schedule from one end of the country to the other, passing through many metropolitan areas in the middle of the night and not during prime-time travel hours.

Source: Rush Loving, Jr., "The Bus Lines Are on the Road to Nowhere," *Fortune* (December 31, 1978), pp. 58-64.

Figure 5-2 depicts the primary components of business strategy. Profiling the main features and characteristics for each "spoke" on the "strategic wheel" ought to yield a fairly thorough overall picture of a firm's present business strategy.

CONDUCTING AN INDUSTRY ANALYSIS

The first thing to understand in conducting an "industry analysis" is that the objective is *not* to just "look for anything one can find" about the industry. For the purposes of evaluating business strategy, industry analysis should be kept trained on four key strategic questions:

FIGURE 5-2
Angles from which to Determine and Evaluate Business Strategy

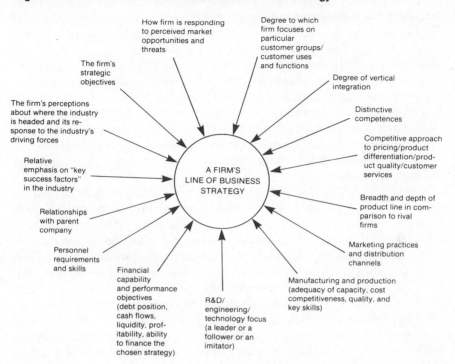

1.   What are the strategically relevant aspects of the industry's structure?
2.   What direction is the industry headed and what forces are driving it in this direction?
3.   What are the underlying economics of the business—most particularly what must a firm know and do well to make money in this business?
4.   What are the strategic issues and problems facing the industry?

The ultimate purposes of an industry analysis are (1) to identify and understand the *key success factors* for competing in the industry and (2) to help select a business strategy that will "best" position the firm in its target market environment.

The Structure of the Industry

Understanding industry structure is the logical starting point for strategic analysis at the business level. As a working definition, we shall use the word "industry" to refer to a group of firms whose products are sufficiently close substitutes for each other that the member firms are drawn into competitive rivalry to serve much the same needs of some or all of the same types of buyers. The raw data for analyzing industry structure are fairly standard: the number of sellers and their relative sizes, who the market leaders are and the extent to which they dominate the market, who the buyers are and the structure of the buying side of the market, what the channels of distribution are from manufacturer to final user, the prevalence of backward and forward integration within the industry, the ease of entry and exit, the size of the industry and its geographical boundaries (local, regional, national, or international), and any other basic characteristics (peculiar to the industry in question) that shape the industry arena in which firms compete. This information provides a general industry overview but, more importantly, it lays the groundwork for a strategic examination of industry structure.

One such examination is *strategic cluster analysis*. This type of analysis stems from the fact that while all firms in an industry do indeed compete with each other, each seller usually competes more intensely with some rivals than with others; in addition, there may exist some important strategic features which are common to some firms but not others. Such characteristics allow for an industry to be subdivided into *strategic clusters*.[1] A strategic cluster can be thought of as a group of similar-type firms—they have many business features in common and they approach the marketplace in the same *general* way (with comparable strategies and with much the same kinds of product line, distribution network, pricing policy, and so on). An industry contains only one strategic cluster when all the member firms approach the market in comparable ways and, at the other extreme, each firm constitutes its own strategic cluster when the market approaches and strategies of every firm all differ in essential respects. The appliance industry, for example, contains three identifiable strategic groups.[2] One cluster (composed of such firms as GE, Hotpoint, and Whirlpool) have broad product lines, heavy national advertising, extensive vertical integration, and an established network of distributors and dealers. Another cluster consists of limited product line or specialist firms (like Amana, Maytag, Kitchen Aid, and Thermidor) which focus on the high-quality, high-price market segment with selective distribution. A third cluster, consisting of firms like Roper and Design and Manufacturing, concentrate on producing unadvertised products for private label.

The concept of strategic clusters is relevant from several industry angles:

1. Because of their similar strategic approaches and business features, firms in the same strategic group tend to be affected by and respond

---

[1] Michael E. Porter, *Competitive Strategy: Techniques for Analyzing Industries and Competitors* (New York: The Free Press, 1980), p. 129.
[2] Ibid., pp. 129-130.

similarly to external events and to the competitive moves of rival firms.[3] Strategic cluster analysis is thus helpful in predicting responses and reactions of the industry to key events and trends.

2. The profit potential of firms in different strategic clusters is often quite different because competitive forces do not have equal impact on different strategic groups.[4] Industry structure analysis can pinpoint groups of firms whose position is tenuous or marginal; firms in marginal groups are candidates for exit or for launching strategic attempts to move into another strategic cluster.

3. Entry barriers depend upon the particular strategic cluster that the entrant seeks to join.[5]

4. Firms in different strategic clusters often enjoy differing degrees of bargaining power with suppliers and/or with customers and they may also face differing degrees of exposure to competition from substitute products outside the industry.[6]

5. The existence of multiple strategic clusters generally increases competitive rivalry in the industry because there is both intragroup and intergroup rivalry and because the greater diversity among competitive strategies tends to increase the likelihood that one or more firms will initiate "aggressive" competitive moves that, in turn, provoke retaliation.[7]

6. The greater the "distance" among the strategic clusters, the more vigorous the competitive skirmishing among the firms tends to be; this is because firms pursuing widely different strategic approaches tend to have quite different ideas about how to compete, thus opening more room for them to misunderstand and/or disagree with each others' tactical moves.[8]

7. Industry trends often have different implications for different strategic clusters.[9] It is worth thinking through each industry trend to explore (a) whether the trend is closing off the viability of one or more strategic groups and, if so, where will firms in the affected groups shift, (b) whether the trend will raise/lower the entry barriers into a cluster and the degree to which competitive pressures in the cluster will be increased/decreased, and (c) how the firms in each cluster will otherwise be affected by the trend and their probable response to the trend.

[3]Ibid., p. 130.
[4]Ibid., pp. 132 and 154.
[5]Ibid., pp. 136-137.
[6]Ibid., pp. 136-137.
[7]Ibid., p. 138.
[8]Ibid., p. 140.
[9]Ibid., pp. 154-155.

In addition, the insights gained from profiling the strategic groups in the industry raises some key questions about the course the firm's business strategy ought to take: Is there opportunity for the firm to employ a strategy that will create a new strategic group (as did Hanes in creating an entirely new group in hosiery with its L'eggs strategy)? Should the firm shift to a more favorably situated strategic cluster? Should the firm pursue a business strategy that will strengthen its position within its present strategic group? Should the firm shift to a new cluster and try to strengthen that cluster's structural position in the industry?

Where the Industry Is Headed—The Driving Forces

Although analysis of industry structure provides a perspective and a framework for developing business strategy, there is a need for further industrywide probing. Industry structures change, often in fundamental ways. Moreover, some industries go through evolutionary phases or stages—development, growth, shakeout, maturity, saturation, and decline, the so-called industry/product life cycle. Understanding where an industry is headed and what forces are driving the changes takes on critical importance in evaluating business strategy. Fundamental changes in the industry affect long-run investment opportunities and they often require firms to make strategic adjustments.

Whether industries can be depended upon to evolve neatly according to the familiar life cycle pattern is debatable.[10] Sometimes industries skip maturity, passing from growth to decline very quickly. Sometimes growth reappears after a period of decline, as has occurred in the radio broadcasting, bicycle, and motorcycle industries. In addition, companies can influence both the length of the growth phase and the rate of industry growth through product innovation and product repositioning.[11] Because of these facets, the duration of the stages varies from industry to industry, and it is often unclear just what stage of the cycle an industry is in. A basic problem with the industry life cycle hypothesis as a *predictor* of where an industry is headed is that it poses only *one* pattern of evolution. In actuality, there can be several patterns and, further, the length of each phase of evolution is variable and uncertain. Nothing in the life cycle hypothesis permits reliable prediction as to when the cycle pattern will hold, when it will not, and how long the phases will last.

Hence, while it is worthwhile to be alert to signs as to where the industry might be in the cycle, it is more fruitful to search out what forces are driving the industry to change. *Industries evolve because some forces are in motion*

---

[10]For a more extended discussion of this point, see Porter, *Competitive Strategy*, pp. 157-162.

[11]For a discussion of how firms can accomplish this, see Theodore Levitt, "Exploit the Product Life Cycle," *Harvard Business Review*, vol. 43, no. 6 (November-December 1965), pp. 81-94.

that create incentives or pressures for change.[12] These can be called *the industry's driving forces.* The driving forces work to push the current industry structure into a new structure and they usually create new kinds of competitive pressures—both of which have implications for business strategy.

There are numerous types of driving forces which can exist to produce evolutionary changes in an industry:[13]

- *Changes in the long-term industry growth rate*—The rate at which an industry is growing is a powerful force for structural and strategic changes. It is a key variable in investment decisions to expand capacity and at least maintain market share; it influences the balance between industry supply and buyer demand; and it affects the intensity of competition. The long-term industry growth rate can change because of (1) changing buyer demographics (this is especially important in consumer goods industries), (2) trends in the need for and usage of the industry's products (rising property theft, for instance, has triggered increased demand for security alarms, safes, guards, and locks), (3) lower prices and/or new availability of substitute and/or complementary products, (4) a leveling off of demand owing to almost complete penetration of the *new* customer market (sales and growth then become a function of replacement demand), and (5) product innovation.

- *Changes in buyer composition*—Increases or decreases in the kinds of customers who purchase the product have potential for changing customer service requirements (credit, technical services, maintenance and repair), creating a need to alter distribution channels, and precipitating broader/narrower product lines, increased/decreased capital requirements, and different marketing practices. The hand calculator industry became a different market requiring different strategies when students and households began to use them as well as engineers and scientists. Trying to ascertain the kinds of industry change to expect should, therefore, include an assessment of potential new buyer segments and their characteristics.

- *Product innovation*—Product innovations can broaden the market, promote industry growth, and enhance product differentiation among rival sellers. When an industry is characterized by rapid product introduction, product innovation is sure to be a key driving force—one that not only shapes what the industry's products are and will be but also impacts manufacturing methods, economies of scale, marketing costs and practices, and distribution. A classic example is the computer industry where new generations of computers are regularly introduced to appeal to new buyer groups (the minicomputers for small businesses

---

[12]Porter, *Competitive Strategy*, p. 162.
[13]Porter, *Competitive Strategy*, pp. 164-183.

and the personal computer for home use are the most recent of these) and to enlarge the "computing power" beyond that of existing products. Other industries where product innovation is a key driving force include copying equipment, cameras and photography equipment, and electronic video games.

- *Process innovation*—Frequent and important technological advances in manufacturing methods can likewise have a powerful impact on an industry. Rapid changes in manufacturing technology can dramatically alter unit costs, capital requirements, minimum efficient plant sizes, the desirability of vertical integration, and experience curve effects. All of these are capable of producing important industry changes and creating a need for revisions in business strategy.

- *Marketing innovation*—The new ways that firms discover to market their products can sometimes revolutionize an industry. The shift in marketing wine from low-key magazine advertising to network television produced major gains in sales for wine and greatly increased the strategic position of large wineries with national distribution vis-a-vis small family wineries specializing in premium wines for local and regional markets. Breakthroughs in the use of new media (advertising movies on TV), introduction of new advertising themes, discovery of new points of difference among products which can be exploited (less sugar or caffeine), the use of new distribution channels (the classic Timex decision to market low-priced watches through drugstores and discount outlets rather than the traditional jewelry store) can widen demand, increase product differentiation, and/or lower unit costs, thus setting in motion new forces to alter the industry and the strategies of participant firms.

- *Entry and exit of major firms*—The entry of Philip Morris into beer and soft drinks and of Coca-Cola into wine proved to be important new driving forces because they resulted in the introduction of new marketing skills and financial resources that were applied to change competition and industry marketing practices. When an established firm from another industry enters a new market, it usually brings with it new ideas and perceptions about how its skills and resources can be innovatively applied. Hence the entry of a large and different type of firm can result in a "new ballgame" with new rules and new key players. Similarly, exit of a major firm changes industry structure by reducing the number of market leaders and perhaps increasing the dominance of the leaders who remain.

- *Diffusion of proprietary knowledge*—As a technology becomes more established and knowledge about it spreads through the conduits of rival firms, suppliers, distributors, and customers, the advantage held by firms with proprietary technology erodes. This makes it easier for new competitors to spring up and, also, for suppliers or customers to integrate vertically into the industry. A well-known example is the technology of aerosol packaging; firms with proficiency in aerosol packaging gradually saw their business position erode as many large consumer marketing companies, armed with growing understanding of aerosol packaging methods, integrated backward to form their own captive filling operations. As time passed and other aerosol users also turned to doing their own filling, the once-strongly entrenched contract fillers found themselves left with the role of meeting emergency demand and in a very adverse bargaining position with large customers for aerosol cans. Even though the contract-filling firms invested in improving filling technology and in trying to invent new aerosol applications to restore their technological advantage, their strategy proved hard to execute and their position weakened substantially over time. Except where strong patent protection effectively blockades the diffusion of an important technology, it is likely that rapid diffusion of proprietary knowledge will be an important driving force for industry change.

- *Changes in cost and efficiency*—In industries where new economies of scale are emerging or where experience curve effects cause unit costs to decline, large firm size becomes a distinct advantage and can cause all firms to adopt volume-building strategies—a "race for growth" emerges as the driving force. Likewise, sharply rising costs for a key ingredient input (either raw materials or necessary labor skills) can cause a scramble to either (a) line up reliable supplies of the input at affordable prices or else (b) search out lower-cost substitute inputs. The impact such cost increases can have is well illustrated by the recent experience of shifting from a condition of plentiful supplies of low-cost energy to a condition of depleting supplies and sharply higher energy costs. The strategic changes for both energy-suppliers and energy-users have been profound.

- *Moving from a differentiated to a commodity product emphasis (or vice versa)*—In some industries there is a tendency for once-highly differentiated products of firms to become more like commodity products as buyers become more sophisticated and base purchasing decisions on better information. This has occurred in gasoline, where the once much-touted brands of the major oil companies are now largely perceived as identical to the products of the small independent retailers; the 3-5 cent per gallon differential between the major brands and the "discount" brands has virtually disappeared. Now the focus is largely on price—the key characteristic of the market for a commodity product. On the other hand, when sellers are repeatedly successful in catering to the needs and tastes of different buyer segments by bringing out new performance features, making style changes, offering options and accessories, and creating image differences via advertising and packaging, then the focus of the whole industry can become one of effective product differentiation (examples include cigarettes, soft drinks, automobiles, and magazine publishing). It is crucial to understand, therefore, whether the forces in motion in the industry are acting to increase or decrease the emphasis upon product differentiation and how business strategy can be tailored accordingly.

- *Regulatory influences and government policy changes*—Regulatory and governmental influences can significantly impact where an industry is headed and the character of the changes taking place. Medicare/Medicaid provisions affect hospital and nursing home operations. Government regulations weigh heavy on the natural gas industry and the trucking industry; a shift to deregulation would quickly become *the* driving force in the trucking industry, calling for far-reaching strategic adjustments of participant firms. Safety and pollution regulations have been key forces in the automobile industry and in the electric utility industry.

- *Reductions in uncertainty and business risk*—An emerging industry is typically characterized by much uncertainty over potential market size, technological bugs, an unproven cost structure, what to do about product development, how to distribute the products and access potential buyers, and what overall strategy to employ. The risk of failure can be high, despite the fact that rapid expansion of the market may for a time allow firms the luxury of employing widely divergent strategies and market approaches (each representing a different "bet" about the future road ahead). Over time, however, the uncertainties get resolved and the poor strategies are abandoned while the successful ones are imitated and improved—an evolutionary process which tends to stiffen competitive pressures. Meanwhile, as uncertainty about the industry's viability and prospects dissipates, new firms may be enticed to enter the industry. Often, the new entrants are larger, established firms with a preference for lower risk ventures that have a proven track record. The entry of bigger firms is especially likely when it becomes clear that the new industry's potential is large and that the existing hurdles can be overcome. As uncertainty and business risk are reduced, those firms which have grown up with the industry must strategically prepare to defend against the potential entry of bigger rivals and to shift to a successful strategy (if earlier judgments about strategy prove wrong).

The preceding discussion of the many different types of driving forces that can prevail in an industry indicates that there is no one way in which industries evolve. The driving forces which dominate an industry and push it in a given direction are variable. They vary from industry to industry and they vary from time to time in a given industry. Hence, analyzing what the driving forces in an industry are, how and why they are causing the industry to head in a given direction, and what the implications are for strategy are integral parts of the process of analyzing and evaluating strategy.

The Underlying Economics of the Business

Every industry has an underlying set of economic characteristics. These economic characteristics consist of such things as capital requirements, the nature of internal cash flows, the cost structure, typical operating profit margins, pricing practices, economies of scale, price-cost relationships at various percentages of capacity utilization, breakeven volumes, and the like. A command of the economics of the business is fundamental to strategy analysis since revenue-cost-profit relationships effectively establish boundaries upon what a firm can and cannot do.

Take the convenience foodstore business, for example. A breakdown of the margins, expenses, and net profit for the representative convenience food store for a recent year showed:

Sales............................	$400,000	100.0%
Cost of goods sold	284,800	71.2
Gross profit margin	115,200	28.8
Expenses:		
Wages and benefits	50,000	12.5
Advertising and promotion	2,800	0.7
Rents and property upkeep	13,200	3.3
Utility costs	12,800	3.2
Other expenses	22,800	5.7
Total expenses	101,600	25.4
Profit before taxes	$13,600	3.4%

A typical investment in an urban convenience store location was about $200,000, the bulk of which represented the cost of acquiring a choice location with adequate parking on a heavily traveled thoroughfare. Convenience stores tended to have about 600 customers daily; on the average, patrons spent about $2 and took 3 to 4 minutes to make their purchase. Convenience store prices were 10 to 15 percent above the levels in most supermarkets, a reflection of the fact that patrons were willing to pay extra for the convenience such stores offered—location, easy access, 24-hour service, popular selections, and quick checkout. Stores generally stock 3,000 items in their 2,400 square foot space and can be staffed with a single clerk. With these underlying economic characteristics, it was generally agreed in the industry that business success hinged upon:

1. *Choosing good store locations*—visible, easily accessible sites on well-traveled routes are essential to drawing an ample clientele.
2. *Selecting the products to stock and merchandising them effectively*—customers expect to find what they are looking for and, in many instances, also make an impulse purchase (factors which make it important to stock popular, high-turnover items and to do a good job of merchandising and positioning them in the store).
3. *Pricing*—given that operating expenses are mostly fixed (not sensitive to changes in sales volume), it is important for prices to be set high enough to produce an average 28-30% gross margin on the mix of goods sold, yet pricing has to be sensitive to any competition from supermarkets.
4. *Operating efficiency*—with only a 28-30% gross margin, sloppy management practices and inefficiencies in store operations can quickly erode the slim 3.0-3.5% pretax profit margin.

The point is this: unless and until an industry analysis produces in-depth understanding of the economics of the business, strategists may fail to accurately perceive one or more of the key factors for success in the business. The *key success factors* in any business point squarely to *what it takes to make money in the business*—that is, what a firm must concentrate on doing well and doing right if it is to capture enough patronage to make the business healthy and attractive. Key success factors suggest the specific kinds of skills and competencies a firm will need to cope with market realities and they indicate which aspects of which functional area activities are the most crucial and why. Key success factors are then a top-priority strategic consideration. At the very least, business strategy must specify how the firm plans to address each key success factor. At the most, key success factors can serve as *the cornerstones* upon which business strategy is built.

While it would be nice to be able to generalize about what the key success factors are, one cannot. They vary from industry to industry and even from time to time within the same industry (as industry conditions and the stage of the life cycle change). And even where two industries may have some of the same kinds of key success factors, the underlying reasons for each factor usually differ as does its role and rank in the overall business scheme. Hence, the nature and importance of the key success factors outlined above for the convenience food industry differ from the key success factors in many other retailing businesses (such as jewelry, tires, gasoline, clothing). And the kinds of key success factors in retailing businesses are not like those in manufacturing businesses. In beer, the keys are brewing quality, distribution, and advertising; in copying equipment, the keys are product innovation and service. In apparel manufacturing, the keys are fashion design and manufacturing efficiency. It is because the subtleties of the key success factors vary significantly across industries and across time that industry analysis is so crucial to strategy evaluation.

Strategic Issue Identification

The last component of industry analysis is to identify and understand the strategic issues and problems confronting the industry. Every industry has its own peculiar mix of issues and problems. Nearly always these have a bearing on strategy evaluation because there is the ever-present question of how adequate the present business strategy is to deal with these industry-related problems and issues. The catalog of strategic issues and problems is a logical product of the three prior parts of the industry analysis. Once a thoroughgoing probe of industry structure, industry direction, and key success factors have been conducted, the strategic issues and problems confronting the industry ought to be easily compiled.

Although the specific strategic issues and problems of an industry vary from situation to situation, the signs to look for and the questions to ask do not vary greatly. Generally, the strategic issues and problems grow out of:

- How well positioned the industry is to deal with emerging opportunities and threats.
- The probability that substitute products (from outside the industry) could erode the industry's economic and competitive position.
- The industry's capability for meeting the future needs of customers, as well as needs *not* presently being met by existing products.
- What the anticipated demographic and population-based changes portend for the size of the market and for competition in the industry.
- Whether there are any reasons to expect major changes in costs or in supply conditions.
- Whether the course of the economy (inflation, unemployment, interest rates, economic growth, and so on) is likely to produce any *unusual* changes in industry conditions, industry direction, and competitive intensity.
- Changes in government policies.

Sizing up how an industry will "solve" its current problems/issues and what options exist for dealing with anticipated problems/issues is inherently subject to alternative judgment. Different people may view the same industry situation and reach different judgments about what the chief problems/issues are and what the implications are for strategy. Nonetheless, judgmental differences based on serious analysis are a more tolerable condition than flying blind with no explicit consideration of the strategic issues looming just ahead. At the very least, assumptions can be made explicit and the "hard to call" areas explored fully for the various probable scenarios. The various outcomes can be tested for their sensitivity to changes in the underlying assumptions. And *environmental scanning* activities can be regularly conducted as an early warning detector of future strategic issues and problems.[14]

ANALYZING COMPETITION AND KEY COMPETITORS

Industry analysis sets the stage for the second phase of business-level strategy evaluation—assessing the impact of competition and key competitors' strategies on an organization's choice of business strategy. Here three questions are paramount:

1. What are the forces driving competition in the industry?
2. How and why do the competitive approaches of rival firms differ?
3. What are the competitive positions and relative strengths of key rivals—what are their strategies, how well are they working, and why are some rivals doing better than others?

This phase of the strategy evaluation process is fundamental because competitive forces shape strategy and because the strategies of rival firms shape competitive forces. Thus, it is often useful for a firm, in searching out its optimal strategic position in a market, to consider a strategy that either builds defenses against competitive forces or that puts it in market niches where these forces are weak.

The Driving Forces of Competition

Even though each industry tends to have its own special style of competition and set of competitive pressures, there are enough similarities to permit generalizations about the main sources and forces of competition across industries. An excellent conceptual model for analyzing competition in an industry is shown in Figure 5-3. Nearly always, the principal *driving competitive force* in an industry consists of the interplay of the strategic moves and countermoves of rival firms. But, in addition, there are four other important sources of competitive pressure: (1) whether the participant firms are confronted with competitive threats from the substitute

---

[14]*Environmental scanning* is a term used to describe a broad-ranging, mind-stretching effort to monitor and interpret social, political, economic, and technological events in an attempt to gain an early warning of emerging trends and conditions that could have an impact on a firm's operations and strategic plans. Companies which undertake environmental scanning on a fairly continuous and comprehensive level include General Electric, AT&T, Coca-Cola, Ford, General Motors, DuPont, and Shell Oil. For an excellent discussion of the linkage between environmental scanning and strategic planning, see Ian H. Wilson, "Environmental Scanning and Strategic Planning," *Business Environment/Public Policy: 1979 Conference Papers* (St. Louis: American Assembly of Collegiate Schools of Business, 1980), pp. 159-163.

products of firms in other industries, (2) the potential entry of new competitors, (3) the economic power of suppliers, and (4) the economic power of customers. The relative strength and influence of these five forces and the pattern of interaction among them largely determine the nature and intensity of competition in an industry.

FIGURE 5-3
The Forces of Competition

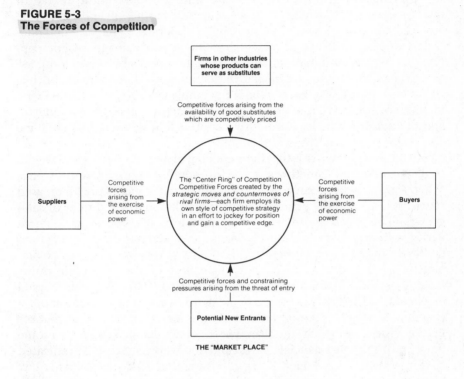

Firms in other industries
whose products can
serve as substitutes

Competitive forces arising from the
availability of good substitutes
which are competitively priced

The "Center Ring" of Competition
Competitive Forces created by the
*strategic moves and countermoves of
rival firms*—each firm employs its
own style of competitive strategy
in an effort to jockey for position
and gain a competitive edge.

Competitive
forces
arising from
the exercise
of economic
power

Suppliers

Competitive
forces
arising from
the exercise
of economic
power

Buyers

Competitive forces and constraining
pressures arising from the threat of entry

Potential New Entrants

THE "MARKET PLACE"

The Competitive Force of Rival Firms' Strategies.   The competitive strategies of rival firms are the center ring of the competitive arena.[15] Every firm aspires to secure a competitive edge over its rivals. However, the challenge is how to achieve an advantage, given that the effectiveness of one firm's strategy hinges in large part on what strategies its rivals use.

What is the "best" strategy for firm A in its struggle for competitive advantage depends partly on firm B's choice of strategy and firm B, in turn, may elect to finetune its strategy in light of A's strategic moves. Thus, the

---

[15]This section is drawn from the discussion in Arthur A. Thompson, "Competition as a Strategic Process," *Antitrust Bulletin*, vol. 25, no. 4 (Winter 1980), pp. 777-803.

motivation of firms to gain an advantage, in conjunction with the interdependence of their strategic approaches to the market, produces an ongoing sequence of strategic moves and countermoves, some offensive and some defensive, on the part of each seller in the market. Each firm's competitive moves and countermoves are an integral part of its overall business strategy for improving its competitive position and for achieving a degree of market success sufficient to justify staying in the business over the long-run. Normally, a firm's competitive strategy incorporates both price and non-price features, with the exact mix being a function of management perceptions as to what combination will have the most desirable market impact, given the prevailing strategies (and anticipated counterstrategies) of rival firms. How long a firm goes without finetuning its strategy or subjecting it to major overhaul is a function of the firm's market successes (or failures) and the durability of its competitive approach in withstanding strategic challenges from rival firms.

But the key point here is that the launching of new competitive strategies triggers a new and sometimes powerful round of competitive pressures. When a firm makes a successful strategic move, it can expect increased rewards, largely at the expense of rivals' market shares and rates of sales growth. The speed and extent of the initiator's strategic encroachment varies with whether the industry's product is standardized or differentiated, the initiator's competence and resources to capitalize on any advantage the strategy has produced, how difficult it is for sellers to shift buyer loyalties, and the ease with which the new strategy initiative can be copied or else blunted. The pressures on rivals to respond are, in addition, a function of whether the initiator is (1) a major firm with considerable market visibility, (2) a fringe firm whose efforts can be ignored for some time, or (3) a firm in financial distress and thus whose strategy is predicated on desperation. For instance, if a firm's strategic offensive is keyed to a low price and quick market penetration but also carries with it a substantial risk that full costs will not be recovered, rivals may judge that the strategy will be short-lived; they may choose to respond or not, depending on their estimates of whether it will be better to meet the low price on a temporary basis or to ride out whatever buyer resistance may be encountered. If the initiating firm finds its move neutralized by rivals' countermoves, then it is challenged to seek out a better strategy not as easily defeated or else remain content with the stalemate it has encountered.

The ease with which a firm's competitive strategy options can be neutralized is a major criterion of strategy selection; there is good reason to gravitate towards competitive strategies which can be neither easily imitated nor easily defeated. Such considerations indicate why it is wise for a firm to push the development of a *distinctive competence* whereby it can employ a strategic approach that is not susceptible to successful imitation. By developing its own special strategic advantage, a firm may be able to gain a distinctive image and reputation for its product offering, thereby insulating itself somewhat from the competitive pressures created by rival firms' strategies.

It may be that only a few firms (large or small) will tend to initiate fresh strategic moves, and they may not do it often. But to the extent that these few are able to impact the market with their strategic initiatives, the give-and-take of strategic move and competitive response spreads and continues.[16] A fresh move may come from a firm with ambitious growth objectives, from a firm with excess capacity, or from a firm under pressure to gain added business. More generally, though, the classic offensive strategies are made by firms that see market opportunities and a chance to improve their profit performance. Such firms, whether they be actual leaders, would-be leaders, or mavericks, will likely be aware of the risks of undertaking a bold strategic move but they also are likely to have confidence, one, that they are shrewd enough to keep ahead of the game and, two, that they will be better off making a bold move than they would be by holding back and letting others take the lead.[17] The defensive responses which follow aggressive moves will not only reflect time lags and uncertainties but their character will also tend to differ according to whether the new offensive consists of a new promotional campaign, introduction of a new product or product variation, a new channel of distribution, or an expansive move towards a new form of horizontal or vertical integration.

Typically the strategies of the participant firms cause the flow of competition to swing first in one direction and then another—in no set pattern and mix. At any given time the central focus of competition might be on one or several of the following: price, new and improved products, a broader product offering, technical sophistication, the adoption of new cost-saving methods of manufacture, customer service, promotion, guarantees, styling, function, economy of use, convenience, and so on—and the focus can shift as new events and moves unfold.

Most of the time, lulls in the competitive storm tend to be temporary, owing to the stream of new strategic opportunities and threats which emerge from the possibilities for product variation, cost-related technological changes, new buyer tastes and preferences, changing demographics and life-styles, shifts in buying power, new product availability, and general economic change. Apart from these market-related variables, periodic changes can be expected in the host of complex institutional factors that mold a firm's strategy choices from the outside and the intrafirm considera-

---

[16]J. M. Clark, *Competition as a Dynamic Process* (Washington: The Brookings Institution, 1961), p. 473. See also Michael E. Porter, *Interbrand Choice, Strategy, and Bilateral Market Power* (Cambridge, Mass.: Harvard University Press, 1976), Chapter 4; and Michael E. Porter, "How Competitive Forces Shape Strategy," *Harvard Business Review*, vol. 57, no. 2 (March-April 1979), pp. 137-145.

[17]Clark, *Competition as a Dynamic Process*, p. 474.

tions which shape strategy from the inside. From a strategy evaluation standpoint, the main thing to remember is that from time to time there will be fresh strategic moves and these are likely to so stir competitive forces as to compel reactions and responses from other firms in the market. This is why the crux of business strategy centers around positioning the firm in its target market environment in ways intended to enhance its distinctive and competitive capabilities relative to rival firms.

It follows from this characterization of competition as a strategic process that competition can assume many forms and shades of intensity. The present strategies of firms in a given industry are just snapshots of an ongoing process whereby markets and competition affect firms' strategies and firms' strategies affect markets and competition. New competitive pressures are regularly created by the neverending sequence of strategic moves and countermoves of participant firms. Changing competitive pressures are thus the norm not the exception.

The Competitive Force of Substitute Products.   All firms selling a particular product are, in a broad sense, in competition with firms producing related substitutes. Steel producers are in competition with aluminum producers—in the case of some customers and end uses. The producers of fiber-glass insulation are in competition with the producers of styrofoam, rock wool, and cellulose insulation. Sugar producers are in competition with the firms which are introducing sugar-free products.

The competitive force of closely-related substitute products impacts sellers in several ways. First, the price and availability of acceptable substitutes for good X places a ceiling on the prices which the producers of good X can charge; at the same time, the ceiling price places a limit on the profit potential for good X.[18] Second, unless the sellers of good X can upgrade quality, reduce prices via cost reduction, or otherwise differentiate their product from its substitutes, they risk a low growth rate in sales and profits owing to the inroads which substitutes may make. The more sensitive the sales of X are to changes in the prices of substitutes, the stronger is the competitive influence of the substitutes.

As a rule, the lower the price and the higher the quality and performance of substitutes, the more intense are the competitive pressures posed by substitute products. One very telling indicator of the strength of competition emanating from the producers of substitutes is their growth rate in sales; other indicators are their plans for expansion of capacity and the profits they are earning.

The Potential for New Entry.   New entrants to a market bring new production capacity, the desire to establish a market niche and a viable market share, and often substantial resources with which to compete.[19] The

[18]Porter, "How Competitive Forces Shape Strategy," p. 142.
[19]Ibid., p. 138.

entry of strong firms can cause a major market shake-up, particularly in the case of established companies which diversify through acquisition into new products and markets (a classic example being Philip Morris' acquisition of Miller Brewing and Seven-Up).

Just how serious the competitive threat of entry is into a particular market depends on two classes of factors: *barriers to entry* and the *expected reaction of existing firms to new entry*. A barrier to entry exists whenever the nature of the market for the product and/or the economics of the business put a potential entrant at a price/cost disadvantage relative to its competitors. There are several major sources of entry barriers:[20]

- *Economies of scale*—The presence of important scale economies deters entry because it forces the potential entrant to commit to entering on a large-scale basis (a costly and perhaps risky move) or else to accept a cost disadvantage (and, consequently, lower profitability). Large-scale entry could result in chronic overcapacity in the industry and/or it could so threaten the market shares of existing firms that they are pushed into aggressive competitive retaliation (in the form of price cuts, increased advertising and sales promotion, and similar such steps) so as to maintain their position; either way, the entrant's outlook is for lower profits. Scale economies may be encountered not just in production, but in research, advertising, selling, financing, in-house servicing of products, and distribution as well.

- *Brand preferences and customer loyalty*—When the products of rival sellers are differentiated, buyers usually have some degree of preference and loyalties to existing brands. This means that a potential entrant must be prepared to spend enough money on advertising and sales promotion to overcome customer loyalties and build its own clientele. Substantial time, as well as money, can be involved. Not only may a new entrant have to budget more funds for marketing than existing firms (which gives existing firms a cost advantage), but also the capital invested in establishing a new brand (unlike the capital invested in facilities and equipment) has no resale or recoverable value, which makes such expenditures a riskier "investment." In addition, product differentiation can entail costs to buyers of switching brands, in which case the new entrant must persuade buyers that the changeover or switching costs are worth incurring; this may require lower prices or better quality-service-performance—again leading to lower profit expectations.

- *Capital requirements*—The larger the total dollar investment needed to enter the market successfully, the more limited is the pool of potential entrants. The most obvious capital requirements are associated with manufacturing plant and equipment, working capital to finance inven-

---

[20]Porter, *Competitive Strategy*, pp. 7-17.

tories, offering credit to customers, establishing a clientele, and bearing startup losses.

- *Cost disadvantages independent of size*—Existing firms may have cost advantages not available to potential entrants, regardless of the entrant's size. These advantages relate to access to the best and cheapest raw materials, possession of patents and unique technological know-how, the effects of the learning curve and the experience curve, having purchased fixed assets at preinflation prices, favorable locations, and availability of financial capital at lower costs.

- *Access to distribution channels*—Where a product is distributed through established market channels, a potential entrant may face the barrier of gaining adequate distribution access. Some distributors may be reluctant to take on a product that lacks buyer recognition. The more limited the number of wholesale and retail outlets and the more that existing producers have these tied up, the tougher entry will be. Potential entrants, to overcome this barrier, may have to lure distribution access by offering better margins to dealers and distributors or by giving advertising allowances and other promotional incentives, with the result that the potential entrant's profits may be squeezed unless and until its product gains market acceptance.

- *Government actions and policies*—Government agencies can limit or even bar entry by instituting controls over licenses and permits. Regulated industries like trucking, radio and television stations, liquor retailing, and railroads all feature government-controlled entry. Entry can also be restricted, and certainly made more expensive, by government safety regulations and environmental pollution standards.

Even if a potential entrant is willing to tackle the problems of entry barriers, it may be dissuaded by its expectations about how existing firms will react to new entry.[21] Will incumbent firms "move over" grudgingly and let a new entrant take a viable share of the market, or will they launch a vigorous, "survival of the fittest" competitive battle for market position— including price cuts, increased advertising, product improvements, and whatever else is calculated to give a new entrant (as well as other rivals) a hard time? A firm is likely to have second thoughts about entry:

- when incumbent firms have previously been aggressive in defending their market positions against entry.
- when incumbent firms possess substantial financial resources with which to defend against new entry.
- when incumbent firms are in a position to use leverage with distributors and customers to keep their business.

---

[21]Porter, "How Competitive Forces Shape Strategy," p. 140.

- when incumbent firms are able and willing to cut prices to preserve their market shares.

- when product demand is expanding slowly, thus limiting the market's ability to absorb and accommodate the new entrant without adversely affecting the profit performance of all the participant firms.

- when it is more costly for existing firms to leave the market than to fight to the death (because the costs of exit are very high, owing to heavy investment in specialized technology and equipment, union agreements which contain high severance costs, or important shared relationships with other products).

Naturally, a potential entrant can only guess about how incumbent firms will react to entry. Reactions to past entry are one obvious indication. So is how existing firms behave competitively toward each other. Sometimes the "personality" of rival firms can provide clues to their probable reaction to entry; relevant personality indicators include (1) the propensity a firm may exhibit to be aggressive or conservative, a leader or a follower, (2) the backgrounds and experiences of their executives, (3) the priority which rival firms have historically given to research and development, advertising, technology, and similar key competitive variables, and (4) the assumptions and perceptions which the managements of rival firms seem to have about themselves and their business, as revealed by speeches and interviews, the kinds of people they recruit, and how they tend to reward their executives.

One additional point needs to be made about the threat of entry as a competitive force: the threat of entry changes as economic and market conditions change. For example, the expiration of a key patent can greatly increase the threat of entry. Technological discovery can create such a scale economy as to virtually bar new entry. The decisions of incumbent firms to increase advertising or strengthen distributor-dealer relations or step up R&D or improve product quality can result in the erection of higher roadblocks to entry. Dramatic price increases which also produce sharply higher profits can enhance the attractiveness and probability of new entry.

The Economic Power of Suppliers.   The competitive impact which suppliers can have upon an industry is chiefly a function of how significant the input they supply is to the buyer.[22] When the input of a particular group of suppliers makes up a sizable proportion of total costs, is crucial to the buyer's production process, or else significantly affects quality of the industry's product, suppliers' *potential* bargaining power and competitive influence over firms in the buying industry tend to be greater. The extent to which this potential impact is realized depends upon a number of factors; in general, a group of supplier firms is more powerful:[23]

---

[22]Ibid., p. 140.
[23]Porter, *Competitive Strategy*, pp. 27-28.

- when the input is, in one way or another, important to the buyer.
- when the supplier group is dominated by a few large firms that are not confronted with intensely competitive conditions.
- when suppliers' respective products are differentiated to such an extent that it is difficult or costly for buyers to switch from one supplier to another.
- when the buying firms are *not* important customers of the suppliers. In such instances, suppliers are not constrained by the fact that their own well-being is tied to the industry they are supplying; hence, they have no big incentive to protect the customer industry via reasonable prices, improved quality, or new products which might well enhance the buying industry's sales and profits.
- when the suppliers of an input do *not* have to compete with the substitute inputs of suppliers in other industries. (For instance, the power of the suppliers of glass bottles to the soft drink bottlers is checked by the ability of the soft drink firms to use aluminum cans and plastic bottles).
- when one or more suppliers pose a credible threat of forward integration into the business of the buyer industry (attracted, perhaps, by the prospect of higher profits than it can earn in its own market).
- when the buying firms display no inclination toward backward integration into the suppliers' business.

The power of suppliers can be an important economic factor in the marketplace because of the impact they can have on customer profits. Powerful suppliers can squeeze the profits of a customer industry via price increases which the latter is unable to pass on fully to its own customers. They can also jeopardize a buyer's profits via reductions in the quality of the inputs—reductions which enhance their own profits at the expense of the buyer's profits.

The Economic Power of Customers.   Just as powerful suppliers can exert a competitive influence over an industry, so also can powerful customers.[24] The relative power of customers tends to be greater:[25]

- when buyers are large and few in number and when they purchase in large quantities. Often large customers are successful in using their volume-buying leverage to obtain important price concessions and other favorable terms and conditions of sale.
- when buyers' purchases are a sizable percentage of the selling industry's total sales.
- when the supplying industry is comprised of large numbers of relatively small sellers.

[24]Porter, "How Competitive Forces Shape Strategy," pp. 140-141.
[25]Porter, *Competitive Strategy*, pp. 24-26.

- when the item being purchased is sufficiently standardized among sellers that not only can buyers find alternative sellers but also they can switch suppliers at virtually zero cost.
- when buyers pose a credible threat of backward integration, being attracted by the prospects of earning greater profits or by the benefits of reliable prices and reliable delivery.
- when sellers pose little threat of forward integration into the product market of buyers.
- when the item being bought is *not* an important input.
- when it is economically feasible for buyers to follow the practice of purchasing the input from several suppliers rather than one.
- when the product/service being bought does not save the buyer money.

A firm can enhance its profitability and market standing by seeking out suppliers and customers who are in a comparatively weak position to exercise adverse power. Especially is this feasible in the case of selecting the customer segments to target one's marketing efforts. Rarely do all buyer segments enjoy equal bargaining power, and some may be more price or quality or service sensitive than others. An example is the automobile tire industry where the major tire manufacturers on the one hand confront very significant customer power in selling original equipment tires to the automobile manufacturers and on the other hand find themselves in position to exercise more of an upper hand when selling replacement tires to individual car owners through their own networks of retail stores. Also, Crown Cork and Seal Co. has been very successful in concentrating its efforts on producing cans for two types of buyers—those who use aerosol cans and those who require cans for products with unique characteristics.

Factors Affecting the Intensity of Competition

In general, any market characteristic which affects strategic rivalry, barriers to entry or exit, the economic power of buyers or sellers, and the price and availability of closely-related substitutes affects the vigor of competition. While there can be a wide range of specific characteristics directly influencing how strong competition will be, certain ones seem to crop up again and again. These are worth enumerating.[26]

Competition tends to increase as the number of rival firms increases and as these firms become more equal in size and capability. The number of firms is important because, up to some point, more firms increase the probability for fresh, creative strategic initiatives and because greater numbers reduce the effects of any one firm's actions upon the others,

---

[26]These characteristics are based upon Porter, "How Competitive Forces Shape Strategy," pp. 142-143.

thereby reducing somewhat the probability of direct retaliation. When rival firms are more equal in size and capability, the chances are better that the firms can compete on a fairly even footing, a feature which makes it harder for one or two firms to "win" the competitive battle and emerge as dominant firms in a position to exercise leadership and some degree of market control.

Market rivalry is usually stronger when demand for the product is growing slowly. In a rapidly expanding market, rivalry is weakened by the fact that there is enough business for everybody. Indeed, it may take all of a firm's financial and managerial resources just to keep abreast of market growth, much less devoting efforts to steal away the customers of its rivals. But when growth slows, expansion-minded firms tend to ignite a battle for market share that often results in a shakeout of the weak and less efficient firms. Market share competition can be counted upon to produce fresh strategic moves and countermoves directly aimed at taking customers away from rival firms.[27]

Competition is more intense when rival firms are tempted to use price cuts or other marketing tactics to boost unit volume. Whenever fixed costs are high and marginal costs are low, firms are under strong economic pressure to produce at or very near full capacity. Hence, if market demand weakens and capacity utilization begins to fall off, rival firms frequently resort to secret price concessions, special discounts, rebates, and other sales-increasing tactics. A similar situation arises when a product is perishable or seasonal or is costly or difficult to store or hold in inventory. It can also occur if an industry is characterized by (1) long lead times in constructing new plant capacity, (2) scale economies which dictate that additions to capacity be made in large increments, or (3) persistent ups and downs in market demand that periodically give rise to excess capacity throughout the industry.

Competition is stronger when the products/services of rival firms are not so strongly differentiated that buyers become locked in by the high costs of switching from one brand to another. Product differentiation *per se* is not a deterrent to competition; indeed, it has the capacity for enlivening rivalry by forcing firms to seek creative new ways of improving their price-quality-service-performance offering. The strategic moves of one firm to differentiate its product may well require important countermoves from rival firms. However, when the nature of product differentiation begins to result in layers of insulation from rivalry—as occurs when switching becomes costly or difficult, then a firm may gain protection from raids

---

[27]In average growth markets, aggressive firms may move to build new plant capacity *ahead* of the time it will be needed so as to discourage others from expansion and thereby capture a greater market share. Should rivals catch on to this tactic and decide to retaliate with capacity additions of their own, the outcome can be a vigorous competitive struggle in which overall industry profitability is reduced. Such situations usually occur in oligopolistic markets where increased market share is a key to increased profits.

on its customers by its rivals. Should this occur, competitive intensity is obviously lessened.

Market rivalry increases in proportion to the size of the payoff from a successful strategic move. The essential idea here is that the greater the potential reward, the more likely some firm will give in to the temptation of a particular strategic move. How big the strategic payoff is varies partly with the speed of retaliation. When competitors can be expected to respond slowly (or maybe even not at all), the initiator of a fresh competitive strategy can reap the benefits in the intervening period and perhaps gain a lead time advantage which is not easily surmounted; the greater the chance this will occur, the greater will the potential benefits justify the risk of eventual retaliation. Firms which have shrewdly assessed the "personality" of each rival firm and which also understand the economics of their rivals' business are in the best position to correctly predict how and when rivals may respond to a given strategic move; such knowledge is advantageous in assessing the potential payoffs of strategic alternatives.[28]

Market rivalry tends to be more vigorous when it costs more to get out of a business than to stay in and compete. The higher are exit barriers (and thus the more costly it is to abandon a market), the stronger the incentive for firms to remain and compete as best they can, even though they may be earning low profits or even incurring a loss. The point here is that the strength and character of competition is affected by factors which determine how the short-run costs of exit stack up against the long-term costs of staying in and trying to become a more successful competitor.

Competition becomes more volatile and unpredictable the more diverse that rival firms are in terms of their strategies, their personalities, their corporate priorities, their resources, and their countries of origin. When rival firms differ on how to compete (whether this be due to different perceptions about the market or different corporate objectives and personalities), their strategies are likely to produce a head-on clash in the marketplace. Moreover, a diverse range of views and approaches enhances the probability that one or more firms will behave as "mavericks" and employ strategies which produce more market flux and uncertainty than would otherwise occur. In such an environment, it is difficult for firms to predict rivals' behavior accurately; the effects of signalling are uncertain; and the comfortable atmosphere of a "fraternity of insiders" does not prevail. Indeed, the mere presence of "outsiders" or mavericks—particularly foreign firms or new entrants—who either do not understand or else

---

[28]It is worth noting here that it is important for a firm to understand the reasons underlying any shifts in the competitive strategies of rival firms. Unless a firm correctly perceives what the intentions of its competitors are, it is less able to develop appropriate moves and countermoves of its own. When rival firms change their competitive strategy, management is thus obliged to ask: What are they up to, why are they doing this, and what do they expect to accomplish? Is this an aggressive move or is it something we should all be doing? The answers are almost certain to be relevant in figuring out the firm's own strategic response.

deliberately ignore conventional methods of competing has considerable potential for creating "a whole new ballgame."

At the same time, firms tend to gear their competitive strategies and counterstrategies in part to their own specific internal priorities, strengths, weaknesses, and financial capabilities; the more these factors are divergent from rival to rival, the more likely that the "right" strategy for one firm is the "wrong" strategy for another. Such diversity is consistent with active competition because it stimulates finetuning and countermoves as buyers respond to one firm's strategy more favorably than to another's. The only exception arises when rival firms pursue individual strategies which are aimed at catering to different types of buyers; then each firm moves deliberately to carve out its own market niche and build up its own customer following in ways that do not directly threaten or overlap with the market segments of its rival. To the extent that each firm limits its competitive energies to only one or a few of these segments, then competition in any one market segment may well be weaker than is suggested by the total number of firms in the overall market.

Sizing Up the Different Competitive Approaches of Rival Firms

Rival firms generally do not follow the same strategy for competing in the marketplace—even though they may hold substantially similar views about the industry and about the forces that are driving competition. This is basically because most industries and markets are large and diverse enough to give firms ample room to pursue distinguishably different competitive strategies but it is also because (1) rival firms' situations are enough different that the "right" strategic approach for one firm can be "wrong" for another and (2) the managers of rival firms arrive at different evaluations of how "best" to try to compete for buyer patronage.

Anytime two or more firms compete as rivals in the same market there arises, more or less automatically, the gut issue of whether to compete head-on with essentially the same strategy or whether to employ a substantially different market approach. Imitative or "me, too" competitive strategies are occasionally the most profitable for firms but usually there are several different strategic groups. Some firms may choose to emphasize a lower price, others a higher quality and/or better service; some may elect to integrate vertically, others may concentrate within a single stage; some may strive to become "full-line" producers whereas others deliberately limit themselves to a narrower offering; some may concentrate R&D expenditures on cost-saving process innovations whereas others press harder for new and better products.

Differences in the market approaches taken by rival firms can be classified according to three basic or *generic types of strategies*:[29]

---

[29]Porter, *Competitive Strategy*, pp. 35–40.

1. *Strategies based on cost leadership*—Cost leadership strategies typically entail aggressive construction of efficient-scale facilities, vigorous pursuit of cost reductions linked to any experience curve effects, tight control of overhead, avoidance of marginally profitable lines and customer accounts, and cost minimization efforts in such areas as R&D, advertising, service, and sales expenses. Much management attention is given to budgets, justification of capital expenditures, and overall cost control. Cost leadership allows a firm to use its lower cost position to earn higher profit margins or to charge a lower price or both. By having a low-cost position relative to rivals, such firms are in excellent position to defend themselves against price competition and to always be in position to be price competitive. Examples of firms which are well-known for their cost leadership strategies are Lincoln Electric in arc welding equipment and supplies, Briggs and Stratton in small horsepower gasoline engines, BIC in ballpoint pens, Black and Decker in tools, Texas Instruments in hand calculators and semiconductors, and Harnischfeger in cranes.

2. *Strategies based on differentiation*—The key to a differentiation strategy is to create a product offering that is unique in some way from those of rivals and that gives the firm a distinctive basis for attracting customer patronage. Differentiation can take many forms: extra customer services (IBM in computers), special product features (Jenn-Air in electric ranges), superior dealer network (Caterpillar Tractor in construction equipment), added quality (Curtis Mathes in television sets), design and styling (Rolex in watches), craftsmanship and engineering (Mercedes-Benz in automobiles), technological superiority (MacIntosh and Yamaha in stereo components), distinctive image (Dr Pepper in soft drinks), and product reliability (Johnson & Johnson in baby care products). Differentiation strategies are attractive to many firms because they promote brand loyalty by customers and a somewhat lower customer sensitivity to price and because they are hard to imitate when keyed to a distinctive competence.

3. *Strategies based on focus or specialization*—A focus strategy can be aimed at a particular buyer group or a selected geographic area or a segment of a broad product line. The thrust of a focus strategy is to specialize in serving a limited target market rather than the whole market, the premise being that by zeroing in on a narrow strategic target the firm can be both more efficient and more effective. As a result, *within its target market* the firm can achieve either differentiation (because it caters directly to the needs of its chosen segment) or lower costs (because of economies that attach to specialization), or both—even though it does not achieve these distinctions industrywide.

This classification scheme may be a useful way of grouping rival firms into strategic clusters and then sizing up the extent to which the various competitive forces impact the firms employing each type of competitive approach.

In evaluating the different competitive approaches being taken by firms in the industry, one needs to be alert for:

- how many firms are following each strategic approach and what degree of success each strategic cluster is enjoying.
- the different impacts that the driving forces of competition have on each strategic approach and any differences in competitive intensity among the clusters.
- the skills and organizational requirements needed to execute each basic type of strategy being followed.
- the relative market shares and competitive strength of the group of firms employing each different type of strategy.

The Strategies of Key Competitors

In evaluating one's own business strategy, it is always worthwhile to examine closely the strategies of one's *closest* competitors. Usually, the strongest rivals a firm has are the other firms in its strategic cluster but on occasions a firm's key competitors include firms from other strategic groups.

The strategies of key competitors are important for two reasons. First, if a firm is to formulate a business strategy capable of winning out over the strategies of rival firms, it is essential to know and understand their strategies. One cannot, after all, expect to survive competitive warfare in the marketplace without being keenly aware of what close rivals are up to. Second, because the strategies of close rivals are highly interdependent (the strategic moves of one rival directly impact the others and may prompt counterstrategies), the strategic positions and degrees of success being enjoyed by close rivals have direct relevance to choosing one's own best strategy. More specifically, a perceptive analysis of rival firms ought to provide useful clues and predictions about (1) how a rival will likely react to competitive forces and to broader market trends and environmental conditions, (2) which rivals might initiate what kinds of fresh strategic moves and why, (3) what each rival would probably do in response to the feasible strategic changes of other firms, (4) the meaning and intent of a new strategic move and how seriously it should be taken, and (5) the reasons why some rivals are doing better than others. All of these things are relevant in formulating a firm's own strategy.

Diagnosing the behavior of key competitors has five dimensions: the priorities and performance objectives of each rival, each rival's assumptions and beliefs about the industry and about its competitors, each rival's current business strategy, the backgrounds and experiences of the rival's managers, and each firm's competitive capabilities.[30] Each is worth considering in some detail.

Rivals' Priorities and Performance Objectives.   Doing the detective work to uncover a rival firm's priorities and performance objectives has several payoffs. It can reveal whether the rival is satisfied with its current performance and thus its current strategy. It can aid in assessing the likelihood of a shift in strategy, the reasons for and seriousness behind such a shift, and the speed and vigor of a rival's response to either changes in market conditons or new strategic moves of other firms. Developing answers to the following questions ought to prove particularly helpful:

1. What inferences can be made about the rival's performance objectives and its attitudes toward risks? Is there any evidence that the rival aspires to be the industry leader in pricing or technological proficiency or market share or product quality or some other aspect?

2. How do the rival's performance objectives in this industry compare with how it compensates business-level managers? with compensation of its sales force?

3. Does the rival have a parent company? If so, what are its performance objectives and how is the rival business unit expected to contribute to them in terms of profitability, growth, and cash flow? Does the parent view this business as one of its main strategic interests or is it a sideline or peripheral business? How does the business fit into the parent's corporate strategy and business portfolio? To what extent does the rival business command financial support and management attention from corporate headquarters? Does corporate management have an emotional attachment to the business?

4. Has the rival been involved in any antitrust actions that could condition its strategic responses or that could constrain its performance objectives? In the same vein, is it constrained by other regulatory, environmental, or social considerations?

5. Is the rival under any new pressures from headquarters, customers, or other competitors to improve its performance? Is the rival's future threatened in any way? Is the rival striving to regain lost ground? Can the rival meet its performance objectives without doing anything dif-

---

[30]The discussion of these five dimensions is based on the presentation by Porter, *Competitive Strategy*, Chapter 3. In addition to the Porter reference, readers may also wish to consult H. Kolff, "How Is Competition Performing," *Long Range Planning*, vol. 12, no. 3 (June 1979), pp. 16-21; Jaime I. Rodriguez and William R. King, "Competitive Information Systems," *Long-Range Planning*, vol. 10, no. 6 (December 1977), pp. 45-50; Derek F. Abell and John S. Hammond, *Strategic Market Planning*, (Englewood Cliffs, N. J.: Prentice-Hall, Inc., 1979), Chapter 2; and Robert Hershey, "Commercial Intelligence on a Shoestring," *Harvard Business Review*, vol. 58, no. 5 (September-October 1980), pp. 22-30.

ferent or without launching a major strategic offensive? Is there reason to believe the rival is reasonably happy with its performance?

Rivals' Assumptions and Beliefs.   Every management operates on assumptions and beliefs about the industry and about how the business ought to be run. How a firm sees itself and its situation is often a good barometer of its strategic thinking. The relevant areas to probe into here are indicated in the following questions: What does the rival appear to believe (based on speeches, advertising claims, representations by its sales force to customers, and so on) about its standing in the marketplace relative to quality, cost, technological proficiency, and image with customers? Has the rival's reputation been traditionally identified with some key competitive aspect which will be strongly held—like superior service, quality of manufacture, product innovation, breadth of product line, or focus on particular products or market segments? Does the management of the rival believe strongly in certain principles or values or ways of doing business that can be counted upon to condition what the rival does or does not do? Do the managers of the rival typically adhere to industry customs or rules of thumb or conventional wisdom (such as "you have to give customers great service," "buyers look for quality and performance not low price," "the key is low-cost manufacture and full utilization of capacity," and "you have to offer a full product line")? What does the rival's management appear to believe about industry trends, future competitive conditions, and the strengths and weaknesses of other firms in the industry? What patterns are evident in the way the rival conducts its business? What has the rival tried that succeeded, what has it tried that failed, and are these experiences likely to shape future strategic moves? What does it believe its competitive strengths and weaknesses are? Does the rival use certain consultants, advertising agencies, banks, or other advisors and are they known for particular techniques and approaches? Why did the rival get into this business, or what reason does it have to stay in the business? How accurate are the rival's perceptions about itself, about its competitive position, and about industry trends and conditions? Is the rival's management prone to misjudge or misestimate market conditions or competitors or the kind of shift in strategy which is needed?

Rivals' Current Business Strategy.   An understanding of each major competitor's current business strategy and the way it is being implemented is fundamental to designing a winning strategy of one's own. It is difficult to outmaneuver one's rivals without first having keen insight into what they are doing in the marketplace. Thus staying on top of the strategic behavior of close rivals and diagnosing why their strategies are or are not working well is a relevant part of one's own strategy-evaluating process.

Insofar as possible, information is needed on the following: What are the distinguishing features of each key rival's apparent business strategy? Is the rival considered to be a leader in some respect (innovation, pricing, quality, service, management know-how) or is it a follower? What strengths and weaknesses are evident? Where does the rival concentrate its efforts in terms of products, customers, and geographic focus? Do the rival's functional area support strategies (especially in the areas of R&D, product development, product quality, and marketing) and the major operating-level strategies (especially as concerns maintaining volume and pricing) appear to be coordinated and working well? What does the rival's organization structure indicate about the priorities and importance attached to the various functional areas and how they are coordinated? Where are key strategy decisions made—in the business-unit itself (where?) or at corporate headquarters? Is the rival's business a free-standing unit or does it have to accommodate the requirements of sister units in the company? Which rivals seem to be gaining or losing ground in the marketplace and why? Are they locked into their present strategies because of facilities commitments or some other factor? What are the implications for our own strategy?

Backgrounds and Experiences of Rival Managers.   One of the most important set of clues about the behavior and strategies of rival businesses can be gleaned from the personal experiences and backgrounds of their managers. Hence while the information may be hard to come by, it is worth exerting an effort to get. The most important areas of inquiry include:

1.   What are the functional backgrounds of the key managers—accounting, finance, sales, production, R&D, and how likely is it that they will feel most comfortable with strategies which emphasize such functional areas? What other businesses have these managers worked in and what strategic approaches were characteristic of those businesses?

2.   What types of strategies have/have not worked for them personally in their previous jobs?

3.   Has the rival's current management been promoted from within (which may suggest continuation of the present strategy) or have those in charge come recently from outside the division or even outside the company? Is the manager in charge a person thought to be "on the way up" or is it someone who is about ready to retire? Is the rival known for selecting managers with a certain personality or educational background or managerial philosophy?

4.   Is there reason to believe that the managers of the rival business will be influenced by some previous major event in their background or experience (a sharp recession, having managed a rapid growth business, a sudden drop in profitability, a severe strike, or a disruption in raw material supply)?

5.   Have any of the rival's managers offered clues about their current thinking in their speeches to securities analysts, program appearances at trade associations, interviews with the media, or conversations with customers? Is there any evidence that they place a high value on

industry leadership in market share or technology, stable pricing, quality manufacture, or on some other strategic feature that may suggest what courses of action they are apt to follow?

Rivals' Capabilities to Compete Effectively.   Perhaps the really key issue about any rival firm is its capacity for competing effectively in the marketplace. Its strengths and weaknesses regarding product line, marketing and selling, dealer distribution network, R&D, engineering, manufacturing, cost and efficiency, financial condition, and managerial competence are all important in determining its ability to respond to competitive moves or to deal with industry trends. Special attention ought to be given to what a rival firm is best and worst at doing and what flexibility it has should a need arise to adapt to a price-cost squeeze, a shift to more emphasis on customer service, extensive product innovation, or some other relevant change in competitive conditions. Also pertinent is an appraisal of the degree to which it is likely to be a major factor in the marketplace over the long haul and why its market standing is likely to increase or decrease.

Pinning Down a Rival's Competitive Moves.   Gaining useful answers to the kinds of questions and issues posed above is not a simple, short-run task. The needed information trickles in bits and pieces and it takes both time and hard work to get a real "feel" for a rival's situation and how its management thinks. But it is a task worth doing and doing systematically. The result can be a good ability to predict:

- how a rival will respond to changes in market trends or economic conditions.

- how satisfied a rival firm is with its present market position and profitability, and thus whether it is likely to initiate a fresh strategic move.

- the most likely moves a rival will make, given its performance objectives, its assumptions and beliefs about the market, its current strategy, its management approach, and its competitive strengths and weaknesses.

- how vulnerable a rival would be to one's own strategic moves.

- how much the rival can be pushed before it will be provoked into retaliation.

- the nature and effectiveness of any such retaliatory action.

Such predictive ability is immensely valuable in choosing one's own best time, place, and method for fighting it out with competitors. Indeed, indepth familiarity with rivals' strategies and how they think is the key to astutely judging which of one's own business strategy options is likely to meet with the greatest market success.

AN ASSESSMENT OF THE FIRM'S OWN
PRESENT BUSINESS SITUATION

With the strategic profile of the industry and the competitive environment now complete, the analytical spotlight shifts to the firm's own business situation. The primary concerns of this third and final portion of the business-level strategy evaluation process are:

1. Identifying and evaluating the firm's internal strengths and weaknesses,

2. Identifying and evaluating the firm's external market opportunities and the strategic threats it faces,

3. Assessing the pluses and minuses in the firm's competitive market position (whether it is gaining ground or losing ground and why),

4. Appraising how well the present business and functional area strategies are working and why, and

5. Pinpointing any special strategic issues and problems unique to the firm and its business.

All five weigh heavy in judging what business strategy has the best "goodness of fit" with the firm's overall situation.

The SWOT Analysis

SWOT is an acronym for a firm's internal Strengths and Weaknesses and its external Opportunities and Threats. A SWOT analysis consists of a candid compilation and appraisal of a firm's strengths, weaknesses, opportunities, and threats. When a SWOT analysis is conducted for strategy evaluation purposes, the emphasis is not on listing *any kind* of strengths, weaknesses, opportunities, and threats but rather on identifying those that are *strategy related*. Figure 5-4 suggests some of the key considerations in compiling a SWOT listing.

However, the SWOT analysis needs to be more than a set of four lists—one for the firm's strengths, one for its weaknesses, one for its opportunities, and one for its threats. Some strategy-related strengths are more important than others and may count for more in the marketplace and in building a successful strategy. Some strategy-related weaknesses can be fatal, while others might not matter much or can be easily remedied. Some opportunities may make more sense to pursue than others. And a firm may find itself much more vulnerable to some threats than to others. Hence it is essential to *evaluate* the SWOT listing in terms of what the implications are for strategy and what adjustments in strategy may need to be explored.

FIGURE 5-4
The SWOT Analysis—with Suggestions of What to Look For

INTERNAL

Strengths	*Weaknesses*
A distinctive competence?	No clear strategic direction?
Adequate financial resources?	A deteriorating competitive position?
Good competitive skills?	Obsolete facilities?
Well thought of by buyers?	Subpar profitability because . . . ?
An acknowledged market leader?	Lack of managerial depth and talent?
Well-conceived functional area strategies?	Missing any key skills or competences?
Access to economies of scale?	Poor track record in implementing strategy?
Insulated (at least somewhat) from strong competitive pressures?	Plagued with internal operating problems?
Proprietary technology?	Vulnerable to competitive pressures?
Cost advantages?	Falling behind in R&D?
Competitive advantages?	Too narrow a product line?
Product innovation abilities?	Weak market image?
Proven management?	Competitive disadvantages?
Other?	Below-average marketing skills?
	Unable to finance needed changes in strategy?
	Other?

EXTERNAL

Opportunities	*Threats*
Enter new markets or segments?	Likely entry of new competitors?
Add to product line?	Rising sales of substitute products?
Diversify into related products?	Slower market growth?
Add complementary products?	Adverse government policies?
Vertical integration?	Growing competitive pressures?
Ability to move to better strategic group?	Vulnerability to recession and business cycle?
Complacency among rival firms?	Growing bargaining power of customers or suppliers?
Faster market growth?	Changing buyer needs and tastes?
Other?	Adverse demographic changes?
	Other?

The Pluses and Minuses in One's Own Competitive Position

In addition to the SWOT analysis, which ranges across all aspects of the firm's situation, the firm needs to conduct an explicit assessment of its competitive market position. The most direct way to do this is simply to *identify* and *evaluate* the pluses and minuses associated with the firm's present competitive standing. Particular attention needs to be given to (1) whether the firm, with its present strategy, is gaining or losing ground in its target markets, (2) whether the firm's position can be expected to improve or deteriorate if the present strategy is continued (allowing for finetuning), and (3) what strategic adjustments can be initiated to improve the firm's strategic positon.

Figure 5-5 illustrates an analytical framework and some factors which merit consideration. Again, more is needed than just a listing of the pluses and minuses. The important thing is to assess the relative importance of each plus and minus and to think through the implications they have for strategy. The end result should be a clearer picture of the business's overall competitive position and competitive strength.

FIGURE 5-5
Identifying the Pluses and Minuses in a Firm's
Competitive Market Position

The Pluses	The Minuses
Strong in particular market segments?	Under attack from key rivals?
Rising market share?	Losing ground to rival firms because . . . ?
A tough, proven competitor?	Below average growth?
A pacesetting or distinctive strategy?	Lacks some key skills to compete effectively?
Growing customer base and customer loyalty?	Short on financial resources?
Above-average market visibility?	A slipping reputation with customers?
In a favorably situated strategic cluster?	Trailing in product development?
Concentrating on fastest-growing market segments?	In a strategic cluster that is destined to lose ground?
Strongly differentiated products?	Weak in areas where there is the most market potential?
Cost-competitive?	Hard-pressed to cope with competitive pressures?
Above-average profit margins?	Inadequate distribution?
Competitive advantages over leaders and key rivals?	A higher-cost producer?
Above-average marketing skills?	Too small to be a major factor in the marketplace?
Above-average technological and innovational capability?	No real distinctive competences?
A creative, entrepreneurially alert management?	A relative newcomer with an unproven track record in this business?
Good market savvy?	A history of poorly-timed or ill-chosen strategic moves?
Capable of capitalizing on opportunities?	Not in good position to deal with emerging threats?
Other?	Other?

How Well Is the Present Strategy Working?

The key indicators of how well a firm's present strategy is working include (1) whether the firm's market share is rising or falling, (2) the size of the firm's profit margins relative to other firms, (3) trends in the firm's net profits and its return on investment, (4) whether the firm's sales are growing as fast as the market is growing, and (5) whether the firm's competitive position is improving or slipping. The signs of strategic success or failure are fairly easy to spot. What is not so easy to understand are the specific reasons underlying the firm's good or not so good strategic performance. These absolutely have to be identified and fully comprehended in order to improve the firm's overall business strategy.

Several considerations are helpful in ferreting out the causes for the degree of business strategy success or failure which a firm has experienced:

- Is the strategy closely linked to the industry's key success factors?

- Is the strategy well matched to the firm's skills and resources?

- Is the strategy timely and in tune with industry trends and the driving forces of competition?

- Is the success of the strategy due to the firm's pioneering or trailblazing strategic approach (such as being the first to act upon or to create new trends)?

- Is any shortfall in performance attributable to bad strategy or to poor implementation and execution?

- Is the firm's strategic performance in any way linked to having (or not having) proprietary technology, a distinctive competence, the good fortune of being in the right place at the right time, the power of a market leader, or the talents and abilities to deal with environmental and competitive changes?

The Firm's Own Strategic Issues and Problems

Because the best strategy for a firm is ultimately a unique game plan reflecting its particular circumstances, it is necessary to factor into the strategy evaluation and selection process those strategy-related issues and problems which are peculiar to the firm. This is largely a case-by-case exercise in which the firm's present strategy has to be evaluated in light of special constraints imposed by the firm's own situation. The important thing to realize here is that the strategic issues and problems which confront a given firm need not coincide exactly with the more general set of industry-wide issues and problems; the differences can make a difference in formulating the firm's own strategic plans.

SIZING UP THE BUSINESS STRATEGY OPTIONS

With the information and conclusions of the foregoing analyses, it ought to be fairly easy to come up with a realistic set of business strategy options. One obvious alternative is always to continue the present strategy, perhaps with minor finetuning. Such a course makes sense when a firm's business-level strategy is not only working well now but is also expected to continue to work well in the immediate future. However, in the event the "continue to follow the same game plan" option is judged unattractive, then two questions need to be posed by the firm's strategists:

1. What can be done to make the present strategy work better and achieve acceptable results?

2. What are the different strategies that fit the firm's situation?

Answering the first question requires an internal appraisal of the business' functional area strategies and how these can be improved to accomplish an overhaul of business-level strategy. Answering the second question requires balancing the different strategies which the firm might optimally like to employ against the constraint of which of these different strategies it is capable of executing well—and with acceptable risk and a prospect of good results.

Searching for the "Right" Competitive Advantage

Given that the acid test of successful business strategy is one of *positioning* the firm in the marketplace where it can be a winner in the ensuing competitive struggle, an important criterion for strategy selection is the magnitude and duration of any competitive advantage which the various strategic options offer. Cost leadership strategies offer the advantage of being in position to sell at a lower price and still earn acceptable profits. Such strategies are appealing when (1) customers are price-sensitive, (2) the offerings of rival firms are essentially identical, standardized, commodity-type products (newsprint, sheet steel, fertilizer, plastic pipe, lumber and bulk commodities), which makes competition solely a cost game, (3) there are not many ways to achieve product differentiation that have much value to buyers, or (4) there are not many differences among buyers (a requirement of differentiation and focus strategies).

Focus strategies offer the advantage of being in position to cater to the special needs of particular types of buyers. Going to a focus strategy has merit (1) when there are distinctly different groups of buyers who either have different needs or else utilize the product in different ways, (2) when rival firms have not attempted to specialize, preferring instead to try to appeal to all types of buyers, or (3) when the firm's resources do not permit it to go after a wide segment of the total market.

Differentiation strategies have the advantage of offering *better value* to customers than rival firms. Efforts to differentiate products or services typically take one of four forms:

1. Strategies based on *technical superiority*.

2. Strategies based on *quality*.

3. Strategies based on giving customers *more supporting services*.

4. Strategies based on the appeal of a *lower price*.

Differentiation strategies are suited for situations where (1) there are many ways to differentiate the product or service and these differences are perceived by some buyers to have value, (2) buyer needs and product uses are diverse, and (3) not many rival firms are following a differentiation strategy. Often, the most attractive avenue for product differentiation is the one least traveled by rival firms—as the saying goes, "never follow the crowd." Also, experience indicates that it is hard to excel in more than one of the four approaches to differentiation simultaneously. To attempt to differentiate in too many ways at once tends to deteriorate into trying to be all things to all people, thus blurring the image the firm presents to its target markets. The best advice in formulating a differentiation strategy is to stress one key value and to develop a distinctive competence in delivering it.

Analyzing Competitive Advantage Options. The matrix shown in Figure 5-6 offers an analytical framework developed by the Boston Consulting Group to help match competitive advantage strategies to prevailing market and competitive conditions.[31] Three premises underlie BCG's competitive advantage analysis: (1) some sort of competitive advantage is necessary for above-average profitability, (2) the number of ways an advantage can be gained and the potential size of the advantage vary by industry, according to certain characteristics, and (3) as industries evolve, so do the nature and magnitude of any competitive advantages. The vertical axis of the matrix is a scale of the number of ways firms have to create a differential competitive advantage. In the restaurant business, firms have many ways to set themselves apart from rivals (location, menu selection, price, atmosphere, meal quality, service) whereas in commodity-type industries the standardized product features make price far and away the most potent competitive weapon. The horizontal axis in Figure 5-6 represents the potential size of the advantage which can be gotten. This, too, varies by industry and by stage of evolution. For example, in an emerging industry, economies of scale often act to give big firms a major advantage over small firms but as that industry consolidates and all firms by necessity invest in efficient, large-scale plants, then the big advantage of large size disappears and competitive advantage opportunities have to be sought in other ways. In commodity-product industries and in other businesses where buyers are not very sensitive to product differences, the size of competitive advantages tends to be very small; the exception is when strategy is keyed to achieving cost leadership and lower price can be used as a competitive weapon.

As shown in Figure 5-6, the plot of the size of the advantage against the number of ways to achieve competitive advantage produces 4 quadrants, each with its own set of dominating competitive features and resulting strategic prescriptions. The content of the 4 cells in Figure 5-6 is self-explanatory; however, one additional point merits emphasis. A competitor

---

[31]This discussion is adapted from an approach used by the Boston Consulting Group as described in Walter Kiechel, III, "Three (or Four, or More) Ways to Win," *Fortune*, October 19, 1981, pp. 181-188.

FIGURE 5-6
Analyzing Competitive Advantage Opportunities

Size of the Competitive Advantage Which Can Be Achieved
(scaled from degrees of "Small" to degrees of "Large")

	Small	Large

Many	*Key Competitive*
	   Feature: Many ways to gain an edge, but the size of the edge counts for little in the marketplace.
	Strategy
	   Prescriptions: Carve out a position and hold it. Emphasize profits *now*. Minimize investment. Be cautious about expansion.
		Key Competitive
		   Feature: A specialized approach to the many market segments is essential and so is creating and protecting the advantage in serving these segments.
		Strategy
		   Prescriptions: Seek a niche. Get in position to serve selected segments. Spend heavily to build and fortify the chosen advantage. Stay ahead of rivals who aspire to gain the same advantage. Watch out for change.

Few	*Key Competitive*
	   Feature: Almost a pure cost-price game; on other factors, all firms are in about equal position. In the absence of price-cost differences, there is a virtual competitive stalemate.
	Strategy
	   Prescriptions: Use aggressive cost reduction strategies. Emphasize ways to improve efficiency. Manage to increase cash flow. Look for diversification opportunities.
		Key Competitive
		   Feature: Only those who get and keep one of the large competitive advantages will survive; usually low cost is the primary advantage that is available. Often, the name of the game is volume.
		Strategy
		   Prescriptions: Pursue economies of scale. Ride the experience curve downward by getting volume up. Go after the customers of weak firms. If weak, get out or look for new ways to compete.

Different Ways a Competitive Advantage Can Be Created (scaled from degrees of "Many" to degrees of "Few")

who unleashes a powerful trend-setting strategy can change the structural character of an industry, establish new competitive rules, and alter the strategic prescriptions. McDonald's strategy transformed the structure and competitive features of the low-volume, single-unit restaurant business during the 1960s and 1970s by literally inventing the fast food business—a high-volume, chain operation keyed to low price, fast service, many locations, and national market coverage. A huge, new segment to the food-away-from-home industry was thus created by a maverick strategy whose spectacular success quickly spawned a raft of new enterprises with imitative-versions of the same basic strategy. Consequently, as an industry's driving forces and competitive rules evolve, an industry can move from one cell to another in Figure 5-6—it is *not* locked into one position.

A somewhat different matrix approach is that used by Strategic Planning Associates and shown in Figure 5-7.[32] Here the variables along the two axes are customer sensitivity to price and customer sensitivity to product differentiation. The issue is how to match the firm's strategy to the various combinations of buyer sensitivity to pricing differences and to product differentiation efforts. The key competitive features and resulting strategic prescriptions (see Figure 5-7) offer further insights into what sorts of competitive approaches fit what sorts of market environments.

The main shortcomings of both matrixes are the same as for all 4-cell matrixes. One, they are not particularly helpful in assessing conditions in the "middle" ranges between high and low or many and few. And, two, the conclusions and prescriptions of matrix analysis are rather general. There are pitfalls in using "standard" game plans for situations which are similar in some respects (price sensitivity, importance of product differentiation, opportunities to gain competitive edges) but are different in other strategically important respects (industry structure and direction, strategic capabilities and positions of the leading firms, the intensity of competitive pressures, the variety among strategic groups, buyer demographics, and so on). As has repeatedly been emphasized, the situation of each industry and each firm is partly unique; these unique features have to be taken into account in formulating strategy. Hence, the generalized strategy prescriptions that spring from matrix analyses such as shown in Figures 5-6 and 5-7 should be viewed as *suggestive* of a general strategic direction and are always subject to being tailored (in major or minor ways) to fit a firm's situation more closely. On those occasions where the unique features in the firm's situation have overriding import, it may be wise to discard the generalized prescriptions altogether.

Screening the List of Strategic Options

Numerous considerations and criteria can be used to separate the stronger candidates from the weaker ones. Looking at the alternatives from the following angles is helpful:

- Which strategy offers the best match with what the company is good at doing? Do any of the alternatives call for greater competence and/or resources than can be mustered? Which strategy takes maximum advantage of the company's strengths?

---

[32]As described by Kiechel, "Three (or Four, or More) Ways to Win," p. 184.

FIGURE 5-7
Matching Strategy to the Competitive Variables of Price
and Product Differentiation

Customer Sensitivity to Differences in the Product
Offerings among Rival Sellers

	High (the differences make a big difference)	Low (the differences don't matter much)
Customer Sensitivity to Price Differences among Rival Sellers — **High**	*Key Competitive Features:* Competition is very active on all fronts; and there are frequent, bold moves by firms to introduce products with new features and/or to alter pricing. Buyers are very discriminating, have little brand loyalty, and shop around for the best overall deal. Key competitive variables can change rapidly. *Strategy Prescriptions:* Adopt a "flexible" strategy. Promote both price and distinctive product features. Push new product development. Be creative and innovative. Prepare for rapid change.	*Key Competitive Features:* A commodity-product business where low cost and low price are the name of the game. Gaining market share is often the key to higher profitability. *Strategy Prescriptions:* Pursue economies of scale. Ride the experience curve downward by getting volume up. Be aggressive in trying to capture market share. Strive for cost leadership.
Low	*Key Competitive Features:* Having the product features that buyers are looking for and appreciate is essential. Must cater to the needs of distinct buyer segments. Success is usually keyed to the right kind of specialization. *Strategy Prescriptions:* Adopt a focus strategy. Differentiate your products from those of rivals. Build a distinctive competence. Avoid blurring the firm's image with a broad coverage strategy (either many product versions or many target segments or, worst of all, both).	*Key Competitive Features:* Very hard to build a meaningful competitive edge; competition is seldom intense. Rivalry is not active and the balance between market demand and market supply govern industry profitability. *Strategy Prescriptions:* Avoid price competition. Promote differences but don't spend much on creating them. Work on improving profit margins by cutting costs and increasing the size of the firm's clientele.

- Which candidate strategies are less attractive from the standpoint of profit outlook or return on investment criteria even though they meet minimum standards? Which option offers the best risk-reward tradeoff?

- Which of the candidate strategies offers the most dominant competitive edge? How vulnerable is each alternative to successful competitive counter-attack?

- How vulnerable are each of the alternatives to market and environmental threats now existing or on the horizon?

- Which strategy appears most capable of succeeding in a variety of market and economic situations? Are any of the alternatives heavily dependent for their success on general economic prosperity and a "sellers' market"? If market conditions are likely to be volatile, which strategy offers the most flexibility and allows contingencies to be built in?

- Which strategy appears best suited to management's philosophy and personality? Should any of the candidate strategies be ruled out because of a conflict with management's sense of social responsibilities or personal values?

- Which option, if successfully executed, would provide the best platform for taking advantage of other market opportunities that might present themselves?

When an alternative scores well on some factors but negatively on others, the net effect is not simply a function of whether there are more pluses than minuses or vice versa. Some criteria are more critical than others—and which ones are the most important vary from case to case.

Ideally, one would like to be able to formulate a business strategy where all or most of the vital considerations were simultaneously optimized.[33] In practice, this objective proves much too utopian. Tradeoffs are inevitably necessary. Trying to minimize risk exposure, for example, nearly always entails a sacrifice of potential profits. Strategic attempts to exploit every opportunity to its fullest can both stretch resources too thin and lead to marching in too many directions at once. The criterion of catering to organizational strengths can divert attention from the need to shore up organizational weaknesses. Moreover, compromises are necessary in order to fashion a strategy which meets the needs of various coalition groups in the management hierarchy (marketing, manufacturing, finance) and which also is consonant with the interest of exogeneous groups (stockholders, labor, consumers, government, the general public). Hence, which strategy is "best" from one angle seldom turns out to be the "best" from other pertinent angles.

---

[33]The discussion in this paragraph applies to corporate strategy evaluation as well as to business strategy evaluation.

In the final analysis, strategic decisions, both at the corporate level and the business level, boil down to a matter of managerial and business judgment. Even after a lengthy and exhaustive strategic evaluation, management is often confronted with choosing among several close alternatives rather than merely confirming a clearcut choice. Very rarely is the issue of what to do so cut-and-dried as to eliminate the judgment/choice problem. Facts and analysis by themselves usually do not resolve the problem of conflicts and inconsistencies. For this reason, intuition, personal experience, judgment, qualitative trade-offs, value preferences, intangible situational factors, and compromise of opinion are an integral part of the process of arriving at a choice of strategy. And no formula or how-to-do-it description is ever likely to take their place.

Three elements of the strategy selection problem frequently assume a pivotal import in reaching a decision:

(1) the risk/reward trade-off,

(2) timing the strategic move, and

(3) contribution to peformance and objectives.

Risk/Reward Considerations.   The relevance of the profitabilty versus risk trade-off is obvious. Risk-averters will be inclined toward "safe" strategies where external threats appear minimal, profits adequate but not spectacular, and in-house resources ample to meet the task ahead. Quite often, such firms insist upon following a financial approach that emphasizes internal financing rather than debt-financing; likewise they may opt to defer major financial commitments as long as possible or until the effects of uncertainty are deemed minimal. They may view pioneering-type innovations as "too chancy" relative to proven, well-established techniques, or else they may simply prefer to be followers rather than leaders. In general, the risk-averter places a high premium on "conservative" strategies which minimize the downside risk.

On the other hand, eager risk-takers lean more toward opportunistic strategies where the payoffs are greater, the challenges more demanding, and the glamour more appealing—despite the pitfalls which may exist. Innovation is preferred to imitation. Aggressive action ranks ahead of defensive conservatism. A confident optimism overrules pessimism. The organization's strengths, not its weaknesses, serve as a chief criterion for matching strategy and organizational capability.

Timing Considerations.   Timing issues are partly a function of the risk-reward situation. For instance, where uncertainty is high, the risk-averter's tendency is to proceed with extreme caution or to stall. A defensive stance is likely to emerge. In contrast, the risk-taker is willing to move early and assume a trail-blazing role. Yet, the timing dilemma goes deeper than the risk/reward trade-off and a preference for an active or reactive style. It also relates to whether market conditions are ripe for the strategies being contemplated. A "good" strategy undertaken at the wrong time can spell failure. Chrysler Corp. had this experience in 1974-1975 when it decided to put more emphasis on full-size, family cars and compete head-on with General Motor's Chevrolet Impala and full-sized Pontiacs, Buicks, and Oldsmobiles. Chrysler redesigned its Plymouth, Dodge, and Chrysler cars along the styling lines of GM's medium-priced models but, unfortunately for Chrysler, they had barely hit the market when the Arab oil boycott and the subsequent steep climb in gasoline prices made customers wary of "big" cars. Chrysler found itself not only stuck with the high costs of having restyled its line of cars but also without an appealing selection of small cars to offer the growing number of economy-minded buyers.

In addition, there are several other timing-related issues which bear on strategy selection.[34] One pertains to the lead time between action and result and any difficulties which may ensue if the lead time is "too long" or "too short." In a closely related vein, whether management's attention is focused principally on the short-run or the long-run can prompt the selection of a strategy geared towards improving performance in whichever time interval is preferred. Still another involves whether the magnitude and rate of investment funding required to support a given strategy fits in with the organization's overall financial structure and cash flow requirements. Inasmuch as strategic investments commonly entail a stream of expenditures rather than a single lump-sum expenditure, the timing of the components may favor the selection of one strategy over another, especially if other factors are not decisive.

Contribution to Performance and Objectives.   Frequently, the real problem of strategy selection originates as a response to unsatisfactory performance. Thus it makes sense that the choice of strategy is heavily governed by the expected contribution to achieving high-priority performance objectives.

ILLUSTRATION CAPSULE 18
Strategy Evaluation: An Example of How It Pays Off

> As an example of what the performance payoff can be when management takes the time to do a serious job of evaluating and reformulating business strategy, consider the case of a small manufacturer of industrial plastics (sales of $60 million). Acquired the previous year by a much larger diversified company, it suffered a serious business downturn and reported profits well below the corporate ROI target. According to one analyst:
>
> Source: Carter F. Bales, "Strategic Control: The President's Paradox," *Business Horizons*, vol. 20, no. 4 (August 1977), pp. 18-19. Quoted with permission.

---

[34]Seymour Tilles, "Making Strategy Explicit," in H. Igor Ansoff, *Business Strategy* (New York: Penguin Books, 1970), p. 197.

ILLUSTRATION CAPSULE 18 *(continued)*

The division had never developed a formal strategy, but management cherished ambitions of building the division into a major producer of commodity and specialty plastics. On the commodity plastics side, division management had counted on finding new applications in the construction industry. On the assumption that new Occupational Safety and Health Administration (OSHA) plant regulations would force at least a few of its competitors out of the market, it was planning an aggressive marketing program. In this way, management thought it could enlarge the division's operating base and eventually justify and "base load" a new world-scale plant to replace two older, relatively inefficient facilities. Meanwhile, on the specialty side, sales of the division's 200-odd patented plastics were limping badly, and a score of new items added over the past two years had so far failed to take off as expected.

It is not surprising that corporate headquarters was worried. Top management knew that the profit decline since 1974 was due partly to the rising price of one major raw material, a petroleum derivative, and partly to the deteriorating production economics of their old plants. They were less confident about the division's strategic assumptions. What if customers should begin shifting to substitute materials? And what if the maturation of some commodity plastics markets should lead to a more cyclical pattern of demand? Faced with these questions, corporate management decided to invest in a formal strategy development effort.

The initial situation analysis was an eye opener. First, division management's optimism about the commodity end of the business turned out to be ill founded: the specialty plastics side was clearly more promising. An analysis of end-use markets, coupled with detailed projections of likely profit economics, pointed to a slow-growing but genuine opportunity in selected segments. But to capitalize on that opportunity, the product line and marketing effort would have to be modified.

Accordingly, management decided to convert the division, over a five-year period, from a minor factor in many sectors of the industrial plastics market to a strong competitor on a much narrower front. The specialty product line would be tailored to customer requirements, the sales force upgraded and the marketing approach refocused. As demand for the specialty line grew, the division would gradually withdraw from the commodity business. At the same time, exposure and risk would be reduced by closing the older of the two manufacturing plants, by cutting working capital and by eliminating near-term capital expenditures.

Eighteen months after these decisions were made, the division had already realized profit improvements of better than $4 million, almost doubling its profits and performing well above the corporate ROI target. It did so well, in fact, that a proposal to replace the remaining manufacturing plant with a modern, efficient facility had already been approved. The division's profitable new strategy had four characteristics that are present in most high-payoff strategies:

ILLUSTRATION CAPSULE 18 *(continued)*

It focused on the sectors of highest potential yield. The plastics division concentrated on the most profitable and exploitable product families and types, customer industries and specific customers, and channels of distribution. Analysis showed that well over half of the division's 200 specialty plastics lines were making a marginal contribution to fixed costs or actually losing money. Nearly forty had been competing in markets where they were clearly inferior; for example, one that was being pushed for outdoor application did not stand up well to weathering. And the many colors offered often meant short, uneconomic production runs.

By pruning unprofitable products and consolidating product recipes, the division reduced its line to thirty-three items that had above-average performance characteristics and were targeted at end-use markets where competition was not yet severe and demand was likely to grow. Prices were increased, based on the price differential with the nearest competitive material and the calculable effect on the customer's production costs. A special surcharge was instituted on low-volume purchases of nonstandard colors.

It balanced profit payoff and business risk. In its drive for expanded market share in the commodity sector, the plastics division had unwittingly embraced a high-risk strategy. Despite its precarious position as a marginal competitor, it had failed to plan for such contingencies as a proposed federal regulation that could have wiped out one major product application. Moreover, it would have sharply increased its financial exposure had it proceeded with the proposal to replace the two obsolete plants.

Management carefully examined a range of alternatives before settling on the strategy offering the most acceptable combination of risk and payoff. Risk was reduced by withdrawing from the commodity business, while the phaseout of the older factory shrank the asset base and cut working capital. To put the strategy on a pay-as-you-go basis, specific financial and market development objectives were set up for specialty plastics, and replacement of the second plant was tied to their attainment. At the same time, a targeted sales effort and a tough manufacturing cost reduction program were launched.

It emphasized both feasibility and consistency. Surprisingly often, businesses plan market and sales initiatives, product development programs and the like that are unrealistic or incompatible. The plastics division, for example, had been trying to penetrate the specialty market with a sales force that knew how to sell only commodity plastics to a few high-volume customers. Unable to help with new applications, they soon lost the few prospects that turned up for the specialty line. The new strategy, in contrast, explicitly identified target customers and analyzed their potential, and laid out programs for upgrading the sales force and providing applications support.

Again, though the division was plagued with cost problems and loaded with new products it couldn't sell, its R&D staff had been hard at work

ILLUSTRATION CAPSULE 18 *(concluded)*

developing new specialty products. But four out of the twelve new products under development were technological long shots, and the total potential market for the rest was estimated at less than $50 million. Under the new strategy, a watchdog group of managers—from marketing, customer applications assistance and R&D—was set up to keep all new product and applications projects geared to the new market priorities.

It specified tasks, responsibilities, and timetables. Specific goals, responsibilities and completion dates were assigned to each major product group and business function for three years ahead. Volume, profit and market share objectives were translated into specific targets such as the percentage of trial customers to be converted into repeat purchasers and the amount and timing of price increases by product and customer. Performance criteria were established for successive six-month progress reviews, and contingency moves were mapped out, based on the results in hand and the market and competitive situation as each checkpoint was reached.

THE ACT OF STRATEGIC COMMITMENT

The final component of strategy selection is the commitment decision. In fact, a strategic choice cannot be said to have been made until money and manpower have been committed. The act of commitment is what takes the issue of the strategic decision out of the category of an alternative and activates the chosen strategy to official organizational status. Commitment entails (1) directing some part of the organization to undertake the strategy selected, (2) assigning responsibility for implementing the strategic plan to the appropriate personnel, (3) allocating the resources necessary for implementation, (4) clarifying exactly where and under what circumstances implementation is to be undertaken, and (5) specifying the time interval for implementation. In effect, then, strategic commitment supplies answers to the obvious implementation issues of *who, where,* and *when* and thus lays a foundation for launching the task of putting the chosen strategy into place.

Two concluding points. First, the process of evaluating strategic alternatives and arriving at a choice of strategy has elements of ambiguity. There are no infallible rules or procedures which, if followed to the letter, will lead to the "right" strategy choice. Strategy selection cannot be reduced to a precise, formula-like, analytic process. Intangible situational factors, astute entrepreneurship, and creativity must be judiciously interwoven with the quantifiable, concrete realities of a competitive marketplace. Thus, there is no substitute for the exercise of managerial business judgment and, consequently, no way of posing a strategy formulation methodology that will "guarantee" an effective strategic choice. In short, strategy selection is a managerial responsibility, not a technique. The process is not susceptible to a step-by-step "how to" set of answers. One can, at most, offer guidelines, indicate pitfalls, and pose some of the right kinds of questions to ask.

Second, everything that was said earlier (Chapter 4) about the process of corporate strategy formulation being incremental and evolutionary, the result of trial and error and gradually accumulated understanding, applies equally to business strategy evolution and formulation. Rarely is there an all-inclusive grand formulation of the total business strategy. Instead, the evaluation and reformulation of business strategy evolves from ongoing events and is the product of learning from the successes and failures of the firm's own strategy, observing how well other firms' strategies are working, gaining firsthand experience with the marketplace and competitive actions of rivals, building awareness of the changing winds of competition and industry direction, sensing the buildup of new driving forces, observing customer reactions and behavior, acquiring a "feel" for the strategically-relevant factors, sifting through the pros and cons of the firm's strategic options and building a consensus on what course to follow. Thus while there are certainly times when strategy is intensely evaluated and major reformulations occur, the supporting analysis and the actions taken generally have roots in many past events and experiences, both internal and external. Formulating, evaluating and reformulating business strategy, as for corporate strategy, is a product of many steps and few giant analytical leaps and brainstorms.

SUGGESTED READINGS

Buchele, Robert B., "How to Evaluate a Firm," *California Management Review*, vol. 4, no. 1 (Fall 1962), pp. 5-17.

Frohman, Alan L. and Domenic Bitondo, "Coordinating Business Strategy and Technical Planning," *Long-Range Planning*, vol. 14, no. 6 (December 1981), pp. 58-67.

Gilmore, Frank, "Formulating Strategy in Smaller Companies," *Harvard Business Review*, vol. 49, no. 3 (May-June 1971), pp. 71-81.

Henry, Harold W., "Appraising Company's Strengths and Weaknesses," *Managerial Planning* (July/August 1980), pp. 31-36.

Kaiff, H., "How Is Competition Performing?" *Long Range Planning*, vol. 12, no. 3 (June 1979), pp. 16-21.

Lunneman, Robert E. and John D. Kennell, "Short-Sleeve Approach to Long-Range Planning," *Harvard Business Review*, vol. 55, no. 2 (March-April 1977), pp. 141-50.

Porter, Michael E., "How Competitive Forces Shape Strategy," *Harvard Business Review*, vol. 57, no. 2 (March-April 1979), pp. 137-45.

Porter, Michael E., *Competitive Strategy: Techniques for Analyzing Industries and Competition* (New York: The Free Press, 1980).

Rodriguez, Jaime I. and William R. King, "Competitive Information Systems," *Long Range Planning*, vol. 10, no. 6 (December 1977), pp. 45-50.

South, Stephen E., "Competitive Advantage: The Cornerstone of Strategic Thinking," *Journal of Business Strategy*, vol. 1, no. 4 (Spring 1981), pp. 15-25.

Wall, Jerry, "What the Competition Is Doing? Your Need to Know," *Harvard Business Review*, vol. 52, no. 6 (November-December 1974), pp. 22 ff.

READING

Competitive Advantage: The Cornerstone of Strategic Thinking*

STEPHEN E. SOUTH

Stephen E. South is Director, Corporate Planning and Development, Clark Equipment Company.

The idea of competitive advantage is not new. What is new is the growing acceptance of this planning concept as a general philosophy of management. In all likelihood, the notion of competitive advantage will provide the guiding philosophy for the predominant management practice of the 1980s: strategic management. As experience at Clark Equipment Company shows, the answers to eight key questions can spell out a winning strategy.

There are signs that a new management philosophy is emerging. As the 1980s begin, a general approach for dealing with the central business challenges of the time is already being incorporated into management practice. From an historical perspective this is to be expected, since in previous decades new management philosophies have evolved to accommodate the fundamental forces which were then influencing business success.

During the coming decade there will be in all likelihood two predominant forces with which management must deal: uncertainty in the business environment and intensity of global competition. While other developments will also be important, these two are likely to shape the prevailing management philosophy of the decade. Under these circumstances it is becoming more and more evident that the idea of competitive advantage—the philosophy of choosing only those competitive arenas where victories are clearly achievable—offers the best general approach for achieving sustained business success. It does so by prescribing a concentrated investment of resources in those enclaves of competitive activity which, because they are sheltered from the changing business environment and protected from intense global competition, offer the best opportunity for continuing profitability and sound investment returns.

This general approach to the management task is more selective than that of previous decades and is providing the underlying philosophy for the

This article is reprinted by permission from the *Journal of Business Strategy*, vol. 1, no. 4 (Spring 1981), pp. 15-25. Copyright © 1981 by Warren, Gorham and Lamont, Inc., 210 South Street, Boston, Mass. All rights reserved.

dominant management practice of the 1980s: strategic management. The process of strategic management is coming to be defined, in fact, as the management of competitive advantage—that is, as a process of identifying, developing, and taking advantage of enclaves in which a tangible and preservable business advantage can be achieved.

This article will first deal with the idea of competitive advantage, how it developed and where it fits in the evolution of management practice. Then we will deal with a key question: Is it achievable in real-life business situations? And, by example, we will demonstrate its value as an effective basis for building strategies and plans. Finally, we will discuss an approach used for instilling this philosophy in a large multinational organization, including group learning exercises used in strategic management workshops conducted around the world.

HOW THE NOTION OF COMPETITIVE ADVANTAGE EMERGED

The idea of competitive advantage emerged in the late 1970s, articulated by McKinsey and Company and based on the success of the Japanese in penetrating world markets under changing business circumstances. It is an interpretation of the approach which brought competitive success to a wide range of Japanese companies. These companies achieved high levels of operating efficiency based in part on cultural differences which are now widely discussed. But they were successful also in artfully selecting competitive arenas in which they could do battle from a position of strength. In short, they succeeded as strategists—winning strategic as well as operating victories.

In a sense the Japanese experience offers a preview of the 1980s, confronted as they were with the necessity of becoming worldwide competitors at a time when world markets were shocked by the uncertainties of oil shortages, recession, rapid escalation of oil and other prices, and floating exchange rates. The Japanese have already experienced and dealt with the forces which are coming to be recognized as the important management challenges of the 1980s. These forces clearly have a direct impact on day-to-day operations, and many tactics have evolved for dealing with the difficulties they create. But they are also impacting the fundamentals of what it takes to make a business successful, necessitating a rethinking of the basics of business success.

RETHINKING BUSINESS SUCCESS

In rethinking the basics of superior performance relative to competitors, managers in Japan and elsewhere have come to distinguish between two fundamental elements of business success: operating effectiveness and competitive position. It is now widely recognized that effective management of operations is not the only key, and that competitive position in an industry is frequently the dominant factor in determining which businesses are most successful.

Competitive position, determined not only by market share but also by manufacturing process, distribution approach, product offering and the like, frequently overwhelms differences in operating effectiveness to determine which competitors are most successful. So while the combination of strong competitive position and effective operations almost always guarantees success, a strong competitive position makes relative success highly likely even if operating performance suffers in comparison with competition. On the other hand, a weak competitive position combined with poor operating effectiveness virtually assures failure relative to competitors. And the chances of offsetting a weak position with more effective operations are questionable at best.

Interestingly, evidence suggests that this has always been an important distinction. But, in a world of slower change and more isolated competitive arenas, competition tended to focus on operations, with competitive positions tending to be very similar except for differences in volume and market share.

RECIPROCAL VERSUS STRATEGIC COMPETITION

Because of this, only recently have we come to recognize that there are really two very different forms of competition. The first and most familiar, and still the most prevalent, is reciprocal competition. In this instance, which most frequently occurs in mature industries, companies compete from very similar strategic positions, relying on operating differences to separate the successful from the unsuccessful.

The new form of competition, effectively pursued by the Japanese, is strategic competition. In this approach the competitive struggle is pursued, first and foremost, on a strategic basis. The choice of market segments, product offering, distribution channels, and manufacturing process becomes the paramount consideration.

COMPETITIVE ADVANTAGE: THE KEY TO STRATEGIC COMPETITION

The notion of competitive advantage suggests that the key to successful strategic competition is the selection of competitive arenas which meet two criteria: First, that they can be sheltered from change in the business environment and, second, that an advantaged position can be achieved as protection from intense global competition. The purpose is not to retreat from competition, but to compete selectively from an advantageous strategic position.

Competitive advantage can be achieved through a number of different avenues:

- By concentrating on particular market segments.
- By offering products which differ from, rather than mirror, the competition.
- By using alternative distribution channels and manufacturing processes.
- By employing selective pricing and fundamentally different cost structures.

In each instance, however, the goal is to establish a clear and favorable differentiation from competitors. This can be achieved in very direct ways, including patent protection or trade barriers, for example, and indirectly through competitor inaction or aggressive pursuit of advantage by a competitor more willing to take risks.

Regardless of the basis for competitive advantage, the central considerations are whether the advantage is tangible and measurable and whether it is preservable, at least for a period of time. In short, a competitive advantage is one which offers the opportunity for sustained profitability relative to competitors rather than a circumstance in which profits are competed away by firms with similar positions fighting for volume and market share.

Strategic Management

The idea of competitive advantage is a powerful one because it identifies what to look for in developing strategies and plans—namely, a fundamentally advantageous position from which to compete. The management approach which it prescribes is a continuing process of identifying, developing, and exploiting advantageous business positions. To accept anything less than a tangible and preservable advantage in the competitive arena, especially during the 1980s, is to virtually insure that sustained business success will be sacrificed to changed business conditions and aggressive global competitors.

IS COMPETITIVE ADVANTAGE REALLY ACHIEVABLE?

With regard to this philosophy of management, or any other for that matter, the key question is not whether the approach appears to fit the needs of the times or is conceptually appealing, but whether it is a practical and useful tool for managing businesses. And in this instance, the specific question is whether it is practical to achieve advantaged competitive positions in real business situations.

From our experience in capital goods businesses at Clark Equipment Company, the answer is yes. The internal consulting group in our corporate planning department has dealt with business situations around the world using competitive advantage as the guiding philosophy for developing strategies and plans. And this experience has convinced us that, at least for many of our businesses, it is possible to achieve tangible and preservable business advantages which can be the basis for sustained profitability relative to competitors.

As suggested earlier, there are two primary considerations in identifying or developing competitive advantage in real-life business situations:

- To select or establish business arenas which are relatively sheltered from the vagaries of environmental change.
- To achieve a protected or advantageous competitive position within that arena.

SHELTERED BUSINESS ARENAS

The first of these considerations tends to be more subjective and subtle, more a matter of degree. However, there are examples of successfully achieving sheltered business situations which are relatively immune from economic, political, and technological change.

An Example: Going Local

In a Latin American subsidiary, for example, a number of steps were taken over the years to shelter the operation from substantial changes in government policy. Early on it was recognized that the only avenue for successfully participating in that market on a continuing basis was to develop an operation indigenous to the country, one which was in concert with the basic aims and interests of the government and which could comfortably adapt to and contribute to changes in policy. This was accomplished through a series of steps, including shared ownership with local investors, local manufacture of virtually all products sold in the market, high local content to provide maximum employment and to develop local suppliers, and export programs to support government trade policies. In short, these steps were taken to establish an operation which was relatively immune from changes in economic policy directed at outsiders and, in that sense, one which was sheltered from some of the uncertainties of that market.

Other Opportunities: Technology and Finance

There are, moreover, other opportunities for developing sheltered business enclaves, including technologically stable product and manufacturing situations which are not susceptible to abrupt technological change, financial structures which can help to neutralize the impact of currency changes, the development of a business mix which neutralizes the impact of economic cycles, and the establishment of a funding mix which minimizes the impact of interest rate cycles. In each case, the common denominator is a deliberate effort to establish a business arena which is not directly vulnerable to major changes in the environment.

ADVANTAGED COMPETITIVE POSITIONS

As these examples suggest, the philosophy of blanket participation in all markets, products, and technologies related to a business can give way to selective participation in those arenas with enough stability to insure profitable return on investment. And this more selective approach carries over to the second consideration in arriving at competitive advantage. That consideration is whether, within a chosen business enclave, there is an opportunity to establish a clearly advantageous business position. This may be accomplished either through a fully protected situation where no competition exists, or one in which competition is present but is clearly at a disadvantage.

Patents and Trade Barriers

The most obvious illustration of a fully protected business position is patent protection. Trade barriers are another avenue for achieving similar levels of protection. In some industries and countries, businesses still enjoy relatively complete protection from imports and few if any local competitors. This provides clearly protected situations with uncontested access to these markets and, importantly, a period of time in which to develop a strong competitive position. Other opportunities for fully protected situations range from high tariffs to single-source contracts.

Early Market Entry

Time can often be as effective in protecting a business position as the presence of an artificial barrier. Early market entry is the most obvious example. There are still many opportunities in world markets for exclusive involvement for extended periods before competitors enter. In countless instances in the capital goods industry, companies have entered markets in which there was little or no competition for five or ten years, and more. These protected positions, achieved through individual company initiative and inaction by competitors, provide an extended period in which to achieve brand identification and customer loyalty, develop distribution networks, achieve manufacturing scale, and to enjoy considerable flexibility in pricing and product offering.

Product Leadership

Product leadership—being the first to introduce a product in a certain class or size range—can also provide a protected position. In one of our North American markets, there was a clear pattern of new product introduction from year to year as competitors launched products with greater and greater capacity in two product classes. Three or four manufacturers led the way and, typically, there was a six-month-to-two-year lag from the time one manufacturer introduced a model until the others followed suit. During that period of time, for that capacity machine, the leader enjoyed a protected business position.

As attractive as protected positions are, they tend to break down over time regardless of whether they are based on government policy, competitor inaction, or other factors. However, they are important not only for the immediate profit opportunity they provide, but also for the opportunity to develop an advantageous position for the longer term. In the case of product leadership, for example, the temporary absence of competition provides the opportunity to gain market share and brand loyalty, which tends to continue over a long period of time. Across the board, the first entrant in a size class tended to maintain a significant share advantage over competition.

Innovative Product Features

There are many other examples, however, of advantageous competitive positions which are not developed under protected circumstances, such as introduction of innovative product features. In one such case relatively competitive machines were available from a number of manufacturers, but the first to introduce a new feature enjoyed an advantageous position for more than two years, with an opportunity for profitability and market share until the others followed suit and neutralized the advantage.

Pricing

Pricing can often be the vehicle for maximizing competitive advantage. In one interesting example,[1] a company holding a small share of industry volume recognized that in certain applications the fuel consumption of its

---

[1] William E. Johnson, "Trade-Offs in Pricing Strategy," *Pricing Practices and Strategy* (The Conference Board, 1977).

product was materially lower than competitors, providing a measurable advantage in operating cost. From this basic advantage, the company was able to establish a price premium for its product which materially improved profitability. Yet, by focusing on these applications and limiting the price advantage to less than the product's true value to the customer, the company was also able to gain market share.

Cost Structure

Price advantage can also frequently be the vehicle for reaping the rewards of an advantageous cost position. The advantage may be based on scale or experience and volume. Advantages are also obtainable through parts commonality and concentration of product lines into fewer models and, of course, through vertical integration. Making fundamental shifts in manufacturing process—for example, shifting from bay-build to moving line—can also achieve significant cost advantage.

Financial Structure

Finally, in addition to product, market, price, and cost-based advantages there are other opportunities which involve parts and service support, financial merchandising, and even the financial structure of the company. The impact of an aggressive financial structure—a highly leveraged balance sheet—on competitive cost position is sometimes overlooked. The willingness to take financial risk through greater leverage can mean that margins and prices can be reduced without sacrificing shareholder profitability relative to competitors. And the price advantage this provides can be the basis for gains in market share.

These are just a few examples which illustrate the range of possibilities for achieving competitive advantage. In some cases, they represent actions which might have been pursued for other reasons, but the important point is to take full advantage of such situations.

INSTILLING THE IDEA THROUGHOUT
AN ORGANIZATION

Our experience in applying the idea of competitive advantage in some of our divisions suggested to us the value of instilling throughout the organization a discipline for critically examining businesses to identify current or future opportunities to achieve advantaged positions.   The vehicle we used to instill this philosophy on a worldwide basis was a series of two-day workshops in strategic management. These sessions involved all general managers, managers of marketing, manufacturing and engineering, controllers and planners. The purposes of these workshops were to:

- Develop a common strategic thought process—a shared way of thinking among the management group of each division which focused on strategic competition and what to do about it.
- Establish an understanding of competitive advantage as the centerpiece of strategic thinking and as the underlying philosophy of strategic management.
- Communicate realistic examples of competitive advantage taken from our businesses.
- Discuss techniques of business analysis which could help in identifying competitive advantage.

THINKING STRATEGICALLY: THE KEY QUESTIONS

The method we used for developing among participants a common strategic thought process based on competitive advantage was a simple framework—or outline—consisting of a series of questions to be answered for individual businesses. This approach was prompted by similar frameworks used in developing military strategy. In fact, strategic thinking is a thought process probably first developed centuries ago by military organizations. And these organizations have found it useful to develop aids to strategic thinking which help them focus on the right issues, suggest a sequence for the thought process, and provide a common frame of reference for discussing and reviewing strategy. The questions which make up our framework serve as aids in developing business strategy, with one question building on another, leading to conclusions regarding the strategies and plans most appropriate for the business.

What Business Am I In?

The approach begins with the question: What business am I in? At least at the outset, the definition can be straightforward. The key elements will be products offered, geographic or other boundaries of the market, and a listing of major competitors. These elements will generally define the current scope of the business, although in some instances it may be necessary to elaborate on technologies involved or other factors. However, there can be more to this question than you might think.

First, some concern usually arises over how narrowly or broadly to define businesses. This is a matter of judgment, but the basic principle is to isolate a unique competitive situation which can be dealt with on a relatively uniform basis.

A second important consideration is whether to define the business as it presently stands or as it can be in the future. For example, a railroad might consider itself to be in the business of providing rail service utilizing a given route structure or, alternatively, as a transportation company employing rail and other modes to transport goods within a geographic area.

The choice of business definition, more than any other element of strategy, depends on the personality, leadership qualities, and vision of the individual general manager. In those instances in which he is pursuing a new and different direction, his definition of the business can itself be the central element of a business strategy.

Regardless of how a business is defined at the outset, however, it is likely to be redefined as actual strategies are considered. Often the definition will be broadened to encompass the full range of available opportunities, which may not have been recognized initially.

What Spells the Difference between Success and Failure?

Once the scope of the business is clear, the next question is: What makes the difference between success and failure in this business? Answering this question involves sorting through all the complexities of the business, and boiling them down to a limited number of factors which will make one competitor more or less successful than the others.

Two approaches can help in arriving at sound answers. In the "top-down" or "macro" approach, one begins by considering those factors which are generally important to the profitability of any business—market share, investment intensity, and the like. Then a broad-gauge comparison of the industry with others helps to narrow the list. Finally, from that broad perspective it is possible to formulate a short list of factors which are keys to success for the specific business in question, based primarily on judgment and industry experience.

The second method, a "bottom-up" or "micro" approach, involves looking more intensively and perhaps more analytically at the particular industry segment in which the business competes. One technique is to compare the way competitors do business and to separate the successful from the unsuccessful, identifying what the first group does or does not do compared to the second. A complementary approach is to focus on the ultimate customer, rethinking his needs and the role the product plays in the economics of his business or in his value system. This is important because prevailing industry practices may, in fact, be missing the mark entirely.

The important thing to keep in mind is that success is relative. A winning strategy is one which places a business among the most successful in its industry segment. Those factors which make the difference between the more and less successful must, therefore, become the focal point for the strategic thought process.

Where Do Competitors Stand?

Identifying these key success factors sets the stage for the next question: Where do I and my competitors stand? For those key factors which really make the difference, what is the true market and competitive situation? The purpose in answering this question is to develop an objective evaluation of the situation.

From the strategic perspective there are two important elements of a business situation: competitive circumstances and the market environment. Two questions need to be asked:

- Relative to competitors, what are my strengths and weaknesses?
- In the marketplace, what are the primary opportunities and threats?

Some factors to consider in answering these questions are product offering, distribution networks, manufacturing processes, technological changes, and political developments.

The analysis of strengths/weaknesses and opportunities/threats is now a relatively conventional approach to situation analysis. In thinking through a basic strategy for the business, however, it is useful to limit this evaluation to those key factors which make the difference between success and failure. For example, if distribution coverage is the key to success, the evaluation of competitors and market changes should focus on implications for the distribution network.

Who Has Competitive Advantage?

From this objective self-analysis some conclusions can be reached to the question: Do I or my competitors have any unique competitive advantages?

The real problem in identifying competitive advantage is to distinguish it from the vague notion that "we are better than they are." Identifying current competitive advantage can begin from the analysis of strengths and weaknesses relative to competitors. But a strength will represent an advantage and a weakness a disadvantage only if it:

- Involves a key success factor.
- Is definable, measurable, and significant.
- Is preservable.

The question of competitive advantage has a second aspect which extends beyond the current situation. That involves identifying potential advantages that can be developed for the future. Assessing future moves, based on opportunities and threats in the market environment, provides a list of possibilities to consider in arriving at a strategy for the future of the business.

How Should I Use My Advantage?

Once competitive advantage has been identified, the question is then: How do I most effectively employ the advantages I have, counter those of my competitors, and develop or acquire greater advantage? Managing a business strategically means continually asking and answering this question in an effective way.

This question not only defines business strategy in a specific way—as the management of competitive advantage—but also identifies the elements necessary for a comprehensive strategy. These include not only a rationale for making the most of current circumstances but also for minimizing competitive inroads and, importantly, for building a position of advantage for the future. Without each of these elements a strategy is incomplete.

Answering the strategy question provides the important ingredient frequently missing from conventional planning approaches: namely, a clear and explicit rationale for achieving competitive success, based on a clearly defined scope for the business, an understanding of those factors which make for success in the industry, an objective assessment of the market and competitive situation, and a clear understanding of competitive advantage.

What Support Will This Strategy Require?

With this rationale in mind the planning question can be asked from a strategic viewpoint: What will this strategy require in terms of product development, marketing, and manufacturing?

This approach differs from the conventional approach to planning because it provides a clear purpose for developing plans. That purpose is to devise a practical way of achieving competitive advantage; that is, a concrete group of actions which will implement the rationale for competitive success. It may involve product specifications which meet needs served ineffectively by competitor products, marketing priorities which focus on market segments in which competitor presence is missing or ineffective, a change to a different manufacturing process, unused by competitors, which provides unique cost or quality advantages, a pricing policy which exploits a competitor price umbrella, or parts and service policy which reflects an advantage in field population. In short, this approach helps to shift the planning effort away from the conscious or unconscious mimicking of competitors.

Is It Worth It?

The next important consideration is the financial question: Is the investment of resources—financial and otherwise—worth it in terms of expected returns and, for the company as a whole, is it affordable? The important point here is that the total investment in a strategy, not simply the capital equipment portion, be subjected to thoughtful analysis as an integral part of the strategic thought process.

A full financial analysis may, however, interrupt the strategic dialogue. But a simple balancing of costs involved and benefits expected, even without being reduced to the common denominator of discounted investment returns, can generally separate the practical from the impractical. The important consideration is to identify all of the major impacts of a strategy. For example, aggressive pricing in a particular market segment must be reflected in lower gross margins. Once the strategic impacts are identified, costs can be weighed against benefits judgmentally, with detailed analysis to follow when appropriate.

Who Will Implement the Plan and How?

The final question, and an important element of strategy is: Who will implement the plan and how? What are the principal goals and objectives individuals must achieve to successsfully implement the strategy? Can they survive the test for competing priorities? This is a crucial question because many strategies and plans fail for lack of effective implementation.

This final question completes the basic elements of thinking through a comprehensive strategy for a business. Taken together, they suggest a sequence for developing, reviewing, and discussing business strategy.

A PRACTICAL EXERCISE IN STRATEGIC THINKING

As an aid to strategic thinking the questions just outlined are simple and straightforward. As a practical matter, however, considerable effort is required to instill this discipline throughout an organization. And the best way to introduce this approach, in our experience, is for individual managers to apply this framework directly to their own businesses in a workshop setting. As a vehicle for doing so we have devised an exercise (Exhibit 1) which serves as a convenient way of recording thoughts and conclusions regarding each of these questions. During the workshops, a moderator elaborates briefly on each question and discusses examples. Individual participants then answer each question as it pertains to their own business, developing a strategy rationale for the business as they proceed.

However, in all but the most autocratic organizations, strategy planning is a collective, not an individual, undertaking. It is a collective process of thinking and communicating which involves not only the general manager, but also managers of major business functions such as engineering, manufacturing, and marketing.

EXHIBIT 1

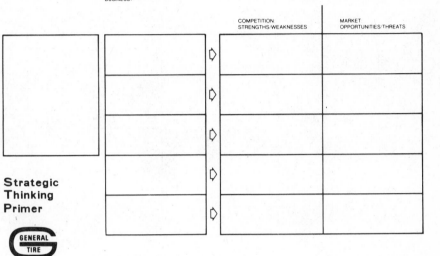

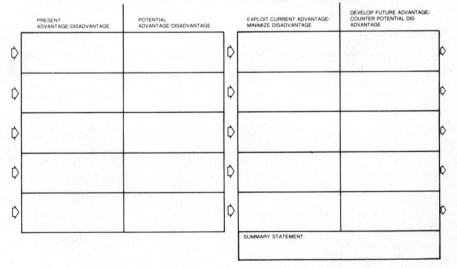

EXHIBIT 1 *(concluded)*

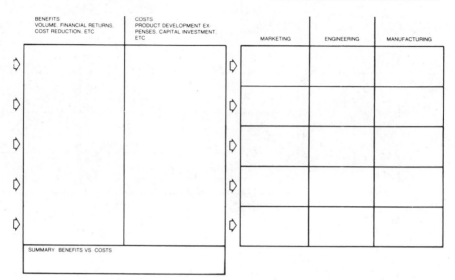

FORECASTS
IS IT WORTH IT AND CAN I AFFORD IT?

BENEFITS
VOLUME, FINANCIAL RETURNS,
COST REDUCTION, ETC

COSTS
PRODUCT DEVELOPMENT EX-
PENSES, CAPITAL INVESTMENT,
ETC

SUMMARY BENEFITS VS COSTS

GOALS AND OBJECTIVES
WHAT MUST BE DONE TO IMPLEMENT THE STRATEGY AND PLANS?

MARKETING	ENGINEERING	MANUFACTURING

PLANS AND PROGRAMS
WHAT WILL THIS STRATEGY REQUIRE IN TERMS OF MARKETING, PRODUCT DEVELOPMENT, MANUFACTURING AND SERVICE/SUPPORT

MARKETING: PRICING, DISTRIBUTION, MARKETING FOCUS, ETC	PRODUCT DEVELOPMENT PRODUCT OFFERING, TIMING, ETC	MANUFACTURING LOCATION/SOURCE, MANUFACTUR-ING PROCESS, ETC	SERVICE/SUPPORT AFTER SALE SUPPORT REQUIREMENTS

Combining Individual and Group Exercises

For this reason, the exercise has been used not only as an individual learning experience but also as a group learning process—again, using a real business situation. The approach is for individual members of a division's management group to first complete the exercise independently. Then a group discussion session is convened. The exercise begins again, starting with the question of business definition. In time, each question is discussed and, where possible, a consensus or common view is developed. This group exercise helps develop a common framework for discussing and arriving at business strategy based on competitive advantage. And it can help to identify issues to be resolved and conflicting perceptions of the business which could hamper implementation of the general manager's strategy.

Of course, no simple framework can do justice to the complex thought process involved in developing a business—or military—strategy. But it can help to focus and channel the process in a constructive way and provide a common language for the planning dialogue.

A common framework for thinking about and communicating strategies is perhaps the central discipline which contemporary planning practice is bringing to business organizations. An approach such as the one just outlined, however, can also provide a useful framework for developing another important planning discipline: the creation of strategies and plans which are soundly based on data, facts, and analysis. And that is the final purpose of the strategic management workshops.

Strategic Management Workshops

The two-day workshops begin with an explanation of the company's planning process. Most of the first morning is devoted to the exercise in strategic thinking, for individuals and then for teams of managers. For the remaining day and a half each of the strategic questions is again discussed. These discussions focus on real-life examples from businesses other than those represented at the workshop, and on techniques of business analysis which can most appropriately be used to arrive at sound answers to these questions. For example, techniques of market analysis ranging from survey research to econometric forecasting are discussed as vehicles for arriving at a sound assessment of the market environment.

A STRATEGIC MANAGEMENT CULTURE

These workshops, then, are a basic vehicle for developing a common strategic perspective among operating managers—a perspective based on competitive advantage as the underlying philosophy of strategic management. The development of such a perspective can contribute greatly to an organization's ability to think strategically about its businesses. And, it can provide a common base of understanding which is central to effective communication on issues of business strategy and, ultimately, to the development of a strong and effective management process. As organizations grow larger, more complex, and more distant from the competitive realities of the marketplace, this understanding—communicated widely through an organization—can help create a management culture focused on achieving competitive success in the turbulent business environment of the 1980s.

REFERENCES

Banks, Robert L., and Wheelwright, Steven G., "Operations vs. Strategy: Trading Tomorrow for Today," *Harvard Business Review*, May-June 1979.

"Effective Strategies for Competitive Success," *The McKinsey Quarterly*, Winter 1978.

Hayes, Robert H., and Wheelwright, Steven G., "The Dynamics of Process-Product Life Cycles," *Harvard Business Review*, March-April 1979.

Johnson, William E., "Trade-Offs in Pricing Strategy," *Pricing Practices and Strategy* (The Conference Board, 1977).

————. *Strategic Leadership: The Challenge to Chairmen* (McKinsey & Co., 1979).

IMPLEMENTING AND ADMINISTERING STRATEGY: ORGANIZATIONAL STRUCTURE AND RESOURCE ALLOCATION

6

.. . organizations are creatures of habit just like people. They are cultures, heavily influenced by the past.

Robert H. Waterman, Jr.

. . . the purpose of formal organizations is to provide a framework for cooperation and to fix responsibilities, delineate authority, and provide for accountability. . . .

Edmund P. Learned

Strategy formulation and strategy implementation have a fundamentally different managerial character. The first has an entrepreneurial focus and the second has an administrative focus. The first emphasizes the abilities to conceptualize, analyze, and judge what constitutes an entrepreneurially effective strategy and what does not, whereas the second depends upon the skills of working through others, instituting internal change, and guiding the activities requisite for executing the strategic plan. In comparison, the task of converting the chosen strategic plan into good results takes a lot more managerial time and energy than does the task of formulating it. And the managerial problems of strategy implementation sweep across a broad administrative front.

THE CENTRAL TASKS OF STRATEGY IMPLEMENTATION AND ADMINISTRATION

Implementing a strategic plan, especially the new and different features it contains, quickly brings the administrative requirements of carrying out the plan to the forefront. In general, every unit of an organization, from headquarters on down to each operating department, has to ask, "what is required for us to implement our part of the overall strategic plan and how can we best get it done?" A thorough answer to this question means examining a host of administrative and operating areas to see what the strategy-related requirements are and how they can be accommodated. Organizationwide commitment to the plan and to what needs to be done to implement it has to be generated. An atmosphere of purposeful change and a culture of "the way we *now* need to do things around here" has to emerge and pave the way for translating the plan into action. There is the issue of whether the present organization is well-suited to implement the chosen strategy and, if not, what changes in structure and key positions may have to be made. Considerable administrative attention will need to be given such critical areas as how to develop and nurture the skills and distinctive competences upon which the strategy is grounded, how much of what kind of resources to allocate to the various organization units, what performance standards to set, how to link the firm's motivation and reward structure directly and clearly to accomplishing the strategic plan, what new or different internal operating policies and procedures to institute, and what kinds of strategically-relevant information to gather and disseminate. Later, management will have to assess how well its implementation efforts are working and make whatever corrective adjustments are indicated.

Because implementing and administering the chosen strategic plan cuts across so many facets of managing and affects the whole management hierarchy from top to bottom, one can easily get bogged down in surveying the ins and outs of each and every one of the administrative requirements that can flow from a comprehensive strategic plan. To circumvent this, we shall keep the spotlight trained on five strategy-related administrative aspects—all of which are central to *the general manager's role in strategy implementation and administration:*

1. Building an organization capable of carrying out the strategic plan.

2. Allocating resources and focusing the energy of the organization on strategic objectives.

3. Galvanizing organizationwide commitment to the chosen strategic plan.

4. Monitoring the progress of strategy implementation and keeping the organization on its strategic course.

5. Exerting strategic leadership and initiating actions to improve how the strategy is being carried out.

These five central tasks, and the key issues relating to each, are shown in Figure 6-1. They will serve as the framework for our survey of the general manager's role as chief administrator of the strategic plan. This chapter covers the first two of these five tasks and Chapter 7 deals with the last three.

BUILDING A STRATEGICALLY CAPABLE ORGANIZATION

Successful strategy execution is assisted when an organization has both the structure and the talent it needs to carry out its strategic plan smoothly and efficiently. Building a capable organization is thus always a top general management priority. From the standpoint of implementing and administering strategy, two organizational issues stand out as dominant:

1. How to match organization structure to the needs of strategy.

2. How to build and nurture the distinctive competence in which the strategy may be grounded and to see, generally, that the organization has the managerial talents and technical skills it needs.

Matching Organization Structure to Strategy

There are few hard and fast rules for just what kind of organization structure to employ for each type of strategy. Every firm's situation is different—it has its own internal "culture" and its own past history. And every strategy is grounded in its own set of key success factors and critical tasks. The only really ironclad imperative is to match the choice of organization structure to the key success factors and critical tasks inherent in the firm's strategy. The following five-sequence procedure serves as a useful guideline for accomplishing the match:[1]

1. Identify the key functions and critical tasks imposed by the strategy.

2. Gain an understanding of the relationships among the strategy-critical functions and tasks and how they, in turn, relate to those that are routine.

3. Group the functions and tasks, both critical and routine, into organizational units, making sure that the *main* organizational building blocks center on the strategically-crucial activities and tasks.

4. Determine the degrees of authority needed to manage each unit, bearing in mind both the benefits and costs of decentralized decision-making.

5. Provide for coordination and integration of the units.

---

[1]LaRue T. Hosmer, *Strategic Management: Text and Cases on Business Policy* (Englewood Cliffs, N.J.: Prentice-Hall, Inc., 1982), Chapter 10 and J. Thomas Cannon, *Business Strategy and Policy* (New York: Harcourt, Brace, & World, 1968), p. 316.

FIGURE 6-1
The Central Tasks of Strategy Implementation and Administration

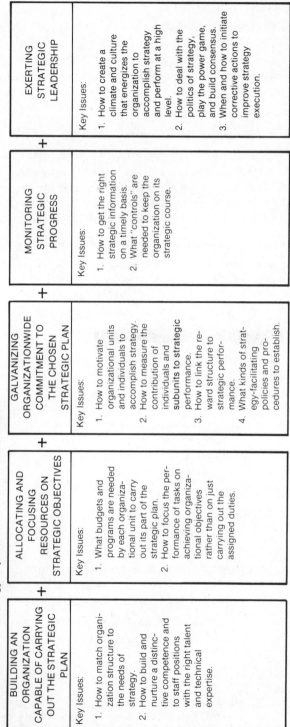

BUILDING AN ORGANIZATION CAPABLE OF CARRYING OUT THE STRATEGIC PLAN	+	ALLOCATING AND FOCUSING RESOURCES ON STRATEGIC OBJECTIVES	+	GALVANIZING ORGANIZATIONWIDE COMMITMENT TO THE CHOSEN STRATEGIC PLAN	+	MONITORING STRATEGIC PROGRESS	+	EXERTING STRATEGIC LEADERSHIP
Key Issues: 1. How to match organization structure to the needs of strategy. 2. How to build and nurture a distinctive competence and to staff positions with the right talent and technical expertise.		Key Issues: 1. What budgets and programs are needed by each organizational unit to carry out its part of the strategic plan. 2. How to focus the performance of tasks on achieving organizational objectives rather than on just carrying out the assigned duties.		Key Issues: 1. How to motivate organizational units and individuals to accomplish strategy. 2. How to measure the contribution of individuals and subunits to strategic performance. 3. How to link the reward structure to strategic performance. 4. What kinds of strategy-facilitating policies and procedures to establish.		Key Issues: 1. How to get the right strategic information on a timely basis. 2. What "controls" are needed to keep the organization on its strategic course.		Key Issues: 1. How to create a climate and culture that energizes the organization to accomplish strategy and perform at a high level. 2. How to deal with the politics of strategy, play the power game, and build consensus. 3. When and how to initiate corrective actions to improve strategy execution.

Identifying the Key Functions and Critical Tasks.   In any organization, some activities and tasks are always more critical to strategic success than others. From a strategy perspective, much of an organization's total work effort is routine and falls under the rubric of administrative good housekeeping and necessary detail (handling payrolls, keeping files and records, processing grievances, taking care of warehousing and shipping, responding to customer inquiries and complaints). Yet, there are usually certain crucial tasks and functions which have to be exceedingly well done for the strategy to be successful. For instance, tight cost control is essential for a firm employing a cost leadership strategy in a commodity business where margins are low and price-cutting is a widely-used competitive weapon. However, for a marketer of high-quality, luxury items, the critical tasks may be manufacturing craftsmanship, distinctive styling, and sophisticated promotional appeal. The critical tasks and key functions vary according to the particulars of a firm's strategy and the requirements for competitive success in the marketplace.

In identifying what an organization's key functions and critical tasks are, two questions can usefully be posed: "What functions and activities need to be performed extra well and on time for the strategy to succeed?" and "In what areas of the firm's business would malperformance seriously endanger or undermine strategic success?"[2] The answers to these two questions should point squarely at those functions and tasks which dominate the economics of the firm's business and which shape whether the firm will be able to compete successfully in its target markets.

Understanding the Relationships among Activities.   Before the various critical and routine activities can be grouped into logical organizational units, one must first understand the strategic relationships that prevail among them. Activities can be related by the flow of material through the production process, by the type of customer served, by the distribution channels used, by the technical skills and know-how needed to perform them, by a strong need to centralize authority over them, by the sequence in which tasks must be performed, and by geographic location, to mention some of the most obvious ways. Such relationships are important because one (or more) of the ways that tasks are related usually becomes the basis for grouping them into organizational units.

If the needs of strategy are to drive organization design, then the relationships to look for are those that link one piece of the strategy to another. Thus, a diversified firm that is in several manufacturing businesses, each with its own strategy, might be well advised *not* to put all of its manufacturing activities in one single manufacturing unit but, instead, to separate them and align each manufacturing unit according to line of business so that

---

[2]Peter F. Drucker, *Management: Tasks, Responsibilities, Practices* (New York: Harper & Row Publishers, 1974), pp. 530 and 535.

manufacturing strategy can be tailored to fit business strategy. As another example, consider a bank whose strategy is aimed at catering more to commercial loans than to personal loans; the bank's lending activities might then usefully be subdivided into a commercial loan department and a personal loan department rather than grouped together under a single loan department. In this instance, the ruling criterion in designing the bank's organization structure is not the common function of lending money (whether it be to commercial businesses or individuals) but rather separating the lending function by customer group to better meet the needs of strategy.

Grouping Activities into Organization Units.   The chief guideline here is to make key functions and crucial tasks the *main* building blocks in the organization structure. The rationale is simple and powerful: if activities that are crucial to strategic success are to get the attention and visibility they need and deserve, then they have to occupy a central position in the organization structure. When key functions and critical tasks take a structural backseat to routine and less important activities, there is a natural political tendency for them to be given fewer resources and accorded less significance than they actually have. On the other hand, when they form the core of the whole organization structure, their role and priority in the overall scheme of things is highlighted and institutionalized. A general manager can seldom give a stronger signal as to what is strategically important than by making key functions and critical tasks the most prominent organizational building blocks and, further, assigning them a high position in the organizational pecking order.

Determining the Degree of Authority and Independence to Give Each Unit.   How much authority and decision-making latitude to give each organization unit, especially line of business units, is crucial. In the case of line of business units, one alternative is to supply the managerial backup needed from other existing organizational units; another option is to let it be self-sufficient and have its own managerial staff to do the job of administration. The pros and cons of decentralization, while partly economic, mainly depend on what the appropriate managerial level is at which to make the principal decisions that confront the business unit and the most workable means of aligning corporate strategy and line of business strategy. Within a line of business unit, the question of authority generally is governed by how much need there is for coordination between the functional areas and how the general manager decides to pull separated activities into a unified whole.

Several generalizations about parcelling out authority across the various units can be offered. Activities and organizational units with a key role in strategy execution should never be made subordinate to routine and non-key activities. Revenue-producing and results-producing activities should never be made subordinate to internal support or staff functions. The general rule is that a unit's role in contributing to strategic success should determine its rank and placement in the hierarchy of authority.

Providing for Coordination among the Units.   Providing for coordination of the activities of organizational units is accomplished mainly through positioning them in the hierarchy of authority. Managers higher up in the pecking order generally have broader authority over several organizational units and, thus, more clout to coordinate, integrate, and otherwise arrange for the cooperation of the units under their supervision. General managers are, of course, the final point of coordination because of their position of authority over the whole unit. Besides positioning organizational units along the vertical scale of managerial authority, a general manager can also achieve coordination of strategic efforts through informal meetings, project teams, special task forces, standing committees, formal strategy reviews, and annual strategic planning and budgeting cycles. And, additionally, the formulation of the strategic plan itself can serve a coordinating role; the whole process of negotiating and deciding upon the objectives and strategies of each organizational unit and making sure that the different pieces of the strategic plan join together suitably acts to coordinate the role and contribution of each organizational unit.

The Structure Follows Strategy Thesis.   The practice of consciously matching organization design and structure to the particular needs and requirements of strategy is a fairly recent management development and it springs from research evidence about the actual experiences of firms. The landmark study is Alfred Chandler's *Strategy and Structure*.[3] According to Chandler, changes in an organization's strategy bring about new administrative problems which, in turn, require a new or refashioned structure if the new strategy is to be successfully implemented. In more specific terms, Chandler found that structure tends to follow the growth strategy of the firm—but often not until inefficiency and internal operating problems provoke a structural adjustment. His studies of seventy large corporations revealed a sequence consisting of new strategy creation, emergence of new administrative problems, a decline in profitability and performance, a shift to a more appropriate organizational structure, and then recovery to more profitable levels and improved strategy execution. Chandler found this sequence to be oft-repeated as firms grew and modified their corporate strategies. He cites DuPont's experience as a classic example:

---

[3](Cambridge, Mass.: M.I.T. Press, 1962). Although the stress here is on matching structure to strategy, it is worth noting that structure can and does influence the choice of strategy. As was discussed in Chapter 2, a "good" strategy must be doable. When an organization's present structure is so far out of line with the requirements of a particular strategy that the organization would have to be turned upside down and inside out to implement it, then the strategy may, as a practical matter, not be doable and ought not to be given further consideration. In such cases, structure shapes the *choice* of strategy. The point here, however, is that once a strategy is chosen, structure must be made to fit the strategy if, in fact, an approximate fit does not already exist. Any influences of structure on strategy should, logically, come *before* the point of strategy selection rather than after it.

The strategy of diversification quickly demanded a refashioning of the company's administrative structure if its resources, old and new, were to be used efficiently and therefore profitably; for diversification greatly intensified the administrative load carried by the functional departments and the central office. Once the functional needs and the activities of several rather than one product line had to be coordinated, once the work of several very different lines of businesses had to be appraised, once the policies and procedures had to be formulated for divisions handling a wide variety of products, and, finally, once the central office had to make critical decisions about what new lines of business to develop, then the old structure quickly showed signs of strain. To meet the new needs, the new organizational design provided several central offices, each responsible for one line of products. At the new general office, the Executive Committee and staff specialists concentrated on the over-all administration of what had become a multi-industry enterprise. And in transforming the highly centralized, functionally departmentalized structure into a "decentralized," multi-divisional one, the major achievement had been the creation of the new divisions.[4]

The lesson of this example is that the choice of organization *structure does make a difference* in how an organization performs. All forms of organization structure are not equally supportive in implementing a given strategy.

The *structure follows strategy* thesis is undergirded with powerful logic: how the work of an organization is structured is just a means to an end—not an end in itself. Structure is no more than a managerial device for facilitating the implementation and execution of the organization's strategy and, ultimately, for achieving the intended performance and results. Toward this end, the structural design of an organization acts both as a "harness" that helps people pull together in their performance of diverse tasks and as a means of tying the organizational building blocks together in ways that promote strategy accomplishment and improved performance. Without *deliberately* organizing functional responsibilities and activities so as to produce linkages between structure and strategy, the outcomes are likely to be disorder, friction, and malperformance.[5] Consequently, making organization structure supportive of strategy hinges upon the cleverness of the general manager in coming up with *strategically effective ways* of weaving the total work effort together.

How Structure Evolves as Strategy Evolves: The Stages Model

In a number of respects, the strategist's approach to organization building is governed by the size and growth stage of the enterprise, as well as by the key success factors inherent in the organization's business. For instance, the type of organization structure that suits a small specialty steel

---

[4]Chandler, *Strategy and Structure*, p. 113.
[5]Drucker, *Management*, p. 523.

firm relying upon a concentration strategy in a regional market is not likely to be suitable for a large, vertically-integrated steel producer doing business in geographically diverse areas. The organization form that works best in a multi-product, multi-technology, multi-business corporation pursuing a conglomerate diversification strategy is, understandably, likely to be different yet again. Recognition of this characteristic has prompted several attempts to formulate a model linking changes in organizational structure to stages in an organization's strategic development.[6]

The underpinning of the stages concept is that enterprises can be arrayed along a continuum running from very simple to very complex organizational forms and that there is a tendency for an organization to move along this continuum toward more complex forms as it grows in size, market coverage, and product line scope and as the strategic aspects of its customer-technology-business portfolio become more intricate. Four distinct stages of strategy-related organization structure have been singled out.

Stage I.   A Stage I organization is essentially a small, single business enterprise managed by one person. The owner-entrepreneur has close daily contact with employees and each phase of operations. Most employees report directly to the owner, who makes all the pertinent decisions regarding objectives, strategy, daily operations, and so on. As a consequence, the organization's strengths, vulnerabilities, and resources are closely allied with the entrepreneur's personality, management ability and style, and personal financial situation. Not only is a Stage I enterprise an extension of the interests, abilities, and limitations of its owner-entrepreneur but also its activities are typically concentrated in just one line of business. For the most part, today's Stage I enterprise is epitomized by small firms run by "independent businesspersons" who are "their own bosses" and, typically, such firms have a strategy which centers around a single product, market, technology, or channel of distribution.

Stage II.   Stage II organizations differ from Stage I enterprises in one essential respect: an increased scale and scope of operations create a pervasive strategic need for management specialization and force a transition from one-person management to group management. However, a Stage II enterprise, although run by a team of managers with functionally-specialized responsibilities, remains fundamentally a single business operation. This is not to imply, though, that the categories of management specialization are uniform among large, single-business enterprises. In practice, there is wide variation. Some Stage II organizations prefer to divide strategic responsibilities along classic functional lines—marketing,

---

[6]See, for example, Malcolm S. Salter, "Stages of Corporate Development," *Journal of Business Policy*, vol. 1, no. 1 (Spring 1970), pp. 23-27; Donald H. Thain, "Stages of Corporate Development," *The Business Quarterly* (Winter 1969), pp. 32-45; Bruce R. Scott, "The Industrial State: Old Myths and New Realities," *Harvard Business Review*, vol. 51, no. 2 (March-April 1973), pp. 133-148 and Alfred D. Chandler, *Strategy and Structure*, Chapter 1.

production, finance, personnel, control, engineering, public relations, procurement, planning, and so on. In other Stage II companies functional specialization is keyed to distinct production units; for example, the organizational building blocks of a vertically-integrated oil company may consist of exploration, drilling, pipelines, refining, wholesale distribution, and retail sales. In a process-oriented Stage II company, the functionally sequenced units aim primarily at synchronizing the flow of output between them.

Stage III.   Stage III embraces those organizations whose operations, though concentrated in a single field or product line, are large enough and scattered over a wide geographical area to justify having *geographically decentralized* operating units. These units all report to corporate headquarters and conform to corporate policies but they are given the flexibility to tailor their unit's strategic plan to meet the specific needs of each respective geographic area. Ordinarily, each of the semi-autonomous operating units of a Stage III organization is structured along functional lines. The key difference between Stage II and Stage III, however, is that while the functional units of a Stage II organization stand or fall together (in that they are built around one business and one end market), the operating units of a Stage III firm can stand alone (or nearly so) in the sense that the operations in each geographic unit are not rigidly tied to or dependent on those in other areas. Characteristic firms in this category would be breweries, cement companies, and steel mills having production capacity and sales organizatons in several geographically separate market areas. Corey and Star cite Pfizer International as being a good example of a company whose strategic requirements in 1964 made geographic decentralization propitious:

> With sales of $223 million in 1964, Pfizer International operated plants in 27 countries and marketed in more than 100 countries. Its product lines included pharmaceuticals (antibiotics and other ethical prescription drugs), agriculture and veterinary products (such as animal feed supplements and vaccines, and pesticides), chemicals (fine chemicals, bulk pharmaceuticals, petrochemicals and plastics), and consumer products (cosmetics and toiletries).
>
> Ten geographic Area Managers reported directly to the President of Pfizer International and exercised line supervision over Country Managers. According to a company position description, it was "the responsibility of each Area Manager to plan, develop, and carry out Pfizer International's business in the assigned foreign area in keeping with company policies and goals."
>
> Country Managers had profit responsibility. In most cases a single Country Manager managed all Pfizer activities in his country. In some of the larger, well-developed countries of Europe there were separate Country Managers for pharmaceutical and agricultural products and for consumer lines.
>
> Except for the fact that New York headquarters exercised control over the to-the-market prices of certain products, especially prices of widely used pharmaceuticals, Area and Country Managers had considerable autonomy in

planning and managing the Pfizer International business in their respective geographic areas. This was appropriate because each area, and some countries within areas, provided unique market and regulatory environments. In the case of pharmaceuticals and agriculture and veterinary products (Pfizer International's most important lines) national laws affected formulations, dosages, labeling, distribution, and often price. Trade restrictions affected the flow of bulk pharmaceuticals and chemicals and packaged products, and might in effect require the establishment of manufacturing plants to supply local markets. Competition, too, varied significantly from area to area.[7]

Stage IV.   Stage IV is typified by large, multi-product, multi-unit, multi-market enterprises decentralized by line of business. Their corporate strategies emphasize diversification, concentric and/or conglomerate. As with Stage III companies, the semi-autonomous operating units report to a corporate headquarters and conform to certain firm-wide policies, but the divisional units pursue their own respective line of business strategies. Typically, each separate business unit is headed by a general manager who has profit and loss responsibility and whose authority extends across all of the unit's functional areas except, perhaps, accounting and capital investment (both of which are traditionally subject to corporate approval). Both strategic decisions and operating decisions are thus concentrated at the divisional level rather than at the corporate level. The organizational structure of the business unit may be along the lines of Stage I, II, or III types of organizations. Characteristic Stage IV companies include General Electric, ITT, Procter & Gamble, General Foods, Textron, and DuPont.

Movement through the Stages.   From our perspective, the stages model provides useful insights into why organization structure tends to change in accordance with product-market-technology relationships and new directions in corporate strategy. As firms have progressed from small, entrepreneurial enterprises following a basic concentration strategy to more complex strategic phases of volume expansion, vertical integration, geographic expansion, and product diversification, their organizational structures have evolved from unifunctional to functionally centralized to multi-divisional decentralized organizational forms. Firms that remain single-line businesses almost always have some form of a centralized functional structure. Enterprises which are predominantly in one industry but which are slightly diversified typically have a hybrid structure; the dominant business is managed via a functional organization and the diversified activities are handled through a divisionalized form. The more diversified an organization becomes, irrespective of whether the diversification is along either concentric or conglomerate lines, the more it moves toward some form of decentralized business units.

---

[7]Raymond Corey and Steven H. Star, *Organizational Strategy: A Marketing Approach* (Boston: Division of Research, Harvard University Graduate School of Business Administration, 1971), pp. 23-24.

However, it is by no means imperative that organizations begin at Stage I and move sequentially toward Stage IV.[8] U.S. Rubber (now Uniroyal) moved from a Stage II organization to a Stage IV form without ever passing through Stage III. And some organizations exhibit characteristics of two or more stages simultaneously. Sears, at one time, was decentralized geographically for store operations, personnel, sales promotion, banking, inventory and warehousing, and maintenance, yet centralized for manufacturing and procurement of goods, thus overlapping the organization structures of Stage II and III. Furthermore, some companies have found it desirable to retreat into prior stages after entering a particular stage. For example, the DuPont Textile Fibers Department originated out of five separate, decentralized, fully-integrated fiber businesses—rayon, acetate, nylon, "Orlon," and "Dacron."[9] Many weavers and other industrial users bought one or more of these fibers and used them in significantly different ways that also required different application technologies. According to Corey and Star:

> Customers objected to being solicited by five DuPont salesmen each promoting a different type of synthetic fiber and each competing with the others. Users of synthetic fibers wanted sales representatives from DuPont who understood their product lines and production processes and who could serve as a source of useful technical ideas.[10]

As a consequence, DuPont consolidated all five units into a Textile Fibers Department in an effort to deal more effectively with these customers. The new department established a single multifiber field sales force and set up market programs for four broad market segments—men's wear, women's wear, home furnishings, and industrial products, each of which had a potential demand for all five fibers.

In general, then, owing to the several ways which product-market relationships and strategy may turn, the paths along which an organization's structure may develop are more complex and variable than suggested by a single pattern of moving in sequence from Stage I through Stage IV. Still, it does appear that as the strategic emphasis shifts from small, single-product businesses to large, dominant-product businesses and then on to concentric or conglomerate diversification, a firm's organizational structure evolves, in turn, from one-man management to large group functional management to decentralized, line-of-business management. This is substantiated by the fact that about 90 percent of the *Fortune 500* firms (nearly all of which are diversified to one degree or another) have a divisionalized organizational structure with the primary basis for decentralization being line of business considerations.

---

[8]For a more thorough discussion of this point, see Salter, "Stages of Corporate Development," pp. 34-35.

[9]Corey and Star, *Organization Strategy*, p. 14.

[10]Ibid.

One final lesson that the stages model teaches is worth iterating. A reassessment of organization structure and authority is always useful whenever strategy is changed.[11] A new strategy is likely to entail modifications in what the critical tasks and key activities are. If these changes go unrecognized, the resulting mismatch in strategy requirements and organization design creates an opening for strategic performance to be unnecessarily short of its potential.

The Strategy-Related Pros and Cons of Alternative Organization Forms

There are essentially six strategy-related approaches to organization: (1) functional specialization, (2) geographic organization, (3) departmentalization keyed to differences in processing stage, market channel, or customer class, (4) decentralized business/product divisions, (5) strategic business units, and (6) matrix structures featuring *dual* lines of authority and strategic priority. Each form relates structure to strategy in a different way and, consequently, has its own set of strategy-related pros and cons.

The Functional Organization Structure.   A functional organization structure tends to be effective whenever a firm's critical tasks and key activities revolve around well-defined skills and areas of specialization. In such cases, in-depth specialization and focused concentration on performing functional area tasks and activities can enhance both operating efficiency and the development of a distinctive competence. Generally speaking, organizing by functional specialities promotes full utilization of the most up-to-date technical skills and helps a business capitalize on the efficiency gains to be had from using specialized manpower, facilities, and equipment. These are strategically important considerations for single-business organizations, dominant-product enterprises, and vertically-integrated firms, and accounts for why they usually have some kind of centralized, functionally specialized structure.

However, just what form the functional specialization will take varies according to customer-product-technology considerations. For instance, a technical instruments manufacturer may be organized around research and development, engineering, production, technical services, quality control, marketing, personnel, and finance and accounting. A municipal government may, on the other hand, be departmentalized according to purposeful function—fire, public safety, health services, water and sewer, streets, parks and recreation, and education. A university may divide its organizational units up into academic affairs, student services, alumni relations, athletics, buildings and grounds, institutional services, and budget control. A typical functional structure is diagrammed in Figure 6-2.

---

[11]For an excellent documentation of how a number of well-known corporations revised their organization structure to meet the needs of strategy changes and specific product/market developments, see Corey and Star, *Organization Strategy*, Chapter 3.

FIGURE 6-2
A Functional Organization Structure (manufacturing company)

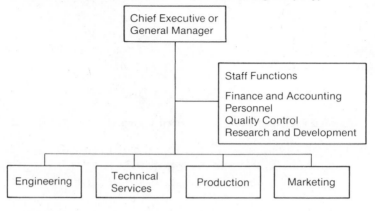

Advantages	Disadvantages
Enhances operating efficiency where tasks are routine and repetitive.	Poses problems of functional coordination.
Preserves centralized control of strategic results.	Can lead to interfunctional rivalry, conflict, and empire building.
Allows benefits of specialization to be fully exploited.	May promote overspecialization and narrow management viewpoints.
Simplifies training of management specialists.	Limits development of general managers.
Promotes high emphasis on craftsmanship and professional standards.	Forces profit responsibility to the top.
Well suited to developing a distinctive competence.	Functional specialists often attach more importance to what's best for the functional area than to what's best for the whole business.
Often fits the needs of business-level strategy.	

The Achilles heel of a functional structure is proper coordination of the separated functional units. Functional specialists, partly because of their training and the technical nature of their jobs, tend to develop their own mindset and ways of doing things. The more that functional specialists differ in their perspectives and their approaches to task accomplishment, the more difficult it becomes to achieve both strategic and operating coordination between them. They neither "talk the same language" nor have an adequate understanding and appreciation for one another's problems and approaches. Each functional group is more interested in its own "empire" and sets its priorities accordingly (despite the lip service given to cooperation and "what's best for the company"). This, in turn, can create a time-consuming administrative burden on a general manager in terms of resolving cross-functional differences, enforcing joint cooperation, and opening lines of communication. In addition, as will be discussed below, a purely functional organization is ill-suited for multi-business organizations; it works well within a single business but not across businesses.

Geographic Forms of Organization.   Organizing according to geographic areas or territories is a rather common structural form for large-scale enterprises whose strategies need to be tailored to fit the particular needs and features of different geographical areas. As indicated in Figure 6-3, geographic organization has its advantages and disadvantages but the

FIGURE 6-3
A Geographic Organizational Structure

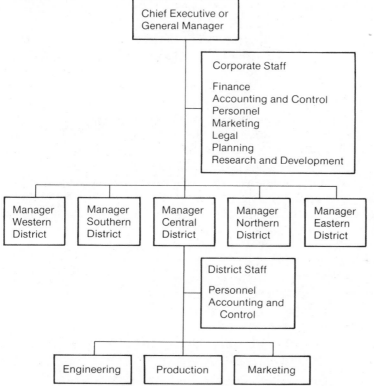

Advantages	Disadvantages
Allows tailoring of strategy to needs of markets.	Greater difficulty in maintaining consistent and uniform company-wide practices.
Delegates profit/loss responsibility to lowest strategic level.	Requires a larger management staff, especially general managers.
Improves functional coordination within the target market.	Leads to duplication of staff services.
Takes advantage of economies of local operations.	Poses a problem of headquarters control over local operations.
Area units make an excellent training ground for higher-level general managers.	

chief reason for its popularity is that, for one reason or another, it promotes improved performance.

In the private sector, a territorial structure is typically utilized by chain store retailers, cement firms, railroads, airlines, the larger paper box and carton manufacturers, and large bakeries and dairy products enterprises; the member companies of American Telephone and Telegraph which make up the Bell Telephone System all represent geographically decentralized units. In the public sector, such organizations as the Internal Revenue Service, the Small Business Administration, the federal courts, the U.S. Postal Service, the state troopers, the Red Cross, and religious groups have adopted territorial departmentation in order to be directly accessible to geographically dispersed clienteles.

Process, Market Channel, or Customer-Based Organization. Grouping an enterprise's activities according to production stages, market channels, or customer groups fits situations where business strategy is grounded in achieving operating economies or in catering to distinct buyer segments. A metal parts manufacturer may find it operationally efficient to subdivide in series, thus having foundry, forging, machining, finishing, assembly, and painting departments. Firms with a diverse clientele may find it strategically useful to break their distribution and marketing activities down into subgroups to permit different strategic approaches to each buyer/channel category. For example, some years ago Purex Corp. decided that neither product nor territorial units were as well-suited to its strategy as was a market channel form of organization because having different units for each channel allowed it to focus separately on selling to supermarket chains and to drug chains. United Way drives are typically organized into a number of individual solicitation units with each assigned to canvass a particular segment of the community—commercial establishments, industrial plants, unions, local schools, county government, city government, hospitals, and agriculture. There are various departments of the federal government set up expressly for veterans, senior citizens, the unemployed, small businesses, widows and dependent children, the poor, and others. Figure 6-4 illustrates organizing by process, by market channel, and by customer category.

Decentralized Business Units. Grouping activities along business and product group lines has been a clear-cut trend among diversified enterprises for the past half-century, beginning with the pioneering efforts of DuPont and General Motors in the 1920s. Separate business/product divisions emerged because diversification made a functionally-specialized manager's job incredibly complex. Imagine the problems a manufacturing executive would have if put in charge of, say, 50 different plants using 20 different technologies to produce 30 different products in 8 different businesses/industries. In a multi-business enterprise, the needs of strategy virtually dictate that the organizational sequence be corporate to line-of-business to functional area within a business rather than corporate to functional area (aggregated for all businesses). The latter produces a nightmare in making sense out of business strategy and achieving functional area coordination of line-of-business strategy. From a business strategy implementation standpoint, it is far more logical to group all the different activities that belong to the same business under one organizational roof, thereby creating line-of-business units (which, then, can be subdivided into whatever functional subunits that suits the key activities/ critical tasks make-up of the business). The outcome not only is a structure which fits strategy but also a structure which makes the jobs of managers more "do-able."

Strategic Business Units.   In the really large, diversified companies, the number of decentralized business units can be so great that the span of control is too much for a single chief executive. Then, it may be useful to group those which are related and delegate authority over them to a senior executive who reports directly to the chief executive officer. While this imposes another layer of management between the divisional general managers and the chief executive, it may nonetheless improve strategic planning and top management coordination of diverse business interests. This explains both the popularity of the group vice-president concept among conglomerate firms and the recent trend toward the formation of *strategic business units*.

A strategic business unit (SBU) is a grouping of business divisions where the criterion for grouping is based on some important strategic element common to each. At General Electric, a pioneer in the concept of decentralized strategic business units (SBUs), 48 divisions were reorganized into 43 SBUs; in one case, three separate divisions making various food preparation appliances were combined as a single SBU serving the "housewares" market.[12] At Union Carbide 15 groups and divisions were decomposed into 150 "strategic planning units" and then regrouped and combined into 9 new "aggregate planning units." At General Foods SBUs were originally defined on a product line basis but were later redefined according to menu segments (breakfast foods, beverages, main meal products, desserts, and pet foods). These examples suggest that how management chooses to define its SBUs depends largely on managerial judgment and pragmatic considerations. In general, though, the aim is to include within a single SBU those products and activities which share an important strategic relationship—whether it be with regard to similarity in manufacturing, or use of the same distribution channels, or overlap in customers and target markets, or some other pertinent strategic feature.

The managerial value of the concept of SBUs is that it provides diversi-

---

[12]William K. Hall, "SBUs: Hot, New Topic in the Management of Diversification," *Business Horizons*, vol. 21, no. 1 (February 1978), p. 19.

FIGURE 6–4
Process, Market Channel, and Customer-Based Forms of Organization

A. Process organization

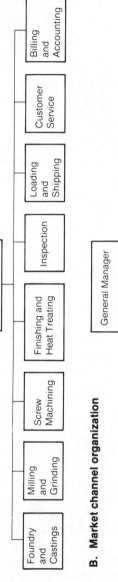

B. Market channel organization

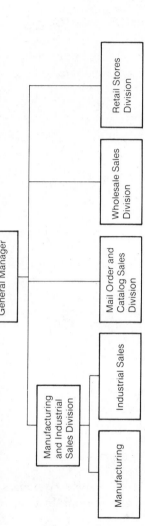

C. Customer organization

```
                    ┌─────────────────┐
                    │ Director of Welfare │
                    │     Services      │
                    └─────────────────┘
         ┌──────────┬──────────┬──────────┬──────────┬──────────┐
┌────────┐ ┌────────┐ ┌────────┐ ┌────────┐ ┌────────┐ ┌────────┐
│Old Age │ │Widows  │ │Handi-  │ │Unem-   │ │Low     │ │Medical │
│Assist- │ │and     │ │capped  │ │ployed  │ │Income  │ │Assist- │
│ance    │ │Orphans │ │and     │ │        │ │and     │ │ance    │
│        │ │        │ │Disabled│ │        │ │Food    │ │        │
│        │ │        │ │        │ │        │ │Stamps  │ │        │
└────────┘ └────────┘ └────────┘ └────────┘ └────────┘ └────────┘
```

Advantages

Structure is tied to performance of key activities.

Facilitates achievement of operating economies derived from use of specialized departments.

Allows strategy to be closely linked to any key differences in channels and/or customer groups.

Disadvantages

Encourages presssure for special treatment.

Poses problems of how to coordinate interdepartmental activities.

May lead to uneconomically small units or underutilization of specialized facilities and manpower as demand shifts from unit to unit.

FIGURE 6-5
A Decentralized Business/Division Type of Organization Structure

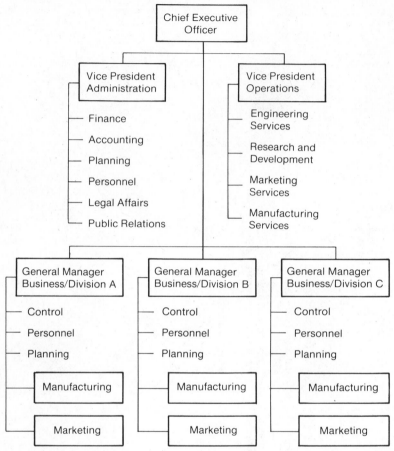

Advantages

Offers a logical and workable means of decentralizing responsibility and delegating authority in diversified organizations.

Puts responsibility for business strategy in closer proximity to each business's unique environment.

Allows critical tasks and specialization to be organized to fit business strategy.

Frees CEO to handle corporate strategy issues.

Creates clear profit/loss accountability.

Disadvantages

Leads to proliferation of staff functions, policy inconsistencies between divisions, and problems of coordination of divisional operations.

Poses a problem of how much authority to centralize and how much to decentralize.

May lead to excessive divisional rivalry for corporate resources and attention.

Raises issue of how to allocate corporate-level overhead.

fied companies with a practical rationale for organizing what they do and with a workabie approach to staying on top of the strategic performance of diverse operating units. It is particularly helpful in reducing the complexity of dovetailing corporate strategy and business strategy and in developing focused product/market business strategies on a decentralized basis. Figure 6-6 illustrates the SBU concept of organizing diversification where each SBU is headed by a "group" vice president—see also Illustration Capsule 19.

FIGURE 6-6
An SBU Type of Organization Structure

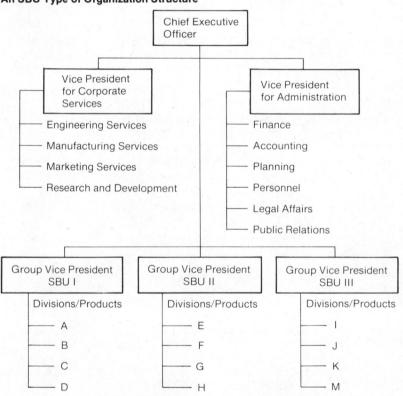

Advantages	Disadvantages
Provides a logical basis for top management to maintain close watch over divisional operations.	Adds another layer to top management.
Improves coordination between divisions with similar strategies, markets, and management problems.	The role and authority of the group vice president is often ambiguous and fleeting.

ILLUSTRATION CAPSULE 19
Structuring Diversification: The Troublesome Role of the Group Executive

A recent survey showed that 70 percent of the *Fortune 500* firms used some form of a group vice-president structure in managing diversification. This percentage was up sharply from 39 percent a few years previous. Yet, nearly two-thirds of the group executives working in these companies view their jobs as more or less a "can of worms." The reasons given are interesting for what they reveal about the management problems of diversified organizations:

1. Some group vice presidents find themselves as being little more than a high-priced courier between the chief executive and the division heads.

2. The group head is in a no-man's land between operating units that expect maximum autonomy and presidents who judge his performance by the profits and losses of those same operating units. As a consequence, the group head is like an army corps commander, responsible for sector achievement but having limited control over limited resources.

3. The group vice president must walk a line between giving division managers enough elbow room to be effective entrepreneurs and maintaining enough control to keep corporate headquarters comfortable. The manager who is not politically expert at walking this line tends to be regarded as "the gestapo" by the divisions and "a nursemaid" by the CEO.

4. Although the job of group vice president is often seen as a logical progression on the way to corporate president, in many companies a group vice president either moves up, sideways, or out within five years. It is not the type of job that many people make a career out of.

5. For executives who enjoy "doing" rather than "coordinating and overseeing," the nebulous role of a group head is frustrating. It requires a low profile and behind the scenes influence, as opposed to being in the thick of the action. Recognition for performance gets blurred; credit for success tends to go first to the chief executive, then to the division head, and last to the group vice president.

From a corporate perspective, having a layer of group vice-presidents to help the CEO direct and coordinate a growing, diversified company is almost a creation of necessity. The more operating divisions an enterprise has, the more important it becomes to have them report to someone besides the chief executive. So far, no more logical way has been devised than a group structure.

While it is generally agreed that there is a legitimate need for a group vice president type structure in diversified companies, there are wide differences on what the group vice president position should be like. At Textron group managers are regarded as "counselors" while at AMF a group head is held

Source: "The Frustrations of the Group Executive," *Business Week*, September 25, 1978, pp. 102ff.

ILLUSTRATION CAPSULE 19 *(concluded)*

totally responsible for division performance. The prevailing view seems to be that, as a minimum, the group vice president should (1) have heavy line responsibility for allocating financial resources within his group, (2) be brought into corporate operating committees, and (3) exercise primary responsibility for defining and directing the group's marketing, sales, and advertising priorities. This means that the chief executive must be willing to relax his own supervision over the divisions and to delegate a meaningful role to the group executive. In addition, it is important for the CEO to not deal directly with the divisions in a manner which undercuts the group manager's role and authority.

Experience indicates that the key to making the job of group vice president both attractive and effective is in finding the middle ground in terms of delegating power to the divisions while at the same time fully utilizing the talents and energies of senior executives at the group level. Companies that find the right balance between the desire for autonomy at the division level and holding the group vice president at least partly accountable for division performance and group performance seem to be the most satisfied with the group vice president approach.

Matrix Forms of Organization. A matrix form of organization is a structure with two (or more) channels of command, two lines of budget authority, two sources of performance and reward, and so forth. The key feature of the matrix is that product (or business) and functional lines of authority are overlaid (to form a matrix or grid) and managerial authority over the employees in each unit/cell of the matrix is shared between the product manager and the functional manager—as shown in Figure 6-7. In a matrix structure, subordinates have a continuing dual assignment: to the business/product and to their base function.[13] The outcome is a compromise between functional specialization (engineering, R&D, manufacturing, marketing, accounting) and product specialization (where all of the specialized talent needed to produce and sell a given product are assigned to the same divisional unit).

A matrix type organization is a genuinely different structural form and represents a "new way of life." One reason is that the unity of command principle is broken; two reporting channels, two bosses, and shared authority create a new kind of organizational climate. In essence, the matrix is a conflict resolution system through which strategic and operating priorities

---

[13]A more thorough treatment of matrix organizational forms can be found in Jay R. Galbraith, "Matrix Organizational Designs," *Business Horizons*, vol. 15, no. 1 (February 1971), pp. 29-40.

FIGURE 6-7
Matrix Organization Structures

A. A defense contractor

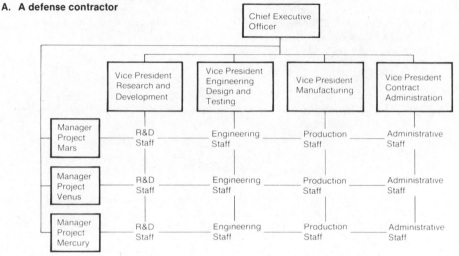

B. A college of business administration

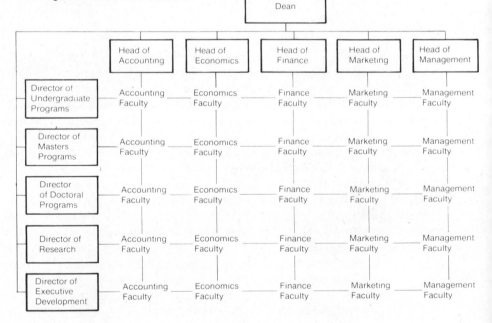

are negotiated, power is shared, and resources are allocated internally on a "strongest case for what is best overall for the unit" type basis.[14]

The list of companies using some form of a matrix includes General Electric, Texas Instruments, Citibank, Shell Oil, TRW, Bechtel, and Dow Chemical. Its growing popularity is founded on some solid business trends. Firms are turning more and more to strategies that add new sources of diversity (products, customer groups, technology) to their range of activities. Out of this diversity are coming product managers, functional managers, geographic area managers, business-level managers, and SBU managers—*all* of whom have important *strategic* responsibilities. When at least two of several variables (product, customer, technology, geography, functional area, and line of business) have roughly equal strategic priorities, then a matrix organization can be an effective structural form. A matrix form of organization allows for the management of multiple sources of diversity by creating multiple dimensions for strategic management, with each dimensional manager being responsible for one dimension of strategic initiative. The matrix approach thus allows *each* of several strategic priorities to be managed directly and to be represented in discussions of how the total enterprise (or business unit) can best be managed. In this sense, it helps middle managers make trade-off decisions from a general management perspective.[15] Further, because a manager is assigned line responsibility for attending to an explicit area of strategic concern, a matrix organization can facilitate management response to a rapidly emerging strategic priority.

Combination and Supplemental Methods of Organization.   The preceding structural designs are not always sufficient to handle the diversity of situations which complex organizations face. One additional option is to mix and blend the six basic organization forms, matching structure to strategy piece-by-piece and unit-by-unit. Another is to supplement a basic organization design with special-situation devices. Three of the most frequently used ones are:

1.   The *project manager* or *project staff* approach, where a separate, largely self-sufficient subunit is created to oversee the completion of a special activity (setting up a new technological process, bringing out a new product, starting up a new venture, consummating a merger with another company, seeing through the completion of a government contract, supervising the construction of a new plant). [16] Project man-

---

[14]An excellent critique of matrix organizations is presented in Stanley M. Davis and Paul R. Lawrence, "Problems of Matrix Organizations," *Harvard Business Review*, vol. 56, no. 3 (May-June 1978), pp. 131-142.

[15]Ibid., p. 132.

[16]For a more complete treatment of project management, see C.J. Middleton, "How to Set Up a Project Organization," *Harvard Business Review*, vol. 45, no. 2 (March-April 1976), pp. 73-82; George A. Steiner and William G. Ryan, *Industrial Project Management* (New York; The MacMillan Company, 1968); Ivar Avots, "Why Does Project Management Fail," *Califor-*

agement has become a relatively popular means of handling "one-of-a-kind" situations having a finite life expectancy and where the normal organization is deemed unable or ill-equipped to achieve the same results in addition to regular duties. On occasions, however, "temporary" projects have proved worthy of becoming made "ongoing," thus resulting in either the elevation of the project unit to "permanent" status or a parceling out of the project's functions to units of the regular organization.

2. The *task force* approach, where a number of functional specialists are brought together to work on unusual assignments of a problem-solving or innovative nature. Special task forces provide increased opportunity for creativity, open communication across lines of authority, tight integration of specialized talents, expeditious conflict resolution, and common identification for coping with the problem at hand. However, according to Drucker, team organization is more than a temporary expedient for dealing with nonrecurring special problems; he argues that the team is a genuine design principle of organization and is especially good for such permanent organizing tasks as top-management work and innovating work.[17]

3. The *venture team* approach, whereby a group of individuals is formed for the purpose of bringing a specific product to market or a specific new business into being. Dow, General Mills, Westinghouse, and Monsanto have used the venture team approach as a regenesis of the entrepreneurial spirit. One difficulty with venture teams is if and when to transfer control of the project back to the regular organization and the problems of discontinuity and shifting managerial judgments which result.[18]

Perspectives on Matching Strategy and Structure

The foregoing discussion brings out two points: (1) there is no such thing as a perfect or ideal organization design and (2) there are no universally applicable rules for matching strategy and structure. There is room for organizations with similar strategies to have significantly different organization structures. What suits one type of strategy can be totally wrong for another. Structures that worked well in the past may not be as suitable for the future. Experience shows that firms have a habit of regularly outgrow-

nia Management Review, vol. 12, no. 1 (Fall 1969), pp. 77-82; C. Reeser, "Human Problems of the Project Form of Organization," *Academy of Management Journal,* vol. 12, no. 4 (December 1969), pp. 459-67; R. A. Goodman, "Ambiguous Authority Definition in Project Management," *Academy of Management Journal,* vol. 10, no. 4 (December 1969), pp. 395-407; and D. L. Wilemon and J. P. Cicero, "The Project Manager-Anomalies and Ambiguities," *Academy of Management Journal,* vol. 13, no. 3 (September 1970), pp. 269-82.

[17]Drucker, *Management,* pp. 564-71.

[18]Philip Kotler, *Marketing Management: Analysis, Planning, and Control,* 3rd ed. (Englewood Cliffs, N.J.: Prentice-Hall, Inc., 1976), pp. 200-201.

ing their prevailing organizational arrangement—either an internal shake-up is deemed periodically desirable or else changes in the size and scope of customer-business-technology relationships make the firm's structure strategically obsolete. An organization's structure thus is dynamic; changes are not only inevitable but typical.

There is room to quibble over whether organization design should commence with a strategy-structure framework or with a pragmatic consideration of the realities of the situation at hand—the corporate culture, the constraints imposed by the personalities involved, and the way things have been done before. By and large, agonizing over where to begin is unnecessary; both considerations have to be taken into account. However, strategy-structure factors usually have to take precedence if structure is to be firmly built around the organization's strategy-critical tasks, key success factors, and high priority business units. Adapting structure to the peculiar circumstances of the organization's internal situation and personalities is usually done to modify the strategy-structure match in "minor" ways.

No one of the six basic forms of strategy-structure match is indisputably best—even for a particular organization at a single moment of time. All of the basic organizational forms have their strategy-related strengths and weaknesses. Moreover, use of one of the basic organizational forms does not preclude simultaneous use of others; many organizations are large enough and diverse enough to have subunits organized by functional specialty, by geographical area, by process sequence, by market channel, by customer type, by line of business, and by SBU at the same time—there is no need to adhere slavishly to one basic organization type.

ILLUSTRATION CAPSULE 20
Selecting Managers to Fit Each Strategy

There is a growing practice in diversified companies to match a manager's personality and skills to the strategy of the line of business or operating division which the person is assigned to manage. The reason stems from a recognition that a manager, because of his own particular talents, experience, and approach to managing, is better suited for some strategic situations than for others. For instance, an entrepreneurial type manager who has guided a business through the growth stage of the product-industry life cycle and transformed a 5 percent market share into a 25 percent market share might not be the right person to manage the division once demand matures and the division's product line has little growth potential. An entrepreneurial manager's forte is discerning opportunity, capitalizing on existing expansion potential, being creative in product development and innovation, and taking the

Source: "Wanted: A Manager to Fit Each Strategy," *Business Week*, February 25, 1980, p. 166-173.

ILLUSTRATION CAPSULE 20 *(concluded)*

necessary risks to outmaneuver the competition. But in a mature business, the strategic and operating emphasis tends to be on keeping costs to a minimum, improving productivity, increasing cash flows and profit margins, and maintaining competitive position and market share—managerial tasks which an entrepreneurially oriented manager may not be as skilled at or as well-suited personality-wise to tackle. In a sense, assigning an entrepreneurial manager to run a mature or declining business is akin to moving a star offensive halfback into a defensive guard's slot.

A recent *Business Week* article cited several examples where companies have explicitly tried to match managerial talents, personality, and orientation with the requirements of strategy.

General Electric—Using business portfolio matrix analysis, GE has identified three types of strategies as being appropriate for many of the company's products and businesses; the shorthand labels attached to these three strategies are "grow," "defend," and "harvest" (and are based largely on the perceived stage of the business in the product/industry life cycle). In attempting to match managerial talent and style with the needs of strategy, general managers at GE are being classified by their personalities and managerial orientations as "growers," "caretakers," and "undertakers." According to one "GE-watcher," the company is rumored to have a shortage of "growers" but is making a concerted effort to remove the "undertaker" types who are heading up units with a "grow" strategy.

United Vintners (a subsidiary of Heublein)—In 1977 the company split its wine operations into two divisions, forming a premium wine division to stress quality over volume and a standard wine division to emphasize competitive prices and efficient, high volume production. A wine professional, with previous marketing experience, was chosen to head the premium wine business; but as general manager of the standard wines division, the company brought in a personal products manager from Gillette. The former sales staff was also reorganized along quality vs. quantity lines; moreover, in the premium wine group most of the people had wine backgrounds while those in the standard wine business often had backgrounds in consumer products and food companies.

Texas Instruments—According to the manager of strategic planning at TI, "As a product moves through different phases of its life cycle, different kinds of management skills become dominant." Corporate manpower policies reflect belief in this principle and TI takes special pains to match management style and expertise with job needs. TI's president personally reviews the backgrounds and records of the top 20% of TI's managers.

On the other hand, many companies do not accept the idea that strategic performance is improved by a careful matching of strategy and managerial skills. The chairman of Tenneco has expressed a preference for versatile, capable managers: "It doesn't make that much difference to us whether it's a growth business or a stable business per se. Most good managers can run any kind of business."

Tailoring structure (1) to the requirements of a firm's strategy, (2) to all the special circumstances that flow from how the firm has been organized before, (3) to the strengths, experiences, and personalities of key executives, and (4) to all the other relevant considerations argues for a general manager to adopt a *contingency approach* to organization-building.[19] Such an approach is based on the principle that the "best" organizational arrangement is the one that "best" fits the *overall* situation. The benefits of flexibility and catering to all the contingencies notwithstanding, there are still some worthwhile tendencies and lessons which are emerging from the experiences of firms: One, the greater the diversity within an organization's business make-up, the greater the likelihood that the most effective form of organization will be decentralized and multi-divisional, as opposed to centralized and functional. Two, where a given business uses a continuous process or assembly-line type of technology, the structure tends to be functionally-oriented and centralized since common standards of performance and tightly-sequenced integration are crucial. Three, where a firm operates in a tightly regulated environment, firms often employ a more rigid, authoritative, and bureaucratic organization structure because the governmental rules and mechanisms which must be observed leave less room for individualized discretion. Four, where a firm's products are mostly custom-made and/or there is wide variety in the day-to-day work routine and/or the production process is high technology, the structure tends to be decentralized and individual behavior is not tightly circumscribed by authority and procedural requirements. And, finally, the more uncertain and diverse the organization's product-market environment, the more likely it is that firms will utilize a loose, "organic" design with considerable managerial latitude delegated to subordinates, the logic being that structural flexibility is more conducive to adapting organizational subunits to the unique features of their respective sub-environments.[20]

Drucker has summed up the intricacies of organization design thusly:

> The simplest organization structure that will do the job is the best one. What makes an organization structure "good" are the problems it does not create. The simpler the structure, the less that can go wrong.
>
> Some design principles are more difficult and problematic than others. But none is without difficulties and problems. None is primarily people-focused rather than task-focused; none is more "creative," "free," or "more democratic." Design principles are tools; and tools are neither good nor bad in themselves. They can be used properly or improperly; and that is all. To obtain both the greatest possible simplicity and the greatest "fit," organiza-

---

[19]The contingency approach to organization-building was first documented by Jay Lorsch and Paul Lawrence of the Harvard Business School. See, for example, P. R. Lawrence and J. W. Lorsch, *Organization and Environment: Managing Differentiation and Integration* (Boston: Division of Research, Harvard Graduate School of Business Administration, 1967).

[20]Gene W. Dalton, Paul L. Lawrence, and Jay W. Lorsch, *Organization Structure and Design* (Homewood, Illinois: Irwin-Dorsey, 1970), p. 6.

tion design has to start out with a clear focus on *key activities* needed to produce *key results*. They have to be structured and positioned in the simplest possible design. Above all, the architect of organization needs to keep in mind the purpose of the structure he is designing.[21]

Building a Distinctive Competence

A good match between structure and strategy is plainly one key facet of a strategically-capable organization. But an equally dominant organization-building concern is that of staffing the chosen structure with the requisite managerial talent and technical skills—and, most particularly, staffing in a manner calculated to give the firm a distinctive competence in performing one or more critical tasks. The strategic importance of deliberately trying to develop a distinctive competence within an organization stems from the extra contribution which special expertise and a competitive edge make both to performance and to strategic success. To the extent that an organization can build an astutely conceived distinctive competence in its chosen business domains, it creates a golden opportunity for achieving a competitive advantage, gaining market share, and posting a superior record of performance. As indicated in prior chapters, a distinctive competence can take the form of greater proficiency in product development or quality of manufacture or calibre of technical services offered to customers or speed of response to changing customer requirements or cost leadership or any other strategically relevant factor.

However, distinctive competences do not just naturally appear. They have to be consciously developed and nurtured. Consequently, for a distinctive competence to emerge from organization-building actions, general managers have to push aggressively to secure an inventory of technical skills and managerial capabilities in those few select subunits where superior performance of strategically-critical tasks can make a real difference to greater strategic success. Usually, this means (1) giving above-average operating budget support to strategy-critical tasks and activities, (2) seeing that these tasks and activities are staffed with high-calibre managerial and technical talent, and (3) insisting upon high performance standards from these subunits, backed up with a policy of rewarding superior performance. In effect, general managers must take premeditated actions to see that the organization is staffed with enough of the right kinds of people and that these people have the budgetary and administrative support needed to generate a distinctive competence.

Once developed, the strengths and capabilities that attach to distinctive competences become logical cornerstones for successful strategy implementation as well as for the actual strategy itself. Moreover, really distinc-

---

[21]Drucker, *Management*, pp. 601-2.

tive internal skills and capabilities are not easily duplicated by other firms; this means that any differential advantage so gained is likely to have a lasting strategic impact and thus help pave the way for above-average performance over the long-term. Conscious general management attention to the task of building strategically relevant internal skills and strengths into the overall organizational scheme is therefore one of the central tasks of organization building and effective strategy implementation.

ALLOCATING AND FOCUSING RESOURCES ON STRATEGIC OBJECTIVES

Keeping an organization squarely on the strategy implementation path requires that the general manager assume a central role in directing the resource allocation process. Not only must a general manager oversee "who gets how much" but this must also be followed up with an equal concern for "getting the biggest bang for the buck." Two issues thus stand out:

1. What budgets and programs are needed by each organizational unit to carry out its part of the strategic plan.
2. How to focus the energies of people on achieving organizationwide objectives as opposed to just carrying out their assigned duties.

How well a general manager resolves these two issues shapes whether the organization will be results-oriented and kept pointed in the direction of strategy accomplishment or whether it gets bogged down and wanders off the path of "making it happen."

Allocating Resources: Budgets and Programs

Little discussion is needed to establish the role of budgets and programs in the strategy implementation process. Obviously, organizational units must have the resources needed to carry out their part of the strategic plan. This includes having enough of the right kinds of people and having enough operating funds for them to carry out their work. And, obviously, each subunit must program its activities to meet its objectives; this means deciding upon the duties and content of jobs, setting up the flow and sequences of various jobs and activities, establishing schedules and deadlines for accomplishment, and, in general, parcelling out assignments for exactly who is responsible for what and by when. Budgets and programs go hand in hand. Programs lay out detailed, step-by-step action plans, and budgets specify the costs of the planned activities.

The range of strategy-related resource allocation issues which confront general managers go across the whole landscape. A sampling of some of the more important ones include:

- How many extra dollars to allocate to a business unit which is trying to rebuild and reposition itself after having just gone through a period of slack demand and competitive weakness.

- How much to budget for advertising and promoting a major new item in the firm's product line.

- What extra resources will be needed to manage a newly-acquired subsidiary and to establish systems for reporting the subsidiary's financial performance on a regular basis.

- What extra R&D expenditures are needed to accommodate a new outbreak of rapid technological developments.

- What additional resources will be needed to increase manufacturing capacity by X percent.

- What changes in resource allocation are implied by a shift in emphasis from product A to product B.

- What are the resource allocation implications of shifting from a "grow and build" strategy to a "maintain and hold" strategy.

- What will it cost to build a distinctive competence in providing technical support services to customers.

- How much funding will it take to increase recruitment of new entry-level engineers by 50%.

How well a general manager resolves strategy-related resource allocation decisions of this magnitude can, quite clearly, either promote or impede the process of strategy implementation and execution. Too little funding deprives subunits of the capability to carry out their piece of the strategic plan. Too much funding is a waste of organizational resources and reduces financial performance. Both outcomes argue for a strong general management role in the budgeting process and in reviewing the programs and proposals of strategy-critical subunits within the organization.

Focusing Work Efforts on Strategic Objectives

As previously indicated, successful strategy implementation and execution is assisted when critical tasks and key activities are linked directly and clearly to accomplishing the strategic plan. Matching structure to strategy provides one valuable linkage. Defining jobs and assignments in terms of the strategic results to be accomplished (as well as in terms of the duties and functions to be performed) adds another, and equally important, linkage.

The value of defining jobs and assignments in terms of what is to be accomplished is that it makes the work environment results-oriented and performance-oriented. From a strategy perspective, what is to be accomplished is (1) carrying out the strategy and (2) achieving the target levels of organization performance. When an organization's attention and its energies are kept firmly trained on executing strategy and achieving the agreed-upon objectives, the chances for accomplishing the strategic plan are decidedly greater.

The question, then, is how to keep the organization trained on achieving the right strategic results as opposed to routinely carrying out duties and functions in hopes that the byproduct will be strategic success. Making the right things happen rather than hoping they will happen is, of course, what "managing with objectives" is all about. The approach has a simple, powerful logic: An organization's objectives *are* the priorities for achievement; they define precisely what is to be accomplished and they suggest where work efforts should be directed. Organizationwide objectives get translated into line of business objectives and on down to functional area, operating-level, and job-specific objectives via the strategy formulation process (where the hierarchy of objectives is matched against the hierarchy of strategies). Done correctly, the outcome is a top-to-bottom understanding of what each organization unit and each person needs to accomplish and what their expected role and contribution to the strategic plan is. Then, and here's the key part, each person's and each organization unit's performance must be measured and evaluated in terms of whether or not the objectives are actually achieved. This means that "doing a good job" is defined in terms of "achieving the agreed-upon objectives." While other things besides achieving the agreed-upon objectives may count for something in the reward structure, they do not count nearly as much—and it is this feature that gets the attention of the organization and keeps people's energies trained on achieving the target levels of performance.

ILLUSTRATION CAPSULE 21
How "Managing with Objectives" Assists Strategy Implementation

The following remarks of a vice-president of marketing for a small candy manufacturer illustrate how strategy-critical tasks, jobs, and work assignments can be defined in terms of the results to be accomplished. Observe how the vice-president uses quotas and budgets to keep sales efforts trained on achieving the target market results, thereby promoting strategy implementation.

Basically I'm trying to operate so my people will grow along with the company. I set high standards. I know they won't all be met, but at least people will know what I'm looking for. I expect a subordinate to have ideas and to have plans on what he wants to do and how. I may differ with him, and I'll explain why I think another way is better, but I don't penalize

ILLUSTRATION CAPSULE 21 *(concluded)*

---

people for doing things their own way. What I want is results, and if a man has his own way, that's O.K.

Our regional men and brokers have quotas and also specific objectives to reach in each market. I ask them to set a quota for themselves, partly to get their appraisal of a market and partly so I can appraise their motivation and judgment. I don't want them to promise pie in the sky, but neither do I want to see them aiming low to be sure of hitting it and getting a bonus.

We give each regional manager a discretionary fund to spend as he pleases. It's only $5,000, but it is important in a couple of ways. For one thing the way a man uses it helps me appraise his judgment. Second, it makes him a much more important part of the organization. The brokers look to him to use some of the money for promotions in their territory—so it helps the regional man get the broker's cooperation. And don't forget that it's the strength of our distribution that has let us grow rapidly on so little money.

All this field work is done within the general framework of corporate marketing objectives. We write these up and send them out to each broker and regional man. Each month we send him a rundown on how he is doing compared to the objectives (based on information from the IBM reports). At the end of the year we go over the plan and each unfulfilled objective with every man. We try to determine if we were unrealistic, if it was unavoidable, or if it was a lack of something on his part. It isn't done to crucify someone; we want our objectives and quotas to be realistic or they are worse than useless. We want each man to believe he can hit them, so it's important that we all understand why they weren't reached.*

What do you think of this application of "managing with objectives?" If one rejects use of managing with objectives, then what other ways are available for linking work activity directly to accomplishment of the strategic plan? How dependable are these other ways? When the jobs of salespersons are functionally defined as calling on X customers per week and putting in at least 40 hours of selling activity each week, can one safely assume that overall sales targets will be met? How important is it, then, to combine a description of the duties and functions to be performed with a description of what results are to be achieved? And which description is more important to strategy implementation—the functions to be performed or the results to be achieved?

*As quoted in George A. Smith, Jr., C. Roland Christensen, Norman A. Berg, and Malcolm S. Salter, *Policy Formulation and Administration*, Sixth Edition (Homewood, Ill.: Richard D. Irwin, Inc., 1972), pp. 363-364.

For the tool of "managing with objectives" to be of real assistance in implementing and executing the strategic plan, two things must happen. One, the general manager must insist that jobs and assignments are defined primarily in terms of the results to be accomplished and secondarily in terms of descriptions of the duties and functions to be performed. The danger of the latter is that it is very easy for people and organization subunits to become so engrossed in doing their duties and performing their functions that they lose sight of what it is the functions and duties are intended to accomplish in the first place. By defining jobs and activities in terms of what strategic results and objectives are to be achieved, the spotlight is kept on accomplishment of the strategic plan. Two, the general manager must not waver far from the standard that "doing a good job" *equals* "achieving the agreed-upon strategic objectives and performance." Any other standard simply serves to undermine strategy implementation and to channel energies and efforts into other directions.

Using strategic objectives as the ultimate results for work and job assignments therefore begins with the question "What are our objectives and what results do we want to show for our efforts?" If formulation of the strategic plan has been thorough and complete, the answers to this question are explicit in the strategic plan itself or, at least, are reasonably unambiguous in the minds of the managers of each organizational unit. Otherwise, the answers are suggested by the role and contribution expected of the organization unit in accomplishing the strategic plan. Keep in mind that specific objectives and performance targets are needed not only for the organization as a whole but also for each organizational subunit. While there is ample room for the agreed-upon objectives and results to reflect both top-down and bottom-up considerations, the key is to promote understanding and emphasis on what each organizational unit's part is in achieving the target levels of strategic performance. This makes clearer the kind of work and effort that can be strategically productive. It relates departments and functional areas to the strategic needs of the organization as a whole. But most important, it lets people know what is expected of them— from a results perspective instead of from an activity and effort perspective.

Next, it must be asked "What specific activities, work assignments, and jobs are needed to produce the target levels of performance?" The answers here should suggest the skills, technical expertise, staffing, and funding which are needed to reach the established objectives.

Finally, managers have to address "How can jobs and work efforts in my unit be designed around the unit's strategy-related objectives?" Placing the emphasis of job design and work assignments on "what to accomplish" instead of "what to do" is an important difference. As any student knows, just because an instructor conducts his/her classes regularly it cannot be safely assumed that students are learning what they are being taught— teaching and learning are different things, the first is an activity and the second is a result. In any job, doing an activity is not equivalent to achieving the intended objective. Working hard, staying busy, and diligently attending to one's duties do not guarantee results. Hence, the creativity of managers in drawing attention to the right things to shoot for (accomplishing our part of the strategic plan) and creating a results-oriented work environment (where work efforts are aimed squarely at reaching the unit's target performance objectives) is more than incidental. Indeed, figuring out how to make the achievement of strategy-related objectives a "way of life" up and down the whole organization is central to the general manager's task of strategy implementation. The more that organization energies and efforts flow in the direction of strategy execution, the more that strategy implementation stays on track.

SUMMARY

Linking daily activities and work efforts directly and clearly to accomplishing the organization's strategic plan is critical to successful strategy implementation. The two strategy-implementing tasks of the general manager which aim at creating this linkage are (1) building a capable organization and (2) allocating resources and focusing work efforts on strategic objectives. The first task centers around the strategy-critical components of matching of structure to fit the requirements of strategy and staffing each organizational unit with the skills, expertise, and competences it needs to carry out its assigned role in the strategic plan. The second task involves providing organizational units with the budgetary resources and priorities requisite for accomplishing their piece of the overall strategy and then keeping organizationwide attention focused on "what to achieve" (the target strategic objectives) and not letting work efforts aim simply at "what to do."

Admittedly, though, the most telling test of how well a general manager performs these two roles is not the subjectives of the tight fit between structure and strategy or the care with which the total work effort has been subdivided into jobs and then recombined into coordinated action or the degree of reliance upon managing with objectives or the efficiency of internal resource allocation. These things are important but not sufficient. The sufficient condition is that the organization performs up to potential and to expectations. Unless and until the strategy is converted into results, the task of implementation is uncompleted.

SUGGESTED READINGS

Chandler, Alfred D., *Strategy and Structure* (Cambridge: The M.I.T. Press, 1962).

Corey, Raymond E. and Steven H. Star, *Organization Strategy: A Marketing Approach* (Boston: Division of Research, Harvard University Graduate School of Business Administration, 1971), Chapters 2, 3, 4, and 5.

Daniel, Ronald D., "Reorganizing for Results," *Harvard Business Review*, vol. 44, no. 6 (November-December 1966), pp. 96-104.

Davis, Stanley M. and Paul R. Lawrence, "Problems of Matrix Organizations," *Harvard Business Review*, vol. 56, no. 3 (May-June 1978), pp. 131-42.

Drucker, Peter, *Management: Tasks, Responsibilities, Practices* (New York: Harper and Row, 1974), Chapters 41-48.

Hall, William K., "SBUs: Hot, New Topic in the Management of Diversification," *Business Horizons*, vol. 21, no. 1 (February 1978), pp. 17-25.

Leontiades, Milton, *Strategies for Diversification and Change* (Boston: Little, Brown and Co., 1980), Chapters 2, 3, and 6.

Lorange, Peter, *Corporate Planning: An Executive Viewpoint* (Englewood Cliffs, N.J.: Prentice-Hall, Inc., 1980), Chapters 2, 4, and 7.

Lorsch, Jay W. and Arthur H. Walker, "Organizational Choice: Product vs. Function," *Harvard Business Review*, vol. 46, no. 6 (November-December 1968), pp. 129-38.

Mintzberg, Henry, "Organization Design: Fashion or Fit," *Harvard Business Review*, vol. 59, no. 1 (January-February 1981), pp. 103-16.

Peters, Thomas J., "Beyond the Matrix Organization," *Business Horizons*, vol. 22, no. 5 (October 1979), pp. 15-27.

Rumelt, Richard, *Strategy, Structure, and Economic Performance* (Cambridge, Mass.: Harvard University Press, 1974).

Salter, Malcolm S., "Stages of Corporate Development," *Journal of Business Policy*, vol. 1, no. 1 (1970), pp. 23-37.

Scott, Bruce R., "The Industrial State: Old Myths and New Realities," *Harvard Business Review*, vol. 51, no. 2 (March-April 1973), pp. 133-48.

Slocum, John W., Jr. and Don Hellriegel, "Using Organizational Designs to Cope with Change," *Business Horizons*, vol. 22, no. 6 (December 1979), pp. 65-76.

Waterman, Robert H., Thomas J. Peters, Julien R. Phillips, "Structure Is Not Organization," *Business Horizons*, vol. 23, no. 3 (June 1980), pp. 14-26.

READING

Structure Is Not Organization*

ROBERT H. WATERMAN, JR., THOMAS J. PETERS, AND JULIEN R. PHILLIPS

Robert H. Waterman, Jr. is a Director, Thomas J. Peters a Principal, and Julien R. Phillips an Associate in the San Francisco office of McKinsey & Company. Mssrs. Waterman and Peters are co-leaders of McKinsey's Organizational Effectiveness practice.

The Belgian surrealist Rene Magritte painted a series of pipes and titled the series *Ceci n'est pas une pipe*: this is not a pipe. The picture of the thing is not the thing. In the same way, a structure is not an organization. We all know that, but like as not, when we reorganize what we do is to restructure. Intellectually all managers and consultants know that much more goes on in the process of organizing than the charts, boxes, dotted lines, position descriptions, and matrices can possibly depict. But all too often we behave as though we didn't know it; if we want change we change the structure.

Early in 1977, a general concern with the problems of organization effectiveness, and a particular concern about the nature of the relationship between structure and organization, led us to assemble an internal task force to review our client work. The natural first step was to talk extensively to consultants and client executives around the world who were known for their skill and experience in organization design. We found that they too were dissatisfied with conventional approaches. All were disillusioned about the usual structural solutions, but they were also skeptical about anyone's ability to do better. In their experience, the techniques of the behavioral sciences were not providing useful alternatives to structural design. True, the notion that structure follows strategy (get the strategy right and the structure follows) looked like an important addition to the organizational tool kit; yet strategy rarely seemed to dictate unique structural solutions. Moreover, the main problem in strategy had turned out to be execution: getting it done. And that, to a very large extent, meant *organization*. So the problem of organization effectiveness threatened to prove

*This article is reprinted from *Business Horizons*, vol. 23, no. 3 (June 1980), pp. 14-26. Copyright ©1980, by the Foundation for the School of Business at Indiana University. Reprinted by permission.

The authors offer special acknowledgement and thanks to Anthony G. Athos of Harvard University, who was instrumental in the development of the 7-S framework and who, in his capacity as our consultant, helped generally to advance our thinking on organization effectiveness.

circular. The dearth of practical additions to old ways of thought was painfully apparent.

OUTSIDE EXPLORATIONS

Our next step was to look outside for help. We visited a dozen business schools in the United States and Europe and about as many superbly performing companies. Both academic theorists and business leaders, we found, were wrestling with the same concerns.

Our timing in looking at the academic environment was good. The state of theory is in great turmoil but moving toward a new consensus. Some researchers continue to write about structure, particularly its latest and most modish variant, the matrix organization. But primarily the ferment is around another stream of ideas that follow from some startling premises about the limited capacity of decision makers to process information and reach what we usually think of as "rational" decisions.

The stream that today's researchers are tapping is an old one, started in the late 1930s by Fritz Roethlisberger and Chester Barnard, then both at Harvard (Barnard had been president of New Jersey Bell). They challenged rationalist theory, first—in Roethlisberger's case—on the shop floors of Western Electric's Hawthorne plant. Roethlisberger found that simply *paying attention* provided a stimulus to productivity that far exceeded that induced by formal rewards. In a study of workplace hygiene, they turned the lights up and got an expected productivity increase. Then to validate their results they turned the lights down. But something surprising was wrong: productivity went up again. Attention, they concluded, not working conditions per se, made the difference.

Barnard, speaking from the chief executive's perspective, asserted that the CEO's role is to harness the social forces in the organization, to shape and guide values. He described good value-shapers as *effective* managers, contrasting them with the mere manipulators of formal rewards who dealt only with the narrower concept of *efficiency*.

Barnard's words, though quickly picked up by Herbert Simon (whom we'll come back to later), lay dormant for thirty years while the primary management issues focused on decentralization and structure—the appropriate and burning issue of the time.

But then, as the decentralized structure proved to be less than a panacea for all time, and its substitute, the matrix, ran into worse trouble, Barnard's and Simon's ideas triggered a new wave of thinking. On the theory side, it is exemplified by the work of James March and Karl Weick, who attacked the rational model with a vengeance. Weick suggests that organizations learn—and adapt—very slowly. They pay obsessive attention to internal cues long after their practical value has ceased. Important business assumptions are buried deep in the minutiae of organizational systems and other habitual routines whose origins have been long obscured by time. March goes further. He introduced, only slightly facetiously, the garbage can as an organizational metaphor. March pictures organizational learning and decision making as a stream of choices, solutions, decision makers, and opportunities interacting almost randomly to make decisions that carry the organization toward the future. His observations about large organizations parallel Truman's about the Presidency: "You issue orders from this office and if you can find out what happens to them after that, you're a better man than I am."

Other researchers have accumulated data which support this unconventional view. Henry Mintzberg made one of the few rigorous studies of how senior managers actually use time. They don't block out large chunks of time for planning, organizing, motivation, and controlling as some suggest they should. Their time, in fact, is appallingly but perhaps necessarily fragmented. Andrew Pettigrew studied the politics of strategic decision and was fascinated by the inertial properties of organizations. He showed that organizations frequently hold onto faulty assumptions about their world for as long as a decade, despite overwhelming evidence that it has changed and they probably should too.

In sum, what the researchers tell us is: "We can explain why you have problems." In the face of complexity and multiple competing demands, organizations simply can't handle decision making in a totally rational way. Not surprisingly, then, a single blunt instrument—like structure—is unlikely to prove the master tool that can change organizations with best effect.

Somewhat to our surprise, senior executives in the top-performing companies that we interviewed proved to be speaking very much the same language. They were concerned that the inherent limitations of structural approaches could render their companies insensitive to an unstable business environment marked by rapidly changing threats and opportunities from every quarter—competitors, governments, and unions at home and overseas. Their organizations, they said, had to learn how to build capabilities for rapid and flexible response. Their favored tactic was to choose a temporary focus, facing perhaps one major issue this year and another next year or the year after. Yet at the same time, they were acutely aware of their people's need for a stable, unifying value system—a foundation for long-term continuity. Their task, as they saw it, was largely one of preserving internal stability while adroitly guiding the organization's responses to fast-paced external change.

Companies such as IBM, Kodak, Hewlett-Packard, GM, DuPont, and P&G, then, seem obsessive in their attention to maintaining a stable culture. At the same time, these giants are more responsive than their competitors. Typically, they do not seek responsiveness through major structural shifts. Instead, they seem to rely on a series of temporary devices to focus the attention of the entire organization for a limited time on a single priority goal or environmental threat.

SIMON AS EXEMPLAR

Thirty years ago, in *Administrative Behavior*, Herbert Simon (a 1977 Nobel laureate) anticipated several themes that dominate much of today's thinking about organization. Simon's concepts of "satisficing" (settling for adequate instead of optimal solutions) and "the limits of rationality" were, in effect, nails in the coffin of economic man. His ideas, if correct, are crucial. The economic man paradigm has not only influenced the economists but has also influenced thought about the proper organization and administration of most business enterprises—and, by extension, public administration. Traditional thought has it that economic man is basically seeking to maximize against a set of fairly clear objectives. For organization planners the implications of this are that one can specify objectives, determine their appropriate hierarchy, and then logically determine the "best" organization.

Simon labeled this the "rational" view of the administrative world and said, in effect, that it was all right as far as it went but that it had decided limits. For one, most organizations cannot maximize—the goals are really not that clear. Even if they were, most business managers do not have access to complete information, as the economic model requires, but in reality operate with a set of relatively simple decision rules in order to *limit* the information they really need to process to make most decisions. In other words, the rules we use in order to get on with it in big organizations limit our ability to optimize anything.

Suppose the goal is profit maximization. The definition of profit and its maximization varies widely even within a single organization. Is it earnings growth, quality of earnings, maximum return on equity, or the discounted value of the future earnings stream—and if so, at what discount rate? Moreover, business organizations are basically large social structures with diffuse power. Most of the individuals who make them up have different ideas of what the business ought to be. The few at the top seldom agree entirely on the goals of their enterprise, let alone on maximization against one goal. Typically, they will not push their views so hard as to destroy the social structure of their enterprise and, in turn, their own power base.

All this leaves the manager in great difficulty. While the research seems valid and the message of complexity rings true, the most innovative work in the field is descriptive. The challenge to the manager is how to organize better. His goal is organization effectiveness. What the researchers are saying is that the subject is much more complex than any of our past prescriptive models have allowed for. What none has been able to usefully say is, "OK, here's what to do about it."

THE 7-S FRAMEWORK

After a little over a year and a half of pondering this dilemma, we began to formulate a new framework for organizational thought. As we and others have developed it and tested it in teaching, in workshops, and in direct problem solving over the past year, we have found it enormously helpful. It has repeatedly demonstrated its usefulness both in diagnosing the causes of organizational malaise and in formulating programs for improvement. In brief, it seems to work.

Our assertion is that productive organization change is not simply a matter of structure, although structure is important. It is not so simple as the interaction between strategy and structure, although strategy is critical too. Our claim is that effective organizational change is really the relationship between structure, strategy, systems, style, skills, staff, and something we call superordinate goals. (The alliteration is intentional: it serves as an aid to memory).

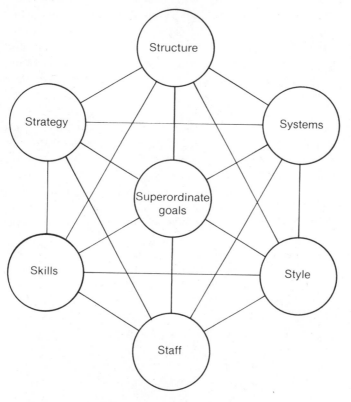

Our central idea is that organization effectiveness stems from the interaction of several factors—some not especially obvious and some underanalyzed. Our framework for organization change, graphically depicted in the exhibit above, suggests several important ideas:

- First is the idea of a multiplicity of factors that influence an organization's ability to change and its proper mode of change. Why pay attention to only one or two, ignoring the others? Beyond structure and strategy, there are at least five other identifiable elements. The division is to some extent arbitrary, but it has the merit of acknowledging the complexity identified in the research and segmenting it into manageable parts.

- Second, the diagram is intended to convey the notion of the interconnectedness of the variables—the idea is that it's difficult, perhaps impossible, to make significant progress in one area without making progress in the others as well. Notions of organization change that ignore its many aspects or their interconnectedness are dangerous.

- In a recent article on strategy, *Fortune* commented that perhaps as many as 90 percent of carefully planned strategies don't work. If that is so, our guess would be that the failure is a failure in execution, resulting from inattention to the S's. Just as a logistics bottleneck can cripple a military strategy, inadequate systems or staff can make paper tigers of the best-laid plans for clobbering competitors.

- Finally, the shape of the diagram is significant. It has no starting point or implied hierarchy. A priori, it isn't obvious which of the seven factors will be the driving force in changing a particular organization at a particular point in time. In some cases, the critical variable might be strategy. In others, it could be systems or structure.

Structure

To understand this model of organization change better, let us look at each of its elements, beginning—as most organization discussions do—with structure. What will the new organization of the 1980s be like? If decentralization was the trend of the past, what is next? Is it matrix organization? What will "Son of Matrix" look like? Our answer is that those questions miss the point.

To see why, let's take a quick look at the history of structural thought and development. The basic theory underlying structure is simple. Structure divides tasks and then provides coordination. It trades off specialization and integration. It decentralizes and then recentralizes.

The old structural division was between production and sales. The chart showing this was called a functional organization. Certain principles of organization, such as one-man/one-boss, limited span of control, grouping of like activities, and commensurate authority and responsibility, seemed universal truths.

What happened to this simple idea? Size—and complexity. A company like General Electric has grown over a thousandfold in both sales and earnings in the past eighty years. Much of its growth has come through entry into new and diverse businesses. At a certain level of size and complexity, a functional organization, which is dependent on frequent interaction among all activities, breaks down. As the number of people or businesses increases arithmetically, the number of interactions required to make things work increases geometrically. A company passing a certain size and complexity threshold must decentralize to cope.

Among the first to recognize the problem and explicitly act on it was DuPont in 1921. The increasing administrative burden brought about by its diversification into several new product lines ultimately led the company to transform its highly centralized, functionally departmental structure into a decentralized, multidivisional one. Meanwhile, General Motors, which has been decentralized from the outset, was learning how to make a decentralized structure work as more than just a holding company.

However, real decentralization in world industry did not take place until much later. In 1950, for example, only about 20 percent of the *Fortune 500* companies were decentralized. By 1970, 80 percent were decentralized. A similar shift was taking place throughout the industrialized world.

Today three things are happening. First, because of the portfolio concept of managing a business, spun off from General Electric research (which has now become PIMS), companies are saying, "We can do more with our decentralized structure than control complexity. We can shift resources, act flexibly—that is, manage strategically."

Second, the dimensions along which companies want to divide tasks have multiplied. Early on, there were functional divisions. Then came product divisions. Now we have possibilities for division by function, product, market, geography, nation, strategic business unit, and probably more. The rub is that as the new dimensions are added, the old ones don't go away. An insurance company, for example, can organize around market segments, but it still needs functional control over underwriting decisions. The trade-offs are staggering if we try to juggle them all at once.

Third, new centralist forces have eclipsed clean, decentralized divisions of responsibility. In Europe, for example, a company needs a coherent union strategy. In Japan, especially, companies need a centralized approach to the government interface. In the United States, regulation and technology force centralization in the interest of uniformity.

This mess has produced a new organization form: the matrix, which purports, at least in concept, to reconcile the realities of organizational complexity with the imperatives of managerial control. Unfortunately, the two-dimensional matrix model is intrinsically too simple to capture the real situation. Any spatial model that really did capture it would be incomprehensible.

Matrix does, however, have one well-disguised virtue: it calls attention to the central problem in structuring today. That problem is not the one on which most organization designers spend their time—that is, how to divide up tasks. It is one of emphasis and coordination—how to make the whole thing work. The challenge lies not so much in trying to comprehend all the possible dimensions of organization structure as in developing the ability to focus on those dimensions which are currently important to the organization's evolution—and to be ready to refocus as the crucial dimensions shift. General Motors' restless use of structural change—most recently the project center, which led to their effective downsizing effort—is a case in point.

The General Motors solution has a critical attribute—the use of a temporary overlay to accomplish a strategic task. IBM, Texas Instruments, and others have used similar temporary structural weapons. In the process, they have meticulously preserved the shape and spirit of the underlying structure (e.g., the GM division or the TI Product Customer Center). We regularly observe those two attributes among our sample of top performers: the use of the temporary and the maintenance of the simple underlying form.

We speculate that the effective "structure of the eighties" will more likely be described as "flexible" or "temporary"; this matrix-like property will be preserved even as the current affair with the formal matrix structure cools.

Strategy

If structure is not enough, what is? Obviously, there is strategy. It was Alfred Chandler who first pointed out that structure follows strategy, or more precisely, that a strategy of diversity forces a decentralized structure.[1] Throughout the past decade, the corporate world has given close attention to the interplay between strategy and structure. Certainly, clear ideas about strategy make the job of structural design more rational.

By "strategy" we mean those actions that a company plans in response to or anticipation of changes in its external environment—its customers, its competitors. Strategy is the way a company aims to improve its position vis-a-vis competition—perhaps through low-cost production or delivery, perhaps by providing better value to the customer, perhaps by achieving sales and service dominance. It is, or ought to be, an organization's way of saying: "Here is how we will create unique value."

As the company's chosen route to competitive success, strategy is obviously a central concern in many business situations—especially in highly competitive industries where the game is won or lost on share points. But "structure follows strategy" is by no means the be-all and end-all of organization wisdom. We find too many examples of large prestigious companies

---

[1] Alfred D. Chandler, Jr., *Strategy and Structure: Chapters in the History of the American Industrial Enterprise* (Cambridge, Mass.: MIT Press, 1962).

around the world that are replete with strategy and cannot execute any of it. There is little if anything wrong with their structures; the causes of their inability to execute lie in other dimensions of our framework. When we turn to nonprofit and public-sector organizations, moreover, we find that the whole meaning of "strategy" is tenuous—but the problem of organizational effectiveness looms as large as ever.

Strategy, then, is clearly a critical variable in organization design—but much more is at work.

Systems

By systems we mean all the procedures, formal and informal, that make the organization go, day by day and year by year: capital budgeting systems, training systems, cost accounting procedures, budgeting systems. If there is a variable in our model that threatens to dominate the others, it could well be systems. Do you want to understand how an organization really does (or doesn't) get things done? Look at the systems. Do you want to change an organization without disruptive restructuring? Try changing the systems.

A large consumer goods manufacturer was recently trying to come up with an overall corporate strategy. Textbook portfolio theory seemed to apply: Find a good way to segment the business, decide which segments in the total business portfolio are most attractive, invest most heavily in those. The only catch: Reliable cost data by segment were not to be had. The company's management information system was not adequate to support the segmentation.

Again, consider how a bank might go about developing a strategy. A natural first step, it would seem, would be to segment the business by customer and product to discover where the money is made and lost and why. But in trying to do this, most banks almost immediately come up against an intractable costing problem. Because borrowers are also depositors, because transaction volumes vary, because the balance sheet turns fast, and because interest costs are half or more of total costs and unpredictable over the long term, costs for various market segments won't stay put. A strategy based on today's costs could be obsolete tomorrow.

One bank we know has rather successfully sidestepped the problem. Its key to future improvement is not strategy but the systems infrastructure that will allow account officers to negotiate deals favorable to the bank. For them the system *is* the strategy. Development and implementation of a superior account profitability system, based on a return-on-equity tree, has improved their results dramatically. "Catch a fish for a man and he is fed for a day; teach him to fish and he is fed for life": The proverb applies to organizations in general and to systems in particular.

Another intriguing aspect of systems is the way they mirror the state of an organization. Consider a certain company we'll call International Wickets. For years management has talked about the need to become more market oriented. Yet astonishingly little time is spent in their planning meetings on customers, marketing, market share, or other issues having to do with market orientation. One of their key systems, in other words, remains *very* internally oriented. Without a change in this key system, the market orientation goal will remain unattainable no matter how much change takes place in structure and strategy.

To many business managers the word "systems" has a dull, plodding, middle-management sound. Yet it is astonishing how powerfully systems changes can enhance organizational effects that so often ensue from tinkering with structure.

Style

It is remarkable how often writers, in characterizing a corporate management for the business press, fall back on the word "style." Tony O'Reilly's style at Heinz is certainly not AT&T's, yet both are successful. The trouble we have with style is not in recognizing its importance, but in doing much about it. Personalities don't change, or so the conventional wisdom goes.

We think it important to distinguish between the basic personality of a top-management team and the way that team comes across to the organization. Organizations may listen to what managers say, but they believe what managers do. Not words, but patterns of actions are decisive. The power of style, then, is essentially manageable.

One element of a manager's style is how he or she chooses to spend time. As Henry Mintzberg has pointed out, managers don't spend their time in the neatly compartmentalized planning, organizing, motivating, and controlling modes of classical management theory.[2] Their days are a mess—or so it seems. There's a seeming infinity of things they might devote attention to. No top executive attends to all of the demands on his time; the median time spent on any one issue is nine minutes.

What can a top manager do in nine minutes? Actually, a good deal. He can signal what's on his mind; he can reinforce a message; he can nudge people's thinking in a desired direction. Skillful management of his inevitably fragmented time is, in fact, an immensely powerful change lever.

By way of example, we have found differences beyond anything attributable to luck among different companies' success ratios in finding oil or mineral deposits. A few years ago, we surveyed a fairly large group of the finders and nonfinders in mineral exploration to discover what they were doing differently. The finders almost always said their secret was "top-

[2]Henry Mintzberg, "The Manager's Job: Folklore and Fact," *Harvard Business Review*, July/August 1975: 49-61.

management attention." Our reaction was skeptical: "Sure, that's the solution to most problems." But subsequent hard analysis showed that their executives *were* spending more time in the field, *were* blocking out more time for exploration discussions at board meetings, and *were* making more room on their own calendars for exploration-related activities.

Another aspect of style is symbolic behavior. Taking the same example, the successful finders typically have more people on the board who understand exploration or have headed exploration departments. Typically they fund exploration more consistently (that is, their year-to-year spending patterns are less volatile). They define fewer and more consistent exploration targets. Their exploration activities typically report at a higher organizational level. And they typically articulate better reasons for exploring in the first place.

A chief executive of our acquaintance is fond of saying that the way you recognize a marketing-oriented company is that "everyone talks marketing." He doesn't mean simply that an observable preoccupation with marketing is the end result, the final indication of the company's evaluation toward the market-place. He means that it can be the lead. Change in orientation often starts when enough people talk about it before they really know what "it" is. Strategy management is not yet a crisply defined concept, but many companies are taking it seriously. If they talk about it enough, it will begin to take on specific meaning for their organizations— and those organizations will change as a result.

This suggests a second attribute of style that is by no means confined to those at the top. Our proposition is that a corporation's style, as a reflection of its culture, has more to do with its ability to change organization or performance than is generally recognized. One company, for example, was considering a certain business opportunity. From a strategic standpoint, analysis showed it to be a winner. The experience of others in the field confirmed that. Management went ahead with the acquisition. Two years later it backed out of the business, at a loss. The acquisition had failed because it simply wasn't consistent with the established corporate culture of the parent organization. It didn't fit their view of themselves. The will to make it work was absent.

Time and again strategic possibilities are blocked—or slowed down— by cultural constraints. One of today's more dramatic examples is the Bell System, where management has undertaken to move a service-oriented culture toward a new and different kind of marketing. The service idea, and its meaning to AT&T, is so deeply embedded in the Bell System's culture that the shift to a new kind of marketing will take years.

The phenomenon at its most dramatic comes to the fore in mergers. In almost every merger, no matter how closely related the businesses, the task of integrating and achieving eventual synergy is a problem no less difficult than combining two cultures. At some level of detail, almost everything done by two parties to a merger will be done differently. This helps explain why the management of acquisitions is so hard. If the two cultures are not integrated, the planned synergies will not accrue. On the other hand, to change too much too soon is to risk uprooting more tradition than can be replanted before the vital skills of the acquiree wither and die.

Staff

Staff (in the sense of people, not line/staff) is often treated in one of two ways. At the hard end of the spectrum, we talk of appraisal systems, pay scales, formal training programs, and the like. At the soft end, we talk about morale, attitude, motivation, and behavior.

Top management is often, and justifiably, turned off by both these approaches. The first seems too trivial for their immediate concern ("Leave it to the personnel department"), the second too intractable ("We don't want a bunch of shrinks running around, stirring up the place with more attitude surveys.")

Our predilection is to broaden and redefine the nature of the people issue. What do the top-performing companies do to foster the process of developing managers? How, for example, do they shape the basic values of their management cadre? Our reason for asking the question at all is simply that no serious discussion of organization can afford to ignore it (although many do). Our reason for framing the question around the development of managers is our observation that the superbly performing companies pay extraordinary attention to managing what might be called the socialization process in their companies. This applies especially to the way they introduce young recruits into the mainstream of their organizations and to the way they manage their careers as the recruits develop into tomorrow's managers.

The process for orchestrating the early careers of incoming managers, for instance, at IBM, Texas Instruments, P&G, Hewlett-Packard, or Citibank is quite different from its counterpart in many other companies we know around the world. Unlike other companies, which often seem prone to sidetrack young but expensive talent into staff positions or other jobs out of the mainstream of the company's business, these leaders take extraordinary care to turn young managers' first jobs into first opportunities for contributing in practical ways to the nuts-and-bolts of what the business is all about. If the mainstream of the business is innovation, for example, the first job might be in new-products introduction. If the mainstream of the business is marketing, the MBA's first job could be sales or product management.

The companies who use people best rapidly move their managers into positions of real responsibility, often by the early- to mid-thirties. Various active support devices like assigned mentors, fast-track programs, and carefully orchestrated opportunities for exposure to top management are hallmarks of their management of people.

In addition, these companies are all particularly adept at managing, in a special and focused way, their central cadre of key managers. At Texas Instruments, Exxon, GM, and GE, for instance, a number of the very most senior executives are said to devote several weeks of each year to planning the progress of the top few hundred.

These, then, are a few examples of practical programs through which the superior companies manage people as aggressively and concretely as others manage organization structure. Considering people as a pool of resources to be nurtured, developed, guarded, and allocated is one of the many ways to turn the "staff" dimensions of our 7-S framework into something not only amenable to, but worthy of practical control by senior management.

We are often told, "Get the structure 'right' and the people will fit" or "Don't compromise the 'optimum' organization for people considerations." At the other end of the spectrum we are earnestly advised, "The right people can make any organization work." Neither view is correct. People do count, but staff is only one of our seven variables.

Skills

We added the notion of skills for a highly practical reason: it enables us to capture a company's crucial attributes as no other concept can do. A strategic description of a company, for example, might typically cover markets to be penetrated or types of products to be sold. But how do most of us characterize companies? Not by their strategies or their structures. We tend to characterize them by what they do best. We talk of IBM's orientation to the marketplace, its prodigious customer service capabilities, or its sheer market power. We talk of DuPont's research prowess, Procter & Gamble's management capability, ITT's financial controls, Hewlett-Packard's innovation and quality, and Texas Instruments' project management. These dominating attributes, or capabilities, are what we mean by skills.

Now why is this distinction important? Because we regularly observe that organizations facing big discontinuities in business conditions must do more than shift strategic focus. Frequently they need to add a new capability, that is to say, a new skill. The Bell System, for example, is currently striving to add a formidable new array of marketing skills. Small copier companies, upon growing larger, find that they must radically enhance their service capabilities to compete with Xerox. Meanwhile Xerox needs to enhance its response capability in order to fend off a host of new competition. These dominating capability needs, unless explicitly labeled as such, often get lost as the company "attacks a new market" (strategy shift) or "decentralizes to give managers autonomy" (structure shift).

Additionally, we frequently find it helpful to *label* current skills, for the addition of a new skill may come only when the old one is dismantled. Adopting a newly "flexible and adaptive marketing thrust," for example, may be possible only if increases are accepted in certain marketing or distribution costs. Dismantling some of the distracting attributes of an old "manufacturing mentality" (that is, a skill that was perhaps crucial in the past) may be the only way to insure the success of an important change program. Possibly the most difficult problem in trying to organize effectively is that of weeding out old skills—and their supporting systems, structures, etc.—to ensure that important new skills can take root and grow.

Superordinate Goals

The word "superordinate" literally means "of higher order." By superordinate goals, we mean guiding concepts—a set of values and aspirations, often unwritten, that goes beyond the conventional formal statement of corporate objectives.

Superordinate goals are the fundamental ideas around which a business is built. They are its main values. But they are more as well. They are the broad notions of future direction that the top management team wants to infuse throughout the organization. They are the way in which the team wants to express itself, to leave its own mark. Examples would include Theodore Vail's "universal service" objective, which has so dominated AT&T; the strong drive to "customer service" which guides IBM's marketing; GE's slogan, "Progress is our most important product," which encourages engineers to tinker and innovate throughout the organization; Hewlett-Packard's "innovative people at all levels in the organization"; Dana's obsession with productivity, as a total organization, not just a few at the top; and 3M's dominating culture of "new products."

In a sense, superordinate goals are like the basic postulates in a mathematical system. They are the starting points on which the system is logically built, but in themselves are not logically derived. The ultimate test of their value is not their logic but the usefulness of the system that ensues. Everyone seems to know the importance of compelling superordinate goals. The drive for their accomplishment pulls an organization together. They provide stability in what would otherwise be a shifting set of organization dynamics.

Unlike the other six S's, superordinate goals don't seem to be present in all, or even most, organizations. They are, however, evident in most of the superior performers.

To be readily communicated, superordinate goals need to be succinct. Typically, therefore, they are expressed at high levels of abstraction and may mean very little to outsiders who don't know the organization well. But for those inside, they are rich with significance. Within an organization, superordinate goals, if well articulated, make meaning for people. And making meanings is one of the main functions of leadership.

CONCLUSION

We have passed rapidly through the variables in our framework. What should the reader have gained from the exercise?

We started with the premise that solutions to today's thorny organizing problems that invoke only structure—or even strategy and structure—are seldom adequate. The inadequacy stems in part from the inability of the two-variable model to explain why organizations are so slow to adapt to change. The reasons often lie among our other variables: systems that embody outdated assumptions, a management style that is at odds with the stated strategy, the absence of a superordinate goal that binds the organization together in pursuit of a common purpose, the refusal to deal concretely with "people problems" and opportunities.

At its most trivial, when we merely use the framework as a checklist, we find that it leads into new terrain in our efforts to understand how organizations really operate or to design a truly comprehensive change program. At a minimum, it gives us a deeper bag in which to collect our experiences.

More importantly, it suggests the wisdom of taking seriously the variables in organizing that have been considered soft, informal, or beneath the purview of top management interest. We believe that style, systems, skills, superordinate goals can be observed directly, even measured—if only they are taken seriously. We think that these variables can be at least as important as strategy and structure in orchestrating major change; indeed, that they are almost critical for achieving necessary, or desirable, change. A shift in systems, a major retraining program for staff, or the generation of top-to-bottom enthusiasm around a new superordinate goal could take years. Changes in strategy and structure, on the surface, may happen more quickly. But the pace of real change is geared to all seven S's.

At its most powerful and complex, the framework forces us to concentrate on interactions and fit. The real energy required to redirect an institution comes when all the variables in the model are aligned. One of our associates looks at our diagram as a set of compasses. "When all seven needles are all pointed the same way," he comments, "you're looking at an *organized* company."

IMPLEMENTING AND ADMINISTERING STRATEGY: COMMITMENT, CULTURE, AND POLITICS

7

. . . . managerial ability is generally tied quite closely to the particular industry setting in which it develops and operates. A good manager's intuitions, like those of a good card player, come from his long experience with the special rules, technology, and markets of a particular industry.

Joel Dean and Winfield Smith

Nothing makes a prince so much esteemed as the undertaking of great enterprises and the setting of a noble example in his own person.

N. Machiavelli

In the previous chapters we examined two of the central general management tasks in implementing strategy, namely building a capable organization and focusing resources and energies on strategy accomplishment. In this chapter we explore the three remaining central tasks: galvanizing organizationwide commitment to strategic accomplishment, monitoring strategic progress, and exerting strategic leadership. The first two tasks embraced structure, staffing, and resource allocation issues; the last three involve the day-to-day aspects of strategy execution, including motivation and reward, measuring organization and individual performance, instituting strategy-related policies and procedures, implementing strategic controls, gathering information about strategic progress, and exercising whatever leadership is needed to keep strategy implementation on course. These are important because they establish an internal climate and culture for strategy accomplishment.

GALVANIZING ORGANIZATIONWIDE COMMITMENT TO THE STRATEGIC PLAN

The general manager's task of generating, maintaining, and otherwise ensuring organizationwide commitment to strategy implementation and execution has at least four main parts:

1. Motivating organizational units and individuals to accomplish the strategic plan.
2. Measuring and evaluating the strategic performance of subunits and the total organization.
3. Linking the reward structure to actual strategic performance.
4. Establishing policies and procedures to facilitate and reinforce strategy implementation.

Motivating the Organization to Accomplish Strategy

Obviously, it is important for organizational subunits and individuals to be committed to implementing and accomplishing the strategic plan. Solidifying organizationwide commitment to putting the strategic plan in place, as with anything else that needs doing, is typically achieved via motivation, incentives, and the rewarding of good performance. The range of options for getting people and organizational subunits to push hard for successful strategy implementation is almost unlimited, but it is virtually certain that the option chosen will need to make it in the overall best interests of everyone concerned to do as good a job of strategy implementation as circumstances permit. Typically, this means heavy dependence on the standard reward-punishment mechanisms—salary raises, bonuses, stock options, fringe benefits, promotions (or fear of demotions), assurance of not being "sidelined" and ignored, praise, recognition, criticism, tension, fear, more (or less) responsibility, increased (or decreased) job control or autonomy, the promise of attractive locational assignments, and the bonds of group acceptance. As the foregoing suggests, motivational incentives can be positive or negative in nature. They may also be intrinsic, as in the case of the increased self-respect and gratification which comes with achieving strategic objectives or making the strategy work as planned.

The prevailing view is that a good motivational system allows for blended fulfillment of both organizational and personal objectives. No doubt this is a useful guideline. But, in practice, it is a ticklish task to gear the size of an individual's rewards to a corresponding contribution to organization objectives; rewards may be excessive, target achievement levels set too low, or contributions unrecognized and mismeasured. More often, though, the opposite is true, as suggested by the way Harold Geneen, former president and chief executive officer of ITT, allegedly combined the use of money, tension, and fear:

> Geneen provides his managers with enough incentives to make them tolerate the system. Salaries all the way through ITT are higher than average—Geneen reckons 10 percent higher—so that few people can leave without taking a drop. As one employee put it: "We're all paid just a bit more than we think we're worth." At the very top, where the demands are greatest, the salaries and stock options are sufficient to compensate for the rigors. As some said, "He's got them by their limousines."
>
> Having bound his men to him with chains of gold, Geneen can induce the tension that drives the machine. "The key to the system," one of his men explained, "is the profit forecast. Once the forecast has been gone over, revised and agreed on, the managing director has a personal commitment to Geneen to carry it out. That's how he produces the tension on which the success depends." The tension goes through the company, inducing ambition, perhaps exhilaration, but always with some sense of fear: what happens if the target is missed?[1]

It goes without saying that if and when a general manager's use of rewards and punishments induces too much tension, anxiety, and job insecurity that the results can be counterproductive. Yet, it is doubtful whether it is ever useful to completely eliminate tension, fear, anxiety, pressure, and insecurity from the strategy implementation process; there is, for example, no evidence that "the quiet life" is highly correlated with superior strategy implementation and strategic success. On the contrary, high-performing organizations usually require an endowment of ambitious people who relish the opportunity to climb the ladder of success, who have a need for stimulation (or who want to avoid boredom), and who thus find some degree of job-related stress and pressure useful in order to satisfy their own drives for personal recognition, accomplishment, and self-satisfaction. There almost has to be some pressure and job insecurity surrounding the consequences of strategic failure else few people will attach much significance to the strategic plan.

The conventional view is that a general manager's push for strategy implementation should incorporate more positive than negative motivational elements, the thesis being that when cooperation is positively enlisted rather than negatively strong-armed people tend to respond with more enthusiasm and more effort. Nevertheless, how much of which incentives and motivational approaches to use depends on how hard the task of strategy implementation will be in light of all the obstacles to be

---

[1] Anthony Sampson, *The Sovereign State of ITT* (New York: Stein and Day, Publishers, 1973), p. 132.

overcome. Suffice it to say that a general manager will have to do more than just talk to everyone about how important strategy implementation is to the organization's future well-being. Talk, no matter how inspiring, seldom commands people's best efforts for long. Ensuring sustained, energetic commitment to strategy thus is certain to entail resourceful use of both positive and negative motivational incentives. And it is a task that a general manager must do consciously and deliberately. The more that a manager understands what motivates subordinates and the more that motivational incentives are relied upon to implement and execute strategy, the greater will be the organization's commitment to carrying out the strategic plan.

ILLUSTRATION CAPSULE 22
The Mysteries of Motivation

The eminently successful Paul W. Bryant, head football coach at The University of Alabama, tells of the time he unwittingly motivated a team just prior to game time:

When I was at Kentucky I got booed one night by a group of students who came to the train to see us off for a game with Cincinnati. I had fired some of our star players and they didn't like that. And we'd lost three of our first five games and they didn't like that either, which I can understand. I didn't like it myself. In fact, I hated it. For a young coach—which I was then—so keyed up I couldn't get to work in the morning without vomiting along the way, it was not exactly heaven on earth. The Cincinnati game took on added importance.

Cincinnati had fine teams then, coached by Sid Gillman, who has been a big name in the pros and is with the Houston Oilers now. What I'm about to say should not be taken as a lack of respect for Sid. You have to appreciate that my collar was tighter than it is now.

We got to the stadium at Cincinnati and I sensed something was wrong. When we went out to warm up for the game there was nobody in the stands. Just a few handfuls scattered around. I thought for a minute I was in the wrong place. When we finished our warm-up and the Cincinnati team still hadn't made an appearance, I said to Carney Laslie, one of my original assistant coaches, "What's that no-good conniving smart-aleck"—meaning the eminent Coach Gillman—"up to now? What the hell is that damn thief trying to pull?"

Carney just shook his head. He was as dumbfounded as I was.

I ordered the team back into the locker room—and then it *dawned* on me. I'd screwed up the schedule. We were an hour early.

Source: Paul W. Bryant and John Underwood, *Bear: The Hard Life and Good Times of Alabama's Coach Bryant* (Boston: Little, Brown and Company, 1974), pp. 3-4, 6-7.

ILLUSTRATION CAPSULE 22 *(concluded)*

I was too embarrassed to tell what I knew. I just walked around, up and down the aisles where the players sat waiting, my big old farmer's boots making the only noise in there. I couldn't think of anything to say, so I didn't say a word. For an hour I clomped up and down. Finally, when I'd used up enough time I delivered a one-sentence pep talk, the only thing I could think to say:

"Let's go."

They almost tore the door down getting out. Cincinnati was favored that day, but it was no contest. We won, 27-7.

Bryant tells of a second instance when coaching at Texas A&M where an approach he tried worked on one occasion but apparently failed when someone else tried it.

They'd been dead all week in the practice before the SMU game, and I wondered, what could we do? What was left to try? I'd run out of ways to motivate them. Elmer Smith, one of my assistants, said he remembered one time when he was playing for Ivan Grove at Hendrix College. Grove woke him up at midnight and read him something about how a mustard seed could move a mountain if you believed in it, something Norman Vincent Peale, or somebody, had taken from the Bible and written in a little pamphlet. It impressed me.

I didn't tell a soul. At 12 o'clock on Thursday night I called everyone on my staff and told them to meet me at the dormitory at 1 o'clock. When they got there, I said, OK go get the players real quick, and they went around shaking them, and the boys came stumbing in there, rubbing their eyes, thinking I'd finally lost my mind. And I read 'em that little thing about the mustard seed—just three sentences—turned around, and walked out.

Well, you never know if you are doing right or wrong, but we went out and played the best game we'd played all year. SMU should have beaten us by 40 points, but they were lucky to win, 6-3. In the last minute of play we had a receiver wide open inside their 20-yard line, but our passer didn't see him.

Several years after that, Darrell Royal called me from Texas. He was undefeated, going to play Rice and worried to death. He said he'd never been in that position before, undefeated and all, and his boys were lazy and fatheaded, and he wanted to know what to do about it.

I said, "Well, Darrell, there's no set way to motivate a team, and the way I do it may be opposite to your way but I can tell you a story." And I gave him that thing about the mustard seed. He said, by golly, he'd try it.

Well, I don't know whether he did or not, but I remember the first thing I wanted to do Sunday morning was get that paper and see how Texas made out. Rice won, 34-7.

Measuring and Evaluating Strategic Performance

Measuring and evaluating strategic performance are central to the job of every general manager. Measurement and evaluation are essential to knowing where the organization is in terms of its strategic plan. The most relevant strategy-related performance measures to use are the objectives contained in the strategic plan. A comprehensive strategic plan contains performance targets for the organization as a whole, for each line of business, for each functional area within a business, and for each operating-level unit. Whether these targets are attained on schedule serves as a direct measure of strategic performance. If the strategic plan does not contain a full set of explicit objectives at each level of the organizational hierarchy, then specific performance measures need to be agreed upon early in the strategy implementation phase.

The importance of spelling out the objectives to be attained for the organization as a whole, for each major subunit, and ultimately, through the efforts of lower level managers, for each job has been repeatedly emphasized. The degree to which an organization's culture and climate is performance-and-results-oriented hinges directly on the general manager's defining and enforcing the performance standards expected at each organization level. Indeed, when a general manager *fails* to (1) insist upon the establishment of strategic objectives and performance targets at each organizational level, (2) set timetables for strategy accomplishment, (3) assign responsibility for producing the target results, and (4) evaluate the performance of subunits and individuals in terms of the agreed-upon objectives and deadlines, then the stage is set for a shortfall in strategy execution and strategy accomplishment. The need to measure performance in terms of the target results specified in the strategic plan is essential—it is the step that elevates the strategic plan to a position of real priority, rather than something which is put together and then forgotten or ignored when "the real decisions" are made and when the time comes to decide who has "done a good job" and who has not.

Usually a number of performance measures are used at each level; rarely will a single measure suffice. At the corporate and line of business levels, the typical performance measures include profitability (measured in terms of total profit, return on equity investment, return on total assets, return on sales, gross profit margins, operating profit, and so on), market share, growth rates in sales and profits, competitive position and competitive strength, short-and long-run prospects, and such other measures as fit the situation. At the functional and operating levels, the measures are of course narrower and more specific. In the manufacturing area the strategy-relevant performance measures may focus on unit manufacturing costs, productivity increases, meeting production and shipping schedules, quality control, the number and extent of work stoppages due to labor disagreements and equipment breakdowns, and so on. In the marketing area, the measures may include unit selling costs, the increases in dollar sales and unit volume, the degree of sales penetration of each target customer group, increases in market share, the success of newly-introduced products, customer complaints, advertising effectiveness, and the number of new customers acquired. While most performance measures are quantitative in nature, there are always several which have elements of subjectivity—improvements in labor-management relations, whether employee morale is up or down, whether customers are more or less satisfied with the quality of the firm's products, what impact advertising is having, how much could have been saved if raw material purchases had been timed differently, how efficient the clerical staff is, and so on.

The Importance of a Results-Orientation and a Spirit of High Performance. As stated in the opening paragraphs of the book, successful enterprises are nearly always characterized by a strong results-oriented culture and by an emphasis on high standards of performance. The ability to instill high levels of commitment to strategic success and to create an atmosphere where there is constructive pressure to perform is one of the most valuable general management traits. When an organization performs consistently at or near peak capability, the outcome is not only improved strategic success but also an organizational climate where the emphasis is on excellence and achievement—a spirit of high performance pervades.

Such a spirit of performance, sometimes referred to as "morale," should not be confused with whether employees are "happy" or "satisfied" or whether they "get along well together." An organization whose approach to "human relations" and "dealing with people" is not grounded in high standards of performance actually has poor human relations and a management that is liable to produce a mean spirit.[2] Certainly, there is no greater indictment of an organization than that of allowing or fostering an atmosphere in which the outstanding performance of a few people becomes a threat to the whole group and a source of controversy, backstabbing, and attempts to enforce safe mediocrity.

For an organization to be instilled with and sustain a spirit of performance, it must maintain a focus on achievement and on excellence. It must strive at developing a consistent ability to produce results over prolonged periods of time. It must succeed in utilizing the full range of rewards and punishment (pay, promotion, assignments, tension, pressure, job security, and so on) to establish and enforce standards of excellence. As the example in Illustration Capsule 23 shows so well, a strong results orientation and a spirit of high performance greatly contribute to execution of the strategic plan.

---

[2] Peter F. Drucker, *Management: Tasks, Responsibilities, Practices,* (New York: Harper and Row, Publishers, 1974), p. 455.

ILLUSTRATION CAPSULE 23
Tandem Computers: An Example of Creating a Spirit of High Performance

There is no set way to approach the task of motivating employees, instilling a results-oriented work environment, and solidifying employees' commitment to strategy accomplishment. Different companies do it differently, and some have experienced better results than others. One of the apparent successes is Tandem Computers, an 8-year old company with $300 million in sales in 1981 and labeled as one of the bright stars on *Fortune's Second 500* list.

Tandem Computers is a leading producer of modular, expandable, multiple processor computing systems designed so that failure of no one module can substantially affect system operations—Tandem calls it the "nonstop computing system" that is fail-safe. Tandem's nonstop computer system can support thousands of terminals in on-line, non-stop conditions, thus preserving data integrity, reliability, and system flexibility. According to Tandem, "no one else has this capability." Key applications are in businesses in which computer "down time" can have serious consequences: electric power monitoring, emergency vehicle dispatching, back office transaction processing for financial institutions, on-line order entry, credit verification, and inventory control.

Tandem's main operations are in California's famous Silicon Valley where many other electronics firms are located. The Silicon Valley is noted for the fierceness with which area companies compete for talent; demand for talented employees is so high that assembly people, operators, and engineers can literally walk across the street and get a job with another company the next day. The Valley's high-technology companies are constantly "pirating" employees from each other's staffs. Moreover, many of the most creative people are unique personality types, sometimes labeled as "semi-freakies" and "pseudo-hippies," and are products of the California culture of the 1960s and early 1970s, with a preference for openness, spontaneity, nonjudgmental acceptance, brotherhood, freedom, and expressiveness.

The Tandem Gospel

As conceived largely by cofounder-president James G. Treybig, pronounced Try-big, Tandem Computers' approach to dealing with its high-technology employees in the Silicon Valley culture represents "the convergence of capitalism and humanism," and incorporates a blend of ideology and incentives. The ideology centers around Treybig's five cardinal principles for running a company:

1. All people are good.

2. People, workers, management and company are all the same thing.

3. Every single person in a company must understand the essence of the business.

Source: Based on information reported in Myron Magnet, "Managing by Mystique at Tandem Computers," *Fortune* (June 28, 1982), pp. 84-91.

ILLUSTRATION CAPSULE 23 *(continued)*

4. Every employee must benefit from the company's success.

5. You must create an environment where all of the above can happen.

These principles are pushed in a continual stream of orientation lectures, breakfast meetings, newsletters, a company magazine, and periodic communications with employees—the content of which is predicated on and inspired by a company manual entitled *Understanding Our Philosophy*. All employees are given a copy of the latter and are put through a two-day indoctrination course.

As an example of how conventional platitudes are instilled with new meaning, Treybig took the oft-said phrase "all employees should be treated with respect" and translated it at Tandem into "You never have the right at Tandem to screw a person or to mistreat them. It's not allowed . . . No manager mistreats a human without a fear of their job." This statement is given teeth by giving any aggrieved employee ready access to anyone in the company—"guilty" managers have been fired.

In indoctrinating employees to the Tandem philosophy, pains are taken to explain the essence of the company's business, to give them a companywide perspective, and to go through the company's five-year plan. In *Understanding Our Philosophy* is a roadmap-size chart, which took Treybig two weeks to draw up, showing how a performance breakdown in one area spills over into lower performance in other parts of the company. While the main purpose of the big picture approach is to explain what various groups in the company are doing and how it all fits together and, thus, to point people in the direction of strategy accomplishment, it also helps boost employee enthusiasm and loyalty. As one of the company founders put it, "People really get a great kick out of being part of the team and trusted with the corporate jewels."

Another key part of Tandem's philosophy is that companies can be overmanaged. According to Treybig, "most people need less management than you think." At Tandem, top management control is not accomplished with numerous reviews, meetings, and reports but rather with giving employees a full understanding and appreciation of the company's business concepts and managerial philosophy. Supervision is loose and flexible. Employees are encouraged to exercise freedom and creativity. They speak in glowing terms about how the company has helped them "grow;" the importance of personal growth is emphasized in Tandem's corporate creed.

Company literature speaks of efforts to foster not just the welfare of employees but also their spouses and "spouse equivalents." Most employees respond positively to all this, describing Tandem's management as "people-oriented."

Tandem's Incentive Package

Undergirding the ideology and philosophy is a package of reinforcing incentives and practices. *Every* employee participates in the company's stock

ILLUSTRATION CAPSULE 23 *(continued)*

option plans. As of mid-1982, an employee who had been with the company since its stock began to be traded publicly in 1977 had received stock options worth almost $100,000. At the company's 1981 Halloween costume party (which was so well attended that the crowd filled most of a large warehouse), the company announced the granting of a 100-share stock option to each of 3,000-plus employees. Even with Tandem's rapid growth three out of five new managers have risen from within the company's ranks.

An abundance of attention is paid to employees' working conditions and amenities. Working hours are kept flexible and no one punches a time clock, the philosophy being, "We don't want to pay people for attendance but for output." The company has built a swimming pool, jogging trails, spaces for yoga classes and dance-exercise, and a basketball court. There are periodic company-supplied weekend barbecues for employees working overtime. Employees get six-week sabbatical leaves every four years. Recently, the company's female employees sponsored an "Incredible Hulk" contest for male employees (the red satin sash prize was won by the vice-president for software development). On Friday afternoons at 4:30, the company conducts its weekly beer bust (attended by about 60% of the employees).

Treybig is seen regularly at the beer busts, once coming in a cowboy hat and boots. Associates note that Treybig deliberately does and says things for their shock value. The result, says one vice-president, is that "a lot of people when they meet Jim for the first time think he's a bullshitter, just shuckin' and jivin'." Yet, beneath the rhetoric and philosophy are some hardnosed policies.

Enhanced Loyalty and Commitment

Managers are pushed to hire new employees who are smarter and more qualified than they are. Normally, only experienced and proven applicants are seriously considered (to help Tandem gain access to new ideas and the best talent available). Interviews are very thorough, sometimes running 20 hours. Managers, not the personnel department, do the hiring, and prospective co-workers play a big role in the selection process. One employee observed, "A manager will never hire somebody his people don't think is good. Basically, he says will you work with this person, and you say yes or no." Employees are paid a $500 bonus for referring prospective candidates who subsequently are employed over 90 days. The hiring system exposes new employees to the Tandem culture before their first day on the job and endeavors to convey the feeling that they have been chosen by an exacting process. Tandem believes that such an initiation builds dedication because, by being ordeals, people tend to place a higher value on what has cost them a lot.

The results have been impressive. Tandem's productivity figures are among the highest in the industry. The work culture is one of commitment, hard work, loyalty, self-esteem, creativity, learning, personal growth, light

ILLUSTRATION CAPSULE 23 *(concluded)*

supervision, and self-discipline. Many employees are convinced that their jobs are filling their innermost goals of self-realization. Several employee comments about the company's approach and its effects are telling:

I don't think someone who thought Tandem was just a job would work out, because Tandem expects commitment.

I feel like I'm accomplishing something with myself.

I speak to my manager about once a month—that's how often my manager manages me.

It's progressive. It's ahead of the times. I don't know what's right or wrong. I know that it's very unique. It sure feels right to me; it fits in with the way I like to see people treated.

It is also true, however, that part of what makes this approach work at Tandem Computers is its close fit with the situation. Tandem has one basic product and one clearly defined market. Most of its parts and components are supplied by subcontractors. Everything is cleaned by a contract janitorial service. What manufacturing Tandem does itself is skilled assembly and massive testing—activities which are conducted in quiet, airy rooms more like labs than factories. Most employees are well-trained, highly-skilled, self-disciplined, and intelligent enough to work well without close supervision. Much of Tandem's work activity is creative and highly technical, and workers need freedom and solitude to perform well. Good performance is handsomely rewarded (although some of the stock options are carefully calibrated to make leaving the company before 4 years very expensive). Rapid growth and financial success have funded the payment of generous benefits, created numerous promotion opportunities, and otherwise helped to make Tandem's unique blend of ideology and incentive work well up to this point. In addition, Tandem's management is strong and the company dominates its market niche via careful product engineering, attention to manufacturing, and skill in marketing—aspects which are also critical in the computer business.

Irrespective of whether the Tandem gospel could be successful in other companies (and it may not continue to work as well at Tandem if growth slows and the company's fortunes slacken), the Tandem experience does spotlight the value of deliberately creating a corporate culture that is in close alignment with strategy. When this occurs, organizationwide commitments to strategy and to results are substantially enhanced.

An important aspect of creating a results-oriented organizational culture is removing people who consistently render poor or mediocre performance. Aside from the organizational benefits, low or mediocre per-

formers should be reassigned for their own good—people who find themselves in a job they cannot handle are usually frustrated, anxiety-ridden,
harassed, and unhappy.[3] Moreover, subordinates have a right to be managed with competence, dedication, and achievement; unless their boss
performs well, they themselves cannot perform well.[4] In general, then, a
general manager is obliged to remove managers who fail to perform; they
should be reassigned, or in extreme cases dismissed, so as not to undercut
either the implementation of strategy or the careers of subordinates. One
well-known proponent of this approach was General George C. Marshall,
Chief of Staff of the U.S. Army in World War II.[5] Marshall reportedly said,
"I have a duty to the soldiers, their parents, and the country, to remove
immediately any commander who does not satisfy the highest performance standards." He repeatedly upheld this duty, actually removing a
number of commanders from assignments. But when he did, he followed it
up with the recognition that, "It was my mistake to have put this or that man
in a command that was not the right command for him. It is therefore *my*
job to think through where he belongs."

The toughest cases, of course, concern the need to reassign people who
have given long and loyal service to the organization but who are past their
prime and unable to deal effectively with demanding situations. The
decision in such cases should be objectively based upon what is best for the
company—which usually means removing the person from his or her job.
Yet, it can be done in a compassionate and human fashion. When Henry
Ford II was trying to revive Ford Motor Company after WWII, he felt that
none of the nine top management people in one key division were competent enough to handle new jobs created by reorganization.[6] Not one was
appointed to the newly-created positions. But while their incompetence
was undisputed and it would have been easy to fire them, the fact remained
that they had served loyally through trying periods. Ford took the position
that while no one should be allowed to hold a job he could not perform in
superior fashion, neither should anyone be penalized for the mistakes of the
previous regime. So, the nine men were assigned as experienced technicians and experts to jobs they could be expected to do well. As things
turned out, seven of the men did well in their new assignments—one so well
that he was later promoted into a more important job than he originally
held. The other two failed; the older one was given early retirement and the
younger one was dismissed. A management that is concerned with building
excellent organizational spirit takes the cases of loyal nonperformers seriously because, while they are (or should be) few in number, they have a
major impact on morale and how their cases are handled tells others in the

---

[3]Ibid., p. 457.
[4]Ibid.
[5]As cited by Peter Drucker, *Management*, p. 458.
[6]This example is drawn from Peter F. Drucker, *Management*, p. 459.

organization much about management's character and the importance placed on high performance standards.

A second aspect of creating a results-oriented climate concerns the extent to which an organization is pointed towards attaining strategic objectives as opposed to carrying out daily routines and solving existing problems.[7] An organization is prone to have higher morale and an acceptance of challenge when *top* priority is given to converting the strategic plan into results. Concentrating first on solving problems and what has to be done today tends to detract from an organization's momentum and to put it on "hold" until the problems at hand are solved and all the necessary details are under control. In contrast, an attitude of "damn the torpedoes, full steam ahead" works to keep the attention of the organization focused on generating the greatest impact on results and performance—an orientation which promotes strategy implementation and strategic success.

Creating a results-oriented atmosphere requires conscious avoidance of some traits and approaches to dealing with subordinates. As Drucker has pointed out so well, there are a number of personal characteristics in a manager which undermine a spirit of high performance:[8]

- a lack of integrity,
- a lack of character,
- cynicism,
- emphasizing the negative aspect of what subordinates cannot do (their weaknesses) rather than the positive aspects of what they can do (their strengths),
- being more interested in "who is right?" than "what is right?",
- being afraid of strong (high-performing) subordinates,
- not setting high standards for one's own work, and
- valuing intelligence more highly than integrity.

The most important trait to be sure to display is a fair-minded and sincere concern for generating the agreed-upon results and achieving the strategic objectives on schedule. This does not mean taking an "at all costs" approach but it does mean taking a "top priority" approach to strategy accomplishment. It also means exhibiting the traits of honesty and integrity in all of one's dealings—without these the respect of subordinates will not be forthcoming.

Linking the Reward Structure to Actual Strategic Performance

If strategy accomplishment is to be a really top priority activity, then the whole reward structure must be linked *explicitly* and *tightly* to actual

---

[7]Ibid., pp. 460-61.
[8]Ibid., p. 462.

strategic performance. Decisions on salary increases, on promotions, and on who gets which key assignments are a general manager's *foremost* attention-getting, commitment-generating devices. How a general manager parcels out the rewards signals who is getting ahead and who is not, who is climbing up the ladder fastest, and who is perceived as doing a good job. They signal what sort of behavior and performance management wants, values, and rewards. Such decisions seldom escape the closest scrutiny of every member of the organization. If anything, an organization will overreact to these kinds of management decisions. What management may view as an innocuous move to solve an interpersonal conflict or to bypass an organizational obstacle may be interpreted as a sign that management wants one kind of behavior while preaching another. Hence, general managers must be ever alert to their decisions on placement, pay, and promotion. They should be based on a factual record of performance as measured against explicit objectives and targets—never on "potential" or friendship or expediency or casual opinions. They should reflect careful thinking, clear policy and procedures, and high standards of fairness and equity.

Once strategic objectives and deadlines are established and agreed-upon as doable, then they must become the *real* basis for evaluating individual efforts and the performance of organizational units. To prevent undermining and undoing the whole "managing with objectives" approach to strategy implementation, a general manager must insist that contributions to the strategic plan be documented and compared against the target objectives. The reasons for any deviations have to be explored fully to determine whether the causes are attributable to managerial miscalculation and misjudgment or to circumstances beyond management control. In short, managers have to be held accountable for carrying out their assigned part of the strategic plan and their rewards have to be based on the caliber of their strategic accomplishments (allowing for both the favorable and unfavorable impacts of uncontrollable, unforseeable, and unknowable circumstances).

One precaution is worth urging. There is sometimes a tendency to acknowledge all activities and efforts as virtuous, worthy, and important to continue. However, working hard is not the same as working smart. Long hours and great efforts can be misplaced and misdirected. Hence, when results are not commensurate with the resources and energies being expended, the time is right to scrutinize whether to overhaul the activity or, if circumstances warrant, to phase it out. An opportunity exists to shift resources and energies into either more productive approaches or into altogether different activities. The time for evaluating actual performance can thus be a time for appraising whether the organization is (1) doing things right and (2) doing the right things.

The Role of Strategy-Related Policies and Procedures

As chief administrator of the strategic plan, it is incumbent upon a general manager to establish whatever internal policies and procedures are needed to guide, support, and communicate how the strategy is to be implemented. Changes in strategy generally dictate at least some changes in how internal activities are conducted and administered. The process of changing from the old ways to the new ways has to be initiated and managed. Asking people to alter actions and practices always "upsets" the internal order of things somewhat. It is normal for pockets of resistance to emerge and, certainly, questions will be raised about the *how* as well as the whys of change. The role of new and revised policies and procedures is to promote these internal shifts and to bring people's actions, behavior, and administrative practices into closer alignment with the new strategy. The idea is to develop "standard operating procedures" that will (1) facilitate strategy implementation and (2) counteract any tendencies for parts of the organization to resist or reject the chosen strategy. Policies and procedures, when designed around the needs of strategy implementation, help enforce strategy implementation and make the general manager's job easier in several noteworthy respects:[9]

1. Policy promotes *uniform handling of similar activities*—a uniformity which facilitates better coordination of work tasks and helps reduce friction arising from favoritism, discrimination, and disparate handling of common functions.

2. Policy places *limits on independent action* and sets boundaries on the kinds and directions of action that can be taken. By making a statement about how things are *now* to be done, policy communicates what is expected and guides the conduct of activities in particular directions.

3. Policy helps *align actions and behavior with strategy* throughout an organization, thereby minimizing zigzag decisions and conflicting practices and establishing some degree of support, regularity, stability, and dependability in how the organization is attempting to make the strategy work.

4. Policy acts as an *automatic decision maker* by formalizing organizationwide answers to previously made management decisions about how particular questions and problems should be resolved; policy thus becomes a guide for handling future such problems or issues as they

---

[9]This listing is adapted from Richard H. Buskirk, *Business and Administrative Policy* (New York: John Wiley & Sons, 1971), pp. 145-150.

recur without them being passed up repeatedly through higher management echelons again and again.[10]

5. Policy offers a *predetermined answer to routine problems* and gives managers more time to cope with nonroutine matters; in this way decisions pertaining to both ordinary and extraordinary problems are greatly expedited—the former by referring to established policy and the latter by drawing upon a portion of the manager's time.

6. Existing policies afford managers *a mechanism for insulating* themselves from hasty and ill-considered requests for operating changes. The prevailing policy can always be used as a reason (or excuse) for not yielding to emotion-based, expedient, or temporarily valid arguments to alter procedures and practices.

From a strategy perspective, policy is (or should be!) subordinate to and supportive of accomplishing the strategic plan since it signals what should and should not be done to further strategy implementation and the attainment of strategic objectives. In this sense policies can serve as internal guidelines for carrying out strategy. They can act to help institutionalize and operationalize the chosen strategy and to orient day-to-day activities in the direction of efficient strategy execution. Examples of policies and procedures which can be used to facilitate strategy implementation include:

1. A retail grocery chain giving store managers the authority to buy fresh produce locally when they can get a better buy, rather than ordering from the regional warehouse.

2. An oil company's deciding to lease the properties and buildings for its service station operations so as to stretch the capital available for new stations over a wider geographic area.

3. A graduate school of business, as part of its strategy to get into the "top 20," deciding not to admit to its MBA program any applicant who does not have at least two years of business experience as well as a B-plus average on all undergraduate coursework.

4. A hospital's requiring all patients to make a $100 cash deposit upon being admitted, as part of its plan for maintaining financial solvency.

---

[10]The automatic decision-making function of policy should not be interpreted as advocating all matters be settled by searching through an omnibus policy manual for the proper policy to apply to a situation, and if a suitable one is not found forcing the application of something close. Policies are not designed to be rigidly applied without the exercise of judgment. Exceptions and situations with unique twists always arise, and all who apply policies are expected to recognize when a policy should be bent to fit the circumstances.

See also the views of H. Edward Wrapp, "Good Managers Don't Make Policy Decisions," *Harvard Business Review*, vol. 45, no. 5 (September-October 1967), p. 95.

Some policies, of course, are purely administrative rather than strategic and amount to little more than "work rules," as in the case of statements specifying the length of coffee breaks and the methods for obtaining reimbursement for travel expenses. Others may border on being operating level strategy ("policies" to spend a fixed percentage of revenues on advertising). Still others may provide vital support to an organization's strategic plan—for example, General Motor's policy of trying to standardize as many parts as possible in producing its many different models of Chevrolets, Pontiacs, Buicks, Oldsmobiles and Cadillacs was aimed at achieving greater mass production economies and minimizing the working capital tied up in parts inventories.

The point here, though, is that there is a definite role for policies and procedures in the strategy implementation process. Wisely constructed policies and procedures can help enforce strategy implementation by channeling actions, behavior, decisions, and practices in directions which promote strategy accomplishment. Checking out the alignment between existing policies and strategy is thus a central part of the strategy implementation process. Failure to examine existing policies and procedures from a strategy perspective runs the risk that some existing policies will act as burdensome obstacles or hurdles to overcome and that those who have a vested interest in these policies may be able to thwart or even defeat the strategic plan (either because they disagree with the strategy or because their thinking is colored by an administrative and bureaucratic mindset rather than a strategic results and performance mindset). Consciously instituting new and revised policies and procedures that guide behavior and build organization commitment to the strategic plan is, consequently, an important tool of strategy implementation.

MONITORING STRATEGIC PROGRESS

In presiding over the strategy implementation process, a general manager has got to stay on top of what strategic progress is being made. Is the strategy being put in place on schedule? Are preliminary results favorable? Are newly established policies and practices being followed and are they effective? What problems are being encountered? What solutions are being developed to overcome these problems? There are two aspects to the central task of monitoring the strategy implementation process:

1. How to get the right strategy-critical information on a timely basis.
2. What "controls" are needed to keep the organization on its strategic course.

These two go hand-in-hand. Having timely information is essential to truly *managing* what is going on.

Information about the progress of strategy implementation comes from many sources: oral conversations with subordinates, periodic written reports, statistical reporting of operating results, feedback from customers, the reactions of rival firms, the flow of gossip and rumors through the grapevine, what is being said "out in the field"—in general, the flow of formal and informal information through all the different channels of communication. However, not all of this information is trustworthy. The content of formal written reports to the general manager may represent "the truth but not the whole truth." "Bad news" may be covered up or not reported at all. Some subordinates are reluctant to be the bearers of bad news in hopes that a delay will give them room to turn things around. As information flows up an organization, there is a tendency for it to get "censored" and "sterilized" to the point that it may fail to reveal strategy-critical information. Hence, general managers have to guard against major surprises by (1) making sure that they have accurate information and a "feel" for the existing situation and (2) instituting a system of management controls and reporting.

A conscious effort to access strategy-critical information and to institute strategic-specific controls is necessary because the regular organization network, by itself, is seldom "tight" enough to allow a general manager to stay fully abreast of how serious the obstacles are to achieving the strategic plan and the priorities being given to agreed-upon objectives. Organizational subunits have their own substrategies which can be at least slightly deflected from the overall organizational strategy. Moreover, individuals have their own career goals and needs, as well as their own perceptions of strategy and their own reasons for disagreeing with appropriateness of parts (or all!) of the strategic plan. Internal politics and rivalry among subunits and professional groups introduce still other possibilities for misdirection. Such happenings and considerations are all quite normal—even in high-performing organizations manned by people of competence and goodwill who agree with and support the chosen strategy. As a consequence, the work of individuals and subunits has to be monitored beyond just the "controls" of budgets, the reward structure, and established policies and procedures.

In trying to specify just what information is really needed to monitor strategic progress and in setting up strategy-specific controls, a general manager may wish to bear in mind the following guidelines:[11]

1. Information and reporting systems should be economical and involve only the *minimum* amount of information needed to give a reliable picture of what is going on. In general, the less effort and fewer check

---

[11]Peter F. Drucker, *Management*, pp. 498-504; Harold Koontz, "Management Control: A Suggested Formulation of Principles," *California Management Review*, vol. 2, no. 2 (Winter 1959), pp. 50-55; and William H. Sihler, "Toward Better Management Control Systems," *California Management Review*, vol. 14, no. 2 (Winter 1971), pp. 33-39.

points which have to be created to chart strategic progress, the better and more effective the control design; too many checks and balances are unwieldy and costly.

2. The information gathered should emphasize strategically meaningful variables (sales volume, product mix, market standing, productivity rates) or symptoms of potentially significant developments (lower profit margins, higher rates of turnover and absenteeism). Temptations to supplement strategy-critical data with other "interesting" information which is marginally related to strategic performance and results should be avoided.

3. Statistical information should report the variables being measured in ways which reveal the real structure of the situation and which are grounds for action. For example, reporting the *number* of grievances per thousand employees does not indicate the *importance* of the grievances in terms of the impacts on morale and productivity.

4. Reports and statistical data-gathering should be geared to provide information on a timely basis—not too late to take corrective action nor so often as to overburden.

5. The type and flow of information and statistics should be kept simple. Voluminous data and complicated reports are likely to misdirect and obscure because of the attention that has to be paid to mechanics, procedures, and interpretive guidelines instead of to the really critical variables. Moreover, the information reported should be in a form that is tailored to the recipient's needs.

6. Information and reporting systems should be instituted for the purpose of taking corrective action rather than just providing interesting information. It is debatable whether reports or studies should receive wide distribution ("for your information"), but they should without fail reach the persons who can take action by virtue of their position in the decision structure.

7. Information and reports should, for the most part, aim at flagging the "exceptions"; this allows management to zero in on the significant departures from norm.

Statistical information gives the general manager a feel for the numbers; reports and meetings provide a feel for new developments and the problems that exist; and personal contacts and conversations add a feel for the people dimension. All are good barometers of the overall tempo of performance and which things are on and off track. Identifying deviations from plan and problem areas to be addressed are prerequisites for initiating actions to either improve implementation or finetune strategy.

An example of the power and control that comes from having the right information at the right time is described in Illustration Capsule 24.

ILLUSTRATION CAPSULE 24
United Airline's System of Management Controls

As early as the mid-1950s, United Airlines had a computer-assisted system of reporting and controls which resulted not only in the chief executive officer having a profit and loss statement every 24 hours but also provided operating heads with up-to-the-hour information on how to respond to weather and passenger load patterns. According to an article in *Nation's Business* by Philip Gustafson:

The statement has its birth every day in the statistical production room at United's Denver operating base. Passenger and cargo volumes, collected from each flight, are combined at the end of the day. The results are wired to United's Chicago offices ready for processing at 8:30 A.M. Economic research employees apply revenue rates predetermined by experience and expense rates based on current operating budget requirements to the previous day's volume appearing on the wire. Within an hour, an operating profit or loss is estimated and passed on to top management.

The daily report shows the day's operating profit or loss along with a month and year to date accumulation. Also, daily revenue passenger-miles and the passenger load factor are given. Data are broken down in such a way as to give the passenger department information on which to decide whether to put more planes on the Chicago to San Francisco run or advertise to get additional passengers.

An intrinsic part of United's reporting system is what company executives like to call "the room with the 14,000-mile view." This is an information and planning center at Denver which is the business world's equivalent of the military briefing room. Facts funneled daily into this center present a clear picture of operations throughout United's 80-city system.

In keeping with the idea of expansive vision, the room has glass walls on one side. Modern white plastic chairs are grouped before a map of the United States, 8 feet high and 20 feet wide, on which United's routes are outlined. Colored lights (red for weather, green for maintenance, and white for passengers) at major terminals show current operating conditions. If the red light glows steadily, for example, it means adverse weather; if it is flashing, the weather is marginal. Electric clocks above the map show the time in each zone through which United operates.

The room is designed to provide management with operational facts in the most convenient form. Data, such as mileage flown, delays at terminals by type of plane and total number of departures, are posted on lucite panels, flanking the map. Dozens of supplementary charts deal with payload volumes and load factors, weather, actual performance as compared with schedule and related information.

Source: Philip Gustafson, "Business Reports: How to Get Facts You Need," *Nation's Business*, vol. 44, no. 8 (August 1956), pp. 78-82.

ILLUSTRATION CAPSULE 24 *(concluded)*

Daily at 8:30 A.M., MST, United's operations executives meet in the room for a 14,000-mile view. Four briefing specialists review operations of the past 24 hours and outline what the next 24 are expected to bring. The opening summary is presented by a meteorologist who analyzes the decisive factors in yesterday's weather conditions from the Atlantic seaboard to the Hawaiian islands. He then gives his forecast for the next 24 hours, accenting developments which may affect operations.

A mechanical specialist follows with information on the status of the company's fleet. He reports the number and types of aircraft withdrawn from service for overhaul and comments on the progress of various engineering projects at the San Francisco base.

A traffic specialist then gives a resume of the previous day's performance in terms of any customer service problems which arose. Approximately 750 plane departures are scheduled daily. Those which deviate from schedule are spotlighted for management study to prevent possible recurrence.

The remaining gaps in the 14,000-mile view are filled in by a flight operations specialist who discusses the availability of equipment, and weather outlook on the line. The session then adjourns. Immediately afterwards, some department chiefs may call their staffs together to act on particular facets of the day's operating plan.

EXERTING STRATEGIC LEADERSHIP

The litany of good strategic management is simple enough: formulate a sound strategic plan, implement it, execute it to the fullest, *win!* It's clearly something that's "easier said than done." Having the leadership skills to take charge, be a "spark plug," ramrod things through, be one of the "movers and shakers" in the organization, and get things done by coaching others to do it are not easy skills to acquire. Moreover, a general manager has many different leadership roles to play: chief entrepreneur, chief administrator, crisis-solver, taskmaster, figurehead, spokesman, resource allocator, negotiator, motivator, inspirationist, policymaker, and so on. No one leadership style or technique tends to suffice for all the different situations general managers face. Sometimes it is useful to be authoritarian and hardnosed; at other times being a perceptive listener and a compromising decision-maker works best; and on still other occasions a strongly participative, collegial approach is called for.

In general, the problem of managerial leadership is one of diagnosing the situation at hand and choosing from any of several ways to handle it. The hoped-for effect, of course, is to raise organizational performance to higher levels while, at the same time, allowing people to grow and develop to their fullest. Three strategy-related leadership issues stand out:

1. How to create an overall climate and culture in which the organization is "energized" to accomplish strategy and perform at a high level.

2. How to deal with the politics of strategy formulation and implementation and "play the power game."

3. When and how to push corrective actions to improve strategy execution and overall strategic performance.

Creating a Climate for Strategy Accomplishment

Every organization is a unique culture. It has its own special history of how the organization has been managed, its own set ways of approaching problems and conducting activities, its own mix of managerial personalities and styles, its own established patterns of "how we do things around here," its own experiences of how changes have been instituted—in other words, its own climate, atmosphere, and organization personality. This says something important about the leadership task of orchestrating strategy implementation: *anything so fundamental as implementing and executing the chosen strategic plan involves moving the whole organizational culture into alignment with strategy.* The optimal condition is a culture and a spirit of performance so in tune with strategy that execution of the game plan can be truly powerful. As one observer noted:

> It has not been just strategy that led to big Japanese wins in the American auto market. It is a culture that enspirits workers to excel at fits and finishes, to produce moldings that match, and doors that don't sag. It is a culture in which Toyota can use that most sophisticated of management tools, the suggestion box, and in two years increase the number of worker suggestions from under 10,000 to over 1 million with resultant savings of $250 million.[12]

Experience at the consulting firm of McKinsey & Co. suggests that an organization's culture is the product of seven broad variables: (1) strategy, (2) structure, (3) the systems and the "mindsets" used to tackle key activities, (4) the styles and behavior of management, (5) the mix and make-up of staffing (engineers vs. skilled technicians vs. blue-collar labor vs. office and clerical employees vs. age vs. male and female vs. length of service, and so on), (6) the degree to which people in the organization have (or don't have) common values (not only with respect to the organization and its future but also as concerns personal goals and personal values) such that there are bonds of compatibility and a *shared* spirit of who we are and where we are headed, and (7) the organization's chief skills, capabilities, and distinctive competence.[13] The idea is that when there is a "goodness of fit" among

---

[12]Robert H. Waterman, Jr., "The Seven Elements of Strategic Fit," *Journal of Business Strategy*, vol. 2, no. 3 (Winter 1982), p. 70.

[13]Ibid., pp. 69-71. McKinsey has diagrammed these into what it calls the 7-S Framework (the seven S's are strategy, structure, systems, style, staff, shared values, and skills—so labeled to promote recall).

these seven determinants of an organization's culture, conditions are ripe to translate sound strategy into sustained success. As chief entrepreneur, it is the general manager's responsibility to chose a strategy that can be executed given the corporate culture. As chief administrator of the strategic plan, it is the general manager's leadership task once strategy is chosen to bring the corporate culture into alignment with strategy and keep it there.

The variables of corporate culture are a useful perspective from which to check out the climate for strategic success. Given the chosen strategic plan, are the other variables of corporate culture aligned to support the strategy and make execution doable? Which ones will have to be changed to create a better fit? Can these changes be made with a reasonable prospect of success? If the answer is no, then reformulation of the strategic plan is indicated. If the answer is yes, then management has to (1) address how to make the needed changes and (2) consider how long it will take for the changes, once initiated, to bear fruit (an overnight transformation is not possible!).

Very likely, managerial actions taken to modify corporate culture will need to be both *symbolic* and *substantive*. The general manager's leadership role is essential here. In addition to being out front, personally keynoting the push for new attitudes and communicating widely and often the reasons for new approaches, the general manager has to convince the organization that more than cosmetics is involved. Talk has to be backed up by substance and real movement. The actions taken have to be credible, highly visible, and serve as unmistakable signals to the whole organization of the seriousness of management's commitment to a new climate and culture. Some quick successes in re-orienting the way some things are done helps highlight the value of the new order, thus making enthusiasm for the changes contagious. However, figuring out how to get some instant results is usually not as important as having the will and patience to mold the parts of the organization into a solid, competent team which is *psychologically committed* to superior strategy execution.

Creating an organizational culture which is fully harmonized with the strategic plan offers a strong challenge to a general manager's administrative leadership abilities. The first step is to be consciously alert to the importance of shaping the organization's habits, mindsets, and personality variables to fit the needs of strategy. The second step is to use the available opportunities to make incremental changes that improve the alignment of culture and strategy. Such opportunities crop up regularly in many forms: the periodic need to create new managerial positions and fill those that become vacant; the appearance of a new problem that paves the way for making a desirable policy change; coming to the support of those proposals of subordinates which have positive culture-impacts; visibly rewarding individuals and subunits which exhibit the desired traits and spirit of performance; and taking advantage of the annual budgetary process to shift resources from one area to another. Step three is to insist that the actions and decisions of subordinate managers be in keeping with the deliberate creation of the desired culture and organizational bonds. Step four is to proactively build and nurture the organization's *psychological* and *attitudinal* commitment to strategy, so as to produce a *tempermental fit* between culture and strategic mission and make achieving the strategic plan almost like a crusade.

The Politics of Strategy and Playing the Power Game

All organizations are political. The drives and ambitions of individuals to climb the ladder of career achievement and success, the conflicts and coalitions that evolve in translating strategies into action and objectives into results, and the hierarchical divisions of responsibility and authority combine to guarantee the existence of a political atmosphere. Positions of power and weakness are inevitable and the people involved are neither likely to be indifferent to power relationships nor passive in their own maneuvering and use of power. Jockeying for position is a normal activity. After all, careers, material rewards, prestige, and egos are at stake, much less the organization's own success and well-being.

Like it or not, a general manager has to be tuned into the internal political environment. On occasions, the arguments advanced to support competing viewpoints may be shaped more by ambition and internal political considerations than by "objective" analysis; conceivably, unscrupulous actions and unethical behavior may arise, together with selfish attempts to "feather one's own nest." One cannot assume that virtue and goodwill will prevail nor that the soundest course of action will emerge with everyone's wholehearted support. This is not to say that organizations are a political jungle with primary emphasis on political maneuvering and thinking up new power plays. But political considerations do abound and "rational choices" often give way to the politics of consensus and compromise. There are many decisions which reflect the political influence wielded by individuals and groups within the organization.

It would be naive to presume that a general manager can effectively formulate and implement strategy without being perceptive about internal politics and being adept at playing the power game.[14] There is politics involved in formulating the strategic plan. Inevitably, key individuals and groups will form coalitions around the issues of which direction the organization should be headed, with each group pressing the benefits and potential of its own areas. Political considerations enter into which strategic

---

[14]For further discussion of this point see Abraham Zaleznik, "Power and Politics in Organizational Life," *Harvard Business Review*, vol. 48, no.3 (May-June 1970), pp. 47-60; R. M. Cyert, H. A. Simon, and D. B. Trow, "Observation of a Business Decision," *Journal of Business* (October 1956), pp. 237-48; and James Brian Quinn, *Strategies for Change: Logical Incrementalism* (Homewood, Ill.: Richard D. Irwin, Inc., 1980).

objectives will take precedence and which lines of business in the corporate portfolio will have top priority in resource allocation. Internal politics is a factor in building a consensus for which business strategy alternative to employ and in settling upon the role and contribution of each functional area in supporting line of business strategy.

Likewise, there is politics in implementing strategy. Typically, internal political considerations enter into decisions affecting organization structure (whose areas of responsibility need to be reorganized, who reports to whom, who has how much span of control over subunits), the choice of individuals to fill key positions and head up strategy-critical activities, and which organizational units get the biggest budget increases. As a case in point Quinn cites a situation where three strong managers who fought each other constantly formed a potent coalition to resist a reorganization scheme to coordinate the very things that caused their friction.[15]

In short, politics and political behavior are an integral part of building organizationwide enthusiasm and support for the strategic plan and in gaining consensus on the various mechanics of how to implement strategy. Indeed, having astute political skills is a definite, and maybe even a *necessary*, asset in managing the whole strategic process. There is a clear-cut imperative for a general manager to understand how the organization's power structure works, who it is that wields true power and influence in the executive ranks, who are the individuals whose opinions often carry a lot of weight, which groups and individuals are "activists" and which are "defenders of the status quo," who can be helpful in a "showdown" or key decision, which direction the political winds are blowing on a given issue, and, in almost every situation, having a "feel" for what the politics are. On key issues and major decisions especially does one need to be sensitive to the politics of managing coalitions and building a consensus on which way to go. As the chairman of a major British corporation expressed it:

> I've never taken a major decision without consulting my colleagues. It would be unimaginable to me, unimaginable. First, they help me make a better decision in most cases. Second, if they know about it and agree with it, they'll back it. Otherwise, they might challenge it, not openly, but subconsciously . . . .[16]

Having a nosecount of the support one can muster when the going gets tough is important if for no other reason than the fact that one can fight only so many losing battles.

Middle-level general managers need to be particularly adept at organizational politics because of their "in-between" position. Corporate-level executives, for instance, nearly always evaluate business-level general managers primarily on the financial performance of the business unit; they

---

[15]Quinn, *Strategies for Change*, p. 68.
[16]This statement was made by Sir Alastair Pilkington, Chairman, Pilkington Brothers, Ltd.; the quote appears in Quinn, *Strategies for Change*, p. 65.

tend to be far more impressed with good results than with the details of how the results are produced. Their notion of getting the job done consists primarily of the general manager achieving the agreed-upon business-unit results in accord with the general prescriptions of corporate strategy and the general directives of corporate policy.[17] But in the course of translating these general corporate requirements into concrete action to be followed by first-level managers and technical unit heads within the business unit, the business-level manager is vulnerable to heavy flak from both sides. He is caught between pressure from above for results to make his boss look good and the need for the goodwill and cooperation of his own subordinates (plus other organizational subunits on which he must rely for support) in order to improve the business' performance. It is difficult for him to shift blame or make excuses when things do not work out well. Hence, he is thrust into walking a political tightrope, seeking compromise and workability between the expectations of subordinates (whose cooperation is required) and the priorities of superiors (whose approval is needed to get ahead). If he wants to maintain the loyalty and respect of subordinates, he must represent their interests and be willing "to go to bat" for them when the occasion demands. Yet, in going to bat as leader and chief spokesman for the organization unit he heads up, he must realize also his obligations to be a "team player" from a corporate-level perspective. One has to choose carefully when to push hard in representing the interests of the business-unit and when to bend these interests to fit corporate-level priorities.

At the top management level, the politics of strategy centers chiefly around stimulating options, nurturing support for strong proposals and killing the weak ones, guiding the formation of coalitions on particular issues, and building consensus and commitment. A recent study of strategy management in 9 large corporations showed that the political tactics of successful executives included:[18]

- Letting weakly-supported ideas and proposals die through inaction.
- Establishing additional hurdles or tests for strongly supported ideas which the general manager views as unacceptable but which are best not opposed openly.

---

[17]In like manner, other types of "middle" managers are seldom told how to get their jobs done in specific terms. The guidelines they receive from higher-ups regarding increasing sales or profits, carving out a bigger market share, or getting by on a smaller budget are mostly general and, so long as organizational policies are observed, the boss's attitude is most likely to be "I don't care how you do it, just get it done—and on time." In other words, the specifics are delegated to the next level down and it ends up the middle manager's job to figure out how what strategies and concrete actions will be needed to generate the desired results. It is the middle manager, more than anyone else, who translates financial, sales, production, and strategic objectives into a day-to-day operating plan and, then, communicates it in functional-specialist language to the technical, detail-oriented, first-line supervisors.

[18]Quinn, *Strategies for Change*, pp. 128-145.

- Keeping a low political profile on unacceptable proposals by getting subordinates to say "no" rather than letting them come on up to the general manager for a decision.

- Letting most negative decisions come from a group consensus that the general manager merely confirms, thereby reserving one's own personal vetoes for big issues and crucial moments.

- Doing a lot of chatting and informal questioning to stay abreast of how things are progressing and to know when to step in to intervene.

- Leading the strategy but not dictating it—giving few orders, announcing few decisions, depending heavily on informal questioning and seeking to probe and clarify until a consensus emerges.

- Rewarding key thrusts that succeed, generously and visibly.

- Assigning responsibility for a major new thrust to someone who is strongly identified with it and whose future is linked to its success.

- Staying alert to the symbolic impact of one's actions and statements, lest a false signal stimulate proposals and movements in unwanted directions.

- Ensuring that all major power bases within the organization have representation in or access to top management.

- Interjecting new faces and new views into considerations of major changes, so as to preclude those who are primarily involved from coming to see the world the same way and then acting as systematic screens against other views.

- Minimizing one's own political exposure on issues which are highly controversial and in circumstances where opposition from major power centers can trigger a "shootout."

ILLUSTRATION CAPSULE 25
Playing the Power Game the Machiavellian Way

Niccolo Machiavelli, in his classic *The Prince*, presented a manual of methods and tactics in the acquisition and use of power. *The Prince* is full of straightforward, bitter truths about the drive for power and the realities of human motivation. Some say that *The Prince* is diabolical; others call it insightful and utterly realistic in its portrayal of human nature. Whatever adjectives one chooses to apply, there is no denying it as one of the most influential books ever written.

Although Machiavelli's study of power politics was addressed specifically to political rulers, the lessons apply equally well to management. Indeed, if in

ILLUSTRATION CAPSULE 25 *(continued)*

reading the excerpts below one will simply substitute "manager" for "prince" (or its equivalent), then the relevance of Machiavelli to modern management can be readily approached:

. . . men must either be cajoled or crushed; for they will revenge themselves for slight wrongs, while for grave ones they cannot. The injury therefore that you do to a man should be such that you need not fear his revenge.

. . . in taking possession of a state the conqueror should well reflect as to the harsh measures that may be necessary, and then execute them at a single blow, so as not to be obliged to renew them every day; and by thus not repeating them, to assure himself of the support of the inhabitants, and win them over to himself by benefits bestowed. . . . Cruelties should be committed all at once, as in that way each separate one is less felt, and gives less offense; benefits, on the other hand, should be conferred one at a time, for in that way they will be more appreciated.

. . . he who, contrary to the will of the people, has become prince by favor of the nobles, should at once and before everything else strive to win the good will of the people, which will be easy for him, by taking them under his protection.

. . . it is much more safe to be feared than to be loved, when you have to choose between the two.

. . . there are two ways of carrying on a contest; the one by law, and the other by force. The first is practiced by men, and the other by animals; and as the first is often insufficient, it becomes necessary to resort to the second. . . . It being necessary then for a prince to know well how to employ the nature of the beasts, he should be able to assume both that of the fox and that of the lion; for while the latter cannot escape the traps laid for him, the former cannot defend himself against the wolves. A prince should be a fox, to know the traps and snares; and a lion, to be able to frighten the wolves; for those who simply hold to the nature of the lion do not understand their business.

. . . a prince should seem to be merciful, faithful, humane, religious, and upright, and should even be so in reality; but he should have his mind so trained that, when occasion requires it, he may know how to change to the opposite.

. . . For the manner in which men live is so different from the way in which they ought to live, that he who leaves the common course for that which he ought to follow will find that it leads him to ruin rather than to safety. For a man who, in all respects, will carry out only his professions of good, will be apt to be ruined among so many who are evil. A prince therefore who desires to maintain himself must learn to be not always good, but to be so or not as necessity may require. . . . For all things considered, it will be found that some things that seem like virtue will lead

ILLUSTRATION CAPSULE 25 (continued)

you to ruin if you follow them; while others, that apparently are vices, will, if followed, result in your safety and well-being.

. . . the dispositions of people are variable; it is easy to persuade them to anything, but difficult to confirm them to that belief. And therefore a prophet should be prepared, in case the people will not believe any more, to be able by force to compel them to that belief.

. . . The worst that a prince may expect of a people who are unfriendly to him is that they will desert him; but the hostile nobles he has to fear, not only lest they abandon him, but also because they will turn against him. For they, being more farsighted and astute, always save themselves in advance, and seek to secure the favor of him whom they hope may be successful.

We must bear in mind . . . that there is nothing more difficult and dangerous, or more doubtful of success, than an attempt to introduce a new order of things in any state. For the innovator has for enemies all those who derived advantages from the old order of things while those who expect to be benefited by the new institutions will be but lukewarm defenders. This indifference arises in part from fear of their adversaries who were favored by the existing laws, and partly from the incredulity of men who have no faith in anything new that is not the result of well-established experience. Hence it is that, whenever the opponents of the new order of things have the opportunity to attack it, they will do it with the zeal of partisans, while the others defend it but feebly, so that it is dangerous to rely upon the latter.

. . . a prince cannot depend upon what he observes in ordinary quiet times, when the citizens have need of his authority; for then everybody runs at his bidding, everybody promises, and everybody is willing to die for him, when death is very remote. But in adverse times, when the government has need of the citizens, then but few will be found to stand by the prince. And this experience is the more dangerous as it can only be made once.

A wise prince, therefore, will steadily pursue such a course that the citizens of his state will always and under all circumstances feel the need of his authority, and will therefore always prove faithful to him.

A prince . . . should always take counsel, but only when he wants it, and not when others wish to thrust it upon him; in fact, he should rather discourage persons from tendering him advice unsolicited by him. But he should be an extensive questioner, and a patient listener to the truth respecting the things inquired about, and should even show his anger in case any one should, for some reason, not tell him the truth.

It is obvious from the above quotations that a practicing Machiavellian divorces morals from power politics; indeed, moral considerations have no place in the Machiavellian system of power politics except where an evil

ILLUSTRATION CAPSULE 25 *(concluded)*

> reputation would be a political detriment. To many people, this is shocking if
> not abhorrent. But even if your own moral code totally rejects a Machiavel-
> lian use of power, the issue still remains what to do in your dealings with
> people who are Machiavellian in their attempts to acquire and use power.
> How would you deal with such a person? Do you not, in fact, know people
> who in your own experience are Machiavellians? What would your strategy
> be if you were one of the intended "victims?"

The politics of strategy implementation is especially critical in attempting to introduce a new strategy against the support enjoyed by the old
strategy. Except for crisis situations where the old strategy is plainly revealed as out-of-date, it is usually bad politics to push the new strategy via
attacks on the old strategy.[19] Bad-mouthing old strategy can easily be
interpreted as an attack on those who formulated it and those who supported it in the enterprise's climb to its present success. Besides, the former
strategy and the judgments behind it may have been well-suited to the
organization's earlier circumstances, and the people who made these
judgments may still be in positions where support for the new strategy is
important. In addition, a wise general manager will recognize that there are
a variety of legitimate views as to what can and should be done in the
present circumstances; the new strategy and/or the plans for implementing
it may thus not have been the first choices of others and lingering doubts
may remain. Consequently, in trying to surmount resistance, nothing is
gained by "knocking" the views of those who argued for alternative approaches. Such attacks are likely to produce alienation instead of cooperation.

In a very real sense, most strategic decisions and most strategic thrusts in
large enterprises emerge as part of an evolving, continuous political
consensus-building with no precise beginning or end.[20] This reality argues
strongly for a general manager to be extremely sensitive to organizational
politics and power relationships and to use the political process as a major
tool in formulating and implementing strategy.

To summarize, then, the general manager's leadership task in bringing
the full force of an organization behind a strategic plan calls for assessing
and dealing with the most important centers of potential support and
opposition to new strategic thrusts.[21] One needs to secure the support of
key people, co-opt or neutralize serious opposition and resistance when
and where necessary, and learn where the zones of indifference are.

---

[19]Ibid., pp. 118-119.
[20]Quinn, *Strategies for Change*, p. 205.
[21]Ibid., p. 119.

Leading the Process of Making Corrective Adjustments

No strategic plan and no scheme for strategy implementation can foresee all the events and problems that will arise. Adjusting-actions and error-corrections are therefore a normal and necessary part of strategic management. Whereas the specifics of what to do always have to be tailored to the organization's situation, something can be said about when and how to undertake corrective adjustments.

Consider, first, the case of where a need arises to *react* and *respond* to problems involving either the strategy or its implementation. The process of what to do starts with an evaluation of whether immediate action needs to be taken or whether time permits a more deliberate response. In a crisis, the approach of general managers typically is to wield a heavy hand in pushing key subordinates to gather as much information as time permits and to formulate recommendations for consideration, personally presiding over extended discussions of the pros and cons of proposed responses, and trying to build a *quick* consensus among members of the executive "inner circle." If no consensus emerges or if several key executives remain divided in their views, the burden falls on the general manager to choose the response and urge "best efforts" support of it.

In the more frequent cases where time permits a full-fledged evaluation, general managers seem to prefer a process of incrementally solidifying commitment to a response.[22] The approach seems to be one of consciously:

1. Staying flexible and keeping a number of options open.
2. Asking a lot of questions.
3. Gaining in-depth information from specialists.
4. Encouraging subordinates to participate in developing alternatives and proposing solutions.
5. Getting the reactions of many different people to proposed solutions, as a test of their potential and political acceptability.
6. Seeking to build commitment to a response by gradually moving toward a consensus solution.

The governing principle seems to be to make a final decision as late as possible so as to (1) bring as much information to bear as is needed, (2) let the situation clarify enough to know what to do, and (3) allow the various political constituencies and power bases within the organization to move toward a consensus solution. Executives are often wary of committing themselves to a major change too soon because it discourages others from asking questions that need to be raised.

Corrective adjustments to strategy need not be just reactive, however. *Proactive* adjustments constitute a second approach to improving strategy

---

[22]Ibid., pp. 20-22.

or its implementation. The distinctive feature of a proactive posture is that adjusting-actions arise out of management's own drives and initiatives for better performance as opposed to forced reactions. Successful strategy managers have been observed to employ a variety of proactive tactics:[23]

1. Commissioning studies to explore and amplify areas where they have a "gut feeling" or sense a need exists.

2. Shopping ideas among trusted colleagues and putting forth trial concepts.

3. Teaming people with different skills, interests, and experiences and letting them push and tug on interesting ideas to expand the variety of approaches considered.

4. Seeking multiple contact points with a variety of people inside and outside the organization to sample viewpoints, probe, and listen, thereby trying to get early warning signals of impending problems/issues and deliberately short-circuiting all the careful screens of information flowing up from below. (As Peter McColough, the chairman and CEO of Xerox expressed it, ". . . if something bothers me, I don't rely on reports or what other executives may want to tell me. I'll go down very deep into the organization, to certain issues and people, so I'll have a feeling for what they think . . . before I see [memos] they go through 15 hands, and I know what that can do to them."[24]

5. Stimulating proposals for improvement from lower-levels, encouraging the development of competing ideas and approaches, and letting the momentum for change come from below, with final choices being postponed until it is apparent which option best matches the organization's situation.

6. Seeking options and solutions that go beyond just extrapolations from the status quo.

7. Accepting and committing to partial steps forward as a way of building up comfort levels before going on ahead.

8. Managing the politics of change so as to promote managerial consensus-building and to solidify management's commitment to whatever course of action is chosen.

Both the reactive and proactive approaches exhibit commonality in the *process* of deciding what adjusting-actions to take; the sequence seems to be one of sensing needs, gathering information, amplifying understanding and awareness, putting forth trial concepts, developing options, exploring the pros and cons, testing proposals, generating partial solutions, building a

[23]Ibid., Chapter 4.
[24]As quoted in "Personal Management Styles," *Business Week* (May 4, 1974), p. 43.

managerial consensus, and formally adopting the agreed-upon course of action.[25] This points to a key feature of strategic management: the job of a general manager in formulating and implementing strategy is not one of steering a clear-cut, linear course of carrying out the original strategy intact according to some preconceived and highly detailed implementation plan. Rather, it is one of creatively (1) adopting and reshaping strategy to unfolding events and (2) employing analytical-behavioral-political techniques to bring internal activities and attitudes into alignment with strategy. As shown in Figure 1-2, the process is iterative, with much looping and recycling to finetune and adjust in a continuously evolving process whereby the conceptually-separate acts of strategy formulation and strategy implementation blur and join together.

A STRATEGY IMPLEMENTATION CHECKLIST

The managerial aspects of implementing and executing a strategic plan are plainly expansive. Virtually every aspect of administrative work comes into play—organizing, staffing, budgeting, motivating, reporting, coordinating, and consensus-building. Because the set of organization circumstances under which strategy is implemented and executed is situation-specific and one-of-a-kind, it is easier to pinpoint the questions to be raised and the things to be considered than it is to give specific answers on what to do. These questions and considerations, distilled from the discussions in Chapters 6 and 7, are presented in the form of a checklist in Table 7-1.

TABLE 7-1
Questions and Issues in Implementing Strategy

A. Building a Capable Organization

  1. Is the organization structure matched to the needs of strategy?

  2. Have key activities and strategy-critical tasks been correctly identified and do they serve as major building blocks in the organization structure?

  3. Does each organization unit know what it must do to implement and accomplish its part of the strategic plan?

  4. Are the separate activities of functional areas coordinated into a cohesive whole?

  5. Have positions been staffed with adequate managerial and technical talent? Does the organization have (or is in the process of acquiring) the skills and expertise it needs to carry out its strategy? What skills are missing? What strategy-critical skills are weakest?

---

[25]Quinn, *Strategies for Change*, p. 146.

TABLE 7-1 (continued)

6. Has authority to make decisions been put in the right place?

7. What success has the organization had in creating a distinctive competence? Are current efforts in this direction adequate?

B. Allocating Resources and Focusing Energies on Strategic Objectives

1. Do key activities and strategy-critical tasks appear to be adequately financed and staffed? Is funding of these areas "top priority"?

2. Are new strategic thrusts adequately funded? What areas appear underfunded?

3. Are financial resources ample to implement strategy? Is cash flow a problem? Can adequate long-term capital be acquired? Are actions being taken to produce a match between strategy and internal resources and capabilities?

4. Do functional area and operating-level managers understand what performance and time schedule is required of them to make implementation successful?

5. Is the organization's attention trained on achieving strategic objectives as opposed to being more focused on the details of day-to-day operations? Have efforts been made to define duties and functions in terms of meeting strategy-related targets? Do individuals and groups have a strong sense of what is expected of them—from a strategy perspective as well as from an activity and effort perspective?

6. To what extent is the organization results-oriented? Is the emphasis more on "what to do" or on "what to accomplish"?

C. Galvanizing Organizationwide Commitment to the Strategic Plan

1. Have efforts been made to motivate groups and individuals to accomplish strategy? Is motivation a problem? Is there a spirit of high performance and achievement?

2. Have timetables been set for achieving performance targets? Has responsibility for producing the target results been assigned? Have standards of performance been agreed upon and communicated at each level in the management hierarchy?

3. Is the performance of individuals and subunits being explicitly evaluated in terms of agreed-upon objectives and deadlines?

4. Is the reward structure explicitly and tightly linked to actual strategic performance? Do those who produce results get rewarded better than those who just try hard and/or work long hours?

5. Are policies and procedures *supportive* of strategy accomplishment?

TABLE 7-1 *(concluded)*

---

6. Are parts of the organization resisting or rejecting the chosen strategy? What efforts are being made to surmount this resistance?

D. Monitoring Strategic Progress

1. Is strategy-critical information available to top management on a timely basis? Do "surprises" appear regularly?

2. Does top management have a good "feel" for how well strategy implementation is progressing? Do they know what problems are being encountered? Do they know if newly established practices and policies are working well?

3. Do managers have a good grip on the strategic changes that are taking place? Are controls and reporting systems adequate? Are problem areas being dealt with?

E. Exerting Strategic Leadership

1. Has top management worked to create a climate in which the needs of strategy are aligned with the corporate culture? Does the organization attitude and temperament fit the strategy? Are needed changes being made?

2. To what extent is management proactively trying to mold the organization's habits, mindsets, and cultural variables to match strategy?

3. Have the chosen strategic direction and strategic thrusts been made politically acceptable within the organization? Do strong pockets of resistance exist? Has management done a good job of managing the politics of strategy and building a consensus on direction and new thrusts?

4. Is top management's leadership style and internal political skills adequate for the situation? Do key managers appear to have the right temperament and personalities to implement the strategy successfully?

5. Do the major details of strategy implementation appear to be thought through? Is the strategy or its implementation flexible enough to accommodate adjusting-actions and error corrections?

6. In view of the firm's strengths and weaknesses and the challenges it faces, what are the odds that the strategy can be implemented with an attractive degree of success?

SUGGESTED READINGS

Adizes, Ichak, "Mismanagement Styles," *California Management Review*, vol. 19, no. 2 (Winter 1976), pp. 5-20.

Doz, Yves L. and C. K. Prahalad, "Headquarters Influence and Strategic Control in MNC's," *Sloan Management Review*, vol. 23, no. 1 (Fall 1981), pp. 15-29.

Drucker, Peter F., *Management: Tasks, Responsibilities, Practices* (New York: Harper & Row, Publishers, 1974), Chaps. 16-19 and 33-39.

Fielder, Fred E., "The Contingency Model—New Directions for Leadership Utilization," *Journal of Contemporary Business*, vol. 3, no. 4 (Autumn 1974), pp. 65-80.

Hall, Jay, "To Achieve or Not: The Manager's Choice," *California Management Review*, vol. 18, no. 4 (Summer 1976), pp. 5-18.

Herzberg, Frederick, "One More Time: How Do You Motivate Employees," *Harvard Business Review*, vol. 51, no. 3 (May-June 1973), pp. 162-80.

Koontz, Harold, "Management Control: A Suggested Formulation of Principles," *California Management Review*, vol. 2, no. 2 (Winter 1959), pp. 50-55.

Machiavelli, N., *The Prince* (New York: Washington Square Press, 1963).

McClelland, David C. and Burnham, David H., "Power Is the Great Motivator," *Harvard Business Review*, vol. 54, no. 2 (March-April 1976), pp. 100-110.

Morse, John J. and Lorsch, Jay W., "Beyond Theory Y," *Harvard Business Review*, vol. 48, no. 3 (May-June 1970), pp. 61-68.

Quinn, James Brian, *Strategies for Change: Logical Incrementalism* (Homewood, Ill.: Richard D. Irwin, Inc., 1980), Chapter 4.

Robbins, Stephen P., "Reconciling Management Theory with Management Practice," *Business Horizons*, vol. 20, no. 1 (February 1977), pp. 38-47.

Rockart, John F., "Chief Executives Define Their Own Data Needs," *Harvard Business Review*, vol. 57, no. 2 (March-April 1979), pp. 81-93.

Roche, W. J. and MacKinnon, N. L., "Motivating People with Meaningful Work," *Harvard Business Review*, vol. 48, no. 3 (May-June 1970), pp. 97-110.

Tannenbaum, Robert and Schmidt, Warren H., "How to Choose a Leadership Pattern," *Harvard Business Review*, vol. 51, no. 3 (May-June 1973), pp. 162-80.

Tichy, Noel M., Charles J. Fombrun, and Mary Anne Devanna, "Strategic Human Resource Management," *Sloan Management Review*, vol. 23, no. 2 (Winter 1982), pp. 47-61.

Tosi, Henry L., John R. Rizzo, and Stephen J. Carroll, "Setting Goals in Management by Objectives," *California Management Review*, vol. 12, no. 4 (Summer 1970), pp. 70-78.

Vancil, Richard F., "What Kind of Management Control Do You Need," *Harvard Business Review*, vol. 51, no. 2 (March-April 1973), pp. 75-86.

Webber, Ross A., "Career Problems of Young Managers," *California Management Review*, vol. 48, no. 3 (May-June 1970), pp. 47-60.

Zaleznik, Abraham, "Power and Politics in Organizational Life," *Harvard Business Review*, vol. 51, no. 2 (March-April 1973), pp. 75-86.

READING

Strategic Human Resource Management*

NOEL M. TICHY, CHARLES J. FOMBRUN, MARY ANNE DEVANNA

Noel M. Tichy is Associate Professor of Organizational Behavior at The University of Michigan. Charles J. Fombrun is Assistant Professor of Management at the Wharton School, the University of Pennsylvania. Mary Anne Devanna is Research Coordinator of the Center for Research in Career Development and Associate Director of the Strategy Research Center at Columbia University's Graduate School of Business.

Technological, economic, and demographic changes are pressuring organizations to use more effective human resource management. While sagging productivity and worker alienation have popularized management tools such as quality circles and profit sharing plans, the long-run competitiveness of American industry will require considerably more sophisticated approaches to the human resource input that deal with its strategic role in organizational performance.

Recent attacks on American business have stressed the short-run financial outlook of its management and its distinctly callous treatment of workers. The Japanese organization, on the other hand, is seen as the prototype of the future, as its planning systems center on worker loyalty.

This article, however, argues that we should not evaluate the Japanese organization per se. Rather, we should focus on human resource management in terms of its strategic role in both the formulation and the implementation of long-run plans. The strategic human resource concepts and tools needed are fundamentally different from the stock in trade of traditional personnel administration. This article, therefore, stresses the strategic level of human resource management at the expense of some of the operational concerns of the standard personnel organization. Several companies are described as examples of sophisticated American organizations that have instituted strategic human resource management as an integral component of their management process. Specifically, this article presents a framework for conceptualizing human resource managment; links human resource management to general strategic management; and describes some current applications of human resource management as a strategic tool in achieving corporate objectives.

Strategic Management

Three core elements are necessary for firms to function effectively:

1.   Mission and Strategy.   The organization has to have a reason for being, a means for using money, material, information, and people to carry out the mission;

2.   Organization Structure.   People are organized to carry out the mission of the organization and to do the necessary tasks;

3.   Human Resource Management.   People are recruited into the organization to do the jobs defined by the division of labor. Performance must be monitored, and rewards must be given to keep individuals productive.

Figure 1 presents these basic elements as interrelated systems that are embedded in the work environment. In the past, human resource management has been largely missing from the general strategic management process. Thus, our aim here is to help make human resource management an integral part of the strategic arena in organizations.

Strategy is defined as a process through which the basic mission and objectives of the organization are set and a process through which the organization uses its resource to achieve its objectives. In turn, structure reflects "the organization of work into roles such as production, finance, marketing, and so on; the recombining of the roles into departments or divisions around functions, products, regions, or markets and the distribution of power across this role structure."[1] The structure of the organization embodies the fundamental division of labor, describes the basic nature of the jobs to be done, and aggregates them into groups, functions, or businesses. It also defines the degree of centralized control that top management holds over the operating units.

Strategy Follows Structure

In his historical study of American industry, Chandler provided a convincing argument that the structure of an organization follows from its strategy.[2] He identified four major strategies that resulted in structural or organizational design changes. They are: (1) expansion of volume; (2) geographic dispersion; (3) vertical integration; and (4) product diversification. Each of these strategies is followed by a structural transformation from function through to product forms. But while Chandler's work focused attention on the structural supports needed to drive a strategy and on the use of the organization's formal design in the implementation of a

---

[1]See A. Chandler, *Strategy and Structure: Chapters in the History of American Industrial Enterprise* (Cambridge, MA: MIT Press, 1962).

[2]Ibid.

strategy, he did not discuss the role of the human resource systems in the implementation process.

FIGURE 1
Strategic Management and Environmental Pressures

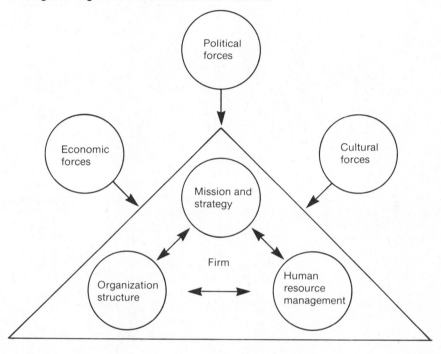

Strategy, Structure, and Human Resource Management

The addition of human resource management to the strategic arena was presented by Galbraith and Nathanson who expanded on Chandler's analysis.[3] They focused on such issues as fitting performance measures to the strategy and structure as well as to rewards, career paths, and leadership styles. Table 1 modifies and expands upon their work to illustrate how strategy, structure, and human resource management systems fit together; the fundamental strategic management problem is to keep the strategy, structure, and human resource dimensions of the organization in direct alignment. In the rest of this article, we will discuss some of the human resource management concepts and tools that are needed to describe completely the strategic management role.

---

[3]See J. Galbraith and D. Nathanson, *Strategy Implementation: The Role of Structure and Process* (St. Paul, MN: West Publishing, 1978).

TABLE 1
Human Resource Management Links to Strategy and Structure

Strategy	Structure	Human Resource Management			
		Selection	Appraisal	Rewards	Development
1. Single product	Functional	Functionally oriented: subjective criteria used	Subjective: measure via personal contact	Unsystematic and allocated in a paternalistic manner	Unsystematic largely through job experiences: single function focus
2. Single product (vertically integrated)	Functional	Functionally oriented: standardized criteria used	Impersonal; based on cost and productivity data	Related to performance and productivity	Functional specialists with some generalists; largely through job rotation
3. Growth by acquistion: (holding company) of unrelated businesses	Separate, self-contained business	Functionally oriented, but varies from business to business in terms of how systematic	Impersonal; based on return on investment and profitability	Formula-based and includes return on investment and profitability	Cross-functional but not cross-business

4.	Related diversification of product lines through internal growth and acquisition	Multidivisional	Functionally and generalist oriented; systematic criteria used	Impersonal; based on return on investment, productivity, and subjective assessment of contribution to overall company	Large bonuses; based on profitability and subjective assessment of contribution to overall company	Cross-functional, cross-divisional, and cross-corporate divisional; formal
5.	Multiple products in multiple countries	Global organization (geographic center and world-wide)	Functionally and generalist oriented; systematic criteria used	Impersonal; based on multiple goals such as return on investment, profit tailored to product and country	Bonuses; based on multiple planned goals with moderate top management discretion	Cross-divisional and cross-subsidiary to corporate; formal and systematic

Source: Adapted from J. Galbraith and D. Nathanson, *Strategy Implementation: The Role of Structure and Process* (St. Paul, Minn.: West Publishing Co., 1978).

Human Resource Policies: A Context

A number of fundamental organizational policies provide the context for considering human resource management. These policies vary from organization to organization and tend to limit or constrain the actual design of a human resource system. While they are not the focus of this article, they are identified as important contextual issues that organizations must consider along the way. These policies are:

1. **Management Philosophy.**   Basic policy that influences the overall design of a human resource system is the organization's management philosophy, i.e., its "psychological contract" with employees. An organization typically specifies the nature of the exchange with its employees. On one end of the spectrum is "a fair day's work for a fair day's pay," a purely extrinsic *quid pro quo* contract. Many U.S. blue-collar jobs fit this description. At the other extreme is the contract that stresses "challenging, meaningful work in return for a loyal, committed, and self-motivated employee," an intrinsically oriented contract. Some of the Scandinavian companies committed to quality of work life are positioned at this end of the spectrum. Such organizations typically develop people from within and seldom go to the external labor market to fill job openings.

A second policy decision involving management philosophy is the extent to which the organization is "top down" or "bottom up" driven. In a top down organization, the human resource system centralizes all key selection, appraisal, and reward and development decisions. A bottom up system encourages widespread participation in all activities.

2. **Reliance on Development or Selection.**   Organizations vary in the degree to which they weight the impact of these two factors of performance. Some companies do almost no training or development. Other companies, such as AT&T, invest heavily in development. A company such as GE ascribes to a management philosophy that stresses both careful selection and development.

3. **Group versus Individual Performance.**   The human resource systems can be geared toward collective, group-based performance or individual performance, or toward some mixture of the two. When the emphasis is on group performance, the selection must take into account social compatibility; the appraisal system must be group focused; and rewards must provide incentives for the work group.

The Human Resource Cycle

In light of these policies, we may now focus on four generic processes or functions that are performed by a human resource system in all organizations—selection, appraisal, rewards, and development. These four processes reflect sequential managerial tasks. Figure 2 represents them in terms of a human resource cycle. Clearly the dependent variable in Figure 2 is performance: the human resource elements are designed to impact performance at both the individual and the organizational levels.

FIGURE 2
The Human Resource Cycle

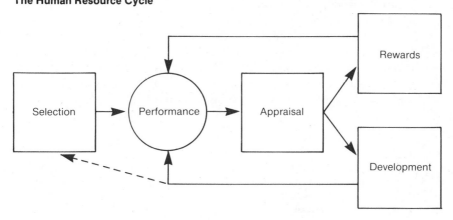

Performance, in other words, is a function of all the human resource components: selecting people who are best able to perform the jobs defined by the structure; motivating employees by rewarding them judiciously; training and developing employees for future performance; and appraising employees in order to justify the rewards. In addition, performance is a function of the organizational context and resources surrounding the individual. Thus, strategy and structure also impact performance through the ways jobs are designed, through how the organization is structured, and through how well services or products are planned to meet environmental threats and opportunities.

In order to put these functions in the various contexts of the organization, we rely upon Robert Anthony's distinction among the three levels of managerial work: the strategic level, the managerial level, and the operational level.[4]

The strategic level deals with policy formulation and overall goal setting; its objective is to position effectively the organization in its environment. The managerial level is concerned with the availability and allocation of resources to carry out the strategic plan. To be in the business(es) specified by the strategic plan, the company must decide what its capital,

----

[4]See R. Anthony, *Planning and Control Systems: A Framework for Analysis* (Boston, MA: Division of Research, Graduate School of Business Administration, Harvard University, 1965).

informational, and human resource needs are. At the operational level, the day-to-day management of the organization is carried out. (Operational activities are ideally carried out under the umbrella of the managerial plan.)

Table 2 illustrates the kinds of activities associated with these three levels for each generic component of the human resource cycle. For example, in the selection/placement area, operational level activities include the annual staffing and recruitment plans. Managerial selection is more concerned with manpower planning for the intermediate future. For instance, a company that is about to open two plants in different parts of the country would want to know the kinds of people the company will need and how it should go about finding the people to run the plants. Strategic selection is concerned with identifying who can best run the business(es) in the long run.

Selection, Promotion, and Placement Process

The selection, promotion, and placement process includes all those activities related to the internal movement of people across positions and to the external hiring into the organization. The essential process is one of matching available human resources to jobs in the organization. It entails defining the organization's human needs for particular positions and assessing the available pool of people to determine the best fit.

Three strategic selection concerns are paticularly salient. The first involves devising an organization-wide selection and promotion system that supports the organization's business strategy. For example, if a company will be diversifying over a ten-year period, it is most likely that the types of people needed to run the new business will be different than they had been in the past. Thus, a redesign in the selection process will be required. This process is taking place in the oil industry as it launches its twenty-year diversification effort.

The second strategic concern requires creating internal flows of people that match the business strategy. Companies that diversify or change their strategic direction need to alter traditional promotional patterns in order to move new types of people into key positions. AT&T's move into the competitive electronic communication and knowledge business has necessitated their developing internal promotion systems for profit-driven people who are able to innovate and deal with competitive markets. This is a major change from the regulated telephone monopoly that was service oriented, that was low on innovation, and that was not managed competitively where profit was regulated.

The third strategic concern is matching key executives to the business's strategy. There is a growing interest in meshing strategic planning with executive skills. This is especially true in companies that are using a product

TABLE 2
Human Resource Activities

Management Level	Selection	Appraisal	Rewards (Compensation and Fringe Benefits)	Development
Strategic	Specify characteristics of people needed to run business in long term Alter internal and external systems to reflect future	In long term, what should be valued? Develop means to appraise future dimensions Early identification of potential	In world as it might be in long term, how will work force be rewarded? Link to the long-term business strategy	Plan developmental experiences for people running business of the future Systems with flexibility to adjust to change Develop long-term career paths
Managerial	Longitudinal validation of selection criteria Development of recruitment marketing plan New markets	Validated systems linking current and future potential Assessment centers for development	Five-year compensation plans for individuals Cafeteria-style fringe packages	General management development programs Organization development Foster self-development
Operational	Staffing plans Recruitment plans Day-to-day monitoring systems	Annual or more frequent appraisal system(s) Day-to-day control systems	Wage and salary administration Benefit packages	Specific job skill training On-the-job training

portfolio analysis approach to strategic management. The Boston Consulting Group's (BCG's) portfolio matrix is the most common and simplest formulation. Using the BCG approach, there is a set of prescribed business practices for managing each type of business. Several examples of companies already committed to using senior executive selection as a strategic management tool are presented below:

General Electric.   GE uses a more complex portfolio matrix with nine cells. Yet the underlying concepts are based on the same product life cycle notions represented in the BCG matrix. GE defines its products in terms of the kinds of management practices required for success. Thus, its products are defined as "growers" for wildcats, "defenders" for stars, "harvesters" for cash cows, and "undertakers" for dogs:

> Its [GE] general managers are being classified by personal style or orientation as "growers," "caretakers," and "undertakers." . . . They [GE] have a shortage of growers but they are making a great effort to remove the undertaker types who are heading up growth businesses. The lighting business is mainly mature but we [GE] just designated international operations as a growth area to our five year forecast. . . . John D. Hamilton, the manager responsible for manpower planning says he and the executive manpower staff at corporate headquarters looked at the whole pool of corporate talent. They decided to move in a manager who had an industrial rather than a lighting background, but who seemed to show entrepreneurial flair.[5]

Corning Glass Company.   At Corning, an extensive effort is under way to assess the company's top 100 executives for such qualities as entrepreneurial flair. The goal is to have a clearer profile of the organization's pool of executive talent specified in terms of capabilities for managing different parts of the BCG matrix. An example of this process occurred in December 1979:

> Corning reshaped its electronic strategy, deciding that the market was starting to expand again, and that it needed a growth oriented manager. It placed a manufacturing specialist who had shown a great deal of flair in working with customers in the top marketing slot for electronics, and says Shafer, "It looks like he's turning it around."[6]

Chase Manhattan Bank.   During the period between 1975 and 1980, the bank underwent major managerial changes. A key to the bank's successful turnaround from a troubled bank in the mid-seventies was its careful strategic level selection and placement of executives. Historically, at Chase, as is the case with banking in general, senior level positions were filled based on the historical precedent; the old boy networks played a major role. Furthermore, the tradition was to reward those with banker skills and not those with managerial skills, which were implicitly consid-

---

[5]See *Business Week*, 25 February 1980, p. 173.
[6]Ibid., p. 166.

ered to be of less importance. But under the stress of serious performance problems, Chase Manhattan Bank had to reexamine these practices. As a result, a very systematic effort was launched to strategically manage senior selection and placement decisions. For example, "When the trust manager retired, corporate management decided that the department, whose operation had been essentially stable, should focus on a more aggressive growth strategy. Instead of seeking a veteran banker, Chase hired a man whose experience had been with IBM" because it was felt that he would bring a strong marketing orientation to the trust department, which the new strategy required.[7]

Texas Instruments.   At TI, there is an explicit attempt to match management style to product life cycles. "As a product moves through different phases of its life cycle, different kinds of management skills become dominant."[8] The mismatch of managerial style to the product life cycle can be quite serious. For example, a risk-taking entrepreneurial manager who is in charge of a cash cow business is likely to reduce the profitability of the business by trying to "grow" the business and take risks. On the other hand, putting a cost-cutting, efficiency-oriented manager in charge of a growth business can stifle innovation and prevent the business from acquiring market share. TI feels that, in the past, it did not pay adequate attention to the match between product life cycle and managerial style. As a result, TI feels it lost its early lead in integrated circuits. During the growth stage, TI had a "cash cow manager in charge rather than a grower or entrepreneurial type."[9] The result was that "tighter controls were introduced, but TI failed to recognize that a research orientation was really what the Integrated Department needed at the growth stage. TI has since redoubled its efforts to match management orientation with job needs. Bucy, now president, personally reviews the records of the top TI managers."[10]

Reward Processes

Performance follows the selection process. Once people are in their jobs, they need to be rewarded for good performance. The list of rewards that exist in organizational settings is surprisingly long. The following is a partial list of potential rewards:

- Pay in its various forms: salary, bonuses, stock options, benefits, and perquisites;

- Promotion: both upward mobility and lateral transfers into desirable positions;

---

[7]Ibid., p. 166.
[8]Ibid., p. 168.
[9]Ibid., p. 168.
[10]Ibid., p. 168.

- Management praise;
- Career opportunities: a long-term chance for growth and development;
- Appreciation from customers and/or clients of the organization;
- Personal sense of well-being: feeling good about oneself for accomplishing objectives;
- Opportunity to learn: a chance to expand one's skills and knowledge base;
- Security: a sense of job and financial security;
- Responsibility: providing individuals with a sense of organizational responsibility;
- Respect from coworkers;
- Friendship from coworkers.

Most organizations, however, do not do a very good job of managing these rewards to produce desired organizational behaviors. As a result, the reward system is one of the most underutilized and mishandled managerial tools for driving organizational performance. As can be seen from the human resource cycle in Figure 2, rewards are a major factor in influencing performance. Assuming that the organization can appraise performance, which is not always a good assumption, the organization then has a rationale for allocating rewards based on how well people perform; many times organizations think of rewards only in terms of managing pay.

Thus, a major strategic issue concerning the reward system is how to use it to overcome the tendency toward short-sighted management. The rewards for this year's profits generally turn out to be both financial incentives and promotions. Motivation of senior executives toward long-term strategic goals is difficult, given that the reward system often encourages short-term achievement at the expense of long-term goals. The following excerpt is a statement made in the *New York Times*:

> Though bonuses based on achieving sales or earnings goals have long been common, the emphasis on long term is a new element. Top corporate executives, under pressure from Wall Street and stockholders have been rewarded with bonuses and stock options when immediate profits spurt. The auto industry, for example, is notable for its short term rewards.[11]

It is unreasonable and unwise to recommend that managers be rewarded only for long-term strategic goals, as businesses must perform in the present to succeed in the future. Thus, the reward system should provide balanced support to short-term and long-term strategic goals.

---

[11]See *New York Times*, 24 April 1980.

Balancing Long- and Short-Term Goals

Texas Instruments.   TI has thought long and hard about the use of its reward system for driving the company's short- and long-term goals.

One major part of TI's strategy since the early 1960s has been to adhere rigidly to the "learning curve theory." Simply put, it states that "manufacturing costs can be brought down by a fixed percentage, depending on the product, each time cumulative volume is doubled."[12] The strategy involves constant redesign improvement of the product and of the processes of production so that prices can drop as fast as possible. This strategy was implemented by organizing Product Customer Centers (PCCs), which are decentralized profit centers that could be closely monitored for cost performance. The reward system was closely tied to the PCCs so that managers worked hard to make the learning curve theory operative. However, there were some problems.

The Product Customer Centers and associated reward systems worked against another organizational strategy—the development of innovations for future products. The rewards were structured to drive managers to be overly concerned with short-run efficiencies and not with long-term strategic goals.

The solution to this dilemma was to design a new organization and to drape it over the existing PCC structure. The new organization, which was called Objectives, Strategies, and Tactics (OST), was created to supplement the PCCs, which remained intact. The OST structure was used for the formulation and implementation of strategic long-range plans, and it consisted of the same managers as that of the PCC organization.

Thus, the top managers at TI wear two hats. Wearing one hat, they are bottom line, efficiency-focused managers who work to drive the PCC system and who are rewarded and evaluated for accomplishing the efficiency objectives. Wearing the other hat, the OST one, the managers are involved in working toward a strategic objective that may have a ten- to twenty-year time horizon. Separate monitoring and appraisal systems tied to the OST organization are used to drive performance in the long-term strategic area. For example, a manager may be responsible for PCC efficiency, while, at the same time, he may work in the OST structure toward a strategic objective in the development of products in the computerized auto industry of the future. If 60 percent of his time was allocated to the PCCs and 40 percent of his time to OST, then his compensation would be split to reflect the short-and long-term aspects of the job.

TI also used the reward system to encourage another set of desired strategic behaviors when it discovered that managers tend to set low-risk objectives in order to enhance their chances of receiving a bigger bonus, and thereby stifling their creativity and innovativeness. TI altered the

---

[12]See *Business Week*, 18 September 1978, p. 68.

reward system through a "wild hare" program that provided funding for more speculative programs. Under this program, managers were asked to rank speculative projects on a separate basis. The bonus system was then tied into this process.

Another strategic reward mechanism for fostering organizational innovation is to provide any organization member(s) with a chance to obtain a grant from a pool containing several million dollars to fund innovative projects. The result has been the emergence of informal groups who apply for grants from the innovation pool, called IDEA; these groups then attempt to turn these ideas into viable products.

Management Development

Activities designed to insure that individuals are properly equipped with skills and knowledge to carry out their jobs fall into the management development category. These activities range from simple job training for lower-level employees to long-term development of senior executives. The three major areas of the developmental process are: (1) job improvement: the development of specific job skills and competencies; (2) career planning: a longitudinal focus on individual growth and development in relation to organizational opportunities; and (3) succession planning: the organizational focus on insuring an adequate supply of human resource talent for projected needs in the future based on strategic plans.

At the long-term strategic level, the developmental process includes such activities as management education, job assignments, and the use of mentor relationships. Some of the strategic level developmental concerns are discussed briefly.

Insuring that the organization has an adequate supply of human resource talent at all levels is no easy task, especially when the organization is undergoing rapid strategic changes. The key to this concern is to have a human resource planning system that makes accurate forecasts of needs and of resources available to meet those needs. Such systems, however, are not easily built, and even though most large companies have manpower planning systems, they are often very inadequate as a result of two basic flaws.

The first flaw is that data about people that are fed into the system are very unreliable because managers generally do not appraise employees well. As it now stands, the appraisal process that provides this data is the weakest link in the human resource cycle. Thus, planning systems that are built on these data are also inadequate. In order to plan for the future, it is necessary to have an inventory of current human resources that includes both an assessment of current performance and of the future potential of key individuals.

The second basic flaw is that there is a missing link between human resource planning systems and business strategy. Although many organizations have given lip service to this missing link, the reality is that it has been treated as an afterthought that has usually been delegated to the human resource staff without any line management involvement. As a result, the human resource plan is a paper exercise that is not utilized by the strategic decision makers.

There is a handful of U.S. companies that have strategically managed the development of senior executive talent. Among these companies are General Motors, Exxon, General Electric, Texas Instruments, IBM, and Procter & Gamble. The emphasis has been on carefully developing managers by following such principles as:

1. Sustained interest in and support for management development and succession planning on the part of top management;

2. Efforts to identify young professionals deemed to have potential for top-level management positions;

3. Comprehensive and systematic rewards used for managerial performance;

4. The appraisal includes data from multiple sources and is used in making decisions about management development;

5. Special recruiting efforts to provide appropriate raw materials for general managers of the future;

6. Opportunities for capable young professionals to develop managerial skills early in their careers;

7. Compensation policies and salary administration to help stimulate management development and retain key personnel;

8. Clear developmental objectives and career plans for managers at all levels;

9. Effective coaching from personnel's superiors;

10. Stressing results in the performance appraisal process.

Some companies have been very strategic in developing managers. For example:

Exxon.   The Compensation and Executive Development (COED) system at Exxon is designed to insure a disciplined approach to the development of managerial talent for the company. The system is directed from the top, where the COED committee is headed by the CEO, Clifford Garvin, and is made up of members of Exxon's Board. The committee is in charge of reviewing the development and placement of the top 250 Exxon executives. Meeting nearly every Monday, the COED committee carefully reviews the performance of executives and examines their developmental needs. To insure that there is a continual flow of managerial talent for the company and that all positions have back-up candidates, the committee then compares the performances of all the executives and makes decisions according to their future developmental needs.

There is also a COED system within each of the Exxon subsidiaries, where the president of each subsidiary has his or her own COED committee, which is similar to the one Mr. Garvin heads. Each subsidiary also has a senior level staff for the COED committee: this enables the COED system to reach the top 2,000 or so managers at Exxon.

In discussions with senior Exxon managers, it is rather striking to hear the universal acclaim given the system. Most agree that the system accounts for Exxon's overall success and that it is an excellent system for developing managers.

General Motors.   General Motors is another company with an equally strong tradition of management development that dates back to Alfred Sloan.

> At General Motors, the supreme court of executive review in recent years included the top six executives in the company. . . . During the week-long sessions in the Board room of Detroit headquarters each February and July, they spend long days and nights listening to analysis of more than 600 managers from each of GM's ten vice presidents and group executives. . . . A variety of questions are covered to get an accurate picture of where the individual stands in his career development. . . . We don't have jobs at GM, we have careers. Along with performance, the probing is centered on just what kind of potential the executive may have. Here are some examples. Does the executive seem to be developing at the rate expected? What is the job contributing to the person's ability? Is it rounding out the person as we intended? What should be the next job for this executive? Should it be in another division or involve greater responsibility? If so, who would we put in this executive's place?[13]

Chase Manhattan Bank.   A more targeted use of management development took place at Chase Manhattan Bank. A management development program was designed to support the company's first formal strategic planning process. The two-week program for the top officers of the bank focused on awareness and frameworks needed to support the new strategic planning process. The program had the involvement of the then chairman, David Rockefeller, and the then president, Willard Butcher. Both symbolically and substantively, the program strongly reinforced the importance of the new strategic planning process.

Appraisal Process

Perhaps the least liked managerial activity is doing the annual performance appraisal. The activity is often only a perfunctory paper exercise. Performance appraisals are like seat belts: everyone agrees that they are

---

[13]See *New York Times*, 4 September 1980.

important and that they save lives, yet no one uses them. Similarly, the problem with appraisal systems includes poorly designed procedures, a psychological resistance of managers to give negative evaluations, and a perceived invalidity. The appraisal system, nonetheless, is central to the human resource cycle. It contributes to three essential processes.

1. Rewards can be allocated in relation to performance only through the use of an appraisal system by which performance can be measured. Such appraisal systems range from subjective personal evaluations to impersonal criteria based on profitability, return on investment, market share, and other quantitative measures.

2. Human resource planning relies on valid appraisals. A current inventory of talent can be made only through a valid appraisal process that shows those who have been performing well and those who have not. In addition, future human resource projections must be based on an assessment of the potential of the employees, which is indicated by the appraisal process. Without the data provided by a valid appraisal, such forecasting is impossible, as there is no basis for making predictions.

3. The development process is also built on the appraisal process. Based on an assessment of an individual's performance and potential, both the individual and the organization can plan for future training and development. A weak data base leads to a hit or miss training program and retards the development process.

Relationship to Strategy

A strategic concern for companies is to develop appraisal processes that are supportive of the business strategy. A study by Lorsch and Allen indicated that such a link influences total performance.[14] In this study, the authors compared the appraisal systems in diversified companies to those in integrated companies. They found that the diversified companies placed more emphasis on objective and result measures such as productivity, profit, volume, etc. The integrated firms, however, tended to rely more on operating and intermediate measures, as well as on more subjective evaluation of abilities such as "planning," "controlling," "organizing," and "leadership." The diversified appraisal system worked better because the divisions were more self-contained, having little interdivisional or corporate contact. The integrated companies, on the other hand, had greater interdivisional contact and greater sharing of resources, which made it hard for them to decide who exactly was responsible for how much of the end results. These two simple examples underscore some of the strategic issues involved in matching an appraisal process to the business strategy.

---

[14]See J. Lorsch and S. Allen, *Managing Diversity and Interdependence* (Boston, MA: Division of Research, Harvard Business School, 1973).

The key to an effective appraisal system at the strategic level is the commitment of quality managerial time to systematic examination and evaluation of executive talent. The descriptions of the Exxon and GM development systems, which were discussed earlier, are in part descriptions of their appraisal systems as the two systems are interrelated. But perhaps the company with the best strategic appraisal system is General Electric, where much time and staff work go into appraising the top 600 executives.

General Electric.   The diversification of GE makes the appraisal of managers more complex than that of most other companies. Unlike GM or Exxon who have one major line of business, GE has more than 240 businesses. As a result, GE has developed elaborate approaches to handling the appraisal of key managers.

An example of this is the slate system. The top 600 positions at GE are carefully managed and monitored by the chairman. A special human resource staff that is under the direction of a senior vice president reviews these key executives. This staff works with line managers to develop slates of acceptable candidates for key managerial positions in the company. Positions must be filled from among those on the approved slate; that is, a business head cannot select his own vice president of marketing unless the individual is among those on the official slate list for the position. Although a manager may select an individual who is not on the slate, the decision must ultimately be kicked up the hierarchy at GE to the chairman. However, this kind of selection is frowned upon and thus very few people who are not on the slate are selected for key managerial positions.

One of the services that the human resource staff provides in developing the data base for the slate system is an in-depth executive review of key managers. Highly trained personnel spend several weeks preparing a report on a single executive. The process involves interviews with subordinates, peers, bosses, and even customers of GE to get a composite picture of the individual's strengths, weaknesses, accomplishments, failures, and potentials. These reviews estimate the expected future progress of the individual at GE and give extensive suggestions for further development. The completed report is then reviewed by the individual who can voice disagreement. It then becomes part of the individual's file. (Only forty of these reviews are conducted in a year.)

Implementing Strategic Human Resource Management

In another article, we discussed a methodology for moving a human resource function into the strategic arena.[15] The approach is based on a human resource audit that provides the organization with data on the

---

[15]See M. Haire, "A New Look at Human Resources," *Industrial Management Review* (now *Sloan Management Review*), Winter 1970, pp. 17-23.

internal capacity of the human resource function and data from the line concerning the kind of services the organization needs at the operational, managerial, and strategic levels. As a result of our conducting these audits in several large companies, we developed the following suggestions for making the human resource function more strategic:

The Internal Organization of the Human Resource Function.   The first area of focus is on how to properly organize, staff, and manage the human resource function. This involves:

- Step 1. Identify the portfolio of human resource tasks at the strategic, managerial, and operational level for each human resource element.

- Step 2. Reorganize the human resource function to reflect the operational, managerial, and strategic needs of the business. The *operational level* is best served by a traditional functional personnel department where there are separate units carrying out recruitment, compensation, development, etc. The *managerial level* must be organized to cut across the subfunctions identified at the operational level (recruitment, development, compensation, etc.) by using such design tools as liaison managers, teams, or, under limited conditions, a matrix organizational design. The *strategic level* activities require an elite senior human resource management (individual or team, depending on the size of the organization) that is supported by strong managerial human resource services.

- Step 3. The human resource staff must be trained in the more strategically focused organization. At the operational level, the function must be staffed with technically focused professional personnel and/or with MBAs who are starting out in their careers and who need to learn the nuts and bolts of personnel. At the managerial level, individuals, who possess a more general managerial orientation and background either through actual work experience or through an MBA degree, should be selected from the operational level. Finally, at the strategic level, staffing should be based on selecting human resource executives who have political skills, a broad business orientation, and a broad human resource management background. A proactive stance toward the strategic future of the organization is also required.

- Step 4. The reward and control systems must be altered to support the strategic human resource function. The rewards and controls should reflect specific tasks at each of the three levels. Most personnel reward and control systems are geared toward operational level activities; these should be expanded to reward and control people in terms of the new strategic and managerial level activities.

Linking the Human Resource Function to the Line Organization.   Major changes are also required to link the human resource function to the user organization. Most personnel functions are linked to the operational business activities. With the addition of new managerial and strategic activities, new linking mechanisms will be required:

- Step 1. Provide the business with good human resource data bases. These include environmental scanning of labor marketing and social and economic issues that impact the long-term human resource context of the organization. In addition, data on the internal labor pool are required in both a present and a future context. Internal marketing data on the human resource needs of various user groups in the organization are especially helpful.

- Step 2. Alter the senior management role when it comes to human resource management issues so that these concerns receive quality attention. The managers need to be committed to weighing human resource issues with the same level of attention as that of other functions, such as finance, marketing, and production.

- Step 3. The line organization must alter its incentive and control systems so that the overall human resource function is managed. It will also be necessary for the organization to have ways of measuring the overall performance of the human resource function at the strategic, managerial, and operational levels. This will entail ongoing audits of the human resource function to determine how well it is doing in providing services to its clients. Also adjustments must be made in budgeting or human resource services, as some of these adjustments will require new sources of corporate funding.

These steps are illustrative of what is involved in developing a more strategic human resource function. Obviously, every organization must develop its own answers and a tailored strategic stance in terms of its human resources.

Summary and Conclusions

Human resource management is a major force in driving organizational performance. Thus, when business is castigated and when American industry is unfavorably compared to that of Japan or West Germany, two major factors are underscored: (1) our lack of a long-term perspective in management; and (2) our lack of skill in managing people. Both of these factors can be changed only with a concomitant change in the human resource activities inside our organizations; that is, it requires changes in the way people think and behave. In the final analysis, three concluding points should be made about human resource management:

1. Human resource activities have a major impact on individual performance and hence on productivity and organizational performance.
2. The cycle of human resource activities is highly interdependent. The human resource system is therefore only as strong as its weakest link.

3. Effective strategic management requires effective human resource management.

Additional Readings

M. A. Devanna, C. Fombrun, and N. Tichy, "Human Resource Management: A Strategic Approach," *Organizational Dynamics*, Winter 1981.

J. Galbraith and D. Nathanson, *Strategy Implementation: The Role of Structure and Process* (St. Paul, MN: West Publishing, 1978), p. 118.

B. Henderson, *Henderson on Corporate Strategy* (Cambridge, MA: Abt Books, 1979).

C. Hofer and D. Schendel, *Strategy Formulation, Analytical Concepts* (St. Paul, MN: West Publishing, 1978), p. 42.

T. Peters, "Putting Excellence into Management," *Business Week*, 21 July 1980.

READING

Chief Executives Define Their Own Data Needs*

JOHN F. ROCKART

John F. Rockart is director of the Center for Information Systems Research, Sloan School of Management, Massachusetts Institute of Technology, and a senior lecturer at the Sloan School.

He could have been the president of any one of a number of successful and growing medium-sized companies in the electronics industry. He had spent the previous day working to salt away the acquisition of a small company that fitted an important position in the product line strategy he had evolved for his organization. Most of this day had been spent discussing problems and opportunities with key managers. During both days he had lived up to his reputation of being an able, aggressive, action oriented chief executive of a leading company in its segment of the electronics field.

Unfortunately, the president had chosen the late afternoon and early evening to work through the papers massed on his desk. His thoughts were not pleasant. His emotions ranged from amusement to anger as he plowed through the papers. "Why," he thought, "do I have to have dozens of reports a month and yet very little of the real information I need to manage this company? There must be a way to get the information I need to run this company!"

In effect, he was expressing the thoughts of many other general managers—and especially chief executive officers—whose needs for information are not as clearly determined as are those of many functional managers and first-line supervisors. Once one gets above the functional level, there is a wide variety of information that one might possibly need, and each functional specialty has an interest in "feeding" particular data to a general manager. As in this case, therefore, a massive information flow occurs. This syndrome is spelled out with differing emphases by the recent comments of two other chief executives:

> "The first thing about information systems that strikes me is that one gets too much information. The information explosion crosses and criss-crosses executive desks with a great deal of data. Much of this is only partly digested and much of it is irrelevant . . ."[1]

---

*This article is reprinted from the *Harvard Business Review*, vol. 57, no. 2 (March-April 1979), pp. 81-93. Copyright © 1979 by the President and Fellows of Harvard College. All rights reserved.

[1]Interview with Anthony J.F. O'Reilly, president of H. J. Heinz Co., *M.I.S. Quarterly*, March 1977, p. 1.

"I think the problem with management information systems in the past in many companies has been that they're overwhelming as far as the executive is concerned. He has to go through reams of reports and try to determine for himself what are the most critical pieces of information contained in the reports so that he can take the necessary action and correct any problems that have arisen."[2]

It is clear that a problem exists with defining exactly what data the chief executive (or any other general manager) needs. My experience in working with executives for the past decade or more is that the problem is universally felt—with individual frustration levels varying, but most often high.

In this article, I will first discuss four current major approaches to defining managerial information needs. Next, I will discuss a new approach developed by a research team at MIT's Sloan School of Management. Termed the "critical success factor (CSF) method," this approach is being actively researched and applied today at the MIT center. Finally, I will describe in detail this method's use in one major case as well as provide summary descriptions of its use in four other cases.

CURRENT PROCEDURES

In effect, there are four main ways of determining executive information needs—the *by-product* technique, the *null* approach, the *key indicator* system, and the *total study* process. In this section of the article, I will offer a brief synopsis of each of these and discuss their relative strengths and weaknesses.

By-Product Technique

In this method, little attention is actually paid to the real information needs of the chief executive. The organization's computer-based information process is centered on the development of operational systems that perform the required paperwork processing for the company. Attention is focused, therefore, on systems that process payroll, accounts payable, billing, inventory, accounts receivable, and so on.

The information by-products of these transaction-processing systems are often made available to all interested executives, and some of the data (e.g., summary sales reports and year-to-date budget reports) are passed on to top management. The by-products that reach the top are most often either heavily aggregated (e.g., budgeted/actual for major divisions) or they are exception reports of significant interest (e.g., certain jobs now critical by some preset standard). All reports, however, are essentially by-products of a particular system designed primarily to perform routine paperwork processing.

---

[2]Interview with William Dougherty, president of North Carolina Bank Corporation, *M.I.S. Quarterly,* March 1977, p. 1.

Where the information subsystem is not computer-based, the reports reaching the top are often typed versions of what a lower level feels is useful. Alternatively, they may be the ongoing, periodically forthcoming result of a previous one-time request for information concerning a particular matter initiated by the chief executive in the dim past.

Of the five methods discussed herein, the by-product approach is undoubtedly the predominant method. It leads to the welter of reports noted in the introductory paragraphs of this article. It has the paper-processing tail wagging the information dog.

The approach is, however, understandable. Paperwork must be done and clerical savings can be made by focusing on automating paper-processing systems. It is necessary to develop this class of data processing system to handle day-to-day paperwork. However, other approaches are also necessary to provide more useful management information.

Null Approach

This method is characterized by statements that might be paraphrased in the following way: "Top executives' activities are dynamic and ever changing, so one cannot predetermine exactly what information will be needed to deal with changing events at any point in time. These executives, therefore, are and must be dependent on future-oriented, rapidly assembled, most often subjective, and informal information delivered by word of mouth from trusted advisers."

Proponents of this approach point to the uselessness of the reports developed under the by-product method just noted. Having seen (often only too clearly) that (1) the *existing* reports used by the chief executive are not very useful, and (2) he, therefore, relies very heavily on oral communication, advocates of this approach then conclude that all computer-based reports—no matter how they are developed—will be useless. They look at inadequately designed information systems and curse all computer-based systems.

Proponents of the null approach see managerial use of information as Henry Mintzberg does:

> ". . . it is interesting to look at the content of managers' information, and at what they do with it. The evidence here is that a great deal of the manager's inputs are soft and speculative—impressions and feelings about other people, hearsay, gossip, and so on. Furthermore, the very analytical inputs—reports, documents, and hard data in general—seem to be of relatively little importance to many managers. (After a steady diet of soft information, one chief executive came across the first piece of hard data he had seen all week—an accounting report—and put it aside with the comment, 'I never look at this.')"[3]

[3]See Henry Mintzberg, "Planning on the Left Side and Managing on the Right," *Harvard Business Review*, July-August 1976, p. 54.

To some extent, this school of thought is correct. There is a great deal of information used by top executives that must be dynamically gathered as new situations arise. And, most certainly, there are data that affect top management which are not computer-based and which must be communicated in informal, oral, and subjective conversations.

There are, however, also data that can and should be supplied regularly to the chief executive through the computer system. More significantly, as I will note later on, it is also important to clearly define what informal (*not* computer-based) information should be supplied to a top executive on a regular basis.

Key Indicator System

A clear contender today for the fastest growing school of thought concerning the "best" approach to the provision of executive information is the key indicator system. This procedure is based on three concepts, two of which are necessary and the third of which provides the glamour (as well as a few tangible benefits).

The first concept is the selection of a set of key indicators of the health of the business. Information is collected on each of these indicators. The second concept is exception reporting—that is, the ability to make available to the manager, if desired, only those indicators where performance is significantly different from planned.

The third concept is the expanding availability of better, cheaper, and more flexible visual display techniques. These range from computer consoles (often with color displays) to wall-size visual displays of computer-generated digital or graphic material. A paradigm of these systems is the one developed at Gould, Inc., under the direction of William T. Ylvisaker, chairman and chief executive officer. As *Business Week* reports:

> "Gould is combining the visual display board, which has now become a fixture in many boardrooms, with a computer information system. Information on everything from inventories to receivables will come directly from the computer in an assortment of charts and tables that will make comparisons easy and lend instant perspective.
>
> "Starting this week Ylvisaker will be able to tap three-digit codes into a 12-button box resembling the keyboard of a telephone. SEX will get him sales figures. GIN will call up a balance sheet. MUD is the keyword for inventory.
>
> "About 75 such categories will be available, and the details will be displayed for the company as a whole, for divisions, for product lines, and for other breakdowns, which will also be specified by simple digital codes."[4]

At Gould, this information is displayed on a large screen in the boardroom, and is also available at computer terminals. The data are available in full, by exception, and graphically if desired.

---

[4] "Corporate 'War Rooms' Plug into the Computer," *Business Week*, August 23, 1976, p. 65.

As in most similar key indicator systems I have seen, the emphasis at Gould is on financial data. Daniel T. Carroll, reporting on Gould's system in mid-1976, described the system's "core report."[5] The report, available for each of Gould's 37 divisions, provides data on more than 40 operating factors. For each factor, current data are compared with budget and prior year figures on a monthly and year-to-date basis. The report, as noted by Carroll, is ever changing, but its orientation toward "profit and loss" and "balance sheet" data, as well as ratios drawn from these financial data, is evident.

Total Study Process

In this fourth approach to information needs, a widespread sample of managers are queried about their total information needs, and the results are compared with the existing information systems. The subsystems necessary to provide the information currently unavailable are identified and assigned priorities. This approach, clearly, is a reaction to two decades of data processing during which single systems have been developed for particular uses in relative isolation from each other and with little attention to management information needs. In effect, this approach was developed by IBM and others to counter the by-product method previously noted.

The most widely used formal procedure to accomplish the total study is IBM's Business Systems Planning (BSP) methodology. BSP is aimed at a top-down analysis of the information needs of an organization. In a two-phase approach, many managers are interviewed (usually from 40 to 100) to determine their environment, objectives, key decisions, and information needs. Several IBM suggested network design methods and matrix notations are used to present the results in an easily visualized manner.

The objectives of the process are to develop an overall understanding of the business, the information necessary to manage the business, and the existing information systems. Gaps between information systems that are needed and those currently in place are noted. A plan for implementing new systems to fill the observed gaps is then developed.

This total understanding process is expensive in terms of manpower and all-inclusive in terms of scope. The amount of data and opinions gathered is staggering. Analysis of all this input is a high art form. It is difficult, at best, to determine the correct level of aggregation of decision making, data gathering, and analysis at which to work.

Yet the top-down process tends to be highly useful in most cases. The exact focus of the results, however, can be biased either toward top management information and functional management information or to-

---

[5]Daniel T. Carroll, "How the President Satisfies His Information Systems Requirements," published in *Society for Management Information Systems Proceedings*, 1976.

ward paperwork processing, depending on the bias of the study team. I have not seen a BSP study that gives priority to top executive information in the study's output. The design, cleaning up, and extension of the paper-processing information network is too often the focus of the study team. Each of the four current procedures just discussed has its advantages and disadvantages. The by-product technique focuses on getting paperwork processed inexpensively, but it is far less useful with regard to managerial information. It too often results in a manager's considering data from a single paperwork function (e.g., payroll) in isolation from other meaningful data (e.g., factory output versus payroll dollars).

The null approach, with its emphasis on the changeability, diversity, and soft environmental information needs of a top executive, has probably saved many organizations from building useless information systems. It, however, places too much stress on the executive's strategic and person-to-person roles. It overlooks the management control role of the chief executive, which can be, at least partially, served by means of routine, often computer-based, reporting.[6]

The key indicator system provides a significant amount of useful information. By itself, however, this method often results in many undifferentiated financial variables being presented to a management team. It tends to be financially all-inclusive rather than on-target to a particular executive's specific needs. The information provided is objective, quantifiable, and computer stored. Thus in the key indicator approach the perspective of the information needs of the executive is a partial one—oriented toward hard data needs alone. More significantly, in its "cafeteria" approach to presenting an extensive information base, it fails to provide assistance to executives in thinking through their real information needs.

The total study process is comprehensive and can pinpoint missing systems. However, it suffers, as noted, from all of the problems of total approaches. There are problems concerning expense, the huge amount of data collected (making it difficult to differentiate the forest from the trees), designer bias and difficulty in devising reporting systems that serve any individual manager well.

NEW CSF METHOD

The MIT research team's experience in the past two years with the critical success factors (CSF) approach suggests that it is highly effective in

---

[6]Management control is the process of (a) long-range planning of the activities of the organization, (b) short-term planning (usually one year), and (c) monitoring activities to ensure the accomplishment of the desired results. The management control process thus follows the development of major strategic directions that are set in the strategic planning process. This definition roughly follows the framework of Robert N. Anthony, *Planning and Control: A Framework for Analysis* (Boston: Division of Research, Harvard Business School, 1965).

helping executives to define their significant information needs. Equally important, it has proved efficient in terms of the interview time needed (from three to six hours) to explain the method and to focus attention on information needs. Most important, executive response to this new method has been excellent in terms of both the process and its outcome.

The actual CSF interviews are usually conducted in two or three separate sessions. In the first, the executive's goals are initially recorded and the CSFs that underlie the goals are discussed. The interrelationships of the CSFs and the goals are then talked about for further clarification and for determination of which recorded CSFs should be combined, eliminated, or restated. An initial cut at measures is also taken in this first interview.

The second session is used to review the results of the first, after the analyst has had a chance to think about them and to suggest "sharpening up" some factors. In addition, measures and possible reports are discussed in depth. Sometimes, a third session may be necessary to obtain final agreement on the CSF measures-and-reporting sequence.

Conceptual Antecedents

In an attempt to overcome some of the shortcomings of the four major approaches discussed earlier, the CSF method focuses on *individual managers* and on each manager's *current information needs*—both hard and soft. It provides for identifying managerial information needs in a clear and meaningful way. Moreover, it takes into consideration the fact that information needs will vary from manager to manager and that these needs will change with time for a particular manager.

The approach is based on the concept of the "success factors" first discussed in the management literature in 1961 by D. Ronald Daniel, now managing director of McKinsey & Company.[7] Although a powerful concept in itself for other than information systems' thinking, it has been heavily obscured in the outpouring of managerial wisdom in the past two decades. It has been focused on and clarified to the best of my knowledge only in the published work of Robert N. Anthony, John Dearden, and Richard F. Vancil.[8]

Daniel, in introducing the concept, cited three examples of major corporations whose information systems produced an extensive amount of information. Very little of the information, however, appeared useful in assisting managers to better perform their jobs.

To draw attention to the type of information actually needed to support managerial activities, Daniel turned to the concept of critical success factors. He stated,

---

[7]See D. Ronald Daniel, "Management Information Crisis," *Harvard Business Review*, September-October 1961, p. 111.

[8]See Robert N. Anthony, John Dearden, and Richard F. Vancil, "Key Economic Variables," in *Management Control Systems* (Homewood, Ill.: Irwin, 1972), p. 147.

". . . a company's information system must be discriminating and selective. It should focus on 'success factors.' In most industries there are usually three to six factors that determine success; these key jobs must be done exceedingly well for a company to be successful. Here are some examples from several major industries:

- In the automobile industry, styling, an efficient dealer organization, and tight control of manufacturing cost are paramount.

- In food processing, new product development, good distribution, and effective advertising are the major success factors.

- In life insurance, the development of agency management personnel, effective control of clerical personnel, and innovation in creating new types of policies spell the difference."[9]

Critical success factors thus are, for any business, the limited number of areas in which results, if they are satisfactory, will ensure successful competitive performance for the organization. They are the few key areas where "things must go right" for the business to flourish. If results in these areas are not adequate, the organization's efforts for the period will be less than desired.

As a result, the critical success factors are areas of activity that should receive constant and careful attention from management. The current status of performance in each area should be continually measured, and that information should be made available.

As Exhibit 1 notes, critical success factors support the attainment of organizational goals. Goals represent the end points that an organization hopes to reach. Critical success factors, however, are the areas in which good performance is necessary to ensure attainment of those goals.

Daniel focused on those critical success factors that are relevant for any company in a particular industry. Exhibit 1 updates Daniel's automobile industry CSFs and provides another set of CSFs—from the supermarket industry and a nonprofit hospital.

As this exhibit shows, supermarkets have four industry-based CSFs. These are having the right product mix available in each local store, having it on the shelves, having it advertised effectively to pull shoppers into the store, and having it priced correctly—since profit margins are low in this industry. Supermarkets must pay attention to many other things, but these four areas are the underpinnings of successful operation.

Writing a decade later, Anthony and his colleagues picked up Daniel's seminal contribution and expanded it in their work on the design of management control systems. They emphasized three "musts" of any such system:

"The control system *must* be tailored to the specific industry in which

---

[9]Daniel, "Management Information Crisis," p. 116.

the company operates and to the specific strategies that it has adopted; it *must* identify the 'critical success factors' that should receive careful and continuous management attention if the company is to be successful; and it *must* highlight performance with respect to these key variables in reports to all levels of management."[10]

EXHIBIT 1
How Attainment of Organizational Goals Is Supported by CSFs

Example	Goals	Critical Success Factors
For-profit concern	Earnings per share Return on investment Market share New product success	Automotive industry: Styling Quality dealer system Cost control Meeting energy standards
		Supermarket industry: Product mix Inventory Sales promotion Price
Nonprofit concern	Excellence of health care Meeting needs of future health care environment	Government hospital: Regional integration of health care with other hospitals Efficient use of scarce medical resources Improved cost accounting

While continuing to recognize industry-based CSFs, Anthony et al. thus went a step further. They placed additional emphasis on the need to tailor management planning and control systems to both a company's particular strategic objectives and its particular managers. That is, the control system must report on those success factors that are perceived by the managers as appropriate to a particular job in a particular company. In short, CSFs differ from company to company and from manager to manager.

Prime Sources of CSFs

In the discussion so far, we have seen that CSFs are applicable to any company operating in a particular *industry*. Yet Anthony et al. emphasized that a management control system also must be tailored to a particular *company*. This must suggest that there are other sources of CSFs than the industry alone. And, indeed, there are. The MIT team has isolated four prime sources of critical success factors:

---

[10]Anthony, Dearden, and Vancil, "Key Economic Variables," p. 148.

1. *Structure of the Particular Industry.*   As noted, each industry by its very nature has a set of critical success factors that are determined by the characteristics of the industry itself. Each company in the industry must pay attention to these factors. For example, the manager of *any* supermarket will ignore at his peril the critical success factors that appear in Exhibit 1.

2. *Competitive Strategy, Industry Position, and Geographic Location.* Each company in an industry is in an individual situation determined by its history and current competitive strategy. For smaller organizations within an industry dominated by one or two large companies, the actions of the major companies will often produce new and significant problems for the smaller companies. The competitive strategy for the latter may mean establishing a new market niche, getting out of a product line completely, or merely redistributing resources among various product lines.

    Thus for small companies a competitor's strategy is often a CSF. For example, IBM's competitive approach to the marketing of small, inexpensive computers is, in itself, a CSF for all minicomputer manufacturers.

    Just as differences in industry position can dictate CSFs, differences in geographic location and in strategies can lead to differing CSFs from one company to another in an industry.

3. *Environmental Factors.*   As the gross national product and the economy fluctuate, as political factors change, and as the population waxes and wanes, critical success factors can also change for various institutions. At the beginning of 1973, virtually no chief executive in the United States would have listed "energy supply availability" as a critical success factor. Following the oil embargo, however, for a considerable period of time this factor was monitored closely by many executives—since adequate energy was problematical and vital to organizational bottom-line performance.

4. *Temporal Factors.*   Internal organizational considerations often lead to temporal critical success factors. These are areas of activity that are significant for the success of an organization for a particular period of time because they are below the threshold of acceptability at that time (although in general they are "in good shape" and do not merit special attention). As an example, for any organization the loss of a major group of executives in a plane crash obviously would make the "rebuilding of the executive group" a critical success factor for the organization for the period of time until this was accomplished. Similarly, while inventory control is rarely a CSF for the chief executive officer, a very unusual situation (either far too much or far too little stock) might, in fact, become a high-level CSF.

Like Organizations, Differing CSFs

Any organization's situation will change from time to time, and factors that are dealt with by executives as commonplace at one time may become critical success factors at another time. The key here is for the executive to clearly define at any point in time exactly those factors that are crucial to the success of his particular organization in the period for which he is planning.

One would expect, therefore, that organizations in the same industry would exhibit different CSFs as a result of differences in geographic location, strategies, and other factors. A study by Gladys G. Mooradian of the critical success factors of three similar medical group practices bears this out.[11] The medical group practices of the participating physicians were heterogeneous with regard to many of these factors. Each group, however, was well managed with a dynamic and successful administrator in charge.

Mooradian defined the CSFs through open-ended interviews with the administrator of each group practice. She then asked the managers to define their critical success factors and to rank them from most important to least important. Finally, to verify the factors selected, she obtained the opinions of others in the organization.

EXHIBIT 2
Critical Success Factors for Three Medical Group Practices

	Clinic 1	Clinic 2	Clinic 3
Most important	Government regulation	Quality and comprehensive care	Efficiency of operations
	Efficiency of operations	Federal funding	Staffing mix
	Patients' view of practice	Government regulation	Government regulation
	Relation to hospital	Efficiency of operations	Patients' view of practice
	Malpractice insurance effects	Patients' view of practice	Relation to community
	Relation to community	Satellites versus patient service	Relation to hospital
		Other providers in community	
Least important		Relation to hospital	

Exhibit 2 shows the administrators' key variables for the three group practices, ranked in order as perceived by the managers of each institution.

---

[11]Gladys G. Mooradian, "The Key Variables in Planning and Control in Medical Group Practices," unpublished master's thesis (Cambridge, Mass.: MIT, Sloan School of Management, 1976).

It is interesting to note that several of the same variables appear on each list. Several variables, however, are unique to each institution. One can explain the difference in the CSFs chosen by noting the stages of growth, location, and strategies of each clinic:

- The first medical group is a mature clinic that has been in existence for several years, has a sound organization structure, and has an assured patient population. It is most heavily concerned with government regulation and environmental changes (such as rapidly increasing costs for malpractice insurance), which are the only factors that might upset its highly favorable status quo.

- The second group practice is located in a rural part of a relatively poor state. It is dependent on federal funding and also on its ability to offer a type of medical care not available from private practitioners. Its number one CSF, therefore, is its ability to develop a distinctive competitive image for the delivery of comprehensive, quality care.

- The third clinic is a rapidly growing, new group practice, which was—at that point in time—heavily dependent for its near-term success on its ability to "set up" an efficient operation and bring on board the correct mix of staff to serve its rapidly growing patient population.

In looking at these three lists, it is noticeable that the first four factors on the mature clinic's list also appear on the other two lists. These, it can be suggested, are the all-encompassing industry-based factors. The remaining considerations, which are particular to one or the other of the practices but not to all, are generated by differences in environmental situation, temporal factors, geographic location, or strategic situation.

CSFs at General Manager Level

To this point, I have discussed CSFs strictly from the viewpoint of the top executive of an organization. Indeed, that is the major focus of the MIT research team's current work. It is, however, clear from studies now going on that CSFs, as might be expected, can be useful at each level of general management (managers to whom multiple functions report). There are significant benefits of taking the necessary time to think through—and to record—the critical success factors for each general manager in an organization. Consider:

- The process helps the manager to determine those factors on which he or she should focus management attention. It also helps to ensure that those significant factors will receive careful and continuous management scrutiny.

- The process forces the manager to develop good measures for those factors and to seek reports on each of the measures.

- The identification of CSFs allows a clear definition of the amount of information that must be collected by the organization and limits the costly collection of more data than necessary.

- The identification of CSFs moves an organization away from the trap of building its reporting and information system primarily around data that are "easy to collect." Rather, it focuses attention on those data that might otherwise not be collected but are significant for the success of the particular management level involved.

- The process acknowledges that some factors are temporal and that CSFs are manager specific. This suggests that the information system should be in constant flux with new reports being developed as needed to accommodate changes in the organization's strategy, environment, or organization structure. Rather than changes in an information system being looked on as an indication of "inadequate design," they must be viewed as an inevitable and productive part of information systems development.

- The CSF concept itself is useful for more than information systems design. Current studies suggest several additional areas of assistance to the management process. For example, an area that can be improved through the use of CSFs is the planning process. CSFs can be arrayed hierarchically and used as an important vehicle of communication for management, either as an informal planning aid or as a part of the formal planning process.

Let me stress that the CSF approach does not attempt to deal with information needs for strategic planning. Data needs for this management role are almost impossible to preplan. The CSF method centers, rather, on information needs for management control where data needed to monitor and improve existing areas of business can be more readily defined.

Illustrative CSF Example

Let us now turn to an example of the use of this approach. The president referred to at the start of this article is real. He is Larry Gould, former president of Microwave Associates, a $60-million sales organization serving several aspects of the microwave communication industry.[12] When he first looked carefully at the "information" he was receiving, Gould found that some 97 "reports" crossed his desk in a typical month. Almost all were originally designed by someone else who felt that he "should be receiving this vital data."

---

[12]Since this was originally written, Gould has assumed the position of chairman of the board of M/A-COM, Inc., a holding company of which Microwave Associates is a subsidiary.

However, the reports provided him with virtually nothing *he* could use. A few gave him some "score-keeping data," such as the monthly profit statement. One or two others provided him with bits and pieces of data he wanted, but even these left major things unsaid. The data were either unrelated to other key facts or related in a way that was not meaningful to him.

The concept of critical success factors sounded to him like one way out of this dilemma. He therefore, with the MIT research analyst, invested two two-and-a-half-hour periods in working through his goals, critical success factors, and measures. First, he noted the objectives of the company and the current year's goals. Then, he went to work to assess what factors were critical to accomplish these objectives.

Factors & Measures

The seven critical success factors Gould developed are shown in Exhibit 3, along with from one to three prime measures for each factor (although he also developed some additional measures). The reader should note that this specific set of CSFs emerged only after intensive analysis and discussion. At the end of the first meeting, nine factors were on Gould's list. By the end of the second meeting, two had been combined into one, and one had been dropped as not being significant enough to command ongoing close attention.

Most of the second interview session centered on a discussion of the measures for each factor. Where hard data were perceived to be available, the discussion was short. Where softer measures were necessary, however, lengthy discussions of the type of information needed and the difficulty and/or cost of acquiring it often ensued. Yet convergence on the required "evidence" about the state of each CSF occurred with responsible speed and clarity in each case. Some discussion concerning each CSF and its measures is perhaps worthwhile. Consider:

1. *Image in Financial Markets.*   Microwave Associates is growing and making acquisitions as it seeks to gain a growth segment of the electronics industry. Much of the company's growth is coming from acquisitions. Clearly, the better the image on Wall Street, the higher the price-earnings ratio. The measure of success here is clear: the company's multiple vis-a-vis others in its industry segment.

2. *Technological Reputation with Customers.*   Although Microwave Associates has some standard products, the majority of its work is done on a tailor-made, one-shot basis. A significant number of these jobs are state-of-the-art work that leads to follow-on production contracts. To a

very large extent, buying decisions in the field are made on the customer's confidence in Microwave's technical ability. Sample measures were developed for this CSF. The two measures shown in this exhibit are at the opposite extremes of hard and soft data. The ratio of total orders to total bids can be easily measured. While this hard measure is indicative of customers' perception of the company's technical ability, it also has other factors such as "sales aggressiveness" in it.

The most direct measure possible is person-to-person interviews. Although this measure is soft, the company decided to initiate a measuring process through field interviews by its top executives. (Other measures of this CSF included field interviews by sales personnel, assessment of the rise or fall of the percentage of each major customer's business being obtained, and so forth.)

3. *Market Success.*   On the surface, this CSF is straightforward. But, as shown by the measures, it includes attention to *current* market success, as well as the company's progress with regard to significant *new* market opportunities (e.g., the relative rate of growth of each market segment, opportunities provided by new technology, and relative—not just absolute—competitive performance).

EXHIBIT 3
CSFs Developed to Meet Microwave Associates' Organizational Goals

Critical Success Factors	Prime Measures
1. Image in financial markets	Price/earnings ratio
2. Technological reputation with customers	Orders/bid ratio Customer perception interview results
3. Market success	Change in market share (each product) Growth rates of company markets
4. Risk recognition in major bids and contracts	Company's years of experience with similar products "New" or "old" customer Prior customer relationship
5. Profit margin on jobs	Bid profit margin as ratio of profit on similar jobs in this product line
6. Company morale	Turnover, absenteeism, etc. Informal feedback
7. Performance to budget on major jobs	Job cost budget/actual

4. *Risk Recognition in Major Bids and Contracts.*   Because many of the jobs accepted are near or at the state of the art, controlling the company's risk profile is critical. As noted in the exhibit, a variety of factors contribute to risk. The measurement process designed involves computer algorithm to consider these factors and to highlight particularly risky situations.

5. *Profit Margin on Jobs.* When profit center managers have low backlogs, they are often tempted to bid low to obtain additional business. While this procedure is not necessarily bad, it is critical for corporate management to understand the expected profit profile and, at times, to counter lower-level tendencies to accept low-profit business.

6. *Company Morale.* Because of its high-technology strategy, the company is clearly heavily dependent on the esprit of its key scientists and engineers. It must also be able to attract and keep a skilled work force. Thus morale is a critical success factor. Measures of morale range from hard data (e.g., turnover, absenteeism, and tardiness) to informal feedback (e.g., management discussion sessions with employees).

7. *Performance to Budget on Major Jobs.* This final CSF reflects the need to control major projects and to ensure that they are completed on time and near budget. Adverse results with regard to timeliness can severely affect CSF #2 (technological perception), and significant cost overruns can similarly affect CSF #1 (financial market perception). In general, no single job is crucially important. Rather, it is the *profile* of performance across major jobs that is significant.

Reports & Subsystems

Given the foregoing CSFs and measures, the next step was to design a set of report formats. This step required examination of both existing information systems and data sources.

For the soft, informal, subjective measures, this process was straightforward. Forms to record facts and impressions were designed so as to scale (where possible) perception and highlight significant soft factors.

For some of the hard computer-based measures, existing information systems and data bases supplied most of the necessary data. However, in every case—even where *all* data were available—existing report forms were inadequate and new reports had to be designed.

Most important, however, two completely new information subsystems were needed to support the president's CSFs. These were a "bidding" system and a vastly different automated "project budgeting and control" system. (Significantly, each of these subsystems had been requested many times by lower-level personnel, who needed them for more detailed planning and control of job bidding and monitoring at the product-line manager and manufacturing levels). Subsequently, these subsystems were placed at the top of the priority list for data processing.

In summarizing the Microwave case, it is clear that the exercise of discovering information needs through examination of the chief executive's critical success factors had a number of specific benefits. All of the seven general advantages of the CSF method for information systems development previously noted applied to some extent. However, the importance of each of these varies from organization to organization. At Microwave, the most striking advantages were:

- The conscious listing (or bringing to the surface) of the most significant areas on which attention needed to be focused. The process of making these areas *explicit* provided insights not only into information needs, but also into several other aspects of the company's managerial systems.

- The design of a useful set of *reports* to provide the information needed for monitoring ongoing operations at the executive level. (There clearly were other data needed—i.e., for developing strategy, dealing with special situations, and so on.) The CSF route, however, focused on the data needed for the ongoing "management control" process, and this need was significant at Microwave.

- The development of *priorities* for information systems development. It was clear that information needed for control purposes by the chief executive should have some priority. (It also highlighted priorities for other management levels.)

- The provision of a means of hierarchical *communication* among executives as to what the critical factors were for the success of the company. (Too often, only goals provide a major communication link to enhance shared understanding of the company and its environment among management levels.) This hierarchical approach provided another—and we believe more pragmatic and action-oriented—means of communication. At Microwave, there is a current project aimed at developing and sharing CSFs at the top four management levels.

Other Case Examples

The critical success factors developed in four other cases provide useful additional background for drawing some generalizations about the method and executive information needs. These CSFs are arrayed in Exhibit 4.

Major Oil Company

The chief executive of this centralized organization responded quickly and unhesitatingly concerning his critical success factors. His goal structure was oriented toward such traditional measures as increasing return on investment, increasing earnings per share, and so forth. Yet he felt there were two major keys to profitability in the future. One was to improve relationships with society as a whole and with the federal government in particular. The other was the urgent need to provide a broader base of earnings assets in petroleum-shy future decades.

As a result of this view of the world, the CEO had initiated major

EXHIBIT 4
CSFs in Four Cases

Chief Executive of a Major Oil Company	President of a Store Furnishings Manufacturer	Director of a Government Hospital	Division Chief Executive of an Electronics Company
1. Decentralize organization.	1. Expand foreign sales for product lines B and C.	1. Devise method for obtaining valid data on current status of hospital operations.	1. Support field sales force.
2. Improve liquidity position.	2. Improve market understanding of product line A.	2. Devise method for resource allocation.	2. Strengthen customer relations.
3. Improve government/business relationships.	3. Redesign sales compensation structure in three-product lines.	3. Manage external relationships.	3. Improve productivity.
4. Create better social image.	4. Improve production scheduling.	4. Get acceptance of concept of regionalization by all hospitals.	4. Obtain government R&D support.
5. Devlopes new ventures.	5. Mechanize production facilities.	5. Develop method for managing regionalization in government.	5. Develop new products.
	6. Strengthen management team.	6. Strengthen management support, capability, and capacity.	6. Acquire new technological capability
		7. Improve relationship with government department central office.	7. Improve facilities
		8. Meet budgetary constraints.	

programs to develop new ventures and to decentralize the organization. To facilitate the acquisition process, emphasis was placed on cash flow (liquidity) as opposed to reported earnings. In addition, prime attention was given to understanding and improving external relationships.

All of these efforts are reflected in the company's critical success factors shown in Exhibit 4. Progress in each of these areas is monitored weekly. CSFs #1, #3, and #4 are reported on with regard to both actions taken and the appropriate executive's subjective assessment of results attained. Liquidity measures are provided by computer output. New venture success is now assessed by a combination of hard and soft measures.

Store Furnishings Manufacturer

This midwestern company has three major product lines. The largest of these is a well-accepted but relatively stable traditional line on which the company's reputation was made (product line A). In addition, there are two relatively new but fast-growing lines (B and C). The president's preexisting information system was a combination of monthly financial accounting reports and several sales analysis reports.

The president's critical success factors directly reflected the changing fortunes of his product lines. There was a need to concentrate on immediate foreign penetration (to build market share) in the two "hot" lines. At the same time, he saw the need to reassess the now barely growing line on which the company was built three decades ago.

Equally significant, whereas direct selling had been the only feasible mode for the traditional line, the new lines appeared to respond heavily to trade advertising to generate both leads and, in some cases, direct-from-the-factory sales. Because margins are relatively tight in this competitive industry, one factor critical to the company's success with this new product structure, therefore, was a redesign of the sales compensation structure to reflect the evidently diminished effort needed to make sales in the new lines.

A similar need for cost-consciousness also dictated attention to the CSFs of production scheduling efficiency and productivity improvements through the increasing mechanization of production facilities. Finally, strengthening the management team to take advantage of the opportunities presented by the new product lines was felt to be critical by this president.

The analysis of CSFs in this case indicated a need for two major changes in formal information flow to the present. Subsequently, a far more meaningful production reporting system was developed (to support CSF #4), and a vastly different sales reporting system emphasizing CSFs #2 and #3 was established.

Government Hospital

The CSFs for the director of a government hospital reflect his belief in the need for his organization to radically restructure itself to adapt to a future health care environment perceived as vastly different. He believes that his hospital and his sister government agency hospitals must provide specialized, cost-conscious, comprehensive health care for a carefully defined patient population. Moreover, this care will have to be integrated with that provided by other government hospitals and private hospitals within the region of the country in which his hospital exists.

The director's critical success factors are thus, as shown in Exhibit 4, concerned primarily with building external links and managing cooperation and resource sharing within the set of eight government agency hospitals in his region. The director is also concerned with the development of adequate data systems and methods to manage effective and efficient use of scarce medical resources.

The organization currently has only minimal management information—drawn in bits and pieces from what is essentially a financial accounting system designed primarily to assure the safeguarding and legal use of government funds. The director's desire to get involved in a CSF-oriented investigation of management information needs grew from his despair of being able to manage in the future environment with existing information.

The MIT research team is currently conducting a study involving CSF-based interviews with the top three levels of key managers and department heads in the hospital. Their information needs are heavily oriented toward external data and vastly improved cost accounting.

Major Electronics Division

This decentralized electronics company places return-on-investment responsibility on the top executive of a major division. His first two CSFs indicate his view of the need for an increasing emphasis on marketing in his traditionally engineering-oriented organization. As Exhibit 4 shows, his CSFs #3, #6, and #7 are oriented toward the need for more cost-effective production facilities.

Equally important is his attention to new product development (CSF #5) in a fast-moving marketplace. In conjunction with this, CSF #4 reflects his view that a healthy portfolio of government R&D contracts will allow a much larger amount of research to be performed, thereby increasing the expected yield of new ideas and new products. Thus he spends a significant share of his time involved in the process of assuring that government research contracts are being avidly pursued (although they add relatively little to his near-term bottom line).

Efforts to improve the information provided to this division manager have revolved primarily around making more explicit the methods of measuring progress in each of these CSF areas. More quantitative indexes have proved to be useful in some areas. In others, however, they have not improved what must be essentially "subjective feel" judgments.

SUPPORTIVE CSF INFORMATION

Previously, I discussed the advantages (both general and specific to one case) of using the CSF process for information systems design. Additionally, some important attributes of the types of information necessary to support the top executive's CSFs can be drawn from the five examples. Consider:

- Perhaps most obvious, but worth stating, is the fact that traditional financial accounting systems rarely provide the type of data necessary to monitor critical success factors. Financial accounting systems are aimed at providing historical information to outsiders (e.g., stockholders and others). Only very occasionally is there much overlap between financial accounting data and the type of data needed to track CSFs. In only one of the companies studied was financial accounting data the major source of information for a CSF, and then for only one factor. However, the need for improved cost accounting data to report on CSFs was often evident.

- Many critical success factors require information external to the organization—information concerned with market structure, customer perceptions, or future trends. Approximately a third of the 33 CSFs in the five examples fit this description. The data to support these CSFs are not only unavailable from the financial accounting system but, in the majority of cases, are also unavailable as a by-product of the organization's other usual day-to-day transaction-processing systems (e.g., order entry, billing, and payroll). The information system must therefore be designed, and the external information consciously collected from the proper sources. It will not flow naturally to the CEO.

- Many other CSFs require coordinating pieces of information from multiple data sets that are widely dispersed throughout the company. This is perhaps best noted in the Microwave case, but it is a recurrent feature in all companies. This situation argues heavily for computer implementation of data base systems that facilitate assessing multiple data sets.

- A small but significant part of the information concerning the status of CSFs requires subjective assessment on the part of others in the organization, rather than being neatly quantifiable. About a fifth of the status measures at the companies studied require subjective assessment. This is significant managerial data, and top executives are used to these soft but useful status measures.

(However, it should be noted, many more of the measures at first devised were subjective. It takes considerable work to find objective measures, but in more instances than originally perceived, suitable objective measures are available and can be developed.)

- Critical success factors can be categorized as either the "monitoring" or the "building" type. The more competitive pressure for current performance that the chief executive feels, the more his CSFs tend toward monitoring current results. The more that the organization is insulated from economic pressures (as the government hospital was) or decentralized (as the oil company was becoming), the more CSFs become oriented toward building for the future through major change programs aimed at adapting the organization to a perceived new environment.

In all cases that I have seen thus far, however, there is a mixture of the two types. Every chief executive appears to have, at some level, both monitoring and building (or adapting) responsibilities. Thus a great deal of the information needed will not continue to be desired year after year. Rather, it is relatively short-term "project status" information that is needed only during the project's lifetime. Periodic review of CSFs will therefore bring to light the need to discontinue some reports and initiate others.

READING

Headquarters Influence and Strategic Control in MNCs*

YVES L. DOZ AND C. K. PRAHALAD

Yves L. Doz is associate professor of business policy at INSEAD in Paris, France. C. K. Prahalad is associate professor of policy and control in the Graduate School of Business Administration at The University of Michigan

Competing successfully in global industries often requires global strategies. To implement a global strategy, it may be necessary for the headquarters to influence the direction of subsidiary strategy.[1] In some cases, subsidiary dependence on headquarters for key human, financial, technological, and managerial resources may provide headquarters with the needed leverage to exercise considerable influence. Often, however, a tradition of subsidiary self-sufficiency and autonomy limits drastically the influence of headquarters. In such circumstances, when the MNC has become *fragmented* into separate subsidiaries, rebuilding headquarters influence becomes much more difficult. Short of substantive dependence, headquarters can gain influence over time through the development of an *organizational context*.

In this second article, we analyze how a series of administrative mechanisms can be used by headquarters to gain control over subsidiary operations and to influence their strategies over time. We first review the mechanisms and discuss the considerations involved when using these mechanisms. The second section of this article presents a simple model of how selected mechanisms can be used in sequence to establish headquarters control. We then present examples of companies we studied in detail to illustrate, analyze, and contrast instances of successful establishment of headquarters control with unsuccessful attempts.

Mechanisms for Headquarters Control

In our first article, we argued that an organization can be considered the sum of four orientations—cognitive, strategic, power, and administrative—all of which are interrelated. Effective headquarters influence in shaping a global competitive strategy requires not only changes in cognitive and strategic orientations but also shifts in the thrust of resource

*This article is reprinted from the *Sloan Management Review*, vol. 23, no. 1 (Fall 1981), pp. 15-29. Copyright © 1981 by the Sloan Management Review Association. All rights reserved.

[1]L. G. Franko, *The European Multinationals* (London: Harper & Row, 1976); P. J. Buckley and R. I. Pearce, "Overseas Production and Exporting by the World's Largest Enterprises—A Study in Sourcing Policy," *International Investment*, September 1977; N. Owen, "Scale Economies in the EEC: An Approach Based on Int·a EEC Trade," *European Economic Review*, February 1976, pp. 143-63.

allocation choices. This, in turn, requires changes in power within the organization. Effective implementation of the new programs implied by changed resource allocation choices usually requires changes in administrative control mechanisms. In other words, all four orientations have to change if headquarters control is to be effective.

Administrative mechanisms can influence all four orientations. For instance, in the changes we analyzed, these mechanisms over time could shift the context of subsidiary decisions from an exclusive concern with national priorities to an active search for integrated global strategies. Such shifts can be obtained by affecting the information available to managers, their perceptions of criteria for success, and the way conflicts are resolved between subunits of the organization. Although the mechanisms used may vary from company to company, a typical list of mechanisms used by headquarters to gain influence is provided in Table 1.

Three Types of Mechanisms

The following mechanisms help to accomplish the prerequisites in the acquisition of headquarters control: (1) *data management mechanisms* structure and provide data that are pertinent to the global performance of the company; (2) *managers' management mechanisms* shift the expectations of managers and their perceptions of self-interest from subsidiary autonomy to international business performance; (3) *conflict resolution mechanisms* resolve the conflicts triggered by the necessary tradeoffs among national subsidiaries, which must be made since effective global strategies usually mean that some subsidiaries are likely to benefit more than others.

General Characteristics of Mechanisms

In choosing the mix of mechanisms to be used and the ordering and timing of their introduction, top managers must consider the characteristics of these mechanisms.

1.   **Organizational Orientations Affected.**   Not all mechanisms affect all four orientations equally. Key management appointment affects primarily the power orientation. Therefore, appointing individuals who are more enterprising, stronger-willed, or more skillful at eliciting personal loyalties and commitments and at building a power base as worldwide business managers is likely to move the organization toward increased headquarters influence over subsidiary strategy. At the same time, managers should pick as subsidiary managers those who are likely to exhibit more administrative and less entrepreneurial personal traits. Such asymmetry in personality traits usually results in asymmetry in power; whereas, two entrepreneurial personalities pitched one against the other would probably clash in a sterile power struggle, and they would be unable to develop

TABLE 1
A Typical Repertoire of Administrative Mechanisms to Carry Out a Strategic Shift

I. Data Management Mechanisms	*II. Managers' Management Mechanisms*	*III. Conflict Resolution Mechanisms*
1. Information systems	1. Choice of key managers	1. Decision responsibility assignments
2. Measurement systems	2. Career paths	2. Integrators
3. Resource allocation procedures	3. Reward and punishment systems	3. Business teams
4. Strategic planning	4. Management development	4. Coordination committees
5. Budgeting process	5. Patterns of socialization	5. Task forces
		6. Issue resolution processes

jointly a consistent resource allocation focus or to manage a clear imple-mentation process.

Other mechanisms may affect several orientations more directly (e.g., information systems). By supplying varied information, or information packaged in diverse ways, information systems may affect the cognitive dimension. Information systems also affect the strategic dimension at least insofar as a strategic orientation may look better or worse against one set of data or another. Since selective access to information provides power within an organization, how the information systems shape the information flows also affects the power dimension.

2.   **Strength and Symbolic Value of Mechanisms.**   Mechanisms give signals of various strength and symbolic value to middle managers in the organization. Headquarters' desires to acquire control, evidenced by a stream of administrative and managerial changes, usually lead middle managers to try to read clues in each new mechanism, to assess its strength, and to give it a symbolic interpretation.

The decision to create an intersubsidiary "coordination" committee, for instance, is, in itself, a relatively weak mechanism. What is important is how the committee is used. A skillful top management may vary the use of such a committee almost from meeting to meeting. Such a committee may also be dissolved on short notice without major difficulties.

However, appointing a highly respected senior executive to worldwide product line coordination is a much stronger and a more portentous move because the symbolic value of such a move is considerable; it cannot be reversed easily without top management losing face. Even more significant are shifts in patterns of career paths; they take years to be effectuated and even more to be reverted. The costs of mistakes may be extremely high: wastage of managerial talents, power struggles, resignations, and high emotional and personal costs to the managers involved. Senior executive appointments and explicit "interpreted" shifts in career paths directly affect the perceived power relationships and are extremely strong signals of change. Contrary to a committee appointment, they also signal a clear shift in *direction* (the direction of change is as critical as the *extent* of change).

Other mechanisms, such as strategic planning procedures, may not have the same strength as the mechanisms described, but they may legitimize the use of stronger mechanisms by selectively changing the cognitive orientations or by fostering an awareness of selected strategic opportuni-ties or difficulties while leaving other issues unchanged.

3.   **Selectivity.**   Some mechanisms may have the capacity to deter-mine selectively across a range of decision issues—the balance between subsidiary autonomy and headquarters control. This is important because tensions between economic and political imperatives (discussed in the first article) often find no lasting one-time solution and must be continuously

managed. Some decisions are better left to the subsidiaries, and effective representation of national perspectives ought to be maintained even if headquarters control is established. Headquarters influence must not result in full power given to worldwide business executives to the exclusion of subsidiary managers and regional executives.

Some companies have developed elaborate decision-making grids, in which the respective powers of headquarters and subsidiaries are spelled out according to the type of decision involved.[2] Some other companies use coordinators as filtering agents: L.M. Ericsson is such an example.[3] Career paths, conversely, cannot be very selective; they represent major choices based on broad considerations and do not allow for fine-tuning without giving confusing signals to managers who are sensitive to patterns in promotions.

4.   Continuity.   Some mechanisms may be discarded easily at no cost and on short notice. Discarding others may imply very high personal costs for the involved managers. Obviously, the time horizon of various mechanisms also differs widely. Task forces may be seen as temporary mechanisms leading to quick results. Major change in strategic planning procedures may take years to yield results as do shifts in career patterns.

Some mechanisms may involve high continuity in less visible ways. Views held by individual managers, which support specific resource allocation proposals and discard others, are shaped over a period of time by perceptions of benefits and risks, by the development of careers, and by the building of personal track records. Though the formal approval criteria for projects may be changed easily, as can the format of these proposals, the views that actually kill a proposal or propel it toward corporate approval cannot. Therefore, it is critical for top management to consider carefully the time required for a mechanism to bear results and the delays involved in shifting the focus of a mechanism from subsidiary autonomy to headquarters control.

5.   Need for Top Management's Ongoing Support.   Mechanisms offer no substitute for top management direct involvement and personal leadership. Yet, mechanisms differ in the extent to which they require ongoing top management support. First, direction (the change actually impacted to an orientation) usually depends on top management. The

[2]C. K. Prahalad and Y. L. Doz, "Strategic Control: The Dilemma of Headquarter-Subsidiary Relationships" (paper prepared for the International Research Symposium on Headquarter-Subsidiary Relationships in Transnational Corporations. Stockholm School of Economics, June 2-4, 1980).

[3]This is a critical issue. For many multinational businesses, it is extremely difficult to make a one-time commitment to a strategic direction. Thus, mechanisms that increase the ability of the organization to tradeoff flexibly among conflicting demands on the strategy of a multinational firm are extremely important. An analysis of these aspects is presented in the companion article. See C. K. Prahalad and Y. L. Doz, "An Approach to Strategic Control in MNCs," *Sloan Management Review,* Summer 1981, pp. 5-13; See also, Y. L. Doz, *Multinational Strategic Management: Economic and Political Imperatives* (forthcoming), ch. 11 in particular.

existence of a mechanism merely provides an action channel for headquarters but does not impart a sense of direction. For example, headquarters involvement in promotions within subsidiaries does not imply per se headquarters control, unless headquarters also creates consistent patterns in career paths that sustain a global strategy.

Most other mechanisms need to be set and monitored by top management. Top management monitoring may involve seemingly trivial but such critical tasks as ensuring that committee meeting dates do not exclude systematically certain members or checking that managers actually receive the data specified by information systems. Some mechanisms may require comparatively little top management involvement in their day-to-day operations, but they imply great care in their design and in the initiation of their use.

Specific Characteristics of Mechanisms

Space limitations prevent us from detailing the five characteristics for each typical mechanism—organizational orientations affected; strength of signal and symbolic value; selectivity; continuity; and need for top management's ongoing support. However, a simplified summary comparing the characteristics of selected mechanisms is presented in Table 2. The importance of each characteristic for each mechanism is simply indicated on a low-medium-high scale according to the analysis of the role of the mechanism in the companies we observed in detail.

Appropriate Use of Mechanisms

It is important to note that not all sixteen mechanisms described may be available to top management of any particular company. Some mechanisms may be so critical to corporation unity as to be "taboo"; that is, no single manager has the power to change them. In some cases, a particular mechanism may be a central part of a common corporate ideology or culture dating back to the company's founders. In other cases, a mechanism may be the outcome of prior power conflicts or bargains among senior managers, and thus it represents the cornerstone of internal stability. Changing this mechanism would reopen old wounds, revive internecine conflicts, and break a power equilibrium.

Concretely, this leads to recognition of the historical diversity of corporations: a mechanism that works very well in one organization may not work at all in another, or else it may trigger negative unintended consequences. The repertoire of means available to a manager in a particular situation is thus only a subset of the mechanisms identified here.

The challenge for top management, beyond the skillful use of each mechanism, is to decide when to use which mechanism and in what

TABLE 2
Major Attributes of Selected Control Mechanisms

Mechanisms	Organizational Orientations Affected	Strength and Symbolic Value of Mechanisms	Selectivity	Continuity	Need for Top Management's Ongoing Support
I. Data Management					
1. Information systems	Cognitive Strategic Power	Variable*	High	Low	Low
2. Measurement systems					
Business performance	Cognitive	Medium	Medium	Medium	Low
Managers' performance	Power	High	Medium	Medium	Low
3. Resource allocation procedures					
Content	Strategic	Low	High	Low	Low
Impetus	Power	High	High	High	Medium
Approval	Administrative	High	High	Low	High
4. Strategic planning	Strategic	Variable*	Low	High	Medium
5. Budgeting process	Administrative	High	Low	Low	Low
II. Managers' Management					
1. Choice of key managers	Power	Strong	Low	High	Medium
2. Career paths	Power	Strong	Low	High	High
3. Reward and punishment systems	Power	Strong	Low	Medium	High

4. Management development	Strategic Cognitive	Variable*	High	Medium	Medium
III. Conflict Resolution					
1. Decision responsibility assignments	Administrative	High	High	Medium	High
2. Integrators	Cognitive	Low	High	Low	High
3. Business teams	Cognitive	Low	Low	Medium	High
4. Cognitive	Low	High	Low	High	
5. Task forces	Strategic	Variable*	High	Low	High
6. Issue resolution processes	Strategic	Variable*	High	Low	High

*Variable means that the strength and symbolic value of the mechanism rest mainly on how the mechanism is set and managed.

sequence. The historical nature of large corporations as social and political systems ensures that there is no universal guide to prescribe the use of mechanisms. Studying successful and unsuccessful attempts by MNC headquarters to gain managerial control over their subsidiaries may, however, lead to some insights and to the formulation of some general propositions.

The Development of Headquarters Control over Subsidiaries

In comparing how top managers in several companies built and used headquarters control mechanisms, our purpose is not simply to describe but also to provide insight into skillful or clumsy use of these mechanisms. These attempted changes fall into three categories: (1) purposive changes that have been carried out; (2) stalled changes; and (3) abortive changes.[4] We will first develop a model of successful change, and then analyze areas in which some companies face major difficulties.

Successful Changes

Successful instances of headquarters gaining control over subsidiary strategies shared some important characteristics. They all started with the appointment of a key executive (who was respected and who enjoyed a high level of legitimacy within the organization) to a new position with a broad charter to improve performance through the coordination of subsidiary activities. The driving logic behind such coordination was usually to decrease costs by avoiding duplications of product development efforts and by producing individual components and products in larger volume, thereby taking advantage of economies of scale and experience. Tough competitive pressures made this approach legitimate.

This appointment was followed by a phase—during which the new executive acted on the cognitive orientation of managers abroad—that led to the explicit consideration of strategic issues from a regional to a global perspective. This was done mostly through the creation of business teams and various types of coordinating or planning committees. In one case (General Motors and its European components business in 1971-73), this was achieved by intensive personal contacts between the new executive and operating managers. These coordination and conflict resolution mechanisms made it legitimate to consider possible strategic changes. The precise explicit consideration of a strategic shift required new data, which, in turn, often triggered changes in the information systems.

---

[4]Two of the companies studied have opted for anonymity and are labeled as Delta and Gamma; the identity of the other companies is undisguised. Reference will be made in the text to detailed descriptions or analyses of these companies (published elsewhere) to which the reader may turn to gain a deeper sense for the process and satisfy himself or herself that our capsule summaries do justice to the detailed data.

At least a year into this process, minor responsibility assignment changes started to be made in favor of headquarters control. At first, these were changes that the subsidiaries could easily agree to, such as central export coordination at Delta or the relocation of GM overseas operations staffs to Detroit.

At Delta, export coordination was useful to establish national production programs and improve plant utilization. At GM, subsidiaries had been complaining that the relatively ineffective "overseas" central staffs were a barrier between them and corporate headquarters or U.S. divisions.[5] Both changes were welcomed by subsidiary managers. These responsibility assignment changes consolidated the position of the new executive. Other apparently minor changes were made, e.g., technology transfer coordination or joint R&D programs between subsidiaries.

Only late in the change process were strong power or authority changes made; that is, changes in resource allocation procedures, shifts in career paths, and significant status changes (e.g., the move of GM's major foreign subsidiaries to full divisional status). The change process can be divided into three broad stages:

Stage I: Variety Generation.   Broad cognitive and strategic variety are developed at this stage and subsidiary managers are closely involved in the process. Strategic questions are raised and explicit consideration of strategic change becomes legitimate. This stage closes with changes to the data management mechanisms. These changes provide for multiple cognitive and strategic orientations and generate precise business or product data across subsidiaries so alternative strategies may be analyzed. Yet, complete strategies are seldom elaborated. Integration strategies are proposed in a functional operation context (manufacturing, for example).

Stage II: Power Shift.   When skillfully managed, this stage consists of a series of relatively minor reallocations of decision and implementation authority. Each reallocation is made legitimate by the cognitive and strategic shifts explored in Stage I (variety generation). Individually, no stage is very portentous, and subsidiary managers are unlikely to make a stand against them. Cumulatively, however, these minor changes increase the power of the new executive. At the end, he or she exercises substantive control on exports, technology transfers, plant specification, capacity utilization, and raw material procurement. The new executive now manages many key dependencies of the national subsidiaries.

Stage III: Refocusing.   By this stage, some of the benefits of headquarters control begin to materialize. The shift has acquired legitimacy and

---

[5]For detailed data on Delta, see C. K. Prahalad, "The Strategic Process in a Diversified Multinational Corporation" (unpublished doctoral dissertation, Harvard University, 1975); for detailed data on General Motors, see Y. L. Doz, "Strategic and Organizational Changes in International Automobile Manufacturers," in *The Incidence of the External Environment on the Global Automotive Industry*, P. Friedenson, ed. (Cambridge, England: Cambridge University Press, forthcoming); see also, Y. L. Doz, *General Motors' Overseas Operations-Europe* (ICCH, forthcoming).

the executive has attained the power to implement major changes. Only at this stage are strong mechanisms used, such as sweeping changes in decision responsibility patterns or visible changes in career paths. Finally, some of the variety introduced in the data management mechanisms early in the change process may be eliminated. These mechanisms may be refocused and narrowed down to areas critical to headquarters control and integration strategies. The process is summarized in Figure 1.

FIGURE 1
A Process of Headquarters Control Development

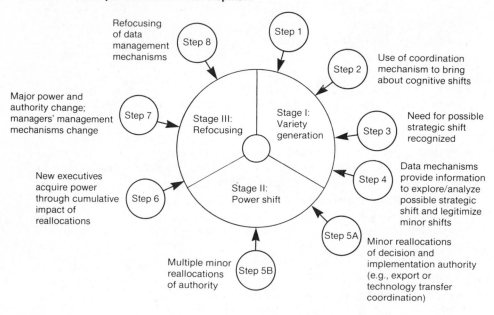

It is important to recognize the time needed by such changes. In the cases we studied, the development and use of conflict resolution mechanisms to bring about a cognitive change and the explicit consideration for strategic changes took about a year. Minor changes in decision responsibility assignments took another year. Managers' management change mechanisms were used only in the third year or later. Shifts took about three years, on average, to be completed.

Why such slow progress? Each mechanism requires some time to become effective: the mere communication of changes, the scheduling of meetings or the use of the mechanism for the first time, and, above all, the maintenance of the mechanisms' credibility to operating managers took much time.

Managers approached change incrementally. Mechanisms were introduced one at a time, and feedback was obtained on their effectiveness before further ones were added or before existing ones were reset. Many mechanisms have a relatively long time horizon, and feedback could be obtained only slowly. Considering these difficulties and the desire to avoid sudden radical reorganizations, the changes at Delta and GM proceeded at a remarkable pace. By comparing these successful changes with less successful ones, we can further shed light on the key aspects of the change process outlined in Figure 1.

Stalled Changes

The examples of European truck maker IVECO and of Corning Glass show some of the difficulties faced during the acquisition of control by headquarters over subsidiaries.[6] The international operations of Corning were built upon high technology applications of glass products, from television tubes or oven-resistant glass to optical lenses and laboratory glassware. Until the late 1960s, subsidiaries had remained autonomous. Most had started as joint ventures or as independent European companies that Corning later acquired. IVECO started as a joint venture between Fiat and Klockner Humbolt Deutz (KHD), with truck manufacturing operations in three European countries (Italy, Germany, and France) and sales and service subsidiaries throughout Europe. IVECO's goal was to achieve low-cost through large-scale production to compete effectively against Daimler Benz, the largest full-line European truck producer.

Both these companies initiated the change process in ways rather similar to Delta and GM (e.g., Corning's top management developed some sense of a need for better coordination between U.S. domestic and European operations). Strategic shift in both companies started with the appointment of a key executive, but it was quickly stalled for lack of consistent use of administrative mechanisms.

Corning Glass.   Latent problems had existed at Corning since an earlier split of responsibility had occurred between the corporate and international levels. When Corning took majority control of European subsidiaries, attempts to implement a uniform reporting system for legal reasons made subsidiary managers even more resistant to headquarters control. Export coordination followed with some success as in the case of Delta. An attempt to coordinate technology transfers (again as in the case of Delta) failed: the new European area manager could not, by himself, coordinate technology transfers across many different product lines. In contrast to Delta, he was not in charge of U.S. operations, and he had little leverage over U.S. domestic divisions. Recognizing part of that difficulty, Corning's

---

[6]For a description of IVECO, see "Strategic and Organizational Changes in International Automobile Manufacturers"; for a description of Corning Glass, see C. A. Bartlett and M. Y. Yoshino, Corning Glass Works International (A) (ICCH #9-379-051).

European area manager appointed three international business managers to coordinate U.S. and European operations by broad product categories ("consumer," "electrical," and "science and medical" products). However, the subsidiary managers were not immediately involved in any form of intersubsidiary business teams: that involvement only came about a year later. This contrasts to Delta or GM where such teams were set up almost immediately (a worldwide product team at Delta and an overseas planning committee at GM).

In the meantime, a number of data management mechanisms were used at Corning but without much consistency. At any one subsidiary, product interdependencies left much room for judgmental cost allocations among products. Not all subsidiary managements reached comparable judgments. Further, the actual need for a global strategy varied between products, and this variation was not fully recognized by the international business managers. One of them attempted to integrate operations in cookware products that were very sensitive to national market differences. Conversely, another business manager decided to "rely on the subsidiaries" and give them full autonomy in the electrical products area where integration was needed. As a result, subsidiary managers saw no well-defined, legitimate strategy that could provide a basis for headquarters' attempts to gain managerial control. Therefore, they saw these attempts as being illegitimate and inconsistent. Since the differences among products were not analyzed systematically, both subsidiary managers and international business managers used different products to show that each side was "right." Thus, the process did not legitimize decision responsibility and power changes, and it ground to a halt in 1974.[7]

The change process had stalled around Steps 3 and 4, as defined in Figure 1: indiscriminate use of coordination mechanisms (Step 2) resulted in poor definition of the need for strategic shift. Imprecise use of data mechanisms (Step 4) made the reallocation of authority (Steps 5A and 5B) impossible. Changes were not made legitimate, and belated attempts to involve subsidiary managers in "World Business Boards" failed.

The business slump of 1975, combined with the realization that the "World Business Boards" were ineffective in bringing further change, led to a top management decision to call in outside consultants. The various businesses were analyzed and categorized according to the need for a globally integrated strategy for each to compete successfully. A subsequent series of meetings between top management and subsidiary executives led to the definition and acceptance of "decision grids," which de-

---

[7]For a detailed account of a very similar situation, see M. Beer and S. M. Davis, "Creating a Global Organization: Failures along the Way," *Columbia Journal of World Business*, Summer 1978; for a discussion of some of the issues involved in bringing in coordinators, see Y. L. Doz, *GTE's International Division* (ICCH #2-379-061).

tailed the decision-making process on a number of issues according to the analysis done by the consultants. International staffs also merged with domestic staffs (similar to the case of GM). Further changes were made in the accounting, planning, and budgeting systems to provide for complete clarity and for dual comparisons: results reported by country could be directly related to results reported by product. By the late 1970s, Corning Glass had evolved into a complex multinational matrix in which the extent of headquarters control varied with product lines and functions. In the last two years, 1980-81, functional management has been given increasing emphasis.[8]

In summary, inconsistency, illegitimacy, and inadequate ordering in the use of administrative mechanisms prevented the acquisition of headquarters control at Corning in 1974-75.

IVECO.   At IVECO, the process was also stalled and consultants were called in. IVECO had been created at the initiative of a senior Fiat executive who became president of the new company. The company comprised former Italian and French truck manufacturing subsidiaries of Fiat and the former Magirus truck division of Klockner Humboldt Deutz, who received 20 percent of IVECO's shares in exchange for the merger.

The new president quickly created IVECO intersubsidiary functional coordination committees, which were chaired by corporate coordinators. A management advisory committee was also created under his chairmanship; it consisted of IVECO's corporate coordinators and the managing directors of the three national companies (in Italy, France, and Germany). In the first few months of IVECO's existence, these committees agreed upon an intersubsidiary engineering and manufacturing rationalization plan. Massive new investments controlled by headquarters supported this plan and provided IVECO's top management with much leverage over the subsidiaries.

Yet, once the most desperate needs for rationalization had been fulfilled, implementation of the plan slowed down. The data management mechanisms were too crude, or imprecise, to justify fully further changes. Accounting data, for instance, were not precise enough to provide accurate cost information. The planning process did not take hold because the managers of national subsidiaries lacked the irrefutable data to agree on further steps. Whereas, several mechanisms—the president's leadership, the competitive need to rationalize product engineering and production, and major new investments—permitted rapid change of the cognitive and strategic orientations, the change mechanisms were too weak (or ambiguous) to complete the strategic redirection. The administrative dimension

---

[8]For a description of subsequent events at Corning, see C. A Bartlett and M. Y. Hoshino, *Corning Glass Works International* (B), (C), and (D) (ICCH #s 9-379-052,41.)

did not change, and beyond the initial appointment of a powerful president, the reallocation of power did not take place.[9]

The lack of sophistication in the design and in the use of data management mechanisms was a major stumbling block (see Step 4 in Figure 1). Latent conflicts, which initially had been suppressed by the strong leadership of IVECO's first president, were played out against the setting of the data management mechanisms, and they were given much symbolic value. As a result, these mechanisms remained imprecise. The imminent retirement of the president neutralized the one major source of legitimacy for the change. The fuzziness of the data and the source of conflict they represented made further formal changes in authority almost impossible. This led to a deadlock.

By aligning the cognitive, strategic, and power orientations with the formal authority structure, a functional approach suggested by consultants greatly simplified the task of management. This approach provided power abruptly to key executives (Step 6 in Figure 1) and refocused the four orientations toward Europe-wide competitiveness. The most reluctant national subsidiary managers were given major responsibilities, and thus they were coopted into the new structure.

Contrast of Stalled Changes.   The process at IVECO contrasts to that at Corning because the early involvement of IVECO subsidiary managers and effective use of several conflict resolution mechanisms permitted the cognitive and strategic orientations to shift. Little product diversity, relative to Corning, and severe competition also made a centrally directed strategy more obvious to all managers. Yet, the relative lack of clarity and precision in the data management mechanism prevented the shift from being completed. Once obvious measures were completed and the large corporate investments were made (about three years into the process), the shift ground to a halt. Early changes in responsibility had been limited to the specialization of plants and engineering centers. In other words, IVECO's shifts stopped later in the process than did Corning's, but they were even more abrupt.

Abortive Attempts to Gain Headquarters Control

Forces embedded in managerial mechanisms may push toward subsidiary autonomy, often by supporting major businesses that require extensive national responsiveness and close host government relationships. For example, Brown Boveri has had national subsidiaries established since the early 1900s, serving predominantly national electric utilities. In fact, most of these subsidiaries have found themselves twice on opposite sides of a

---

[9]For a more detailed description of the evolution of IVECO, see Y. L. Doz, "IVECO (A) and (B)" (INSEAD mimeographed cases, forthcoming).

world war. Given these characteristics and a very small Swiss domestic market, Brown Boveri's management had long assumed that little basis existed for substantive headquarters control. The only exception they felt was in two areas: management of technology and coordination of export sales.[10]

Gamma Company (a disguised identity) was in a rather similar position. Until the 1970s, its success had been based on subsidiaries replicating the parent's manufacturing facilities while remaining autonomous in operating them and in marketing their production. Though government-controlled customers were not as critical to Gamma as they were to Brown Boveri, Gamma was active in numerous sectors where government's influence was intense: pharmaceuticals, data processing, instrumentation, etc.

In both companies, most administrative mechanisms supported national autonomy. Each national company was a self-contained profit center as was each business within the national company. There was very little managerial movement across countries; career progression took place within each national company. Almost all the top managers of Brown Boveri Company (BBC) were from the power system group, and they were very sensitive to the need for national subsidiary autonomy. Within Gamma, major countries' managers clearly enjoyed more status than did product group managers. The very strong managers' management mechanisms thus fully supported the national orientation. Against that array of strong mechanisms favoring national responsiveness, the difficulties for headquarters to acquire control over certain businesses needing a global strategy become clear.

Brown Boveri.   At BBC, intersubsidiary business and product teams had been set up since 1970. There were sixteen business teams, each responsible for a major business (e.g., electrical motors) and over 100 product teams, one for each major product line (e.g., low voltage breakers). These teams were responsible for developing worldwide business strategies. Several corporate staff groups were also created in 1970—marketing, planning, and finance. The corporate marketing staff coordinated exports from the national subsidiaries. The planning and finance staff groups were less active in a coordinating role.

In the late 1960s, the small motor business (with sales mostly to industrial users) came under severe price competition from Japanese and Eastern European low price imports. European competitors, such as Leroy Somer, had developed very large scale plants to reduce their costs.

In a cognitive or strategic sense, the solution to the profit crisis in BBC's motor business was obvious: BBC had to rationalize motor production among the national subsidiaries to exploit economies of scale and to bring

---

[10]For an analysis of Brown Boveri's operations, see Y. L. Doz, *Government Control and Multinational Strategic Management* (New York: Praeger, 1979), ch. 8.

its costs in line with that of its major competitors. A plan was evolved in 1972: its rationale was obvious to all managers concerned.

Yet, the plan was never fully implemented.[11] The change mechanisms never fully supported the development of headquarters control. Only the business and product teams and the corporate marketing staff (in its role as export coordinator) supported the change, and only the cognitive and strategic orientations were affected directly. All other mechanisms remained unchanged, and thus they reinforced the status quo and the power of the national managements.

Further, the cognitive and strategic orientations of the subsidiaries' top managers were shaped by their major businesses, for which rationalization was politically unfeasible. Since the motor business only accounted for a small part of sales volume, it drew little top management attention in the subsidiaries, and its exposure to intense foreign competition was not fully recognized. In the eyes of the subsidiary managers, the potential profits in the motor business were not sufficient to outweigh the concern over establishing a precedent that would encroach on their autonomy. (Furthermore, the managers argued against considering the motor business separately from other businesses since they sometimes used the offer to establish a motor assembly plant in developing countries as a basis for gaining export orders for large power systems).

Though the difference in the need for a global strategy between motors and other BBC businesses was clearly recognized at headquarters from the outset (in contrast to Corning where consultants had to carry out detailed studies to make these differences unequivocal), this distinction was never applied in the selective use of administrative mechanisms. The motor business coordinator thus faced an impossible situation. He lacked the power and the authority necessary to offset the pressure for the status quo created by nearly all other mechanisms, and in particular the strong bias in favor of national autonomy of all the managers' management mechanisms. By 1977, the global rationalization remained incomplete and had contributed little to improve the competitive position of the motor business in the long run.

Gamma.   The situation at Gamma is quite parallel to that at Brown Boveri. Beyond sectors in which government involvement is intense, Gamma is active in many sectors where price competition is intense, economies of large scale are significant, and host government interest is relatively low. Since the 1960s, when the company was formally organized as a product country matrix, attempts have been made, with great difficulty, to integrate European engineering and manufacturing activities. These attempts were not fully supported by data management mechanisms and managers' management mechanisms. Sophisticated approaches

---

[11]See Y. L. Doz, Brown Boveri & Cie. (ICCH #4-378-115).

to data management and a large headquarter bureaucracy have been developed but have not matched the needs of the businesses well, particularly in periods of sudden exchange rate and business cycle fluctuations.

Some successes were scored, however. Businesses for which the need for a global strategy was most blatant were rationalized first, e.g., mass manufactured products. But subsidiary managers grew increasingly reluctant as more and more businesses were rationalized. Managers' management mechanisms have remained in favor of countries. For example, no managing director of a large subsidiary would have considered it a promotion to be asked to head a worldwide product group. The large corporate staffs did not enjoy the unreserved esteem of the national subsidiary managers.

The test case for the Gamma Company was the rationalization of business X (which we studied in-depth). Resistance by subsidiary management was facilitated by growing host government interest in X. The weakness of the data management mechanisms and the bias in favor of the status quo of the managers' management mechanisms became fully evidenced in this case, and rationalization went little further than it had gone for BBC's small motor business.

The lack of success of BBC and Gamma illustrates two key points in the acquisition of control:

1. Interdependencies across businesses and the varying needs for central strategies among them need to be recognized explicitly and addressed very early when headquarters attempt to gain control.
2. Whatever mechanisms that exist prior to the shift are likely to be set in favor of national subsidiary autonomy. Certain strong mechanisms may be very difficult to redirect successfully early in a change process (none of the processes we observed shifted the reward and punishment systems abruptly). Nonetheless, these mechanisms need to be loosened or their impact needs to be recognized. Relatively neutral conflict management mechanisms can play a key role but cannot be relied upon to effectuate a change when facing strong biased mechanisms (e.g., career paths).

In terms of the change process summarized in Figure 1, the coordination mechanisms at Brown Boveri and Gamma were not strong enough to offset strong unchanged mechanisms. Thus the change process never really got under way, except in the limited instances when the contemplated change served the immediate interest of the acting subsidiary (e.g., the Swiss operating company of Brown Boveri was able to end electrical motor production), or somehow drew unanimity among the involved subsidiaries. Though the need for a possible strategic shift was intellectually recognized (Step 3 in Figure 1), this recognition was not translated into administrative changes. Only major changes that usually come late in the process (e.g., at Step 7) could have overcome the difficulties. In neither case were such changes made. Lack of top management involvement may have prevented them.

At both BBC and Gamma, top management was largely collegial, and national subsidiary managers (with their national constituencies) played a key role in corporate decision making. Though they recognized the need for headquarters control in some businesses, it was difficult for them to erode their own power base and compromise their legitimacy. In other words, there was no strong, independent, headquarters management. Headquarters management was hardly distinguishable from the collection of national managements. The power of "corporate" managers, as individuals, was drawn from national constituencies.

Conclusion

Strategic change—from national to global strategy—can take effect only through the acquisition of headquarters control over subsidiary operations. Successful acquisition of control by headquarters involves changes in the cognitive and strategic orientations of subsidiary managers. When perceptions of a crisis are shared, the crisis itself changes cognitive and strategic orientations. A repertoire of administrative mechanisms is available to headquarters management to shift cognitive and strategic orientations.

Successful acquisition of control by headquarters, on an ongoing basis, also requires changes in the balance of power between headquarters and subsidiaries. To some extent, environmental changes that require increased headquarter control may trigger power shifts: these changes may increase the importance of interdependencies among subsidiaries or between headquarters and subsidiaries.[12] They create a substantive need for headquarters control. Yet, in almost all cases, power shifts can be effectuated only when they appear legitimate to the great majority of the managers involved. Changes in cognitive and strategic orientations create legitimacy for change. Power change, in the cases we observed, is not a sudden upheaval; it is achieved through apparently minor authority changes in the making of specific decisions, starting with the changes most easily acceptable to subsidiaries.

However, the change process is vulnerable to poor analysis of the need for substantive control and to inadequately established legitimacy for change. Failure to create legitimacy may result from the lack of need for

---

[12]D. J. Hickson et al., "A Strategic Contingencies' Theory of Intraorganizational Power," *Administrative Science Quarterly* (1971): 216-229; G. R. Salancick and J. Pfeffer, "Who Gets Power and How They Hold on to It: A Strategic Contingency Model of Power," in *Organizational Dynamics*, Winter 1977, pp. 3-21; J. Pfeffer, *Power in Organization* (Marshfield, MA: Pitman, forthcoming).

substantive control, a lack of control mechanisms, a confused use of mechanisms, and inattention to existing counteracting mechanisms. This does not necessarily mean that no change takes place, but managed purposive adaptation becomes impossible.[13]

Most clearly, the need for substantive control (or the ability to achieve such control given environmental conditions) varies between industries as it also varies with the competitive position of a firm in its industry.[14] These differences, based on industry characteristics and competitive positions, make a careful differentiation between businesses of a diversified multinational necessary. Differences between countries, in the same business, also need to be recognized. To a large extent, the difficulties at Corning can be traced back to a poor understanding of the substantive need for headquarters control on a business by business basis.

Early involvement of subsidiary managers in a series of product teams may provide a forum to explore the need for strategic control. Brown Boveri's managers, with their focused structure of numerous business and product teams, could gain an understanding of these differences. Corning could not do this credibly with either one area coordinator for all product lines or three "business coordinators," each in charge of a very wide product line. As a result, efforts were made to acquire control where control was not strategically justified.

Once the need for headquarters control is identified, mechanisms must be built, or existing mechanisms must be used, to support the acquisition of control. IVECO had to resort to a structural change because it lacked such mechanisms. The need for headquarters control was identified early, and very significant action was taken (rationalization plan). Implementation, which followed, was facilitated initially by massive new investments. Yet, after the first successful efforts, the lack of clear mechanisms made the completion of a power shift difficult.

At Corning and IVECO, the confused, imprecise use of existing mechanisms (e.g., accounting and budgeting processes) further complicated the change process. Clarity in the use of data management mechanisms is extremely important. Data management mechanisms must allow precise consideration of an action from both the perspective of headquarters and of subsidiaries. Imprecision makes almost all positions tenable. Confusion calls for power plays and conflicts. In both companies, the change process did not affect the power and authority dimensions sufficiently to take hold, and consultants were called in to complete the change.

---

[13]Examples of adaptive, unmanaged "bottom-up" change processes are reported elsewhere. See, for example, P. Mathias, "The Role of Logistics System Strategic Change: The Case of the Multinational Corporation" (unpublished doctoral dissertation. Harvard Graduate School of Business Administration, 1978).

[14]For a discussion of these points, see Y. L. Doz, "Strategic Management in Multinational Companies," *Sloan Management Review*, Winter 1980, pp. 27-46.

Finally, at both BBC and Gamma, strong existing mechanisms that worked contrary to the desired change were ignored. Though the need for control was clear at BBC in the case of small motors, lack of differentiation in managers' management mechanisms made change impossible. This led subsidiary managers to look for strategic alternatives they could handle on their own.

In sum, an intellectual understanding of strategy (shifts in cognitive and strategic orientations) does not lead to action. To result in action, this understanding must be translated into managerial mechanisms that change the power relationships within the firm. This may be achieved by the cumulative impact of minor reallocations of responsibility and authority that cumulatively change the pattern of dependence relationships within the firm. As a result, the distinction between strategy formulation and strategy implementation is not very useful for a manager in a complex organization. What can be accomplished organizationally sets limits on what is feasible as a strategy.

APPENDIX

Research Methodology

The research project on which this and the previous companion article was based lasted a total of six years. In 1974, following the pilot study of a diversified materials and chemicals company, a small sample of companies that were in the process of shifting from subsidiary autonomy to headquarters control and centralized strategy making was studied in detail. These companies were: L.M. Ericsson, Brown Boveri & Cie., General Telephone and Electronics, General Motors, Gamma (disguised European diversified MNC), Nippon (disguised Japanese multinational), Ford Motor Co., Corning Glass Works, IVECO, Alcan, and Massey Ferguson. Some of these companies were studied by doctoral students. The evolution of each company was documented through internal company documents and interviews with involved executives at headquarters and at subsidiaries. Interviews numbered between twenty and sixty per company. In some cases, such as GM, IVECO, or Corning, events were followed as they unfolded, since the researchers got involved before the shift was completed.

Detailed descriptions of the various evolutions were then written and checked with managers in the particular company for accuracy and completeness. Some of these descriptions have been published as cases; others will be as they are released by the companies.

From these descriptions were developed chronological protocols identifying the sequence and timing in the area of managerial mechanisms, their intent, and their results. In turn, the general propositions presented in these articles are the researchers' conceptualization of the structural data offered by the protocols and the company descriptions.

CASE ANALYSIS: ITS ROLE AND METHOD

Appendix **A**

I keep six honest serving men
(They taught me all I knew);
Their names are What and Why and When
And How and Where and Who.

Rudyard Kipling

Management is an action-oriented activity. It requires doing to achieve proficiency. Managers succeed or fail not so much because of what they know as because of what they do. A person cannot expect to succeed as a manager and become a "professional" simply by studying excellent books on management—no matter how thoroughly the text material is mastered nor how many As are earned at exam time. Just like a golfer needs to practice at being a better golfer, a person who aspires to become a manager can benefit from practicing at being a manager.

PRACTICING MANAGEMENT VIA CASE ANALYSIS

In academic programs of management education, students practice at being managers via case analysis. A *case* sets forth, in a factual manner, the conditions and circumstances surrounding a particular managerial situation or series of events in an organization. It puts the readers at the scene of the action and familiarizes them with the situation as it prevailed. It may include descriptions of the industry and its competitive conditions, the organization's background, its products and markets, the attitudes and personalities of the key people involved, production facilities, the work climate, the organizational structure, the marketing methods, and the external environment, together with whatever pertinent financial, production, accounting, sales, and market information upon which management had to depend. It may concern any kind of organization—a profit-seeking business, or a public service institution.

The essence of the student's role in the case method is to diagnose and size up the organization's situation and to think through what, if anything, should be done. The purpose is for the student, as analyst, to appraise the situation from a managerial perspective, asking: What factors have contributed to the organization's success (or failure)? What problems are evident? How serious are they? What managerial skills are needed to deal effectively with the situation? What actions need to be taken? What facts and figures support my position?

It should be emphasized that most cases are *not* intended to be examples of right and wrong, or good and bad management. The organizations concerned are selected neither because they are the best or the worst in their industry nor because they are average or typical. The important thing about a case is that it represents an actual situation where managers were obligated to recognize and cope with the problems as they were.

WHY USE CASES TO PRACTICE MANAGEMENT?

> A student of business with tact
> Absorbed many answers he lacked.
> But acquiring a job,
> He said with a sob,
> "How *does* one fit answer to fact?"

The foregoing limerick was offered some years ago by Charles I. Gragg in a classic article, "Because Wisdom Can't Be Told," to illustrate what might happen to students of management without the benefit of cases.[1] Gragg observed that the mere act of listening to statements and sound advice about management does little for anyone's management skills. He contended it was unlikely that accumulated managerial experience and wisdom could effectively be passed on by lectures and readings alone. Gragg suggested that if anything has been learned about the practice of management, it is that a storehouse of ready-made answers does not exist. Each managerial situation has unique aspects, requiring its own diagnosis and understanding as a prelude to judgment and action. In Gragg's view and in the view of other case method advocates, cases provide aspiring managers with an important and valid kind of daily practice in wrestling with mangement problems.

The case method is, indeed, *learning by doing.* The pedagogy of the case method of instruction is predicated on the benefits of acquiring

---

[1]Charles I. Gragg, "Because Wisdom Can't Be Told," in M. P. McNair, ed, *The Case Method at the Harvard Business School* (New York: McGraw-Hill Book Company, 1954), p. 11.

managerial "experience" by means of simulated management exercises (cases). The biggest justification for cases is that few, if any, students during the course of their college education have an opportunity to come into direct personal contact with different kinds of companies and real-life managerial situations. Cases offer a viable substitute by bringing a variety of organizations and management problems into the classroom and permitting students to assume the managers' roles. Management cases therefore provide students with a kind of experiential exercise in which to test their ability to apply their textbook knowledge about management.

OBJECTIVES OF THE CASE METHOD

As the foregoing discussion suggests, using cases as an instructional technique is intended to have four student-related results:[2]

1. Helping you to acquire the skills of putting textbook knowledge about management into practice.

2. Getting you out of the habit of being a receiver of facts, concepts, and techniques and into the habit of diagnosing problems, analyzing and evaluating alternatives, and formulating workable plans of action.

3. Training you to work out answers and solutions for yourself, as opposed to relying upon the authoritative crutch of the professor or a textbook.

4. Providing you with exposure to a range of firms and managerial situations (which might take a lifetime to experience personally), thus offering you a basis for comparison when you begin your own management career.

If you understand that these are the objectives of the case method of instruction, then you are less likely to be bothered by something that puzzles some students: "What is the answer to the case?" Being accustomed to textbook statements of fact and supposedly definitive lecture notes, students often find that discussions and analyses of managerial cases do not produce any "*answer.*" Instead, issues in the case are discussed pro and con. Various alternatives and approaches are evaluated. Usually, a good argument can be made for more than one course of action. If the class discussion concludes without a clear consensus, some students may, at first, feel frustrated because they are not told "what the answer is" or "what the company actually did."

However, case descriptions of managerial situations where answers are not clear-cut are quite realistic. Organizational problems whose analysis

---

[2]Ibid., pp. 12-14; and D. R. Schoen and Philip A. Sprague, "What Is the Case Method?" in M. P. McNair, ed., *The Case Method at the Harvard Business School* (New York: McGraw-Hill Book Company, 1954), pp. 78-79.

leads to a definite, single-pronged solution are likely to be so oversimplified and rare as to be trivial or devoid of practical value. In reality, several feasible courses of action may exist for dealing with the same set of circumstances. Moreover, in real-life management situations when one makes a decision or elects a particular course of action, there is no peeking at the back of a book to see if you have chosen the best thing to do. No book of provably correct answers exists; in fact, the first test of management action is *results*. If the results turn out to be "good," the decision may be presumed "right," if not, then, it was "wrong." Hence, the important thing for a student to understand in case analysis is that it is the managerial exercise of identifying, diagnosing, and recommending that counts rather than discovering "the right answer" or finding out what actually happened.

To put it another way, *the purpose of management cases is not to learn authoritative answers to specific managerial problems but to become skilled in the process of designing a workable (and, hopefully, effective) plan of action through evaluation of the prevailing circumstances.* The aim of case analysis is not for you to try to guess what the instructor is thinking or what the organization did but, rather, to see whether you can support your views against the counterviews of the group or, failing to do so, whether you can accept the merits of the reasoning underlying the approaches of others. Therefore, *in case analysis you are expected to bear the strains of thinking actively, of making managerial assessments which may be vigorously challenged, and of defending your analysis and plan of action.* Only in this way can case analysis provide you with any meaningful practice at being a manager.

In sum, the purpose of the case method is to initiate you in the ways of thinking "managerially" and exercising responsible judgment. At the same time, you should use cases to test the rigor and effectiveness of your own approach to the practice of management and to begin to evolve your own management philosophy and management style.

PREPARING A CASE FOR CLASS DISCUSSION

Given that cases rest on the principle of learning by doing, their effectiveness hinges upon *you* making *your* analysis and reaching *your* own decisions and then in the classroom participating in a collective analysis discussion of the issues. If this is your first experience with the case method, you may have to reorient your study habits. Since a case assignment emphasizes student participation, it is obvious that the effectiveness of the class discussion depends upon each student having studied the case *beforehand*. Consequently, unlike lecture courses where there is no imperative of specific preparation before each class and where assigned readings and reviews of lecture notes may be done at irregular intervals, *a case assignment requires conscientious preparation before class*. You cannot, after all, expect to get much out of practicing managing in a situation with which you are totally unfamiliar.

Unfortunately, though, there is no nice, proven procedure for studying cases which can be recommended to you. There is no formula, no fail-safe step-by-step technique that we can recommend. Each case is a new situation and you will need to adjust accordingly. Moreover, you will, after a time, discover an approach which suits you best. Thus, the following suggestions are offered simply to get you started.

A first step in understanding how the case method of teaching/learning works is to recognize that it represents a radical departure from the lecture/discussion/problem classroom technique. To begin with, members of the class do most of the talking. The instructor's role is to solicit student participation and guide the discussion. Expect the instructor to begin the class with such questions as: What is the organization's strategy? What are the strategic issues and problems confronting the company? What factors have contributed most to the organization's successes? Its failures? Is management doing a good job? Are the organization's objectives and strategies compatible with its skills and resources? Typically, members of the class will evaluate and test their opinions as much in discussions with each other as with the instructor. But irrespective of whether the discussion emphasis is instructor-student or student-student, members of the class carry the burden for analyzing the situation and for being prepared to present and defend their analysis in the classroom. Thus, you should expect an absence of professorial "here's how to do it," "right answers," and "hard knowledge for your notebook"; instead, be prepared for a discussion involving what do *you* think, and what do *you* feel is important.[3]

Begin your analysis by reading the case once for familiarity. An initial reading should give you the general flavor of the situation and make possible preliminary identification of issues. On the second reading, attempt to gain full command of the facts. You may wish to make notes about apparent organizational objectives, strategies, policies, symptoms of problems, root problems, unresolved issues, and roles of key individuals. Be alert for issues or problems which are not necessarily made explicit but which nevertheless are lurking beneath the surface. Read between the lines and do not hesitate to do some detective work on your own. For instance, the apparent issue in the case might be whether a product has ample market potential at the current selling price while the root problem is that the method being used to compensate salespeople fails to generate adequate incentive for achieving greater unit volume. Needless to say, a sharp, clear-cut "size-up" of the company and its external environment is an essential function of management; one cannot propose improvements in

---

[3] Schoen and Sprague, "What Is the Case Method?" p. 80.

strategy or in its implementation until the company's situation has been diagnosed.

To help diagnose the situation, put yourself in the position of some manager or managerial group portrayed in the case and get attuned to the organizational environment within which the manager or management group must make decisions. Try to get a good feel for the "personality" of the company, the management, and the organizational climate. This is essential if you are to come up with solutions which will be both workable and acceptable in light of the prevailing environmental constraints and realities. Do not be dismayed if you find it impractical to isolate the problems and issues into distinct categories which can be treated separately. Very few and significant real-world management problems can be neatly sorted into mutually exclusive areas of concern.

Most important of all, you must arrive at a solid evaluation of the company, based on the information in the case. Developing an ability to evaluate companies and size up their situations is *the key* to case analysis. How do you evaluate a company? There is no pat answer. But in general you need to identify the firm's strategy, evaluate its business portfolio, size-up its competitive position and financial condition, pinpoint external threats and opportunities as well as internal strengths and weaknesses, and assess its future potential. For more specific suggestions consult Chapters 4 and 5.

Uppermost in your efforts, strive for defensible arguments and positions. Do not rely upon just your opinion; support any judgments or conclusions with evidence! Use the available data to make whatever relevant accounting, financial, marketing, or operations analysis calculations are necessary to support your assessment of the situation. Crunch the numbers!

Lastly, be wary of accepting *everything* stated in the case as "fact." Sometimes, information or data in the case will be conflicting and/or opinions contradictory. For example, one manager may say that the firm's organizational structure is functioning quite effectively, whereas another may say it is not. It is your task to decide whose view is more valid and why. Forcing you to make judgments about the validity of the data and information presented in the case is both deliberate and realistic. It is deliberate because one function of the case method is to help you develop your powers of judgment and inference. It is realistic because a great many managerial situations entail conflicting points of view.

Once you have thoroughly diagnosed the company's situation and weighed the pros and cons of various alternative courses of action, the final step of case analysis is to decide what you think the company needs to do to improve its performance and to set forth a workable plan of action. This is a crucial part of the process of case analysis since diagnosis divorced from corrective action is sterile; but bear in mind that proposing solutions and jumping to a conclusion are not the same thing. One is well-advised to avoid the infamous decision-making pattern: "Don't confuse me with the facts. I've made up my mind."

On a few occasions, some desirable information may not be included in the case. In such instances you may be inclined to complain about the lack of "facts." A manager, however, uses more than facts upon which to base his or her decision. Moreover, it may be possible to make a number of inferences from the facts you do have. So, be wary of rushing to include as part of your recommendations "the need to get more information." From time to time, of course, a search for additional facts or information may be entirely appropriate but you must also recognize that the organization's managers may not have had any more information available than that presented in the case. Before recommending that action be postponed until additional facts are uncovered, be sure that you think it will be worthwhile to get them and that the organization can afford to wait. In general, though, try to assess situations based upon the evidence you have at hand.

Again, remember that rarely is there a "right" decision or just one "optimal" plan of action or an "approved" solution. Your goal should be to find a practical and workable course of action which is based upon a serious analysis of the situation and which appears to you to be right in view of your assessment and weighing of the facts. Admittedly, someone else may evaluate the same facts in another way and thus have a different "right" solution, but since several good plans of action can normally be conceived, you should not be afraid to stick by your own analysis and judgment. One can make a strong argument for the view that the "right" answer for a manager is the one which he or she can propose, explain, defend, and make work when it is implemented.

THE CLASSROOM EXPERIENCE

In experiencing class discussions of management cases, you will, in all probability, notice very quickly that you will not have thought of everything in the case that your fellow students think of. While you will see things others did not, they will see things you did not. Do not be dismayed or alarmed by this. It is normal. As the old adage goes, "two heads are better than one." So, it is to be expected that the class as a whole will do a more penetrating and searching job of case analysis than will any one person working alone. This is the power of group effort and one of its virtues is that it will give you more insight into the variety of approaches and how to cope with differences of opinion. Second, you will see better why sometimes it is not managerially wise to assume a rigid position on an issue until a full range of views and information has been assembled. And, undoubtedly, somewhere along the way you will begin to recognize that neither the instructor nor other students in the class have all the answers, and even if they think they do, you are still free to present and hold to your own views. The truth in the saying that "there's more than one way to skin a cat" will be seen to apply nicely to most management situations.

For class discussion of cases to be useful and stimulating you need to keep the following points in mind:

1. The case method enlists a maximum of individual participation in class discussion. It is not enough to be present as a silent observer; if every student took this approach, then there would be no discussion. (Thus, do not be surprised if a portion of your grade is based on your participation in case discussions.)

2. Although you should do your own independent work and independent thinking, don't hesitate to discuss the case with other students. Managers often discuss their problems with other key people.

3. During case discussions, expect and tolerate challenges to the views expressed. Be willing to submit your conclusions for scrutiny and rebuttal. State your views without fear of disapproval and overcome the hesitation of speaking out.

4. In orally presenting and defending your ideas, keep in mind the importance of good communication. It is up to you to be convincing and persuasive in expressing your ideas.

5. Expect the instructor to assume the role of discussion leader; only when the discussion content is technique-oriented is it likely that your instructor will maintain direct control over the discussion.

6. Although discussion of a case is a group process, this does not imply conformity to group opinion. Learning respect for the views and approaches of others is an integral part of case analysis exercises. But be willing to "swim against the tide" of majority opinion. In the practice of management, there is always room for originality, unorthodoxy, and unique personality.

7. In participating in the discussion, make a conscious effort to *contribute* rather than just talk. There *is* a difference.

8. Effective case discussions can occur only if participants have "the facts" of the case well in hand; rehashing information in the case should be held to a minimum except as it provides documentation, comparisons, or support for your position.

9. During the discussion, new insights provided by the group's efforts are likely to emerge, thereby opening up "the facts" to reinterpretation and perhaps causing one's analysis of the situation to be modified.

10. Although there will always be situations in which more technical information is imperative to the making of an intelligent decision, try not to shirk from making decisions in the face of incomplete information. Wrestling with imperfect information is a normal condition managers face and is something you should get used to.

11. Ordinarily, there are several acceptable solutions which can be proposed for dealing with the issues in a case. Definitive, provably correct answers rarely, if ever, exist in managerial situations.

12. In the final analysis, learning about management via the case method is up to you; just as with other learning techniques, the rewards are dependent upon the effort you put in to it.

PREPARING A WRITTEN CASE ANALYSIS

From time to time, your instructor may ask you to prepare a written analysis of the case assignment. Preparing a written case analysis is much like preparing a case for class discussion, except that your analysis, when completed, must be reduced to writing. Just as there was no set pattern or formula for preparing a case for oral discussion, there is no ironclad procedure for preparing a written case analysis. With a bit of experience you will arrive at your own preferred method of attack in writing up a case and you will learn to adjust your approach to the unique aspects that each case presents.

Your instructor may assign you a specific topic around which to prepare your written report. Common assignments include (1) identify and evaluate company X's corporate strategy; (2) in view of the opportunities and risks you see in the industry, what is your assessment of the company's position and strategy? (3) how would you size up the strategic situation of company Y? (4) what recommendation would you make to company Z's top management? and (5) what specific functions and activities does the company have to perform especially well in order for its strategy to succeed?

Alternatively, you may be asked to do a "comprehensive written case analysis." It is typical for a comprehensive written case analysis to emphasize three things:

1. Identification,

2. Analysis and evaluation, and

3. Presentation of recommendations.

You may wish to consider the following pointers in preparing a comprehensive written case analysis.[4]

Identification.   It is essential that your paper reflect a sharply focused diagnosis of strategic issues and key problems and, further, that you demonstrate good business judgment in sizing up the company's present situa-

---

[4]For some additional ideas and viewpoints, you may wish to consult Thomas J. Raymond, "Written Analysis of Cases," in M. P. McNair, ed., *The Case Method at the Harvard Business School* (New York: McGraw-Hill Book Company, 1954), pp. 139-63. In Raymond's article is an actual case, a sample analysis of the case, and a sample of a student's written report on the case.

tion. Make sure you understand and can identify the firm's corporate strategy. You would probably be well advised to begin your paper by sizing up the company's situation, its strategy, and the significant problems and issues which confront management. State the problems/issues as clearly and precisely as you can. Unless it is necessary to do so for emphasis, avoid recounting facts and history about the company (assume your professor has read the case and is familiar with the organization!).

Analysis and Evaluation.   Very likely you will find this section the hardest part of the report. Analysis is hard work! Study the tables, exhibits, and financial statements carefully. Check out the firm's financial ratios, its profit margins and rates of return, its capital structure and decide how strong the firm is financially. (Table A-1 contains a summary of various financial ratios and how they are calculated.) Similarly, look at marketing, production, managerial competences, and so on, and evaluate the factors underlying the organization's successes and failures. Decide whether it has a distinctive competence and, if so, whether it is capitalizing upon it. Is the firm's strategy working? Why or why not? Assess opportunities and threats, both internally and externally. Determine whether objectives, strategies, and policies are realistic in light of prevailing constraints. Look at how the organization is hedging its risks. Evaluate the firm's competitive position. Review the material in Chapters 4 and 5 to see if you have overlooked something—you may also want to review the checklist in Table A-1.

In writing your analysis and evaluation, bear in mind that:

1. You are obliged to offer supporting evidence for your views and judgments. Do not rely upon unsupported opinions, overgeneralizations, and platitudes as a substitute for tight, logical argument backed up with facts and figures.

2. You should indicate the key factors which are crucial to the organization's success or failure; i.e., what must it concentrate on and be sure to do right in order to be a high performer.

3. While some information in the case is established fact, other evidence may be in the form of opinions, judgments, and beliefs, some of which may be contradictory or inaccurate. You are thus obligated to assess the validity of such information. Do not hesitate to question what seems to be "fact."

4. You should demonstrate that your interpretation of the evidence is both reasonable and objective. Be wary of preparing an analysis which omits all arguments not favorable to your position. Likewise, try not to exaggerate, prejudge, or overdramatize. Endeavor to inject balance into your analysis. Strive to display good business judgment.

Recommendations.   The final section of the written case analysis should consist of a set of recommendations or plan of action. The recom-

TABLE A-1
A Summary of Key Financial Ratios, How They Are Calculated, and What They Show

Ratio	How Calculated	What It Shows
Profitability ratios:		
1. Gross profit margin	$$\frac{\text{Sales} - \text{Cost of goods sold}}{\text{Sales}}$$	An indication of the total margin available to cover operating expenses and yield a profit.
2. Operating profit margin	$$\frac{\text{Profits before taxes and before interest}}{\text{Sales}}$$	An indication of the firm's profitability from current operations without regard to the interest charges accruing from the capital structure.
3. Net profit margin (or return on sales)	$$\frac{\text{Profits after taxes}}{\text{Sales}}$$	Shows aftertax profits per dollar of sales. Subpar-profit margins indicate that the firm's sales prices are relatively low or that its costs are relatively high or both.
4. Return on total assets	$$\frac{\text{Profits after taxes}}{\text{Total assets}}$$ or $$\frac{\text{Profits after taxes} + \text{interest}}{\text{Total assets}}$$	A measure of the return on total investment in the enterprise. It is sometimes desirable to add interest to aftertax profits to form the numerator of the ratio since total assets are financed by creditors as well as by stockholders; hence it is accurate to measure the productivity of assets by the returns provided to both classes of investors.
5. Return on stockholders' equity (or return on net worth)	$$\frac{\text{Profits after taxes}}{\text{Total stockholders' equity}}$$	A measure of the rate of return on stockholders' investment in the enterprise.
6. Return on common equity	$$\frac{\text{Profits after taxes} - \text{preferred stock dividends}}{\text{Total stockholders' equity} - \text{par value of preferred stock}}$$	A measure of the rate of return on the investment which the owners of common stock have made in the enterprise.
7. Earnings per share	$$\frac{\text{Profits after taxes} - \text{preferred stock dividends}}{\text{Number of shares of common stock outstanding}}$$	Shows the earnings available to the owners of common stock.

TABLE A-1 *(continued)*

Ratio	How Calculated	What It Shows
Liquidity ratios:		
1. Current ratio	$$\frac{\text{Current assets}}{\text{Current liabilities}}$$	Indicates the extent to which the claims of short-term creditors are covered by assets that are expected to be converted to cash in a period roughly corresponding to the maturity of the liabilities.
2. Quick ratio (or acid test ratio)	$$\frac{\text{Current assets} - \text{inventory}}{\text{Current liabilities}}$$	A measure of the firm's ability to pay off short-term obligations without relying upon the sale of its inventories.
3. Inventory to net working capital	$$\frac{\text{Inventory}}{\text{Current assets} - \text{current liabilities}}$$	A measure of the extent to which the firm's working capital is tied up in inventory.
Leverage ratios:		
1. Debt to assets ratio	$$\frac{\text{Total debt}}{\text{Total assets}}$$	Measures the extent to which borrowed funds have been used to finance the firm's operations.
2. Debt to equity ratio	$$\frac{\text{Total debt}}{\text{Total stockholders' equity}}$$	Provides another measure of the funds provided by creditors versus the funds provided by owners.
3. Long-term debt to equity ratio	$$\frac{\text{Long-term debt}}{\text{Total stockholders' equity}}$$	A widely used measure of the balance between debt and equity in the firm's overall capital structure.
4. Times-interest-earned (or coverage ratios)	$$\frac{\text{Profits before interest and taxes}}{\text{Total interest charges}}$$	Measures the extent to which earnings can decline without the firm becoming unable to meet its annual interest costs.
5. Fixed charge coverage	$$\frac{\text{Profits before taxes and interest}}{\text{Total interest charges} + \text{lease obligations}}$$	A more inclusive indication of the firm's ability to meet all of its fixed charge obligations.

TABLE A-1 *(continued)*

Ratio	How Calculated	What It Shows
Activity ratios:		
1. Inventory turnover	$$\frac{\text{Sales}}{\text{Inventory of finished goods}}$$	When compared to industry averages, it provides an indication of whether a company has excessive or perhaps inadequate finished goods inventory.
2. Fixed assets turnover	$$\frac{\text{Sales}}{\text{Fixed assets}}$$	A measure of the sales productivity and utilization of plant and equipment.
3. Total assets turnover	$$\frac{\text{Sales}}{\text{Total assets}}$$	A measure of the utilization of all the firm's assets; a ratio below the industry average indicates the company is not generating a sufficient volume of business given the size of its asset investment.
4. Accounts receivable turnover	$$\frac{\text{Annual credit sales}}{\text{Accounts receivable}}$$	A measure of the average length of time it takes the firm to collect the sales made on credit.
5. Average collection period	$$\frac{\text{Accounts receivable}}{\text{Total sales} \div 365}$$ or $$\frac{\text{Accounts receivable}}{\text{Average daily sales}}$$	Indicates the average length of time the firm must wait after making a sale before it receives payment.
Other ratios:		
1. Dividend yield on common stock	$$\frac{\text{Annual dividends per share}}{\text{Current market price per share}}$$	A measure of the return to owners received in the form of dividends.
2. Price-earnings ratio	$$\frac{\text{Current market price per share}}{\text{Aftertax earnings per share}}$$	Faster growing or less risky firms *tend* to have higher price-earnings ratios than slower growing or more risky firms.
3. Dividend payout ratio	$$\frac{\text{Annual dividends per share}}{\text{Aftertax earnings per share}}$$	Indicates the percentage of profits paid out as dividends.

TABLE A-1 *(concluded)*

Ratio	How Calculated	What It Shows
4. Cash flow per share	$\dfrac{\text{Aftertax profits} + \text{depreciation}}{\text{Number of common shares outstanding}}$	A measure of the discretionary funds over and above expenses available for use by the firm.

Note: Industry-average ratios against which a particular company's ratios may be judged are available in *Modern Industry* and *Dun's Reviews* published by Dun & Bradstreet (14 ratios for 125 lines of business activity), Robert Morris Associates' *Annual Statement Studies* (11 ratios for 156 lines of business), and the FTC-SEC's *Quarterly Financial Report* for manufacturing corporations.

mendations should follow directly from the analysis. If they come as a surprise, because they are logically inconsistent with or not related to the analysis, the effect of the discussion is weakened. Obviously, any recommendations for action should offer a reasonable prospect of success. *Be sure that the company is financially able to carry out what you recommend*; also your recommendations need to be workable in terms of acceptance by the persons involved, the organization's competence to implement them, and prevailing market and environmental constraints. Unless you feel justifiably compelled to do so, do not qualify, hedge, or weasel on the actions that you believe should be taken. Furthermore, state your recommendation in sufficient detail to be meaningful. Avoid using panaceas or platitudes such as "the organization should implement modern planning techniques" or "the company should be more aggressive in marketing its product." State *specifically* what should be done and *make sure your recommendations are operational.* For instance, do not stop with saying "the firm should improve its market position"; continue on with exactly *how* you think this should be done. And, finally, you should indicate how your plan should be implemented. Here, you may wish to give some attention to leadership styles, psychological approaches, motivational aspects, and incentives that may be helpful. You might also stipulate a timetable for initiating actions, indicate priorities, and suggest who should be responsible for doing what. For example, "Have the manager take the following steps: (1)_____, (2)_____, (3)_____, (4)_____.

In preparing your plan of action, remember that there is a great deal of difference between being responsible, on the one hand, for a decision which may be costly if it proves in error and, on the other hand, expressing a casual opinion as to some of the courses of action which might be taken when you do not have to bear the responsibility for any of the consequences. A good rule to follow in designing your plan of action is to *avoid recommending anything you would not yourself be willing to do if you were in management's shoes.* The importance of learning to develop good judgment in a managerial situation is indicated by the fact that while the same information and operating data may be available to every manager or executive in an organization, it *does* make a difference to the organization which person makes the final decision.[5]

It should go without saying that your report should be organized and written in a manner that communicates well and is persuasive. Great ideas amount to little unless others can be convinced of their merit—this takes effective communication.

KEEPING TABS ON YOUR PERFORMANCE

Every instructor has his or her own procedure for evaluating student performance so, with one exception, it is not possible to generalize about grades and the grading of case analyses. The one exception is that grades on case analyses (written or oral) almost never depend entirely on how you propose to solve the organization's difficulties. The important elements in evaluating student performance on case analyses consist of (a) the care with which facts and background knowledge are used, (b) demonstration of the ability to state problems and issues clearly, (c) the use of appropriate analytical techniques, (d) evidence of sound logic and argument, (e) consistency between analysis and recommendations, and (f) the ability to formulate reasonable and feasible recommendations for action. Remember, a hard-hitting, incisive, logical approach will almost always triumph over seat-of-the-pants opinions, emotional rhetoric, and platitudes.

One final point. You may find it hard to keep a finger on the pulse of how much you are learning from cases. This contrasts with lecture/problem/ discussion courses where experience has given you an intuitive feeling for how well you are acquiring substantive knowledge of theoretical concepts, problem-solving techniques, and institutional practices. But in a case course, where analytical ability and the skill of making sound judgments are less apparent, you may lack a sense of solid accomplishment, at least at first. Admittedly, additions to one's managerial skills and powers of diagnosis are not as noticeable or as tangible as a loose-leaf binder full of lecture notes. But this does not mean they are any less real or that you are making any less progress in learning how to be a manager.

To begin with, in the process of hunting around for solutions, very likely you will find that considerable knowledge about types of organizations, the nature of various businesses, the range of management practices, and so on has rubbed off. Moreover, you will be gaining a better grasp of how to evaluate risks and cope with the uncertainties of enterprise. Likewise, you

---

[5]Gragg, "Because Wisdom Can't Be Told," p. 10.

will develop a sharper appreciation of both the common and the unique aspects of managerial encounters. You will become more comfortable with the processes whereby objectives are set, strategies are initiated, organizations are designed, methods of control are implemented and evaluated, performance is reappraised, and improvements are sought. Such processes are the essence of strategic management and learning more about them through the case method is no less an achievement just because there is a dearth of finely calibrated measuring devices and authoritative crutches on which to lean.

LIST OF SUGGESTED
CASES

Appendix B

The following is a list of cases that can be used to supplement and illustrate the material found in this book. All the cases can be ordered through Harvard Business School Case Services by listing the case title and case number and sending to:

Harvard Business School Case Services
Soldiers Field Post Office
Boston, Mass 02163

I.   The General Manager: Tasks, Functions, Style of Managing

Jim Heavner Story (A)(B), 38 pp. [9-479-037,038]

A story of the development of an entrepreneur, his core group, and his organization from a small radio to a multi-divisional company. Organizational and personnel challenges of each stage of growth and development are highlighted. [TN(Teaching Note) 5-480-052].

Haskett Computer Services, 34 pp. [9-378-221]

The president of a computer service company is attempting to formulate a corporate strategy for his firm. Major issues are management of change, growth strategy, and organizational structure.

Fred Fischer, 4 pp. [9-480-045]

Introduces the tasks of the general manager. Describes how an individual's background and characteristics contribute to his accumulation of influence in a position of relatively little formal authority.

Jem Productions (A)(C), [9-379-600,602,604]

Describes Jim Minarik's first year of activity as Business Manager of Penn State University's Undergraduate Student Government. The "C" case is four years later as Jim searches for a replacement. [TN 5-379-601,603,605]

Dexter Corporation, 31 pp. [9-379-112]

Describes the increasing involvement of the corporate level of a diversi-fied firm with individual businesses. The president is considering how the business segments should be identified in organization structure because he must deal with an apparently unsuccessful business.

Corning Glass Works: International (A)(B)(C), 54 pp. [9-379-051,052,053]

Introduces the company and its business, tracing the change in organiza-tional systems and structure as Corning shifts its overseas business strategy.

Crown Cork and Seal Co., Inc., 27 pp. [9-378-024]

The case concerns the formulation of corporate strategy for a firm that is facing immediate threats from competition and the environmentalists. The user can formulate new objectives for the company. [TN 5-378-108]

Head Ski Company, 37 pp. [6-313-120]

Describes the development of the company along with the personal values of its president Howard Head.

Tensor Corporation, 24 pp. [9-370-041]

Discusses the rapid growth of a new company with a new and very hot product—the Tensor lamp. A characterization of the management style and values of the president, Jay Monroe.

II.   Strategy Formulation and Evaluation

Dennison Manufacturing Co. (A)(B)(C), 14 pp. [6-313-119,284]

Corporate and divisional viewpoints on the formulation of strategy for a paper converting firm with $100 million in sales.

Stanford Court Condominiums, 32 pp. [9-379-066]

A developer, working on an initial project, must decide whether to proceed. The project is a mixed condominium and rental unit develop-ment. Market and competitive information is supplied.

Tennessee Valley Authority and the Peabody Coal Company, 22 pp. [9-379-038]

The nation's largest producer of electric power must decide whether to enter a bid for the purchase of nation's largest coal company.

Gelco Corporation, 31 pp. [9-379-029]

A rapidly growing firm is considering the purchase of a small vehicle leasing firm in the U.K. The chairman and CEO must review the proposed acquisition.

Mead Corporation: Strategic Planning, 31 pp. [9-379-070]

Describes an elaborate planning system in a large diversified company. A divisional level proposed plan must be evaluated in light of the overall corporate plan.

Barnwell Nuclear Fuel Plant (A)(B), 17 pp. [9-379-143,144]
Describes the steps leading to the building of the Barnwell Nuclear Fuel Plant and the problems in securing its operating license. The case deals with the issue of how an apparently cooperative and successful relationship between a company and the government could lead to such a fiasco.

Chain Saw Industry in 1974, 32 pp. [9-379-157]
Describes the structure of the chainsaw industry in 1974, when it is on the threshold of a major period of growth. Data are provided on each significant competitor.

Chain Saw Industry in 1978, 29 pp. [9-379-176]
Describes the evolution of the industry since 1974. Illustrates issues in industry evolution, the forces causing evolution, and the strategic issues raised by evolution.

National Container Corp (A)(B), 33 pp. [9-379-626,627]
A manager thinks his subordinate is engaged in a price fixing conspiracy in which the manager may be implicated because of his negligence. Should he feign ignorance or investigate his suspicions? [TN 5-379-636]

Marlin Firearms Co., Inc., 29 pp. [6-371-186]
Successful firearms company is confronted by new foreign competition and the possibility of gun control legislation plans for the future. Data are provided on competition, markets, processes, and organization.

III.   Strategy Implementation and Administration

Centurion Court Clubs, Inc., 20 pp. [9-379-180]
Presents the business plan for a new venture into the growing racquetball industry. Data on growth is given and the CEO details his plan for expansion. The issue of the case is to evaluate the implementation plan.

Zurn Industries, Inc., 28 pp. [9-379-100]
Presents current position, problems and opportunities of company which has grown from about $10 million to $300 million in about 15 years.

Allied Chemical Corp. (A), 22 pp. [9-379-137]
Describes Allied, the chemical industry, and the effects of the Kepone problem. The executive must implement a plan to deal with the Toxic Substances Control Act. [TN 5-380-171]

Texas International Airlines, Inc. (A)(B)(C), 37 pp. [9-379-206,207,208]
Discusses a decision concerning pricing strategy in a rapidly changing regulatory environment. The "B" and "C" case ask for a revised strategy in light of an initial success.

Outdoor Outfitters, Ltd., 8 pp. [9-379-608]
A young company is experiencing growing pains. Taken over by new

management, the part-time sales personnel resist changes and attempt to retain the status quo. [TN 5-379-609]

Cumberland Gasket Co., Inc., 11 pp. [9-379-632]

Division manager must formulate and implement a strategy to deal with manufacturing asbestos which may prove to be harmful to his employees. However, there is no substitute for the parts the company manufactures out of asbestos.

Munson Electric Co., 37 pp. [9-379-644]

A medium sized U.S. company is faced with the task of expanding its manufacturing facilities in Canada. Data are provided on two competing locations.

Asheville Foundries, Inc. (A), [9-379-663]

Management is faced with closing a large casting foundry because of poor performance as well as an OSHA citation. Several different alternatives are presented for strategic analysis.

J. I. Case Company, 35 pp. [9-309-270]

Large manufacturer of farm equipment is traced over three different administrations with differing policies, implementing actions, and results achieved.

Aerosol Techniques Inc., 32 pp. [9-313-155]

Discusses in depth a large company involved in aerosol packaging. An implementation plan is needed in light of competitive pressures and a changing marketplace.

CML Group, Inc., 37 pp. [9-371-426]

Examines the influence of corporate management upon the operations of acquired divisions. Reviews in detail the activities of the president vis-a-vis CML's four acquired divisions. Decision focus is provided by a major investment decision facing one division.

INDEX

This book has been set Varityper in 10 and 9 point Caledonia, leaded 2 points. Chapter numbers are 24 point Caledonia and chapter titles are 16 point Caledonia. The size of the type page is 27 by 46 picas.